AF820285

Using Microsoft® Word 97

— Eric Maloney and Joshua C. Nossiter —

QUE®

Using Microsoft Word 97

Copyright© 1996 by Que® Corporation.

All rights reserved. Printed in the United States of America. No part of this book may be used or reproduced in any form or by any means, or stored in a database or retrieval system, without prior written permission of the publisher except in the case of brief quotations embodied in critical articles and reviews. Making copies of any part of this book for any purpose other than your own personal use is a violation of United States copyright laws. For information, address Que Corporation, 201 W. 103rd Street, Indianapolis, IN 46290. You may reach Que's direct sales line by calling 1-800-428-5331.

Library of Congress Catalog No.: 96-71428

ISBN: 0-7897-0956-2

This book is sold *as is*, without warranty of any kind, either express or implied, respecting the contents of this book, including but not limited to implied warranties for the book's quality, performance, merchantability, or fitness for any particular purpose. Neither Que Corporation nor its dealers or distributors shall be liable to the purchaser or any other person or entity with respect to any liability, loss, or damage caused or alleged to have been caused directly or indirectly by this book.

98 97 96 6 5 4 3 2 1

Interpretation of the printing code: the rightmost double-digit number is the year of the book's printing; the rightmost single-digit number, the number of the book's printing. For example, a printing code of 96-1 shows that the first printing of the book occurred in 1996.

All terms mentioned in this book that are known to be trademarks or service marks have been appropriately capitalized. Que cannot attest to the accuracy of this information. Use of a term in this book should not be regarded as affecting the validity of any trademark or service mark.

Screen reproductions in this book were created using Collage Plus from Inner Media, Inc., Hollis, NH.

Composed in *ITC Century*, *ITC Highlander*, and *MCPdigital* by Que Corporation.

Credits

President
Roland Elgey

Publishing Director
Lynn E. Zingraf

Editorial Services Director
Elizabeth Keaffaber

Managing Editor
Michael Cunningham

Director of Marketing
Lynn E. Zingraf

Acquisitions Editor
Martha O'Sullivan

Senior Product Development Specialist
Lorna Gentry

Production Editor
Mark Enochs

Technical Editor
Ed Hanley

Technical Specialist
Nadeem Muhammed

Editorial Assistant
Virginia Stoller

Book Designer
Ruth Harvey

Cover Designer
Dan Armstrong

Production Team
Stephen Adams
Michael Beaty
Debra Bolhuis
Marcia Brizendine
Kevin Cliburn
Wil Cruz
Jennifer Earhart
Jason Hand
Daniel Harris
Bob LaRoche
Kelly Maish
Casey Price
Erich Richter
Kaylene Riemen
Laura Robbins

Indexer
Tim Tate

For my mother, whose typewriter never missed a word.—Eric Maloney

About the Authors

Eric Maloney received his master's degree in journalism from the University of Oregon. He entered computer magazine publishing in 1980 as a copy editor for Kilobaud Microcomputing and has been the editor in chief of three magazines: *80 Micro*, *PC Resource*, and *LAN Technology*. Currently, Eric is a contributing editor for *Maximize* and *DOS World*, for whom he writes articles on a variety of topics. He also teaches writing courses part-time in the journalism department at Keene State College.

Joshua C. Nossiter received a B.A. in English from Dartmouth University and an MBA in Finance from Columbia University. He's worked in broadcasting in California and in public finance on Wall Street, and is the author of books on WordPerfect and Excel. Josh is also a novelist. He wrote his first book with a typewriter, and has used just about every generation of word processing software since. He lives in San Francisco with his two children, where he's at work on new novels and computer books.

We'd Like to Hear from You!

As part of our continuing effort to produce books of the highest possible quality, Que would like to hear your comments. To stay competitive, we *really* want you, as a computer book reader and user, to let us know what you like or dislike most about this book or other Que products.

You can mail comments, ideas, or suggestions for improving future editions to the address below, or send us a fax at (317) 581-4663. For the online inclined, Macmillan Computer Publishing has a forum on CompuServe (type **GO QUEBOOKS** at any prompt) through which our staff and authors are available for questions and comments. The address of our Internet site is **http://www.mcp.com** (World Wide Web).

In addition to exploring our forum, please feel free to contact me personally to discuss your opinions of this book: on CompuServe, I'm at **75703,3251** and I'm **lgentry@que.mcp.com** on the Internet.

Thanks in advance—your comments will help us to continue publishing the best books available on computer topics in today's market.

Lorna Gentry
Senior Product Development Specialist
Que Corporation
201 W. 103rd Street
Indianapolis, Indiana 46290
USA

NOTE **Although we cannot provide general technical support, we're** happy to help you resolve problems you encounter related to our books, disks, or other products. If you need such assistance, please contact our Tech Support department at 800-545-5914 ext. 3833.

To order other Que or Macmillan Computer Publishing books or products, please call our Customer Service department at 800-835-3202 ext. 666.

Contents at a Glance

Table of Contents

Introduction

Part I: What's the Good Word?

1 What You Need to Know to Get Started

Part II: Editing Your Work

5 How to Delete, Move, Copy, and Change Your Text

6 My Grammar and Speling Ain't So Good

11 Turning the Tables

12 Word Documents Are Never Out of Style

Part IV: Be Your Own Publisher

13 Columns, the Pillars of Sturdy Documents

14 Borders, Colors, and Typographical Tweaks

15 Picture This! Documents with Graphics

Part V: Organizational Tools

21 Customizing Word

22 Mail Merge, for Homemade Mass Mailings

Part VII: Word and the Rest of the World

23 Pony Express It's Not: Sending Data In and Out of Word

Introduction

In the early days of personal computers, a word processor wasn't much more than a souped-up typewriter. Its main attraction was that you could edit your documents and save them for later use. Frills such as spell checkers, fonts, macros, and even simple menus were kept to a minimum to preserve the computer's valuable but scant resources.

Alas, the golden age of simplicity is over. No longer are word processors content to let you just sit down and start writing. They've become massive and complex pieces of software that challenge you to conquer them.

Take Word, for example. Its tantalizing arrays of shiny buttons and blinking lights are endless. Menus have commands that have dialog boxes with options that have icons that lead to more menus. Word does everything but feed the cat and put out the milk bottles.

The problem is not with Word itself. In the world of computers, power usually begets complexity. The problem is that most of us don't have the need (or the time) to learn about everything Word offers. We're too busy with our everyday work. All we want to do is produce attractive documents with a minimum of fuss. Leave the vari-dimensional, multi-matrixed, hexadecimal-friendly composition generators to the software gurus.

What this book is all about

The goal of this book is to return simplicity to word processing. We'll do this by showing you the easiest way to handle your most common tasks. We'll help you pick through Word's flea market of features to find only the items you really need.

We won't beat you blind with endless lists of commands you'll never use. We won't waste your time with dozens of obscure keyboard combinations that you'll never remember. And we won't wear you out with descriptions of every option in every menu and dialog box. We'll give you only the best, leaving the rest for you to investigate on a rainy day.

Exploring the unknown

When we refer to Word's most important features, we don't just mean the obvious ones. Naturally, we've got plenty on how to manage files, edit documents, and format type. But we're also going to explore some of Word's lesser-known features that, while they might not jump out at you as Day-Glo icons, can be invaluable writing tools.

For example, Word's grammar checker produces readability statistics. The information these obscure numbers provide can be a powerful aid in helping you improve your writing skills. Word's documentation doesn't tell you how to use these statistics, but we do.

Something old, something new

This book pays special attention to Word's most important new features and commands. While Word 97 strongly resembles its predecessor, Word for Windows 95, many of its new features are notable. Specifically, we'll show you:

- How to use Word's workgroup capabilities, including its new Version command and revamped Track Changes and Comment features
- How you can access the Internet directly from Word
- How you can use Word to create Web pages
- How to get the most out of Office Assistant, Word 97's new tool for getting online help
- How to create tables with Word's expanded set of table commands
- How to use Word's improved Autotext features to create and save frequently used text
- How to use a plethora of new toolbars

For those of you who are upgrading from Word 2 and Word 6, you'll want to pay special attention to sections of the book that show you:

- How to use Word's long file names
- When not to use Word's long file names
- How to use file management features that let you easily move, copy, and delete documents

- How to use Windows 95's system of folders for saving your Word documents
- How to use Word's feature-packed dialog boxes

Working with others: Word's the word

Of all the changes in Word 97, the features designed to accommodate workgroups are the ones that will affect the most users. In fact, these features are so important Microsoft has put them into a new Reviewing toolbar, and we've added a chapter titled "All Together Now—Using Word in Your Workgroup."

Users no longer are working in isolation at their individual workstations; they need to share their documents with others. Word has new and improved commands that let many users work on a single document with ease and efficiency.

For example, Word now lets you save many versions of a document in a single file. When you send a report or proposal to another person in your workgroup, all of the earlier versions are readily available from the File menu. Gone are the hassles of saving and maintaining an individual file for each new version of a document.

Also, Microsoft has beefed up Word's Annotations feature, now called Comments. Not only is it easier to add notes to a document, but other users can read them more quickly and efficiently with a new Reviewing toolbar.

Finally, it's easier in Word 97 to track and mark changes to a document, as well as later review, accept, and reject those changes.

World Wide Word

The other significant addition to Word 97 is its Internet accessiblity.

For starters, you can load your Web browser directly from Word 97. This provides convenient, one-click access to your favorite search tools and Web sites.

And Word 97 now can prepare documents for publication on the Web. You don't even need to understand Hypertext Markup Language; just prepare your document the way you want it to look, and Word 97 automatically inserts the HTML code. "The Word on the Web" gives you an overview of

Word's Web features, including a tutorial on how to use Word's Web Page wizard to create your own home page.

The solution finder

Many computer books provide solutions in search of a problem. Our strategy is the opposite. We identify common problems and then give you the simplest solutions. You'll discover two major advantages to this approach.

First, getting the information you need is easier. You don't have to wade through lots of material that doesn't apply directly to the task at hand.

Second, you don't need to read the book sequentially. You can learn how to check your spelling in Chapter 6 without having to read all of Chapters 1 through 5.

If you're a curious sort, you'll also find that the book's design lends itself to indiscriminate browsing. Just pick a page at random, and there's a good chance you'll learn a new trick or technique.

What's inside

Now that we've gotten all of the philosophical musings out of the way, let's look at what you'll learn from this book.

Part I: What's the Good Word?

Chapters 1 through 4 show you the easiest way to start writing in Word. Here is where you'll learn how to find your way around the screen; how to create a document; how to name, save, and open documents; and how to use Word's extensive online Help files.

Part II: Editing Your Work

What's the easiest way to delete, move, and copy text? We'll show you in Chapters 5 through 7, along with how to use the spelling and grammar checkers and how to prepare your documents for printing.

Part III: Live Fast, Die Young, and Leave a Good-Looking Document

Chapters 8 through 12 cover what you need to know to make your documents more attractive. Topics include how to create simple and attractive tables, how to use styles to automate your formatting, and how to format type, paragraphs, and blocks.

Part IV: Be Your Own Publisher

Here's where we get to the sizzle: creating fancy documents such as brochures and newsletters. Chapters 13 through 15 show you how to put text in columns, how to choose and use type and borders, and how to insert pictures and objects into your documents.

Part V: Organizational Tools

Chapters 16 and 17 cover outlines and how to deal with large documents more efficiently, while Chapter 18 tells you all about Word's new file management features.

Part VI: Advanced Topics

When you get bored with the easy material, turn to Chapters 19 through 22 to find out how to use Word's graphics makers; make your own toolbars, menus, and macros; and use form letters and mail merge. You'll also learn how to share files with other Windows programs.

Part VII: Word and the Rest of the World

Here's where you'll find the new chapters on workgroups and the Internet. Chapter 24 covers issues related to preparing documents for use by others, including how several users can work on a document at the same time. Chapter 25 discusses Word's new Internet features: how to make the Word-Web connection and how to create Web pages without having to become an HTML programmer.

Nuggets of information

Throughout this book, you'll find a variety of special devices that we use to give you special information.

TIP **Tips describe shortcuts and secrets that show you the best way to** get a job done.

CAUTION **Cautions warn you about potential problems that might arise from** a particular action.

Q&A ***Do you have a question?***

We try to anticipate and answer questions or problems you might have about Word's features and procedures.

Plain English, please!

Here we translate **computer terms** and **jargon** into English.

In addition, you'll run across text that is in a different typeface:

A `special typeface` indicates what you see on your screen.

Bold is for new terms or text that you type.

When you see an underlined letter in a command, press the Alt key plus that letter to execute the command. For example, press Alt+F to display the File menu.

Finally, we've created a special icon to indicate important features that are new to Word 97.

Sidebars: entertainment and information

Sidebars are detours from the main text. They usually provide background or interesting information that is relevant but not essential reading.

A Word on the Web

Information on the Internet and World Wide Web will often appear in these special sidebars.

Part I: What's the Good Word?

1

What You Need to Know to Get Started

In this chapter:

- **In the beginning: how to create a new document**
- **Open sesame! Getting a file from your disk**
- **What's in a document name?**
- **Exiting Word**

You don't need to be a computer genius to use Word. Learn these basics, and you'll be producing simple documents before you even finish this chapter . . . .

It seems like every computer book has a chapter titled, "What You Need to Know to Get Started." Then, it proceeds to detail every-thing you *don't* need to know about IRQs, file allocation tables, upper memory blocks, and other technical arcana. You'd probably have more fun memorizing tax tables.

This chapter is different. For starters, we don't know any technical arcana. But even if we did, you wouldn't need it to get Word running. While Word *looks* imposing, it's pretty much designed for human consumption.

Setting Up Word for Windows

When you install Word, Setup adds Microsoft Word to the Windows Programs menu. You run Word by clicking the Start button, then choosing Programs, Microsoft Word, as shown in Figure 1.1.

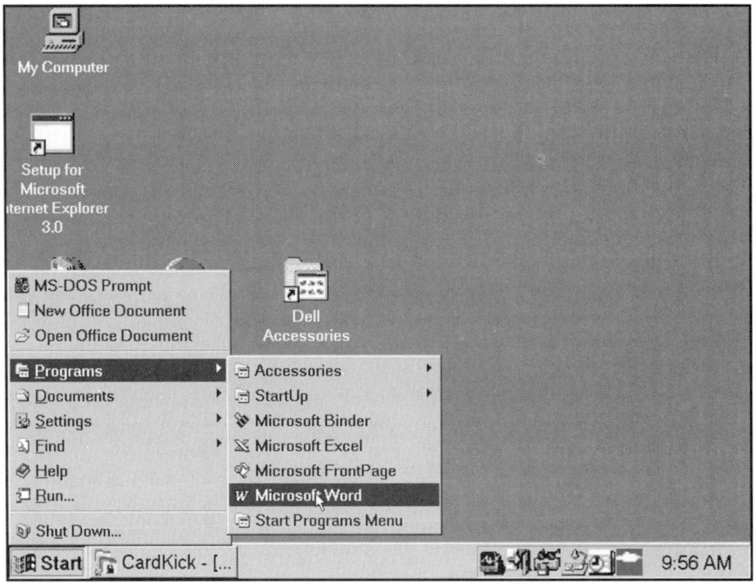

Fig. 1.1
Word sets up shop in the Microsoft Office menu. Click Microsoft Word to run the program.

TIP **Run Setup if you find that Word is missing a component. Make** sure you have your installation disks or CD-ROM ready.

What's what in Word

The Word 97 screen is divided into three basic areas: the bars above the document window, the document window, and the bar below the document window.

The Microsoft Office Shortcut Bar includes buttons for Office programs and features

*The **title bar** tells you what document you're working on*

*The **menu bar** gives you access to your commands. Click the command with your mouse or press Alt and the underlined letter.*

Click the buttons on the Formatting toolbar to change how your text looks

*Click the buttons on the **Standard toolbar** to run common commands*

Use the ruler to change your margin and tabs

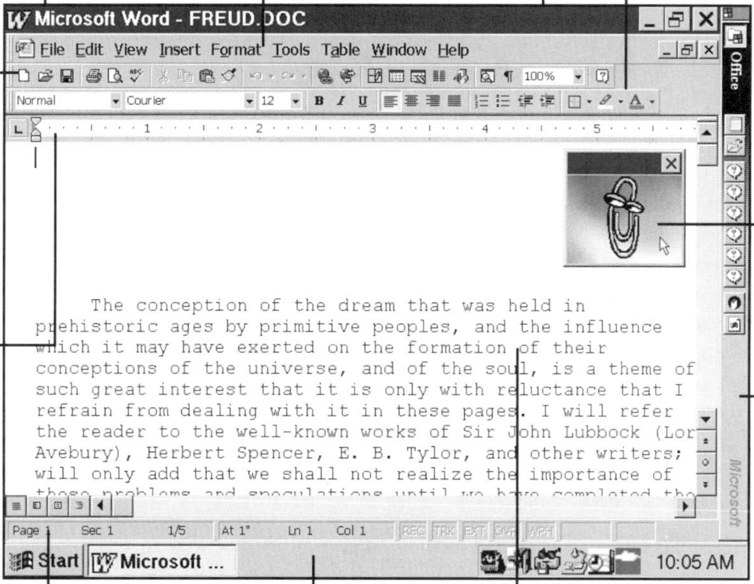
Microsoft Word - FREUD.DOC
File Edit View Insert Format Tools Table Window Help
Normal
Courier
12
100%
Office
The conception of the dream that was held in
prehistoric ages by primitive peoples, and the influence
which it may have exerted on the formation of their
conceptions of the universe, and of the soul, is a theme of
such great interest that it is only with reluctance that I
refrain from dealing with it in these pages. I will refer
the reader to the well-known works of Sir John Lubbock (Lor
Avebury), Herbert Spencer, E. B. Tylor, and other writers;
will only add that we shall not realize the importance of
Page 1 Sec 1 1/5 At 1" Ln 1 Col 1
REC TRK EXT OVR WPH
Start
Microsoft ...
10:05 AM
Microsoft

Click the Office Assistant to get help on Word's features and functions

The scroll bars let you use your mouse to move to parts of the document you can't see

The status bar shows you the line, column, and page on which your insertion point sits; it also displays important messages as you work

The Windows 95 taskbar lets you switch to other programs and folders

The document window is where you type your text. You can open several document windows at the same time.

The Word screen

You'll need some time to become familiar with the basic Word screen. There's a lot to learn. Perhaps more important, there's a lot *not* to learn. Mastering Word depends on how well you can filter nonessential features and focus on the relatively few you'll need to get started.

The previous graphics page shows the main areas of the screen. Let's take a quick look at each of these areas so you have an idea of where to go for what.

The menu bar

The menu bar gives you access to your essential commands. You display a menu by clicking once the option, or by pressing the Alt key plus the underlined letter (for example, press Alt+F for the File menu).

Plain English, please!

Throughout this book, you'll find references to the **Alt** and **Ctrl** keys. These labels stand for **alternate** and **control**, respectively. Alt and Ctrl don't do anything by themselves; you use them in combination with other keys (and sometimes each other) to run commands or perform other actions. For example, you can press Alt+E to view the Edit menu, or Ctrl+S to save a file.

When you use the Alt key, you can press and release it and then press the second key, or you can press Alt and the second key together. However, when you use the Ctrl key, you must hold it down while you press the second key.

Figure 1.2 shows the results of choosing the File menu.

To run a command from a menu, slide the bar insertion point to the command and its icon and click once with your mouse button. If you're using the keyboard, press the underlined letter (for example, press O for Open).

TIP **Some menu commands are followed by a key combination; for** example, Ctrl+O for Open. These are keyboard shortcuts that let you bypass the menu. Take a few minutes to learn them; they'll save you a lot of time. If a menu command is preceded by an icon, it means you'll also find the icon on one of Word's toolbars.

New to Word 97: Icons for commands that are on Word's toolbars are also displayed in Word's menus.

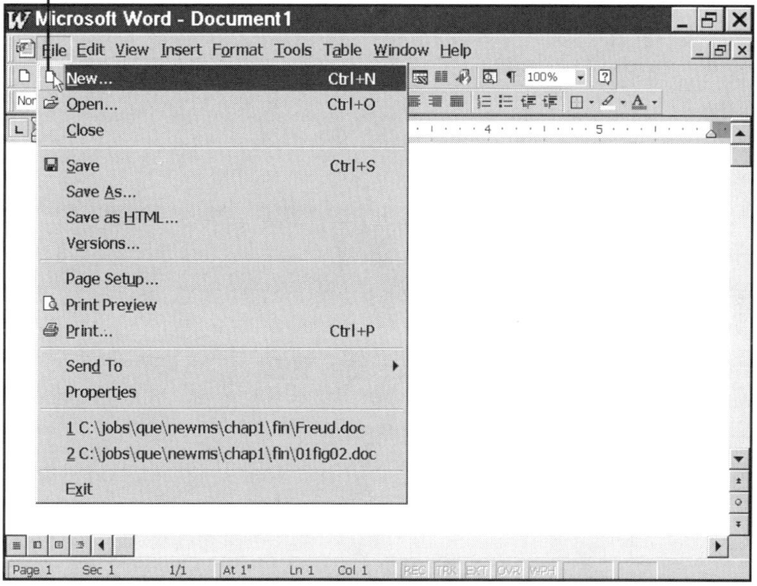

Fig. 1.2
Drop down a menu from the menu bar by clicking the menu item once with the mouse, or by pressing Alt plus the underlined letter (in this case, Alt+F).

Q&A ***Why are some of my menu commands followed by three periods and others by an arrow?***

When you choose a command that is followed by periods—File, New, for example—Word opens a dialog box that lets you select command options. Choosing a command followed by an arrow—such as View, Toolbars—opens a submenu.

The shortcut menu

You can save trips to the menu bar by clicking your right mouse button and calling up a shortcut menu, like the one shown in Figure 1.3. The shortcut menu changes depending on what part of the window you click and what you're doing at the time. The menu in Figure 1.3, which appears when you're working on text in the document window, includes selected commands from the Edit and Format menus.

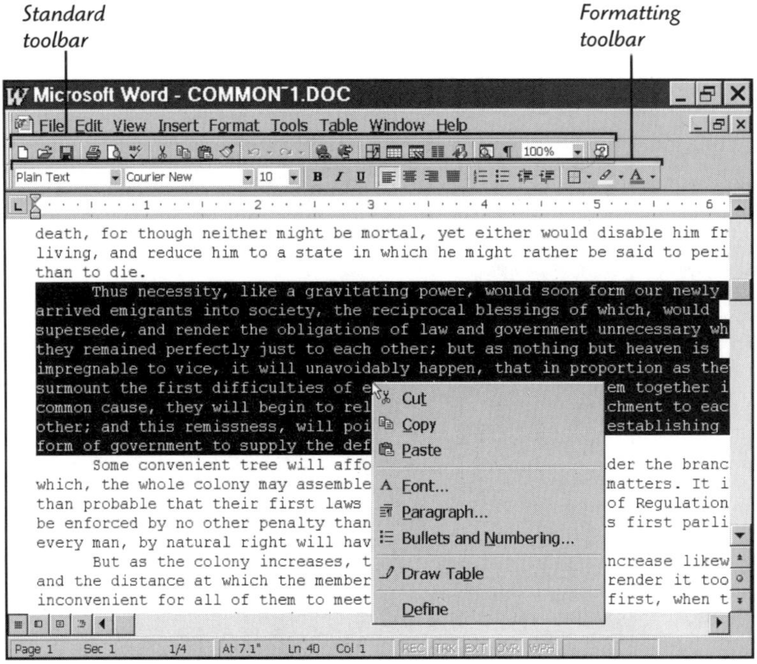

Fig. 1.3
Click the right mouse button to get a shortcut menu. This is the one you get when you click selected text in the document window. Other types of shortcut menus appear when you click other parts of the screen.

Q&A ***Some of my menus have options that are gray, and nothing happens when I click them. Are they unavailable in my version of Word?***

They're available; they're just not active because they can't be used at the moment. For example, in Figure 1.3, the Windows Clipboard is empty, so the Paste command is dormant and therefore grayed out.

The Standard toolbar

The Standard toolbar is the first row of buttons directly beneath the menu bar. It gives you mouse-powered shortcuts to common commands. For example, instead of choosing File, Open from the menu bar to start a new document, click the Open icon (which looks like an open file folder) on the Standard toolbar.

When you become more familiar with Word, you can remove the buttons you seldom use and replace them with others of your choosing.

Some of the icons are self-explanatory, but others are somewhat inscrutable. For example, what's that globe with two blue arrows under Table in Figure

1.3? To find out, just touch the icon with your pointer, and a little box called a **ScreenTip** pops up with the words Web Toolbar.

The following graphics page briefly explains what the Standard toolbar buttons do.

Inside the Standard toolbar

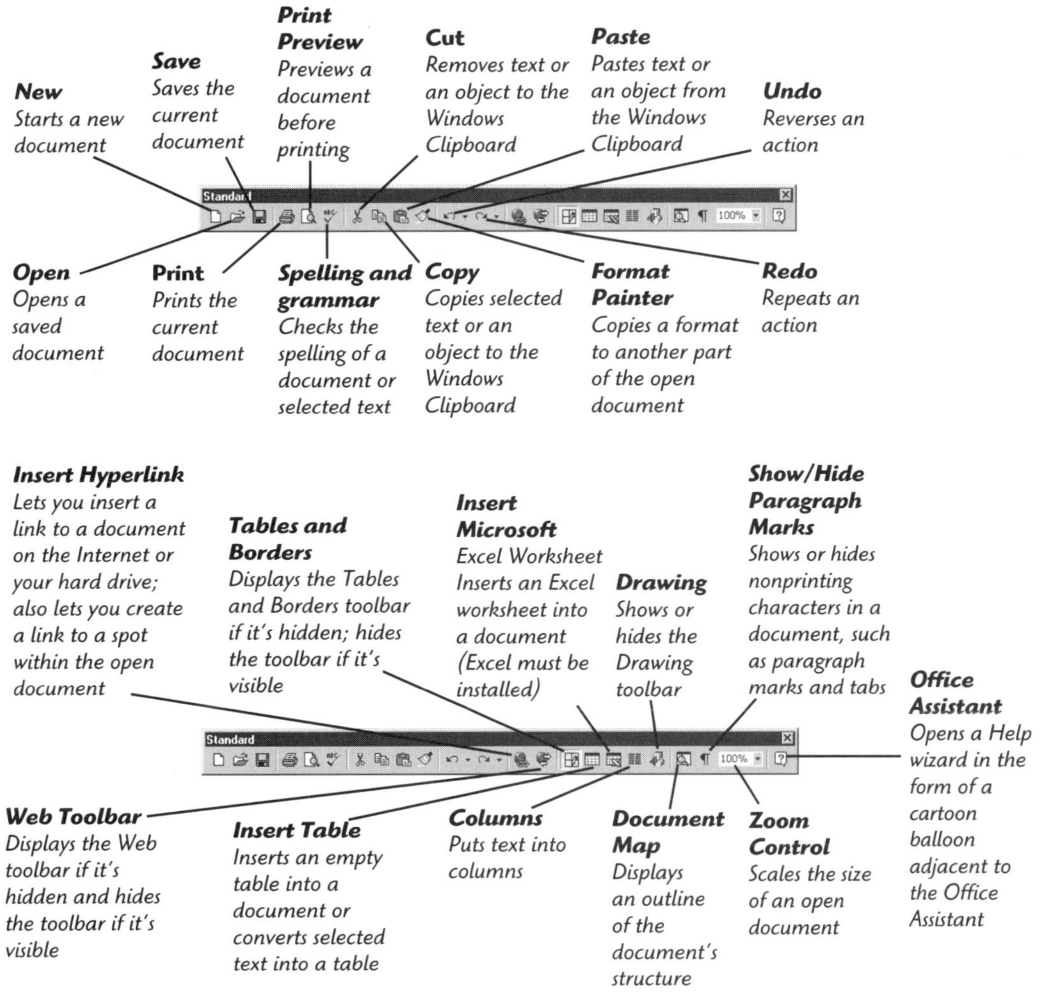

New Starts a new document
Save Saves the current document
Print Preview Previews a document before printing
Cut Removes text or an object to the Windows Clipboard
Paste Pastes text or an object from the Windows Clipboard
Undo Reverses an action
Standard
Open Opens a saved document
Print Prints the current document
Spelling and grammar Checks the spelling of a document or selected text
Copy Copies selected text or an object to the Windows Clipboard
Format Painter Copies a format to another part of the open document
Redo Repeats an action
Insert Hyperlink Lets you insert a link to a document on the Internet or your hard drive; also lets you create a link to a spot within the open document
Tables and Borders Displays the Tables and Borders toolbar if it's hidden; hides the toolbar if it's visible
Insert Microsoft Excel Worksheet Inserts an Excel worksheet into a document (Excel must be installed)
Drawing Shows or hides the Drawing toolbar
Show/Hide Paragraph Marks Shows or hides nonprinting characters in a document, such as paragraph marks and tabs
Office Assistant Opens a Help wizard in the form of a cartoon balloon adjacent to the Office Assistant
Standard
Web Toolbar Displays the Web toolbar if it's hidden and hides the toolbar if it's visible
Insert Table Inserts an empty table into a document or converts selected text into a table
Columns Puts text into columns
Document Map Displays an outline of the document's structure
Zoom Control Scales the size of an open document

The Formatting toolbar

The Formatting toolbar gives you easy access to commands that change the appearance of your document. The following graphics page gives you a quick look at the toolbar buttons and what they do.

Inside the Formatting toolbar

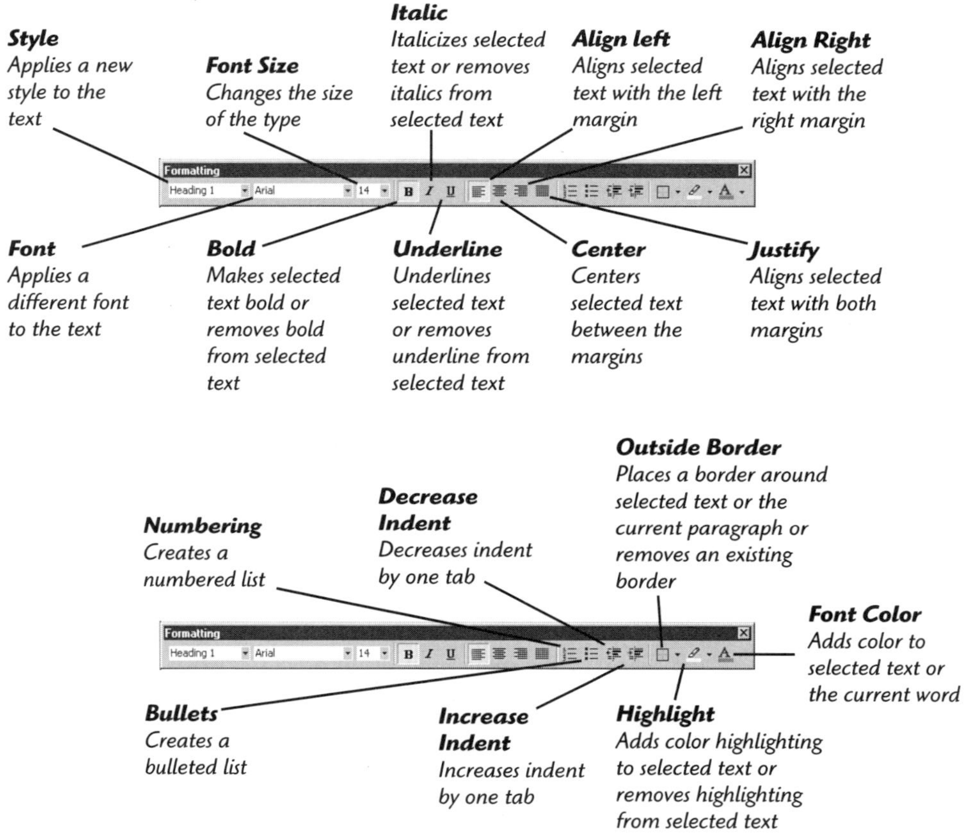
Style Applies a new style to the text
Font Size Changes the size of the type
Italic Italicizes selected text or removes italics from selected text
Align left Aligns selected text with the left margin
Align Right Aligns selected text with the right margin
Formatting
Heading 1
Arial
14
Font Applies a different font to the text
Bold Makes selected text bold or removes bold from selected text
Underline Underlines selected text or removes underline from selected text
Center Centers selected text between the margins
Justify Aligns selected text with both margins
Outside Border Places a border around selected text or the current paragraph or removes an existing border
Decrease Indent Decreases indent by one tab
Numbering Creates a numbered list
Font Color Adds color to selected text or the current word
Formatting
Heading 1
Arial
14
Bullets Creates a bulleted list
Increase Indent Increases indent by one tab
Highlight Adds color highlighting to selected text or removes highlighting from selected text

You'll spend a lot of time with this toolbar after you've learned how to create documents and want to spiff them up. But you can learn quite a few tricks on your own right now simply by clicking the various toolbar buttons, typing some text, and watching what happens.

TIP **Most of the buttons on the Formatting toolbar toggle on and off.** For example, if you want boldface, click the Bold button and start typing. When you want to revert to regular text, just click the Bold button again.

The Web toolbar

Best of 97

If you're on the World Wide Web, you'll like the new Web toolbar. It lets you log on to your favorite Web site or search the Web without leaving the confines of Word.

To use the toolbar, you must be able to access the Internet and have a browser, such as Microsoft's Internet Explorer 3.0, installed.

We're discussing the Web toolbar here because of the significant role it plays as a new feature, but if you don't need Internet access for your everyday work, ignore or hide this toolbar (you'll learn how to hide toolbars in a moment). You'll find information about how you can use Word's Internet-related features throughout this book, and you'll find complete instructions for Internet access in Chapter 25.

The roving toolbars and menu bar

Your toolbars and menu bar don't have to be at the top of the screen. You can put them anywhere in the Word window.

To move a bar to either side of the document window or to the bottom of the window, click the two dark gray lines, called the **handle**, at the far left end of the bar. Hold down the mouse button. The bar becomes bordered by a dotted line. Drag the bar to where you want it, then release the mouse button.

To move the menu bar or a toolbar inside the document window, use the same drag-and-drop method. The bar becomes a floating object that you can put anywhere on the screen (see Figure 1.4).

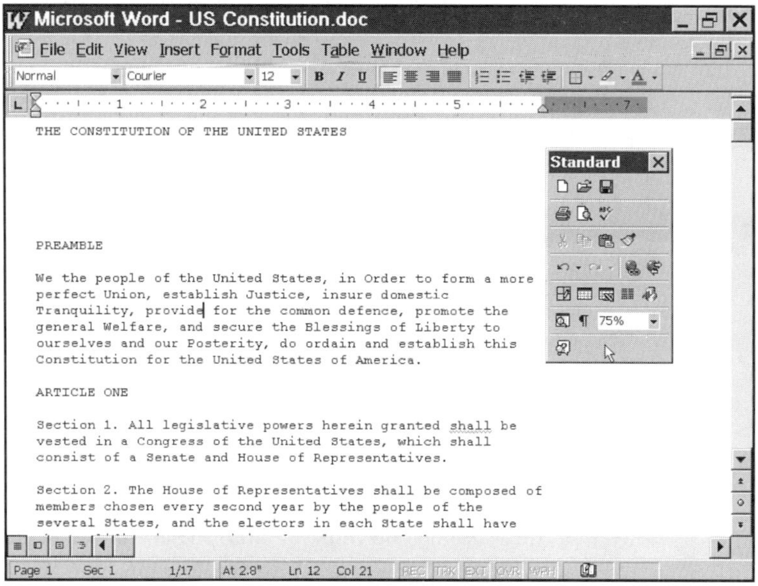
Microsoft Word - US Constitution.doc
File Edit View Insert Format Tools Table Window Help
Normal
Courier
12
THE CONSTITUTION OF THE UNITED STATES
Standard
75%
PREAMBLE
We the people of the United States, in Order to form a more perfect Union, establish Justice, insure domestic Tranquility, provide for the common defence, promote the general Welfare, and secure the Blessings of Liberty to ourselves and our Posterity, do ordain and establish this Constitution for the United States of America.
ARTICLE ONE
Section 1. All legislative powers herein granted shall be vested in a Congress of the United States, which shall consist of a Senate and House of Representatives.
Section 2. The House of Representatives shall be composed of members chosen every second year by the people of the several States, and the electors in each State shall have
Page 1 Sec 1 1/17 At 2.8" Ln 12 Col 21

Fig. 1.4
You can float the menu bar or a toolbar by dragging it into your document window.

To change the shape of a floating bar, eclick and drag the borders. To restore a bar to its original position, click the title bar or a gray space and drag it to the top of the window.

You'll probably want to keep the toolbars where they are until you've become familiar with them. But eventually, you'll find that for some jobs, a floating toolbar makes the toolbar more accessible and the document window larger.

Q&A ***These toolbar buttons look awfully small. Can I make them bigger?***

Sure. Choose View, Toolbars, Customize from the main menu. Word displays the Customize dialog box. Click the Options tab, choose Large buttons, and click Close.

Tons of toolbars

For the sake of simplicity, most of the sample screens in this book show only the Standard and Formatting toolbars. But Word has many other toolbars, including ones for creating tables and borders, drawing, and reviewing document revisions.

You can display or hide these toolbars as you need them. Choose View, Toolbars from the main menu or right-click a visible toolbar. Word pops up a list of toolbars. Put a check mark next to the ones you want Word to display. You can put these toolbars above the ruler or float them in the document window.

The ruler

If you're old enough to remember using a typewriter in typing class, the ruler should be familiar. It looks and acts a lot like the margin scale that sits behind a typewriter's platen. You use it for much the same thing—to set margins, tabs, and indents.

Q&A ***I don't have a ruler. How do I get one?***

Don't worry, it's only hiding. Choose View from the menu bar and choose Ruler.

Questions? Get help fast!

If Word is new to you, the feature you'll probably use most in the beginning is the Office Assistant. Microsoft has conveniently placed the Assistant in its own little window; when you click the window, Word displays a Help dialog balloon (see Figure 1.5). We'll take a close look at Word's Help functions in Chapter 3, but here are a few basics to get you started.

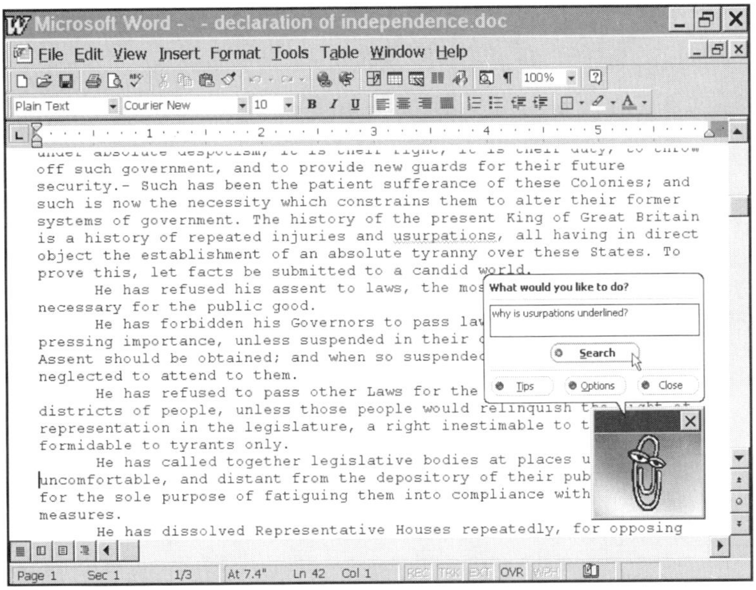
Microsoft Word - declaration of independence.doc
File Edit View Insert Format Tools Table Window Help
100%
Plain Text
Courier New
10
off such government, and to provide new guards for their future
security.- Such has been the patient sufferance of these Colonies; and
such is now the necessity which constrains them to alter their former
systems of government. The history of the present King of Great Britain
is a history of repeated injuries and usurpations, all having in direct
object the establishment of an absolute tyranny over these States. To
prove this, let facts be submitted to a candid world.
What would you like to do?
why is usurpations underlined?
Search
Tips
Options
Close
He has called together legislative bodies at places u
uncomfortable, and distant from the depository of their pub
for the sole purpose of fatiguing them into compliance with
measures.
He has dissolved Representative Houses repeatedly, for opposing
Page 1 Sec 1 1/3 At 7.4" Ln 42 Col 1 REC TRK EXT OVR WPH

Fig. 1.5
Click the Office Assistant window to display a Help dialog box. To make your life easier, Word lets you ask questions in plain English.

To get help on a specific topic, type a question in the text box and choose Search. Word displays a menu of possible topics from which you then choose.

Choose Tips to pop up a tip on how to use Word more effectively. Magically, Word usually provides help on whatever you happen to be doing in your document.

The Options button lets you configure the Assistant. Here's where you go to hide the Assistant if it starts to drive you crazy, choose what kinds of tips you want Word to display, and even pick a new animated character from a gallery of goofy cartoons.

If you hide the Assistant, you can display it again by pressing the F1 key or clicking the Office Assistant button on the Standard toolbar.

The view buttons

Moving to the bottom of the page, we have the view buttons, which are to the far left of the horizontal scroll bar (the gray bar just beneath the document window). These give you one-click access to four ways of viewing your document (Normal, Online Layout, Page Layout, and Outline). They're the same as the first four commands on the menu bar's View menu. Stick with Normal view unless you have a specific reason to choose one of the others.

The status bar

Next, we come to the status bar near the bottom of the screen (see Figure 1.6). Don't be fooled by its location; you'll find yourself referring often to this bar for important information about the current document.

Fig. 1.6
The status bar gives you basic information about the current document.

The status bar shown in Figure 1.6 displays this information:

- `Page 1`: The current page number.

- `Sec 1`: The section you're in. This becomes important only when you start dividing large documents into sections. Until then, it will always say Sec 1.
- `1/3`: The first number is the current page; the second is the total number of pages in the document.
- `At 6"`: Where your insertion point is, in inches, from the top of the page.
- `Ln 33`: Where your insertion point is, in lines, from the first line on the page.
- `Col 1`: Where your insertion point is, in characters, from the beginning of the line.

A word about modes

The five abbreviations at the right end of the status bar are called **mode indicators**. These indicators usually appear as gray buttons with chiseled gray lettering.

These buttons tell you when certain Word features are turned on or off. For example, if you press the Insert key, you change from Insert mode to Overtype mode, and the letters OVR (Overtype) turn black, as they are in Figure 1.5. If the Help for WordPerfect feature is turned on, the letters WPH (WordPerfect Help) are black.

The REC (Record Macro), TRK (Track Changes), and EXT (Extend Selection) buttons are for advanced uses, and you can ignore them for now.

TIP **To move from Insert to Overtype mode or vice versa, double-click** the OVR button on the status bar. Similarly, double-clicking the other mode buttons either switches modes or calls up a dialog box that lets you set options for that mode.

The Windows taskbar

The Windows taskbar shown beneath the Word window on the graphics page is a part of Windows, not Word. It gives you one-click access to other programs you have running at the same time, as well as to the Start button.

Whether the taskbar appears on your screen depends on how you've got Windows set up. If the taskbar is not visible, you can make it so by moving the mouse pointer to the border at the bottom of the Word window until it turns into a two-headed arrow, clicking your mouse button, and pulling the border up like a window shade. To hide the taskbar, do the opposite.

If you can't find the taskbar at the bottom of the Word window, try looking at the sides and the top. The taskbar is movable, so it won't be in the same place on all computers.

Most of the screens in this book do not show the taskbar.

Insertion points and other moving objects

The two most important moving objects on the screen are the **insertion point** and the **mouse pointer**.

Word's insertion point is a blinking, vertical bar that marks the spot where you're typing. When you press a key, Word inserts the character after the insertion point.

You can move the insertion point around the document using the arrow keys and the Page keys, or with the mouse. More on navigating your document in a moment.

The mouse pointer

The mouse pointer is a bit of a shape-shifter; it changes shape and function depending on where you are on the screen and what you're doing. Inside the document window, it looks like an I-bar. If you click the mouse button in your text, the insertion point moves to where the I-bar is located.

The mouse pointer changes to the familiar arrow when you move parts of the screen other than the document window. The pointer can also assume other guises for special tasks, such as when you're dragging text or moving borders. You'll learn more about these other shapes as we go along. Table 1.1 lists some of the more common pointers you're likely to encounter.

Table 1.1 Some well-appointed pointers

Pointer Shape	What It Means
	You can move the insertion point to a new place in the text or select text and graphics. This **I-beam** marks the point where the insertion point will be placed.
	You can select objects outside the document window, such as toolbar icons, menu items, and dialog box buttons.
	You can select blocks of text from the space to the left of the left margin; you can also select a table cell from the space between the left border and the cell text.
	You can click and drag in the direction the arrow is pointing to stretch or shrink an object.
	You can drag and drop selected text.

The end-of-document marker

When you're in Normal view, you'll see what looks like an insertion point lying on its back underneath the last line of the document. The only time this end-of-document marker has any real use is when you need to see how many blank lines you've got between the last line of your text and the end of the document.

Choose your weapon!

Some people like using the mouse, while others prefer the keyboard. Each method has its advantages.

The mouse is easier to use because you don't have to remember a sequence of instructions or key combinations; you just point and click. On the other hand, key combinations are sometimes quicker because you don't have to take your hands off the keyboard when you're typing.

Recognizing that we live in a multifarious culture, the people at Microsoft generously accommodate both preferences. In fact, they give you four ways to handle Word's most common and important tasks:

- You can click the toolbar button.
- You can click the menu bar.
- You can press the Alt key plus the underlined letter of the menu item and then the underlined letter of the command.
- You can use a keyboard combination.

The following table gives you the four options for Word's most-used commands. If you want to be a truly adroit Word whacker, learn them all. With practice, you'll instinctively use the method that's quickest and easiest, depending on what you're doing.

To do this...	Click this icon	Or choose this command	Or press these keys	Or use these keyboard shortcuts
Get new file		File, New	Alt+F, N	Ctrl+N
Open file		File, Open	Alt+F, O	Ctrl+O
Save file		File, Save	Alt+F, S	Ctrl+S
Print file		File, Print	Alt+F, P	Ctrl+P
Undo		Edit, Undo	Alt+E, U	Ctrl+Z
Cut		Edit, Cut	Alt+E, T	Ctrl+X
Copy		Edit, Copy	Alt+E, C	Ctrl+C
Paste		Edit, Paste	Alt+E, P	Ctrl+V
Spelling and Grammar		Tools, Spelling and Grammar	Alt+T, S	F7

TIP **You can learn keyboard shortcuts more quickly by displaying them** in your ScreenTips. Go to the Customize dialog box (choose View, Toolbars, Customize from the main menu). Under the Options tab, put a check mark next to Show Shortcut Keys in ScreenTips and choose Close. From now on when you touch a button, Word shows the name of the button and, if one is available, the corresponding keyboard shortcut.

Word to the max

Let's take a look at how to manipulate the window itself. After all, windows wouldn't be windows if you couldn't expand, shrink, move, size, dematerialize, and otherwise bend them to your will (see Figure 1.7).

Fig. 1.7
The screen elements that you'll work with most are shown here.

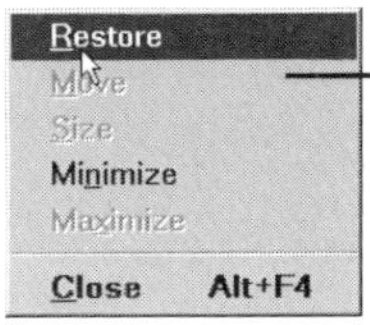

Restore
Move
Size
Minimize
Maximize
Close Alt+F4

When you click the Word Control Menu button, Word pops up a menu you can use to manipulate the window from the keyboard. For a quick shortcut, double-click to exit Word altogether.

When you have an open document, click here to display the Document Control menu. Double-click to close just this document.

You can manipulate either the ***application window*** *(Word itself) using the top set of buttons, or the* ***document window*** *(your current document) using the bottom set of buttons. The screen elements that you work with the most are shown here.*

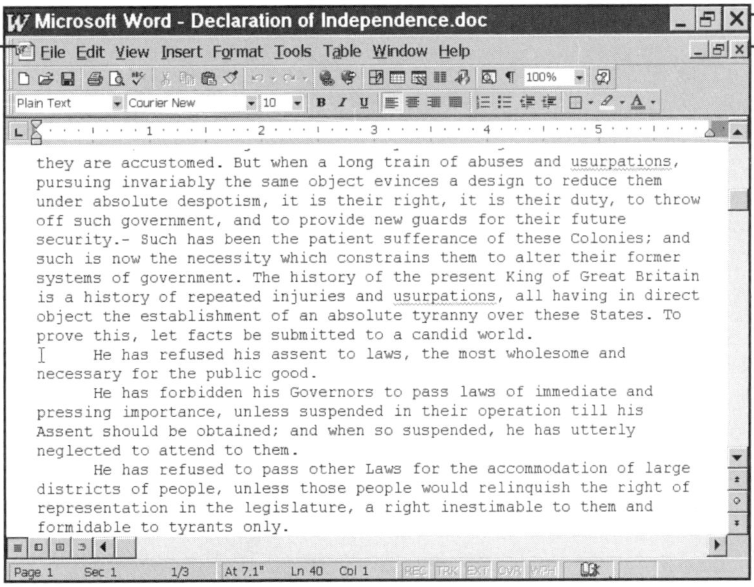

Microsoft Word - Declaration of Independence.doc
File Edit View Insert Format Tools Table Window Help
100%
Plain Text
Courier New
10
they are accustomed. But when a long train of abuses and usurpations, pursuing invariably the same object evinces a design to reduce them under absolute despotism, it is their right, it is their duty, to throw off such government, and to provide new guards for their future security.- Such has been the patient sufferance of these Colonies; and such is now the necessity which constrains them to alter their former systems of government. The history of the present King of Great Britain is a history of repeated injuries and usurpations, all having in direct object the establishment of an absolute tyranny over these States. To prove this, let facts be submitted to a candid world.
He has refused his assent to laws, the most wholesome and necessary for the public good.
He has forbidden his Governors to pass laws of immediate and pressing importance, unless suspended in their operation till his Assent should be obtained; and when so suspended, he has utterly neglected to attend to them.
He has refused to pass other Laws for the accommodation of large districts of people, unless those people would relinquish the right of representation in the legislature, a right inestimable to them and formidable to tyrants only.
Page 1 Sec 1 1/3 At 7.1" Ln 40 Col 1 REC TRK EXT OVR WPH

Word Control
Click this button or press Alt+space bar for a menu that gives you options for sizing and moving the Word window.

Document Control
Click this button to open the Document Control menu, which lets you move or resize the window for just that document.

Minimize Word
What happens when you Minimize depends on how you have Windows 95 set up. If your taskbar is visible, your Word window disappears, but Word remains as a button on the taskbar. You restore Word by clicking the taskbar button.

If your taskbar is not visible, Word simply vanishes. You can recall it by pressing Alt+Tab.

Minimize Document
Same deal. Click the Minimize Document button to tuck just this document away until you're ready for it; Word itself (and any other open documents) stay put.

Maximize Word
If Word is not maximized (that is, it doesn't fill your entire screen), this button is a **Maximize button**. Click it to make Word fill the entire screen and cover any other open windows.

Maximize Document
If your document is not maximized, click this button to make the document fill the entire Word window (whether or not Word itself is maximized).

Restore Word
If Word *is* maximized, click this button to return the Word window to its previous size and shape. For example, if Word had been sized to take half a screen but now takes the entire screen, click the Restore button to return Word to half a screen.

Restore Document
The Restore Document button returns the document window to whatever size it was before it was maximized.

Close Word
Click the Close button to exit Word and any open documents.

Close Document

If you want to close this document but leave Word running for later use, click the lower X button.

Changing your document window

You can manipulate your document window separately from your Word window.

Your document window has its own Control menu box, at the far left of the menu bar. When you click it, you get a menu from which you can size and move the document window.

You can also click the Maximize/Restore button at the other end of the menu bar.

Naming your document

Working with an untitled document is a dangerous practice. If the power should go out or if someone trips over the cord and unplugs your computer, you could lose your document. Get in the habit of naming and saving your file immediately.

We'll examine file-saving and file-naming options in Chapter 4. For now, though, let's look at the quick-and-dirty way to name your file.

Press Ctrl+S to pop up the Save As dialog box (see Figure 1.8). Word suggests a file name in the File Name text box.

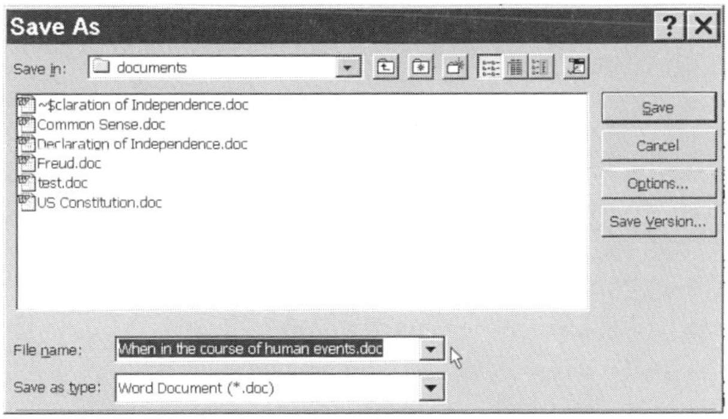

Fig. 1.8
Press Ctrl+S for the Save As dialog box. Word automatically gives a new file a file name based on the first characters of text.

If the document is empty, the suggested file name is `Doc1.doc`. If `Doc1.doc` already exists, Word suggests the next default name, `Doc2.doc`, and so on.

If the document contains text, the suggested file name consists of the first 234 characters and spaces of the document, unless Word first encounters a non-alphanumeric character or an end-of-paragraph marker.

In Figure 1.8, for example, the file name is comprised of the characters up to the comma following "events."

Click Save to accept the suggested file name. If you want a different file name, just type it into the File Name text box. The suggested file name disappears when you begin typing.

Bailing out

When you and Word have had enough of each other, close it either by clicking twice on the Control menu box at the far left of the title bar, clicking the Close button in the upper right corner, or pressing Ctrl+F4. Word asks you if you want to save your open documents. Choose Yes to save them, and No to exit Word.

2

Creating a Document: First Steps

In this chapter:

- **Doing the write thing: rules for typing and formatting**
- **On the move with arrow keys, scroll bars, and other navigational tools**
- **If you've got to go, Go To**
- **How do I get more of my document on the screen?**
- **Inserting and deleting text—the basics**
- **Let Word format your document using templates and wizards**

Starting a new document in Word isn't much more complicated than starting one with a typewriter and paper . . . .

A new word processor is easier to learn than just about any other type of program you can buy. You don't need to know any special codes, languages, conventions, or rules to get going; you just start typing. A word followed by a word followed by another word eventually leads you to sentences, paragraphs, and, yes, entire documents.

Of course, you do need to learn at least a few rules if you want attractively formatted text. But the basics are rooted so much in common sense that you'll probably understand most of them intuitively. If you've ever laid hands on a keyboard, you've won half the battle.

The basic rules of typing and formatting

Your first document doesn't have to be anything fancy—perhaps a letter to Mom or a list of this weekend's errands. Feel free to experiment with the keyboard. Try typing short sentences, long paragraphs, lines of characters without spaces, and lines of spaces without characters.

For now, stay away from the Ctrl, Alt, and function keys (F1 through F12). Word uses many of these keys to run commands and open dialog boxes, some of which you might not understand how to use yet. We'll discuss these special keys throughout this book.

Q&A ***Oops! I accidentally pressed some keys that took me out of my document and someplace strange. How do I get back to my document?***

If you happened to open a dialog box, just click the Cancel button or press the Esc key. If you're in a menu or a text box (such as the Style, Font, and Font Size boxes on the Standard toolbar), press the Esc key.

If you press a bunch of keys and the computer beeps at you when you press the Enter key, just press the Esc key a couple of times. You should be able to regain control of your keyboard.

As you fill your screen with text, pay special attention to the behavior of your keyboard. Note what keys result in what action. Then read the following information about the keyboard and see how much you found out for yourself.

CAUTION **As you use keyboard combinations more regularly, you're likely** to encounter one of the Alt key's little foibles: If you press and release it without pressing another key, your keyboard might seem as if it's locked up. For example, if you press Alt with the intent of displaying a menu (Alt+F for File, for instance), change your mind, release the key, and press Delete, nothing happens. Other keys that apparently "freeze" your keyboard include Insert, Home, End, Page Up, Page Down, and Backspace. To regain control of your keyboard, press the Alt key again or the Esc key.

The Enter key: the end of paragraphs as we know them

The Enter key (or Return key on some keyboards) is the same as the carriage return on a manual typewriter, only without the sound of the little bell and the "ka-chunk" of the carriage-return lever. In Figure 2.1, the Enter key is indicated by the paragraph mark (¶).

On a typewriter, you have to return the carriage after every line. Not so with Word. When Word can't fit any more text on a line, it automatically drops subsequent text to the next line. (This is called **word wrap** in word processing parlance.) You need to press Enter only at the end of a complete paragraph, as shown in the body of the letter in Figure 2.1.

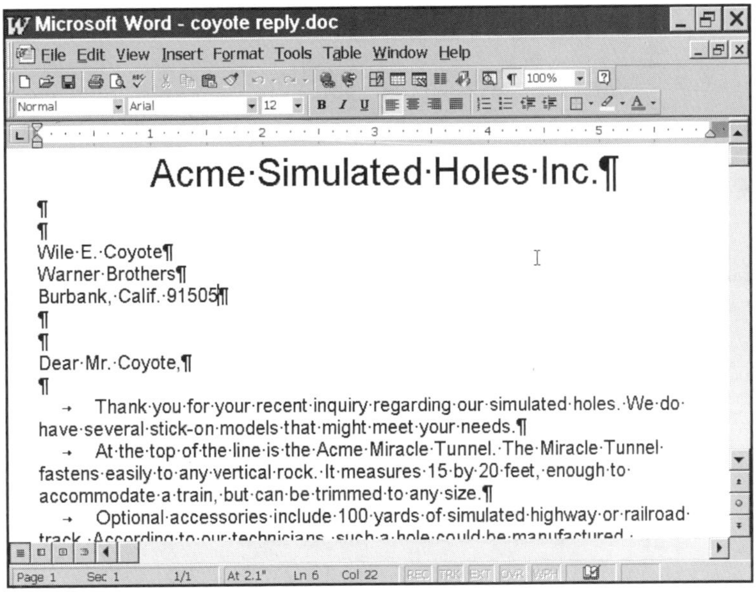

Fig. 2.1
Press the Enter key, represented in this document by the paragraph mark (¶), to end a paragraph or each item in a list, and to insert blank lines.

You press the Enter key for two other reasons: to end a short line, such as those in the address in Figure 2.1, and to insert a line space, such as between the address and the salutation.

CAUTION **Don't press the Enter key at the end of each line in a paragraph.** If you insert carriage returns manually, you will be unable to properly format and edit your document later.

Q&A ***I want to double space my document. How do I do it without pressing the Enter key twice after each line?***

Word has a number of ways to vary the amount of space between lines, and we'll go over them in detail in Chapter 9, "Formatting Paragraphs and Blocks." The quick and easy way to double space is to press Ctrl+2 and start typing. When you want to go back to single space, press Ctrl+1.

What about the IntelliMouse?

Best of 97

If you own Microsoft's new IntelliMouse, you'll have access to a few new Word 97 features that are unavailable to users of a regular mouse.

The IntelliMouse looks the same as the old mouse, with one exception: It includes a wheel between the two buttons. This wheel has two main purposes: It lets you scroll the document without using the vertical scroll bar, and you can enlarge or shrink the document without using Zoom Control on the Standard toolbar.

We'll review these functions in the sections on browsing and zooming in this chapter.

The Tab key: new paragraphs and text alignment

The Tab key works like the one on a typewriter and serves much the same purpose. The tabs in Figure 2.1 are represented by bold right arrows (→). The Tab key has two main uses:

- To indent the first line of a new paragraph, as in the body of the memo shown in Figure 2.1
- To align text in a simple table

When you begin a new document, Word gives you tab stops at half-inch intervals. These default stops appear as tiny lines on the gray area between the ruler and the document. (Don't confuse them with the dots and lines on the ruler itself, which are 1/8-inch markers.) You'll learn later how to set and clear tab stops.

TIP ¶ **To display the paragraph, tab, and space symbols you see in** the document in Figure 2.1, click the Show/Hide Paragraph Marks button on the Standard toolbar.

The basic rules of moving around the screen

You'll undoubtedly want to make corrections, changes, and additions as you type, which means that you need to move your insertion point around the screen. The arrow keys are the most obvious tools, but by themselves, they can move the insertion point only one character or line at a time. You'll find it far more efficient to use Word's many shortcuts that let you leap over text to get to where you want to go more quickly.

TIP **You should practice using the arrow keys automatically and** without peeking, even if you're a confirmed mouser. The mouse has lots of uses, but the arrow keys are better for moving short distances.

Q&A ***The keys on the number pad have arrows, but when I press them, all I get are numbers. How do I make the arrows work?***

Num Lock is on; press the Num Lock key to turn it off. This also activates the keys that have labels such as Home, End, Ins, and Del. Press the Num Lock key again to reactivate the number pad.

Ctrling your destiny

The arrow keys begin to shine when you combine them with the Ctrl key. Try moving your insertion point with these keyboard shortcuts:

One word forward	Ctrl+right arrow
One word back	Ctrl+left arrow
To start of paragraph	Ctrl+up arrow
To start of next paragraph	Ctrl+down arrow

The Home and End keys

The Home and End keys take you to the beginning and end of a line, respectively. *Learn these keys.* Their functions might seem trivial now, but you'll be surprised at how often you need to go from one side of your document to the other.

The Home and End keys become doubly important when you learn to combine them with the Ctrl keys. Use these combinations:

To top of document	Ctrl+Home
To bottom of document	Ctrl+End

Pinpoint accuracy with the mouse

The mouse pointer is a good tool for moving to a place in the middle of your document. Just position the pointer where you want to put the insertion point and click the mouse button.

Moving around in big documents

Arrow keys and simple key combinations are effective ways of moving around the part of the document you can see. But they're not so great for documents that are longer than a page or two.

How do you move quickly through three or four pages? Go from page 2 to page 20 in a single bound? Or find that elusive heading somewhere between pages 12 and 18 without hitting the down arrow line after tedious line?

Word gives you a variety of rapid-transit options. For convenience, we'll divide them into two categories: browsers and pointers.

Browsers are like the arrow buttons on your TV remote control, letting you surf through pages of text at a time.

Pointers, on the other hand, are like the remote's number pad, letting you go directly to a specific spot in your document.

Browsing your document

Use the keyboard's Page Up and Page Down keys to move up or down one screen. The actual number of lines you move varies, depending upon your type size and screen configuration.

The insertion point stays in the same position relative to the top of the screen. If it's on the fifth line from the top on the current screen, it'll be on the fifth line from the top on the next one.

In addition, you can use the Ctrl and Page keys to move your insertion point to the top of the previous or next page. Use these combinations:

To first line of previous page	Ctrl+Page Up
To first line of next page	Ctrl+Page Down

Using the mouse to browse

When you use the Page keys, the insertion point moves with you. If you want to keep your insertion point where it is while you browse, use the **vertical scroll bar**.

The vertical scroll bar is the long gray bar to the right of your document window (see Figure 2.2). Inside is a sliding box called a **scroll box**. Click anywhere above the scroll box to move up one screen and anywhere below the box to move down one screen. The text moves through your document window while your insertion point stays where you left it.

Click the scroll bar arrows to move a line at a time. Unlike when you use the arrow keys, the insertion point stays where you left it. To return to your insertion point, press one of the arrow keys. To move to a new spot on the current screen, point and click with your mouse.

For your browsing pleasure

Best of 97

In previous versions of Word, the vertical scroll bar restricted you to moving by the line, screen, or page. Not any more. In Word 97, you can use the Select Browse Object button, near the bottom of the vertical scroll bar, to choose your own unit by which you wish to move.

Fig. 2.2
The vertical scroll bar lets you use your mouse to move lines or screens at a time.

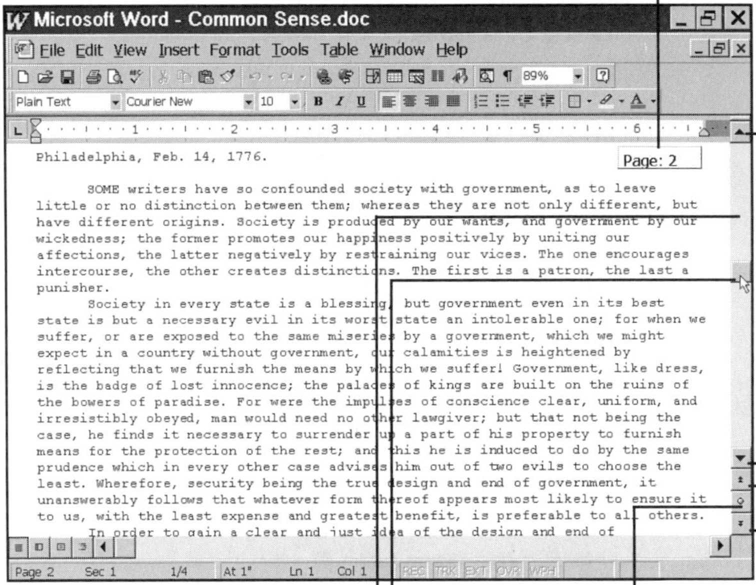
Microsoft Word - Common Sense.doc
File Edit View Insert Format Tools Table Window Help
Plain Text
Courier New
10
89%
Page: 2
Philadelphia, Feb. 14, 1776.
Page 2 Sec 1 1/4 At 1" Ln 1 Col 1
REC TRK EXT OVR WPH
Word shows the page number when you click the scroll box
Click the scroll bar arrows to move one line at a time
Click the Previous and Next buttons to move to the previous or next item selected from the Select Browse Object menu. If you have not selected an item, these buttons take you to the previous or next page.
Click once above or below the scroll box to scroll your document a screen at a time
Click and drag the scroll box to move rapidly to another page in your document
Click the Select Browse Object button to display a menu of items by which you may browse with the Previous and Next buttons

You won't need Select Browse Object to navigate short, simple documents. But it will become a valuable scrolling tool as your documents become longer and more complex.

Let's say, for example, that one day you write a 120-page report made up of 45 parts, each with its own heading. Select Browse Object gives you an easy way to move from one heading to the next.

To see how Select Browse Object works, click the Select Browse Object button near the bottom of the vertical scroll bar. Word displays a small window of icons representing such items as edits, fields, comments, footnotes, and tables. To scroll by headings, click the Browse by Heading icon. Thereafter, clicking the Previous and Next buttons takes you to the previous and next headings, respectively.

If you don't select an item by which to move, the Previous and Next buttons move you one page at a time.

TIP **To move quickly to another page in your document, click the** scroll box and drag it. As you move the scroll box down the vertical scroll bar, Word sequentially displays the page numbers in a ScreenTip. When you reach the page you want, release the mouse button, and Word takes you to that page.

Q&A ***Why is there a scroll bar on the bottom of my screen? When would I need to scroll a document horizontally?***

You use the horizontal scroll bar for extra-wide documents. For example, you might have a document that you're printing lengthwise in which the right margin is out of view. Or if you enlarge your document view with Zoom Control on your Standard toolbar, your text might become too big to fit in the document window. You use the horizontal scroll bar the same way you do the vertical scroll bar.

Another mouse trick

Here's another way to move quickly through your document with the mouse. Place your mouse pointer in your document, hold down the mouse button, and drag up or down the screen. The text you scan becomes highlighted.

When you reach your destination, release the mouse button and click it again or press the right or down arrow. To return to where you started, release the mouse button and press the left or up arrow.

There's an IntelliMouse in the house!

Best of 97

Several of the simpler scrolling functions are built into the IntelliMouse, saving you the trouble of clicking the scroll bar with your mouse pointer.

- To scroll a few lines at a time, rotate the IntelliMouse wheel forward or backward. The number of lines will depend on the size of your type and your Zoom Control settings.
- If you want to scroll continuously through your document—a technique called panning—hold down the wheel button. Your mouse pointer turns

into a double-headed arrow called the **origin mark**. Drag the pointer above or below the origin mark. Your pointer will change into a heavy black arrow pointing in the direction you're scrolling. Once your document starts scrolling, you don't need to continue to move your mouse; just keep the wheel button down. Move the pointer away from the origin mark to speed scrolling and toward the origin mark to slow it down.

- You don't need to hold down the wheel button if you don't want to; the IntelliMouse also lets you **autoscroll**. Quickly press the wheel button and release it. Your origin mark appears in your vertical scroll bar. Scroll your document the same way you would if you were panning.

Pointers: stopping on a dime with Go To

The larger the document, the less effective the scroll bars and keyboard. What you need is Word's transporter beam, Go To.

The Edit, Go To command lets you go directly to any part of the document. You execute Go To by pressing the F5 key or Ctrl+G, double-clicking any part of the status bar to the left of the mode buttons, or clicking the Select Browse Object button and choosing the Go To icon. Word displays the Go To panel of the Find and Replace dialog box (see Figure 2.3).

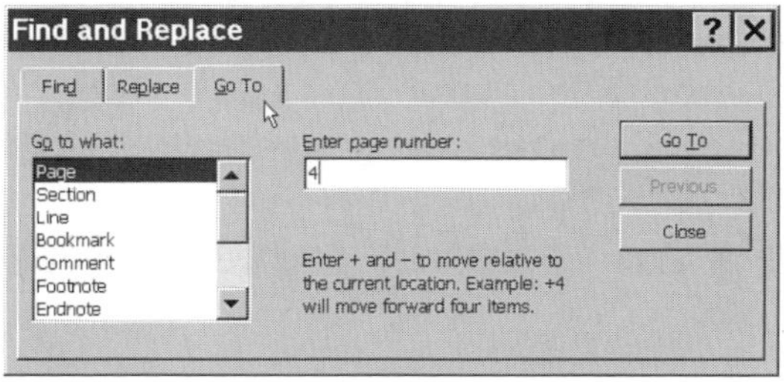

Fig. 2.3
Go To lets you beam directly to any place in your document. Here, selecting Go To moves the insertion point to the top of page 4.

The Go To What selection box gives you a list of items in your document to which you can jump. If you're a beginner, you probably will find Page and Find the most useful. Go To will become much more powerful when you've learned how to take advantage of such features as bookmarks, sections, comments, and headings.

For now, let's see how Go To moves you to a specific page. You simply type the number of the page you want to go to in the Enter Page Number box. The Next button changes into a Go To button. Click this button or press "Enter," and Word takes you to the top of the target page. You can enter another page number and go to new pages from this location, or you can click the Close button to close the dialog box.

TIP **Go To is great for finding a specific line in a long list. For example,** if you choose Line in the Go To What box and type **188** in the Enter Line Number box, Word takes you to line 188 of the document.

Labeling parts of a document with Bookmarks

Remember the college professor who lectured from a text that had about fifty bookmarks sticking out of it? Word has an electronic equivalent, appropriately called a **bookmark**. Like their little paper counterparts, you use Word's bookmarks to quickly flip to parts of your document.

You use a bookmark to name a piece of text; a heading, table, or page, for example. You then use the Go To command to move your insertion point to that bookmark. In Figure 2.4, choosing the bookmark `article12` and clicking Go To moves the insertion point to the location with that name.

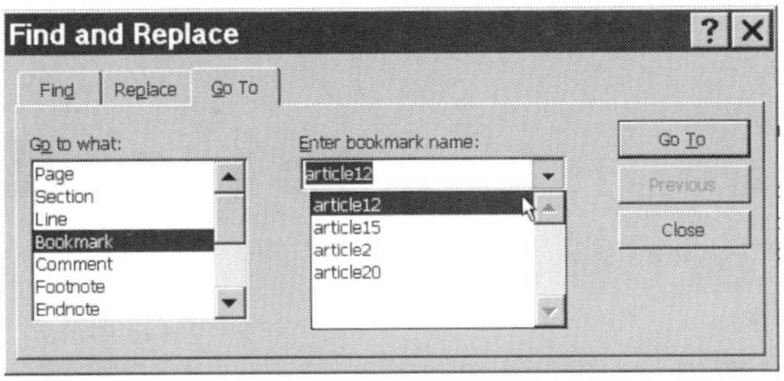

Fig. 2.4
In this Go To panel, choosing Go To moves the insertion point to a section of the document named `article12`.

Creating a bookmark in your document is easy. Go to the place in your document where you want the bookmark. Choose Insert, Bookmark from the menu bar. In the Bookmark dialog box, type a label in the Bookmark Name text box and click Add (see Figure 2.5). (Word won't accept spaces in a bookmark name.)

Use your bookmarks to:

- Mark your place when you close a document.
- Mark text that you want to revise later.
- Mark tables and text that you need to get to quickly.

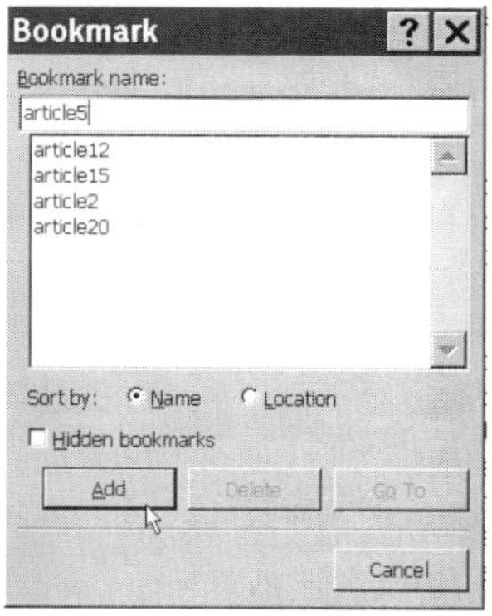

Fig. 2.5
Create a bookmark by choosing Insert, Bookmark and typing a label in the Bookmark Name text box.

TIP **If you're trying to step through a whole bunch of bookmarks in a** document, returning to the Go To panel for each one gets tedious fast. There's a way to jump to the next bookmark with one mouse click. When you choose the first bookmark you want to go to, the Previous and Next arrows in the vertical status bar change to blue. Thereafter, clicking one of the arrows takes you to the previous or next bookmark, until you use Go To to find some other item or choose another object with the Select Browse Object button.

Panoramic screens: how to get a larger view of your document

If typewriters have an advantage (besides the compelling aroma of ribbon ink), it's that you can see the entire page of a document. In contrast, scanning a page in Word is a little like watching a big-screen movie one-eyed through a toilet paper tube. You can focus on detail, but it's tough to get an idea of what the particulars will look like when they're combined into one image.

Word has a couple of tools that can help you overcome this tunnel vision. You can increase the size of your document window and decrease the size of your type. Do both, and you can nearly triple the number of lines on your screen.

Fill the screen with your document window

To expand your document window, choose View, Full Screen from the menu bar. All of your menus and bars disappear (see Figure 2.6). A window labeled Full Screen appears in the lower right-hand corner. Click the Close Full Screen button or press Alt+C to return to your previous screen setup.

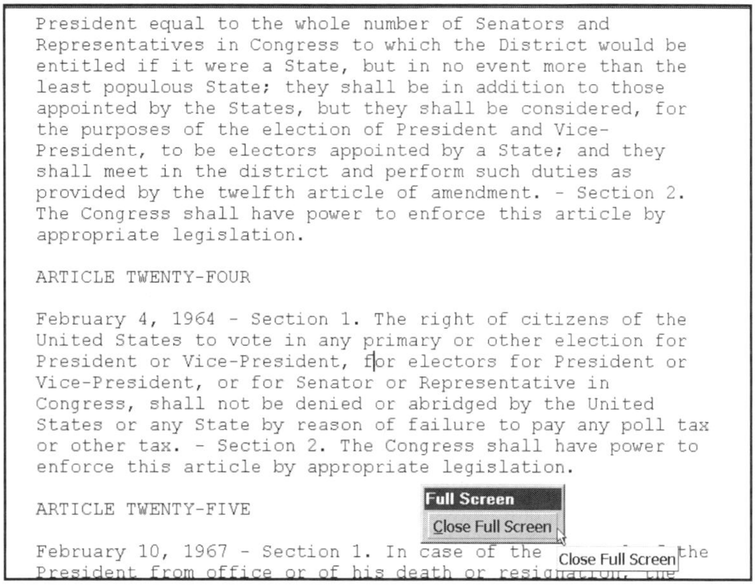

President equal to the whole number of Senators and Representatives in Congress to which the District would be entitled if it were a State, but in no event more than the least populous State; they shall be in addition to those appointed by the States, but they shall be considered, for the purposes of the election of President and Vice-President, to be electors appointed by a State; and they shall meet in the district and perform such duties as provided by the twelfth article of amendment. - Section 2. The Congress shall have power to enforce this article by appropriate legislation.

ARTICLE TWENTY-FOUR

February 4, 1964 - Section 1. The right of citizens of the United States to vote in any primary or other election for President or Vice-President, for electors for President or Vice-President, or for Senator or Representative in Congress, shall not be denied or abridged by the United States or any State by reason of failure to pay any poll tax or other tax. - Section 2. The Congress shall have power to enforce this article by appropriate legislation.

ARTICLE TWENTY-FIVE

February 10, 1967 - Section 1. In case of the ... the

Fig. 2.6
If you choose View, Full Screen, you hide everything except your document. Click the Close Full Screen button to bring it all back.

Q&A *When I'm in a full screen, how am I supposed to access my menu?*

You can display the menu bar by touching the top of the screen with your mouse pointer. When you move your pointer back into the document window, the menu bar disappears again. The menus are also available from the keyboard; Alt+F for the File menu, for example.

Reduce the size of the page

You can reduce the size of the page to as little as 10 percent of the original. Of course, this much shrinking will cause your document to nearly disappear. But a more modest reduction is readable for short periods of time.

This trick is useful when you need to move blocks of type around or if you want to view a large table or picture.

On the Standard toolbar at the far right, you'll see a box called `Zoom Control`, usually with `100%` in it (refer to Figure 2.5). Click this box, and type a smaller percentage or choose one from the list.

Figure 2.7 combines Full Screen with Zoom Control set to 75 percent. In this case, the type is 12-point Courier. Your typeface and point size will determine how much you can reduce a page and still read it.

Fig. 2.7
By combining Full Screen with a reduced page, you can get nearly a full page on the screen. Touch the top of the screen to display the menu bar.

TIP **Using Zoom Control to change the view of a page doesn't affect** how the printed document will look.

IntelliZooming with the IntelliMouse

If you use an IntelliMouse, there's a faster way to zoom your document. Press the Ctrl key and rotate the wheel button, down to shrink the document and up to enlarge it. Each wheel rotation shrinks or enlarges the document by 10 percent.

Deleting and inserting text made easy

Somewhere, there's a parallel dimension in which people always write perfect sentences and never make typing errors. Words like "fix" and "correct" don't exist. But in our flawed universe, changing what we've written is a fact of life.

Word includes a variety of editing tools for those of us with fumbling fingers and stammering brains. For now, we'll concern ourselves with the most basic methods for deleting and inserting text. We'll discuss alternative and advanced techniques in more detail in Chapter 5, "How to Delete, Move, Copy, and Change Your Text."

Deleting characters

The two keys you use most often to delete a few characters at a time are Backspace and Delete.

The **Backspace** key erases the character you just typed. It also erases tabs and paragraph markers.

The **Delete** key erases the character that follows the insertion point. It, too, erases tabs and paragraph markers.

We'll talk about key combinations that delete words, lines, and blocks of text in Chapter 5.

The Insert key and the Overtype mode

The Insert key moves you between Insert and Overtype modes. When you're in Insert mode and press a key, Word inserts the character to the left of the insertion point. When you're in Overtype mode and press a key, Word *replaces* the character that follows the insertion point with the new character.

You can move between the two modes by clicking the mode indicator on the status bar, although pressing the Insert key is usually faster.

You can tell which mode you're in by the OVR mode indicator on right end of the status bar. When the letters OVR are gray, you're inserting; when they're black, you're overtyping.

TIP **Use the Insert mode and switch to Overtype mode only when you** need to. You're less likely to accidentally type over existing text.

Starting a second document

Today's compact-disc players are changers that can hold many CDs, any of which you can play at any time. Similarly, Word can hold many documents, all available when you need them.

The easiest way to start a new document is to click the New button on the Standard toolbar or press Ctrl+N. A fresh page opens immediately.

You can also choose File, New from the menu bar. This is a bit trickier, but offers more options. When you choose File, New, Word presents you with the New dialog box shown in Figure 2.8. The icon labeled Blank Document in this dialog box represents a generic document. Clicking it is the same as clicking the New button on the Standard toolbar.

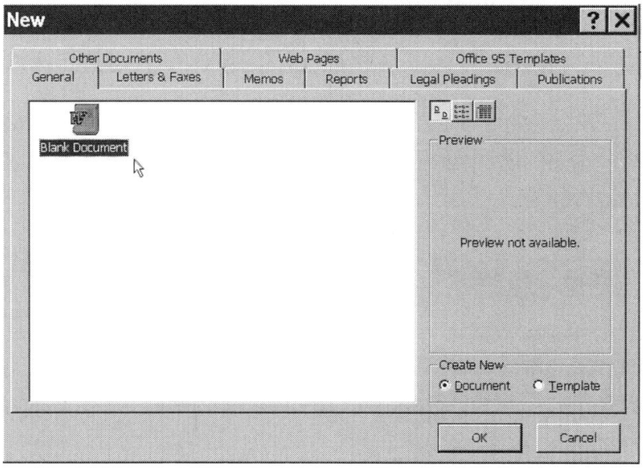

Fig. 2.8
The New dialog box lets you start a new document, even if you already have one open.

TIP **When you open a new document, the first one tucks itself away** until you recall it. You move between the two documents by pressing Ctrl+F6. You can also choose Window from the menu bar to display a list of all your open documents. Display any document by pressing the number that precedes it.

Formatting documents with templates and wizardry

Word can't do your writing for you. But it does give you a variety of prefab forms that can save you the trouble of formatting generic documents such as letters and résumés. You don't have to worry about setting your margins, where to put your text, or what typeface you want. Just click and type; Word does the grunt work.

You open a form from the New dialog box. For example, if you click the Other Documents tab, you can choose from among the forms shown in Figure 2.9.

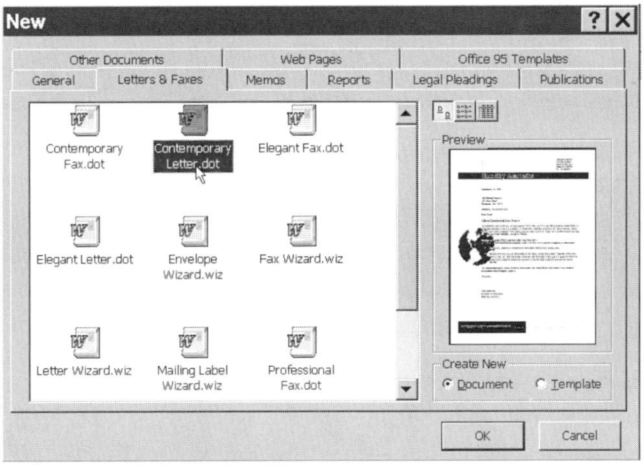

Fig. 2.9
Word gives you a variety of preformatted forms that spare you the drudgery of preparing documents from scratch.

Word gives you two types of forms—templates and wizards.

Templates

A **template** is a preformatted document in which you fill in blanks or replace dummy text. For example, if you choose the Contemporary Résumé template, Word presents you with the résumé for someone named Deborah Greer (see Figure 2.10). Word tells you where to type your address and career objective, and you replace the rest of the information with your own (unless, of course, you *are* Deborah Greer).

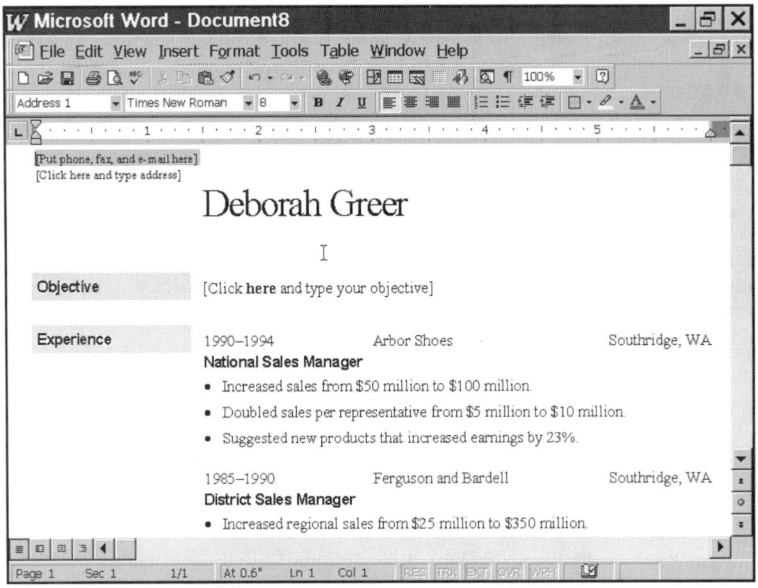

Fig. 2.10
The Contemporary Résumé template. Fill in the blanks and insert your own text to create a résumé that's formatted and ready to print.

Wizards

A **wizard** is a bit more complicated. Essentially, a wizard helps you make your own template by asking you a series of questions about what you want the template to include.

For example, if you choose the Résumé wizard, Word presents you with a menu of categories from which to choose (see Figure 2.11). Click one of the categories on the left side of the screen, or click the Next button to step through the categories one by one.

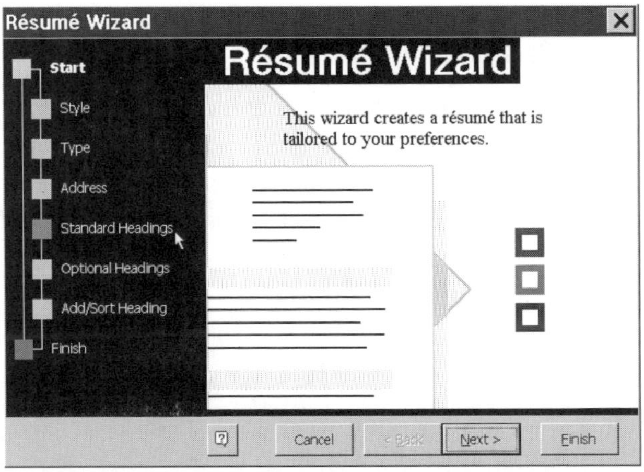

Fig. 2.11
The Résumé wizard creates a résumé template that includes only the features and formats you want.

When you click a category, the wizard gives you a menu of options. The Standard Headings category, for example, lets you pick the headings you want to include in your résumé (see Figure 2.12).

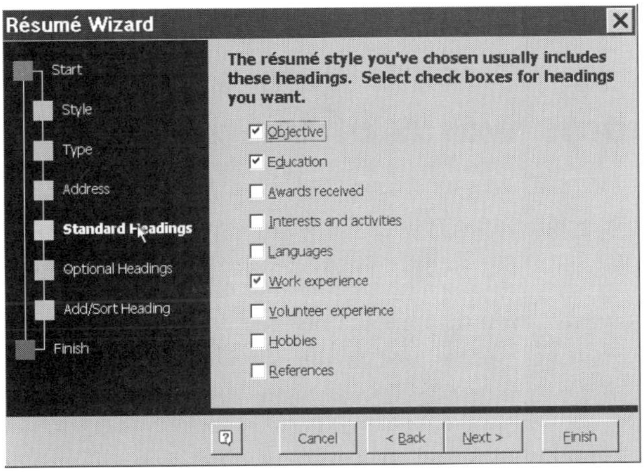

Fig. 2.12
Simply put a check next to the headings you want in your résumé.

When you're done, Word presents you with a template that you can fill in and save as a document (see Figure 2.13). In addition, the Office Assistant gives you options to add a cover letter, change the style of your résumé, or even e-mail the résumé to your future employer.

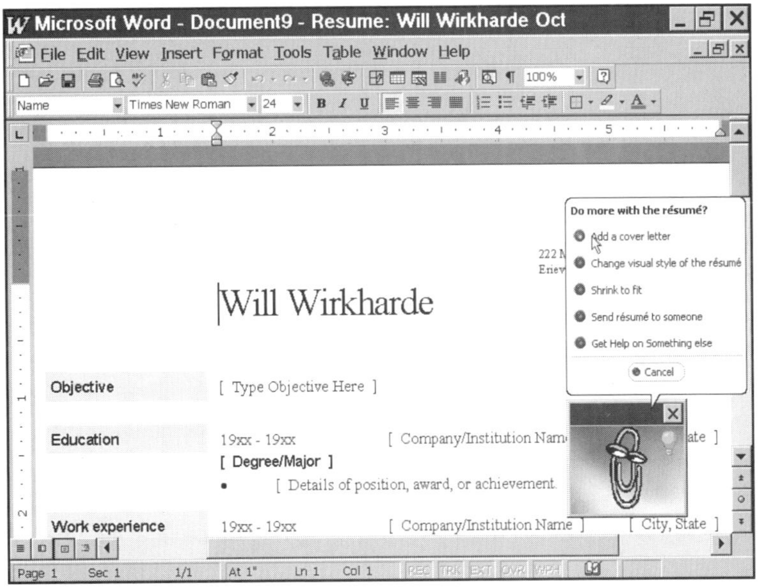

Fig. 2.13
When you're finished with a wizard, Word displays a résumé formatted to your specifications; fill in the blanks and save it.

TIP **If you've created a document that you'd like to modify and reuse,** such as a résumé, save it as a template. Choose File, Save As from the main menu; then choose Document Template (*.dot) in the Save as Type selection box and save the file. Next time you choose File, New, your new template will appear under the General tab.

Some words of caution

Some of Word's templates and wizards, such as those for creating résumés, letters, and press releases, are easy to use. They're also great teachers, giving you examples of interesting formatting tricks and techniques.

However, even the simple ones require you to know the basics of creating, formatting, editing, and saving documents. Read at least the rest of Part I before you start using templates seriously.

Other templates and wizards, particularly those for publications and reports, are for advanced users only. Don't tackle these until you're thoroughly familiar with Word's formatting and editing commands.

The following section describes Word's templates and wizards and indicates their degree of difficulty. You'll get a chance to experiment with some of the more difficult ones later in this book.

3

Need Help? Click Here!

In this chapter:

- The new Assistant: Help when you need it
- What's context-sensitive Help, and how can it help me?
- Tracking down info in Help files
- How do I get around in Help screens?
- In your own words: adding comments to Help
- New! Instant access to Microsoft's Web site

Word's Help system won't tell you the meaning of life, but it will make your life easier by showing you how to use Word's many commands and features . . . .

Many years ago, devoting an entire chapter to a program's Help command would have been overkill. In fact, for some minimalist software, it wouldn't have been possible—there were no Help files.

Not any more. Word's Help is practically a full-blown database program, and you need to learn how to use it to partake of its riches.

When Microsoft started supplementing its manuals with online Help, the company wasn't doing it just to save money. Online Help has many advantages. Most notably, you can use Help's searching and indexing tools to probe Help's extensive files for detailed information. You get to these files through Word 97's new Office Assistant or with the Help command at the far end of the menu bar.

You also can get immediate help for actions you're performing and for items in the Word 97 screen. **Context-sensitive Help** lets you point at the part of the screen you need help with and ask, "What's this?"

The Office Assistant: Not just a cartoon

Best of 97

Microsoft has put Word's help features front and center with a new floating window that contains the Office Assistant. Click anywhere on the Assistant and a dialog box in the form of a balloon pops up. Type in your query, as in Figure 3.1, and choose Search. You can use plain-English sentences, such as "Check my spelling," "How do I check my spelling?" or even, if it's late and you're tired, "Tell me how to check my blankity-blank spelling or I'll break your face!"

The Assistant responds with a list of possible topics based on your query. In Figure 3.2, for example, the second item—"Insert Page Breaks and Control Pagination"—seems most likely to answer the question. Simply click the button next to the topic and Word displays the appropriate Help window.

Q&A ***There's no Office Assistant on my screen. Where is it?***

Lurking in the background. Make it appear by clicking the Office Assistant button on the Standard toolbar. To hide the Assistant, click the Close button on the bar.

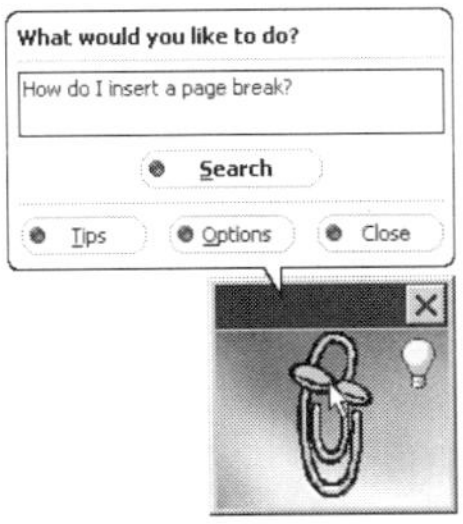

Fig. 3.1
Word 97's new Office Assistant gives you quick access to Word's help features. Click the assistant, type your question, and click Search.

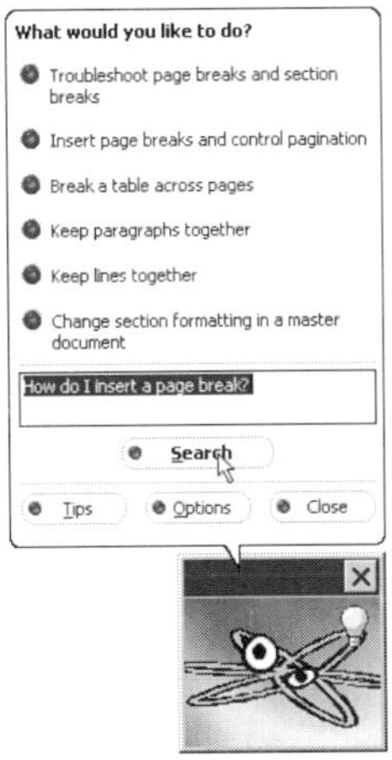

Fig. 3.2
If a number of topics seem to match your query, Assistant gives you a list from which to choose. Click the button next to the entry that seems most likely to answer your question.

Many Helping hands

The Assistant also lets you access several other help features that you'll find useful. You turn them on and off in the Office Assistant dialog box (see Figure 3.3), which you display by right-clicking the Assistant and choosing Options from the shortcut menu. Some of the options won't mean much to you yet, but here's an overview of the more important ones:

Respond to F1 key. Check this if you want the Office Assistant to pop up when you press F1. This is the same as clicking the Office Assistant button on the Standard toolbar. If this option is not checked, pressing F1 displays the Help Topics dialog box, which we'll discuss below.

Move When in the Way. This forces the Assistant to move out of the way when text you're typing is in danger of disappearing behind the Assistant window.

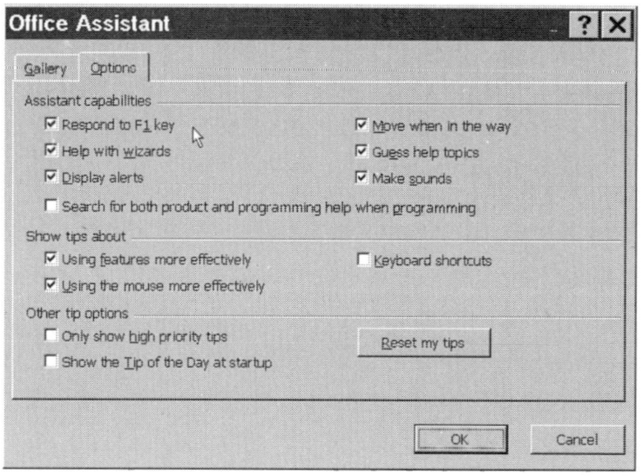

Fig. 3.3
The Office Assistant dialog box lets you tailor the help functions to your needs.

Guess Help Topics. When this is turned on, the Assistant tries to Figure out when you're having trouble with a task and offers to help. Sometimes the Assistant guesses right, and sometimes it guesses wrong. Try the option on for size; if you don't like it, you can always turn it off.

Show the Tip of the Day at Startup. This displays a tip on using Word 97 when you start the program.

The easiest way to find out which options you want is to turn them all on. You can eventually turn off the ones you don't like.

TIP **You can display a tip at any time by clicking the Assistant and** choosing Tips from the dialog balloon. The tip usually relates to a recent action.

Advice when you need it: Context-sensitive Help

Context-sensitive Help lets you get concise information that relates specifically to whatever you're doing at the moment. For example, if you're working in the Save dialog box, you get help on saving files. If you want to change your font, you get help on fonts.

Context-sensitive Help is a real time-saver. You don't have to wade through lists and menus looking for the specific item you need help with. And you avoid the frustration that comes when you can't remember the exact term under which the item is listed in Help's (or the manual's) index.

Help on objects in the Word window

To get a description of any object on the screen, press Shift+F1. Word attached a question mark to your mouse pointer. Point the question mark at the object and click again. For example, if you point the question mark at the Save button, then click the Save button, you see the Help screen shown in Figure 3.4.

TIP **Some dialog boxes have a question mark next to the Close button** on the title bar. To get help on an item in the dialog box, click the question mark once, drag it to the item, and click again.

Help on menu commands and shortcut keys

Shift+F1 is an easy way to get help on menu commands. For example, if you want to know what Format, Drop Cap is choose Format from the menu bar, place your pointer on Drop Cap, and press Shift+F1.

You can even get context-sensitive help on keyboard combinations. For example, if you press Shift+F1 and then Alt+I, N, you'll get information on the Footnote command (Insert, Footnote on the main menu).

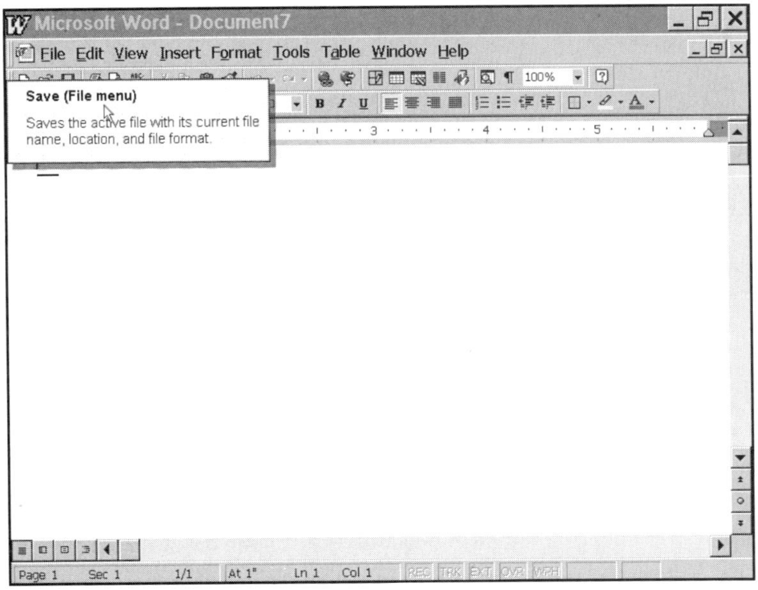

Fig. 3.4
To get help on a toolbar button, press Shift+F1, aim the pointer at the button with which you need help, and click again. Word displays a window that describes the button.

Searching for help

Office Assistant is good for getting quick help on the fly. And context-sensitive Help is the quickest solution when you know the command or button that you need help with. But if you want to do a task and have no idea where to begin, or if you need more comprehensive instructions, it's better to use one of Help's search features.

You start a search by choosing Help, Contents and Index from the menu bar. From the Help Topics dialog box, choose from among three ways to look for information (see the following graphics page).

- **Contents** gives you a table of contents, much like the one you'd find in a book, that groups topics by major category. You can browse through the contents to get an overview of subjects covered in the Help files.
- **Index** lets you search through a list of alphabetical topics.
- **Find** is similar to Index, except that it searches all Help files for any instance of a selected word or partial word.

We'll start with Index, which is the easiest to use.

Q&A ***I don't quite understand how the Help files are organized. Does each of the Help Topics dialog box tabs shown on the graphics page have its own Help files?***

All of Word's Help tabs use the same Help files to get their information; they just give you different ways to search. To more completely understand the way Help is organized—and how you can best use it—read the next few sections.

Index

Let's say you want to learn how to insert a page break. The fastest way is to search the Index for the topic "page break" (refer to the middle figure in the following graphics page).

In the Type The First Few Letters… text box, start typing the word **page**. When you type **p**, the list box takes you to the first entry beginning with "p," which happens to be "page break." Underneath is a list of subtopics. Click twice on "insert" to retrieve the Help screen.

Three ways to get Help

When you choose Help, Contents and Index from the menu bar, Word displays the Help Topics dialog box. The tabs in this dialog box let you choose from among three ways to search for help. In this case, the search is for how to insert a page break in a document.

Browsing through the Contents tab yields the chapter "Page Breaks and Section Breaks" in the book titled *Changing the Appearance of Your Page*.

Searching for the topic "page break" in the alphabetical Index tab takes you to the "page breaks" as soon as you press the "p."

Searching for the words "page break" in the Find tab brings up a number of topics that include the words "page" and "break."

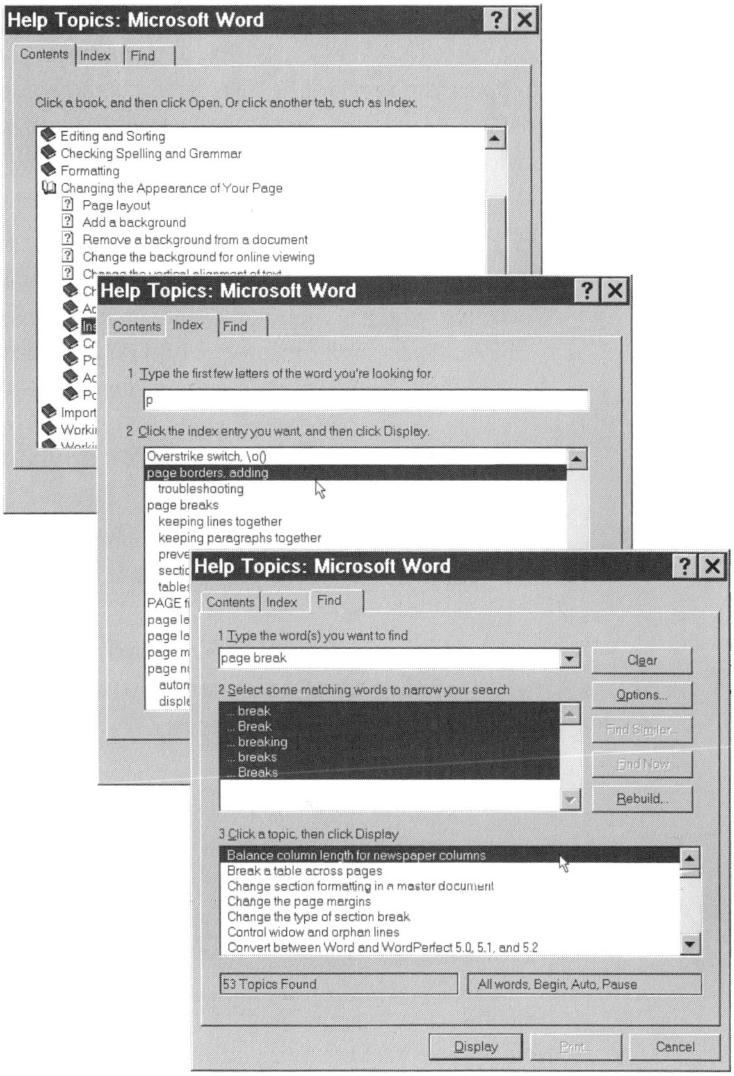

Find

Find is similar to Index, except that it looks for words and phrases rather than for topics. It identifies all occurrences of the search term in all Help files (refer to the bottom figure in previous graphics box).

For example, the Click A Topic... text box lists all entries that include the words "page" and "break."

Find has its drawbacks. As that bottom figure shows, you'll get a lot of help on topics you may not be interested in, and sometimes finding the right Help page is tedious. But Find is better than Index if you have only a general idea of what you're looking for, or if you want to find all references to a topic.

Step-by-step instructions

No matter how you find your topic—the Office Assistant, Index, or Find—Word gives you a screen containing instructions on how to do the task. For example, if you look for information on how to add page numbers, you'll find the Add Page Numbers Help screen shown in Figure 3.5.

Q&A

Is it possible to search for entries that include either "page" or "break"?

Yes. In the Find tab, choose Options. In the Find Options dialog box that appears, click the option called At Least One Of The Words You Typed.

When I click the Find tab, I get a Find Setup Wizard dialog that tells me I have to create a database first. What's going on here?

Not to worry. Find needs to create a word list from Word's Help files before it can do its job. This is a no-muss, no-fuss procedure. Choose the recommended Minimize Database Size. Word gives you on-screen instructions on what to do next. (You can choose Rebuild from the Find dialog box if you want to choose another option later.) Building a database is a one-time-only deal; you won't have to do it again unless you have to reinstall Word.

If the information you need isn't there, scan the topics at the bottom of the Help screen. You get more information on a topic by clicking it.

Fig. 3.5
This Help screen gives you a list of topics on which you can get step-by-step instructions.

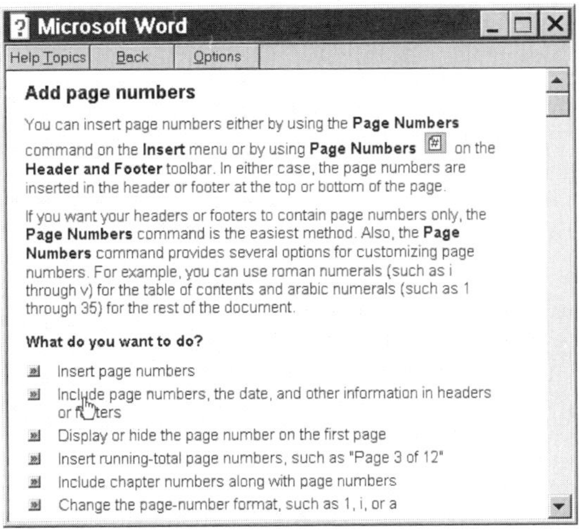
Microsoft Word
Help Topics
Back
Options
Add page numbers
You can insert page numbers either by using the Page Numbers command on the Insert menu or by using Page Numbers on the Header and Footer toolbar. In either case, the page numbers are inserted in the header or footer at the top or bottom of the page.
If you want your headers or footers to contain page numbers only, the Page Numbers command is the easiest method. Also, the Page Numbers command provides several options for customizing page numbers. For example, you can use roman numerals (such as i through v) for the table of contents and arabic numerals (such as 1 through 35) for the rest of the document.
What do you want to do?
Insert page numbers
Display or hide the page number on the first page
Insert running-total page numbers, such as "Page 3 of 12"
Include chapter numbers along with page numbers
Change the page-number format, such as 1, i, or a

We'll look at the Help screen's menu and buttons in a moment.

Tell me about...

Word provides many graphical screens that lead you to general information on a topic. For example, if you search for "page layout" in the Assistant's dialog balloon and click Page Layout, Word displays the screen shown in Figure 3.6.

Fig. 3.6
A graphical Help screen. Touch a topic with the pointer until the pointer turns into a hand, then click.

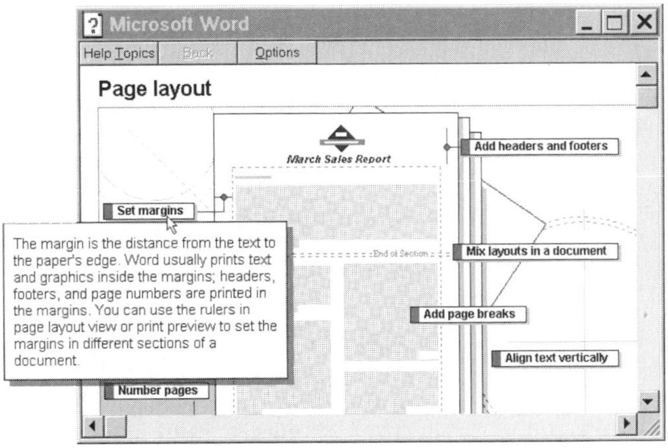
Microsoft Word
Help Topics
Back
Options
Page layout
March Sales Report
Add headers and footers
Set margins
The margin is the distance from the text to the paper's edge. Word usually prints text and graphics inside the margins; headers, footers, and page numbers are printed in the margins. You can use the rulers in page layout view or print preview to set the margins in different sections of a document.
Mix layouts in a document
Add page breaks
Align text vertically
Number pages

Contents

Contents is our final stop in the Help Topics dialog box (refer to the top figure in the previous graphics box). Here, Word takes a much more traditional approach to providing information.

Contents presents a list of general Help subjects, called **books**, each of which is preceded by a closed-book icon. Click twice on a book to open it. A table of contents drops down from the title.

The table of contents can include books, topics (which are preceded by question marks), or both. Double-click a book to get another table of contents, or double-click a topic to get a Help screen.

For example, in the top figure in the previous graphics box, the table of contents for the book titled "Changing the Appearance of Your Page" includes two topics and six other books.

Inside the Help screen

Getting help doesn't have to stop with reading the information and returning to your document. Word's Help screen has several features that you might find useful. For instance, you can print a Help screen, copy the information into a document, and even add your own notes. And many Help screens also include links to other Help screens that have related information.

Q&A ***Can I return to my document without closing the Help window?***

Yes. Click the Help window's Minimize button, click anywhere in the document window, or press Alt+Tab. The Help window will remain in the background. You can bring it back by pressing Alt+Tab.

Options galore

Don't overlook the Options menu, which you get by clicking the Options button or by clicking the right mouse button. From here, you can print, save, and add notes to a Help screen.

Printing a Help screen

Often, it's more convenient to have a printout of a Help topic, so you can tape it to your forehead until you've got the material memorized. Options, Print Topic takes you to the Print dialog box, from where you can send the active Help screen to your printer. (For more information on printing, see Chapter 7, "Prepare to Print!")

Copying a Help screen

Perhaps you'd like to select Help topics for a personal or office manual. You can do it easily with Copy, which lets you copy the contents of a Help screen into a Word file.

Before you undertake such a project, you'll probably want to read about copying text (see Chapter 5, "How to Delete, Move, Copy, and Change Your Text") and formatting documents (see Part III). But here are the basic steps:

1. In the Help screen, choose Options, Copy (nothing apparent will happen, but that's OK).
2. Close the Help screen and start a new Word document.
3. Choose Edit, Paste from the menu or press Ctrl+V.

The text of the Help screen, minus icons and formats, appears in your document.

Q&A ***How do I keep a Help screen from overlapping the part of the document I want to see?***

You can size the Help window any way you want by dragging the borders in and out with the mouse pointer. The new size becomes a permanent part of your Word configuration until you resize it again.

Or you can move a Help window by clicking its title bar and dragging it to another part of the screen.

Q&A ***Whenever I move from a Help screen to my document, the Help screen disappears. How to I keep it visible, so I can refer to it while I'm in the document?***

Simple. From the Options menu in any Help window, select Keep Help On Top, On Top. Thereafter, you can move between the Help window and your document window by clicking inside one or the other, or by pressing Alt+Tab.

Extra help on demand—using the Internet

Word's Help files and books such as this one will give most users all the guidance they'll ever need. But the day comes when most of us run into a problem to which we can't easily find a solution.

Enter Microsoft's Internet Web site. Here you'll find megabytes of useful and esoteric information on a range of Word-related topics, including:

- Answers to tough questions
- Programs and add-ons
- Fixes to software bugs
- Tutorials on how to handle different Word tasks

You don't need to be a Web wiz to use this material. Once you're set up to go online—a topic we cover in Chapter 25, "The Word on the Web"—all you have to do is choose Help, Microsoft on the Web from the main menu and select from the list Word displays.

There's too much on the Web site to cover here, but we can give you a few pointers on where to go and what to expect.

How do I...?

The first place you should check out is Online Support. Your browser will take you to the Microsoft Word Support Wiz ard. Choose one of the available options (for example, "Troubleshooting a Problem"), or click one of the buttons in the left-hand column. Figure 3.7 displays the page you'll see if you click the Read the Feature Articles button.

You choose an item by clicking it. For example, if you want to find out more about macro viruses (refer to Figure 3.7), click Microsoft Word Macro Virus, and Microsoft takes you to the page shown in Figure 3.8.

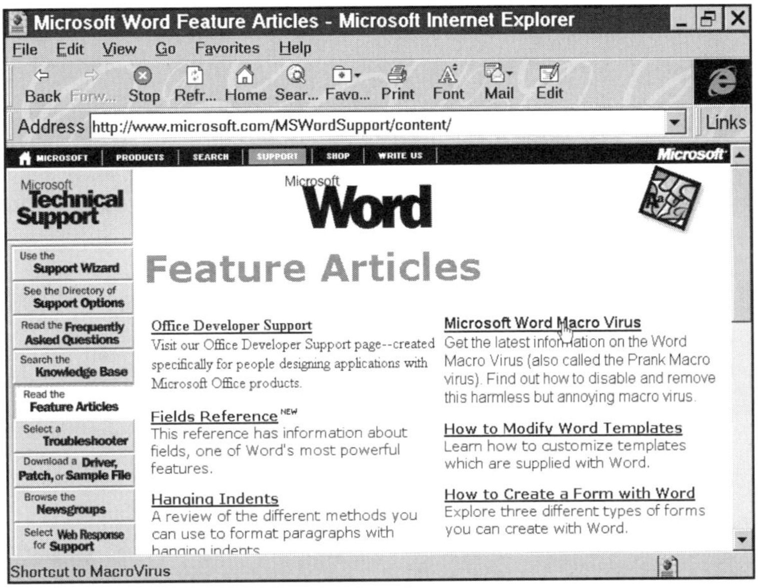

Fig. 3.7
Microsoft's online support page includes tutorials on specific Word tasks, such as creating hanging indents and modifying templates.

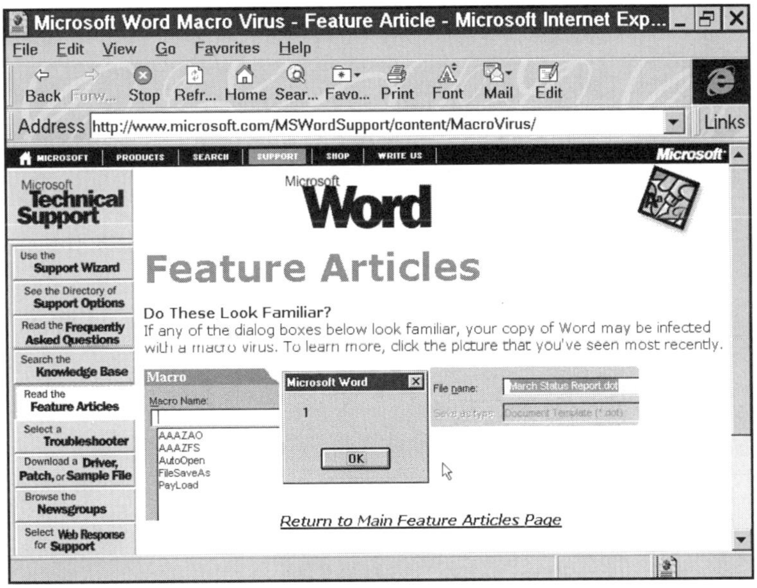

Fig. 3.8
Think you have a macro virus? This Web page shows you how your Word display might be affected.

Just the FAQs, ma'am

Next stop: frequently asked questions, better know as FAQs. A *FAQ* is a collection of typical questions on a specific topic. Got a printer problem? You might find a FAQ on printers that gives you a solution.

Free! Free! Free!

Sometimes a bit of good advice isn't enough: You need a piece of software to solve a problem.

For example, you might have an office mate who doesn't have Word but needs to read and print out your documents. You're tired of converting all your documents to another format, and besides, a lot of your best font and paragraph formatting disappears in the conversion.

The answer is to give him or her Microsoft's free Word Viewer. Choose Help, Microsoft on the Web, Free Stuff. Your browser displays Microsoft's Free Software page, from where you can download the viewer.

Let them hear from you!

Finally, when all else fails, you can aim an e-mail at Microsoft's support staff from the Feedback page. Choose Help, Microsoft on the Web, Send Feedback. You can also use this page to report bugs or tell Microsoft about the one feature you desperately wish they'd include in the next version of Word.

Other helpful Help features

The Help system is far too extensive to describe fully in a few pages. Many of the Help options are best suited for browsing, and the best way to find out what's there is to explore. Here are a few key menu items you might want to check out:

- To find out how to get technical help from Microsoft, go to Contents, open the Getting Help book, and choose "Technical Support." Among other services, you'll get an 800 number that you can use for recorded or faxed replies.
- To get a list of WordPerfect commands and their Word equivalents, open the Switching from WordPerfect book in Contents.

- To get information about your hardware, operating system, memory, and disk storage, choose Help, About Microsoft Word, System Info.
- To learn about keyboard shortcuts, go to Contents, open the Reference Information book, then open the Keyboard Guide book. The list of topics includes everything you need to know, and much more, about how to use the keyboard.
- To find out about Microsoft's Internet site, open the Getting Help book and choose "Connect to Microsoft Technical Resources."

4

Saving and Managing Your Documents

In this chapter:

- **Save your documents early and often!**
- **The name game: using Word's new long file names**
- **Saving documents automatically with AutoRecover**
- **And the password is...**
- **Backup files: Word's safety net**
- **Can I look at a file before I open it?**

Word knows more ways to save than a traveling preacher. Use as many of them as you can; they're your best protection against system crashes . . . .

Most of us learn how to open and close Word documents before the installation disks are cold. Unfortunately, in our zeal to start writing, we often neglect important lessons on other aspects of document management.

There's far more to saving a document than clicking the Save button. How do you protect your open files from system failures? Word lets you save files in ways that minimize your risk. What do you call the file? Using names to organize your files is practically an art. Where do you put the file? Surely, you don't want to put it where you can't find it later.

Word gives you buttons and keyboard shortcuts for many file management tasks, but you should start by learning the File menu (see Figure 4.1). You'll gain a thorough and systematic understanding of Word's many file management options.

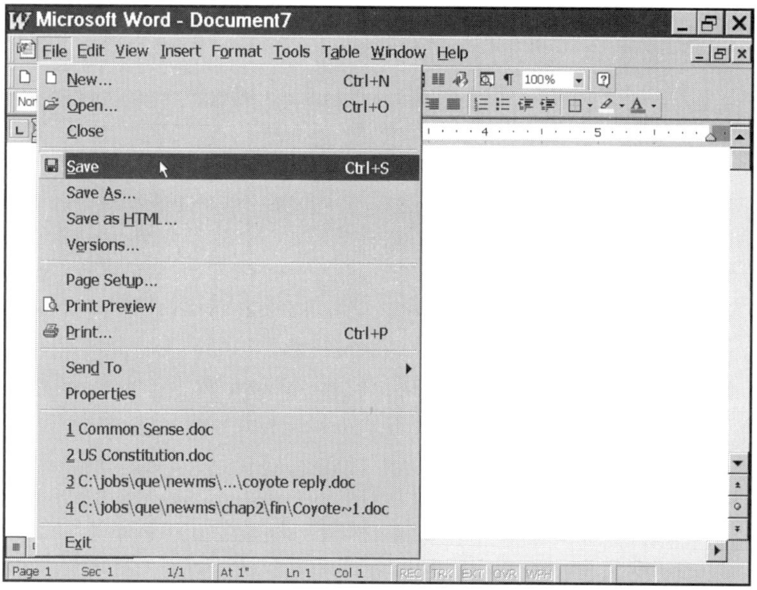

Fig. 4.1
When you choose File from the menu bar, you get this pull-down menu of file management commands.

The file menu contains two options for saving: Save and Save As. You'll need both of them. Let's look at Save first.

Saving files: the basics

Word is designed to let you save files easily and often—and you should. Nothing's more depressing than watching four hours of work disappear because a squirrel jumped on a live wire and brought down the power grid.

So how complicated can saving a file be? Don't you just give the sucker a name and, well, *save* it? It's more involved than you might think.

When you load Word, the title bar shows the name of the file as `Document1`. If you start a second new file, Word calls it `Document2`, and so on. These are not file names, and you should give your file a real name before starting work on your document.

Saving files: a checklist

If you're new to computers, here are a few guidelines for happy file saving:

- Give your document a name and save it immediately—before you even start typing.
- Save your file often. Work under the theory that a meteor is going to hit your house sometime in the next five minutes.
- Copy your documents to floppy disks at least once a day, more often when you're making frequent and substantial changes.
- Use Word's AutoRecover feature to automatically save your file at regular intervals.
- Close your document when you're away from your computer for more than a few minutes.
- *Always* close all files, exit Word, and exit Windows before turning off your computer!

A **file name** is the name you give a document when you save it to disk. A file name consists of a **base name** and an **extension**, which for Word documents is .DOC. The base name and the extension are separated by a period. For example, in the file name BUDGET.DOC, the base name is BUDGET and the extension is .DOC.

If your file name has more than one period, the extension is made up of the characters after the last period. For example, in the file name BUDGET.95.ACTUAL.DOC, the base name is BUDGET.95.ACTUAL and the extension is .DOC. In all, a file name and extension can be 255 characters long, although the extension can't be more than three characters long. (More on Word's long file names in a moment.) You don't need to type the extension; Word adds it automatically.

Choose File, Save to pop up the Save As dialog box shown in Figure 4.2. The suggested file name—in this example, `Doc1.doc`—is highlighted in the File Name text box. Type the new file name (the suggested file name disappears when you start typing) and click OK. The file is now stored on disk.

Fig. 4.2
The Save As dialog box. To replace Word's suggested file name, *Doc1.doc*, type the new file name into the File Name text box.

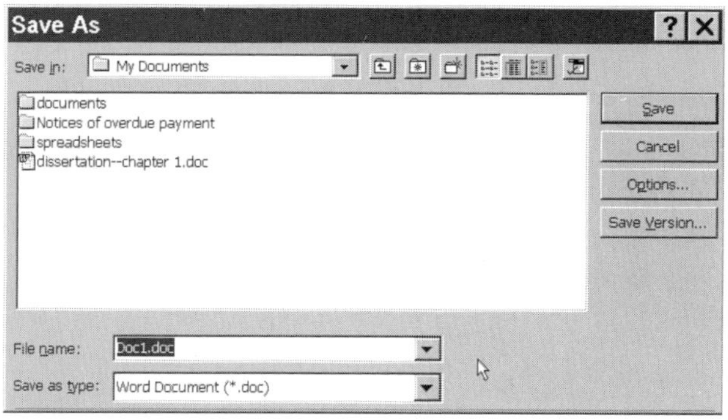

TIP **When you're naming your document for the first time, you** can go directly to the Save As dialog box by pressing Ctrl+S or by clicking the Save button on the Standard toolbar.

The keys to valid file names

Your file names can include letters, numbers, and spaces. You can also use all characters *except* an asterisk (*), forward slash (/), backslash (\), greater-than sign (>), less-than sign (<), question mark (?), quotation mark ("), vertical bar (|), or colon (:)

Experienced PC users take note: Windows 95 accepts a variety of characters that were not valid in Windows 3.1 and its ancestors. These are the period (.), plus sign (+), comma (,), semicolon (;), equal sign (=), and brackets ([]).

Despite Word's willingness to let you use all sorts of character combinations, your best plan is to stick with letters and numbers. Use symbols only if you have a good reason to, such as to separate elements in your file name.

Q&A ***What if I want an extension other than .DOC?***

Put the entire file name in quotation marks; for example, "REPORT.PRN."

TIP **You name folders following the same rules you use to name files.**

Saving a document to an existing file name

What if you want to replace a file on your disk with a document you've just created? That's easy. When you're in the Save As dialog box, click the file name in the list box directly below Save In, then click Save. You can tell which files are word documents by the Word icon to the left of the file name (`Dissertation—Chapter 1` in Figure 4.2).

Word asks you if you want to replace the existing file. Click Yes to save, No to return to the Save As dialog box, and Cancel to return to the document.

The file to which you've saved the document becomes the default file name.

CAUTION **When you save a document to an existing file name, you irrevocably** destroy the file you're replacing. It is gone forever. Never overwrite a file unless you're certain you don't need it!

Resaving a file

Once you've saved a document, you can resave it without returning to the Save As dialog box. Click the Save button on the Standard toolbar or press Ctrl+S. Word lets you know it's saving the file by changing the mouse pointer to a folder with pages dropping into it and displaying a horizontal meter in the status bar. Both of these displays mean, "Hold on a minute, I'm busy doing something."

Saving to another file name

When you want to save a document but give it a new name, choose File, Save As. You get the same Save As dialog box shown in Figure 4.2. The current file name appears in the File Name text box. Just type the new name and click Save.

Saving to another file type

"I need a copy of the Hopper report," says Smithers. "Oh—and can you give it to me in Windows Write 3.0 format?"

Gulp. You've just learned how to create Word for Windows documents, and now you're supposed to make Windows Write documents, too?

Not to worry. You don't need to know a thing about Write to meet Smithers' request. Word can save a document to a file that's Write-ready. It can also save documents for WordPerfect and other versions of Word. You can even save a document in a universal format that nearly any other word processor on the planet can open.

> **"*Plain English, please!***
>
> When Word saves a file, it doesn't simply store your text. The file also includes instruction codes that control how your document looks. For example, one code might say, "We want bold text here," another, "Let's change the type size to 10 points," and so on. Together, these codes are called Word's **format**.
>
> A file that contains text but no codes goes by a variety of names, including **text**, **unformatted text**, and **plain text**.
>
> Occasionally, you'll hear a technically oriented user refer to **ASCII files**. (ASCII stands for American Standard Code for Information Interchange.) Don't be fooled by the jargon; the person probably wants a text file. "

File types for the millions

You save a file in another format using the Save As Type drop-down box in the Save As dialog box (see Figure 4.3).

The text box probably reads `Word Document`, which is the option for Word 97 documents. Click the text box, choose the new file type, and click Save.

> **TIP** **Chapter 24, "All Together Now—Using Word in Your Workgroup,"** tells you more about how to share documents with people using other versions of Word. Chapter 22, "Mail Merge, for Homemade Mass Mailings," provides information on how to save files for use by database managers and by other types of software.

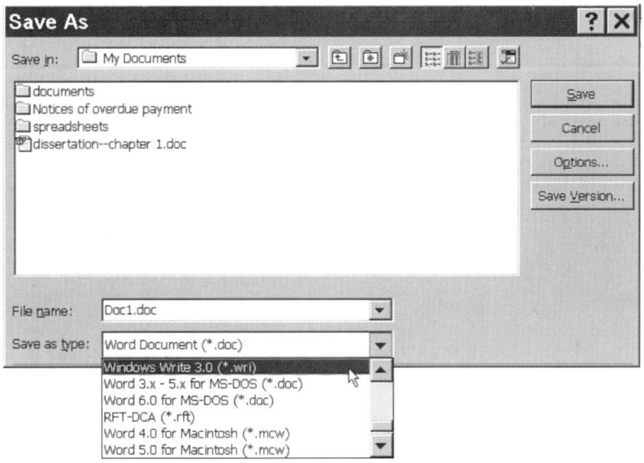

Fig. 4.3
The Save As Type drop-down box lets you save a file to other formats, including ones that other versions of Word can use.

What's HTML?

Word 97's File menu has a new option called Save to HTML that lets you save a document in a format that lets you publish it on the World Wide Web.

HTML stands for Hypertext Markup Language, and it consists of special codes that control how a Web page will look and behave. If you're curious about what this code looks like, save a document using Save to HTML, then choose View, HTML Source from the main menu.

Save to HTML is the same as choosing HTML document in the Save as Type selection box of the Save As dialog box.

You don't need to concern yourself with saving HTML files unless you plan to use Word 97 to prepare Web pages. See Chapter 25, "The Word on the Web," for details.

Saving to a floppy disk

Networks have become a force in the workplace, but the floppy disk is still a popular vehicle for moving files from one computer to another.

To save a Word document to a floppy disk, make sure you have a disk in the floppy drive, then click the Save In box. A tree drops down, similar to the one shown in Figure 4.4. Move the cursor to the floppy drive (in this case, A:) and click it. Name the file and save it.

Here's an alternative that's sometimes quicker: Precede the file name in the File Name text box with the drive letter and a colon. For example, instead of typing resume.doc, type a:resume.doc.

You also can copy a saved Word document from your hard drive to drive A: with the shortcut menu. In the Save As or Open dialog box, right-click the file you want to copy and choose Send To, 3 _ Floppy (A) (see Figure 4.5).

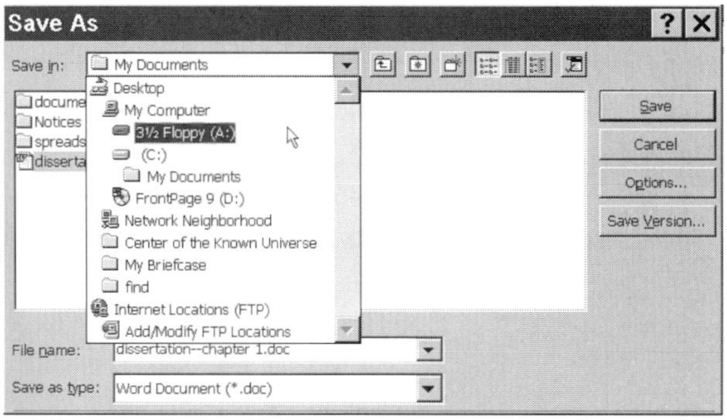

Fig. 4.4
To save to a floppy disk, click the Save In box and select the floppy drive. Make sure you have a disk in the drive!

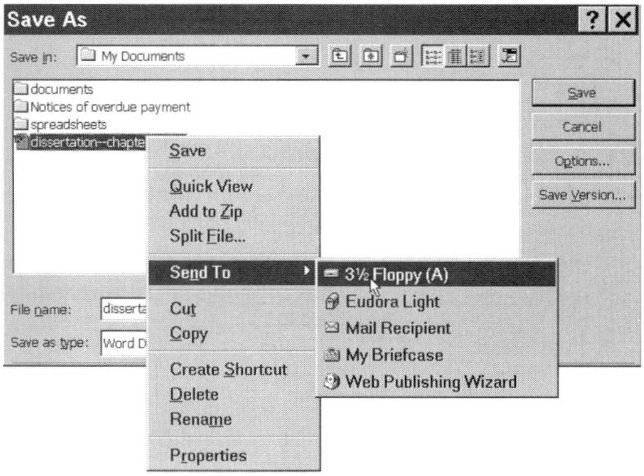

Fig. 4.5
You can quickly copy a document from your hard drive to a floppy disk by using the shortcut menu.

Q&A ***What are these other options—Mail Recipient and My Briefcase—that are on the Send To menu?***

The Mail Recipient option lets you e-mail your document; it's the same as choosing File, Send To, Mail Recipient from the main menu. Chapter 24 provides more information. My Briefcase is a Windows 95 tool that lets you keep files synchronized when you're accessing them from several computers—your desktop and portable PCs, for example. Refer to the Windows 95 Help files for more information on installing and using Briefcase.

The items on the Send To menu are set from Windows 95, and it's possible your menu might differ from the one in Figure 4.5.

Word's crash-protection air bag: AutoRecover

It's happened to all of us. You've just finished three inspired pages of brilliant prose. Exhilarated but exhausted, you leave your desk for a glass of water. Suddenly, the building goes dark—a power failure. As you stand dumbfounded at the cooler, the company wit says, "Sure hope everybody saved their files!" Of course you saved your document—or did you?

No matter how fanatical you are about saving files, the day may come when you'll simply forget. Why take the risk? Word can save your document automatically with a great feature called AutoRecover.

AutoRecover puts your document in a temporary file at intervals you specify. If your computer crashes before you've saved your document, Word tries to recover the file when you run Word again.

TIP **AutoRecover does not save the document to the actual file, so** your changes to the document don't become permanent until you manually save the document to its file name.

To use AutoRecover, click Options from the Save As dialog box (refer to Figure 4.4). Find the check box for Save AutoRecover Info Every and make sure it contains an x. In the text box to the right, enter the interval in minutes (that is, how often you want to AutoRecover the file), then click OK.

Word suggests an AutoRecover interval of ten minutes—fine for most documents. The shorter the interval, the better, but keep in mind that long documents take time to save, and an AutoRecover every few minutes can become intrusive.

TIP **AutoRecover saves all open documents. If the documents are long** and the interval you've set is short, your keyboard might seem to freeze whenever AutoRecover kicks in. You can minimize these delays by closing any documents you're not using.

How to use long file names

If you've used Windows 3.1 and its predecessors, you've probably been frustrated with the fact that you could use only 11 characters in a file name (up to eight in the base name and three in an optional extension, such as LETRTOJM.DOC). Did you name that memo to Ed EDREP821.DOC or RPTEDFIN.DOC? What does the cryptic IV05NSJL.DOC stand for, and what's in the file?

Under Windows 95, Word's rules for naming files are much more liberal, but with freedom comes added responsibility. If you start typing 50-word file names based on whatever pops into your mind, you're going to have major headaches managing your documents.

When to avoid long file names

On the surface, long file names seem to have nothing but advantages. But if you share documents with people who use earlier versions of Word and Windows, your long file names could become someone else's headache.

Most PCs on this planet do not run Windows 95 or Windows NT 3.51. Their operating system is MS-DOS, usually version 6.x, often coupled with Windows 3.1. File names on these computers are limited to 11 characters—an eight-character base and three-character extension. These older systems do not recognize long file names.

To make Windows 95 files compatible with older machines, Windows 95 automatically converts a long file name into an 11-character **alias**. For example, if you save a file as "Actual Expenses for June," Windows gives it the alias ACTUAL~1.DOC.

I am Sparta~1!

This alias becomes the file name when the disk it's on is read by software written for older systems. Thus, when you pass your document to a person using, say, Word 6 and Windows 3.1, he'll see a file called ACTUAL~1, not "Actual Expenses for June."

You don't need a vivid imagination to see the potential problems. The file names that your friends and colleagues see will often bear little resemblance to the ones you created, nor will they always make sense.

Of course, you want to use Windows 95's special features as much as possible. But when you create a document that someone else might open in an earlier version of Windows, you'll do that person a favor by sticking with an 11-character file name.

Play it safe with password protection

You can give your file a password to protect it from the curious. Select Options from the Save As dialog box. In the lower left-hand corner of the Options dialog box that appears, you'll see two text boxes: Password to Open and Password to Modify (see Figure 4.6).

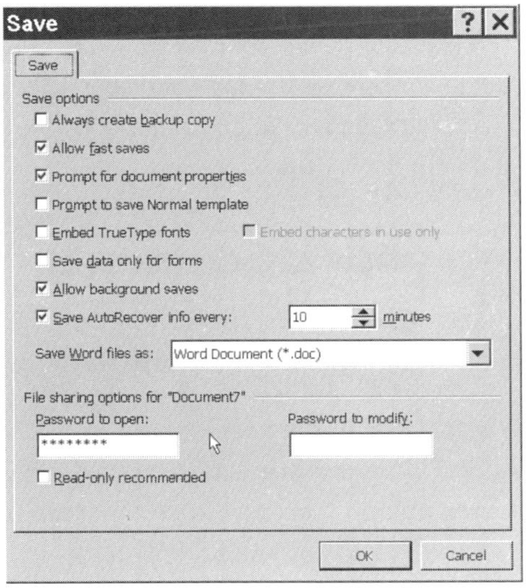

Fig. 4.6
A Password to Open locks the file from anyone who doesn't know the password. A Password to Modify lets other people read the file without the password but not change it.

When you protect a file with a password, anyone who tries to open the file will be presented with a Password dialog box. If you've entered a Password to Open, the person must enter the password to open the file.

If you've entered a Password to Modify, the Password dialog box includes a Read Only button. A user without the password can click this button and open the document, but he or she can't resave the document with the same name to the same folder. Thus, the person has access to the document but can't make changes without saving the document with a new file name or to a different folder.

Type your password into the appropriate text box. Your password can include up to 15 letters, numbers and symbols. When you're done, click the

OK button. Word displays a Confirm Password dialog box; retype the password and choose OK.

Remember your password!

We slothful types tend to use passwords that we can remember easily, such as the name of our dog, our phone number, or (if we're really feeling lazy) "password." These happen to be passwords that virtually any sentient file-cracker will guess. If you're serious about your password, use a nonsense string of letters and numbers at least five characters long (the names of Icelandic cities do nicely, unless you named your dog "Reykjavik").

CAUTION **Once you've protected a file with Password to Open, you won't** be able to open that file without the password. Write down your password and store it in a secure place (and remember where you put it!). Also, don't forget that passwords are case sensitive; that is, "Reykjavik" and "REYKJAVIK" are two different passwords.

Backing up your documents

You can instruct Word to automatically save the previous version of your document to a backup file whenever you save the current version.

A backup can be a godsend if you accidentally save a file with unwanted changes. It also gives you extra protection against file corruption woes. If your hard disk acts up and you can't open the main file, you often can retrieve most of your work by opening the backup.

To make an automatic backup active, select Options from the Save As dialog box and put a check mark in the box next to Always Create Backup Copy under Save Options.

Opening a backup file

Because backup files have the extension .WBK instead of .DOC, you won't see them listed in the Open dialog box. To list your backups, either choose All Files in the Files Of Type list box, or type ***.WBK** in the File Name text box and click Open. You can easily identify a backup file because it is named "Backup of" followed by the name of the original file.

Q&A ***How do I print my document?***

You can get a printout quickly by clicking the Print button on the Standard toolbar. Make sure your printer is turned on. Word bypasses the Print dialog box and sends your document straight to the printer. Chapter 7, "Prepare to Print!" gives you details on printing, including how to preview a document, set your margins, and print envelopes and labels.

Closing a document

Once you're finished with a document, there's no point letting it hang around taking up memory and slowing AutoRecovers. To clear it from your screen, choose File, Close.

If you've made changes to the document since the last time you saved it, Word gives you the option of saving your document before closing it. Closing a document does not close Word or affect other active documents.

Opening a file

You've learned how to create a new file and save it. Now let's talk about how you get it back.

The easiest way to open a file is to click the Open button on the Standard toolbar. You can also choose File, Open or press Ctrl+O. Whatever your option, you'll get the Open dialog box shown in Figure 4.7. It looks a lot like the Save As dialog box, except that Save In becomes Look In and Save As Type becomes Files Of Type. You select a file to open by clicking the file name twice, or by typing the file name in the File Name box.

TIP **Word 97's Open dialog box has a new button, Search the Web,** that lets you open a search page on the World Wide Web for finding documents. By default, Word takes you to a Microsoft page that includes such popular search services as Lycos and Alta Vista, but you can change the page to one of your own choosing. See Chapter 25 for more information on how to use Word with the Web.

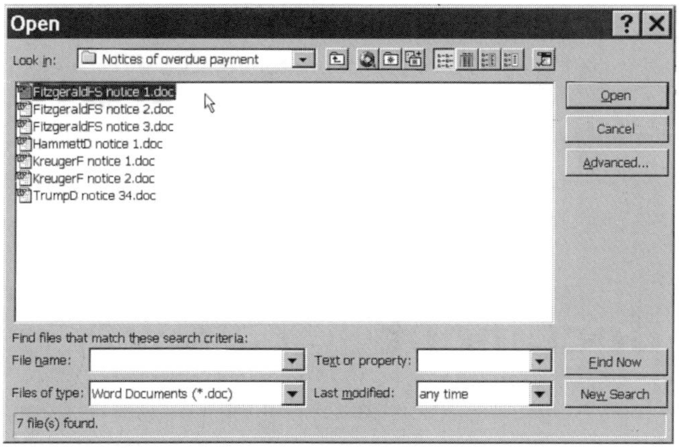

Fig. 4.7
The Open dialog box shows you the Word documents available in the selected folder.

Narrowing your list of files

If your folder begins to fill with documents and other types of files, you can limit which files Word lists in one of several ways.

If you type a string of characters in the File Name text box, Word displays only those files that include those characters. For example, typing **WRI** lists Wright.invoice, Tax.writeoffs, and Orders.wri.

If you want only those files that start with WRI, use the asterisk as a wildcard, like this: **WRI***.

To list files that have a .WRI extension, type ***.WRI**.

> ***Plain English, please!***
>
> Just as a wildcard in poker can represent any card in the deck, a **wildcard** in a file name stands in for any valid file name characters. Word's two wildcards are the asterisk (*) and the question mark (?). The difference is that the asterisk can represent any number of characters, while the question mark can represent only a single character.
>
> For example, the file name REP*5.DOC could represent REP95.DOC, REPORTFOR1995.DOC, or REP5.DOC. The file name REP?5.DOC, on the other hand, can represent only REP95.DOC.

Calling all file types!

If you work exclusively with Word 97 files, they have the .DOC extension, and the Open dialog box shows you all Word documents in the selected directory. But if you want to see files created with other word processors, you have to change the file type.

For example, suppose a coworker gives you a floppy disk that contains a report he wrote in Windows Notepad. You put the disk in your floppy drive, go to the Open dialog box, click the Look In drop-down box, and select drive A:. The list box comes up empty. Did your colleague forget to save the file before handing you the disk?

Probably not. Notepad saves documents with a .TXT extension. Word displays the file name if you click the Files Of Type drop-down box and select Text Only Files (*.txt).

TIP **If you don't know the extension of the file you're looking for,** choose All Files (*.*) in the Files Of Type drop-down box. Click the Details button if you're not sure which are documents and which are other types of files.

Opening several files at once

Word lets you open several documents in a folder at the same time. To select individual files scattered throughout the list, click each separate file while holding down the Ctrl key. Each file becomes highlighted, as shown in Figure 4.8. Then click Open.

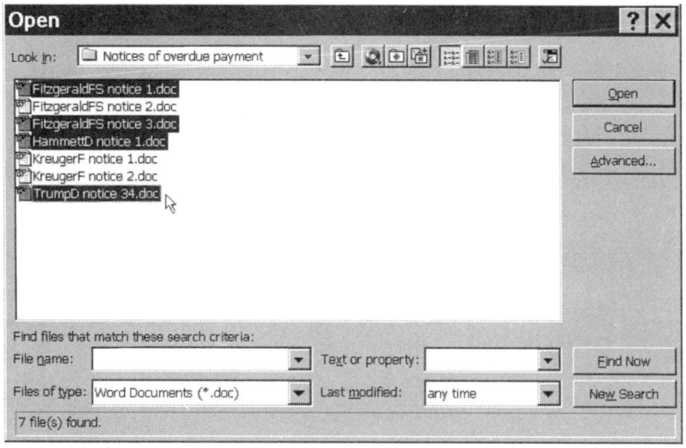

Fig. 4.8
You can open more than one file at the same time by clicking each file while holding down the Ctrl key.

To select contiguous files, click the first file; then, holding down the Shift key, click the last file. Word highlights both files and all files in between.

Opening recent files

Word lets you open documents you've worked on recently without going to the Open dialog box. When you open the File menu on the menu bar, a list of files appears at the bottom. Click the file you want to open or press the number in front of it.

You can change the number of files that appear on this list. Choose Tools, Options from the menu bar and click the General tab. Type a number from between 0 and 9 in the Entries box next to the Recently Used File List option. Make sure, too, that Recently Used File List is checked.

Opening a new file

You've seen how Word creates a new empty file when you first start Word. You can create a file at any time by selecting File, New from the menu bar. Choose the General tab in the New dialog box and click the Blank Document icon to open a generic, unformatted document.

You can bypass the New dialog box by clicking the New button on the Standard toolbar or by pressing Ctrl+N.

Previewing a file

It's not unusual to maintain three or four files that contain different versions of the same document. For example, you might keep several resumes—each one geared toward a slightly different type of job. Rather than open each document until you find the right one, you can use the Preview button in the Open dialog box to peek at them first.

In the Open dialog box, click the name of the file you want to look at and click the Preview button. Figure 4.9 shows Preview in action.

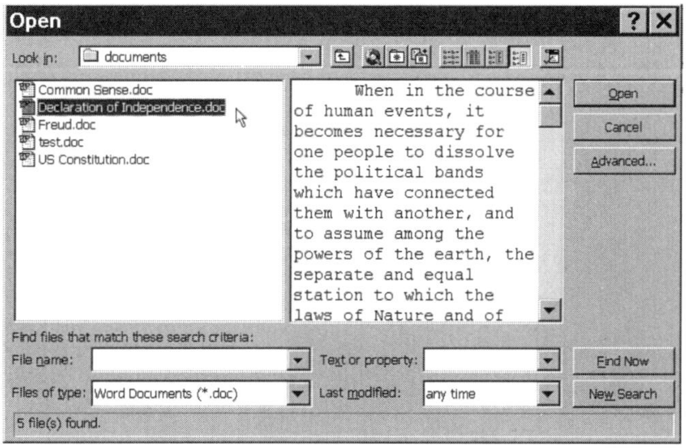

Fig. 4.9
Click the Preview button to peek at the selected file.

Or use Quick View to take a peek

Quick View works a little like the Preview button, letting you get a glimpse of a file before you open it. But Quick View has several important advantages:

- Quick View gives you a bigger picture of the file so you can see what it'll look like when you open it.
- Quick View can preview files in their proper format. For example, in Figure 4.10, Quick View shows a Lotus 1-2-3 spreadsheet as it would appear in Lotus 1-2-3. The Preview window (behind the Quick View window in Figure 4.10) shows the spreadsheet without such features as boldface and gridlines.
- Depending on what viewers you have installed with Windows, Quick View can display files that the Preview window cannot—Quattro Pro spreadsheets, for example. (Be aware, however, that being able to view a file in Quick View does not necessarily mean you will be able to open it in Word.)
- Quick View is a Windows 95 program, not a part of Word. Thus, you can close your Open dialog box and keep the Quick View window active. This lets you move between your document and the Quick View window (using Alt+Tab). You can also keep the window on top of your document, a useful feature when you want to compare an open document with one on disk.

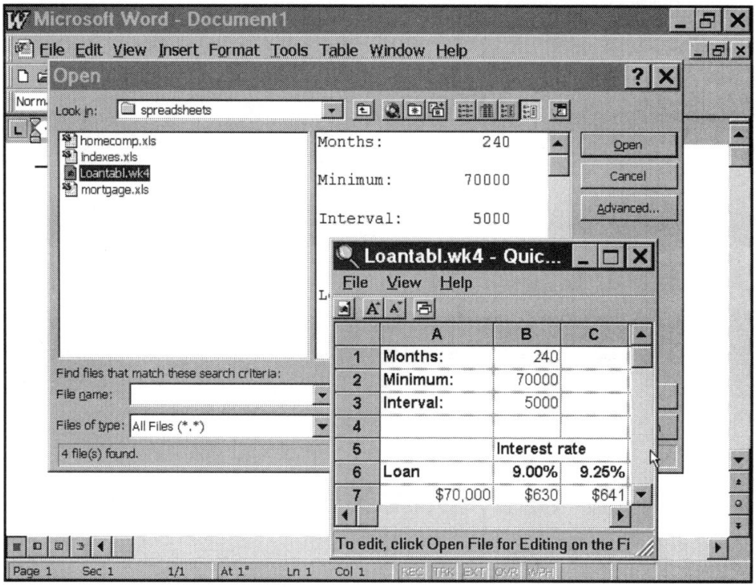

Fig. 4.10
Quick View lets you preview files in a variety of formats. Here, the viewer sneaks a peek at a Lotus 1-2-3 spreadsheet.

Q&A *I can't find Quick View where you said it would be!*

If Quick View is not on your shortcut menu, it's for one of two reasons:

- Quick View isn't installed on your system. Refer to the Windows 95 Help files or manual for information on how to install it.
- You're trying to look at a file whose format Quick View doesn't recognize. For example, Quick View might not appear on the shortcut menu for certain kinds of graphics files.

Part II: Editing Your Work

5

How to Delete, Move, Copy, and Change Your Text

In this chapter:

- **How do I select text?**
- **Quick and easy ways to delete, move, and copy text**
- **Saving time with text libraries—The new, improved AutoText**
- **How to replace text, formats, and special characters**
- **Oops! I didn't mean to do that!**
- **cHANGING the CASE of Words And leTTers**

From hammers to polish, Word has the editing tools that let you pound and buff your document until it's a work of art . . . .

Many of us do not use our word processor's editing functions very efficiently. Walk into any office; odds are most people won't know, for example, how to delete a word or use shortcut keys to move text.

If you're new to word processing, train yourself properly from the start. Learn the best techniques for deleting, copying, and moving text—whether it's with the keyboard or mouse—and do each task the right way until it becomes instinctive.

If, like a self-trained hunt-and-peck typist, you've developed bad habits, now is the time to retool your skills. While you might feel like a wobbly toddler as you pause to ponder your every keystroke and mouse move, you'll soon wow the Word warriors in your office with your flickering fingers and pyrophoric pointer.

You have to select something before you can do anything with it

The key to efficient editing is knowing how to select text. Once you learn the quickest way to choose the words, paragraphs, or blocks you want to edit, the actual editing becomes easy.

To get an idea of how efficient you can be, take a look at Figure 5.1 and imagine that you want to delete the highlighted paragraph.

How would you do this? Well, you can:

1. Click at the start of the paragraph.
2. Hold down the Shift key.
3. Press the right arrow key 335 times until you get to the end of the paragraph.
4. Choose Edit, Cut from the main menu.

Or you can just click twice to the left of the paragraph and press Delete.

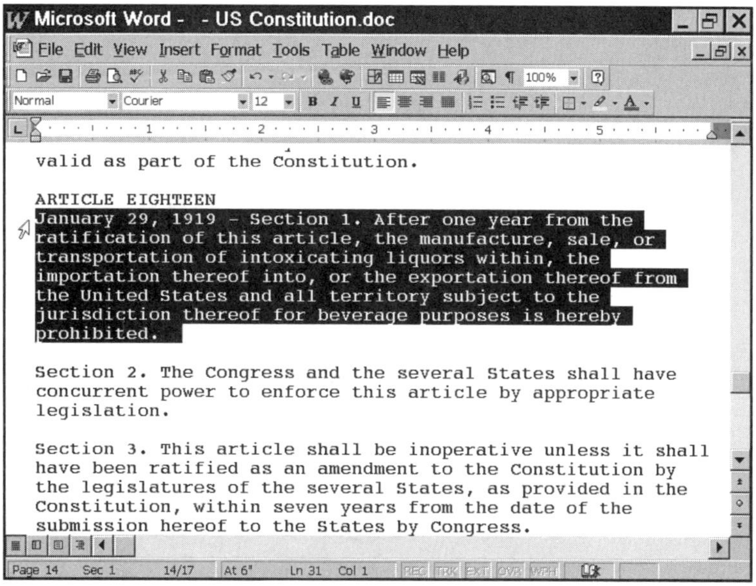
Microsoft Word - - US Constitution.doc
File Edit View Insert Format Tools Table Window Help
Normal
Courier
12
100%
valid as part of the Constitution.
ARTICLE EIGHTEEN
January 29, 1919 - Section 1. After one year from the ratification of this article, the manufacture, sale, or transportation of intoxicating liquors within, the importation thereof into, or the exportation thereof from the United States and all territory subject to the jurisdiction thereof for beverage purposes is hereby prohibited.
Section 2. The Congress and the several States shall have concurrent power to enforce this article by appropriate legislation.
Section 3. This article shall be inoperative unless it shall have been ratified as an amendment to the Constitution by the legislatures of the several States, as provided in the Constitution, within seven years from the date of the submission hereof to the States by Congress.
Page 14 Sec 1 14/17 At 6" Ln 31 Col 1

Fig. 5.1
Deleting a paragraph requires only two mouse clicks and a keystroke.

Word lets you select text by the character, word, line, sentence, paragraph, or document. You can select to the beginning or end of a document. And in most cases, you can use the keyboard or the mouse.

The Word manual includes more than two dozen keyboard and mouse operations, but there's not much point in trying to memorize them. You'll only remember the ones you need, and the odds are you'll need just a few. Once you learn the most important tricks, you can add to your repertoire.

TIP **If you'd like to keep track of the changes you make to a document,** turn on Track Changes by clicking the TRK mode button on the status bar. Word runs a line through text you delete and underlines text you add. Use the Reviewing toolbar (choose View, Toolbar, Reviewing) to accept and reject changes. Chapter 24, "All Together Now—Using Word in Your Workgroup," describes uses for Track Changes and explains how to use the Reviewing toolbar.

Selecting blocks

You can **mark**, or select, any block of text in one of three ways:

- If your insertion point is at the beginning of the block you want to select, put the mouse pointer at the end of the block, hold down the Shift key, and click the mouse button.

- To use the mouse-only technique, click at the beginning of the block and drag the mouse insertion point to the end of the block. Move across the screen to select text word by word; move up or down to select text line by line.
- If you prefer the keyboard, place the insertion point at the beginning of the text. Hold down the Shift key and press the appropriate arrow key. For larger blocks, you can press the Page Up or Page Down key.

Selecting words

The previous methods are best for large blocks, but they're overkill if you just want to select a word or two. It's easier to use these techniques:

- To select a word, click twice anywhere on the word. If you prefer the keyboard, put the insertion point at the beginning of the word and press Ctrl+Shift+right arrow.
- To select several words, click at the beginning of the first word, and hold down the mouse button, and drag the mouse pointer. Word selects the first word character by character, but thereafter selects text word by word. With the keyboard, put the insertion point at the beginning of the word, press Ctrl+Shift, and repeat the arrow as many times as you need to.
- To select from the middle of a word to the end, put the insertion point where you want to start the selection, and press Ctrl+Shift+right arrow. To select to the beginning of a word, use Ctrl+Shift+left arrow.

Selecting lines

A line of text is one that occupies a single line in your document, regardless of punctuation or length. Use these techniques to select lines:

- Select a line by moving your mouse pointer into the space to the left of the line until it points to about 1 o'clock and click once. At the keyboard, place the insertion point at the beginning of the line, and press Shift+End.
- Select multiple lines by clicking the space to the left of the line and dragging the mouse pointer up or down.

- Select to the end of a line by pressing Shift+End. Select to the beginning of a line by pressing Shift+Home.

Selecting sentences

You can select a sentence by clicking twice on the first word and dragging the mouse to the end, but there's an easier way: hold down the Ctrl key and click the sentence.

Selecting paragraphs

A paragraph is all the text between two paragraph marks. Select a paragraph by double-clicking the space next to the paragraph, or triple-clicking inside the paragraph.

Selecting big chunks of text

Sometimes, selecting a few measly sentences or paragraphs isn't enough; you need to cover large expanses of your document fast. Here are a couple of helpful shortcuts:

- Select to the end of your document by pressing Ctrl+Shift+End.
- Select to the beginning of your document by pressing Ctrl+Shift+Home.
- Select the entire document by triple-clicking the space next to your text or by pressing Ctrl+A.

TIP **You can cancel your selected text by clicking anywhere in the text** or by pressing an arrow key.

Okay, my text is selected. Now what?

Once you select your text, you're ready to delete, copy, or move it, or format the text in bold, underline, or italic.

Get rid of it

You delete, or clear, selected text by pressing the Delete or Backspace key.

You can restore deleted text by *immediately* clicking the Undo button on the Standard taskbar, pressing Ctrl+Z, or choosing Edit, Undo Clear from the menu bar.

Moving text with the mouse

Like what you wrote, but decided it would work better somewhere else? Word gives you two ways to move text with the mouse. With the first method, you use two buttons on the Standard toolbar: Cut and Paste.

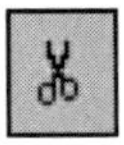

Select your text and click the Cut button. The text disappears, but don't worry—you haven't lost it. Word has stashed the text in a storage bin for later use. Removing text in this manner is called **cutting**, and the storage bin is called the **Clipboard**. We'll cover the Clipboard in more detail in Chapter 22.

Next, position the insertion point where you want to move the text and click the Paste button. Word takes the text out of storage and inserts or **pastes** it at the position of your insertion point.

You can also paste the block by clicking the right mouse button and choosing Paste from the shortcut menu.

Drag-and-drop moving

You can move selected text to any place in your document by pointing to the highlighted block and holding down the mouse button. A small checkered box attaches itself to the pointer as you move the block. Drag the block to its destination and release the button. Word drops the block into its new location.

TIP **If you start dragging your selected text and decide you don't want** to move it after all, move the mouse pointer outside the document window. When it turns into a circle with a line through it, release the button. You also can cancel the move by pressing the Esc key.

Some people prefer the keyboard

To move a block of text with the keyboard, cut it by pressing Ctrl+X, move the insertion point to the point of insertion, and press Ctrl+V.

Can I swap these paragraphs?

You can switch the order of two paragraphs without cutting and pasting. This trick is particularly useful when you want to reorder items in a list.

Put the insertion point anywhere inside the paragraph you want to move (it doesn't have to be highlighted). Press Alt+Shift+up arrow to move it before the previous paragraph. Press Alt+Shift+down arrow to move it after the next paragraph. Note that if you've double-spaced between paragraphs, you need to press the arrow key twice to jump over the extra line.

Copying with the mouse

Copying text is almost the same as moving it, except that the selected block stays where it is.

Click the Copy button on the Standard toolbar instead of the Cut button. Like cutting, copying puts the text on the Clipboard, but Word doesn't delete the selected text.

Move the insertion point to where you want the copied text to appear. Click the Paste button or select Paste from the shortcut menu.

To copy a selected block of text with the drag-and-drop method, first hold down the Ctrl key and point to the selected block; then hold down the mouse button and drag the block to its destination.

Copying with the keyboard

Select the text you want to copy and press Ctrl+C. Move the insertion point to where you want to copy the text and press Ctrl+V.

TIP **When you put a block of text on the Clipboard, you can paste that** text as often as you like. This is a time-saving trick if you have a line of text that you want to repeat several times.

CAUTION **When you cut or copy a block of text to the Clipboard, it replaces** and permanently deletes any text that is already on the Clipboard. If you want to store the block for later use, use AutoText, described later in this chapter.

New muscle for AutoText

Best of 97

The Clipboard is great for simple moves and copies, but what if you want to save a block of text permanently? Something you can insert into a document whenever you need it, such as a greeting in a form letter?

Enter AutoText. This Insert menu command lets you create a library of commonly used text. You can insert the text in any document, at any time, until you remove it from the library. (Word 2 users: AutoText is the same as the Glossary.)

Microsoft has given Word 97's AutoText a lot of new bells and whistles that make it both more powerful and easier to use, but to get the most out of it, you'll need to know something about fields, styles, and templates, all of which we'll cover later in this book. We'll give you the basics now and you can get your advanced degree in AutoTextology later.

Psychic AutoPhenomena

Before you begin to create your own AutoText entries, you should take a look at how it works. Try this experiment:

Start typing the salutation "To Whom It May Concern." By the time you type "To Wh," Word displays the entire string of characters in a ScreenTip, as in Figure 5.2. Press the Enter key or F3. Word inserts the complete salutation. If you don't want to insert the entry, just keep typing, and the ScreenTip disappears.

How does Word know what you're going to type? Simply put, it compares what you're typing to the names of its AutoText entries. When it finds a unique match, it displays the entry. In the previous example, it found a match for "To Wh."

Best of 97

AutoComplete, a new Word97 feature, has the capability to finish a string of text based on the first few characters typed.

"To Whom It May Concern" is one of about 40 AutoText entries that come with Word 97. You can view a complete list by choosing Insert, AutoText from the main menu. The categories include attention lines, salutations, closings, and mailing instructions.

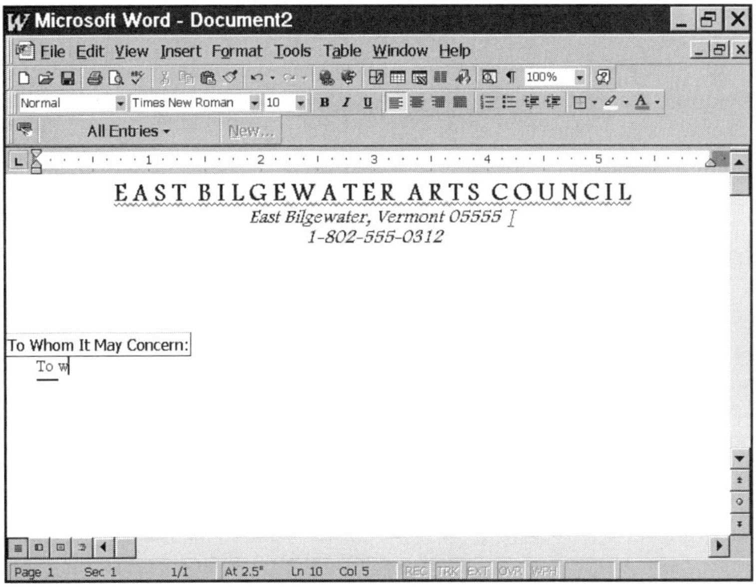

Fig. 5.2
When you type the first few characters of an AutoText name, Word displays the first few words; press F3 to insert the suggested entry.

Q&A *I don't get a ScreenTip when I type an AutoText name. What's wrong?*

The function is turned off. To turn it on, choose Insert, AutoText, AutoText from the main menu. Word displays the AutoText panel of the AutoCorrect dialog box. Put a check next to Show AutoComplete Tip for AutoText and Dates.

TIP **AutoComplete doesn't work just with AutoText entries. It lets** you automatically insert several other items: The current date, a day of the week, a month other than the current one, and your name. AutoText will enter the current date for you, if you just type the first few letters of the month's name. For example, on Christmas Day, typing "Dec" displays a ScreenTip "December"; pressing Enter inserts December. Pressing the spacebar then displays a ScreenTip with the entire date, "December 25, 1996." Press Enter to accept the entry or keep typing to ignore it.

Bellying up to the AutoText toolbar

You'll get comfortable with AutoText more quickly if you use the AutoText toolbar. To display the toolbar, choose View, Toolbars, AutoText from the main menu.

If you want to take a look at AutoText's lists of entries, click the button labeled "All Entries"; you'll see the lists displayed, as shown in Figure 5.3.

The toolbar also is the most convenient way to create a number of AutoText entries from a single document.

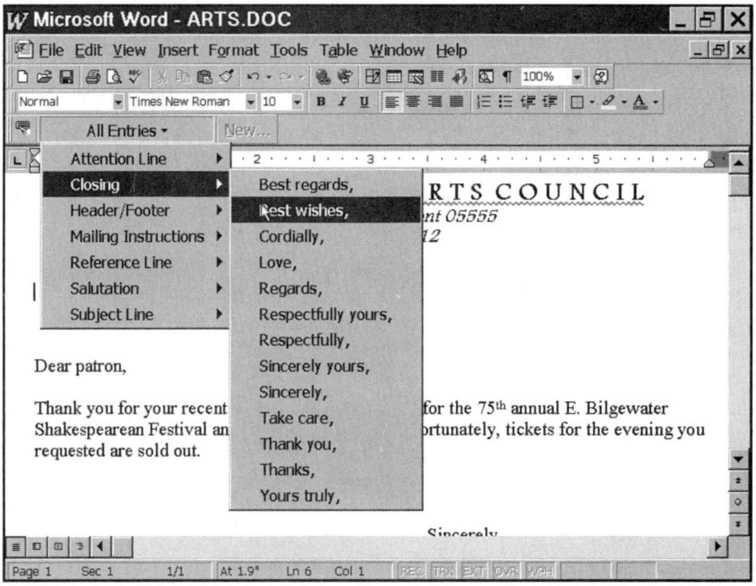

Fig. 5.3
Use the AutoText toolbar to gain easier access to your list of AutoText entries. Word comes with more than 40 entries ready to use.

Create your own AutoText entries

It's time to add some of your own entries to AutoText's library. Say you have a sentence that you want to use in a series of letters. Select the sentence and choose New from the AutoText toolbar. If the toolbar isn't displayed, choose Insert, Autotext, New from the main menu or press Alt+F3. The Create AutoText dialog box appears, as shown in Figure 5.4.

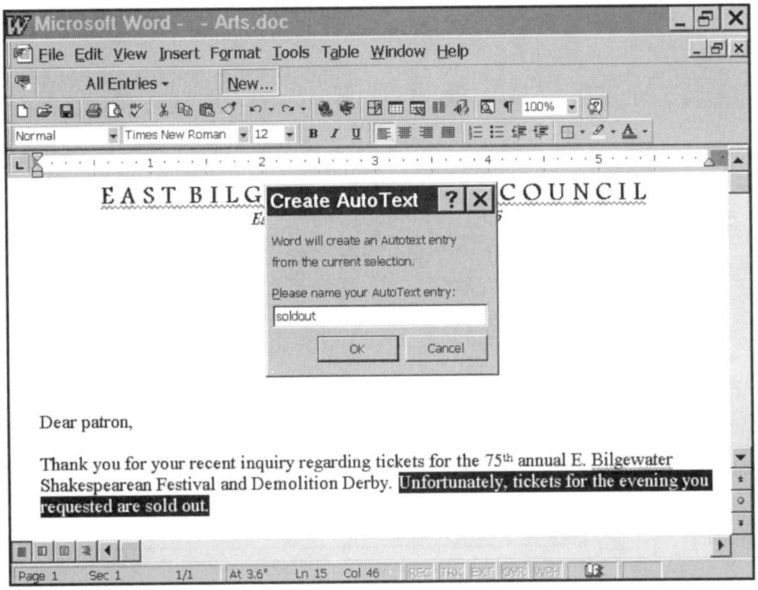
Microsoft Word - - Arts.doc
File Edit View Insert Format Tools Table Window Help
All Entries
New...
100%
Normal
Times New Roman
12
EAST BILG
COUNCIL
Create AutoText
Word will create an Autotext entry from the current selection.
Please name your AutoText entry:
soldout
OK
Cancel
Dear patron,
Thank you for your recent inquiry regarding tickets for the 75th annual E. Bilgewater Shakespearean Festival and Demolition Derby. Unfortunately, tickets for the evening you requested are sold out.
Page 1 Sec 1 1/1 At 3.6" Ln 15 Col 46 REC TRK EXT OVR WPH

Fig. 5.4
AutoText lets you create a permanent library of text blocks that are available to all of your documents.

AutoText gives you an entry name based on the first few words of the text, or you can create your own name. Ideally, the first two or three characters of the name should uniquely identify the entry. Remember: AutoComplete displays a ScreenTip when it has matched what you've typed with an AutoText name. If you have three entries titled "pay me now," "pay me later," and "pay me please," AutoComplete won't know which one you want until you've typed the first letter of the third word.

When you're done, click OK to store the entry.

CAUTION **To ensure that your results match those described here, create** your experimental AutoText entries using Word's Blank Document template (that's the one Word chooses for you when you load Word, or click the New button on the Standard toolbar). Also, make sure Normal appears in the Style selection box on the Formatting toolbar, as in Figure 5.4.

So what's Normal, anyway?

As soon as you create your first AutoText entry, the All Entries menu changes: it now includes a Normal entry. And if you click the Normal button, you'll see the entry titles you created, as seen in Figure 5.5. To explain what happened, we'll have to dip a bit into some semi-technical detail.

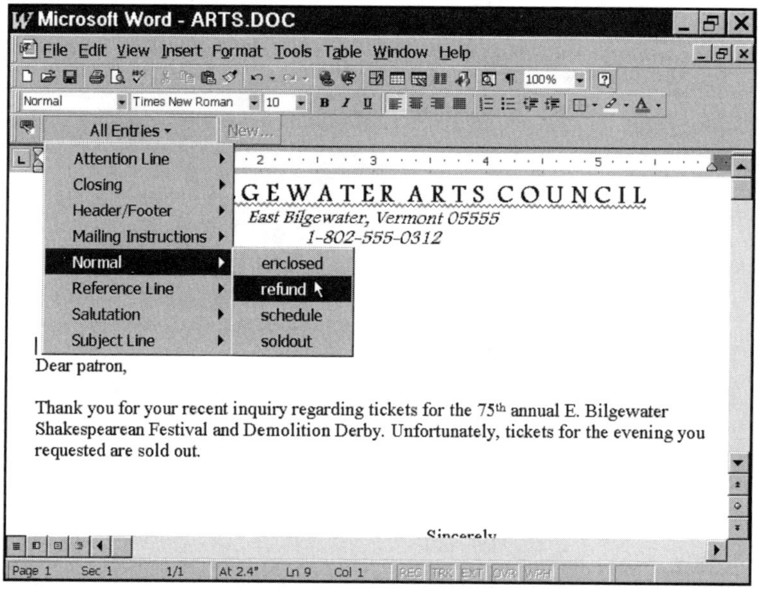

Fig. 5.5
Display a list of your new AutoText entries by choosing Normal from the All Entries menu.

An AutoText entry attaches to the **style** in which it was created. We'll discuss style in detail in Chapter 12. For now, all you need to know is that the toolbar shows the AutoText entries for whatever style is shown in your Style selection box on the Formatting toolbar.

But don't worry; your other AutoText entries are still there. Simply hold down the Shift key as you click the Normal button, and Word displays the All Entries list. (You also can hold down the Shift key as you choose Insert, AutoText from the main menu.)

And if Word shows you the All Entries button, AutoText entries created under the Normal style are avm9lable. Click All Entries and choose Normal; Word displays a submenu listing your Normal AutoText entries.

Tools for the forgetful

What if you don't remember what an AutoText name stands for? Or you forget the AutoText name for an entry you created? Easy: Go to the AutoText panel of the AutoCorrect dialog box (see Figure 5.6). You get there by either clicking the AutoText icon in the AutoText toolbar or choosing Insert, AutoText, AutoText from the main menu.

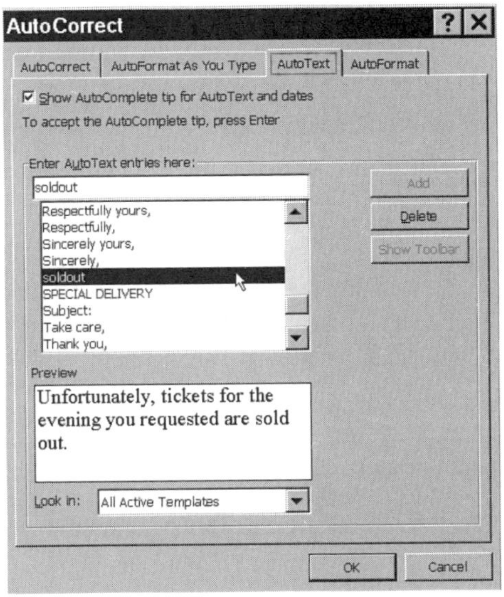

Fig. 5.6
The AutoText panel lets you look at a list of your entries and preview their contents.

The AutoText panel lists all of your entries in the panel beneath Enter AutoText Entries Here. When you select an entry, its contents appear in the Preview panel.

Easy Undoes it

Undo lets you reverse almost any typing or editing—including deletes, cuts, copies, and pastes. The ScreenTip for the Undo button on the Standard toolbar changes to tell you what action you've just taken, as does the Undo command on the Edit menu. For example, if you delete selected text, the ScreenTip and Edit, Undo say Undo Clear. If you paste text, the command is Undo Paste.

Word lets you undo an unlimited number of actions. Click the down arrow next to the Undo button on the Standard toolbar. You'll see a drop-down list box similar to the one in Figure 5.7. Select as many actions as you want undone.

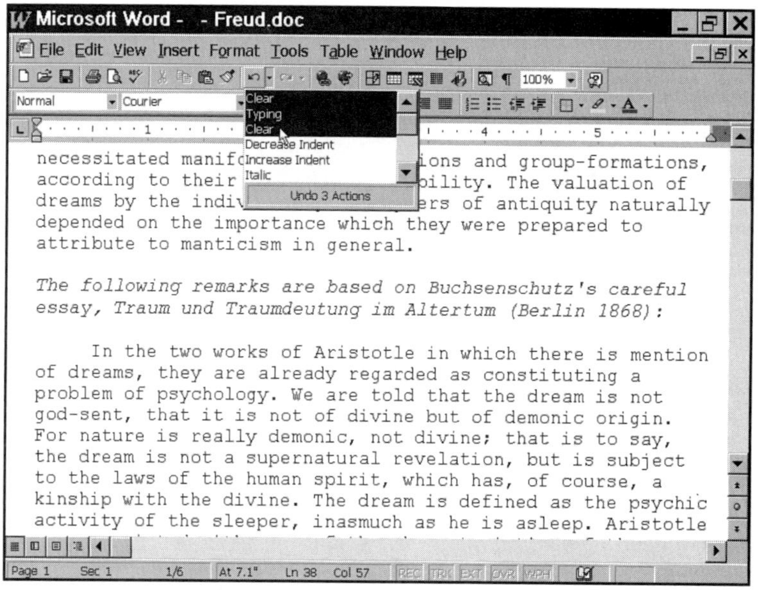

Fig. 5.7
Word's multiple Undo lets you undo deletes, cuts, copies, pastes, and a variety of other actions.

To reverse the undo, press Ctrl+Y or click the Redo button on the Standard toolbar. To redo several undos, click the down arrow next to the Redo button. You'll get a drop-down list box similar to the one for Undo.

CAUTION **You can't undo file commands such as Open, Close, and Save.**

I need to make the same change in a bunch of different places

You've just written a long proposal pitching your company's services to Berwick Manufacturing Co. when a colleague points out that the correct spelling is "Berwyck." You go about the tedious task of scrolling through your document and correcting each misspelling manually. You then spend the rest of the day wondering if you caught every error, comforted by the knowledge that a $3.2 million account is at stake.

Why not let the Replace command do the work for you? Just tell Word to replace every instance of "Berwick" with "Berwyck."

Select Edit, Replace or press Ctrl+H to display the Replace panel of the Find and Replace dialog box. The following graphics page gives you a detailed look at how Replace works.

CAUTION **Find and Replace is a powerful tool, but there are some tricks to** using it successfully. Check out the "Warning! Read this first" section before you use these find and replace techniques in an important document.

To use Find and Replace, open the dialog box and follow these steps:

1. Type the text you want to replace in the Find What text box and the replacement text in the Replace With text box.
2. Choose Find Next or Replace. Word finds the first occurrence of the string in your document and highlights it.
3. To replace the string, click Replace. To skip the string and go to the next occurrence, click Find Next.

   To replace all instances of the text in the document, click Replace All.

CAUTION **Use Undo to reverse a bungled replace. Don't use Replace All** unless you're sure of the results. Replacing strings one at a time is slow and sometimes tedious, but it's safer.

Warning! Read this first

Replace is a powerful command that can lead to unpredictable and distressing results. If you're not careful, you might mangle words without even knowing it.

In particular, be careful of capitalization and strings of text inside words. When you plan a find-and-replace, ask yourself these important questions:

Am I looking for whole words only?

Am I looking for an uppercased word?

Instant Replace

Word's Replace command lets you replace or delete text, formats, and special characters, either one at a time or en masse.

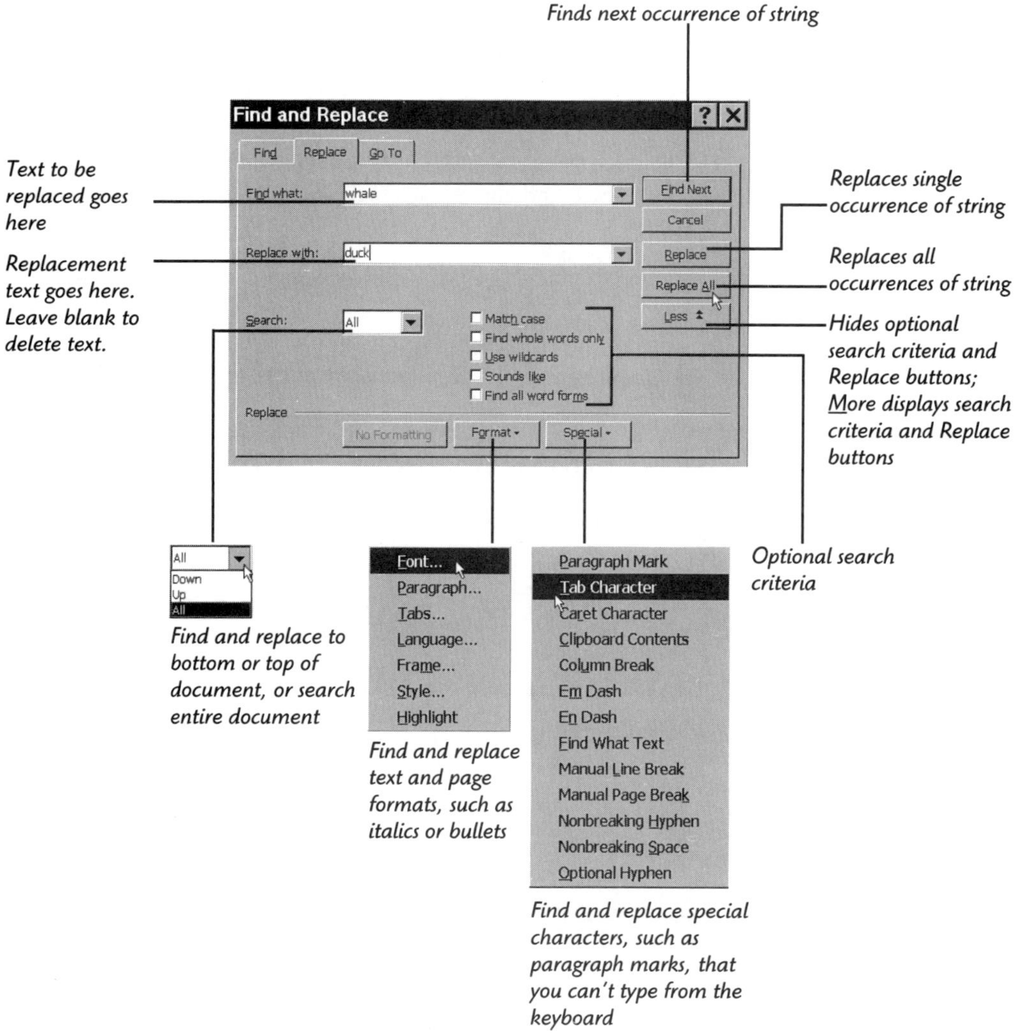

Whole words versus strings

By default, Word searches for *all* instances of a text string, whether it's a whole word or embedded in a larger string. That is, if you look for the abbreviation `mph`, Word also finds `emphatic`, and `camphor`. Replacing `mph` with `miles per hour` also changes `emphatic` to `emiles per houratic` and `camphor` to `camiles per houror`.

To avoid such accidents, check Find Whole Words Only in the Replace panel.

How to match case

Replace also ignores capitalization. For example, `Bill` will find `Bill Clinton` and `please send me the bill`. And if you change `Bill` to `President`, you also change `bill` to `president`.

If you want to find and replace only `Bill`, put a check next to Match Case. When you match case, you must type the replacement text in the proper case.

Form-fitting searches

Word has an interesting option called Find All Word Forms that lets you replace all forms of a noun or verb, not just the form you put into the Find What box. For example, if you replace `goose` with `duck`, Word also replaces `geese` with `ducks`. Or if you replace `go` with `drive`, Word will, for example, even replace the sentence "I'm going out of my mind" with "I'm driving out of my mind." To be on the safe side, replace each occurrence of the word separately with Replace.

Replace as a shortcut for deleting text

You can use Replace to delete all instances of a word. To do that, enter the word in the Find What text box and leave the Replace With text box blank.

Botching such a surgical strike can result in serious damage to your document. Make doubly sure to check the appropriate search criteria in the Replace panel, and use the Find Next and Replace buttons to replace each instance of the string individually.

TIP **Word lets you move between your document and the Find and** Replace dialog box, so you can edit text without interrupting a search or replace. If you're in the dialog box, click the document; if you're in the document, click the dialog box. You can also move between the two by pressing Alt+F6.

Can I replace fonts and formats, too?

Word gives you many options to replace fonts, font styles, and type sizes. While we haven't discussed formatting yet, this simple example should give you an idea of what you can do.

Say that you want to change all italicized text in your document to bold italics. Here's what to do:

1. In the Replace panel, place the insertion point in the Find What box. Delete anything left over from previous replaces.
2. Click Format, and choose Font from the drop-down menu. Word displays the Font panel in the Find Font dialog box, as in Figure 5.8.

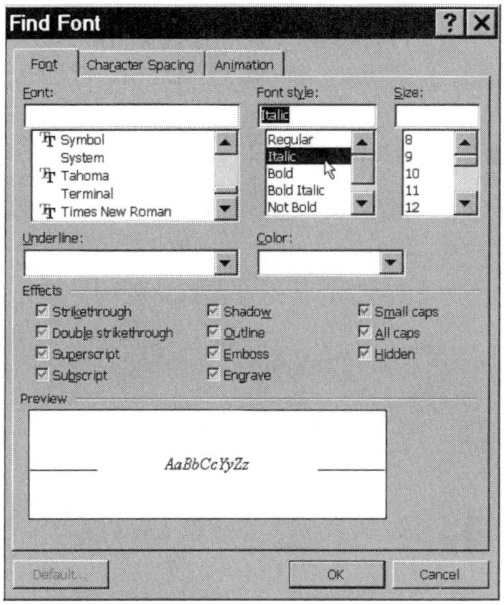

Fig. 5.8
Word is being instructed to look for all instances of italicized words, with the goal of replacing the italics with bold italics.

3. Choose Italic from the list under Font Style and click OK. The words "Format: Italic" appear under the Find What text box.
4. Move the insertion point to the Replace With box.
5. Repeat steps 2 and 3, only choose Bold Italic instead of Italic. The words "Format: Bold, Italic" appear under the Replace With text box.
6. Click OK.
7. Click Replace All.

CAUTION **Don't forget to remove your formatting criteria after you're done** with a search. Otherwise, future word searches are likely to fail, since Word will look for the word only in the format you've specified. In other words, if you look for the word "Duck" in italics, Word won't find "Duck" in regular or bold style. You remove formatting criteria by placing your cursor in the Find What or Replace With text box and choosing No Formatting.

Replacing special characters and codes

As you can replace formats, so can you replace special characters that you can't type from the keyboard, including paragraph marks and tabs.

Figure 5.9 shows you the list box you see when you click Special in the Replace panel. In this case, a tab, represented by `^t`, has already been placed in the Find What text box. Choosing Paragraph Mark puts `^p` in the Replace With text box. The subsequent replace changes all tabs to paragraph marks.

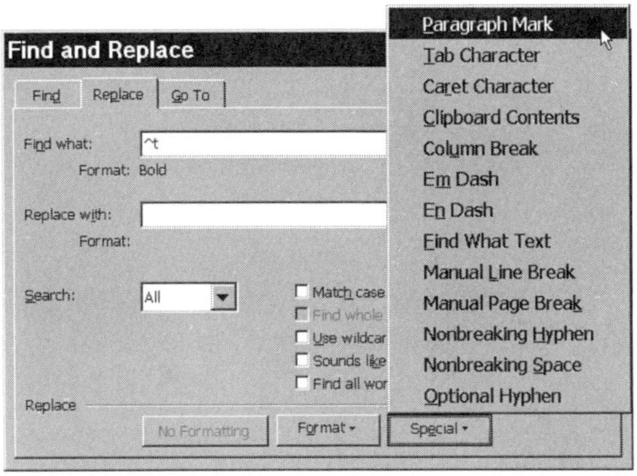

Fig. 5.9
Use Replace to replace special characters that you can't type into the Find What and Replace With text boxes.

Here are some instances in which these special characters are useful:

- *Paragraph Mark.* If you get text from another word processor that has a paragraph mark at the end of each line, you can replace the paragraph marks with spaces. You can also add paragraph indents by changing each paragraph mark to a paragraph mark and a tab.
- *Tab.* You can get rid of paragraph indents by replacing paragraph mark+Tab with a paragraph mark. These appear as `^p^t` and `^p` in the Find What and Replace With text boxes, respectively.

Changing case

You can change the case of selected text by pressing Shift+F3. Word loops you through different combinations of upper- and lowercase letters. For example, if you were to select `you don't have to shout`, Shift+F3 would give you the results in the following table.

Do This...	To Change the Text to This
Press Shift+F3	You Don't Have To Shout
Press Shift+F3 again	YOU DON'T HAVE TO SHOUT
Press Shift+F3 again	you don't have to shout

You also can choose Change Case from the Format menu and choose from the options in the Change Case dialog box.

TIP **To change the case of a word, you don't need to select the word.** Simply put the insertion point anywhere in the word and press Shift+F3.

6

My Grammar and Speling Ain't So Good

In this chapter:

- **Did I spell that rite?**
- **Create your own dictionaries**
- **AutoCorrect: Word's automatic spell-fixer**
- **Use the grammar checker to improve your writing skills**
- **How to use (and *not* use) the thesaurus**

Can't spell? Forgotten what passive voice is? Let Word's spelling and grammar checkers show you the errors of your ways . . . .

Nothing undermines the credibility of a letter or report faster than spelling errors, grammatical blunders, and typos. Most of us know this. But few of us exercise complete command of the English language's many anomalies. No matter how carefully you edit and proofread a document, chances are something will slip past your guard.

Word provides three lines of defense: the spelling checker, AutoCorrect, and the grammar checker. They aren't perfect (they have their own problems handling the language's vagaries), and you should never rely on them alone to check your documents. But they can give you an extra measure of quality control, catching mistakes you overlook and pointing out subtle problems of style and word use.

With previous versions of Word, you usually used the checkers on a finished document. Word 97 includes a new feature that catches mistakes as you make them and lets you make on-the-spot corrections.

Casting a magic spell check

Nearly every first-time Word user heads straight for the spelling checker as soon as he learns how to create a document. Even good spellers find the spelling checker a welcome addition to their arsenal of writing tools.

Word lets you check your entire document, any selected part of a document, or even a single word. Word also lets you modify the spelling checker. You can add words to the dictionary as you go, and you can create special dictionaries for documents that include unusual words and jargon.

Spell checking made easy

Word 97 has a feature that conveniently checks your spelling as you type. When you misspell a word, Word highlights the word with a wavy line, as shown in Figure 6.1.

To fix the error, click the word with the right mouse button. A shortcut menu appears that includes a list of possible replacements. Click the correct spelling.

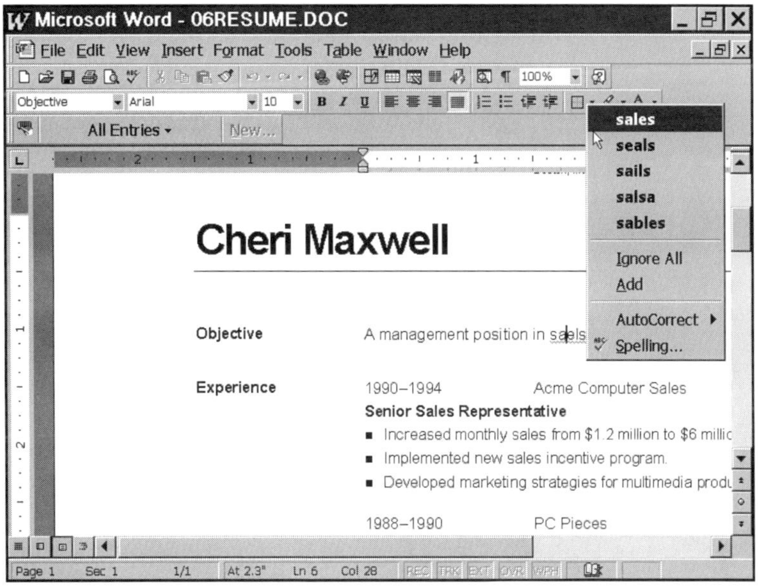

Fig. 6.1
When you turn on Automatic Spell Checking, Word highlights words that aren't in its dictionary. Click the right mouse button if you want to correct the misspelled word.

The shortcut menu also lets you add the word to a supplemental Custom dictionary. For example, in Figure 6.1, right-clicking the word "Chelmsford" and then choosing Add tells the spelling checker that Chelmsford is correct and to no longer highlight it. (You'll learn more about the Custom dictionary and how to create your own special dictionaries later in this chapter.)

If you want the checker to ignore the word for the rest of the document, whether it's right or wrong, choose Ignore All. Word won't try to correct the word, and it won't bug you about it either.

You turn on the spelling checker feature by choosing Tools, Options from the main menu, clicking the Spelling & Grammar tab, and clicking the box next to Check Spelling As You Type.

TIP **You can reverse a spelling change with the Edit, Undo command** or the Undo button on the Standard toolbar.

Running the spelling checker

You've just received a lengthy report that you need to print and photocopy for a meeting in 20 minutes. "Maybe you should proof this first," the department head suggests. "You know how bad my spelling is."

You could turn on AutoCorrect and spend 20 stressful minutes fixing the mistakes manually. Or you could spell check the document in one fell swoop with Word's spelling checker. Word finds all potential misspellings and presents them to you one by one for correction. (You might also suggest that your department head use AutoCorrect from now on.)

To run a spell check, press F7 or click the Spelling button on the Standard toolbar. You can start anywhere in the document. Word checks everything from the insertion point to the end of the document. When it's done, Word gives you the option of checking the beginning of the document.

I just need to check this part

To spell check just a portion of your document, select the text and run the checker. Word spell checks only the text in the defined block.

You can check words, paragraphs, and lines quickly with simple keyboard and mouse combinations. The following table lists the most common types of spell checks.

To Spell Check...	Do This
Whole document	Press F7 or click the Spell button.
Single word	Double-click the word and press F7.
Single line	Click once next to the line and press F7.
Paragraph	Double-click next to the paragraph and press F7.

TIP **If you want to return to where you began your spell check, create** a Bookmark with Insert, Bookmark before you start your check. When Word finishes the check, choose Insert, Bookmark, Go To. For more information on Bookmarks, see Chapter 2, "Creating a Document: First Steps."

Using the Spelling Checker dialog box

When you start a spell check, Word finds the first word it doesn't recognize and displays the Spelling and Grammar dialog box shown in Figure 6.2.

The unrecognized word appears in the Not In Dictionary box. If the dictionary includes possible replacements, it lists them in the Suggestions list box and puts the most likely one at the top.

Fig. 6.2
When the spelling checker finds a misspelled word, it gives you a list of potential corrections to choose from.

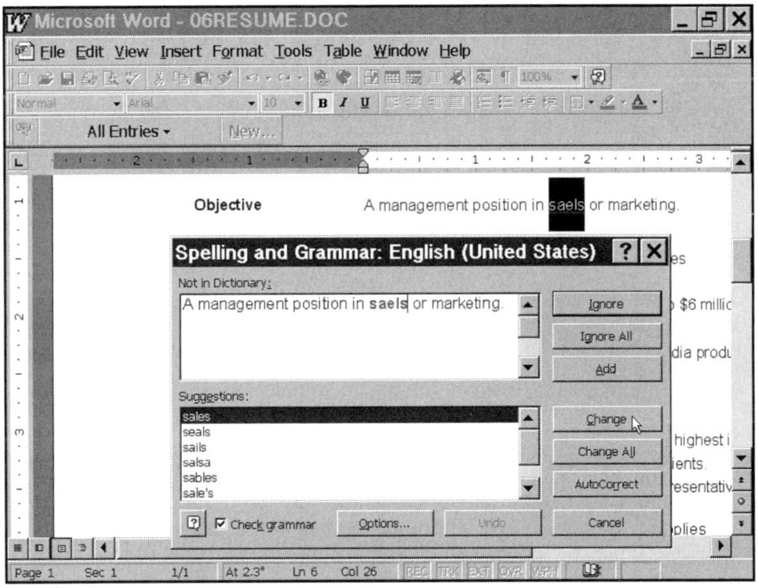

You'll be surprised at how often the spelling checker puts the correct word in the Change To box. For example, in Figure 6.2, the dictionary correctly decided that "saels" was supposed to be "sales" and not "salsa."

To accept the suggested change, click the Change button. If you want another word on the list, double-click it. To delete the word or replace it with one that is not in the Suggestions box, make the correction in the Not in Dictionary box and click Change.

At any point, you can click Change All to change all instances of the word in the document or selected text.

To add the word to your dictionary, click Add.

To keep the word as is, click Ignore. However, the checker will query you on the word if it reappears. If you want the checker to accept the word for the entire document, click Ignore All.

Spelling only, please

In previous versions of Word, the grammar and spelling checkers were separate commands on the Tools menu. Word 97 puts both functions in the same dialog box. By default, you check your spelling and grammar at the same time.

That's fine, but many times you need to check your spelling only. You can speed things up by foregoing the grammar check. Choose either Tools, Options from the main menu and click the Spelling & Grammar tab, or choose Options in the Spelling and Grammar dialog box. Then, in the Spelling & Grammar panel, remove the check mark next to Check Grammar with Spelling (see Figure 6.3).

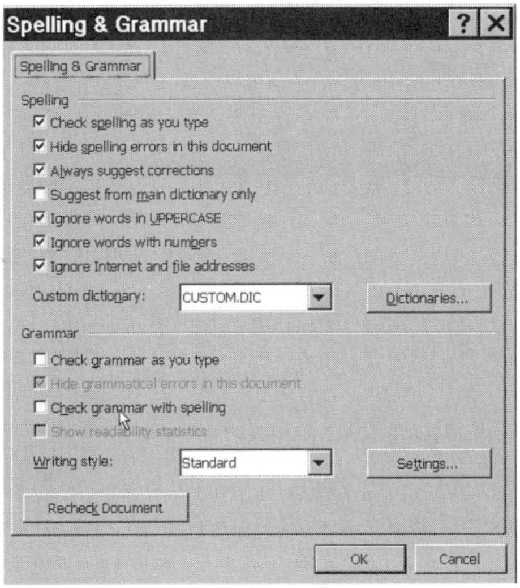

Fig. 6.3
The Spelling & Grammar panel is where you select options for how Word spell and grammar checks your document.

Plain English, please!

Notice in this section that we refer to the Spelling **and** Grammar dialog box, the Spelling **&** Grammar dialog box, and the Spelling & Grammar **panel**. That little ampersand makes a big difference. The Spelling and Grammar dialog box is the one with which you actually check a document, by choosing the button on the toolbar, pressing F7, or choosing Tools, Spelling and Grammar from the main menu (see Figure 6.2).

The Spelling & Grammar dialog box, on the other hand, is the one you get when you choose Options from the Spelling and Grammar dialog box (see Figure 6.3). Within it is the Spelling & Grammar panel, in which you determine how the spelling and grammar checker behaves. Just to make things a little more confusing, you can display the same Spelling & Grammar panel in the Options dialog box, by choosing Tools, Options from the main menu and clicking the Spelling & Grammar tab.

TIP **As you check a document, you can move between the Spelling** and Grammar dialog box and your document by clicking one or the other, or by pressing Alt+F6. This lets you keep the dialog box open while you work. You can use this technique to check several blocks of text without constantly opening and closing the dialog box.

When an error is not an error: adding words to the dictionary

When you add a word that's not in the dictionary, you're actually adding it to a special dictionary called Custom. Word refers to both the regular and Custom dictionaries when it spell checks a document.

You can speed your spell checks by putting names, acronyms, and special terms that you use often in the Custom dictionary. The simplest way is to add your words one by one as the spelling checker flags them. But you can also add words *en masse* by opening and editing the Custom dictionary. Follow these steps:

1. Choose Tools, Options from the menu bar and click the Spelling & Grammar tab. (Do not choose Options from the Spelling and Grammar dialog box; Word won't let you edit the dictionary while a spell check is in progress.)
2. Choose the Dictionaries button. Word displays the Custom Dictionaries dialog box (see Figure 6.4).
3. Select CUSTOM.DIC in the Custom Dictionaries selection box (if it isn't already selected). Do not clear the check box.
4. Click the Edit button. Word opens the dictionary as a Word document.
5. Make your additions, following each by pressing the Enter key.
6. Save the file as you would any document. Word displays an obtuse message telling you that the document might contain formatting you'll lose in Text Only format. That's fine; you want the document in text format, so choose Yes. Then close the document. Word turns off the automatic spelling checker when you edit a dictionary. Don't forget to turn it back on; check Spelling As You Type in the Spelling & Grammar panel (see Figure 6.4).

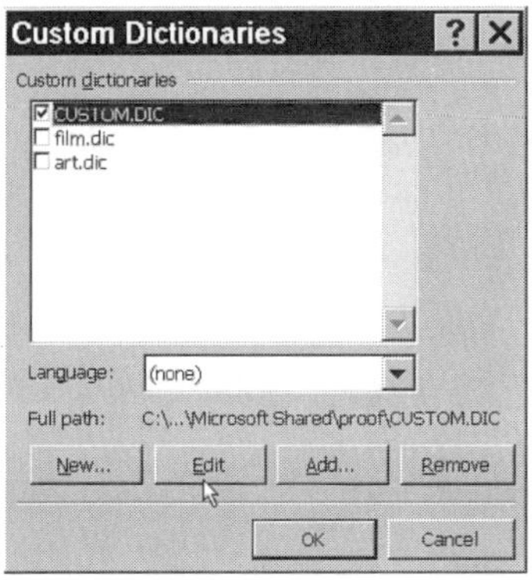

Fig. 6.4
The Custom Dictionaries dialog box lets you add entries to Word's Custom dictionary or create and modify your own special dictionaries.

Create your own dictionaries

Imagine that you're a film critic (aren't we all?) and you're tired of Word suggesting you change "Meryl Streep" to "Merrily Strap." Sure, you could put "Meryl" and "Streep" in your Custom dictionary. But here's an alternative: create a dictionary called Film that includes only actors' names and other film-related terms.

You can use this technique to build a dictionary for any vocation or avocation that has its own lexicon. You can then make that dictionary active only when you need it. Here's how:

1. Choose Tools, Options from the main menu, and then click the Spelling and Grammar tab in the Options dialog box.
2. Click Dictionaries. Word displays the Custom Dictionaries dialog box shown in Figure 6.4.
3. Click New. Word displays a Create Custom Dictionary dialog box that looks like the Open dialog box. The main difference is that Word automatically chooses Dictionary Files (*.dic) in the Save as Type selection box. Change to the Proof subfolder that contains your dictionaries, if you're not already in it.
4. Type the name of the new dictionary in the File Name text box and click Save. Word creates the dictionary file and returns you to the Custom Dictionaries dialog box.

Adding words to your special dictionary

Your custom dictionaries must be activated before you can add to them. Otherwise, when you add a word during a spell check, Word puts it in the Custom dictionary.

Word automatically activates a new custom dictionary when you create it. The dictionary has a check next to it in the Custom Dictionaries list box (refer to Figure 6.4). You can activate up to ten dictionaries, including Custom.

Your active dictionaries appear in the Custom Dictionary selection box in the Spelling & Grammar panel (refer to Figure 6.3). Select the dictionary you want to add to during your spell check and choose OK.

Let Word fix errors as you type

Do you sometimes feel as if you have a small dysfunction in the part of your brain that controls language? One that prevents you from ever remembering how to spell words like "relevant," "harass," and "embarrass?"

And then there's the disconnect between your brain's language center and your fingers. Certain words never come out the way they're supposed to. "Character" comes out as "characater" and "information" as "inforamtion." It's as if your fingers have been cursed by the Voodoo Priest of Annoying Typos.

True, Word's spelling checker alerts you to these errors. But there's a better and more satisfying way to cover your tracks: AutoCorrect. AutoCorrect automatically fixes a misspelling or typo on the spot. If you type "relevent," for example, AutoCorrect immediately replaces it with "relevant."

How to add words to AutoCorrect

AutoCorrect is a list of text strings and their replacements. Word starts you with more than 500 entries. To add to the list, choose AutoCorrect from the Tools menu. Word displays the AutoCorrect panel in the AutoCorrect dialog box. Enter the text you want fixed in the Replace text box and the correction in the With text box; then click Add (see Figure 6.5).

Thereafter, when you type the text that you put in the Replace box, Word immediately replaces it with the correction you entered in the With box.

To start automatic correction, make sure to place a check mark in the Replace Text As You Type check box in the AutoCorrect dialog box.

TIP **You can add to your AutoCorrect list from the Spelling and** Grammar dialog box. After you select the correct word in the Suggestions selection box, click the AutoCorrect button.

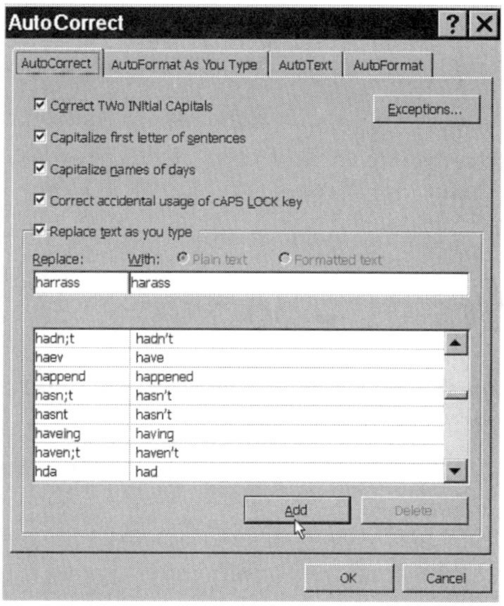

Fig. 6.5
AutoCorrect lets you automatically fix common typos and misspellings.

Teach AutoCorrect some tricks

The uses for AutoCorrect go beyond correcting spelling errors and typos. You can use it to create shortcuts for long text strings and hard-to-type symbols.

Say you write about the Society for the Preservation and Encouragement of Barber Shop Quartet Singing in America (known far and wide as SPEBSQSA). You can use AutoCorrect so that whenever you type **speb**, the full name of the organization is inserted in your text.

The following table lists a few examples of how you can use AutoCorrect creatively:

Replace This	With This
-->	→
NH	New Hampshire
Xerox	photocopy
tel#	1-800-555-1234
Tadz	Tadzhikistan

Q&A ***So what's the difference between AutoCorrect and AutoText?***

They perform much the same function; both instruct Word to insert a string of text in place of a few characters you type. But AutoText prompts you to complete the entry; AutoCorrect completes the entry without prompting. This makes AutoCorrect more convenient for making corrections and other minor changes that don't require your attention.

How to change text into symbols and special characters

Putting "-->" in the Replace text box is simple enough. But how do you get → in the With box?

From your document, choose Insert, Symbol from the menu bar. In the Symbol dialog box, click the Symbols tab and choose Wingdings in the Font drop-down box. Click twice on → to insert the → symbol in your text; then close the Symbol dialog box.

In your document, select the symbol using your Shift and left arrow keys (don't double-click the symbol or you'll return to the Symbol dialog box). Go to the AutoCorrect dialog box. The → symbol appears in the With text box. Type a **-->** in the Replace text box, and then click Add.

> ***Plain English, please!***
>
> For our purposes, **symbols** are characters that don't appear on your keyboard, including specially formatted letters and numbers, dingbats such as astrological signs, and funky bullets.
>
> **Special characters** are a category of symbols that function more as typographic elements; for example, the em dash (—), copyright symbol (©), and single open quote ('). These special characters have their own dialog box to make them easier to find and use. (We discuss symbols and characters in more detail in Chapter 8, "Character Sketches—Formatting Your Type.")

Other AutoCorrections

Most of us type like rhinos wearing mittens. The results often include double capitals, sentences that aren't capitalized, and inadvertent Caps Locks. AutoCorrect has ways to help you handle all of these problems.

Got a lazy Shift-key finger?

If you're a speedy typist, chances are one hand sometimes gets a little ahead of the other and you end up with two capital letters at the beginning of a sentence. AutoCorrect to the rescue. When you select the Correct TWo INitial CApitals check box, Word automatically changes the second capital letter to lowercase (for example, "TWo" becomes "Two"). This option does not affect two-letter acronyms.

You can force Word to accept two initial capitals by undoing the AutoCorrect (press Ctrl+Z or click the Undo button). AutoCorrect adds the double capital to an exceptions list, which you can view or change by choosing Exceptions from the AutoCorrect dialog box and clicking the INitial CAps tab.

Starting sentences with capitals

Either you accidentally use two caps to start a sentence, or you don't use any. Fortunately, AutoCorrect can fix that, too. Word automatically capitalizes the first letter of a sentence when you select the Capitalize First Letter Of Sentences check box. It assumes that you're starting a new sentence if the previous word ends with a terminal punctuation, such as a period or question mark.

The time may come when you'll actually want a sentence to start with a lowercase letter (for example, "e.e. cummings was a poet…"). Rather than go through the bother of turning off Capitalize First Letter Of Sentences, use Undo. Press Ctrl+Z or click the Undo button immediately after the letter changes to uppercase. Word undoes the AutoCorrect and forces the letter to stay in lowercase.

Caps Lock confusion solved!

For many computer users, the most aggravating keyboard screw-up comes when they forget to release Caps Lock. hOW OFTEN DOES IT HAPPEN THAT YOU HAVE TO GO BACK AND CORRECT SENTENCES LIKE THIS AFTER USING CAPS LOCK TO CAPITALIZE A HEADING OR ACRONYM?

Word finally has a solution to the problem. In the AutoCorrect dialog box, select the Correct Accidental Usage Of cAPS LOCK Key check box. When you press Caps Lock to make text uppercase, and then type a word that consists of a small letter followed by capitals, Word automatically reverses the cases. As a bonus, it then releases Caps Lock and puts you back in lowercase.

Grammar Moses

The grammar checker actually checks grammar and style, but the distinction between the two is unimportant for your purposes. Together, they include all those subjects that so engrossed you in your high school English classes—punctuation, passive voice, subject-verb agreement, contractions, prepositions, and so on. In all, the grammar checker can look for 48 different types of problems.

Q&A ***I turned the grammar checker off while using the spelling checker. I've checked my spelling, and now I want to check my grammar—but when I run the checker, I get a message telling me the spelling and grammar check is complete. What do I do?***

Choose Tools, Options, click the Spelling & Grammar tab, and put a check mark next to Check Grammar With Spelling. Run the Spelling and Grammar checker again. Word checks your grammar without rerunning the spelling checker.

Formal or informal?

Before you run the grammar checker, choose which set of rules you want Word to apply: casual, standard, technical, or formal. Choose Tools, Options from the main menu, and click the Spelling & Grammar tab. Choose an option from the Writing Style selection box under the Grammar heading. What are the differences between the four writing styles? We could spend the next 200 pages talking about the nuances of grammar and barely scratch the surface, but here are a few general recommendations:

- Choose Formal if you want to cover all of the grammar rules and most of the style rules. But be warned: the grammar checker will probably query you half a dozen times per sentence (at least, it'll seem that way).
- Choose Standard to enforce most grammar rules but ignore most style rules, such as those governing clichés, jargon, and colloquialisms.
- Choose the For Casual Writing option if you want to keep some of the grammar rules but none of the style rules.
- The Technical option enforces most of the grammar rules and about half of the style rules.

Before you choose your weapon, you probably should look at the grammar and style rules from which Word chooses. Select the Settings button in the Spelling & Grammar panel. Word displays the Grammar Settings dialog box in Figure 6.6. Select the style in the Writing Style selection box; you can see which options are turned on in the Grammar and Style Options list box.

Q&A ***I don't know a relative clause from Santa Claus. Can I get any of this stuff explained to me?***

Sure. Click the question mark in the title bar, drag it to the Grammar and Style Options selection box, and click again. Word displays a Help window, at the bottom of which is a button to click for a grammar and style options list. Click the button, and Word displays a window explaining each rule.

When you run a grammar check using the Casual style option, Word checks for fewer grammar problems than when you choose the Standard or Formal options.

Fig. 6.6
The Grammar Settings dialog box lets you decide what grammar and style rules you want to enforce.

How to use the grammar checker

When the grammar checker runs into a possible error, it displays the Grammar dialog box, as shown in Figure 6.7.

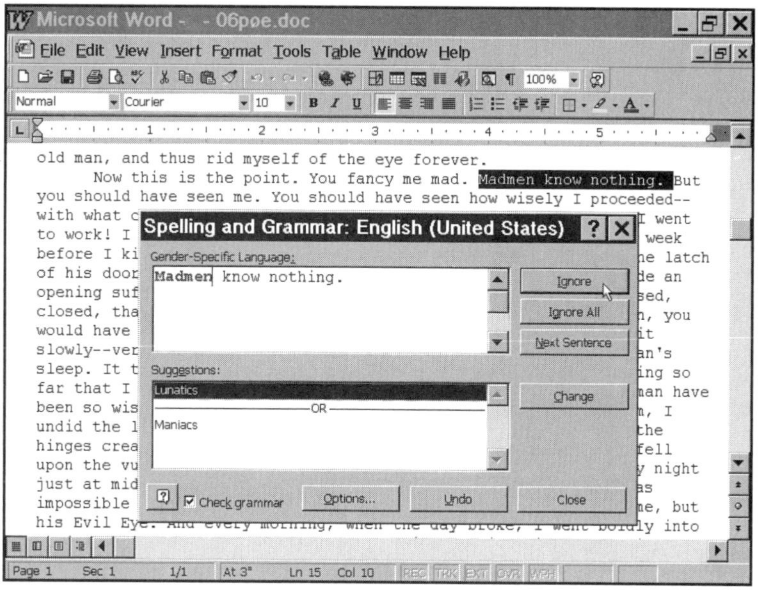

Fig. 6.7
The Grammar dialog box shows you the offending sentence and explains what it thinks the problem is. The grammar checker is not always right.

Figure 6.7 is from Edgar Allan Poe's grammar check of his short story, "The Tell-Tale Heart." In this case, the grammar checker questions whether Ed is being politically correct with his use of the gender-specific word "madman." It shows the entire sentence, with "madman" highlighted, in the upper text box, beneath a heading that summarizes the potential problem. In the lower text box, it suggests non-gender-specific terms that might be more appropriate.

When the grammar checker shows you a potential problem, you can take one of the following actions:

- Ignore the grammar checker's suggestion by clicking Ignore. The checker will go on to the next potential problem.
- Tell the grammar checker to throw out the rule by clicking Ignore All. The checker will skip all further instances of the potential problem for the rest of the document.
- Skip the sentence by clicking Next Sentence.
- Make the grammar checker's suggested change by clicking Change. In Figure 6.7, the checker will replace "madmen" with "lunatics." If you prefer one of the checker's other options, click it and choose Change.
- Make another change to the sentence by editing it in the text box. Delete, insert, and add text using your standard editing tools. For instance, Ed could change "madmen" to "mad people" (he didn't).

Grammar checker overkill

The grammar checker doesn't always hit the mark. It picks more nits than most English teachers know exist—and sometimes, it's flat-out wrong.

For example, the grammar checker will tell you that contractions are unacceptable in formal writing. Many writers and editors disagree. Contractions can be useful because they help make difficult material easier to read.

When you want the checker to stop nagging you about a nonexistent infraction, just tell it to stop by removing the check next to the appropriate item in the Grammar Settings dialog box. Modifying the grammar checker is easy.

How to create your own style

You can modify the existing set of rules, but it's better to keep them as they are and create a new set. Go to the Grammar Settings dialog box (refer to Figure 6.6) and choose Custom from the Writing Style selection box. Then scroll through the list of grammar and style options, and remove the check marks from the boxes next to the rules you don't want.

TIP **At the end of every grammar check, Word displays an information** box called Readability Statistics. Though buried and poorly documented, the Statistics below the Averages and Readability headings can help you refine your writing skills. Turn readability statistics on and off in the Spelling and Grammar panel.

Roget is turning over in his sepulcher

Last among Word's writing aids is its electronic thesaurus. The thesaurus lets you find synonyms for any word. Using it is easy. Place your insertion point on the word and choose Tools, Language, Thesaurus (or press Ctrl+F7). The Thesaurus dialog box pops up, as shown in Figure 6.8.

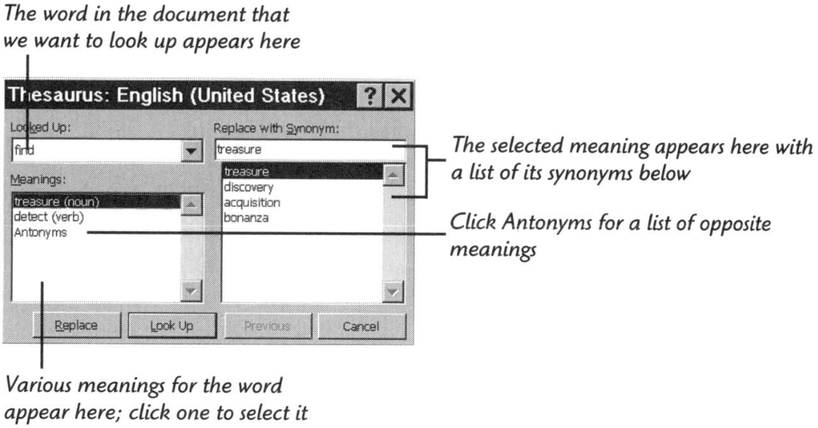
The word in the document that we want to look up appears here
Thesaurus: English (United States)
Looked Up:
find
Replace with Synonym:
treasure
Meanings:
treasure (noun)
detect (verb)
Antonyms
treasure
discovery
acquisition
bonanza
Replace
Look Up
Previous
Cancel
The selected meaning appears here with a list of its synonyms below
Click Antonyms for a list of opposite meanings
Various meanings for the word appear here; click one to select it

Fig. 6.8
The thesaurus lets you find synonyms for a word in your document. Position the insertion point on the word and press Ctrl+F7.

Inside the Thesaurus dialog box

The word for which you want a synonym is automatically inserted in the Looked Up text box. Below it, in the Meanings text box, are the different uses of that word. The meaning that is selected in the Meanings text box is inserted in the Replace With Synonym text box. Underneath is a list of synonyms for that particular meaning.

For example, in Figure 6.8, the word being looked up is "find." In this case, the thesaurus provides synonyms for the noun that means "treasure." Other words for the noun "find" are "discovery," "acquisition," and "bonanza."

To use the Thesaurus dialog box to replace a word with a synonym, follow these steps:

1. Click the appropriate word in the Meanings list; the word appears in the Replace with Synonym text box, and a list of its synonyms appears below it. If you're looking for an antonym, click Antonyms in the Meanings list.
2. To look up any word in either list, click it; then click the Look Up button.

   Continue to click words until the word you want to use is in the Replace with Synonym text box.
3. Click the Replace button to replace the word in Looked Up with the word in Replace With Synonym.

Choosing an option

To automatically replace the word in your document with the one in the Replace with Synonym box, select Replace. You can also choose from these options:

- To look up synonyms for a word in the Replace With Synonym list box, double-click the word, or click the word and choose Look Up.
- To look up synonyms for another word in the Meanings list box ("detect" in Figure 6.8, for example), click the word.
- To look up a new word, type the word in the Replace With Synonym text box and choose Look Up.
- To retrace your steps, click Previous.

7

Prepare to Print!

In this chapter:

- It won't print! How to avoid and solve common printer problems
- What will my document look like? Print Preview reveals all
- Can I print only selected pages or text?
- I need to adjust my page margins
- Special jobs: Easy envelopes and lively labels

Word's vast array of printing tools lets you print documents quickly and easily . . . . >>

We may have thrown out our typewriters, but most of us still need to put our documents on paper. The good news is that today's printers give you good quality at good prices. The bad news is that they're still a pain in the port to set up and operate.

Windows and Word have gone about as far as possible to make printing foolproof. In theory, you should be able to install Word, open a document, choose File, Print, and let 'er rip.

But a printer is like a leash-trained dog. It will behave itself most of the time, but you can't anticipate the cat that unexpectedly leads your baying mutt through the briar patch.

Given the nearly infinite combinations of hardware and software (not to mention cranky networks with shared printers), we can't possibly troubleshoot every malfunction and hold this book to less than 100,000 pages. If you do everything right and your printer still doesn't work, you probably need the help of a highly trained professional, such as your 12-year-old nephew.

Or you can turn to the extensive online Help that Word and Windows 95 provide. We'll tell you where to look a little bit later, once you've taken a crack at printing a few documents.

That said, we'll try to give you some universal advice on common problems as we go along. And if you're new at walking the print dog, read on for some information that might help you avoid a few hard-copy headaches.

Sneak previews: using Print Preview

You can usually tell what a document is going to look like on paper. But when your documents include tables, footnotes, graphics, nonstandard margins, columns, and other formatting, you risk printing documents that don't come out the way you want them to. To save time and paper, use Word's Print Preview command to see a glimpse of the final product.

Open Print Preview by choosing it from the File menu, or by clicking the Print Preview button on the Standard toolbar. Once in the window, you can see an entire document page as it will appear when printed. You can also see how pages of a book will look side by side.

To see how Print Preview works, look at the flyer shown in Figure 7.1. It includes a variety of type treatments that won't fit into the document window. But when the flyer is in a preview window, as shown in Figure 7.2, its type, spacing, and borders are easy to assess. If you don't like how an element looks, close the preview window, edit the document, and then preview it again.

A printer and a prayer

When you install Word, it should detect your printer and make it available to you. But problems inevitably arise. Here are a few questions to ask yourself as you prepare to use your printer for the first time:

Is the printer plugged in and turned on?

Check this first; it's the culprit more often than you think!

Is the printer cable connected snugly to both the printer and the computer?

Printer cables are notorious for loosening at night after the lights are out.

Is the printer online?

Usually, there's an online button and corresponding light on your printer's control panel. Make sure the light's on. Some printers have a small display that says `Ready`.

Does the printer have paper? If the paper is in a tray, is the tray pushed all the way in?

Loose trays are common on laser printers. Also, if your printer has selectable options such as single-sheet or tractor feeding, make sure the right one's selected.

Does the printer that's hooked up to your computer correspond to the printer Word is set up to use?

If, for example, Word expects a Canon Bubble Jet and finds a daisywheel printer, your document won't print as it appears on the screen. Mismatches shouldn't be a concern unless you have more than one printer available (through a network, for example) or you have reason to believe that someone has changed your setup.

To find out what printer Word expects, Choose File, Print. Word shows you the name of the printer in the Print dialog box. If it doesn't match the printer connected to your machine, click the Name text box and see if the right printer is listed.

A mismatched printer doesn't necessarily mean you can't print. You might have a printer that's compatible with the one you have listed in your Print dialog box. The only way to find out is by printing some documents.

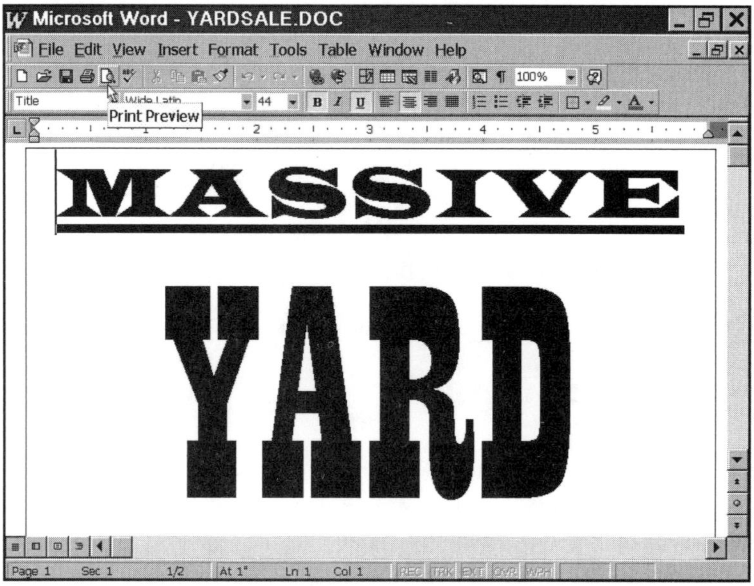

Fig. 7.1
Only part of this yard sale flyer is visible in the document window. Use Print Preview to see how the document will look when printed.

Fig. 7.2
Here's the same flyer as seen in Print Preview.

Q&A ***Do I have to keep switching between Print Preview and Normal view if I want to make editing and formatting changes?***

No. Your editing and formatting commands are still available to you in Print Preview. You can even add the Standard and Formatting toolbars to your Print Preview screen. Choose View, Toolbars from the main menu and click the Standard and Formatting buttons.

To make your Print Preview page large enough to work in, click the Magnifier button on the Print Preview toolbar. Your insertion point turns into a magnifying glass when you place it in the document. Click the mouse button to enlarge the document to 100 percent. After you make your changes to the document, click the mouse button again to reduce the page to its previous size. Click the Magnifier button again to turn off magnification.

Previewing multiple pages

Print Preview lets you display several pages of a document on one screen. Click the Multiple Pages button on the Print Preview toolbar, and sweep the mouse across the pages in the drop-down box to choose the number of pages to be displayed. You can use the Page Up and Page Down keys to page through your document.

When you display more than a handful of pages, they start looking like postage stamps. Don't dismiss these miniature pages just because you can't read them. They can help you identify dense copy, unwanted patches of white space, and poorly placed graphical elements.

The following graphics page describes the buttons on the Print Preview toolbar.

Can I print now?

Enough preparation—let's get down to printing some text. We'll assume for the moment that you've opened a plain document with regular margins and no oddball formatting.

TIP **It's a good idea to save your document before printing, in case** your computer chokes on the document and you have to reboot.

Quick-printing a document

If you want to print a document without going through the Print dialog box, click the Print button on the Standard toolbar. Word sends the entire document posthaste to the printer. (If you want to print only part of the document, you need to use the Print dialog box; see the following graphics page.)

If you turn on background printing, a message telling you what's happening appears on the left-hand side of the status bar, and a printer with pages flying from it appears on the right-hand side. After a few moments, Word prints the open document. (Actually, Word passes the document to Windows, which in turn dishes it out to the printer.) If you turn background printing off, a message box appears in the middle of your screen, and Word prints the document without pause.

Plain English, please!

Background printing lets you continue working while Word prints the document. When you turn off background printing, you have to wait until Word finishes the print job before you can get back to your document. Background printing is slower, so turn it off if you need a long document immediately.

TIP **To turn background printing on or off, choose Tools, Options from** the main menu and click the Print tab. A check in the Background Printing check box means that background printing is turned on.

To cancel the print job before it's done, double-click the animated printer in the status bar.

When to push the panic button

After you send the document to the printer, you might experience a moment of silence, particularly if you have an older printer. On many systems, Word sends the document to a temporary file on the hard drive and the printer must prepare itself to receive the file. Otherwise, if all goes well, your document will emerge from your printer forthwith.

If printer doesn't cough up your document, do *not* try to reprint it. You might end up printing multiple copies. First review the earlier sidebar, "A printer and a prayer," to make sure your printer is ready. Then check your Print dialog box settings to make sure you haven't accidentally sent the document to the wrong place (to a file or another printer, for instance).

Finally, check the **print queue**—a list of documents waiting to be printed—by choosing Settings, Printers from Windows 95's Start menu. Windows displays a window with a list of your installed printers. Double-click the printer you're using. Windows opens another window that shows you what documents are in the queue and each document's status.

If you're still not getting any satisfaction, it's time to jump to Windows' printing and diagnostic tools. Read the next section, "Troubleshooting printer problems with online Help."

CAUTION

Networks can be notoriously slow to print out documents. When several people print at the same time, the documents can line up for processing like cows waiting to be milked. If your document does not print, do not resend it; go to your network administrator for help. Your administrator can also tell you what kinds of delays you can expect under normal circumstances.

Inside the Print dialog box

For anything other than a quick print of the whole document, go to the printing command center, the Print dialog box as shown in Figure 7.3. Press Ctrl+P or select File, Print from the menu bar.

The Print dialog box lets you choose a printer, what you want to print, and how many copies. Make your choices, and then click OK.

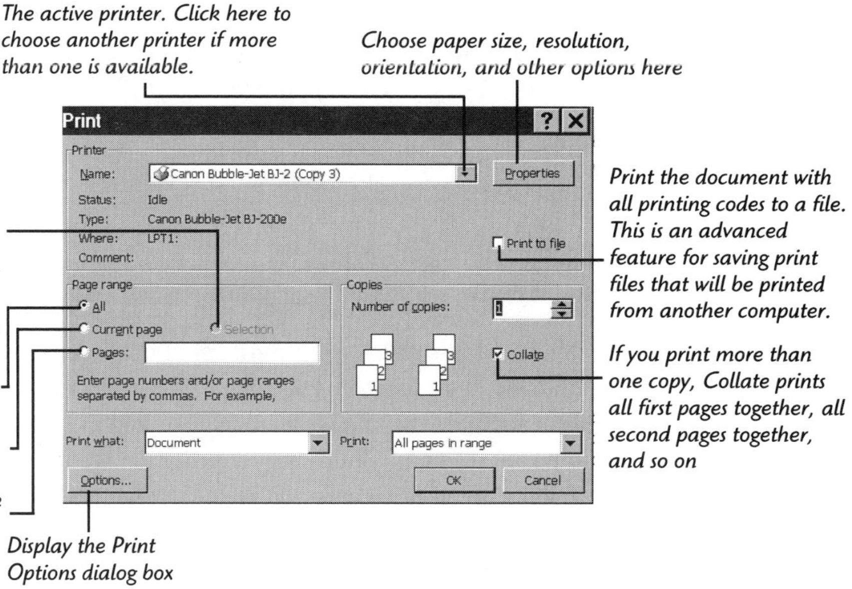

The active printer. Click here to choose another printer if more than one is available.
Choose paper size, resolution, orientation, and other options here
Print selected text or items, such as one paragraph or part of a page. Selection appears grayed out until you select text or an item in your document.
Print all pages
Print page on which insertion point is placed
Print pages listed in the Pages text box
Display the Print Options dialog box
Print the document with all printing codes to a file. This is an advanced feature for saving print files that will be printed from another computer.
If you print more than one copy, Collate prints all first pages together, all second pages together, and so on
Print
Printer
Name:
Canon Bubble-Jet BJ-2 (Copy 3)
Properties
Status: Idle
Type: Canon Bubble-Jet BJ-200e
Where: LPT1:
Comment:
Print to file
Page range
All
Current page
Selection
Pages:
Enter page numbers and/or page ranges separated by commas. For example,
Copies
Number of copies:
Collate
Print what: Document
Print: All pages in range
Options...
OK
Cancel

Fig. 7.3
The Print dialog box.

Troubleshooting printer problems with online Help

Printer problems can be tricky to figure out because the fault might lie with either Word or Windows. Fortunately, both offer informative and thorough Help files to help you diagnose and solve most common printer problems.

Start with Word. Choose Help, Contents and Index to display the Help Topics dialog box. Click the Find tab. Type "Troubleshoot printer" in Type the Word(s) You Want to Find text box. Word displays a list of topics. Click "Troubleshoot printing." Word displays a Help window that lists a number of specific printing problems to choose from, including:

- Nonprinting documents and envelopes
- Text running off the edge of the page
- Nonprinting graphics
- A dimmed Print command on the File menu
- A `Too many fonts` error message

Several of Word's Help screens refer you to Windows' Help files. One of these Windows Help files can actually check out your printer for you and suggest what the problem might be.

Click Help on the Windows 95 or Windows NT Start menu. Choose the Index tab and start to type **print troubleshooting** in the Type The First Few Letters text box. Click the Print Troubleshooting index entry and follow the instructions.

I just want to print a few pages

Often, you don't want to print the entire document. You just need to print the table on page 14, replace page 6, or print the appendix on pages 67 to 75. Word gives you complete control over what you print, using the options under Page Range in the Print dialog box (refer to the earlier graphics page).

> ***How do I print two-sided documents?***
>
> This is a two-step print job. Choose File, Print. In the Print dialog box, choose Print; then choose Odd Pages from the drop-down box. Word prints only the odd pages of your document. Reinsert the paper in your printer so that it will print on the back of page 1 first, the back of page 2 second, and so on. Choose File, Print again. This time, choose Even Pages from the Print drop-down box. Word prints the even pages on the back sides of the odd pages.
>
> One caveat: Some printers don't like paper that's already been printed on. Make sure the paper is flat and that no sheets are clinging together.

Printing files from a disk

You can print a file or several files from the Open dialog box without opening them first.

Select the file to print. If you want to print several files, choose each one by holding down the Ctrl key while you click the left mouse button.

Click the right mouse button and choose Print from the shortcut menu. Word displays the Print dialog box. Select your options and click OK.

Preparing your document for printing

Not all documents print alike. For example, you might need to print a legal document on 8.5 × 14-inch paper, print a wide table sideways, or use wider margins to fit long headings. You can set up your printer to accommodate these different types of print jobs. Here are some common printing problems and how to solve them.

How do I get a different paper size?

If you're printing a document to paper that's other than 8.5 × 11 inches, choose File, Page Setup from the main menu, and click the Paper Size tab in the Page Setup dialog box. Pick the paper you want from the Paper Size drop-down box (see Figure 7.4). The last choice in the box, called Custom Size, lets you define irregular dimensions. Click OK when you're done.

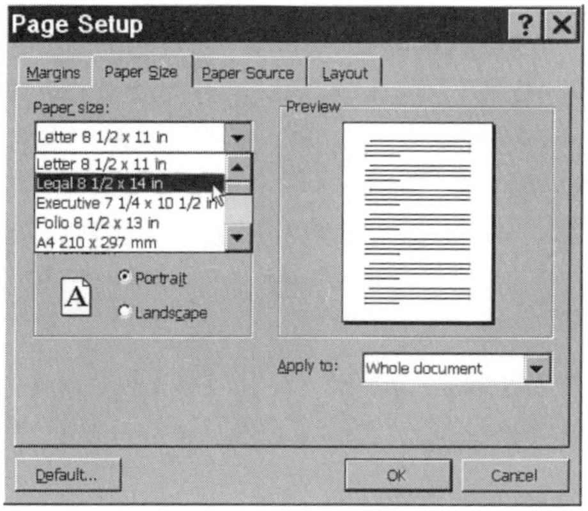

Fig. 7.4
Choose the paper size from the Page Setup dialog box.

I need to print this document sideways

You can print a document in either **portrait** or **landscape** orientation. Which is which? In portrait orientation, the page is longer from top to bottom. In landscape orientation, the page is longer from side to side. Don't worry if you have a hard time remembering these terms; when you choose an orientation in the Page Setup dialog box, Word shows you a sample page.

For documents that are wider than they are long, printing in landscape orientation is the best choice. Choose File, Page Setup from the main menu, and click the Paper Size tab in the Page Setup dialog box. Under Orientation, choose Landscape.

You don't need to adjust your printer to use landscape; your computer does the work of printing the document sideways instead of across.

TIP **The landscape option works with laser, inkjet, and dot-matrix** printers, but not with impact printers.

Adjusting the margins

By default, your text boundaries are 1.25 inches from the left and right page borders and 1 inch from the top and bottom page borders. (We'll look at how to use the ruler to change indents in your document in Chapter 9, "Formatting Paragraphs and Blocks.") You change your margins from Page Setup; for example, if you need more space for a document or want to shift the document image to widen a margin.

Say that your document spills onto a second page by two lines. Here's how to shrink the margins so the document fits on a single page:

1. Choose File, Page Setup from the main menu.
2. Click the Margins tab in the Page Setup dialog box (see Figure 7.5).
3. Decrease the top and bottom margins enough to fit the extra lines. For example, you might change the top margin from 1 inch to 1/2 inch, or both margins from 1 inch to 3/4 inch.

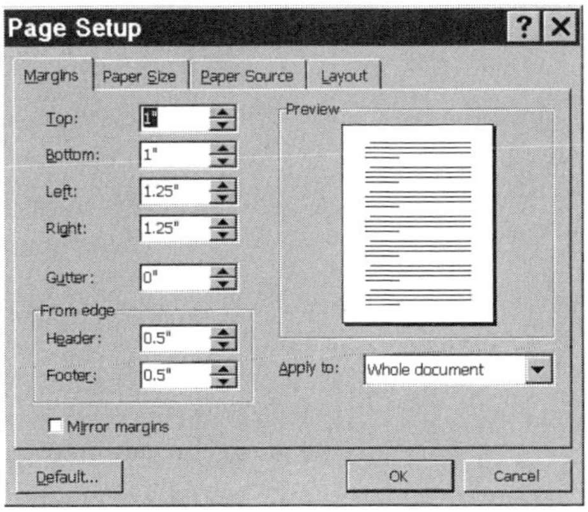

Fig. 7.5
The Page Setup dialog box lets you change your margins to accommodate documents of different sizes.

If your new margins will apply only to new pages in the document, choose This Point Forward in the Apply To list box.

Special print jobs: envelopes

Printing envelopes has always been a chore. You have to set up your printer, configure your word processor, align the envelope, try to print the envelope, unjam the envelope, realign the envelope, print the envelope, throw the envelope away when the address comes out upside down, and repeat the whole process until you get it right.

In the same time, you could hand-address envelopes for the entire Cleveland Symphony Orchestra—and listen to a couple of fugues to boot.

You might be shocked, then, to learn that printing envelopes with Word is almost fun. Maybe not slam-dancing, blues-shouting, bar-walking, let's-have-a-karaoke-party-and-print-envelopes-until-dawn fun, but at least more fun than defrosting your refrigerator.

Here are some of the features that make printing envelopes palatable:

- You can pick the envelope size from a convenient list.
- You can choose how you feed the envelope from a group of graphical buttons.
- You can print the address and return address in any typeface and type size, as well as with such attributes as italics, small caps, and underlining.

May I have the envelope, please?

Choose Tools, Envelopes and Labels from the main menu. Click the Envelopes tab in the Envelopes and Labels dialog box (see Figure 7.6). In the dialog box, fill in the Delivery Address and Return Address text boxes. You also have the option of making the return address permanent, if it isn't already. If you want to exclude the return address for a particular envelope, choose Omit.

Next, you need to tell Word what size envelope you're using. Click Preview, or click the Options button and click the Envelope Options tab. If the Envelope Size text box doesn't show the proper size, click the box and choose the right one from the drop-down list.

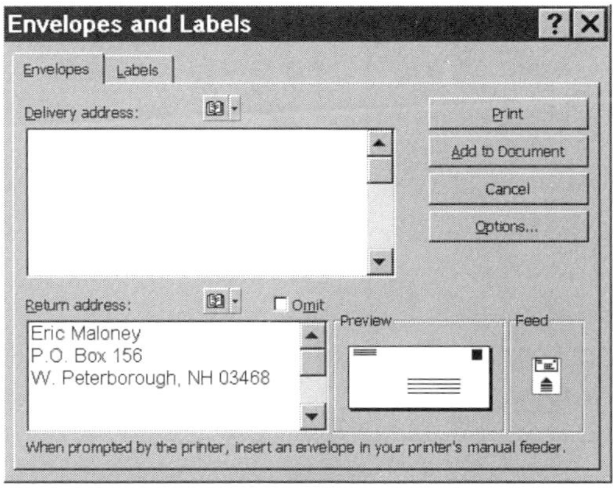

Fig. 7.6
Start your envelope by typing the delivery and return addresses under the Envelopes tab in the Envelopes and Labels dialog box.

Finally, align the envelope in your paper tray the same way it appears in the little graphic under Feed in the lower right-hand corner.

That's it! Just click Print and behold the fruits of your labor.

TIP **Like shoes, envelopes come in standard sizes. For example, a** standard business envelope (4 1/8 x 9 1/2 inches) is a number 10 envelope. Most envelopes you buy at the stationery store have both the dimensions and the number printed on the box.

CAUTION **Check your printer's manual for special instructions on printing** special jobs such as envelopes and labels.

How to fix alignment problems

If your printer chews up your envelope or doesn't print it the way it's supposed to, try putting it in a different way.

Click Feed in the lower right-hand corner of the Envelopes and Labels dialog box; or click the Options button, and click the Printing Options tab.

Choose the new alignment from the box under Feed Method. Click OK, insert an envelope, and print it.

Fun with fonts

If you have a printer that can handle different fonts, you can use them to give your addresses some variety, as shown in Figure 7.7. The return address shown on top is done in a font called Matura MT Script Capitals. The second return address assumes a more corporate look by using Century Schoolbook. The fonts on your computer might be different, but the steps you take to use them are the same.

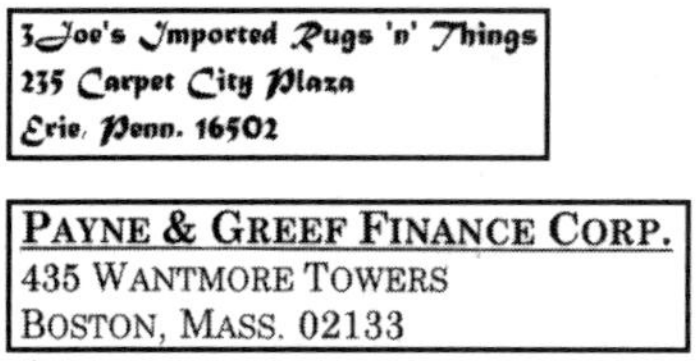

Fig. 7.7
Two examples of envelopes printed with fancy fonts.

Changing fonts is easy. Select the text in the Envelopes and Labels dialog box, click the right mouse button, and choose Font from the context menu. Under the Font tab, choose the typeface, style (bold, italic, or bold italic) and size (see Figure 7.8). You can also pick from among several types of underlines in the Underline drop-down box. (We'll talk more about fonts, styles, and effects in Chapter 8.)

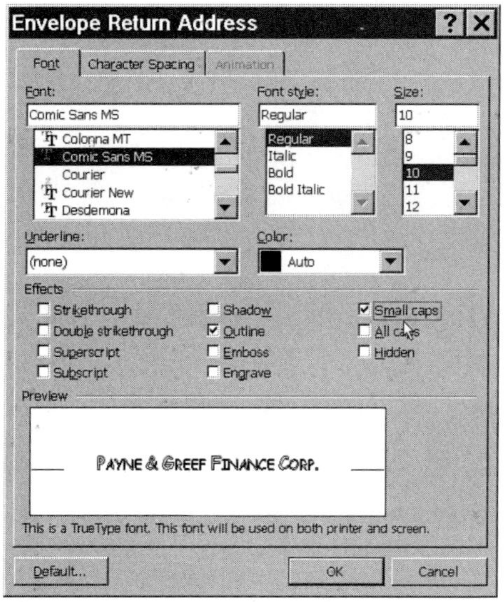

Fig. 7.8
In the Envelope Return Address or Envelope Delivery Address dialog box, choose the Font tab to choose a new font, style, or size.

If you want your final selections to be permanent, click Default. Click OK when you're done; then click OK from the Envelope Options dialog box.

TIP **You can't save an envelope as a separate file, but you can add it** to the top of the current document in its own section by choosing the Add to Document button in the Envelopes and Labels dialog box. This lets you save the envelope and its letter in a single file. If you later want to print the envelope, load the document and choose Tools, Envelopes and Labels from the main menu, as you would if creating a new envelope. Click the Envelopes tab in the Envelopes and Labels dialog box, and you'll find that Word has automatically extracted the delivery and return addresses from the document and placed them in the appropriate text boxes.

Special print jobs: labels

When you think of labels, you probably think of the kind that go on envelopes. But Word lets you print nearly 60 different kinds, including labels for audio and videotape, name tags, and file folders. You can also use the label-printing option to print business cards, rotary cards, and index cards.

Word gives you the dimensions of the label so you know which one to buy.

Word lets you print a single label, a sheet of the same label, or a sheet of different labels. You can also create and save a file of labels for later use.

Let's work from the ground up and start with the single label.

How to print a single label

Choose Tools, Envelopes and Labels, and click the Labels tab (see Figure 7.9). Type the label in the Address box. Under Print, choose Single Label. Word assumes the label is the first one on the sheet in your printer.

If you've already used some of the labels on your sheet, adjust Row and Column accordingly. For example, if the first available label is in the third column of the second row, change the Row spin box to 2 and the Column spin box to 3. Either choose the box and type a new number, or click the arrow keys until the number you want spins into view.

Fig. 7.9
Choose the Labels tab in the Envelopes and Labels dialog box to print single or multiple labels. You can also save labels to use later.

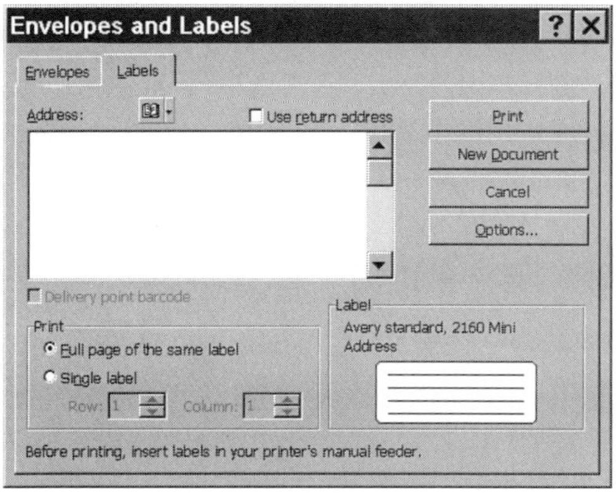

Make sure the label you're set up for is the same as the label in your printer. Word shows you a sample label in the lower right-hand corner.

If you want a different label, click the sample label. In the Label Options dialog box, click Options, or click the sample label in the lower right-hand corner. Scroll the Product Number text box until you find the right one. The dimensions of the label and the label sheet appear in the Label Information box.

The Product Number box gives you stock numbers for Avery labels. If you use something other than Avery labels and you can't find measurements that match, select Label Products and choose MACO Standard or Other. The Product Number box gives you the names of other label-makers' products.

You can see a picture of a label, along with its dimensions and margins, by selecting Details.

TIP **To print return address labels, check Use Return Address under** the Labels tab in the Envelopes and Labels dialog box. Word uses the return address you entered for envelopes. If you haven't entered a return address yet, choose Tools, Options, User Information and enter it in the Mailing Address text box.

How to print multiple labels

To get the most out of multiple labels, you need to know a little about tables, which we discuss in Chapter 11, "Turning the Tables." We'll give you the basics now, and you can return later to polish your label-making skills.

First, make sure you select the right label under the Labels tab in the Envelopes and Labels dialog box. Then choose Full Page Of The Same Label, and click the New Document button.

Word opens what looks like a normal document, but it's really a special document that uses Word's Table feature to format the page for the labels. Also, the document's margins are set for the label sheets you'll be feeding the printer.

To see where the labels are, choose Table, Gridlines. In Figure 7.10, for example, Word has set up a table to handle Avery Standard 2180 Mini File Folder labels.

Fig. 7.10
When you click New Document, Word opens a special document that's formatted for the labels you want to print.

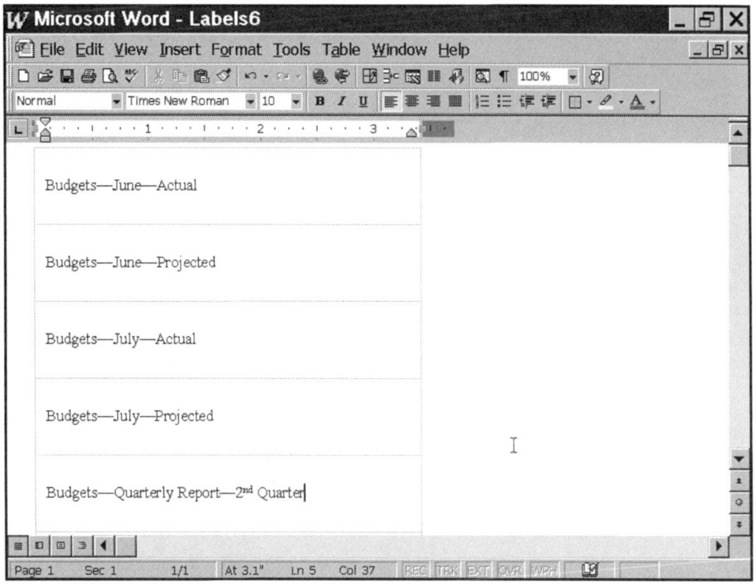

Entering label information

Position your insertion point in the first label and type the information. Press the Enter key after each line. Don't worry about entering too much information; the table keeps you from typing more than the label can hold.

When you're done with the label, press the Tab key to move the insertion point to the next label.

You learn how to edit tables and move around in them in Chapter 11. For now, here's what you need to know:

- Tab moves you to the next label.
- Shift+Tab moves you to the previous label.
- You can move to a label by clicking it with the mouse.
- To add a page to your label document, press the Tab key when you're done with the last label. Word automatically starts a new page and creates its first label.

TIP **Would you like to use fonts and styles for your labels like you can** for envelope addresses? You can play with your type just as you would any other document. Chapter 8 tells you how.

Printing and saving your labels

Your multiple labels are a document that you can print and save like any other document. Just make sure you have your labels in the printer tray before choosing File, Print.

Save your file with the standard Save command, and you can print the same sheet of labels whenever you need it.

TIP **You can save label pages by printing your labels on a blank sheet** of paper first. Hold the sheet against the label page to make sure the labels align properly.

Part III: Live Fast, Die Young, and Leave a Good-Looking Document

8

Character Sketches—Formatting Your Type

In this chapter:

- **Fonts a-plenty: choosing from Word's abundance of types**
- **A few points about type sizes**
- **Subscripts, drop caps, and other typographical trickery**
- **New! Get their attention with animation**
- **Do it this instant! Reformatting text with Format Painter**
- **Can I insert symbols and special characters in my text?**

Word's smorgasbord of types will make your documents easier to read and nicer to look at . . . . >

You wouldn't serve dinner guests plain spaghetti. Sure, it's palatable, but your guests would be a lot more impressed if you added a tasty sauce, a few spices, and maybe even a garnish.

An unadorned Word document often needs the same kind of attention. It may be functional, but is it inviting? Does it hold your reader's interest from beginning to end? Wouldn't a different font here or a bold heading there make your document a bit more flavorful?

Word gives you a variety of ways to change the look of your text. You can `change a font`, underline (or **boldface** or *italicize)* a few words for emphasis, or resize your type. You can apply most of these formats from the keyboard, simply by selecting text and clicking buttons on the Formatting toolbar.

Let's start by looking at the most important ingredient in Word's design kitchen: the font.

The types, they are a-changin'

At first glance, you might think the polished document shown in Figure 8.1 was done by a highly trained layout specialist. Actually, it was done by one of the authors, who knows as much about design as he does about theoretical chemistry.

Creating this document involved no desktop publishing or tricky text formatting. It was done entirely from the Formatting toolbar and Font dialog box, and involved only four actions:

- Changing typefaces
- Changing font styles (bold and italic)
- Changing sizes
- Adding underlining and small capitals

Fig. 8.1
A few simple changes to the text turn a plain document into one that's attractive and more readable.

PROSPECTUS: PSYCHOLOGY 546
I'M OK, YOU'RE BOB

Instructor:	Sue Perego
Class Hours:	Monday through Thursday, 9:30-11:00
Office Hours:	For Bobs, 11:55-noon every fourth Friday
	For others, 11-noon Monday through Thursday

COURSE DESCRIPTION
An exploration of how our names affect our lives. What do you think of people named Bob? If your name's Bob, what do you think of yourself as compared to other Bobs? Why do some Bobs prefer being called Robbie? What happens when two Bobs with name tags meet in an elevator at a Rotary Club function? If Bobs didn't exist, would we have had to invent them? We will analyze the subject from historical, technical, political, and social perspectives.

METHODOLOGY
This course will be a lecture-discussion, with class participation an important component. In addition, we will make a field trip to a half-way house for Bobs, and you will be responsible for at least one project involving original research.

TEXTS
Robertson, Robert, and Roberta Roberts, *Hi! My Name Is Bob*, 4th edition.

ASSIGNMENTS

Nov. 14	Midterm
Nov. 21	Project proposal due
Dec. 15	Project due
Dec. 18	Final Exam

We'll take a look at how we can change the body type in Figure 8.1. This will introduce you to the relevant part of the Formatting toolbar, where much of the work is done.

Selecting and changing the body type

In its original incarnation, the document was written in 10-point Times New Roman, the standard format for all new Word documents created with the Normal template. That's the template Word uses when you click the New button on the Formatting toolbar or press Ctrl+N. Figure 8.2 shows a portion of the original text.

Fig. 8.2
This is the way the document in Figure 8.1 began. Use the Formatting toolbar to change the way your type looks.

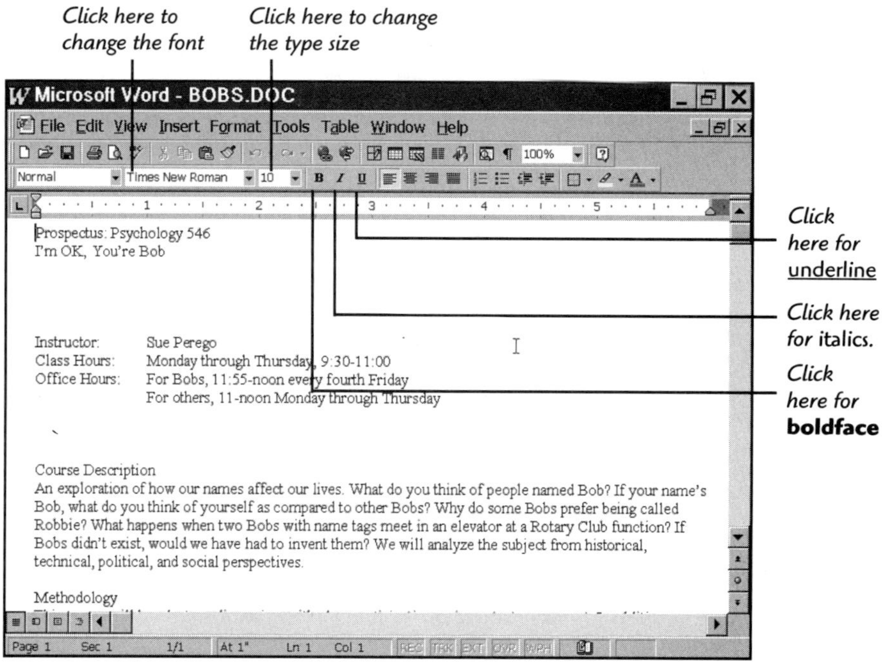
Click here to change the font
Click here to change the type size
Click here for underline
Click here for italics.
Click here for boldface
Microsoft Word - BOBS.DOC
File Edit View Insert Format Tools Table Window Help
Normal
Times New Roman
10
Prospectus: Psychology 546
I'm OK, You're Bob
Instructor: Sue Perego
Class Hours: Monday through Thursday, 9:30-11:00
Office Hours: For Bobs, 11:55-noon every fourth Friday
For others, 11-noon Monday through Thursday
Course Description
An exploration of how our names affect our lives. What do you think of people named Bob? If your name's Bob, what do you think of yourself as compared to other Bobs? Why do some Bobs prefer being called Robbie? What happens when two Bobs with name tags meet in an elevator at a Rotary Club function? If Bobs didn't exist, would we have had to invent them? We will analyze the subject from historical, technical, political, and social perspectives.
Methodology
Page 1 Sec 1 1/1 At 1" Ln 1 Col 1

Here's how to change body type, using the part of the Formatting toolbar shown in Figure 8.2:

1. Select the entire document by pressing Ctrl+A.
2. Choose the Font Size text box in the Formatting toolbar by clicking the down arrow. Choose a new size from the drop-down text box or type it in the box. Sizes are given in points (more on that later).
3. Choose the Font text box by clicking the down arrow, then choose a new font.

Plain English, please!

A **font**, or **typeface**, is a set of letters, numbers, symbols, and punctuation marks that have the same general look. Some examples of fonts include Times New Roman, Arial, and Courier.

Q&A ***How can I see what characters are available for a particular font?***

From The Windows Start menu, choose Settings, Control Panel and choose Fonts. Windows displays a folder of all fonts available on your system. Double-click the font you want to look at, and you'll get a sampling of text and numbers in different sizes.

Changing selected elements

The steps for changing the blocks of text, headings, and other elements are the same: just select the text and change it. For example, if you want to make your text bold, like the main heading in Figure 8.1, do the following:

1. Select the paragraphs you want to change.
2. Choose bold by clicking the Bold button on the Formatting toolbar or by pressing Ctrl+B.

Q&A ***Do I have to start each document with 10-point Times New Roman?***

No, you can start new documents with any font and size you want. Choose Format, Font from the main menu. Select the font and size you want and click the Default button. Choose Yes when Word asks you if you want to change the default. The next time you quit Word, your new default will automatically be saved. If you want the default to apply only to new documents you create during your current session, you can have Word prompt you to save the new default. Choose Tools, Options from the main menu, click the Save tab, choose Prompt To Save Normal Template, and click OK. When you close Word, it will give you the chance to cancel your new default.

The Font dialog box

We took care of the body text in Figure 8.2 using the Formatting toolbar exclusively. While the toolbar is better for quick changes, especially when you know what you want, the Font dialog box does much more. For example, the Font dialog box is where you find small caps like the ones used for the headings in Figure 8.1.

Choose Format, Font to display the Font dialog box (see Figure 8.3).

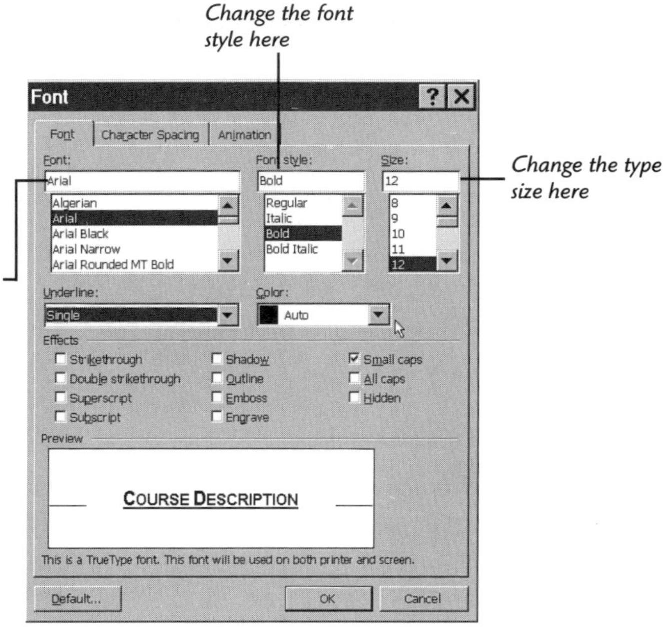

Fig. 8.3
The Font dialog box includes all of the essential text-formatting tools.

The Font dialog box has one big advantage over setting preferences using the toolbar—the Preview box in the lower right-hand corner. The Preview box lets you see what your choices look like before you use them.

The Font dialog box gives you several type treatments that aren't available on the Formatting toolbar. These include four types of underlines, subscripts and superscripts, small caps, and strikethrough. We'll look more closely at these functions a little later.

Q&A ***Some of my fonts just give me a lot of garbage characters. Is there something wrong with them?***

No need to adjust your set. These are special fonts that consist mostly of symbols. These fonts include Monotype Sorts, MT Extra, Symbol, and Wingdings. You usually insert these symbols using the Insert, Symbol command, which we'll discuss toward the end of this chapter.

TIP **If you change your font without first selecting text, the new font** applies to whatever text you type from the current insertion point position.

Choosing the best font for the job

Your first step when you format a document is to decide if Times New Roman is the font that's appropriate for the work you're doing. It's fine for columnar material, short reports, and other documents that need to pack a lot of information in a small space. But for books, manuals, reports, and letters, in which more space between letters and words helps make the material more readable, consider something more stylish.

To look at the fonts you have available, choose Format, Font from the main menu to display the Font dialog box. Choose the Font tab. The names of the fonts appear in the Font text box. When you select a font name, the Preview box shows you what the font looks like. You can preview fonts in rapid succession by scrolling through the text box with the up- and down-arrow keys.

Your fonts might be different from the ones shown in Figure 8.3. Your selection partly depends on what software you have installed. Also, some printers can't print some fonts; other printers come with packages of their own fonts.

TIP **You can save time experimenting with fonts if you create and** print a document with examples of all your typefaces. Post a copy next to your computer for quick reference.

A word about TrueType and other font mysteries

Windows and Word come with a variety of Microsoft fonts called **TrueType fonts**. They're the ones preceded by a TT in the Font text box. TrueType fonts have two important characteristics that other fonts sometimes lack:

- You can enlarge or shrink them to most any size and get good results.
- What you see on the screen is what you get from the printer.

But your font list might include many fonts that do not come from Microsoft. They don't always behave. For example, a font might not display properly, or the font you get on the screen might not match the one you get on paper.

CAUTION **Hundreds, perhaps thousands, of fonts are available for the taking** from the Internet, bulletin boards, and user groups. Resist the temptation to become a font collector. Most of them not only are useless or duplicates, but they take a surprising amount of disk space. A mere 200 fonts might occupy as much as six megabytes. Choose a few good serif and sans serif body types and a few complementary display types, and forego the rest.

Display types, plain and simple

Most of Word's fonts are display types. They're designed to be big and bad, with the goal of attracting attention rather than enhancing readability. You can use display types to put together effective flyers and notices, such as the yard sale flyer in Figure 8.4, which started out looking like this:

MASSIVE
YARD
SALE
Two days
Three families
6,234,567,090 items
(Almost) no offers refused!
Sat. & Sun., 9-4, 1234 Lassiter St.

As you can see, this flyer is nothing more than a glorified document. Putting it together involves no desktop publishing or tricky text formatting—just the tools you use to spruce up body type.

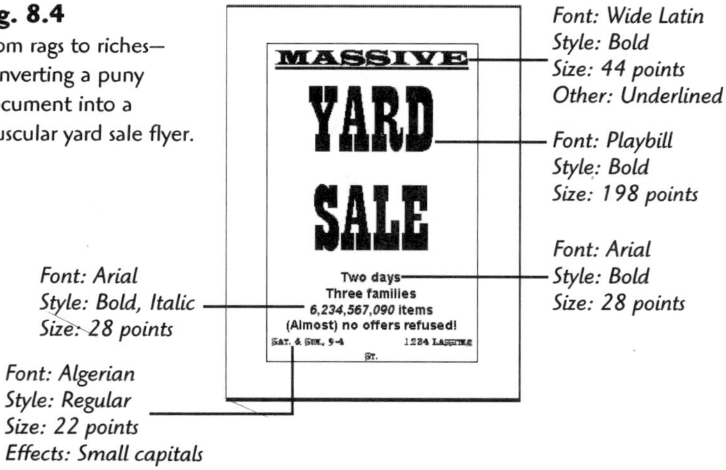

Fig. 8.4
From rags to riches—converting a puny document into a muscular yard sale flyer.

Formatting display type, such as the word "MASSIVE" in the flyer, takes only a few steps:

1. Select the text that you want to format.
2. Choose the Font text box and change the font (for example, "MASSIVE" in Figure 8.5 is in Wide Latin).
3. Choose the Font Size text box and change the size ("MASSIVE" in Figure 8.5 is 44 points).

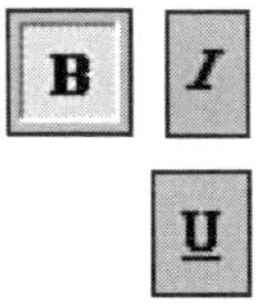

4. Choose your font styles by clicking the Bold, Italic, or Underline button on the Formatting toolbar ("MASSIVE" in Figure 8.5 is in bold and underlined).

Making a point about size

A **point** is the unit printers use to measure the size of the type. There are 72 points in an inch, so a 12-point type is about 1/6 of an inch. However, some 12-point types appear to be smaller than other 12-point types because the characters themselves take less space.

When you choose a size for your body type, you need to think about two factors: readability and space. The smaller the type, the harder it is to read but the more you get on a page. There are three important rules governing type size:

- The longer the line of type, the larger the type size should be. If you're using letter-size paper, for example, anything less than 12 points is hard to read.
- Go to a larger type size only if you have a special reason for doing so, such as for overhead transparencies or documents that will be posted.
- Use a smaller type for columns, particularly if they're justified. Otherwise, Word might have trouble inserting spaces between letters and characters, and you'll end up with type that looks squeezed or too spread out. Newspapers generally use an 8- or 9-point type.

The changing face of type

We've looked at how to change fonts and font sizes. Next on the agenda are font styles—bold, italic, and bold italic. We'll also take up underlining here. The Underline button is on the Formatting toolbar, and underline serves the same purpose as a style, although Microsoft doesn't consider it to be a style.

You can add bold, italic, or underlining to any text. You can also use them in any combination. Just select the text and click the appropriate button on the Formatting toolbar. If you prefer the keyboard, press Ctrl+B for bold, Ctrl+I for italic, and Ctrl+U for underlining.

TIP **Microsoft has added five types of underlines to Word, bringing the** total to nine: single, words only, double, dotted, thick, dash, dot dash, dot dot dash, and wave. The Underline button on the Formatting toolbar gives you a single underline. To use one of the other types, highlight the text, choose Format, Font from the main menu, and select from the Underline text box.

Special effects

Last, and in many ways least, we come to special effects such as strikethrough and superscripts.

These options are not on the Formatting toolbar. To use them, select your text and choose Format, Font. Check the effect under the Effects heading in the middle of the Font dialog box (refer to Figure 8.3).

You'll probably never need most of these effects, but they're good to know about, just in case:

- **Strikethrough** runs a line through a portion of text, ~~like this~~.
- ~~**Double strikethrough**~~, as its name implies, runs two lines through a portion of text.
- **Superscript** gives you a raised character often used in mathematical formulas, such as $A^2+B^2=C^2$.
- **Subscript** gives you the lowered character used in text to reference a footnote, such as Footnote$_1$.

- **Hidden** hides selected text from being displayed or printed. You use hidden text for notes and comments that you don't want in the printed document.

  You can display hidden text by choosing Tools, Options, clicking the View tab, and checking Hidden Text under Nonprinting Characters. Word displays hidden text with a dotted underline.

- **Small caps** turns lowercase letters into SMALL CAPITAL LETTERS that are about the size of the letters they replace. Uppercase letters stay uppercase, as in the subheadings in Figure 8.1.

- **All caps** look the same as ALL UPPERCASE. The differences are technical and don't matter enough to get into here. The Shift key is the easier alternative to get uppercase letters.

Refer to Figure 8.5 for examples of the following effects, all of which are new in Word 97:

- Shadow puts a shadow behind your type, making it seem to float above the page. Your type has to be pretty big for Shadow to be effective. It looks good with Braggadaccio.

- Outline scoops the innards out of your characters. It's difficult to read in large doses; use it to add emphasis to single words. Outline also is more effective with sans serif types; serif types tend to be too thin.

- Emboss and Engrave are fancy effects that are supposed to make your documents look like wedding invitations. Great if you really are doing wedding invitations, but, like Shadow and Outline, generally hard to read and effective only in small doses.

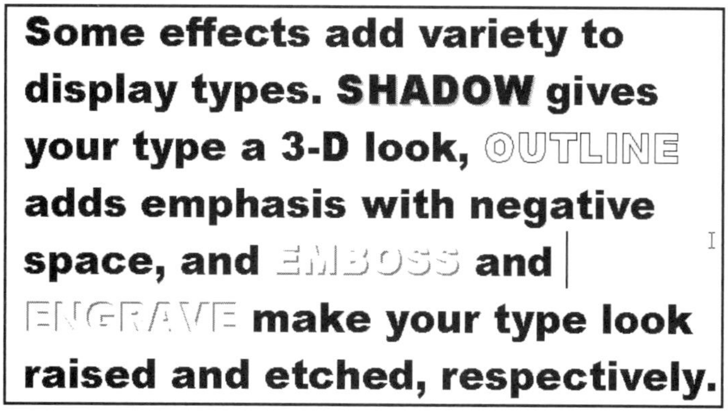
Some effects add variety to display types. SHADOW gives your type a 3-D look, OUTLINE adds emphasis with negative space, and EMBOSS and ENGRAVE make your type look raised and etched, respectively.

Fig. 8.5
Word 97 has four new effects that can give headings and display types a different look.

Drop caps

Occasionally, a document will be broken into sections, but each section won't have its own heading. To distinguish one section from another, try beginning each one with a **drop cap**—a large capital letter (or an entire word of large capital letters) that starts a paragraph.

To insert a drop cap, place your insertion point anywhere in the sentence. You don't need to select the text unless you want to drop more than one character. Choose Format, Drop Cap from the main menu to display the Drop Cap dialog box. Choose Dropped, which sets the cap inside the text, or In Margin, which positions the cap to the left of the text.

You can change the font of the drop cap in the Drop Cap dialog box; just choose the Font drop-down box and pick your new font. You can also change the font, as well as the style and size, right in the document. Click the letter twice or the space inside the drop cap box three times and make your changes as you would to any other selected text.

Get their attention with animation

Best of 97

Good speakers use gestures and body language to help communicate a message. You can't do that in a document—or can you?

Word 97 has a new Animation feature that actually lets you give your document the equivalent of hand-waving. For example, on a list of project assignments that you've distributed, you might get each person's attention by formatting their name to blink rapidly.

Of course, animation works only on the screen, and the people who receive your animated document have to use Word 97 to see the effects.

You animate text by selecting it and choosing Format, Font from the main menu. Choose the Animation tab in the Font dialog box. You'll see six effects in the Animations selection box:

- Blinking Background makes the background of your text flash rapidly on and off.
- Las Vegas Lights puts a theater-like marquee around selected text.
- Marching Black Ants and Marching Red Ants surround selected text with a moving dotted line.

- Shimmer makes your text look like you're trying to read it through heat rising from a sidewalk.
- Sparkle Text sprinkles your document with New Year's Eve confetti.

Reapplying text treatments—a clever shortcut

If you change formats often in a document, selecting and reformatting each new block can get tedious. Word takes away some of the pain with the Format Painter button on the Standard toolbar. Essentially, the Format Painter borrows the format from one part of your document and applies it to another part of your document.

For example, Figure 8.6 shows a document with 12-point Book Antiqua body text. The name of the first entry, "Northern White Cedar," has been changed to 14-point Arial bold, and the Latin name, *Thuja occidentalis*, has been reduced to 10 points and italicized. The task is to change the second and third entries—four one-line paragraphs in all—to match.

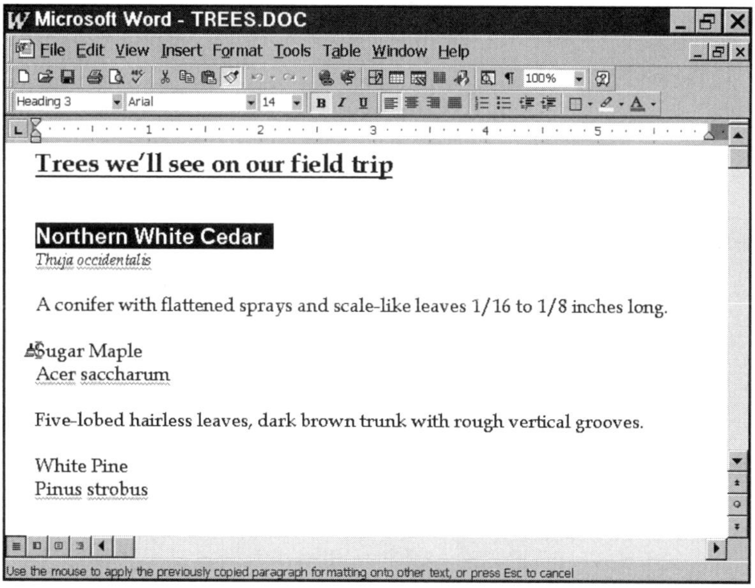
Microsoft Word - TREES.DOC
File Edit View Insert Format Tools Table Window Help
100%
Heading 3
Arial
14
Trees we'll see on our field trip
Northern White Cedar
Thuja occidentalis
A conifer with flattened sprays and scale-like leaves 1/16 to 1/8 inches long.
Sugar Maple
Acer saccharum
Five-lobed hairless leaves, dark brown trunk with rough vertical grooves.
White Pine
Pinus strobus
Use the mouse to apply the previously copied paragraph formatting onto other text, or press Esc to cancel

Fig. 8.6
Format Painter makes it easy to take a style from one part of your document and apply it to another.

Formatting the Sugar Maple and White Pine entries individually involves at least twenty steps. But Format Painter can cut the number of actions in half. Here's the procedure:

1. Place the insertion point anywhere in the paragraph whose format you want to borrow; for example, "Northern White Cedar" in Figure 8.6.

2. Click the Format Painter button on the Standard toolbar.
3. Move your mouse pointer to the left of the paragraph you want to reformat. If the pointer turns into a little paintbrush, keep moving it to the left until it's a standard arrow. (The paintbrush has a specific function that we'll talk about in a minute.)
4. Click the mouse button. Word selects the paragraph and then reformats it.

You can also borrow a format from selected text and apply it to another block of selected text.

Select the text that contains the format you want to borrow. Click the Format Painter button on the Standard toolbar. Move the mouse pointer to the text you want to reformat. The pointer turns into a paintbrush. Holding down the mouse button, run the brush over the text you're reformatting. Word selects the text as you move the brush. Then release the mouse button.

How to reverse formats

You can remove formatting from text—that is, change the text to the formats you started the document with. Select the text whose formats you want to reverse and press Ctrl+spacebar. If you're removing formats for a single word, put the insertion point anywhere in the word.

Ctrl+spacebar removes all formats that you've applied, including fonts, styles, sizes, and effects.

The key word here is "applied"—you must have taken an action from the Formatting toolbar or the Font dialog box. Formats that are part of a paragraph style, which is not the same as a font style, will not be affected. If this sounds confusing, Chapter 12, "Word Documents Are Never Out of Style," should help to clarify matters.

Symbolic victories

You can use symbols in a number of ways to embellish your documents. For example, you might use a pair of scissors along the border of a clip-'n-save coupon, check boxes for checklists, mathematical symbols for your latest theorem explaining the origin of the universe, or your astrology sign for responses to personal ads.

Open dialog box, insert symbol

To insert a symbol, choose Insert, Symbol from the main menu and click the Symbols tab in the Symbol dialog box (see Figure 8.7). Select a font from the Font drop-down box. The symbols for each font appear in the grid below the Font drop-down box.

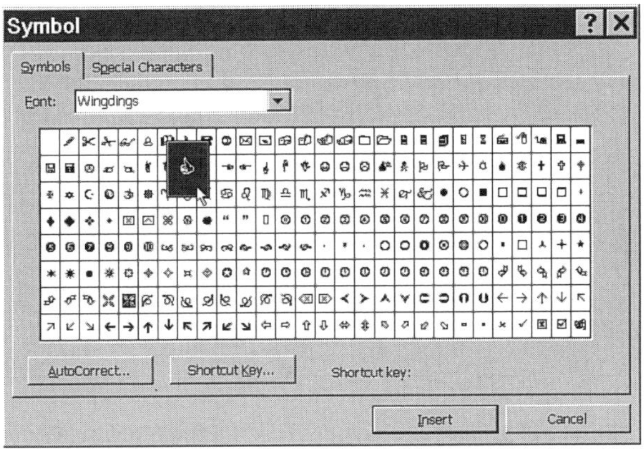

Fig. 8.7
The Symbol dialog box lets you insert a variety of symbols ranging from the practical to the frivolous.

Click a symbol to magnify it (like the thumbs-up symbol shown in Figure 8.7). You can scan the symbols with your arrow keys. When you find the symbol you want to insert, press the Enter key, double-click the symbol, or choose Insert.

TIP **You can move between the Symbol dialog box and your text by** clicking the inactive window with your mouse or by pressing Alt+F6.

How to create a keyboard shortcut

If you've got a symbol that you want to use repeatedly, you'll probably tire of opening the Symbol dialog box for each insertion. The more efficient method is to create a shortcut key. For example, if you assign Ctrl+Alt+X to the check box, you can use that key combination to insert a check box whenever you want.

You create a shortcut by clicking Shortcut Key in the Symbol dialog box. In the Customize dialog box that appears, choose Press New Shortcut Key. In the text box, press Ctrl or Alt, followed by a letter or number (for example, Alt, then M). The string Alt+M appears in the text box.

Word displays a message under the text box that warns you if the key already has a shortcut. If so, press the Backspace key to delete the shortcut and choose another one.

How to add a symbol to your AutoCorrect table

You also can use AutoCorrect to automatically replace a text string with your symbol. Choose AutoCorrect in the Symbols panel. Word displays the AutoCorrect dialog box with the symbol inserted in the With box. Type the string in the Replace box and click OK. For example, you might represent the thumbs-up symbol in Figure 8.10 with the letters "tu." Thereafter, when you type tu followed by a space, Word replaces it with the thumbs-up symbol.

How many keys can you press at one time?

Because Word uses Ctrl and Alt for its own shortcuts, finding an unassigned key isn't always easy. You can increase the number of unassigned keys available to you in one of two ways:

- Use Ctrl and Alt together or with the Shift key; for example, Ctrl+Alt+M and Alt+Shift+L.
- Use a two-part shortcut; for example, Alt+L,C and Alt+L,X. Alt+L becomes the prefix while C becomes the shortcut key. Alt+L,C might give you the check box, while Alt+L,X might insert the box with an X in it.

TIP **To delete, copy, move, or size a symbol, you first need to select it.** Click the symbol or put your insertion point before the symbol, then press Shift+right arrow.

Inserting special characters

You might have noticed in the Symbol dialog box that there's also a tab titled Special Characters. These characters are similar to symbols, only they're more like text: different types of dashes, hyphens, and spaces; copyright, registered trademark, and trademark symbols; ellipses; and a variety of quotation marks. You insert special characters the same way you do symbols.

You can add special characters to your AutoCorrect table the same way you do symbols; refer to the previous section "How to add a symbol to your AutoCorrect table." You'll find that some special characters, such as those for copyright and trademark, are already AutoCorrect entries.

9

Formatting Paragraphs and Blocks

In this chapter:

- **How do I center text?**
- **Indenting paragraphs the easy way**
- **Just put it on my tab stop!**
- **I want to double-space my paragraphs**
- **Right on target with bulleted lists**
- **Highlighting text with boxes and shading**
- **Borders and shading made easier: Three new toolbars**

Tired of documents that are unbroken blocks of gray type? Add some pizzazz with different alignments, indents, and bulleted lists . . . .

Remember the days when TV dads never took off their suits? At dinner, on weekends, or at Beaver's ball game, Ward Cleaver always looked like he was on his way to a business meeting. Ward probably even wore his tie in the shower.

Word is set up to produce documents that Ward would have appreciated: plain type, single-spaced, and aligned unobtrusively against the left-hand margin. But we don't live in a cautious world anymore. While conservative dress still has its place, there's also room for style and even decoration.

Most documents have lists, quoted material, and other blocks of text that deserve (or even demand) to be highlighted. A bulleted list here, a centered head there, and an indented paragraph over there can transform even the blandest document into a more interesting reading experience.

Word has commands and buttons to take care of most paragraph formatting. We'll start with the formatting commands available to you on the Formatting toolbar, shown in Figure 9.1.

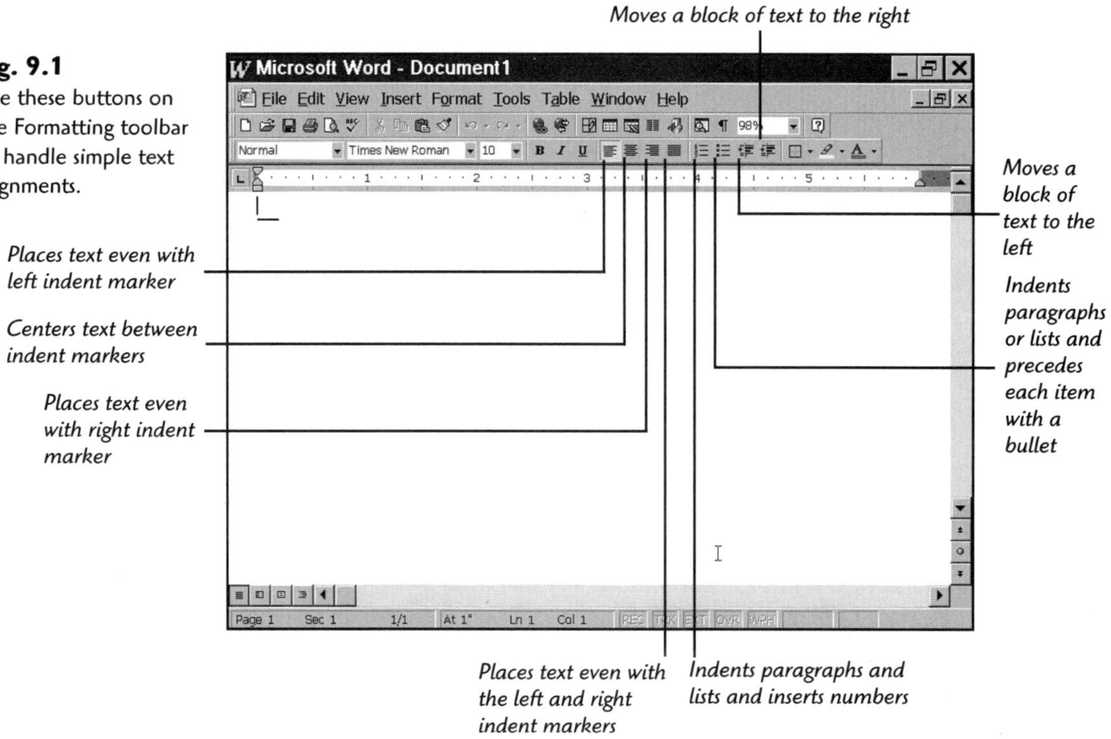

Fig. 9.1
Use these buttons on the Formatting toolbar to handle simple text alignments.

Center, right, and justified alignment

You can use alignments to format part or all of a document. In most cases, however, centering and right alignment are used to give variety to headings and small blocks of text. Use justified type to give body text a neater, more formal look.

The document in Figure 9.2 shows examples of all three alignments. The head is centered, the date is flush right, and the body text is justified.

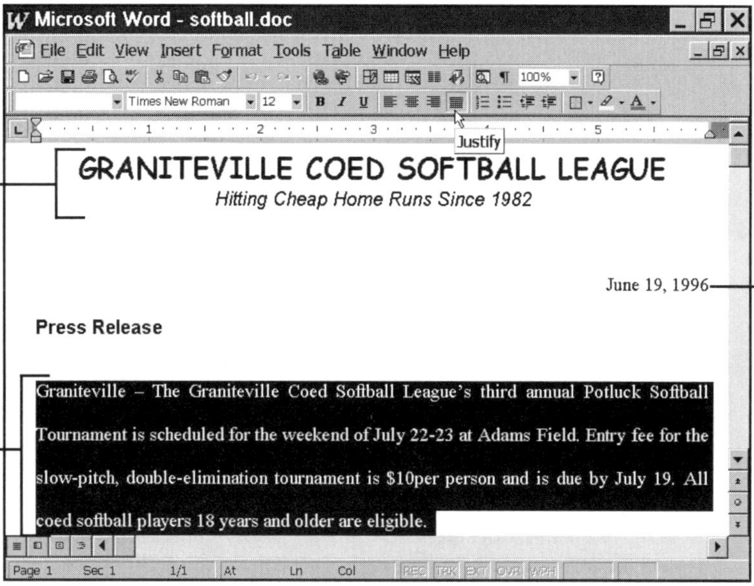
Microsoft Word - softball.doc
File Edit View Insert Format Tools Table Window Help
100%
Times New Roman
12
Justify
GRANITEVILLE COED SOFTBALL LEAGUE
Hitting Cheap Home Runs Since 1982
June 19, 1996
Press Release
Graniteville – The Graniteville Coed Softball League's third annual Potluck Softball Tournament is scheduled for the weekend of July 22-23 at Adams Field. Entry fee for the slow-pitch, double-elimination tournament is $10per person and is due by July 19. All coed softball players 18 years and older are eligible.
Page 1 Sec 1 1/1 At Ln Col REC TRK EXT OVR WPH

Fig. 9.2
Different text alignments separate elements of type and give a document more visual appeal.

Centering automatically aligns text so that it's the same distance from each indent marker

Justified type aligns the left and right sides of text with their respective indent markers

Right alignment brings type against the right indent marker

Here's the easy way to align paragraphs:

To center the heads, select them and click the Center button on the Formatting toolbar.

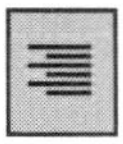

To align the date flush right, place the insertion point anywhere in the line of text and click the Align Right button on the Formatting toolbar.

To justify the body type, select the text and click the Justify button on the Formatting toolbar.

Alignment tricks you should know

Here are a few extra pointers to make text alignment easier:

- You don't need to select a paragraph or line when you realign it; just put the insertion point anywhere in the text you want to realign, then click the appropriate button.
- To align text that you are about to type, choose the alignment you want and start typing.
- The shortcut keys for aligning text are Ctrl+L for flush left, Ctrl+E for align center, Ctrl+R for align right, and Ctrl+J for justification. While the buttons usually are better for fixing alignment in a finished document, the shortcut keys are quicker when you're aligning text as you type it.

Indenting paragraphs made easy

Pages of gray, monolithic text are boring to look at and hard to digest. One solution is to set off the text by indenting it. Figure 9.3 shows examples of the most common types of indents: the *paragraph indent*, the *hanging indent*, and the *negative indent*.

You can get any indent easily by dragging the indent markers on the ruler. Figure 9.4 identifies the markers and other elements of the ruler. When you drag a marker, a dotted line extends the length of the page to help you align your text.

Note that Word gives you two different left indents. The first is for the first line of a paragraph; it's controlled by the first-line indent marker on the top of the ruler. The second is for the rest of the paragraph. You set it with the left indent marker on the bottom of the ruler. You can drag either marker separately, or you can slide them together with the box attached to the indent marker.

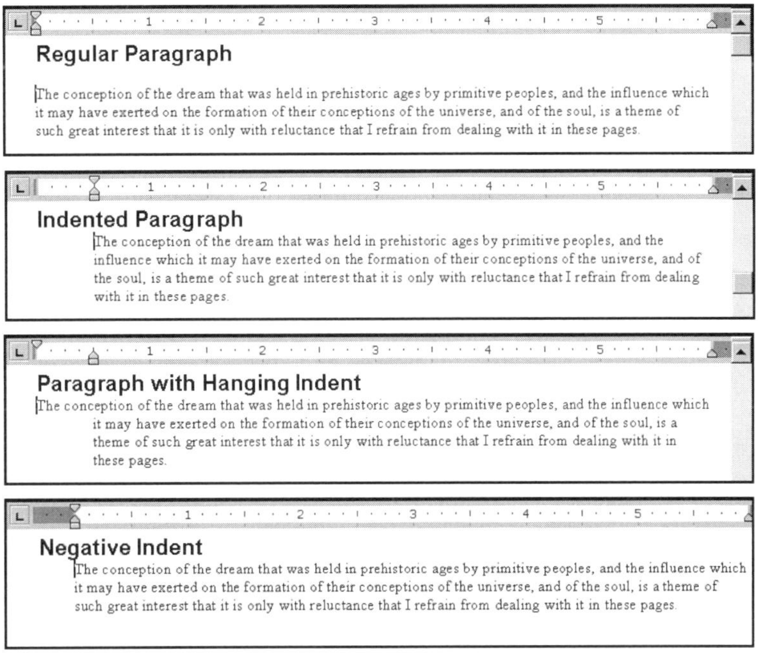

Fig. 9.3
Paragraph indents and their corresponding ruler settings. You can move the ruler markers by dragging them with the mouse. Note the difference between the indented paragraph and the negative indent. With an indented paragraph, the heading is flush with the margin boundary and the text is indented; with a negative indent, the text is flush with the margin boundary and the heading is pushed into the left margin.

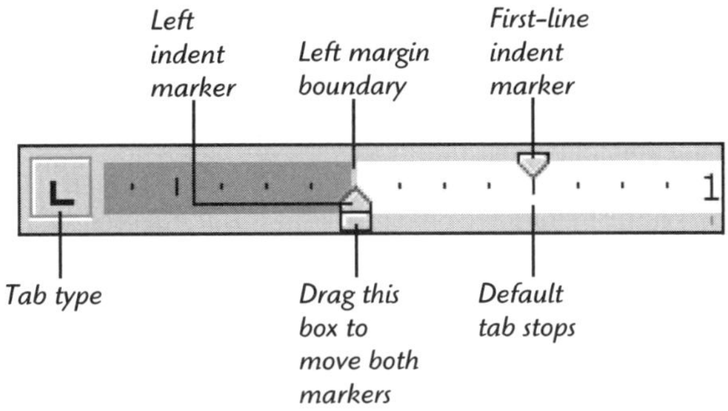

Fig. 9.4
Use the indent markers to create different kinds of paragraph indents.

The paragraph indent

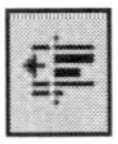

The most convenient way to indent a paragraph is to click the Increase Indent button on the Formatting toolbar. You also can press the Tab key at the beginning of any line in a paragraph, other than the first. Word moves the indent markers to the first tab and indents the selected paragraph accordingly. Word increases the indent by one tab for each subsequent button click.

If you'd rather take the manual approach, you can indent a paragraph by placing the insertion point anywhere in the text and dragging both indent markers to the new location.

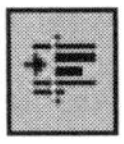

The easiest way to reverse an indent is to click the Decrease Indent button on the Formatting toolbar, or you can press Shift+Tab at the beginning of any line in the paragraph. Also, you can drag the indent markers on the ruler back to the margin boundary.

TIP **To indent more than one paragraph, select the text before you** drag the indent markers. To indent an entire document, select the document first by pressing Ctrl+A.

The hanging indent

Bored with paragraph indents? Try a hanging indent. The difference is that the left indent marker (that's the one on the bottom) is to the right of the first-line indent marker. To create a hanging indent, place the insertion point in the paragraph you want to indent and do either of the following:

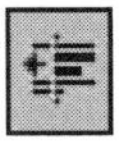

- Click the Increase Indent button on the Formatting toolbar, then drag the first-line indent marker back to where you want the first line of the paragraph to begin. The body of the paragraph hangs down from the first tab.
- Drag the left indent marker to the spot where you want the body of the paragraph to hang.

Meanwhile, on the other end of the ruler...

A paragraph indent is a great way to set off a block of text, but why not go one step further and indent it from the right margin, too? A little bit of space on both sides of a block quote, a list, or important instructional material attracts the reader's eye and balances the design of your page.

To indent text from the right margin, drag the right margin marker as you do the other markers.

A little tab will do you

Tabs were once important for preparing tables and columnar material. But most of these functions have been stolen by Word's Table and Columns commands, which are easier to use and have far more design and editing power.

Still, tabs have their place if you need a simple two- or three-column listing—a price or inventory list, for example, or a schedule of events.

Word places default tab stops at 1/2-inch intervals (they're little gray marks just underneath the ruler). These usually aren't practical for aligning tabular material because they're so close together; you often have to press the Tab key half a dozen times to align your text properly. The more efficient way is to set your own tab stops.

Setting new tab stops

Figure 9.5 shows a simple to-do list. It consists of two columns, the second starting at 3 inches. The start of the second column is marked on the ruler by a tab stop, which looks like a squat, boldfaced L. The default tab stops before the set tab stop are gone.

> ***Plain English, please!***
>
> A **tab stop** is where your insertion point stops when you press the tab key and is marked on the ruler. A **tab**, on the other hand, is what you get when you press the Tab key—the space between your tab stop and where your insertion point was. Tabs are usually hidden, but you can see them by clicking the Show/Hide Paragraph Marks button on the Standard toolbar; they're the bold arrows in Figure 9.5.

Here's what you do to create tabular material:

1. Click the ruler where you want the tab stop. Word inserts the new tab stop and deletes the default tab stops to its left.
2. Start typing your text. When you reach the end of an entry in the first column ("Write summary of objectives" in Figure 9.5, for example), press the Tab key. Your insertion point slides to the tab stop. Type the entry for the second column and press the Enter key.

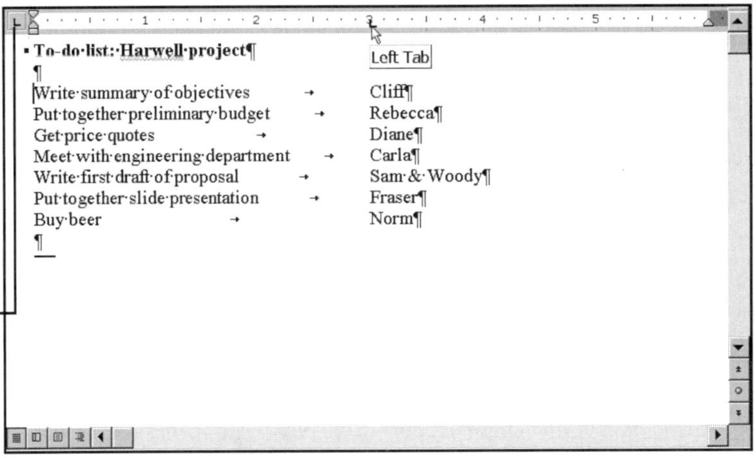

Fig. 9.5
A simple two-column table created with a single tab stop at 3 inches on the ruler.

The Tab Alignment button shows what kind of tab you'll create when you click the ruler—in this case, a left tab

If you decide you want the tab stop somewhere else on the ruler, click it with the mouse and drag it to its new location. To help you align your column, Word drops a dotted line from the tab through your text.

You can insert as many tab stops as will fit on the ruler. However, if you find yourself with a table that has more than two or three simple columns, check out the Word's table feature (see Chapter 11, "Turning the Tables"). It's easier to use and gives you more editing options.

When you reach the end of your table, you can reinstate Word's default tab stops by clicking the tab stop you set and dragging it off the ruler.

Q&A ***How do I set tab stops for a list or table I've already typed?***

Start by selecting the text. Click the ruler where you want the tab stop. Of course, you must have tabs at the appropriate places between columns to align the text.

Q&A ***OK, I created a two-column list following your instructions. So how come the text in the second column doesn't align with the tab stop?***

If you used Word's default tab stops to align your second column of text *before* you set your new tab stop, there's a good chance you have extra tabs. Also, to make your text line up properly, you probably used more tabs in some lines than you did in others. Delete the extra tabs, and you should be set.

Different tabs for different tables

Figure 9.5 uses a left-aligned tab; that is, the text of the second column starts at the tab stop. You can also set tabs for right and center alignment, and for decimals. Figure 9.6 shows examples of right and decimal alignment. Notice that right alignment in the table labeled "Schedule" neatly lines up the times. In the second table, "Costs," decimal alignment lines up the Figures, even the ones that don't have a decimal.

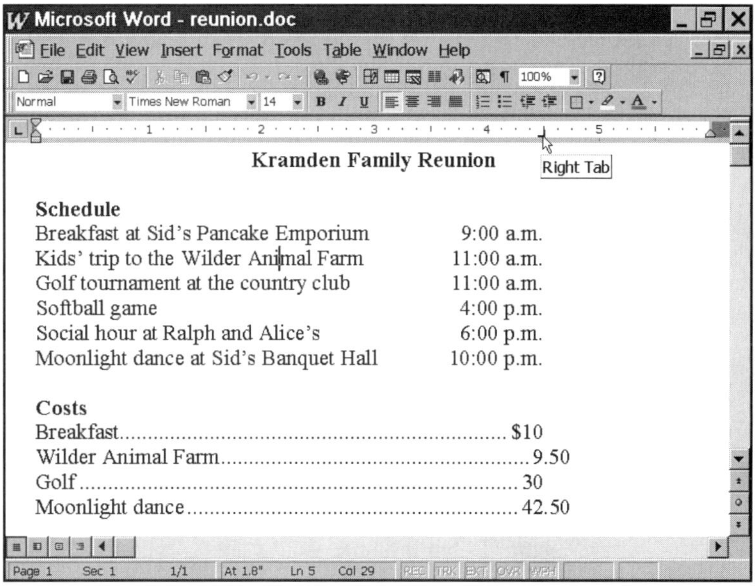

Fig. 9.6
The first table shows an example of how you can use a right-aligned tab to line up lists such as times. The second uses decimal alignment to line up dollar amounts.

Center alignment balances a column so that each entry has equal amounts of text on either side of the tab. You can center-align the middle column of a three-column table to give the table more balance. Center alignment is also effective for columns that consist of single words.

You choose the type of tab stop you want with the Tab Type button at the far left of the ruler. Click the ruler until the tab you want appears. A ScreenTip tells you what type of tab you'll get. Then click the ruler where you want to put the tab stop.

Q&A ***I finished my table, then tried to change a tab stop by dragging it on the ruler. The tab stop changed for only one line! How do I change the tab stops for all of the lines in the table?***

Select the entire table first, then drag the tab stop. When no text has been selected, dragging a tab stop affects only the line on which your insertion point is positioned.

Take me to your dot leaders

Most phone books have little dots that connect each name with its phone number. The dots, collectively called a *leader*, make the listings easier to read.

While you might not be creating a phone book any time soon, you should consider leaders for long lists in which the columns are spread apart; for example, phone lists, indexes, tables of contents, and schedules. The second table in Figure 9.6 shows dot leaders; Word also lets you replace tabs with dashed leaders or a solid underline leader.

If you're creating a new table, set up your leaders after you set your tab stop and before you start typing. If you've already created a table and you want to add leaders, select the table text first. In either case, follow these steps:

1. Right-click a tab stop twice; the Tabs dialog box appears (see Figure 9.7).
2. Under Tab Stop Position, choose the tab stop you want your leader to precede.
3. Under the Leader heading, choose the type of leader you want.
4. Click OK, and Word replaces the tab before the tab stop with the leader.

Word inserts a leader only for the tab stop you've clicked. If you want to use a leader with another tab stop in the same selected text, click Set instead of OK. Select the tab stop from the Tab Stop Position list box, choose another leader, and click Set. When you've got as many leaders as you want, click OK.

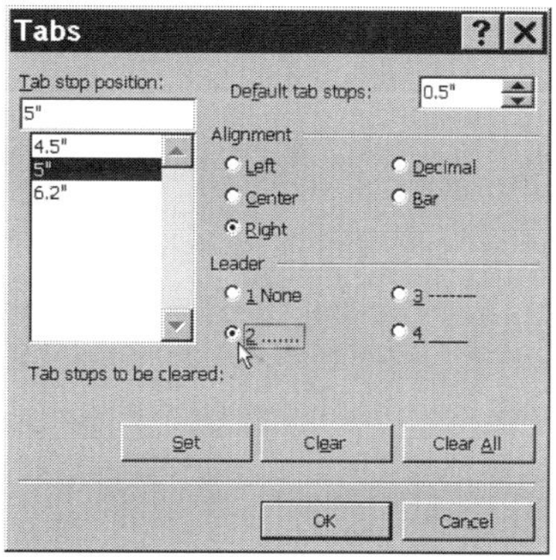

Fig. 9.7
Set and clear tabs from the Tabs dialog box. You can also use this dialog box to insert leaders.

Q&A ***I tried creating leaders in my document, but I don't get any. What am I doing wrong?***

Have you set tab stops to align your tabular material? Leaders don't work with Word's default tab stops.

Clearing tabs

The easiest way to clear a tab stop is to drag it up or down off the ruler. If you want to clear all tab stops, click the Clear All button in the Tabs dialog box (refer to Figure 9.7). Word resets all tabs to the default shown in the Default Tab Stops text box.

Vertical leaps—line and paragraph spacing

Long reports are easier to read if you add space between lines and paragraphs, and Word gives you the commands to do both.

In Figure 9.8, for example, the body text is double-spaced and the space between the indented quotes has been reduced to 6 points.

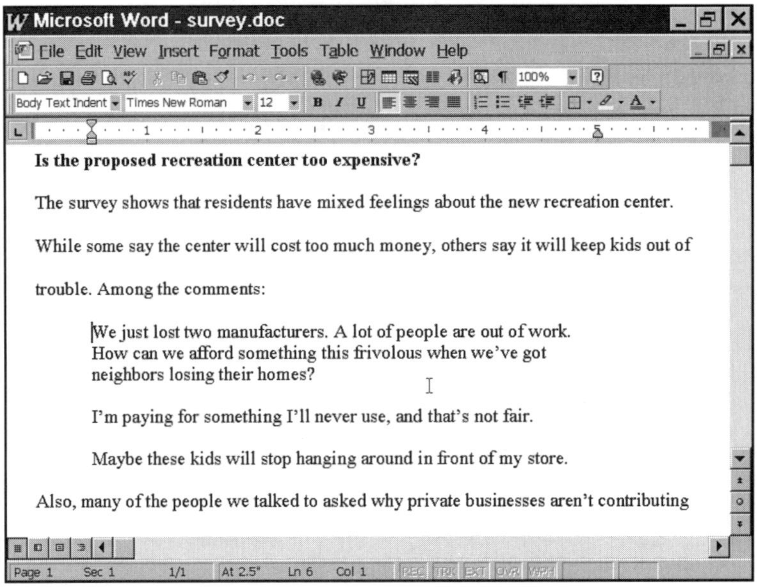
Microsoft Word - survey.doc
File Edit View Insert Format Tools Table Window Help
100%
Body Text Indent
Times New Roman
12
Is the proposed recreation center too expensive?
The survey shows that residents have mixed feelings about the new recreation center.
While some say the center will cost too much money, others say it will keep kids out of
trouble. Among the comments:
We just lost two manufacturers. A lot of people are out of work.
How can we afford something this frivolous when we've got
neighbors losing their homes?
I'm paying for something I'll never use, and that's not fair.
Maybe these kids will stop hanging around in front of my store.
Also, many of the people we talked to asked why private businesses aren't contributing
Page 1 Sec 1 1/1 At 2.5" Ln 6 Col 1
REC TRK EXT OVR WPH

Fig. 9.8
Use line and paragraph spacing to make text more readable and emphasize indented text.

How to adjust line spacing

To double-space paragraphs, press Ctrl+2 before you start typing. Double-space a single paragraph by placing the insertion point anywhere in the text and pressing Ctrl+2. You can also use Ctrl+2 to double-space selected paragraphs. Press Ctrl+1 for single space; press Ctrl+5 for one and a half spaces.

If you want to adjust your spacing to something else—triple space, for instance—use the Paragraph dialog box (see Figure 9.9). Choose Format, Paragraph from the main menu and click the Indents and Spacing tab. Choose the Line Spacing drop-down box and choose Multiple. Type the new spacing in the At text box (for example, type **3** for triple spacing).

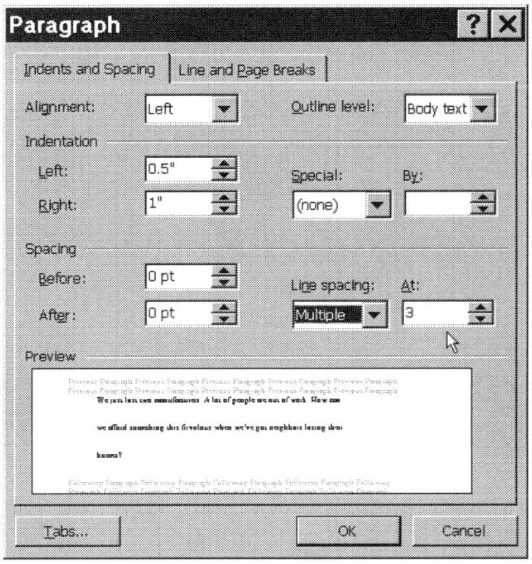
Paragraph
Indents and Spacing
Line and Page Breaks
Alignment:
Left
Outline level:
Body text
Indentation
Left:
0.5"
Right:
1"
Special:
By:
(none)
Spacing
Before:
0 pt
After:
0 pt
Line spacing:
At:
Multiple
3
Preview
Tabs...
OK
Cancel

Fig. 9.9
Use the Paragraph dialog box to adjust the space between lines or paragraphs.

Fine points

You can adjust line and paragraph spacing by the point. This lets you control your spacing with much greater precision. Figure 9.10 shows examples of 10-point Bookman, with line spacing ranging from 6 to 10 points.

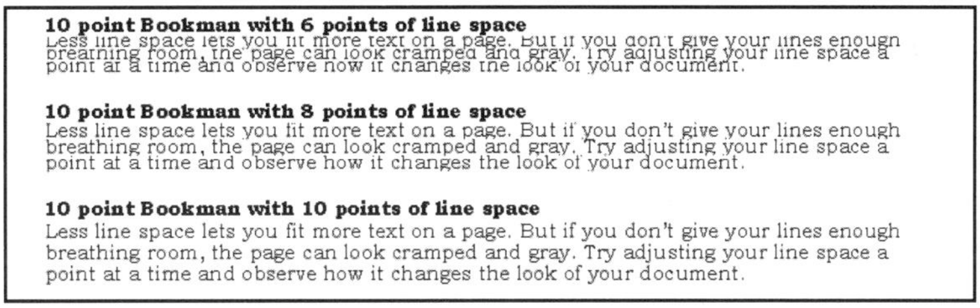
10 point Bookman with 6 points of line space
Less line space lets you fit more text on a page. But if you don't give your lines enough breathing room, the page can look cramped and gray. Try adjusting your line space a point at a time and observe how it changes the look of your document.
10 point Bookman with 8 points of line space
Less line space lets you fit more text on a page. But if you don't give your lines enough breathing room, the page can look cramped and gray. Try adjusting your line space a point at a time and observe how it changes the look of your document.
10 point Bookman with 10 points of line space
Less line space lets you fit more text on a page. But if you don't give your lines enough breathing room, the page can look cramped and gray. Try adjusting your line space a point at a time and observe how it changes the look of your document.

Fig. 9.10
You can adjust line spacing by the point to put more text on a page or give the text more space.

To expand or tighten line spacing by the point, choose Exactly from the Line Spacing drop-down box, and enter the new spacing followed by pt in the At text box (refer to Figure 9.9). For example, to change spacing to 10 points, type **10 pt**.

How to adjust paragraph spacing

Adjust the spacing between paragraphs in the Paragraph dialog box, in the Before and After text boxes under Spacing (refer to Figure 9.9). For example, to get the 6 points shown in Figure 9.8, select the indented paragraphs *except for the last one* and enter **6 pts** in the After text box. You don't select the last indented paragraph to avoid adding space between the indented text and the body text.

Q&A ***I selected a double-spaced paragraph, pressed Ctrl+1, and nothing happened. What did I do wrong?***

¶ There's a good chance the person who wrote the document pressed the Enter key after each line (this is a common mistake among inexperienced users). Click the Show/Hide Paragraph Marks button on the Standard toolbar and look for telltale paragraph markers. Delete all but the one that ends the paragraph.

Bulleted and numbered lists

Bulleted and numbered lists are excellent ways to emphasize points or organize instructional material. Figure 9.11 shows a few simple examples.

Creating a bulleted or numbered list is as easy as aligning text. You can also change the appearance of such lists in several ways, for example:

- You can change the bullet into a special character, such as the check box in the second example in Figure 9.11.
- You can change the font, style, and size of numbers.
- You can change the spacing between the bullets or numbers and the text.

Fig. 9.11
Three types of lists with numbers and bullets.

These are the standard bullets and indents you get when you click the Bullets button

Here the bullets are replaced with check boxes

Click the Numbering button to get this list

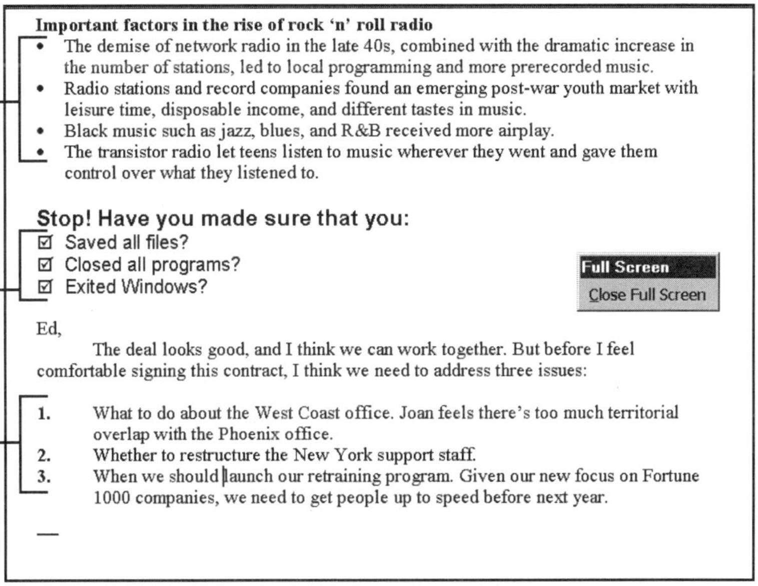
Important factors in the rise of rock 'n' roll radio
• The demise of network radio in the late 40s, combined with the dramatic increase in the number of stations, led to local programming and more prerecorded music.
• Radio stations and record companies found an emerging post-war youth market with leisure time, disposable income, and different tastes in music.
• Black music such as jazz, blues, and R&B received more airplay.
• The transistor radio let teens listen to music wherever they went and gave them control over what they listened to.
Stop! Have you made sure that you:
☑ Saved all files?
☑ Closed all programs?
☑ Exited Windows?
Full Screen
Close Full Screen
Ed,
The deal looks good, and I think we can work together. But before I feel comfortable signing this contract, I think we need to address three issues:
1. What to do about the West Coast office. Joan feels there's too much territorial overlap with the Phoenix office.
2. Whether to restructure the New York support staff.
3. When we should launch our retraining program. Given our new focus on Fortune 1000 companies, we need to get people up to speed before next year.

Lists made easy

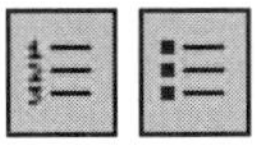

If you're creating a list from scratch, put the insertion point where you want to start the list. Click the Numbering button if the list is numbered, and the Bullets button if the list has bullets.

Word inserts the number or bullet and moves the insertion point to where your text begins. Type the first item on your list. If your text is longer than one line, Word automatically indents your text so that subsequent lines are indented evenly.

Press the Enter key at the end of each item. Word inserts the next number or bullet. When you've finished the last item in the list, press the Enter key twice to switch back to your regular format.

To add numbers or bullets to a list that you've already written, select the text and click the Numbering button or the Bullets button.

Q&A ***How do I get rid of my bullets? I've tried the Delete key, but it doesn't work!***

Highlight the list items and click the Numbering or Bullets button. If you want to delete a single bullet or number, the easiest way is to put your insertion point between the bullet or number and the following text and press the Backspace key.

It's not unusual to create a numbered list and then find you need to change it. Here are a few tricks that will make editing lists easier:

- To insert an item in the middle of a numbered list, put your insertion point at the end of the previous item and press the Enter key. Word starts the next line with the correct number and automatically renumbers the items that follow. Word also renumbers a list if you delete an item.
- To skip numbering a paragraph in the middle of a list, put your insertion point anywhere in the text of the item you don't want numbered and click the Numbering button. From the keyboard, put the insertion point at the beginning of the item and press the Backspace key. Word renumbers the items that follow so they stay in sequence.
- If you want to break a list into two lists, press the Enter key twice after the item that will end your first list. This inserts two blank, unnumbered lines. Put your insertion point on the first line of the second list, click the right mouse button, and choose Bullets and Numbering. Word displays the Numbered panel in the Bullets and Numbering dialog box. Click the Restart Numbering button and choose OK. Word creates a new list, starting with No. 1.

Formatting fandangos

If you get tired of plain old numbers, Word gives you a nearly endless variety of formatting options.

Figure 9.12 gives you an example. The numbers have been replaced with letters preceded by the word "Item," the typeface has been changed to Arial bold, and the space between the letters and the text has been widened.

All of the work was done from the Bullets and Numbering dialog box. Let's walk through the procedure.

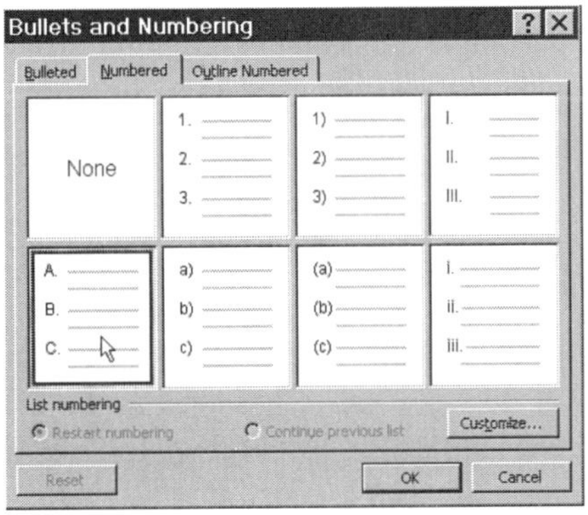

Fig. 9.12
Spice up plain old numbers in a numbered list by adding descriptive text.

Changing the numbers

We'll assume that you're changing an existing list, although you can just as easily choose your options before you start.

Select the numbered text you want to work with and choose Format, Bullets and Numbering from the main menu. On the Bullets and Numbering dialog box that appears, click the Numbered tab (see Figure 9.13). Click one of the six ready-to-go formats (for our example, the first one in the second row).

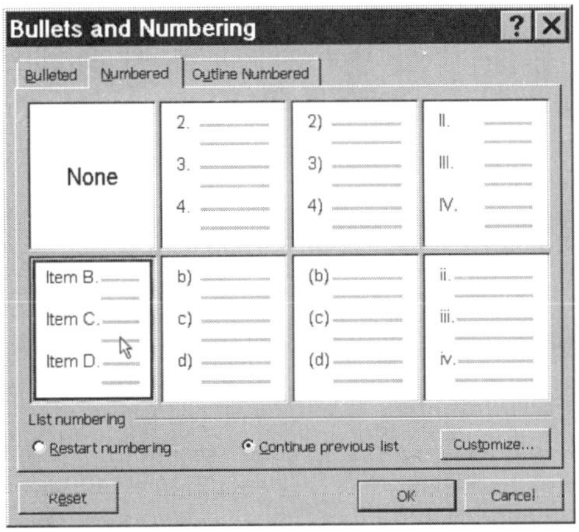

Fig. 9.13
Click the Numbered tab in the Bullets and Numbering dialog box to change the format of a numbered list.

Next, click the Customize button to display the Customize Numbered List dialog box, then make these changes:

- Type the word "Item" before the letter A in the Number Format box.

- Change the value in the Indent At box to 0.7".
- Choose the Font button to display the Font dialog box, select Arial from the Font display box and Bold from the Font Style box, and click OK. (Chapter 8 gives you more information on how to use the Font dialog box.)

Putting together a numbered list often takes some experimenting, so try different combinations and see how they look in the Preview box. If you apply a format that you don't like, you can click the Undo button on the Standard toolbar to bail out.

Hit the bulls-eye with fancy bullets

You don't have quite as many options for playing with bullets, but you can replace them with any character and change their size. Figure 9.14 shows you a few possibilities.

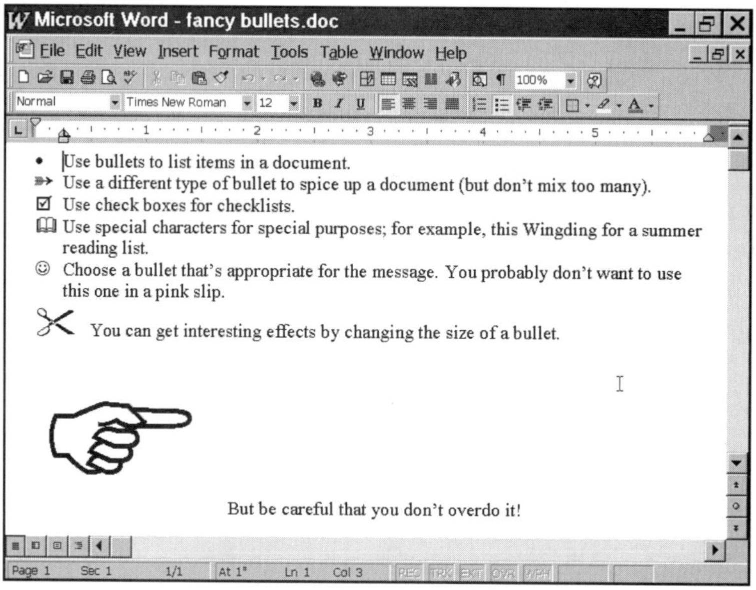
Microsoft Word - fancy bullets.doc
File Edit View Insert Format Tools Table Window Help
Normal
Times New Roman
12
100%
Use bullets to list items in a document.
Use a different type of bullet to spice up a document (but don't mix too many).
Use check boxes for checklists.
Use special characters for special purposes; for example, this Wingding for a summer reading list.
Choose a bullet that's appropriate for the message. You probably don't want to use this one in a pink slip.
You can get interesting effects by changing the size of a bullet.
But be careful that you don't overdo it!
Page 1 Sec 1 1/1 At 1" Ln 1 Col 3

Fig. 9.14
For special effects, replace your plain bullets with symbols.

Choose Format, Bullets and Numbering from the main menu. The Bulleted tab looks like the Numbered tab, with six types of bullets you can choose from.

The real action is in the Customize Bulleted List dialog box (see Figure 9.15). Here's where you change the size of a bullet or pick a new one.

Click the Customize button from the Bulleted panel of the Bullets and Numbering dialog box. To change the font, style, and size of a bullet, choose the Font button and make your changes in the Font dialog box.

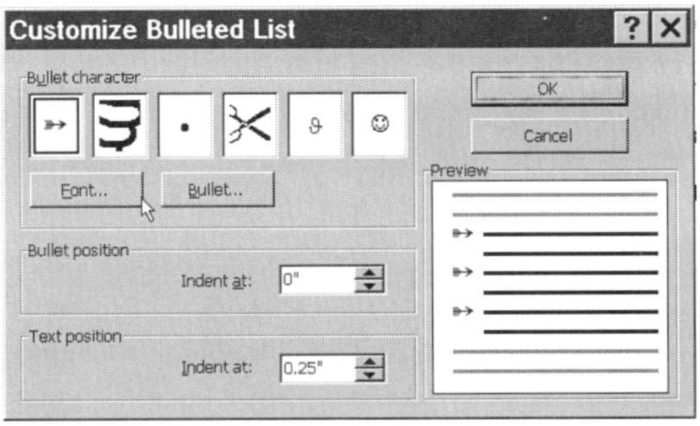

Fig. 9.15
The Customize Bulleted List dialog box lets you change a bullet's size or pick new bullets.

If you want a new bullet, click the Bullet button. Word opens the Symbol dialog box. Click the Font drop-down box and choose a font. Click the symbol you want, then click OK.

For more information on symbols and special characters, see Chapter 8.

CAUTION **Do not try to create a Word document with the intent of later** converting it to HTML format for publication on the World Wide Web. Word will strip out many of your formats, including many bullets and numbers. If you're creating Web pages, start them from scratch as HTML documents. See Chapter 25, "The Word on the Web," for details.

Borderline decisions: how to box paragraphs

Fonts, bullets, indents—these are all devices you can use to emphasize parts of your document. But if you *really* want to set off a block of text, check out Word's borders and shading.

A well-placed border can do for text what a frame does for a painting. It contains the text and separates the document into segments that make the page easier to read. Shading a block does much the same thing with more subtlety.

You can box or shade text using either the Borders and Shading dialog box or the Tables and Borders toolbar. For heavyweight boxers, the toolbar is the fastest way to go, but let's do a little sparring first with the Borders and Shading dialog box, where your options are easier to select.

Boxing lessons

You can border or shade any paragraph. Start by placing your insertion point anywhere in the paragraph you want to format. You can format several paragraphs by selecting them first. In Figure 9.16, for example, the three lines of the letterhead are boxed and shaded.

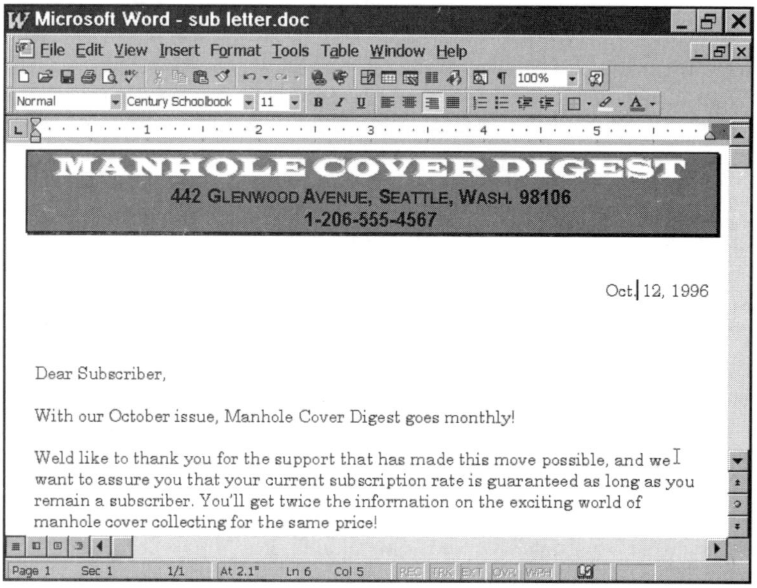
Microsoft Word - sub letter.doc
File Edit View Insert Format Tools Table Window Help
Normal
Century Schoolbook
11
100%
MANHOLE COVER DIGEST
442 GLENWOOD AVENUE, SEATTLE, WASH. 98106
1-206-555-4567
Oct 12, 1996
Dear Subscriber,
With our October issue, Manhole Cover Digest goes monthly!
Weld like to thank you for the support that has made this move possible, and we want to assure you that your current subscription rate is guaranteed as long as you remain a subscriber. You'll get twice the information on the exciting world of manhole cover collecting for the same price!
Page 1 Sec 1 1/1 At 2.1" Ln 6 Col 5 REC TRK EXT OVR WPH

Fig. 9.16
An example of a letterhead with a shadowed box and shading.

Choose Format, Borders and Shading from the main menu and click the Borders tab (see Figure 9.17). You can choose from among three ready-made styles under the Setting heading: Box, Shadow, or Three-D. A box is, well, a box—lines of equal weight on all four sides. If you choose Shadow, Word makes your box look like it's floating, as in Figure 9.16. Three-D gives your box a three-dimensional effect (and you don't even need 3-D glasses to see it).

Next, choose the type of border you want under Style. Word offers a wide range of borders, including single lines, double lines, wavy lines, and dotted lines. If you're creating a Three-D box, a single line won't work; you must choose a multiline style. You can get an idea of what the border will look like in the Border preview box.

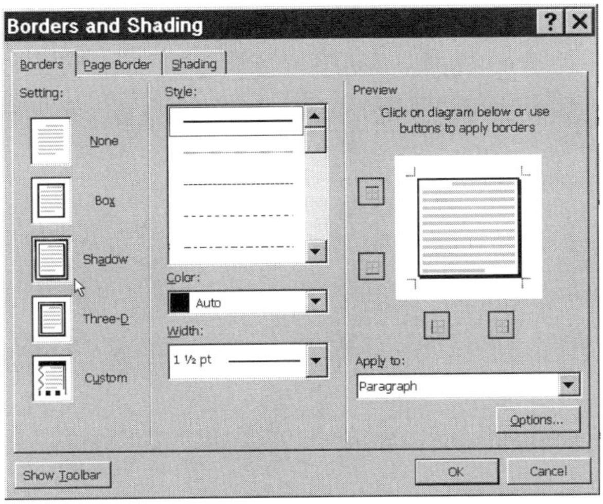

Fig. 9.17
The Borders and Shading dialog box lets you choose the type of border you want.

You can also choose how much space you want between the borders and your text. Choose the Options dialog box to display the Border and Shading Options dialog box. You can adjust the space individually for each border. For most uses, 1 point is about right for the top and borders, and 4 points for the left and right borders.

Opening the border

If your text is feeling claustrophobic and starts clamoring for air, you can open your box by deleting one or more of its sides. Click the border you want to get rid of in the preview box. For example, to give the letterhead in Figure 9.16 top and bottom lines but no sides, click the left and right borders.

Made in the shade

To add a shaded background to your selected text, choose Format, Borders and Shading and click the Shading tab. (You can shade paragraphs without borders, but shades usually look neater when they're boxed.)

Unless you've got a color printer, you most likely will want a shade of gray. Click the appropriate button under the Fill heading (see Figure 9.18). Word displays the percentage of shading (35 percent in Figure 9.18) and also shows you what it will look like in the Preview box. Word gives you a range of choices, from 5 percent to 95 percent. The higher the percent, the heavier the shade.

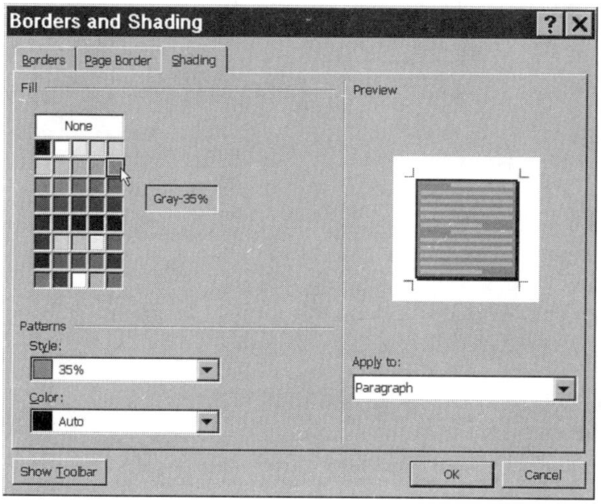

Fig. 9.18
Add shading to a box or paragraph by clicking a color button under Fill.

The shading in Figure 9.16 is set at 45 percent, but it's darker than usual because the title is embossed. You usually don't want to go much above 30 percent; anything heavier begins to overwhelm your text. You might need to experiment to find out what shades are most attractive on your printer.

Q&A ***I'd like to use a color for my fill. Can I shade it the way I can shade grays?***

Yes. After you've chosen your color, click the Style selection box. You'll see a list of percentages—5%, 10%, 12.5%, and so on. Click the percent of shading you want.

Boxer shorts

After you've gone a few rounds in the Borders and Shading dialog box, try using one of Word's Borders and Shading toolbars. Word offers three toolbars, shown in Figure 9.19.

Using the toolbars has two advantages:

- You can select top, bottom, left, and right borders with the first four buttons.
- You can work in your document and click the toolbars when you need them. This lets you change borders and shading without going through the menu bar.

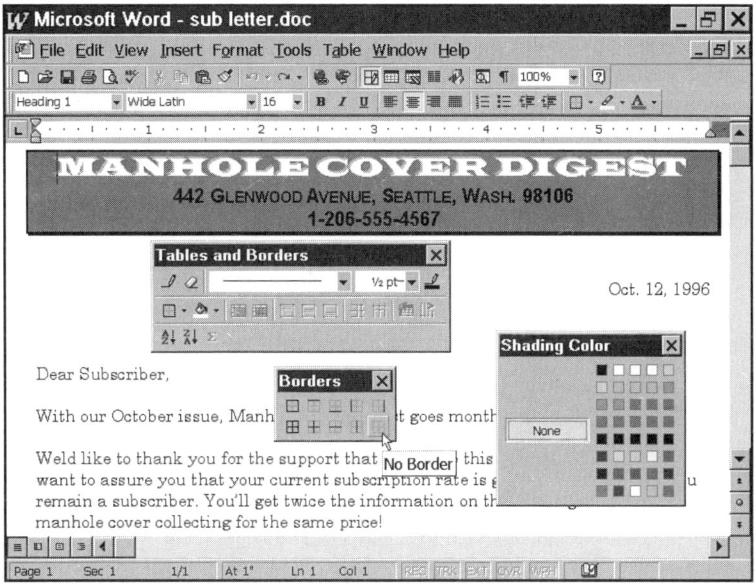
Microsoft Word - sub letter.doc
File Edit View Insert Format Tools Table Window Help
Heading 1
Wide Latin
16
MANHOLE COVER DIGEST
442 GLENWOOD AVENUE, SEATTLE, WASH. 98106
1-206-555-4567
Tables and Borders
Oct. 12, 1996
Shading Color
None
Dear Subscriber,
Borders
With our October issue, Manh
t goes month
We'd like to thank you for the support that
No Border
this
want to assure you that your current subscription rate is
remain a subscriber. You'll get twice the information on th
manhole cover collecting for the same price!
Page 1 Sec 1 1/1 At 1" Ln 1 Col 1

Fig. 9.19
Word has three toolbars that you can use in combination to make borders and shades easier to create.

Choose your toolbar

The Tables and Borders toolbar gives you a complete set of tools for creating both tables and borders. We'll discuss this toolbar in detail in Chapter 11, "Turning the Tables"; for now, ignore the table-related tools and focus on the border tools. Display the Tables and Borders toolbar by clicking the Tables and Borders button on the Standard toolbar.

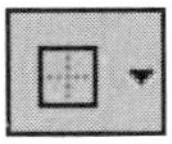

The Borders toolbar lets you quickly select the sides of a paragraph you want bordered. You display it by clicking the arrow next to the Borders button.

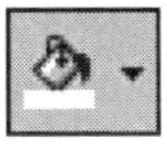

The Shading Color toolbar is the same as the selection box under Fill in the Shading panel of the Borders and Shading dialog box. Display it by clicking the arrow next to the Shading button.

Pull-out toolbars

When you click the arrow next to the Borders or Shading Color toolbar, the toolbar appears as a drop-down menu that looks like a mini-toolbar. Word 97 includes a nifty trick that lets you turn them into floating toolbars.

For example, click the arrow next to the Border button. Touch the mini-toolbar's title bar. Word displays a ScreenTip that reads, "Drag to make this menu float." Click and drag the mini-toolbar into the document window. Use the same technique to float the Shading Color toolbar.

Time to line up your borders

Once you've used the Borders and Shading dialog box to create borders, the toolbars in Figure 9.19 will be pretty much self-explanatory. Here's how to create your border:

1. Select your paragraphs.
2. Pick your Line Style and Line Weight from the Tables and Borders dialog box.
3. Choose the borders you want from the Border dropdown menu or toolbar.

The buttons on the Border toolbar act as toggles. Click a button to create a border; click it again to remove a border.

10

Formatting Your Page

In this chapter:

- **I'd like to start a new page, please**
- **How do I create and format sections?**
- **I want page numbers on my document**
- **Can I keep blocks of text together?**
- **This document needs headers (or footers)**
- **The dating game: adding the date and time**

Give me a break! And while you're at it, how about some footers, page numbers, and dates. . . . .

As you develop more elaborate documents, you may have specific needs that Word's basic formatting tools can't fulfill. How do you create a separate page in the middle of your document? Prevent Word from splitting a block of text or table between two pages? Put a title and page number on each page? We'll take up these topics and more in this chapter.

Divide and conquer: inserting page and section breaks

As documents become larger, they're easier to read if you break them into smaller units. For example, you might want a table on its own page or a report broken into chapters. Sound complicated? It's not. Word's Break command lets you do these things in just a few simple steps. Breaks have another important function—they make formatting and editing easier. For example, if you break your document into sections, you can use a different sequence of page numbers for each section.

> ***Plain English, please!***
>
> A **page break** is the spot where Word ends one page and begins the next one. An **automatic page break** is one that Word inserts when it reaches the end of the page. The break moves as you add or delete text above it. A **manual page break** is one that you insert; it's permanent, regardless of how you change previous text. A **section break** creates a new section, somewhat like the chapter of a book, that you can format separately from other sections.

How to start a new page

When you insert a page break, Word ends the page at that point and starts a new page. Word marks a manual page break in Normal view with a dotted line and the words `Page Break`, as shown in Figure 10.1.

Fig. 10.1
Insert a page break to force Word to start a new page.

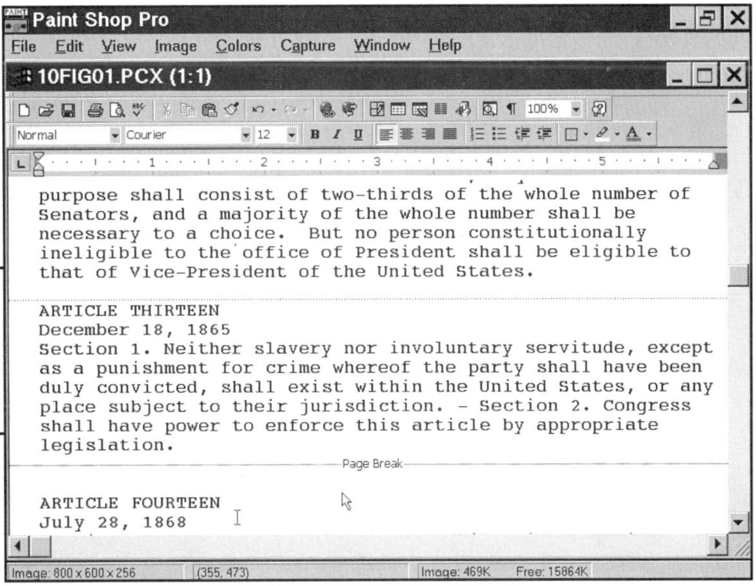
Paint Shop Pro
File Edit View Image Colors Capture Window Help
10FIG01.PCX (1:1)
Normal
Courier
12
100%
purpose shall consist of two-thirds of the whole number of Senators, and a majority of the whole number shall be necessary to a choice. But no person constitutionally ineligible to the office of President shall be eligible to that of Vice-President of the United States.
Automatic page break
ARTICLE THIRTEEN
December 18, 1865
Section 1. Neither slavery nor involuntary servitude, except as a punishment for crime whereof the party shall have been duly convicted, shall exist within the United States, or any place subject to their jurisdiction. - Section 2. Congress shall have power to enforce this article by appropriate legislation.
Manual page break
Page Break
ARTICLE FOURTEEN
July 28, 1868
Image: 800 x 600 x 256
(355, 473)
Image: 469K
Free: 15864K

The easiest way to insert a page break is with the keyboard shortcut Ctrl+Enter. You can also choose Insert, Break from the main menu and then Page Break in the Break dialog box.

Delete a page break by putting the insertion point on it and pressing the Delete key.

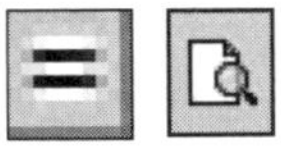

To see how a page break affects your document, choose View, Page Layout from the main menu, or click the Page Layout View button to the left of the horizontal scroll bar. Choose File, Print Preview or click the Print Preview button to see how the break will look in the printed document.

CAUTION **If you insert, delete, or move a lot of text after you insert a** manual page break, be careful of double page breaks—an automatic page break followed by a manual page break with no text between them. You'll get a blank page in the middle of your document.

Breaking a document into sections

At first glance, a section break looks a lot like a page break. Both segment a document, but a section break has several important differences:

- You can do some types of formatting by the section. For example, if you have an extra-long table, you can put it in a section and tell Word to print just that section lengthwise, using landscape orientation.
- You can give each section separate page numbers.
- You can put a new title on each page of a new section in a header or footer.

> ***Plain English, please!***
>
> A **header** is information, such as a title or page number, that Word automatically inserts at the top of each page. A **footer** is the same as a header, except that it appears at the bottom of the page.

How do I start a new section?

To insert a section break, place the insertion point where you want the section to start and choose Insert, Break from the main menu. Under Section Breaks in the Break dialog box, Word gives you the following options:

- *Next Page* starts the new section on the next page.
- *Continuous* inserts a section break that you can format separately, but it does not start a new page.
- *Odd Page* starts the new section on the next odd-numbered page. For example, if you insert a section break on page 41, the new section will start on page 43 and leave page 42 blank. Use this break when you print on both sides of your paper and want your sections to always start on right-hand pages, like the chapters in this book.
- *Even Page* is the same as Odd Page, only the new section starts on the next even-numbered page.

Word marks a section break in Normal view with a double dotted line and the words `Section Break (type), where "type" is the type of section you've created`. Use Page Layout view or Page Preview to see how a break will look in the printed document.

The status bar tells you which section you're working in.

Delete a section break by putting your insertion point on it and pressing the Delete key.

TIP **Use the Go To command to move quickly to the beginning of a** section. Press the F5 function key, choose Section in the Go To What text box, type the section number in the Enter Section Number text box, and click the Go To button. Use the Next and Previous buttons to move from one section to another.

Formatting sections

The Columns and Page Setup dialog boxes have an Apply To text box in which you can tell Word what part of the document you want to format. If you don't have section breaks, your choices are Whole Document or This Point Forward. (If you've selected text, then This Point Forward is replaced by the Selected Text option.) If you have inserted section breaks, Apply To adds This Section as an option.

Section formatting is most useful when you want to print part of your document with different margin settings. In the document in Figure 10.2, for example, the margins for the second section beginning on the right-hand page have been reset to two inches.

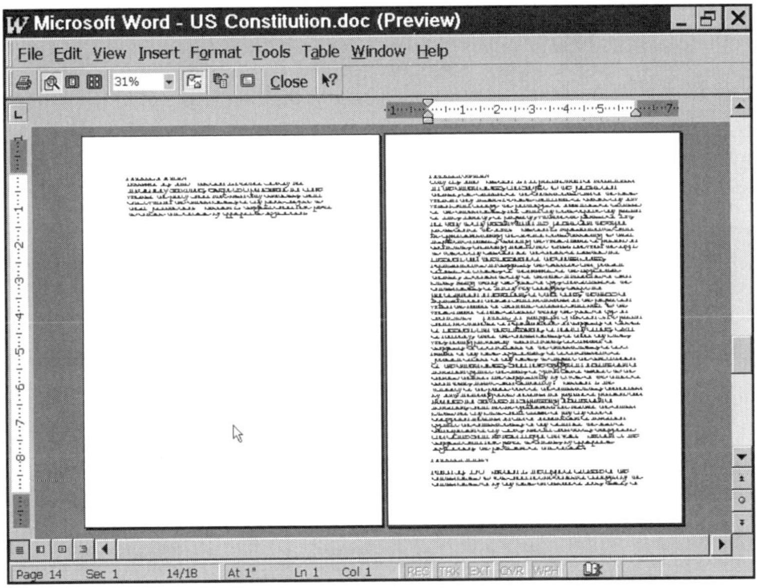

Fig. 10.2
Use section breaks if you want to reset the margins for a particular part of a document.

We'll look more closely at another example—using a new header for a separate section—when we discuss headers and footers later in this chapter.

Can I copy a section break?

You can copy a section break to another part of your document. This is a useful shortcut if, for example, you want to use the same margins in another section.

However, copying section breaks does not work quite the way you might expect. You have to mark and cut the break *after* the section whose format you want to copy. Likewise, you have to paste the break *after* the section whose format you want to change.

Let's say you're working in a document with regular margins set up for portrait printing. In the middle of the document, you create a wide table that you need to print sideways, in landscape orientation. You insert a section break above the table and format section 2 for landscape printing. When you're done, you want to resume typing your document with regular margins. Here's how you do it:

1. Insert a section break after the table. This ends section 2, which contains the table, and starts section 3, in which you'll continue typing your document.
2. Select the section break that separates section 1 and section 2.
3. Copy the section break to the Clipboard by pressing Ctrl+C or clicking the right mouse button and choosing Copy from the shortcut menu.
4. Put your insertion point after the section break that ends section 2 (the section with the table).
5. Paste the first section break by pressing Ctrl+V or clicking the right mouse button and choosing Paste from the shortcut menu.
6. Continue typing your document in the section above your new section break.

TIP **When you create and format a section, Word stores the** formatting information in the section break at the end of the section. If you delete the break, the section *above* the break assumes the format of the section *below* the break. For example, if the second section is set up for landscape printing, deleting the page break changes the first for landscape printing.

Q&A ***I put my section break in the wrong place. How do I move it?***

Select the section break. Click the selected break and hold down the mouse button. A small checkered box appears at the tail of your mouse pointer, and Word displays the message `Move to Where?` in the status bar. Drag the section break to where you want it, and release the mouse button.

Saving and reusing a section format with AutoText

If you have a section format that you use often, save it as an AutoText entry. The section will be available whenever you open a new document.

Select the section break and press Alt+F3. Give the section a name and click OK. To insert the break, start typing the name; when Word displays the full name in a ScreenTip, press the Enter key. (For more about AutoText, see Chapter 5, "How to Delete, Move, Copy, and Change Your Text.")

How to prevent breaks

You can prevent Word from breaking a paragraph that you want to keep in one piece. Put your insertion point in the paragraph. Choose Format, Paragraph from the main menu and click the Line and Page Breaks tab. Select the Keep Lines Together check box. Word will not place an automatic page break within the paragraph.

Word treats the paragraph as an unbreakable block even if you move it to another part of the document, unless you insert a manual page break, a paragraph return, or a section break within the block.

I want these paragraphs to stay on the same page

If you have two paragraphs that you want on the same page, put the insertion point in the first paragraph and choose Format, Paragraph from the main menu. Click the Line and Page Breaks tab and select the Keep With Next check box.

You can use the same method for keeping more than two paragraphs together. Select all but the last paragraph and follow the previous steps.

Headers and footers

Rare is the book, magazine, or long report that doesn't include such text as the title, page number, date, or author on each page. This information—called a *header* when it's on the top and a *footer* when it's on the bottom—serves as an important reference for the reader, who never has to guess where she is in the document or what she's reading. A header or footer also ties the pages of a document together visually, giving each page at least one element in common with all other pages.

Word has a command that lets you insert headers or footers automatically on designated pages. The command is easy to use and comes with a variety of formatting options.

You usually use a header or footer to put a page number, title, or chapter heading on each page. Your header can also include text, the date, the time, or anything else you want.

You format the contents of a header or footer the same way you format body text. You can choose a different font, styles such as bold and italics, alignments such as centering and flush right, and tabs with leaders. You can even give your header or footer a border or shading (see Chapter 9, "Formatting Paragraphs and Blocks," for information on the Borders and Shading command).

" ***Plain English, please!***

A **leader** is a line of dots or dashes that appears between two pieces of text separated by a tab. See Chapter 9 for information on how to create leaders. **"**

For convenience, we'll focus on headers; the steps for creating footers are identical.

Starting your header

To start your header, choose View, Header and Footer from the main menu. Word displays the Header box and the Header and Footer toolbar shown in Figure 10.3.

Type the text you want in the header. You can format the header with Word's Formatting toolbar and main menu. In Figure 10.3, for example, the text has been changed to 14-point Century Gothic and underlined. The page number is moved to the right margin with a tab, and "Page" is formatted for small caps.

Fig. 10.3
You can format the text in your header the same way you do the text in your document.

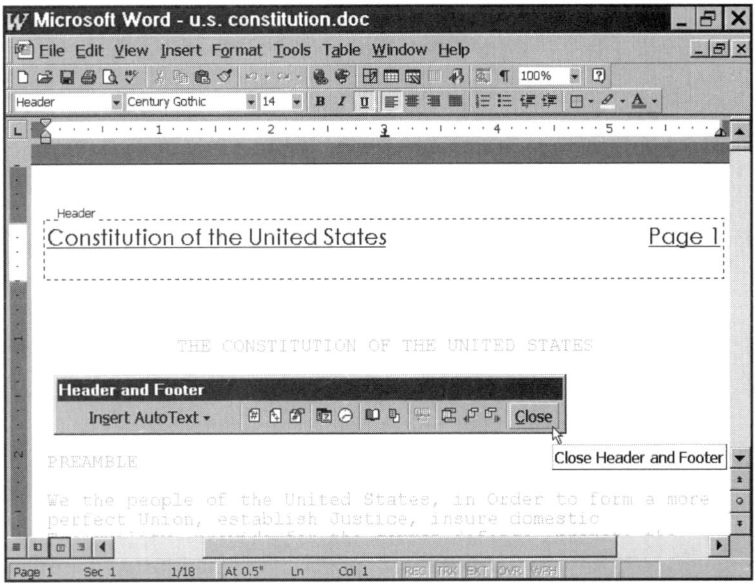

TIP **You can include just about anything in a header or footer that you** can include in your document, including graphics and symbols. See Chapter 16, "Hate Outlines? Outline View May Change Your Mind," for information on pictures and objects; see Chapter 8, "Character Sketches—Formatting Your Type," for more on symbols and special characters.

TIP **Word 97's Header and Footer toolbar has a new Insert AutoText** button that lets you insert AutoText entries from a list. By default, Word displays entries that you're most likely to include in a header, such as "Author, Page #, Date" and "Filename and Path." But you can see all of your AutoText entries by holding down the shift key as you click the Insert AutoText button.

How do I see my new header?

When you're done, click Close on the Headers and Footers toolbar. Don't be alarmed if the headers don't appear in your document; they won't if you're in Normal view. Choose Page Layout from View on the menu bar, or click the Page Layout View button at the beginning of the horizontal scroll bar.

The header appears in light gray. Click the Print Preview button or choose File, Print Preview to see what the header will look like when you print the document.

TIP **To change a header into a footer, choose View, Header and** Footer from the main menu. Select the header text, cut it with Ctrl+X or the Cut button, press the Down arrow, and paste the text with Ctrl+V or the Paste button.

Adding page numbers, dates, and times to a header or footer

To add page numbers, put the insertion point where you want the number in the header or footer and click the Page Numbers button on the Header and Footer toolbar (see the following graphics page). Word inserts a page field. The page number changes automatically for each following page.

Plain English, please!

A **field** is a code that automatically inserts information into a document, header, or footer. For example, the date field inserts the date while the time field inserts the time.

You insert the date or time field by clicking the Insert Date and Insert Time buttons, respectively.

You can instruct Word to update your date and time automatically when you open the document. Choose Tools, Options from the main menu and click the Print tab in the Options dialog box. Choose Update Fields under Printing Options and click OK.

You can update a date or time manually by clicking it with the right mouse button and choosing Update Field from the shortcut menu.

Q&A ***I tried to insert page numbers, but all I get is the word "PAGE" between two squiggly brackets! Why isn't this feature working?***

What you see, {PAGE}, is the name of the field. You can change it to the actual page number in one of two ways. Right-click the field and choose Toggle Field Codes from the shortcut menu.

Close-Up: the Header and Footer toolbar

Page Setup
Click here to change the page setup of the selected sections

Same as Previous
Click here to insert the contents of the previous header or footer

Insert Date
Click here to insert a date field

Show Previous
Click here to show the previous header or footer

Insert Number of Pages
Click here to insert a number of pages field, which reports the number of pages in the document

Close
Click here to close Header/Footer view and return to your document

Insert AutoText
Click here to display a list of AutoText entries commonly used in headers and footers. Press the shift key and click to display a list of all AutoText entries.

Insert Page Number
Click here to insert a page number field

Show Next
Click here to show the next header or footer

Format Page Number
Click here to open the Page Number Format dialog box, which lets you choose how you want your page numbers to appear

Switch between Header and Footer
Click here to switch between the header and footer

Insert Time
Click here to insert a time field

Show/Hide Document Text
Click here to show or hide the text in the document

I don't want a header on the first page

Title and first pages often don't need a header or footer. To force Word to start your header on page 2, click the Page Setup button and choose Different First Page under Headers and Footers and click OK. Word presents you with a blank header; ignore it and click Close on the Header and Footer toolbar.

TIP **To remove a header or footer, delete the text in the header or** footer box, then click Close on the Header and Footer toolbar.

Inserting a new header or footer

When you want a different header or footer for a new section, go to that section and choose View, Header and Footer. Click the Same as Previous button. This deselects the button and gives you a blank header or footer. Enter your new text, then click Close.

CAUTION **It's important to turn off Same as Previous *before* you start your** new header or footer. Otherwise, your previous headers or footers will change to match your new one.

What about page numbers?

If you want only page numbers, you can insert them without using the Headers and Footers command. Choose Insert, Page Numbers from the main menu to display the Page Numbers dialog box (see Figure 10.4).

Fig. 10.4
Use the Page Numbers dialog box to position and align your page numbers.

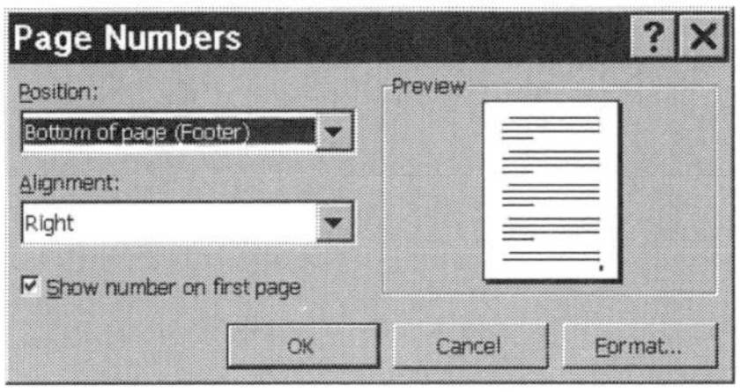

In the Position text box, choose whether you want the page number to appear at the top or bottom of the page. Then choose the alignment—left, center, right, inside, or outside—from the Alignment text box.

If you're printing a two-sided document with facing pages, Outside alternates your page numbers so that they're always close to the outside margin. That is, the number is on the left side of even-numbered pages and the right side of odd-numbered pages. Choose Inside to insert them next to the inside margin.

To hide the page number on the first page of a document, click the Format button in the Page Numbers dialog box and remove the check mark from the Show Number On First Page check box.

TIP **To use Roman numerals for prefaces and introductions, click the** Format button in the Page Numbers dialog box, then choose the Roman numeral format from the Number Format drop-down box.

Dates and times

You can insert the current date or time in one of two ways:

- As plain text
- As a field that updates to reflect the current date or time

In Figure 10.5, the top time is plain text that you can edit like any other text. The bottom time, on the other hand, changes when you click it and choose Update Field from the shortcut menu.

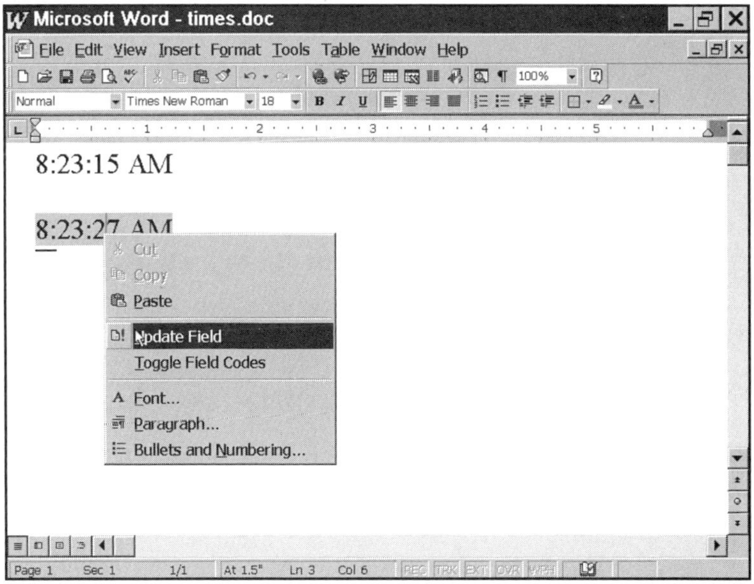

Fig. 10.5
The top time is plain text that remains fixed. The bottom time is a field that updates to the new time whenever you reopen the file or choose Update Field from the shortcut menu.

Choose Insert, Date and Time from the main menu. Word displays the Date and Time dialog box shown in Figure 10.6. Select the format you want from the Available Formats list box. If you want a time or date that can be updated, select the Update automatically check box.

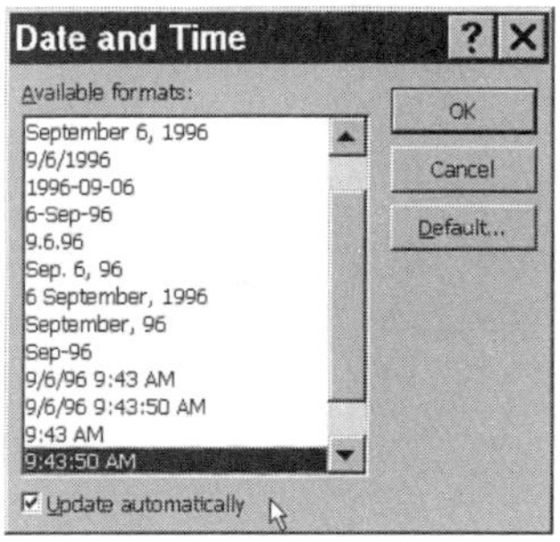

Fig. 10.6
Now when was it I printed this document? Choose the Update automatically check box to help you keep track.

Inserting file names, your name, and other information

How often have you stared at two printed versions of the same report and wondered which one was the most recent? Wouldn't it be nice if you could include information that identifies a document, such as the author, date that the document was created, and the size of the file in which the document was stored? And just to make life a bit easier, how about the document's file name so you could quickly find it on your disk?

Word lets you put this information, and a lot more, in your document. You do it the same way you add the current date and time, by inserting a field. Some of the information, such as the author's name and address, is useful in headers and footers. Other fields, such as the creation date and file name, are appropriate for a cover sheet or at the top of your document.

You can insert any field with the Field command. Put your insertion point where you want the information and choose Insert, Field from the main menu. In the Field dialog box, choose a category from the Categories selection box, then choose a field from the Field Names selection box. Word describes each field at the bottom of the dialog box. When you've found the field you want, click OK, and Word inserts the field in your header or footer.

11

Turning the Tables

In this chapter:

- **Creating a table: one click is all you need**
- **New! Drawing your table by hand**
- **How to insert, delete, and move rows and columns**
- **Table out of order? Try sorting it**
- **How do I add borders and shading?**
- **Squeeze fat tables with vertical heads**
- **AutoFormat—Word's instant table formatter**

Wait a minute! That's about all it takes for Word's Table command to organize anything from a plain list to a boring ledger page into an attractive visual . . . .

In the world of consumer products, "fast" usually means "mediocre." Whether you're talking about instant food, snap-together furniture, or five-minute-a-day exercise machines, you usually lose as much in quality as you gain in speed and convenience.

Word's Table functions buck the trend. Fast? Very. But mediocre? Hardly. Word's Table command is the quintessential combination of speed and power. The first table shown in the graphics page, for example, took less time to set up than it takes to make instant oatmeal.

Word gives you two basic ways to create a table. The first assumes you haven't typed the text yet; that is, you're going to create the table and then fill it in. The second assumes you already have the text typed; in other words, you want to create the table from existing material.

How to create a table from scratch

First, let's look at how you create an empty table:

1 Click the Insert Table button on the Standard toolbar. A panel of squares representing the cells of your table drops down.

2 Drag your mouse across and down the grid until it's the right size. The dimensions appear at the bottom of the grid. In Figure 11.1, for example, the resulting table will be 14 rows deep and four columns wide. The dimensions of your grid might vary depending on where your Insert Table button is located and how much screen space is available.

   For larger tables—up to 63 columns by 32,767 rows—choose Table, Insert Table to display the Insert Table dialog box and enter the appropriate numbers in the text boxes.

3 Click the mouse button again to insert the table.

Word automatically adds a 1/2 point border to your table grid. You're not stuck with this border, and we'll look at how to modify it a little later.

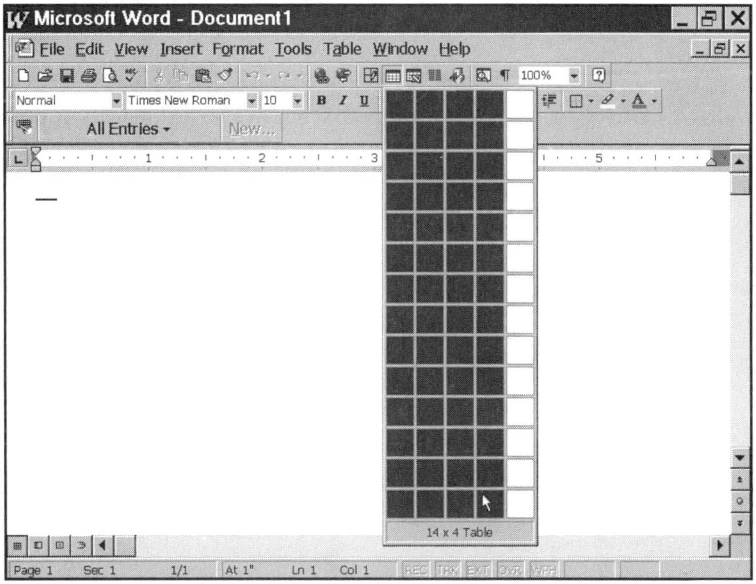

Fig. 11.1
Use the Insert Table button to create a table from scratch. This table will be four columns wide and 14 rows deep.

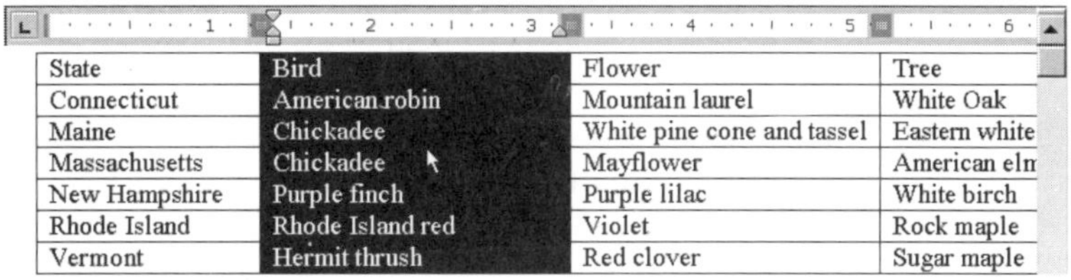

State	Bird	Flower	Tree
Connecticut	American robin	Mountain laurel	White Oak
Maine	Chickadee	White pine cone and tassel	Eastern white
Massachusetts	Chickadee	Mayflower	American eln
New Hampshire	Purple finch	Purple lilac	White birch
Rhode Island	Rhode Island red	Violet	Rock maple
Vermont	Hermit thrush	Red clover	Sugar maple

Fig. 11.2
Word automatically fits your new table to the width of your page.

Don't worry about getting the number of rows or columns right. As we'll see later, they're as easy to add as pressing the Tab key, and not much harder to delete. You'll also learn how to quickly adjust the column widths once you've filled in the table.

Plain English, please!

A **cell** is the location in a table where a row and column intersect. You see a cell on the screen as a box. A table is simply a **grid** made up of many cells. A **border**, discussed later in this chapter, is a line that you add to a table. It remains visible on the screen at all times and appears as part of your printout. **Grid lines** are thin, dotted lines on the screen that outline a table's cells. Grid lines are hidden by borders, and they don't appear on printouts.

The Tables and Borders toolbar

Before we go much further, we need to discuss Word 97's Tables and Borders toolbar. You'll see frequent mentions of it throughout the rest of this chapter, and it appears in many of the figures.

You display the Tables and Borders toolbar by clicking the Tables and Borders button on the Standard toolbar. The page titled "Inside the Tables and Borders toolbar" gives you an overview of what the buttons do.

You can draw it, too

The insert borders button automatically sets all columns to the same width, and it stretches them from one margin to the other. But Word 97 has a new tool that gives you more flexibility when creating a table: Draw Table. This command lets you draw a table by hand much as you would with a pencil on paper.

Draw Table has two major advantages over Insert Table:

- You can set individual column widths as you go.
- You can create a table that's indented from either or both margins; Word automatically adjusts the indent markers on the ruler.

The Draw Table button is on the Tables and Borders toolbar. Draw Table is active by default when you display the toolbar; you'll be able to tell because your mouse pointer turns into a pencil, as in Figure 11.3.

Put the pencil where you want your table to begin, and click the left mouse button; you'll see a small, dotted box dangling from the tip of the pencil. Drag the pencil to where the lower right-hand corner of the table will be, and release the button. A dotted line will extend from the pencil as you drag it. In Figure 11.3, for example, the table will be indented one inch from the left and right margins.

Next, using the same drag-and-drop technique, draw your column lines inside the table. Word again displays a dotted line to show you where you're drawing (see Figure 11.4).

When you're done, click the Draw Table button again to turn it off.

Inside the Tables and Borders toolbar

Draw Table
Lets you hand draw a table, cells, rows, and columns.

Eraser
Erases cell lines in a table and merges cells if the lines aren't bordered; otherwise removes borders.

Line Style
Choose the style of your borders here.

Line Weight
Choose the weight of your borders here.

Border Color
Choose the color of your borders here.

Borders
Lets you select which grid lines you want to add borders to or remove borders from.

Shading Color
Lets you select the color and shade of your table cells.

Merge Cells
Combines selected cells into single cell.

Split Cells
Splits selected cells.

Align Top
Aligns text with the top of a cell.

Center Vertically
Centers text between the top and bottom of a cell.

Align Bottom
Aligns text with the bottom of a cell.

Distribute Rows Evenly
Makes selected rows the same height.

Distribute Columns Evenly
Makes selected columns the same width.

Table AutoFormat
Opens Table AutoFormat dialog box, which lets you apply a preset format to table.

Change Text Direction
Changes direction of text between horizontal and vertical.

Sort Ascending
Sorts entire table in ascending order by selected column.

Sort Descending
Sorts entire table in descending order by selected column.

AutoSum
Inserts a formula that adds contents of cells above or to the left of the cell.

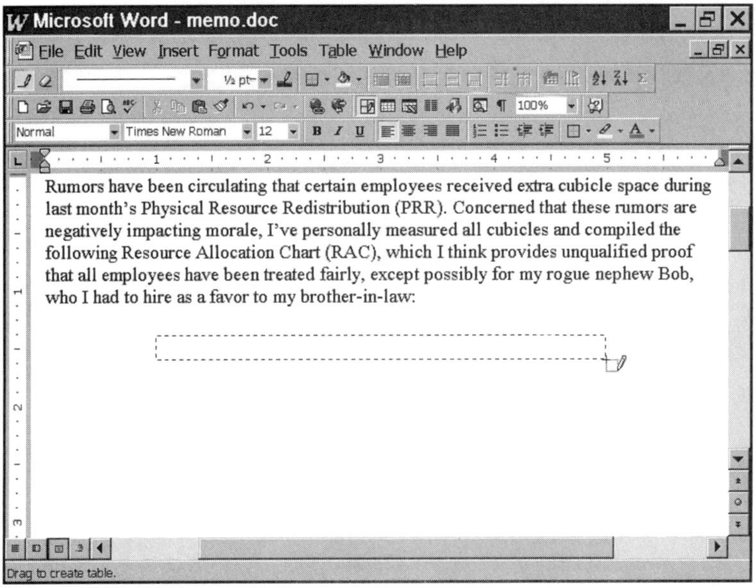
Microsoft Word - memo.doc
File Edit View Insert Format Tools Table Window Help
Normal
Times New Roman
12
100%
Rumors have been circulating that certain employees received extra cubicle space during last month's Physical Resource Redistribution (PRR). Concerned that these rumors are negatively impacting morale, I've personally measured all cubicles and compiled the following Resource Allocation Chart (RAC), which I think provides unqualified proof that all employees have been treated fairly, except possibly for my rogue nephew Bob, who I had to hire as a favor to my brother-in-law:
Drag to create table.

Fig. 11.3 Using Draw Table, you can draw a table simply by dragging and clicking the pencil.

Don't be too concerned about getting your column widths and row heights exactly right. As we'll see later in this chapter, you can easily fine-tune them after you've entered your text.

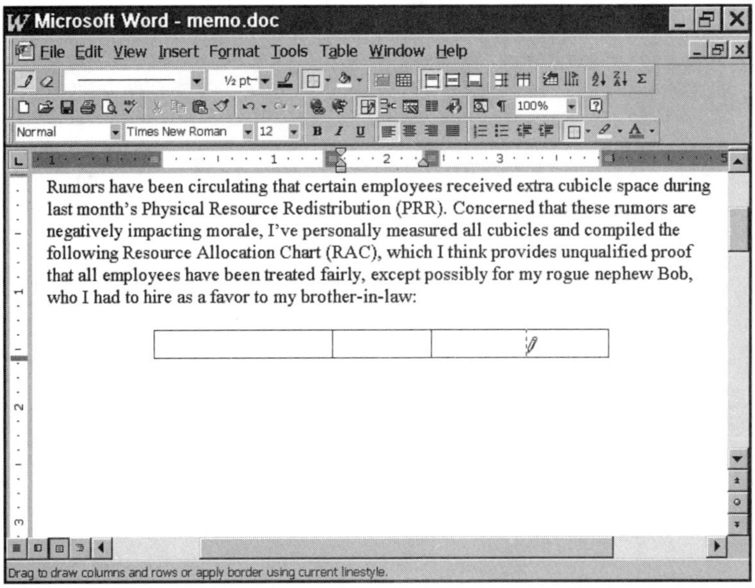
Microsoft Word - memo.doc
File Edit View Insert Format Tools Table Window Help
Normal
Times New Roman
12
100%
Rumors have been circulating that certain employees received extra cubicle space during last month's Physical Resource Redistribution (PRR). Concerned that these rumors are negatively impacting morale, I've personally measured all cubicles and compiled the following Resource Allocation Chart (RAC), which I think provides unqualified proof that all employees have been treated fairly, except possibly for my rogue nephew Bob, who I had to hire as a favor to my brother-in-law:
Drag to draw columns and rows or apply border using current linestyle.

Fig. 11.4 Draw horizontal and vertical lines inside the table to create columns and rows.

TIP **If Word floats your Tables and Borders toolbar in your document** window, you might want to put it above the window to get it out of the way, as in Figures 11.3 and 11.4. Click the title bar and drag the toolbar to its new position.

Getting creative with tables

When you're drawing a table on paper, you can split and combine rows and columns however you want. The same is true with Draw Tables.

In my table, for example, I decided to split the first four columns under Bob's entry into two rows, but leave the fifth column intact. Figure 11.5 shows the results.

What can't it do?

The best way to learn how to use Draw Table is to play with it. Here are a few limitations you should know about before you begin:

- You can't use Draw Table to draw a table around text. Word will insert the table above the paragraph you're trying to draw in. We'll discuss how to create a table from existing text later in this chapter.
- Hand-drawing a table with precise column widths is difficult; Word doesn't give you any guides. Similarly, your row heights might not be exactly what you want. Read on for tips on how to adjust widths and heights.

TIP  **Did you insert an inside border that you don't want any-more?** Use the Erase button on the Tables and Borders toolbar to get rid of it. When you click the button, your mouse pointer turns into an eraser with what looks like a very tiny little sunburst at the bottom corner. Put the burst at one end of the line you're deleting, click the left mouse button, and drag the eraser across the line. When the line has been selected, release the mouse button, and the line disappears. Be aware that text in the cells on either side of the line will merge.

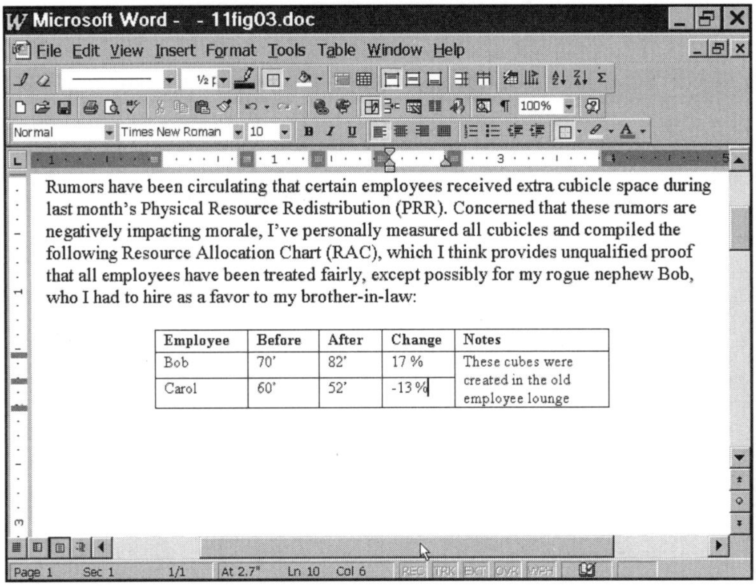

Fig. 11.5
You can split selected rows while leaving others intact, creating rows of different heights.

Creating tables with the Table command

Many users prefer to create their table, fill it in, and tinker with the formatting details later. But if you're the type who likes to get the job done right the first time, you can specify how your table will look before you create it, using the menu commands T<u>a</u>ble, <u>I</u>nsert Table followed by T<u>a</u>ble, Auto<u>F</u>ormat. However, these options probably won't do you much good until you learn how to format your tables manually. Otherwise, you'll be stuck with tables you don't know how to edit or reformat. Finish with the basics first, then we'll tackle the more advanced tricks at the end of this chapter.

How to fill out the table

Place your insertion point in a cell and type your text. When you reach the right grid line of the cell, notice how Word wraps the text to the next line and extends the cell vertically to fit the text. When you're done typing, you have these options:

- Press the Tab key to move to the next cell to the right. You can also use the right arrow key if you're at the end of the text.
- Press Shift+Tab to move to the next cell to the left. The left arrow key also works if you're at the beginning of the text.

- If you're on the last line in the cell, press the down arrow to move down one cell.
- If you're on the first line in the cell, press the up arrow to move up one cell. If you run out of table space, you can add a row to the bottom by placing the insertion point in the lower right-hand cell and pressing the Tab key.
- Press Ctrl+Tab in a cell to insert a normal tab in your text.

How to create a table from text

So far, so good. But what if you've already typed your table, using tabs to make your columns? Do you have to retype or copy the text into the new table? Probably not. If you set your tabs properly, you can select the text and drop the grid lines on top of it.

The key to converting text into a table is to make sure you have only one tab between items in a row. In most cases, this means setting tabs for each column rather than using the default tabs.

Once you've got your tabs right, select the text and click the Insert Table button on the Standard toolbar. If you don't see any gridlines, choose Table, Show Gridlines to display them.

TIP **If you've already set up your columnar material with default tabs** you can fix it without having to create custom tabs. Simply replace all back-to-back tabs with single tabs. Select your text and Choose Edit, Replace from the main menu. Put ^t^t in the Find What box and ^t in the Replace With box (^t represents a tab). Choose Replace All. (Your columns won't line up anymore, but it doesn't matter; the final table will look the way it's supposed to.)

Modifying your table

A new table is rarely perfect. You'll probably need to add, move, or delete rows or columns. These are uncomplicated tasks but require that you know how to select parts of your table.

Selecting columns, rows, and cells

To select a column, position the pointer at the top grid line of the column until it's an arrow pointing down, then click the mouse button (see Figure 11.6).

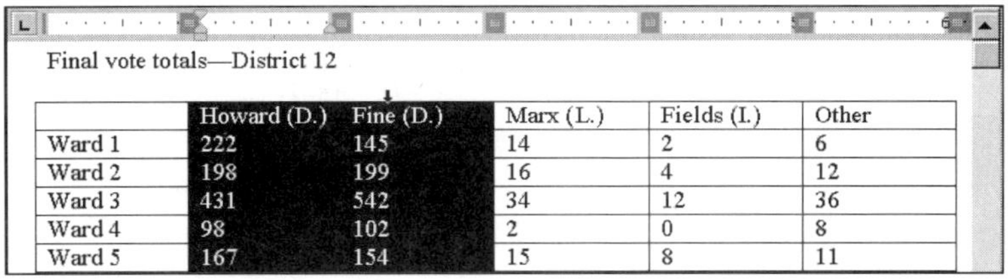
Final vote totals—District 12

	Howard (D.)	Fine (D.)	Marx (L.)	Fields (I.)	Other
Ward 1	222	145	14	2	6
Ward 2	198	199	16	4	12
Ward 3	431	542	34	12	36
Ward 4	98	102	2	0	8
Ward 5	167	154	15	8	11

Fig. 11.6
To select a column, touch the top grid line until your pointer turns into an arrow, then click once. Drag the pointer to select more than one column.

To select several contiguous columns, point to the top of the first column to select it, then click and drag the mouse across the table. You can also select the first column, hold down the Shift key, and click the last column.

To select a row, put the pointer to the left of the row and click once. Drag the pointer down to select several rows.

To select a cell, click the space between the left grid lines of the cell and the text. The entire cell becomes highlighted, as shown in Figure 11.7. Select several contiguous cells by dragging the pointer across the cells.

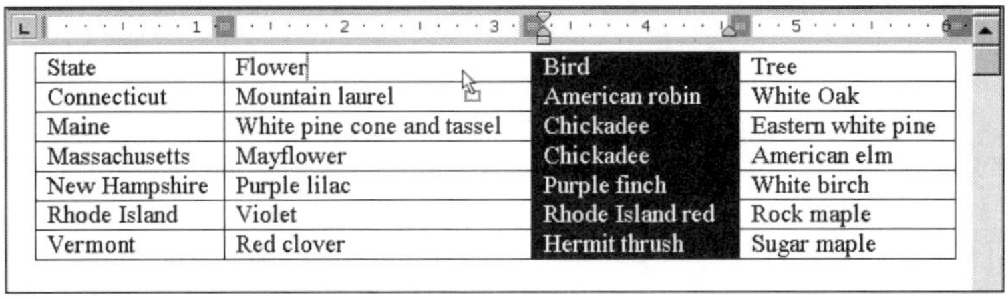
State	Flower	Bird	Tree
Connecticut	Mountain laurel	American robin	White Oak
Maine	White pine cone and tassel	Chickadee	Eastern white pine
Massachusetts	Mayflower	Chickadee	American elm
New Hampshire	Purple lilac	Purple finch	White birch
Rhode Island	Violet	Rhode Island red	Rock maple
Vermont	Red clover	Hermit thrush	Sugar maple

Fig. 11.7
To select a cell, point at the space between the left grid line and the text and click once.

You can also select cells using the keyboard. Put the insertion point at the beginning of the text in the cell and press Shift+Ctrl+down arrow. To select several more cells to the right, press Shift+End for each cell. Use Shift and the appropriate arrow key to move left, up, or down. Here are a few other useful keyboard shortcuts:

- To select the text in the next cell in the row, press the Tab key.
- To select the text in the previous cell in the row, press Shift+Tab.

- To select the current and previous cells in the row, place the insertion point at the beginning of the cell and press Shift+left arrow.

To select the text in a cell, select it as you would regular text; only the text will be highlighted (see Figure 11.8).

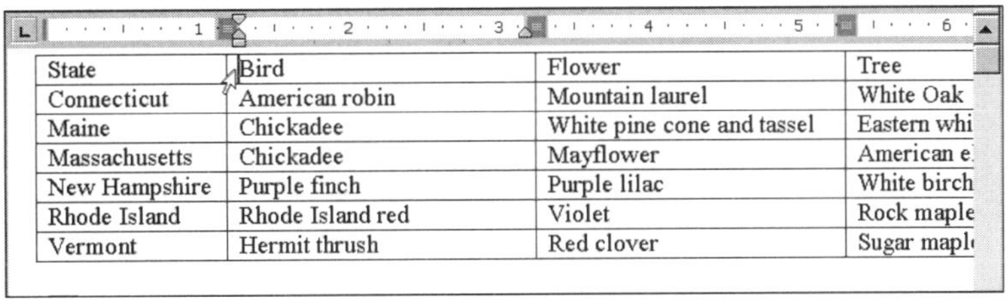

State	Bird	Flower	Tree
Connecticut	American robin	Mountain laurel	White Oak
Maine	Chickadee	White pine cone and tassel	Eastern whi
Massachusetts	Chickadee	Mayflower	American e
New Hampshire	Purple finch	Purple lilac	White birch
Rhode Island	Rhode Island red	Violet	Rock maple
Vermont	Hermit thrush	Red clover	Sugar mapl

Fig. 11.8
Select cell text as you would body text. For example, select a word by double-clicking it.

To select the entire table, hold down the Alt key and double-click anywhere in the table, or choose Table, Select Table from the main menu. You can also press Alt+Num5 (the number 5 on the numeric keypad); make sure that NumLock is off.

TIP **You can select a column or row with the right mouse button the** same way you do with the left mouse button, only a shortcut menu with common table commands also pops up. This saves a step if you're going to perform an action on a single column or row such as cutting, copying, or pasting.

How to change column widths

When you create a table using the Insert Table button, Word automatically sets all columns to the same width and stretches the table from margin to margin. You'll likely want to change the widths of a column or two.

The easiest way to change the width of a single column is to drag the border marker on the ruler with the mouse. But Word gives you three ways to resize. You have to be careful of how the method you choose will affect your other column widths.

In Figure 11.9, the goal is to widen column 3. But the method used for the second example pushes the table beyond the right margin, and the method used for the third example narrows column 4 too much. Only the fourth example has properly formatted columns.

Here are the three options you can choose from:

- If you drag the border marker with the mouse only, the next column to the right changes, as in the second example in Figure 11.9. The table width stays the same.
- If you drag the mouse while pressing the Shift key, all the other columns stay the same width, thus extending the right margin (see the third example in Figure 11.9).
- If you drag the mouse while pressing Ctrl, all columns to the left stay the same, while columns to the right are narrowed to fit the table (see Fig. 11.9). The table width stays the same.

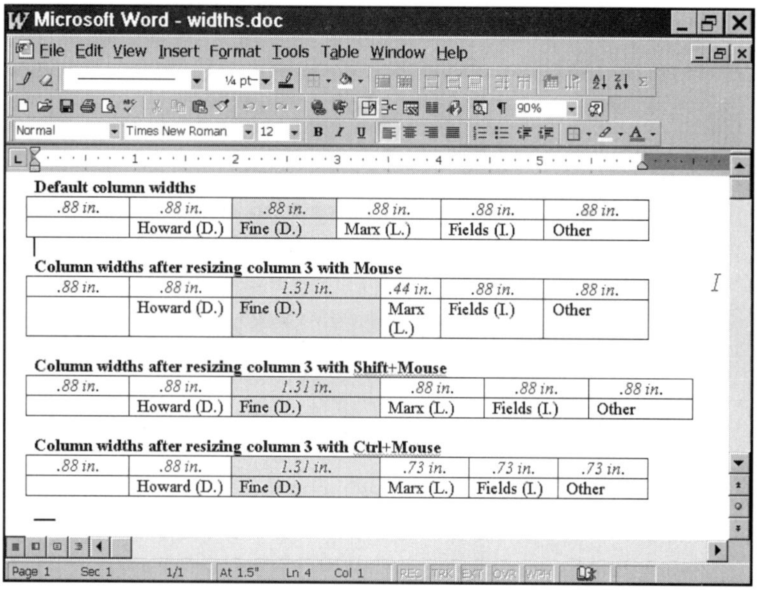

Fig. 11.9
Word gives you three ways to widen a column, each affecting subsequent columns differently.

Q&A ***My ruler isn't showing. How do I change column widths?***

You can change a column's width by dragging the grid line in the table. Select the column, then touch the right grid line with the pointer until it changes into two vertical lines between two arrows, then use the same mouse and keyboard combination as when dragging the border marker.

How to change several columns at once

To change several column widths at the same time, select the columns and choose Table, Cell Height and Width from the main menu. In the Cell Height and Width dialog box that appears, enter the column width in the Width Of Column text box, then click OK.

CAUTION **When you select a column to change its width, make sure the** entire column, not just the top cell, is highlighted. Otherwise, you'll change the width of only the selected cell.

Q&A ***I goofed around with my column widths, and now they're all messed up. How do I change my widths so they're all the same again?***

Select the table and choose the Distribute Columns Evenly button on the Tables and Borders toolbar, or choose Table, Distribute Columns Evenly.

Perfect fit: how to adjust column widths automatically

Wouldn't it be convenient if Word adjusted your column widths automatically? It can, with a command called AutoFit. Word expands or shrinks the columns according to the text they contain.

Here's how to use AutoFit on selected columns:

1. Select the columns whose width you want to adjust.
2. Touch the right grid line of the last selected column until your pointer changes into two vertical lines between two arrows.
3. Double-click the grid line.

You can also use AutoFit from the keyboard. Select the columns you want to adjust. Choose Table, Column Height and Width from the main menu, click the Column tab in the Cell Height and Width dialog box, and click AutoFit.

Changing the width of a single cell

You can change the width of a single cell by selecting the cell and dragging the border markers or grid lines. In Figure 11.10, for example, the selected cell has been widened on either side so that the text will fit without wrapping to a second line.

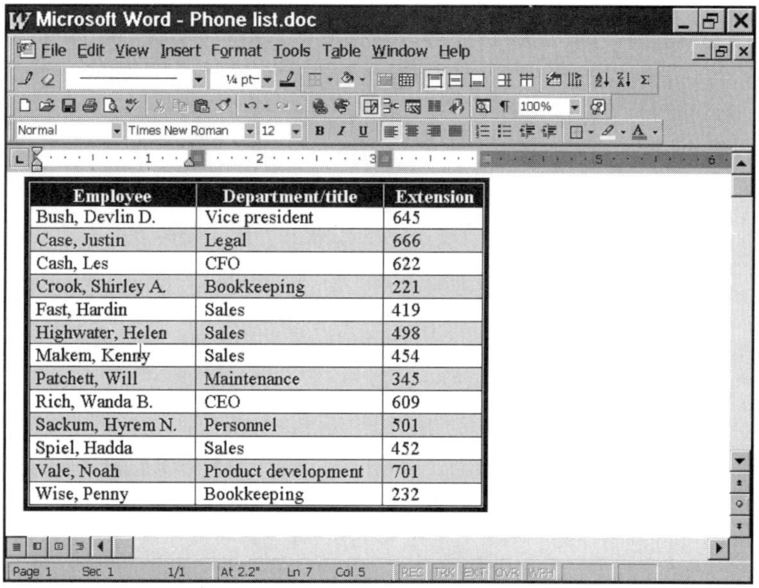

Employee	Department/title	Extension
Bush, Devlin D.	Vice president	645
Case, Justin	Legal	666
Cash, Les	CFO	622
Crook, Shirley A.	Bookkeeping	221
Fast, Hardin	Sales	419
Highwater, Helen	Sales	498
Makem, Kenny	Sales	454
Patchett, Will	Maintenance	345
Rich, Wanda B.	CEO	609
Sackum, Hyrem N.	Personnel	501
Spiel, Hadda	Sales	452
Vale, Noah	Product development	701
Wise, Penny	Bookkeeping	232

Fig. 11.10
To change the width of a single cell, select the cell and drag the border markers or grid lines.

TIP **If you change the widths of many individual cells in a table, some** cells might appear to realign themselves under different columns. In fact, cells remain with their original columns, no matter where they are on the screen. If you need to see which cells make up a column, select the column by clicking its top grid line.

Inserting a row

You can't always know exactly how many rows and columns you need when you create a table. Conveniently, Word gives you more ways to insert rows and columns than you can shake a pointer at. Let's start with how to add rows.

If your insertion point is in the row that will follow the new row, click the Insert Rows button on the Standard toolbar. (The Insert Rows button takes the spot occupied by the Insert Table button when you're not in a table.)

Alternatively, you can place the mouse pointer in the left margin next to the row that will follow the new row, then press the right mouse button; the row is highlighted and Word displays a shortcut menu. Choose Insert Rows from the shortcut menu. Your new row will include any formats contained in your selected row.

Inserting a column

The steps for inserting a column are a lot like those for inserting a row. Select a column and click the Insert Columns button on the Standard toolbar. (The Insert Columns button is in the same place as the Insert Table button, only with a new name and picture and function.)

Alternatively, you can select the column by right-clicking it and choosing Insert Columns from the shortcut menu.

How to insert several rows or columns at once

Once you've inserted a row or column, you can make additional insertions by clicking the Insert Rows or Insert Columns button on the Standard toolbar.

To insert several rows at the same time, select the same number of rows that you want to insert and click the Insert Rows button. For example, to insert six rows, select the six rows below the insertion point and click the Insert Rows button.

The same technique works for inserting several columns. Select the same number of columns that you plan to insert and either click the Insert Columns button or choose Insert Columns from the shortcut menu.

Going, going, gone: deleting rows and columns

Word provides several ways to delete rows or columns, but the easiest method is to select them and then take either of these steps

- Click the right mouse button and choose Delete Rows or Delete Columns from the shortcut menu.
- Choose Table from the main menu, then choose Delete Columns or Delete Rows from the Table menu.

When you delete rows and columns, you erase them completely. If you want to insert them somewhere else in your table or document, then cut them instead. We'll cover cutting and pasting in a moment. (See Chapter 5, "How to Delete, Move, Copy, and Change Your Text," for details on the differences between deleting and cutting.) Select the rows or columns and use one of the following methods:

- Click the right mouse button and choose Copy from the shortcut menu.

- Click the Copy button on the Standard toolbar.
- Press Ctrl+C.

Q&A ***Oops! I accidentally deleted a column. Is it gone forever?***

Not if you deleted it recently. If the deletion was your last action, click the Undo button on the Standard toolbar or press Ctrl+Z. If you've taken some actions since the delete, click the down arrow next to the Undo button on the Standard toolbar. Find Delete Columns in the selection box and click it. Note, however, that Word also undoes all actions above Delete Columns.

Anywhere you want it: moving rows and columns

Once you've got a vegetable garden planted, it's pretty tough moving your rows of plants around. If you decide you really wanted the carrots next to the radishes instead of the lettuce, you just have to wait until next year.

Fortunately, a Word table is a bit more flexible. Moving a row or column is not much more complicated than clicking and dragging.

Let's look at the steps to move a column. (The steps to move a row are nearly identical.) In Figures 11.11 and 11.12, for example, we'll move the Bird column between the State and Flower columns. Here's how to do it:

1. Select the column you want to move by clicking its top grid line.
2. Move your mouse pointer into the column.

3 Hold down the mouse button and move it into the column that follows the point at which you want to insert the column—in this case, the Flower column. A small, dotted box appears at the bottom of the pointer, as in Figure 11.11.

4 Release the mouse button. Figure 11.12 shows the results.

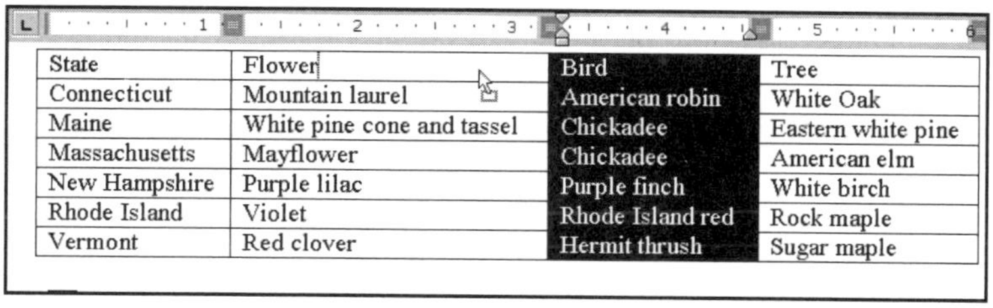

State	Flower	Bird	Tree
Connecticut	Mountain laurel	American robin	White Oak
Maine	White pine cone and tassel	Chickadee	Eastern white pine
Massachusetts	Mayflower	Chickadee	American elm
New Hampshire	Purple lilac	Purple finch	White birch
Rhode Island	Violet	Rhode Island red	Rock maple
Vermont	Red clover	Hermit thrush	Sugar maple

Fig. 11.11 To move a column, select it and move your mouse pointer to the column that it will precede.

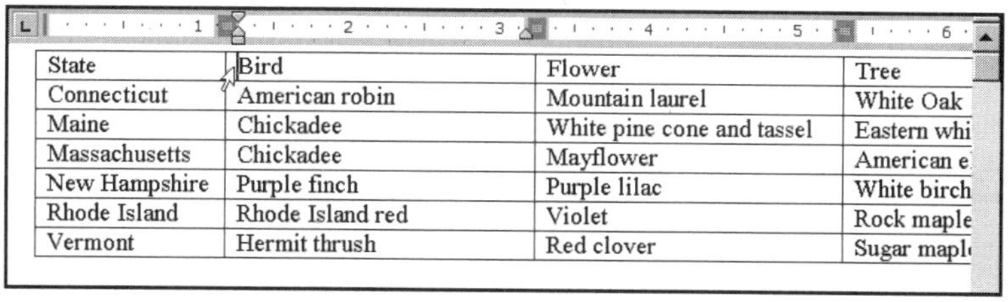

State	Bird	Flower	Tree
Connecticut	American robin	Mountain laurel	White Oak
Maine	Chickadee	White pine cone and tassel	Eastern whi
Massachusetts	Chickadee	Mayflower	American e
New Hampshire	Purple finch	Purple lilac	White birch
Rhode Island	Rhode Island red	Violet	Rock maple
Vermont	Hermit thrush	Red clover	Sugar mapl

Fig. 11.12 When you release the mouse button, Word moves the selected column to its new location.

Moving a row is almost the same:

1 Select the row to move by clicking to the left of the row's left grid line.

2 Hold down your mouse button and put the pointer into the row that will follow the row you're moving. For example, in Figure 11.12, to move the Maine row below Massachusetts, you place the pointer in the New Hampshire row.

3 Release the mouse button.

You move several columns or rows the same way, as long as they're contiguous.

Table out of order? Try sorting it

Sorting is one of the best ways to make a table easier to read. Your personal or office phone list is a perfect example: you'll find "Aadaabandaah, Hubert" a lot quicker if he's at the top of the table and not buried between "Zerph, Meg" and "Kasper, Kenny" somewhere in the middle.

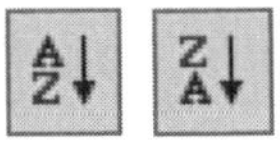

In Word, you sort a table quickly by using the sort buttons on the Tables and Borders toolbar. The table must have a header row—that is, the top row must consist of headings. Put the insertion point in the column by which you want to sort and click either Sort Ascending or Sort Descending. Word sorts starting with the second row of the table.

All sorts of sorts

For more complex sorts, use the Sort dialog box. From here, you can sort tables without headings and sort by several columns (for example, a phone list first by department and then alphabetically within each department).

Put your insertion point anywhere in the table and choose Table, Sort from the main menu. The Sort dialog box appears (see Figure 11.13).

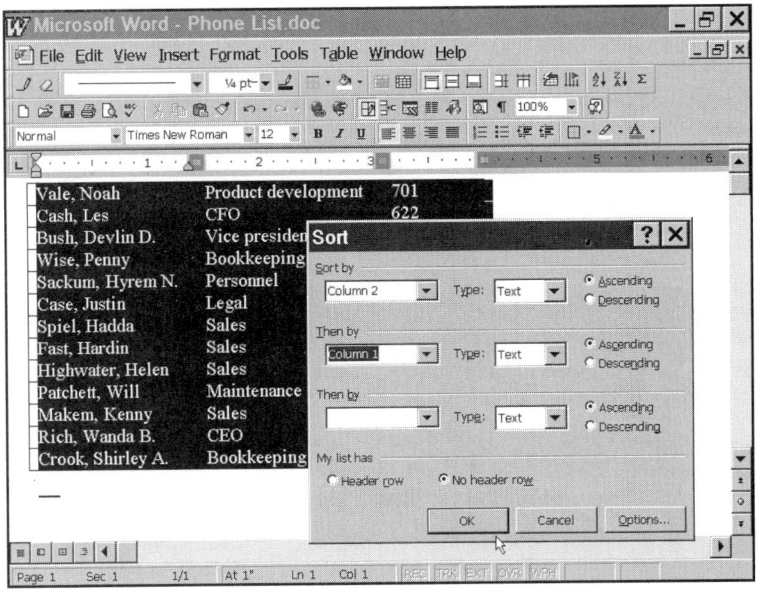

Fig. 11.13
Use Table, Sort to sort a table that has no headings. In this example, the table is sorted first by the second column and then by the first column.

If your table has no headings, choose No Header Row under My List Has. In the Sort By text box, choose the column by which you want to sort the table (Column 2 in Figure 11.13). You can also choose up to two additional columns in the Then By and Then By text boxes. When you finish making your selections, click OK.

If your table has headings, choose Header Row under My List Has. The Sort By and Then By boxes will list the headings instead of the column numbers.

Can I format my table text?

A table is rarely complete without a few extra formatting touches. How about bold headings? Centered text in a column? Or even a bulleted list in a cell? These and most other types of formats you use in regular text are readily available.

To format text in a row, for example, select the row and choose your formatting options.

A new slant on headings

Experienced table-makers know this problem: You've got columns whose headings are very long but whose data in each cell are very short. Until now, you were stuck with unnecessarily wide columns that sometimes stretched beyond the normal right margin. But Word 97 has a new feature that lets you change the direction of your text. You can now contract those tables down to size by running long headings vertically.

Figure 11.14 shows the table from Figure 11.18, only with the regular headings changed from horizontal to vertical. The steps are easy:

1. Select the row you want to change.

2. Click the Change Text Direction button on the Tables and Borders toolbar. Word rotates you through three options: vertical reading from top to bottom, vertical reading from bottom to top, and back to horizontal.

3. When you've picked the direction you want, use AutoFit to automatically narrow the columns.

Note that vertical text appears properly formatted only if you're in Page Layout mode (View, Page Layout).

Fig. 11.14
Use Word 97's new Change Text Direction feature to create vertical headings.

	Howard (D.)	Fine (D.)	Marx (L.)	Fields (L.)	Other
Ward 1	222	145	14	2	6
Ward 2	198	199	16	4	12
Ward 3	431	542	34	12	36
Ward 4	98	102	2	0	8
Ward 5	167	154	15	8	11

Adding borders and shading

Dressing a table doesn't stop with formatting its text. You can embellish the table itself by adding different types of borders and shading.

As Figure 11.15 shows, borders and shading don't have to be just cosmetic. They can make text more readable by subtly blocking off columns and directing the reader's eyes across rows.

Word gives you many options for adding borders and shading to a table. You can use either for the entire table or selected cells, and you can mix different border widths and shading densities.

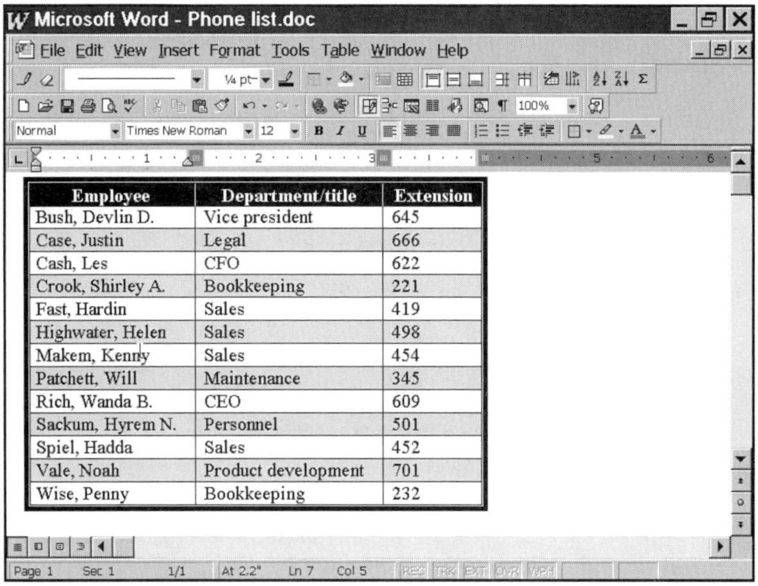

Employee	Department/title	Extension
Bush, Devlin D.	Vice president	645
Case, Justin	Legal	666
Cash, Les	CFO	622
Crook, Shirley A.	Bookkeeping	221
Fast, Hardin	Sales	419
Highwater, Helen	Sales	498
Makem, Kenny	Sales	454
Patchett, Will	Maintenance	345
Rich, Wanda B.	CEO	609
Sackum, Hyrem N.	Personnel	501
Spiel, Hadda	Sales	452
Vale, Noah	Product development	701
Wise, Penny	Bookkeeping	232

Fig. 11.15
Borders and shading improve the appearance of a table and make it more readable.

You can add borders and shading from the Borders and Shading dialog box or with the Tables and Borders toolbar. The techniques are much the same as for bordering and shading paragraphs, which we covered in Chapter 9, "Formatting Paragraphs and Blocks."

The table in Figure 11.15 might seem like a lot of work, but it's not. Most of the borders and shading were added with the Tables and Borders toolbar. Let's go over the steps.

Placing an order for borders

You can modify the borders Word automatically gives a table, but it's often better to start with a clean slate, so the first step is to get rid of the existing borders. Put the insertion point anywhere in the table and select the table by holding down the Alt key and clicking twice. Click the arrow next to the Borders button on the Tables and Borders toolbar. Click the No Border button on the Borders mini-toolbar that drops down (see Figure 11.16).

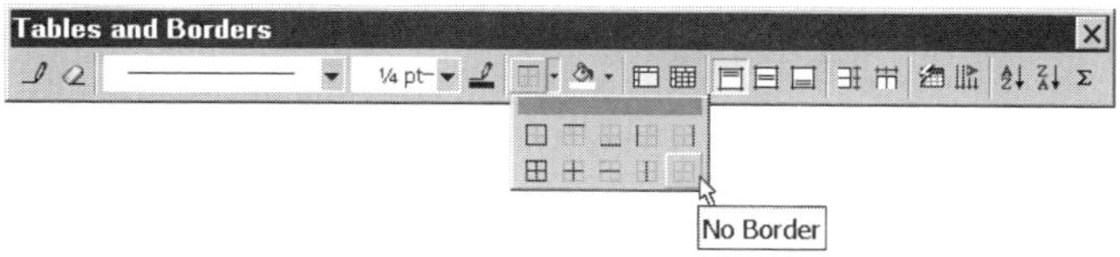

Fig. 11.16
The Border mini-toolbar lets you select your borders, or choose no borders at all.

Next, we'll add the new outside border. Take these steps:

1. Select the table.
2. Click the Line Style box and find the appropriate border.
3. Click the arrow next to the Border button again and click Outside Border from the mini-toolbar that drops down.

Got the hang of it? Then the inside borders should be easy: Select the table, choose the border, and click the Inside Border button from the Border button's mini-toolbar.

Made in the shade

Now for the shading. Because the title row will take some extra work, it's easier to do the telephone entries first. The procedure is similar to that for adding borders. We'll start with the Justin Case entry:

1. Select the row.
2. Click the arrow next to the Shading Color button.
3. A mini-toolbar, like the one for Borders, drops down. Choose a shade from the palate (in this example, 15 percent gray) and click it.

That's it—the first row's done. Luckily, Word provides a shortcut so that you don't have to repeat these steps for all the rows to be shaded. Simply select the next row you want to shade and click the Shading Color button.

When you're done, the table will look like the one in Figure 11.17.

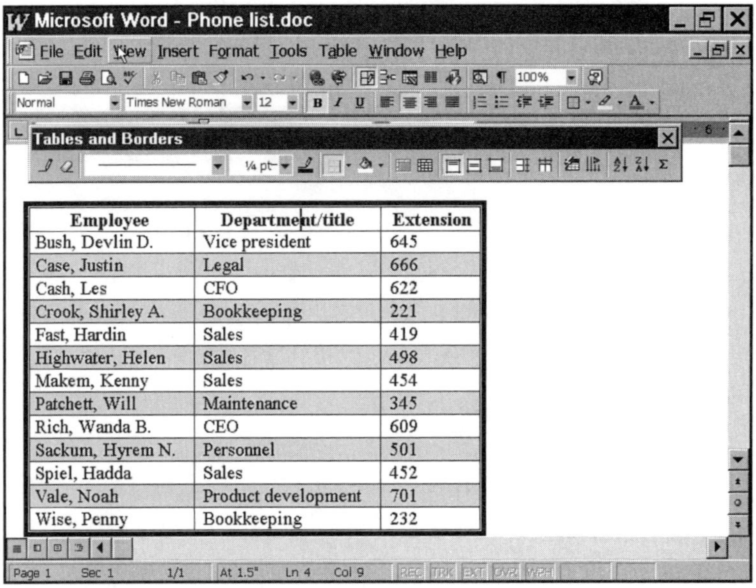

Employee	Department/title	Extension
Bush, Devlin D.	Vice president	645
Case, Justin	Legal	666
Cash, Les	CFO	622
Crook, Shirley A.	Bookkeeping	221
Fast, Hardin	Sales	419
Highwater, Helen	Sales	498
Makem, Kenny	Sales	454
Patchett, Will	Maintenance	345
Rich, Wanda B.	CEO	609
Sackum, Hyrem N.	Personnel	501
Spiel, Hadda	Sales	452
Vale, Noah	Product development	701
Wise, Penny	Bookkeeping	232

Fig. 11.17
The table's almost done; all that's left to format are the headings.

Throwing your titles in reverse

That leaves us with the row of headings. How do we get the reverse type—white on black? Easy. Shade the row the same way you did the others, only select black from the Shading Color palette. Word automatically reverses the type.

But there's still one small detail to take care of. Notice in Figure 11.15 that the borders dividing the headings also are reversed. Here's how it's done:

1. Choose the Border Color button from the Tables and Borders toolbar. A mini-toolbar containing a palette drops down.
2. Choose the white button from the palette. The mouse pointer turns into a pencil.
3. Run the pencil over the two lines that are to be white.
4. When you're done, press Esc to get out of Border Color mode.

AutoFormat—table formatting for the masses

Formatting a table is easy. But the variety of formats, borders, and shades can be bewildering. What are the most attractive borders? How much shading is too much? What's the best way to make a table more attractive while maintaining its readability?

Enter AutoFormat, Word's automatic table formatter. AutoFormat lets you choose from among 37 formats that you can apply to your table. Some of the formats aren't much more than unadorned grids, while others include fancy shading and 3-D effects. Using AutoFormat is like trying to find the best frame for a picture. You can quickly apply a series of formats to your table and then pick the one you like best. The AutoFormat dialog box also lets you choose which parts of the format you want to apply. For example, if you like the format except for the shading, you can remove the shading.

Using AutoFormat

To use AutoFormat, click the Table AutoFormat button on the Tables and Borders toolbar or choose Table, Table AutoFormat from the main menu. Word displays the Table AutoFormat dialog box shown in Figure 11.18.

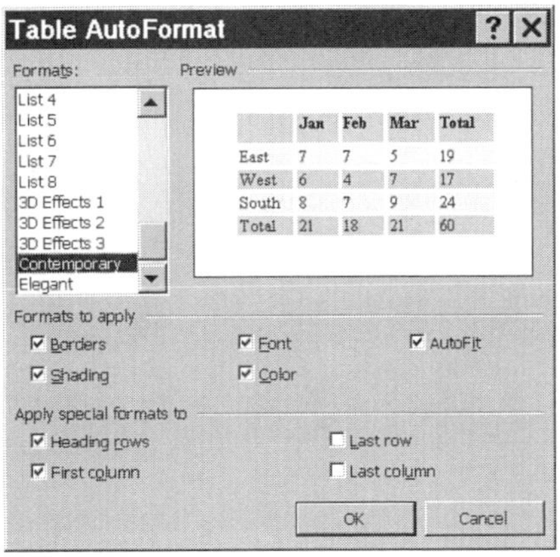

Fig. 11.18
AutoFormat lets you choose from among 37 prefab formats that you can use to create a table.

To select a format, scroll the Formats list box. You can see a sample of each in the Preview box. Select or deselect whatever items you wish under Formats To Apply or Apply Special Formats To. The Preview box changes to reflect your choices.

When you find and adapt the format you want, click OK, and Word automatically formats your table.

Once you've formatted a table with AutoFormat, you can reformat parts of the table manually using the formatting tools we've discussed in this chapter.

12 Word Documents Are Never Out of Style

In this chapter:

- **Just what is a Word style?**
- **How do I use styles?**
- **AutoFormat as you type, for on-the-fly style!**
- **Thanks, but I'd rather AutoFormat selectively**
- **How do I change this style?**
- **I want my own style**

Some people do anything in the name of style. Swallow goldfish, buy fancy cars—you name it. But for a stylish Word document, all it takes is a couple of mouse clicks . . . . . .

Styles change. But good ones, like sensible fashions, endure. Jonathan Swift's Gulliver's Travels reads as clearly to us as it did to his contemporaries, nearly three centuries years ago. Swift had this to say about literary style: "Proper words, in proper places, make the true definition of a style."

That still holds, though if Swift had used Word instead of a quill pen, he might have modified his definition. Word **styles** are formatting elements that you apply to text. You can assemble, name, and save your own styles, or you can use Word's built-in styles. "Proper words, in proper places, with proper formatting," is how Swift might have defined style today.

What do I need to know about styles?

Whenever you write something the old-fashioned way, with pen and paper, you're formatting a document in a particular style—your handwriting (mine is called the "illegible style").

Word does the same thing when you start typing. Any new text is formatted in the Normal style, which is why you see the word Normal in the Style box on the Formatting toolbar. The Normal style is just one of the styles that make up the Normal template (see Chapter 2 for more on templates). Shift+click the Style box drop-down arrow to see all the other styles available in the Normal template, as shown in Figure 12.1.

There are two basic kinds of styles (refer to Figure 12.1):

- **Paragraph styles** are applied to entire paragraphs.
- **Character styles** are applied to selected characters.

Fig. 12.1
The styles for a template are displayed in the Style box; just click a style to apply it to the current paragraph.

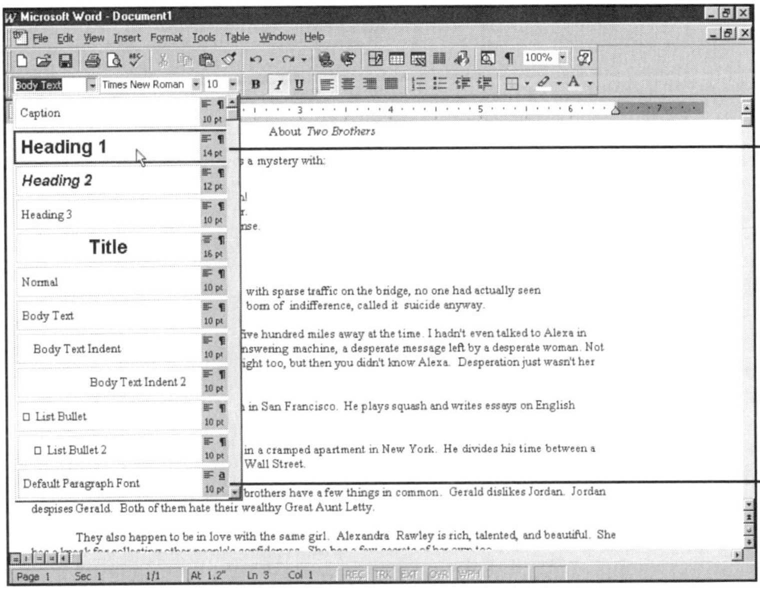

Paragraph styles are indicated by paragraph marks, together with the style's alignment and font size

Character styles are shown with the a

Why use styles in the first place? Apply Word's heading styles to your document headings, and you can generate instant tables of contents, master documents, and even slide shows (see Chapters 17, 19, and 23). Most usefully, a document formatted with heading styles turns into an outline with a single click of the Outline View button! (See Chapter 16 for more about outlines.) Here are some other reasons to use styles:

- Styles are fast. One click applies formatting that would otherwise involve working your way through several commands and dialog boxes. And if you have several paragraphs formatted in the same style, just change the formatting in the style. That changes the formatting of all the paragraphs in that style.
- Styles give your documents consistent formatting. If you format all your headings with the default Heading styles, for example, you avoid the jumbled appearance of documents with too many different formats.
- Styles are versatile. You can create your own mix of fonts and other formatting, name it, and save it as a custom style.

> ***Plain English, please!***
>
> **Formatting** is everything to do with the appearance of text in a document—bold, italicized, indented, and so on. **Styles** are one or more formatting elements that are named and saved, and can then be applied to text. **Templates** are collections of styles and other formatting that you apply to an entire document.

One click, for effortless style

To use any of the paragraph styles listed in the Style box, just position the insertion point anywhere in the paragraph you want to format and click a style. Or select a style and start typing a new paragraph. The entire paragraph, from the first character at the left margin, to the hard return (automatically inserted whenever you press Enter) at the end of the last sentence in the paragraph, is instantly formatted with the font, font size, alignment, and any other formatting commands in that style.

Applying character styles is a little different. You select the words or parts of the word you want to format, then click a character style to apply it.

To apply a different style to the next paragraph, click the style and press Enter.

> **TIP** **Fed up with mousing around in the Style box? Apply a style to a** paragraph, then select the next paragraph you want formatted in the same style. Press Ctrl+Y to apply the style to the selected paragraph. Select additional paragraphs, and every time you press Ctrl+Y, you'll apply the same style again.

Once you've applied a style to a paragraph, you can see exactly what formatting elements make up that style. Press Shift+F1, and your pointer is joined by a question mark. Now click the paragraph you've just styled. A box pops up with details about the character and paragraph formatting you've just applied.

Press Esc to get rid of the question mark and restore the normal cursor. We could have used the Format, Font command to select the font face, size, and attributes of the Normal template's Heading 1 style, but using the style instead saved us a few clicks.

TIP **If you use the Heading styles to format your section headings, you** can generate a fast table of contents based on your headings. Click Insert, Index and Tables, Table of Contents for the Table of Contents tab of the Index and Tables dialog box shown in Figure 12.2.

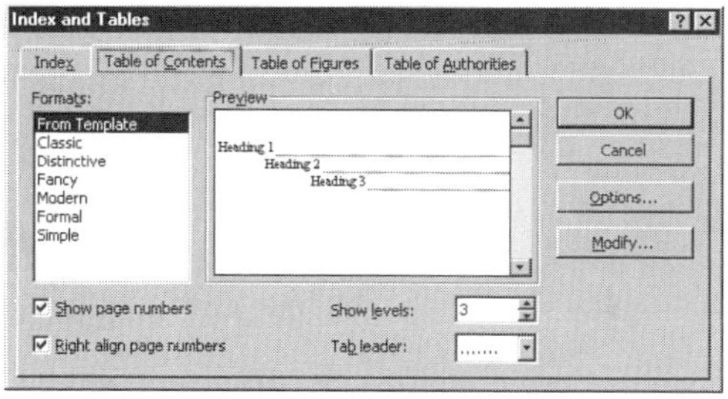

Fig. 12.2
Heading styles let you produce an instant table of contents, formatted any way you like.

Select a format for your table of contents from the Formats list, then click OK. An instant table of contents appears at the insertion point, complete with the styled headings and their page numbers.

AutoFormat, for instant style

Applying a style to a paragraph is like putting up wallpaper on a wall; AutoFormat is more like turning an interior decorator loose on the entire room. This is an unusual interior decorator, though—if you want it to, AutoFormat will format your document as you type! That's like a decorator who follows you around the room, improving your decorating touches as you make them.

To turn on AutoFormat as you type, click Tools, AutoCorrect. Click the AutoFormat As You Type tab in the AutoCorrect dialog box, for the options shown in Figure 12.3.

The Replace As You Type group of options replaces your typed text with AutoFormat formatting and symbols.

TIP **To get an automatic em dash (—), type two hyphens immediately** after your text, and type the next text right after the hyphens. Don't add spaces on either side of the two hyphens.

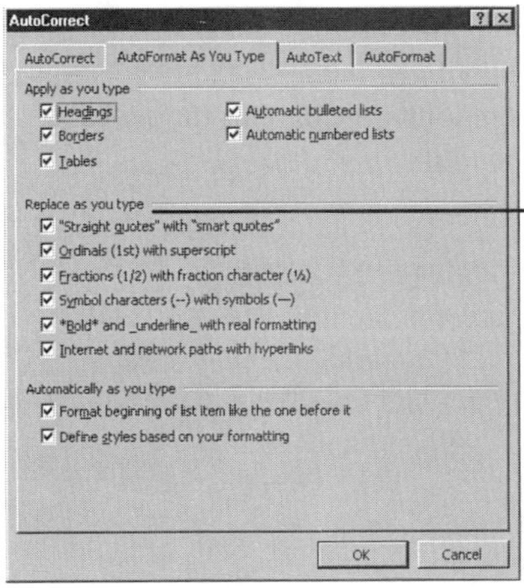

Fig. 12.3
If you find any of these options more annoying than helpful, here's the place to turn them off.

The AutoFormat As You Type feature, for automatic style

Clicking a style in the Style box on the Formatting toolbar to apply heading styles isn't much of a strain, as we've seen. Click the heading, click the style, and you're done.

With AutoFormat As You Type, you can spare yourself even that minimal effort. If you want it to, AutoFormat will supply headings, bulleted and numbered lists, and even solid borders, automatically! Click Tools, AutoCorrect, and click the AutoFormat As You Type tab. If all the options in the Apply as you type group are checked (refer to Figure 12.3), here's what happens:

- For an automatic heading, type a line of text at the left margin. Don't use any punctuation, and capitalize the first letter of the line. Press Enter twice in rapid succession at the end of the line, and the Heading 1 style is automatically applied.

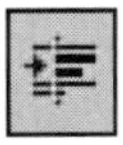

- To get an automatic subheading, press the Tab key or click the Increase Indent button on the Formatting toolbar. Type a line of text with an initial capital and no punctuation. Then press Enter twice in rapid succession at the end of the line. The Heading 2 style is applied automatically. For Heading 3 through Heading 9 styles, just press Tab (or click the Increase Indent button) an additional time for each heading level. For example, for Heading 3, press Tab *twice*, then type your line of text and press Enter twice at the end of the line.

- If you want automatic numbered lists, type **1.** and press the spacebar before the first list item. When you press Enter at the end of the first item, AutoFormat automatically numbers the subsequent lines 2., 3., and so on. Press Enter twice after the last item in the list to turn off automatic numbering.

Q&A ***I can't seem to get these automatic headings to work!***

Automatic headings are handy, but fussy. Your text has to begin with a capital letter, it can't have any punctuation, and automatic headings won't work on consecutive lines; you have to have a line of text in between them. If automatic headings are still giving you trouble, you might find it easier to click the heading style you want in the Style box.

- Need a solid line border? Type three dashes (---) and press Enter. Instant border, courtesy of AutoFormat As You Type.
- For automatic bulleted lists, type an asterisk (*) and press the spacebar before the first bulleted item. AutoFormat As You Type converts the asterisk to a bullet when you press Enter at the end of the line, and automatically bullets the next line. Press Enter twice after the last bulleted item to turn off automatic bullets.

Figure 12.4 shows you the formatting magic AutoFormat As You Type can work on a document.

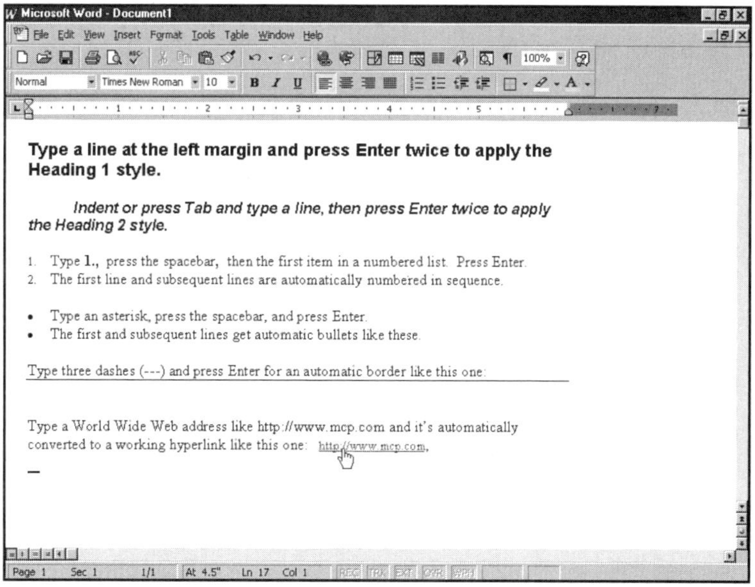
Microsoft Word - Document1
File Edit View Insert Format Tools Table Window Help
Normal
Times New Roman
10
Type a line at the left margin and press Enter twice to apply the Heading 1 style.
Indent or press Tab and type a line, then press Enter twice to apply the Heading 2 style.
1. Type 1., press the spacebar, then the first item in a numbered list. Press Enter.
2. The first line and subsequent lines are automatically numbered in sequence.
• Type an asterisk, press the spacebar, and press Enter.
• The first and subsequent lines get automatic bullets like these.
Type three dashes (---) and press Enter for an automatic border like this one:
Type a World Wide Web address like http://www.mcp.com and it's automatically converted to a working hyperlink like this one: http://www.mcp.com.
Page 1 Sec 1 1/1 At 4.5" Ln 17 Col 1

Fig. 12.4
If your documents are peppered with headings, lists, and borders, AutoFormat As You Type will save you a few nanoseconds.

If you don't like what AutoFormat As You Type has done after you type something, click the Undo button on the toolbar.

Turn network and internet addresses into instant Hyperlinks

AutoFormat As You Type may seem magical, but the magic is thoroughly up to date. Here's the ultimate rabbit in this feature's hat: type a World Wide Web address like **http://www.mcp.com**, press the spacebar, and AutoFormat As You Type converts it to a working hyperlink, automatically.

Click the link after the AutoFormat As You Type conversion, and if you've installed the Microsoft Internet Explorer, you'll connect to the Web and go straight to the address you've typed. **mcp.com**, by the way, is the Macmillan Computer Publishing page on the World Wide Web. If you care to read a library of online books, read about the authors of this book, and lots more, pay it a visit.

For those on a network, AutoFormat As You Type also converts network addresses to network links. Just type a document's full network path name, and a press of the spacebar will forge an automatic Hyperlink.

> ***Plain English, please!***
>
> **Hyperlinks** are like cross-references in an encyclopedia—they direct you to another page (or document) with related information. Hyperlinks are automatic though: click the links and you travel immediately to other documents on the Internet or a local network.

How do I AutoFormat existing text?

AutoFormat As You Type is an amazing feature. Most users will find it pretty handy. Others (I'm neutral on this) may find it a distracting pain. If you fall into the latter category, just deselect the options you don't want in the AutoFormat As You Type tab of the AutoCorrect dialog box.

Even those who like AutoFormat As You Type may have existing documents that haven't benefited from AutoFormat's formatting tricks. Others can take advantage of AutoFormat's convenience by applying it manually and selectively.

To AutoFormat an existing document, open the document and click Format, AutoFormat. That pops up the AutoFormat dialog box shown in Figure 12.5.

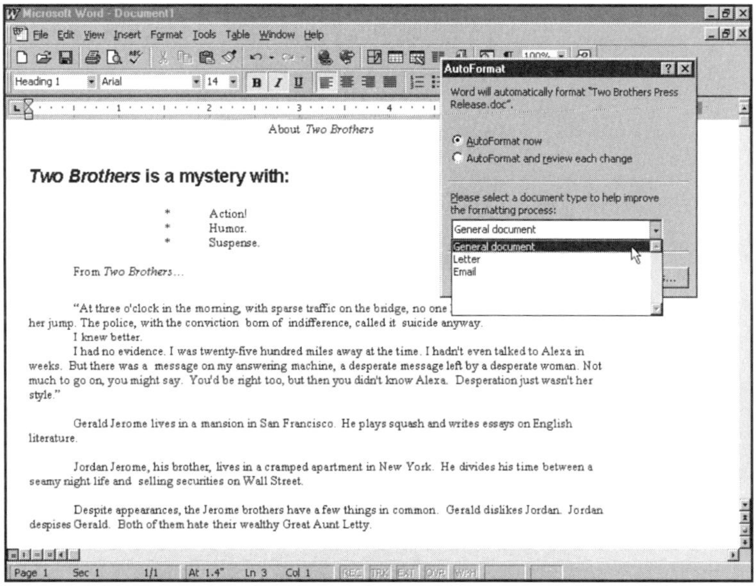
Microsoft Word - Document1
File Edit View Insert Format Tools Table Window Help
Heading 1
Arial
14
AutoFormat
Word will automatically format "Two Brothers Press Release.doc".
AutoFormat now
AutoFormat and review each change
Please select a document type to help improve the formatting process:
General document
General document
Letter
Email
About Two Brothers
Two Brothers is a mystery with:
* Action!
* Humor.
* Suspense.
From Two Brothers…
"At three o'clock in the morning, with sparse traffic on the bridge, no one
her jump. The police, with the conviction born of indifference, called it suicide anyway.
I knew better.
I had no evidence. I was twenty-five hundred miles away at the time. I hadn't even talked to Alexa in weeks. But there was a message on my answering machine, a desperate message left by a desperate woman. Not much to go on, you might say. You'd be right too, but then you didn't know Alexa. Desperation just wasn't her style."
Gerald Jerome lives in a mansion in San Francisco. He plays squash and writes essays on English literature.
Jordan Jerome, his brother, lives in a cramped apartment in New York. He divides his time between a seamy night life and selling securities on Wall Street.
Despite appearances, the Jerome brothers have a few things in common. Gerald dislikes Jordan. Jordan despises Gerald. Both of them hate their wealthy Great Aunt Letty.
Page 1 Sec 1 1/1 At 1.4" Ln 3 Col 1

Fig. 12.5
What sort of document do you have? Take your pick in the AutoFormat dialog box.

Choose a document type, select AutoFormat Now, and Word analyzes every paragraph in your document. AutoFormat then automatically applies what it decides are the appropriate styles to each paragraph. Headings get the Headings styles, titles are styled as Titles, body text as Body Text, and so on.

AutoFormat performs a few other tricks:

- Copyright, trademark, and registration mark symbols that you've indicated with a (c), (tm), or (r) are replaced with ©, ™, and ®.

- Extra spaces and paragraph and tab marks are cleared. They can creep into documents when you inadvertently hit the spacebar, Enter, or Tab keys when you don't mean to. As you continue to type, they get buried in the text, which can result in odd-looking spacing in the final draft. AutoFormat decides which of these marks are unnecessary and wipes them out. Click the Show/Hide Paragraph Marks button on the Standard toolbar to display the paragraph marks in your document.
- Numbered list numbers and homemade bullets are replaced with Word's automatic varieties. Since you've probably created those lists

with the Bullets and Numbering buttons on the Formatting toolbar anyway (which produce automatic numbers and bullets), this AutoFormat feature may not be too helpful.

- AutoFormat also replaces straight quotation marks, the kind you produce from the keyboard (") with the curly opening and closing SmartQuotes (“ and ”).

I'd rather control what AutoFormat does with my document

You might find it handier to AutoFormat selectively, and review each change AutoFormat makes. Accept or reject the changes individually, or accept or reject them all, it's your choice.

To AutoFormat a document and exercise some control over what AutoFormat does:

1. Position the insertion point anywhere in the document and click Format, AutoFormat. That pops up the AutoFormat dialog box shown in Figure 12.5. Choose AutoFormat and review each change.

> **TIP** **If you don't want to AutoFormat the whole document, select the** text you do want formatted first. AutoFormat perform its tricks on only the selected text.

2. Click OK, and AutoFormat gives your document a makeover. When the makeover is completed, the AutoFormat dialog box pops up again.

3. If you like the look of what AutoFormat's done, click Accept All in the AutoFormat dialog box. If you hate it, click Reject All to return your document to its former appearance. Otherwise, click Review Changes for the Review AutoFormat Changes dialog box.

4. Click Find to review the first AutoFormat change. Click Reject if you don't like it, or Find again to leave it and go to the next formatting alteration. Work your way through the entire document if you want to, rejecting or finding each change. Most AutoFormat changes will be of interest only to the most punctilious (see Figure 12.6).

Fig. 12.6
Some might mourn the absence of leading white space; most won't care. Just click Find to skip to the next format change.

On a color screen, AutoFormat shows the original formatting in red, and the improvements in blue

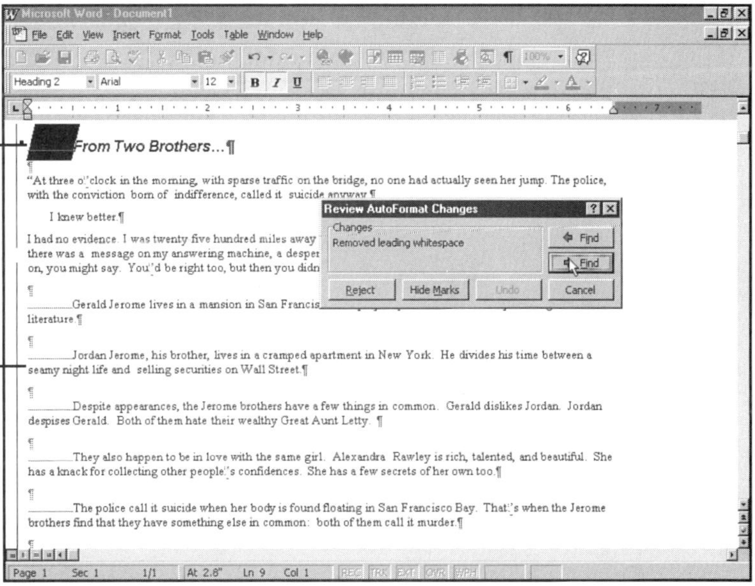
Microsoft Word - Document1
File Edit View Insert Format Tools Table Window Help
Heading 2
Arial
12
From Two Brothers...¶
"At three o'clock in the morning, with sparse traffic on the bridge, no one had actually seen her jump. The police, with the conviction born of indifference, called it suicide anyway.¶
I knew better.¶
Review AutoFormat Changes
Changes
Removed leading whitespace
Find
Find
Reject
Hide Marks
Undo
Cancel
Jordan Jerome, his brother, lives in a cramped apartment in New York. He divides his time between a seamy night life and selling securities on Wall Street.¶
Despite appearances, the Jerome brothers have a few things in common. Gerald dislikes Jordan. Jordan despises Gerald. Both of them hate their wealthy Great Aunt Letty.¶
They also happen to be in love with the same girl. Alexandra Rawley is rich, talented, and beautiful. She has a knack for collecting other people's confidences. She has a few secrets of her own too.¶
The police call it suicide when her body is found floating in San Francisco Bay. That's when the Jerome brothers find that they have something else in common: both of them call it murder.¶
Page 1 Sec 1 1/1 At 2.8" Ln 9 Col 1

TIP **Using the Find button in the Review AutoFormat Changes dialog** box to search for every single AutoFormat alteration can get old fast. To speed things up, click the document to activate it. Then use the keyboard or the scroll bars to scroll through the document. Eyeball the AutoFormat changes. If you see one you don't like, select it, then click Reject in the AutoFormat dialog box.

5 When you're done, click the X (Close) button in the upper right corner of the Review AutoFormat Changes dialog box. That returns you to the AutoFormat dialog box. If you're satisfied, click Accept All.

6 If you still don't like the document's appearance, click Style Gallery for some major alterations. You get the Style Gallery dialog box, with a preview of the document and a list of document templates. Click any of the templates in the Template list and view the results in the Preview window.

7 When you preview the different template styles in the Style Gallery dialog box, the document's actual formatting doesn't change; it's more like viewing an object through different colored lenses. Sample as many as you like.

8. If you find a template you want, click OK. The styles from that template are copied to the current document. If none of them appeal to you, just click Cancel.

9. When you're happy with the way things look, save your document to preserve the formatting changes, and you're done.

I want my own Style

Each of Word's templates, including the Normal template you start out with when you first run the program, comes with its own styles. They can be modified with different fonts and font styles (like **bold** or *italics*), and with different spacing and alignments—indents, for example, or centering. Or create your own style, name it, and save it.

Modified or newly created styles are saved in the active document. If you want to use your own styles in other documents as well, just copy them to a template.

How do I change this style?

Want a Heading 2 style subheading, but hate the default font? Just modify the style with a different font. To change a style in the active document:

1. Select the paragraph formatted in the style you want to change. Make sure the style name is displayed in the Style box when you do this; if it's not, click the paragraph, then select it.

2. Make your formatting changes; use the Formatting toolbar to apply boldface or italics, center or right-align the text, or change the font.

3. Click the style name in the Style box on the Formatting toolbar and press Enter. That pops up the Modify Style dialog box shown in Figure 12.7.

4. Select the option called Update The Style to Reflect Recent Changes and click OK. That modifies the style with the changes you've made. The next time you apply that style, you'll apply the redefined version with your alterations included.

Changing the font of the Heading 2 style (refer to Figure 12.7) changed the font for all the paragraphs formatted in that style throughout the document.

Fig. 12.7
If you change your mind, select the Reapply The Formatting Of The Style To The Selection? option to restore the style's original formatting.

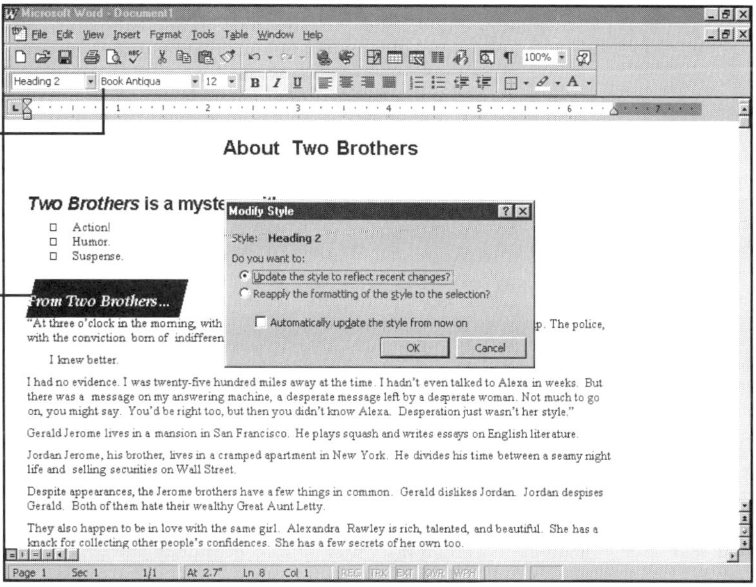
Microsoft Word - Document1
File Edit View Insert Format Tools Table Window Help
Heading 2
Book Antiqua
12
100%
About Two Brothers
Two Brothers is a myste
Action!
Humor.
Suspense.
From Two Brothers...
Modify Style
Style: Heading 2
Do you want to:
Update the style to reflect recent changes?
Reapply the formatting of the style to the selection?
Automatically update the style from now on
OK
Cancel
"At three o'clock in the morning, with
with the conviction born of indifferen
p. The police,
I knew better.
I had no evidence. I was twenty-five hundred miles away at the time. I hadn't even talked to Alexa in weeks. But there was a message on my answering machine, a desperate message left by a desperate woman. Not much to go on, you might say. You'd be right too, but then you didn't know Alexa. Desperation just wasn't her style."
Gerald Jerome lives in a mansion in San Francisco. He plays squash and writes essays on English literature.
Jordan Jerome, his brother, lives in a cramped apartment in New York. He divides his time between a seamy night life and selling securities on Wall Street.
Despite appearances, the Jerome brothers have a few things in common. Gerald dislikes Jordan. Jordan despises Gerald. Both of them hate their wealthy Great Aunt Letty.
They also happen to be in love with the same girl. Alexandra Rawley is rich, talented, and beautiful. She has a knack for collecting other people's confidences. She has a few secrets of her own too.
Page 1 Sec 1 1/1 At 2.7" Ln 8 Col 1 REC TRK EXT OVR WPH

I selected a different font, Book Antiqua, for the paragraph in the Heading 2 style

You can modify character styles the same way. Just select the characters in a particular character style and make your changes. Click the style name in the Style box, press Enter, then redefine the style as we did above.

Birth of a Style: creating a new style

When mere alterations aren't enough, create your own style. You might, for example, want all your document titles in the same custom style. It's easy to do; just create a style called Custom Title.

To create your own style:

1 Select a paragraph and format it. Change fonts, font size, add shading, whatever you like.

Q&A ***Why doesn't this new style seem to have all the formatting I added?***

When you create a paragraph style, the formatting you use applies to the whole paragraph. You can't, for example, italicize part of a paragraph and save it as a style. You can always go back to the paragraph later and add more formatting, like italics, to particular words or phrases.

2 Click the style name of the selected paragraph in the Style box.

3 Type a new name for your style. The new text overwrites the old name. Press Enter, or click anywhere outside the Style box, and your new style is born, as shown in Figure 12.8.

Fig. 12.8
You can call your style anything you want. Just don't use a backslash, curly braces, semicolons, or asterisks.

Click here to type in the new style name

Here's the current paragraph, with a box border and a font change

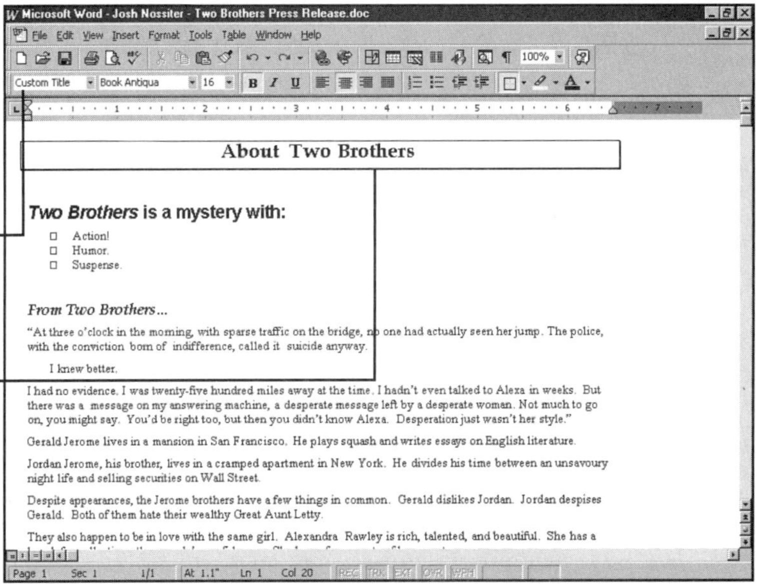
Microsoft Word - Josh Nossiter - Two Brothers Press Release.doc
File Edit View Insert Format Tools Table Window Help
100%
Custom Title
Book Antiqua
16
About Two Brothers
Two Brothers is a mystery with:
Action!
Humor.
Suspense.
From Two Brothers...
"At three o'clock in the morning, with sparse traffic on the bridge, no one had actually seen her jump. The police, with the conviction born of indifference, called it suicide anyway.
I knew better.
I had no evidence. I was twenty-five hundred miles away at the time. I hadn't even talked to Alexa in weeks. But there was a message on my answering machine, a desperate message left by a desperate woman. Not much to go on, you might say. You'd be right too, but then you didn't know Alexa. Desperation just wasn't her style."
Gerald Jerome lives in a mansion in San Francisco. He plays squash and writes essays on English literature.
Jordan Jerome, his brother, lives in a cramped apartment in New York. He divides his time between an unsavoury night life and selling securities on Wall Street.
Despite appearances, the Jerome brothers have a few things in common. Gerald dislikes Jordan. Jordan despises Gerald. Both of them hate their wealthy Great Aunt Letty.
They also happen to be in love with the same girl. Alexandra Rawley is rich, talented, and beautiful. She has a
Page 1 Sec 1 1/1 At 1.1" Ln 1 Col 20 REC TRK EXT OVR WPH

The style whose name you eradicated to make room for the new name is unaffected by the change.

I want that new style in my other documents

You'll only want one title in a document. But you might want to reuse that title style in your other documents. Trouble is, when you open a new document, you won't see your new style. It's only saved in the active document.

If you want your style in other documents as well, copy it to the Normal template:

1 Click Format, Style for the Style dialog box, then click Organizer in the Style dialog box to pop up the Organizer dialog box.

2 Select the style you want to copy on the In [document name] list, as shown in Figure 12.9.

Fig. 12.9
The list on the left shows the styles in the active document; the To list displays the current template.

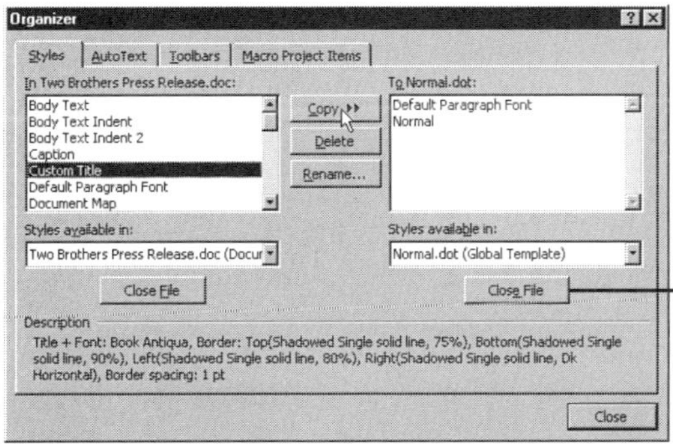

Click here to summon up a different template or document to copy your style to

3 Click Copy to copy the new style to the Normal template.

With your new style copied to the Normal template, it'll be available in all your documents. If you want to copy the style to a different template, or to another document, click the Close File button under the To list (refer to Figure 12.9).

The button turns into an Open File button. Click it again, and you get the Open dialog box. Double-click the document or template you want to copy to, then click the Copy button in the Organizer dialog box.

TIP **To display all the available templates in the Open dialog box, click** the Up One Level button on the Open dialog box toolbar. That displays the parent Msoffice folder in the Look In box. Then click the Files Of Type drop-down arrow and select Document Templates.

Part IV: Be Your Own Publisher

13 Columns, the Pillars of Sturdy Documents

In this chapter:

- **I need columns, fast!**
- **How do I change column widths?**
- **These columns are unbalanced**
- **Can I leave some text out of these columns?**

Columns enliven the page and make text more readable. To be a successful columnist in Word, all you do is point and click . . . .

Columns hold things up. One ancient architectural form uses columns, or posts, to support a horizontal beam, called a lintel. Greek temples were built on the post and lintel principal; so was the Lincoln Memorial in Washington.

Documents, like buildings, should be structurally sound. Long lines of text across the page can cause a reader's interest to sag. Columns prevent that by breaking up the page. And just as in architecture, too many columns on a page can be too much of a good thing. Word makes it easy to adjust column sizes and numbers. Propped up with a few columns, Word documents never sag.

Quick newspaper columns, for more readable documents

By dividing text up into columns, newspapers make it easy for the eye to scan a lot of information quickly. With headlines and subheads as guides, newspaper columns turn a reader's eyes into powerful search tools. Formatting your Word documents with columns confers the same benefits on your own readers.

How do I set this text in newspaper columns?

Newspaper columns, in which the text automatically flows from the bottom of one column to the top of the next, are easy to work with and easy to read. They're also what you get when you click the Columns button on the Standard toolbar.

TIP **Write your text with the normal left and right margins first, before** you turn on columns. Applying columns to existing text is much easier than composing text inside columns.

To apply columns to a document:

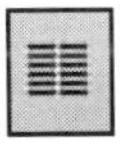

1. Click the Columns button on the Formatting toolbar. That gets you a palette of four columns. Point at the first column on the left, and drag across to select the number of columns you want to use, as shown in Figure 13.1.

Fig. 13.1
As you drag across the Columns button palette, you highlight each selected column.

TIP **If you continue to drag past the fourth column, the columns** palette expands to six columns. Just remember that the more columns you use, the skinnier they get.

2. Release the mouse button, and your document is formatted in as many columns as you selected. Word switches to Page Layout view automatically so that you can see the columns, as shown in Figure 13.2.

In Normal view, Word displays all your text in one column, no matter how many columns you've actually inserted. That's why Word switches you to Page Layout view when you apply columns.

Because you can't display multiple columns in Normal view, it's easier to write and edit your document first, and then apply columns to the finished text. You *can* write and edit in Page Layout view, but you might find Word a mite sluggish.

Fig. 13.2
Formatting documents in Word columns is a simple click-and-drag operation.

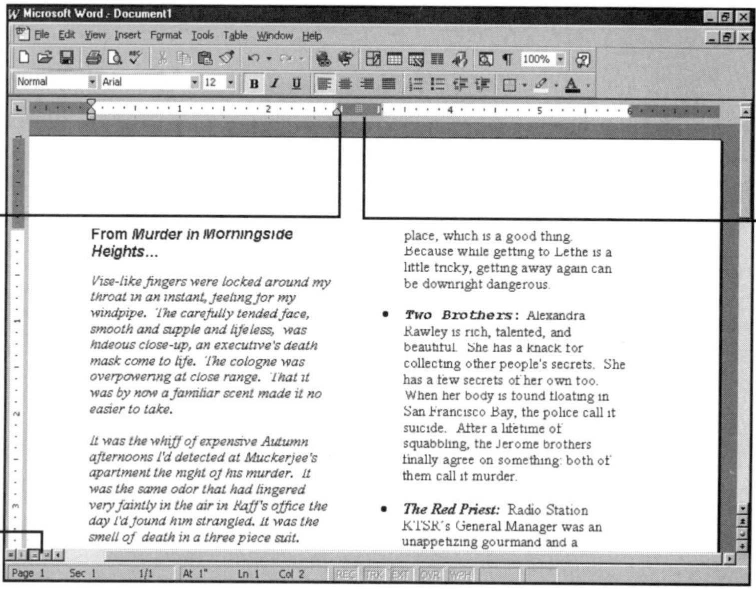
Microsoft Word - Document1
File Edit View Insert Format Tools Table Window Help
Normal
Arial
12
100%
From Murder in Morningside Heights...
Vise-like fingers were locked around my throat in an instant, feeling for my windpipe. The carefully tended face, smooth and supple and lifeless, was hideous close-up, an executive's death mask come to life. The cologne was overpowering at close range. That it was by now a familiar scent made it no easier to take.
It was the whiff of expensive Autumn afternoons I'd detected at Muckerjee's apartment the night of his murder. It was the same odor that had lingered very faintly in the air in Raff's office the day I'd found him strangled. It was the smell of death in a three piece suit.
place, which is a good thing. Because while getting to Lethe is a little tricky, getting away again can be downright dangerous.
Two Brothers: Alexandra Rawley is rich, talented, and beautiful. She has a knack for collecting other people's secrets. She has a few secrets of her own too. When her body is found floating in San Francisco Bay, the police call it suicide. After a lifetime of squabbling, the Jerome brothers finally agree on something: both of them call it murder.
The Red Priest: Radio Station KTSR's General Manager was an unappetizing gourmand and a
Page 1 Sec 1 1/1 At 1" Ln 1 Col 2 REC TRK EXT OVR WPH

If indented paragraphs don't look right in columns, drag the indent marker to the left

Word automatically switches to Page Layout view when you apply columns

Column markers appear on the ruler in between each column

How do I adjust these columns?

When you format text in columns, a *column marker* appears on the ruler in between each column (refer to Figure 13.2). You drag the column marker to adjust both the width of the columns and the amount of space in between each column.

Change the column width...

To adjust column widths, point at the dimpled center of the column marker. The pointer turns into a two-headed arrow. Now drag left or right to widen or narrow the columns on either side of the marker, as shown in Figure 13.3.

The dimpled center of the column marker

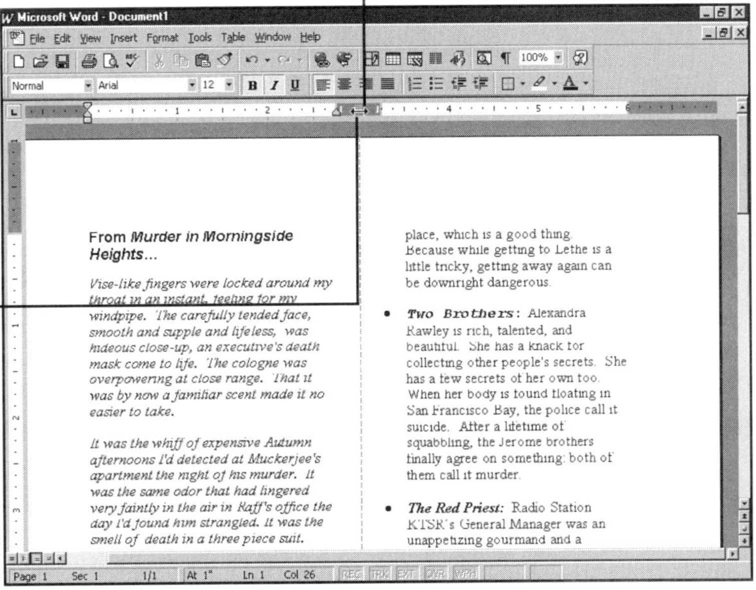
Microsoft Word - Document1
File Edit View Insert Format Tools Table Window Help
Normal
Arial
12
100%
From *Murder in Morningside Heights*...
Vise-like fingers were locked around my throat in an instant, feeling for my windpipe. The carefully tended face, smooth and supple and lifeless, was hideous close-up, an executive's death mask come to life. The cologne was overpowering at close range. That it was by now a familiar scent made it no easier to take.
It was the whiff of expensive Autumn afternoons I'd detected at Muckerjee's apartment the night of his murder. It was the same odor that had lingered very faintly in the air in Raff's office the day I'd found him strangled. It was the smell of death in a three piece suit.
place, which is a good thing. Because while getting to Lethe is a little tricky, getting away again can be downright dangerous.
Two Brothers: Alexandra Rawley is rich, talented, and beautiful. She has a knack for collecting other people's secrets. She has a few secrets of her own too. When her body is found floating in San Francisco Bay, the police call it suicide. After a lifetime of squabbling, the Jerome brothers finally agree on something: both of them call it murder.
The Red Priest: Radio Station KTSR's General Manager was an unappetizing gourmand and a
Page 1 Sec 1 1/1 At 1" Ln 1 Col 26 REC TRK EXT OVR WPH

Fig. 13.3
As you widen the column on one side of the marker, the column on the other side narrows.

The pointer turns into a double-headed arrow; drag to adjust column widths

Or adjust the space in between the columns

In printer's jargon, the white space in between columns is called the *gutter*. A little white space in between columns makes your page more readable, but don't overdo it. As you increase the space between the columns, the columns themselves get skinnier.

If you look closely at a column marker, you'll see two indented surfaces on either side of the dimpled center. To adjust the space in between the columns, point at either indented surface on the column marker. The pointer changes into a double-headed arrow. Now drag to the left or right to increase or decrease the space in between the columns.

If you drag those indented sides of the column marker far enough, the marker shrinks to a gray sliver. Just drag it out again if you decide you want a wider gutter.

Precision columns are a two-button drag

Dragging column markers makes for fast column and gutter width adjustments. But what if you need exact measurements? Precision page-layout artists can set up columns and gutters to within a hundredth of an inch.

Just press both the left and right mouse buttons at the same time as you drag the column markers. The ruler displays the exact column and gutter widths, as shown in Figure 13.4.

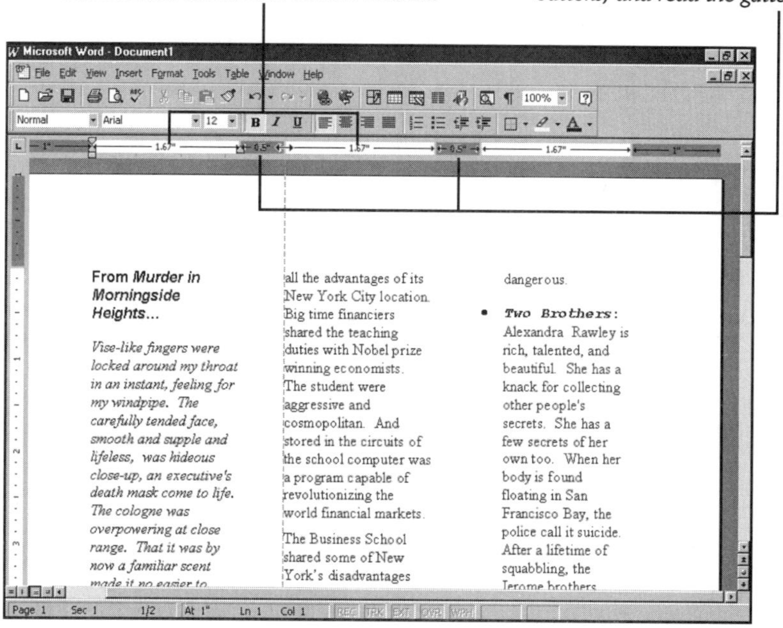
Drag the column marker's dimpled center with both mouse buttons, and note the width measurement between the columns
Drag either indented end of the column marker with both mouse buttons, and read the gutter width here
Microsoft Word - Document1
From Murder in Morningside Heights...
Vise-like fingers were locked around my throat in an instant, feeling for my windpipe. The carefully tended face, smooth and supple and lifeless, was hideous close-up, an executive's death mask come to life. The cologne was overpowering at close range. That it was by now a familiar scent
all the advantages of its New York City location. Big time financiers shared the teaching duties with Nobel prize winning economists. The student were aggressive and cosmopolitan. And stored in the circuits of the school computer was a program capable of revolutionizing the world financial markets.
The Business School shared some of New York's disadvantages
dangerous.
Two Brothers: Alexandra Rawley is rich, talented, and beautiful. She has a knack for collecting other people's secrets. She has a few secrets of her own too. When her body is found floating in San Francisco Bay, the police call it suicide. After a lifetime of squabbling, the

Fig. 13.4
For a tightly formatted page, where every fraction of an inch counts, two-button dragging is the way to go

TIP **Find it awkward to drag with both mouse buttons? Press Alt as you** drag a column marker with the left mouse button. The Alt+drag combination gives you the same display as two-button dragging.

These columns are out of balance!

Here's a minor bother you're likely to run into with columns: even though your text fills an entire page, when it's formatted in columns, one column is shorter than the others. To see if your columns came out with uneven lengths, click the Print Preview button.

Figure 13.5 illustrates the problem.

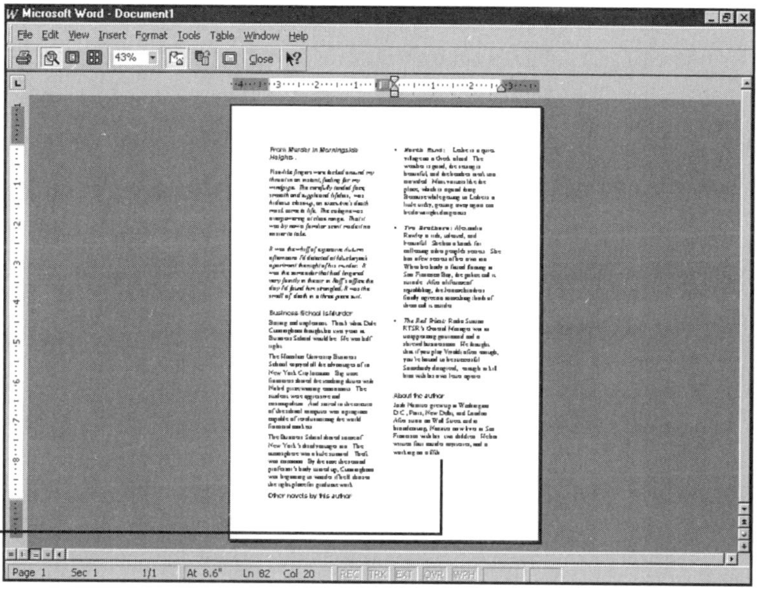

Fig. 13.5
Print preview mode shows you if your columns are unbalanced.

For two balanced columns, put your section break at the end of the second column

There's a fast fix. To balance your columns:

1 If you're not already in it, switch to Page Layout view so you can see what you're doing. Position the insertion point after the last of the columns you want to balance—if you have two columns, click after the period of the last sentence in the second column (see Figure 13.5).

2 Click Insert, Break for the Break dialog box shown in Figure 13.6.

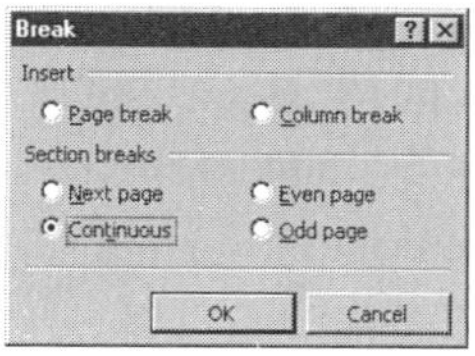

Fig. 13.6
Section breaks are used to divide the page into sections with different formatting.

3 Click the Continuous option button, then click OK. Your columns get adjusted to equal lengths.

In some cases, the second column may be about one line shorter than the first. Unless your columns happen to have exactly the same number of lines, this minor discrepancy is unavoidable. If you want to start a new page after your balanced columns, put the insertion point at the end of the last column and click Insert, Break, Page Break, OK.

Q&A ***Why won't my columns balance?***

You've gone through the steps to balance your columns, and they won't balance! Frustrating, but fixable. There are three possible causes:

- Paragraph formatting can prevent columns from balancing. To fix it, click Format, Paragraph, and click the Line and Page Breaks tab. Clear all the check boxes in the Pagination group of options and click OK.
- You might find that the top of the last column begins one line below the top of the column to the left of it. That means you've got a paragraph mark at the bottom of the next-to-last column. Click the Show/Hide Paragraph Marks button on the Standard toolbar and delete the offending paragraph mark.
- If you've converted the document from another word processor or an earlier version of Word, choose Tools, Options. That gets you the Options dialog box. Click the Compatibility tab in the Options dialog box, then clear the Don't Balance Columns For Continuous Section Starts check box. If that doesn't fix the problem, select the Suppress extra line spacing at bottom of page option. Click OK when you're done.

What else can I do with columns?

Setting up your page in columns is a snap, as we've seen. But what if you want only some of the page in columnar format? Maybe you'd like to add a headline all the way across the top of the page. And while dragging the column markers can give you columns of unequal width, getting the widths just right can be a bit of a drag. There's a shortcut for doing that, and those other items are easily taken care of too.

I don't want the whole page in columns

Some text works better in lines that go from the left to the right margin than in columns. And a page that has both columns and regular text draws attention to each kind. To format only part of the page in columns, just select the text you *do* want in columnar format, click the Columns button on the toolbar, and select the number of columns you want.

If you've already set up the page in columns, then you decide to offset some of the page by formatting it as ordinary left-to-right margin text, here's how to do it:

1 Select the text you want outside the columns.

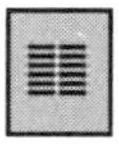

2 Click the Columns button and select one column.

3 When you release the mouse button, the selected text is formatted from the left to the right page margins, as shown in Figure 13.7.

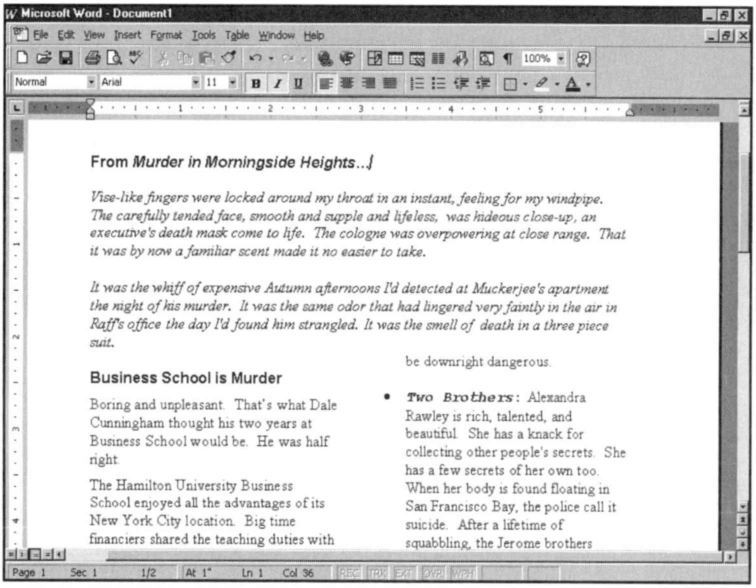
Microsoft Word - Document1
File Edit View Insert Format Tools Table Window Help
Normal
Arial
11
100%
From Murder in Morningside Heights...
Vise-like fingers were locked around my throat in an instant, feeling for my windpipe. The carefully tended face, smooth and supple and lifeless, was hideous close-up, an executive's death mask come to life. The cologne was overpowering at close range. That it was by now a familiar scent made it no easier to take.
It was the whiff of expensive Autumn afternoons I'd detected at Muckerjee's apartment the night of his murder. It was the same odor that had lingered very faintly in the air in Raff's office the day I'd found him strangled. It was the smell of death in a three piece suit.
Business School is Murder
Boring and unpleasant. That's what Dale Cunningham thought his two years at Business School would be. He was half right.
The Hamilton University Business School enjoyed all the advantages of its New York City location. Big time financiers shared the teaching duties with
be downright dangerous.
Two Brothers: Alexandra Rawley is rich, talented, and beautiful. She has a knack for collecting other people's secrets. She has a few secrets of her own too. When her body is found floating in San Francisco Bay, the police call it suicide. After a lifetime of squabbling, the Jerome brothers
Page 1 Sec 1 1/2 At 1" Ln 1 Col 36 REC TRK EXT OVR WPH

Fig. 13.7
This works best for text at the beginning of the first column or the end of the last column.

If you want columns above and below and right-to-left page margin text in the middle of the page, select the text and format it in one column, as we did in Figure 13.7. You'll probably have some tweaking to do. Heads and subheads may not come out exactly right, or you might have to prune or add a paragraph mark or two.

Changed your mind about pulling that text out of columnar format? Here's the fast way to snap it back into your columns: Click the Show/Hide

Paragraph Marks button on the toolbar. You'll see the Section Break double line after the text you pulled out, as shown in Figure 13.8.

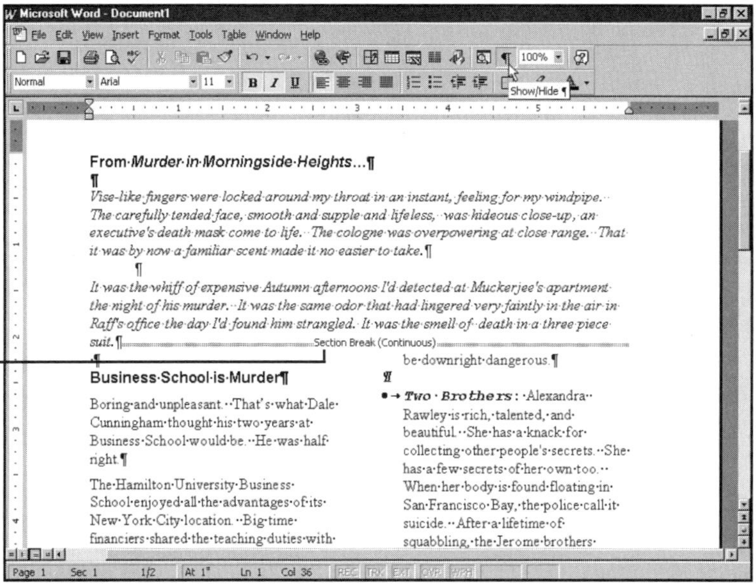
Microsoft Word - Document1
File Edit View Insert Format Tools Table Window Help
Show/Hide ¶
From·Murder·in·Morningside·Heights...¶
Vise-like·fingers·were·locked·around·my·throat·in·an·instant,·feeling·for·my·windpipe.·· The·carefully·tended·face,·smooth·and·supple·and·lifeless,··was·hideous·close-up,·an· executive's·death·mask·come·to·life.··The·cologne·was·overpowering·at·close·range.··That· it·was·by·now·a·familiar·scent·made·it·no·easier·to·take.¶
It·was·the·whiff·of·expensive·Autumn·afternoons·I'd·detected·at·Muckerjee's·apartment· the·night·of·his·murder.··It·was·the·same·odor·that·had·lingered·very·faintly·in·the·air·in· Raff's·office·the·day·I'd·found·him·strangled.·It·was·the·smell·of··death·in·a·three·piece· suit.¶
Section Break (Continuous)
Business·School·is·Murder¶
Boring·and·unpleasant.··That's·what·Dale· Cunningham·thought·his·two·years·at· Business·School·would·be.··He·was·half· right.¶
The·Hamilton·University·Business· School·enjoyed·all·the·advantages·of·its· New·York·City·location.··Big·time· financiers·shared·the·teaching·duties·with·
be·downright·dangerous.¶
Two·Brothers:·Alexandra·· Rawley·is·rich,·talented,·and· beautiful.··She·has·a·knack·for· collecting·other·people's·secrets.··She· has·a·few·secrets·of·her·own·too.·· When·her·body·is·found·floating·in· San·Francisco·Bay,·the·police·call·it· suicide.··After·a·lifetime·of· squabbling,·the·Jerome·brothers·
Page 1 Sec 1 1/2 At 1" Ln 1 Col 36

Fig. 13.8
Columnar and non-columnar text is treated as different sections of a page by Word.

The Section Break double line indicates where columnar text begins

Position the insertion point next to the Section Break double line and press Delete. Your text snaps back into columnar format.

How about a title for these columns?

Putting a title (also called a *banner headline*) across the top of a columnar page is something you may want to do.

If your page isn't formatted in columns yet, just select the text below the title, click the Columns button, and drag for the number of columns you want.

To add a banner headline to a page already formatted in columns, use the same technique we used to pull text out of columns. Type your title at the top of the first column, select it, then click the Columns button and choose a single column. That yanks the selected text out of the column and strings it across the top of the page, just like the title on the front page of a newspaper.

What's the easy way to get columns of unequal width?

Columns of unequal width are a good way to offset different subjects in a document. You might also want columns of unequal width just for variety's sake. While dragging the column markers will do the job, getting your widths exactly right might be a chore.

Here's the fast way to get columns of unequal width:

1 With the insertion point anywhere in the document, click Format, Columns for the Columns dialog box shown in Figure 13.9.

Fig. 13.9
Use the Columns dialog box to get rid of columns too—just click One in the Presets group, then click OK.

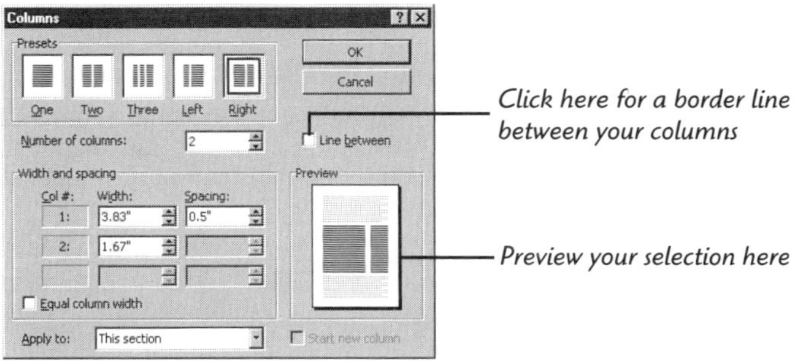

2 Click Left for a left-hand column half the width of the right column, or click Right for a right-hand column half the width of the left column. Then click OK.

I need a newsletter, fast!

Somebody has to do it—churn out the company newsletter, that is. If that somebody happens to be you, save yourself a lot of time and aggravation. Summon up the Word Newsletter Wizard and let the Wiz guide you through the steps of creating a (nearly) instant newsletter.

To get the Newsletter Wizard, Click File, New for the New dialog box. Click the Publications tab and select Newsletter Wizard for a preview of your newsletter, as shown in Figure 13.10.

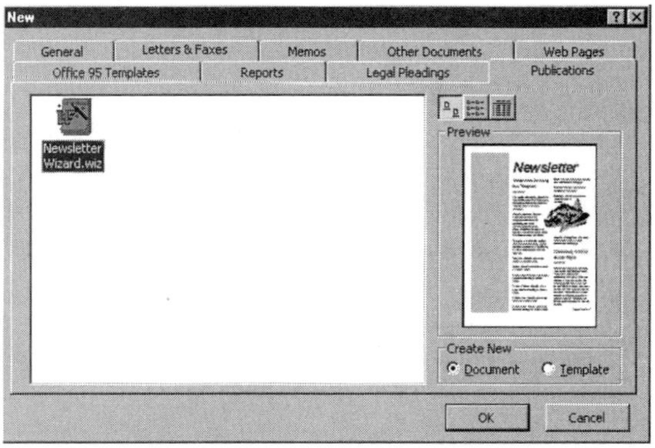

Fig. 13.10
Once you get the hang of columns, you might be tempted to wing your newsletters. Trust me on this: the Wizard is faster.

Double-click the Newsletter Wizard icon to pop up the Wizard. Answer the Wizard's questions, give your newsletter a title, and you'll wind up with the formatted shell of a newsletter. Add your own text and graphics, and you'll be done in plenty of time to find somebody else to do the chore before the next issue.

TIP **If you're planning to post a multi-column newsletter to your local** intranet or the World Wide Web, set up your newsletter in a table, not in columns. Word tables can convert to the World Wide Web HTML format, but columns cannot. See Chapter 11, "Turning the Tables," for more about tables, and Chapter 25, "The Word on Web," for information on converting documents from Word's format to HTML.

14 Borders, Colors, and Typographical Tweaks

In this chapter:

- **How do I jazz up my document with borders?**
- **Linked text boxes hold stories with sequels**
- **Shaded and colors, for snazzy effects!**
- **White space isn't flashy, just readable**
- **How come this big title looks odd?**

From the bold and brash to the quiet and refined, Word has formatting tricks to enhance all kinds of documents. . . .

To a writer, a blank page is an open invitation. For a reader, a page has to have something on it to be inviting. If the writer can catch the reader's eye, odds are the page will be read. One obvious way to grab that first glance is with a page made attractive with borders, colors, and shading. A more subtle approach spaces lines and words so perfectly that the eye can't resist reading them. Word makes it easy to take either approach. Word's special effects won't put you on a best-seller list, but they might draw a little attention to that report you've just written.

All about borders

Borders are lines and boxes that you throw around a paragraph. They can be solid lines, double-lines, broken lines—you name it. Borders go above, below, or to the right or left of a paragraph. You can also put a border all the way around a paragraph, or between two paragraphs.

Use borders to:

- Separate columns, or headings and body text.
- Highlight important passages in a document.
- Add a little visual variety to titles and headings.
- Format tables in attractive and readable ways.
- Create interesting frames around graphic objects.

CAUTION **Borders are not supported in HTML, the World Wide Web format.** Word documents converted to HTML will lose all their borders. See Chapter 25, "The Word on the Web," for information on substituting different effects for formatting lost in HTML conversions.

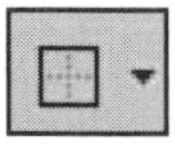

The Borders button on the Formatting toolbar puts a palette of borders at your fingertips (see Figure 14.1). The button itself applies the border it displays, and the display changes to reflect that last border you used. For a different border style, click the arrow next to the Borders button. To apply any of the borders on the palette (except for the Inside Borders—see the following on how to do that), just click a paragraph, click a choice on the Borders palette, and you're done.

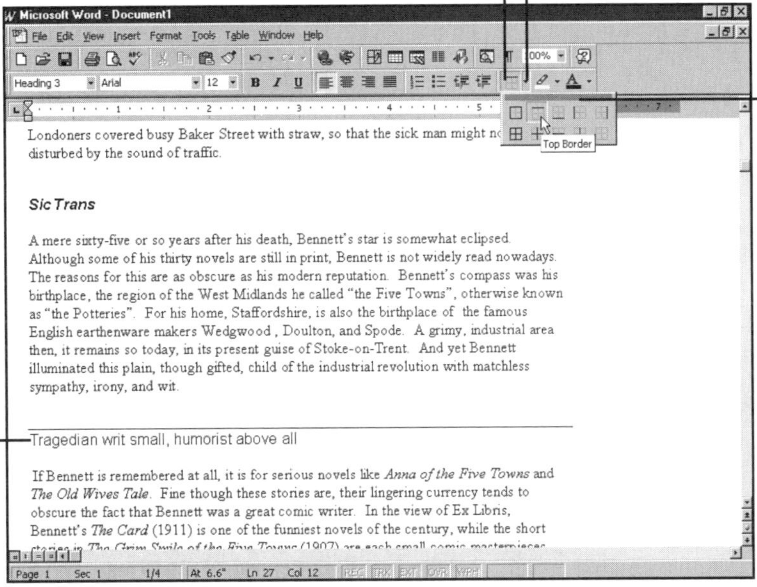
The Borders button displays the last border you used; click it to apply the displayed border
Click the drop-down arrow for the borders palette
Click the paragraph for which you want a border, then click your choice on the palette to apply a border
Drag here to "tear off" the palette and float it on the screen
Microsoft Word - Document1
Top Border
Sic Trans
Tragedian writ small, humorist above all

Fig. 14.1
The Borders palette gives you one-click border shopping.

To get rid of the border again, click the paragraph, click the Borders drop-down arrow, and select No Border on the Borders palette.

How do I add an inside border?

Adding and clearing borders is so easy that you might want to take an experimental approach. Try one, get rid of it, then try another. Keep at it until you achieve exactly the look you want.

For example, here's how to apply an inside border between two paragraphs:

1 Select two adjacent paragraphs.

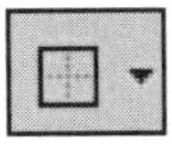

2 Click the Borders button arrow on the Formatting toolbar to pop up the Borders palette and click the Inside Horizontal Border button. The resulting inside border is shown in Figure 14.2.

Fig. 14.2
Inside borders work well for two-paragraph headings.

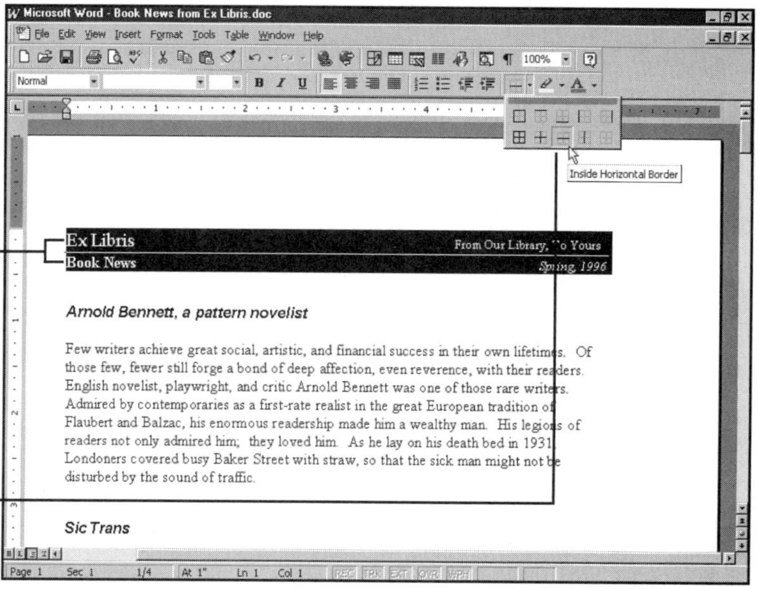
Microsoft Word - Book News from Ex Libris.doc
Inside Horizontal Border
Ex Libris
From Our Library, To Yours
Book News
Spring, 1996
Arnold Bennett, a pattern novelist
Few writers achieve great social, artistic, and financial success in their own lifetimes. Of those few, fewer still forge a bond of deep affection, even reverence, with their readers. English novelist, playwright, and critic Arnold Bennett was one of those rare writers. Admired by contemporaries as a first-rate realist in the great European tradition of Flaubert and Balzac, his enormous readership made him a wealthy man. His legions of readers not only admired him; they loved him. As he lay on his death bed in 1931, Londoners covered busy Baker Street with straw, so that the sick man might not be disturbed by the sound of traffic.
Sic Trans

Select the two paragraphs first

Then click the Inside Horizontal Border choice to apply an inside border between them

Colored borders? Dotted lines? Call up the Tables and Borders toolbar

When you first select a border from the Borders button palette, you get the default line style for your border. That's a solid black line 3/4 of a point thick.

For a different line style, colored or shaded borders, and a variety of line **weights**, or thicknesses, summon up the Tables and Borders toolbar. Click the Tables and Borders button on the Standard toolbar, and the Tables and Borders toolbar snaps into place under the Formatting toolbar.

Q&A ***After I clicked the Tables and Borders button, my pointer turned into a little pencil. Now I can't select anything in the editing window!***

This comes under the heading of "it's not a bug, it's a feature." When you click the Tables and Borders button, the Draw Table tool (that's the little pencil) is activated by default. Clicking in the editing window with the Draw Table tool inserts a table, which is fine if you want a table, not so fine if you want to select text or move the insertion point.

The Draw Table tool is deactivated as soon as you click another button on the Tables and Borders toolbar. Otherwise, click the Draw Table button or press Esc to deactivate the Draw Table tool and restore your pointer to the normal I-beam shape.

Want a different look for your border? Click the Line Style drop-down arrow on the Tables and Borders toolbar and take your pick. There are double lines, dotted, and dashed lines, too, as shown in Figure 14.3.

These tools are used for creating and formatting tables. The eraser's tempting, but it won't work on borders.

The Borders button works just like the one on the Formatting toolbar

Splash color or shades of gray on a paragraph with the Shading button

Take your pick of line thicknesses and colors

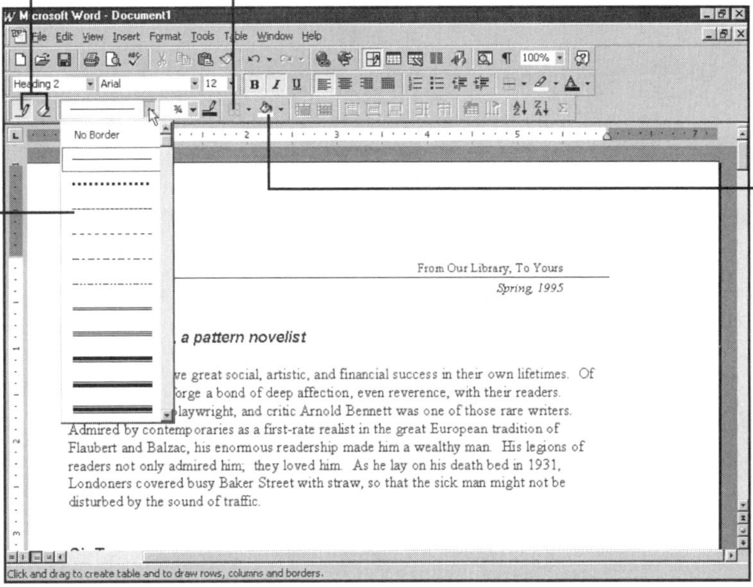
Microsoft Word - Document1
File Edit View Insert Format Tools Table Window Help
Heading 2
Arial
12
100%
No Border
From Our Library, To Yours
Spring 1995
a pattern novelist
ve great social, artistic, and financial success in their own lifetimes. Of
orge a bond of deep affection, even reverence, with their readers.
laywright, and critic Arnold Bennett was one of those rare writers.
Admired by contemporaries as a first-rate realist in the great European tradition of
Flaubert and Balzac, his enormous readership made him a wealthy man. His legions of
readers not only admired him; they loved him. As he lay on his death bed in 1931,
Londoners covered busy Baker Street with straw, so that the sick man might not be
disturbed by the sound of traffic.
Click and drag to create table and to draw rows, columns and borders.

Fig. 14.3
The Tables and Borders toolbar mixes essential tools for—you guessed it—tables and borders.

To apply a different line style, weight, or color to an existing border, click the bordered paragraphs, then make your choices on the Tables and Borders toolbar. Click the Borders button again to reapply that last selected border style with the new formatting. For a new border, select the line style, weight, and color, then apply the border with the Borders button palette.

Q&A *Why can't I see my inside border?*

If you try to apply an inside border to a single paragraph, you won't see it. But if you press Enter to split the paragraph in two, or to begin a new paragraph, the inside border appears. Inside borders are only visible in between paragraphs.

What's the difference between a border line and an underline?

One thing about borders you'll notice right away: they're applied to the entire paragraph. Lines and boxes extend all the way from the left paragraph indent to the right indent. If you want to underline only some of a paragraph, select the text and click the Underline button on the Formatting toolbar. Figure 14.4 shows the difference between selected underlined text and a border applied to an entire paragraph.

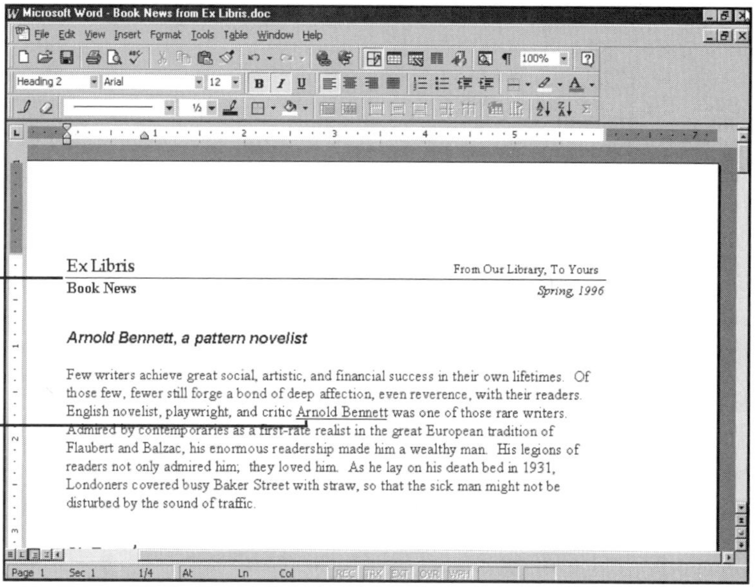
Microsoft Word - Book News from Ex Libris.doc
File Edit View Insert Format Tools Table Window Help
Heading 2
Arial
12
100%
Ex Libris
From Our Library, To Yours
Book News
Spring, 1996
Arnold Bennett, a pattern novelist
Few writers achieve great social, artistic, and financial success in their own lifetimes. Of those few, fewer still forge a bond of deep affection, even reverence, with their readers. English novelist, playwright, and critic Arnold Bennett was one of those rare writers. Admired by contemporaries as a first-rate realist in the great European tradition of Flaubert and Balzac, his enormous readership made him a wealthy man. His legions of readers not only admired him; they loved him. As he lay on his death bed in 1931, Londoners covered busy Baker Street with straw, so that the sick man might not be disturbed by the sound of traffic.
Page 1
Sec 1
1/4
At
Ln
Col
REC
TRK
EXT
OVR
WPH

Fig. 14.4
If you are curious about the difference between borders and underlining, here's the answer: borders are applied to the whole paragraph.

Here's our inside border

This text was selected, then underlined

I don't want a border all the way across the page

Suppose you have a paragraph that extends only part way across the page. You want a border under it, but you don't want a border that extends beyond your text. You could use the Underline button on the Formatting toolbar, except that it gives you the choice of a single thin line under your text, period. Some choice.

TIP **You can change the underline style from the Font dialog box.** Select the text you want underlined, then choose Format, Font. Click the Font tab in the Font dialog box that pops up, and choose an underline style from the Underline drop-down menu. Click OK when you're done.

For more variety, apply a border with your choice of line styles to the paragraph, then adjust the right indent marker to trim the border to fit your text. Figure 14.5 shows you how to do that.

Fig. 14.5
Cutting a border down to size is a simple drag operation.

Drag the right indent marker to the left to fit the border to the text

Click the paragraph, then click the border style or styles you want

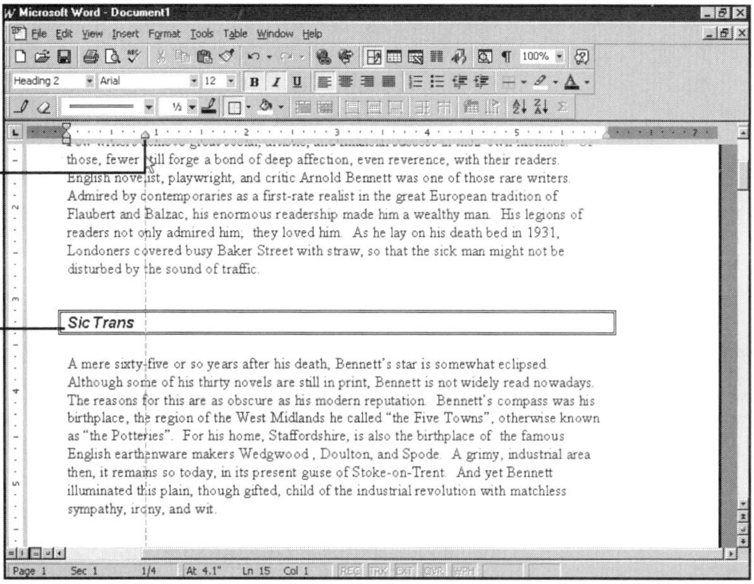
Microsoft Word - Document1
File Edit View Insert Format Tools Table Window Help
Heading 2
Arial
12
100%
those, fewer still forge a bond of deep affection, even reverence, with their readers.
English novelist, playwright, and critic Arnold Bennett was one of those rare writers.
Admired by contemporaries as a first-rate realist in the great European tradition of
Flaubert and Balzac, his enormous readership made him a wealthy man. His legions of
readers not only admired him; they loved him. As he lay on his death bed in 1931,
Londoners covered busy Baker Street with straw, so that the sick man might not be
disturbed by the sound of traffic.
Sic Trans
A mere sixty-five or so years after his death, Bennett's star is somewhat eclipsed.
Although some of his thirty novels are still in print, Bennett is not widely read nowadays.
The reasons for this are as obscure as his modern reputation. Bennett's compass was his
birthplace, the region of the West Midlands he called "the Five Towns", otherwise known
as "the Potteries". For his home, Staffordshire, is also the birthplace of the famous
English earthenware makers Wedgwood , Doulton, and Spode. A grimy, industrial area
then, it remains so today, in its present guise of Stoke-on-Trent. And yet Bennett
illuminated this plain, though gifted, child of the industrial revolution with matchless
sympathy, irony, and wit.
Page 1 Sec 1 1/4 At 4.1" Ln 15 Col 1

When you release the mouse button, you'll see that the border extends only to the right indent marker. With Outside borders, like the one in Figure 14.5, you can also fit the border closer to the text by dragging one of the border lines, as shown in Figure 14.6.

Dragging an outside border line only works within limits. You can't drag a bottom border line past the text inside the border, and you can't drag a right border line to the left much beyond the right indent marker.

If you apply a right border to a short paragraph, the border will look very lonely sitting by itself at the right margin. Just drag the right indent marker to position the border next to the paragraph's text. See Figure 14.7 for a right border dragged alongside a paragraph.

Fig. 14.6
Dragging the right indent marker keeps your borders from extending too far

Drag an outside border line to fit the border closer to (or farther from) the text

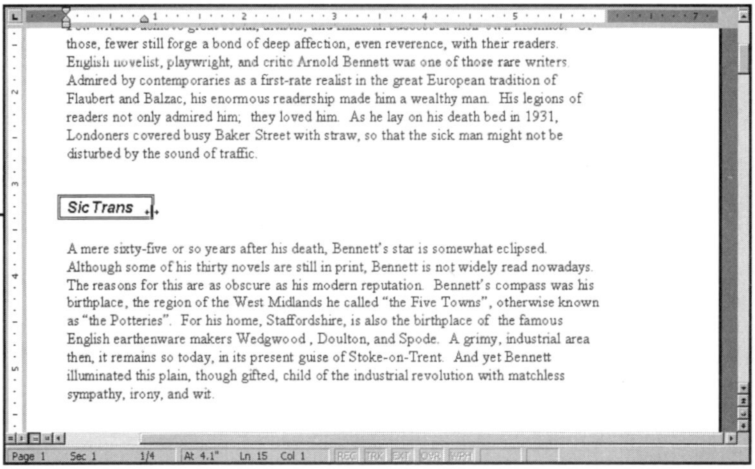
those, fewer still forge a bond of deep affection, even reverence, with their readers. English novelist, playwright, and critic Arnold Bennett was one of those rare writers. Admired by contemporaries as a first-rate realist in the great European tradition of Flaubert and Balzac, his enormous readership made him a wealthy man. His legions of readers not only admired him; they loved him. As he lay on his death bed in 1931, Londoners covered busy Baker Street with straw, so that the sick man might not be disturbed by the sound of traffic.
Sic Trans
A mere sixty-five or so years after his death, Bennett's star is somewhat eclipsed. Although some of his thirty novels are still in print, Bennett is not widely read nowadays. The reasons for this are as obscure as his modern reputation. Bennett's compass was his birthplace, the region of the West Midlands he called "the Five Towns", otherwise known as "the Potteries". For his home, Staffordshire, is also the birthplace of the famous English earthenware makers Wedgwood, Doulton, and Spode. A grimy, industrial area then, it remains so today, in its present guise of Stoke-on-Trent. And yet Bennett illuminated this plain, though gifted, child of the industrial revolution with matchless sympathy, irony, and wit.
Page 1 Sec 1 1/4 At 4.1" Ln 15 Col 1

Too many borders can result in a border incident

Although you have to select paragraphs to apply inside borders, you needn't bother when you apply the other border styles. Just click a paragraph and click a border style on the Borders toolbar.

It's so effortless that you might be tempted to overdo it. As you can see in Figure 14.7, too many borders can spoil the document.

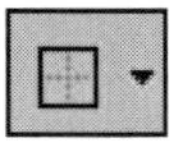

If your document starts to look like the one in Figure 14.7, select the paragraphs with borders and click the No Border button on the Borders palette. That instantly erases unwanted borders.

Q&A ***How do I break out of this box?***

When you add a border and press Enter at the end of the paragraph to start a new one, the border extends to the new paragraph. Right, left, and outside borders expand, and bottom borders get shoved down one line. To avoid that, start the new paragraph first, then apply the border to the previous paragraph. If you've already applied a border and you want a new, borderless paragraph, click the No Border button to clear the border, start the new paragraph, then reapply the border to the previous paragraph.

Fig. 14.7
Click a paragraph, click a border style. What could be easier? But this is a little too much of a good thing.

A right border, positioned next to the short paragraph by dragging the right indent marker

A left border

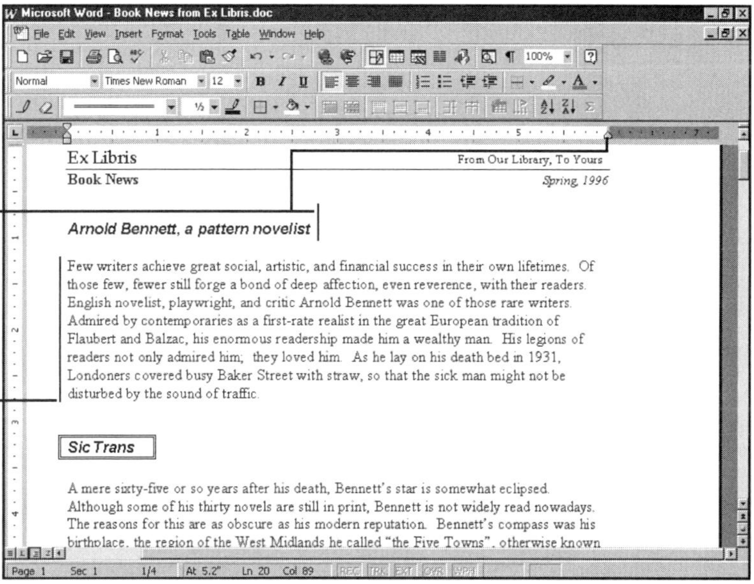
Microsoft Word - Book News from Ex Libris.doc
File Edit View Insert Format Tools Table Window Help
Normal
Times New Roman
12
100%
Ex Libris
From Our Library, To Yours
Book News
Spring, 1996
Arnold Bennett, a pattern novelist
Few writers achieve great social, artistic, and financial success in their own lifetimes. Of those few, fewer still forge a bond of deep affection, even reverence, with their readers. English novelist, playwright, and critic Arnold Bennett was one of those rare writers. Admired by contemporaries as a first-rate realist in the great European tradition of Flaubert and Balzac, his enormous readership made him a wealthy man. His legions of readers not only admired him; they loved him. As he lay on his death bed in 1931, Londoners covered busy Baker Street with straw, so that the sick man might not be disturbed by the sound of traffic.
Sic Trans
A mere sixty-five or so years after his death, Bennett's star is somewhat eclipsed. Although some of his thirty novels are still in print, Bennett is not widely read nowadays. The reasons for this are as obscure as his modern reputation. Bennett's compass was his birthplace, the region of the West Midlands he called "the Five Towns", otherwise known
Page 1 Sec 1 1/4 At 5.2" Ln 20 Col 89

Not-so-dark shadows

Here's a dramatic way to emphasize a paragraph; cast a shadow around it. To get a shadow effect, click the paragraph you want to format, then select Format, Borders and Shading, Borders.

In the Paragraph Borders and Shading dialog box that appears, click Shadow. If you want your paragraph to cast a wider shadow, choose a thicker line style from the Width list, as shown in Figure 14.8.

Fig. 14.8
Check the Preview window for an inkling of the paragraph's appearance.

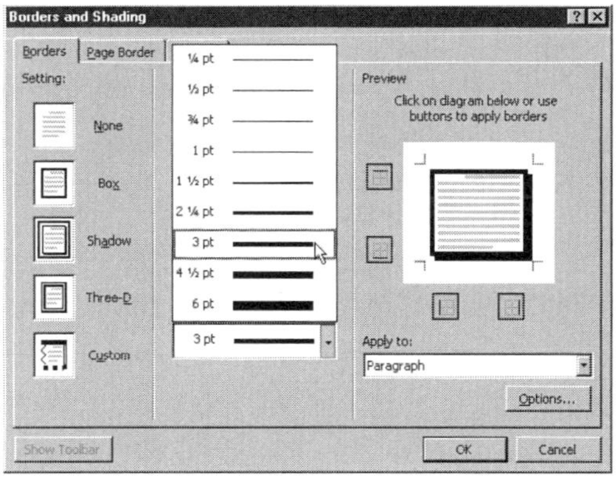
Borders and Shading
Borders
Page Border
Setting:
None
Box
Shadow
Three-D
Custom
¼ pt
½ pt
¾ pt
1 pt
1 ½ pt
2 ¼ pt
3 pt
4 ½ pt
6 pt
3 pt
Preview
Click on diagram below or use buttons to apply borders
Apply to:
Paragraph
Options...
Show Toolbar
OK
Cancel

Figure 14.9 shows a paragraph with a shadow border.

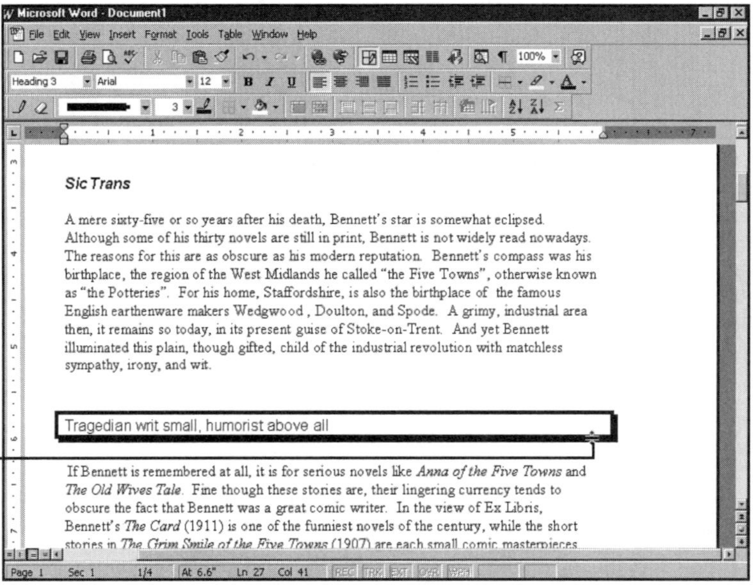
Microsoft Word - Document1
Sic Trans
A mere sixty-five or so years after his death, Bennett's star is somewhat eclipsed. Although some of his thirty novels are still in print, Bennett is not widely read nowadays. The reasons for this are as obscure as his modern reputation. Bennett's compass was his birthplace, the region of the West Midlands he called "the Five Towns", otherwise known as "the Potteries". For his home, Staffordshire, is also the birthplace of the famous English earthenware makers Wedgwood, Doulton, and Spode. A grimy, industrial area then, it remains so today, in its present guise of Stoke-on-Trent. And yet Bennett illuminated this plain, though gifted, child of the industrial revolution with matchless sympathy, irony, and wit.
Tragedian writ small, humorist above all
If Bennett is remembered at all, it is for serious novels like Anna of the Five Towns and The Old Wives Tale. Fine though these stories are, their lingering currency tends to obscure the fact that Bennett was a great comic writer. In the view of Ex Libris, Bennett's The Card (1911) is one of the funniest novels of the century, while the short
Page 1 Sec 1 1/4 At 6.6" Ln 27 Col 41

Fig. 14.9
Shadows create a nifty effect, but I find that a little shadow goes a long way.

Drag here to expand or contract the shadowed box around the paragraph

Shading and color make paragraphs jump off the page

Color printers are pretty common nowadays. If you have one, or if your e-mail system can handle colors, Word makes it easy to splash color on your borders. Even if you don't have a color printer, a combination of shading and a border makes a paragraph stand out:

1 If you don't have the Borders toolbar displayed already, click the Tables and Borders button on the Standard Toolbar, then click the paragraph you want to format.

2 Click the Shading Color drop-down arrow on the Tables and Borders toolbar. A palette of colors and shades appears; click your choice on the palette.

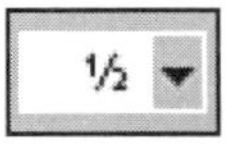
½

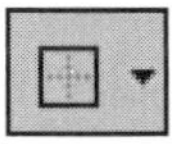

3 Click the Line Weight drop-down arrow and choose a thicker line, then add Top and Bottom borders from the Borders palette. You'll wind up with a paragraph that looks like Figure 14.10.

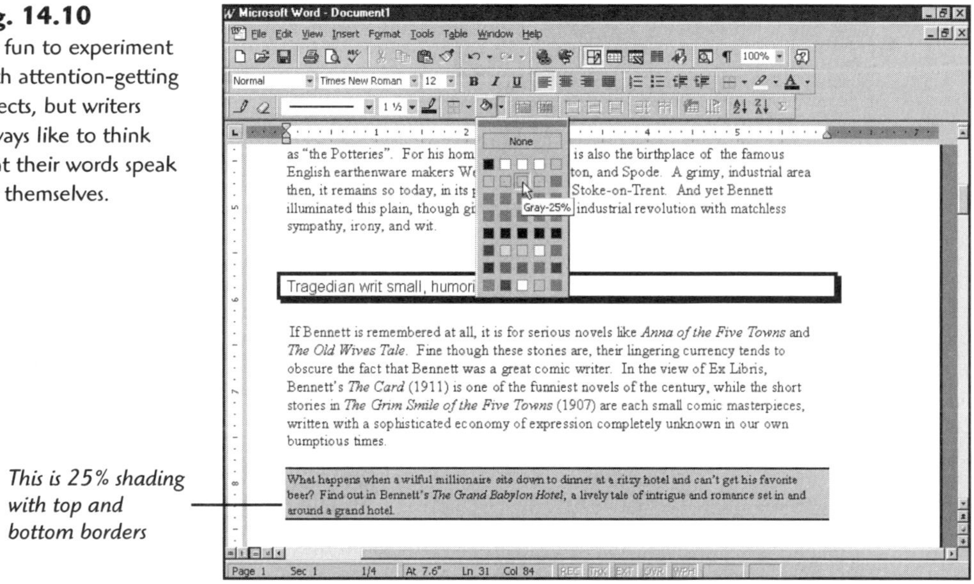
Microsoft Word - Document1
File Edit View Insert Format Tools Table Window Help
100%
Normal
Times New Roman
12
None
Gray-25%
as "the Potteries". For his hom
is also the birthplace of the famous
English earthenware makers W
ton, and Spode. A grimy, industrial area
then, it remains so today, in its
Stoke-on-Trent. And yet Bennett
illuminated this plain, though g
industrial revolution with matchless
sympathy, irony, and wit.
Tragedian writ small, humori
If Bennett is remembered at all, it is for serious novels like Anna of the Five Towns and The Old Wives Tale. Fine though these stories are, their lingering currency tends to obscure the fact that Bennett was a great comic writer. In the view of Ex Libris, Bennett's The Card (1911) is one of the funniest novels of the century, while the short stories in The Grim Smile of the Five Towns (1907) are each small comic masterpieces, written with a sophisticated economy of expression completely unknown in our own bumptious times.
What happens when a wilful millionaire sits down to dinner at a ritzy hotel and can't get his favorite beer? Find out in Bennett's The Grand Babylon Hotel, a lively tale of intrigue and romance set in and around a grand hotel.
Page 1 Sec 1 1/4 At 7.6" Ln 31 Col 84
This is 25% shading with top and bottom borders

Fig. 14.10
It's fun to experiment with attention-getting effects, but writers always like to think that their words speak for themselves.

If you select 80% or more shading and your font color is set to Auto (point at the Font Color button on the Formatting toolbar to check the font color; a ToolTip appears with the current selection), Word automatically switches the font color to white. White text on a dark background makes for a startling effect, but the text might be difficult to read. Try formatting the text in boldface to improve readability.

Q&A *My text looks white on the screen, but it prints as black. Can't I print white text against a shaded background?*

You can. Some printers just need a little help first.

1. Click File, Print. In the Print dialog box, click Properties for the Setup dialog box.
2. Click the Config button in the Setup dialog box, and select the Print as Graphics option on the TrueType Mode drop-down list.
3. Click OK in each dialog box, and your document should print with white text against a shaded background.

This paragraph looks like a sidebar

The shaded paragraph in Figure 14.11 stands out from the rest of the document, in part due to its formatting, but also because the content isn't part of the narrative flow. Passages like that are called **sidebars**, and you see them scattered throughout this book. They're handy for presenting relevant, but ancillary, information.

The Borders toolbar can whip up a quick sidebar (refer to Figure 14.10), but if you want a sidebar you can easily move around the page, and around which you can wrap text, try a Word Text Box. Text Boxes can be sized and formatted any way you like. Text Boxes can also be linked together, so that text begun in one Text Box flows automatically into another when you type past the boundaries of the first box. That's handy if you're laying out a newsletter or report, and you have a sidebar-type story that you want to continue in a box on another page.

To create a Text Box:

1. Click Insert, Text Box. If you're not in Page Layout view, Word switches you automatically, because Text Boxes don't display in Normal View.
2. The pointer turns into a crosshair. Position the crosshair where you'd like your Text Box, and click the left mouse button. That gives you a one-square-inch box. For a different size and shape, put the crosshair at the upper left of where you want your box, and drag to the lower right corner. When you release the mouse button, the box pops up with the insertion point inside it.

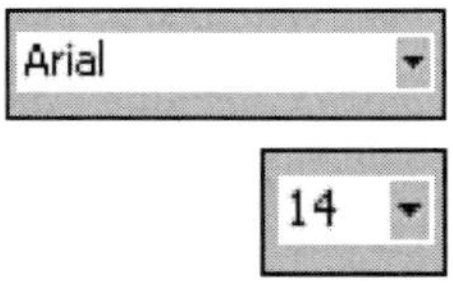

3. Type your text inside the box. All the lines automatically wrap at the box's right margin. Use the Font and Font size buttons on the Formatting toolbar to format the text if you like.
4. If you need to make the box bigger or smaller, click anywhere around the box's border to pop up handles. Drag a handle with the two-headed arrow to expand or shrink the box, as shown in Figure 14.11.

Fig. 14.11
To add or edit the text, just click inside the frame to make the insertion point reappear.

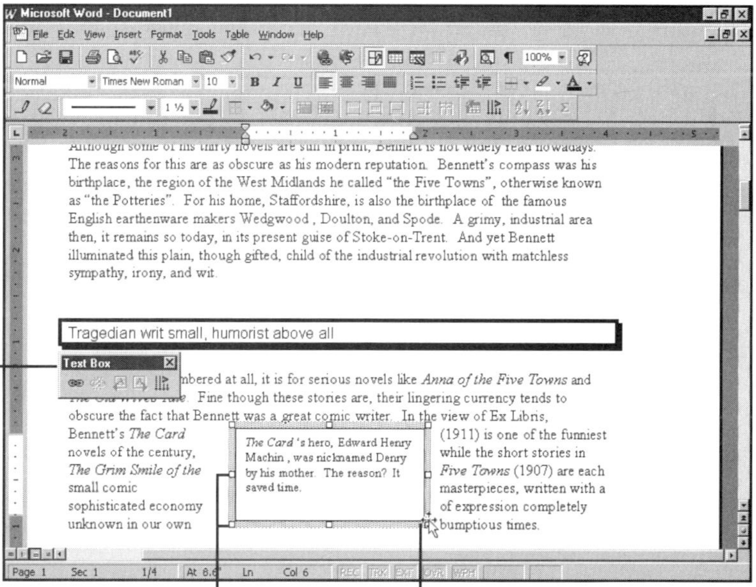
Microsoft Word - Document1
File Edit View Insert Format Tools Table Window Help
Normal
Times New Roman
10
100%
The reasons for this are as obscure as his modern reputation. Bennett's compass was his birthplace, the region of the West Midlands he called "the Five Towns", otherwise known as "the Potteries". For his home, Staffordshire, is also the birthplace of the famous English earthenware makers Wedgwood, Doulton, and Spode. A grimy, industrial area then, it remains so today, in its present guise of Stoke-on-Trent. And yet Bennett illuminated this plain, though gifted, child of the industrial revolution with matchless sympathy, irony, and wit.
Tragedian writ small, humorist above all
Text Box
mbered at all, it is for serious novels like Anna of the Five Towns and
. Fine though these stories are, their lingering currency tends to
obscure the fact that Bennett was a great comic writer. In the view of Ex Libris,
Bennett's The Card
novels of the century,
The Grim Smile of the
small comic
sophisticated economy
unknown in our own
The Card's hero, Edward Henry Machin, was nicknamed Denry by his mother. The reason? It saved time.
(1911) is one of the funniest
while the short stories in
Five Towns (1907) are each
masterpieces, written with a
of expression completely
bumptious times.
Page 1 Sec 1 1/4 At 8.6" Ln Col 6

The Text Box toolbar pops up automatically when you insert a box

Drag any handle to make the box bigger or smaller

Click along here to get the handles

5 If you're creating a sidebar-type box, use the Borders button to add and format borders for text within the box. Sidebars like the ones in this book are often formatted with a top border, or with top and bottom borders. Take your pick from the Borders button palette.

6 To wrap document body text around the box, double-click the box's border to pop up the Format Text Box dialog box. Click the Wrapping tab for the wrap options shown in Figure 14.12.

Fig. 14.12
The Format Text Box dialog offers plenty of options; the one you're most likely to use is Text Wrapping.

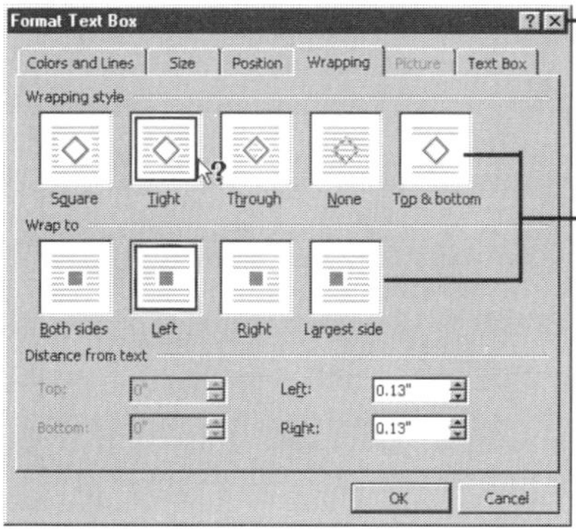
Format Text Box
Colors and Lines
Size
Position
Wrapping
Picture
Text Box
Wrapping style
Square
Tight
Through
None
Top & bottom
Wrap to
Both sides
Left
Right
Largest side
Distance from text
Top:
0"
Bottom:
0"
Left:
0.13"
Right:
0.13"
OK
Cancel

If any of the options aren't clear, click the question mark, then click the option for an explanation

Choose both a Wrapping Style and a side to Wrap to

7 Choose a Wrapping style and the side you'd like text to Wrap to. Try Tight and Left as one possibility; if you don't like the results, return to the Format Text Box dialog and try something else.

8 To change or eliminate the border lines around the box, click the Colors and Lines tab and take your choice among the Line options. If you've added borders to the text within the box, you'll want to get rid of the border lines *around* the box; click the Line Color drop-down arrow and choose No Line to do that.

9 Also on the Colors and Lines tab, click the Fill Color drop-down arrow and make a choice if you want a filled box. When you're finished, click OK in the Format Text Box dialog.

Click anywhere outside the Text Box to get rid of the handles and that fuzzy border. To move the Text Box around the document, point at an edge; your pointer is joined by a four-headed arrow. Now drag the box anywhere you want to.

When you're through typing, formatting, and dragging, you'll wind up with something that looks like Figure 14.13.

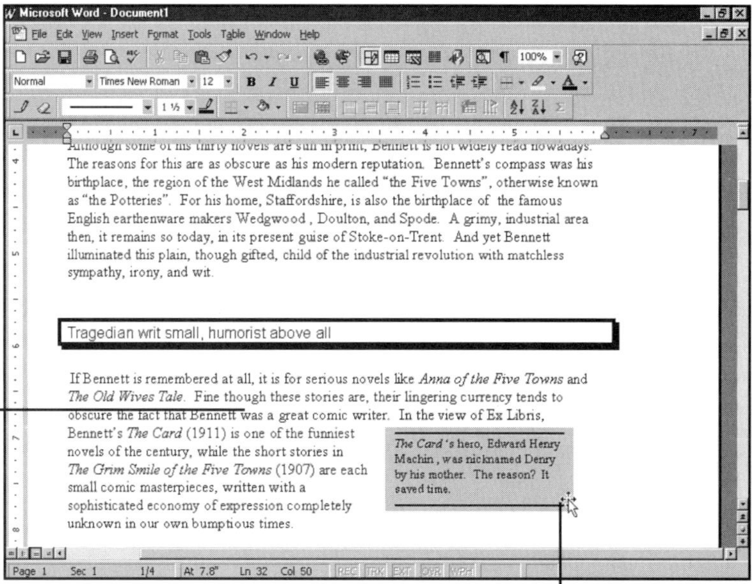
Microsoft Word - Document1
File Edit View Insert Format Tools Table Window Help
Normal
Times New Roman
12
100%
The reasons for this are as obscure as his modern reputation. Bennett's compass was his birthplace, the region of the West Midlands he called "the Five Towns", otherwise known as "the Potteries". For his home, Staffordshire, is also the birthplace of the famous English earthenware makers Wedgwood, Doulton, and Spode. A grimy, industrial area then, it remains so today, in its present guise of Stoke-on-Trent. And yet Bennett illuminated this plain, though gifted, child of the industrial revolution with matchless sympathy, irony, and wit.
Tragedian writ small, humorist above all
If Bennett is remembered at all, it is for serious novels like Anna of the Five Towns and The Old Wives Tale. Fine though these stories are, their lingering currency tends to obscure the fact that Bennett was a great comic writer. In the view of Ex Libris, Bennett's The Card (1911) is one of the funniest novels of the century, while the short stories in The Grim Smile of the Five Towns (1907) are each small comic masterpieces, written with a sophisticated economy of expression completely unknown in our own bumptious times.
The Card's hero, Edward Henry Machin, was nicknamed Denry by his mother. The reason? It saved time.
Page 1 Sec 1 1/4 At 7.8" Ln 32 Col 50

Fig. 14.13
Text Boxes are easy to create, and they're handy for squeezing in extra information.

The Text Box toolbar and the box handles disappear when you click outside the box

Point at an edge and drag with the four-headed arrow to move the box

For text that jumps from box to box, Linked Text Boxes.

We're in the middle of a gripping newspaper story, and right at the climax we read, "Please turn to page D12." Newspapers don't do that to aggravate readers, but for reasons of space (although it is aggravating indeed when the paper leaves out page D12 entirely). A newspaper can cram only so many stories onto the front page, and to fit in as many as possible, front page stories "jump" to the inside pages.

With linked Text Boxes, you can do the same thing in your Word documents. If space is tight on the first page of a newsletter, for example, you can begin the text of a story in a box on page one, link it to a second box on an inside page, and the text will automatically continue into the second box when you fill up the first one.

To create linked Text Boxes:

1. Click Insert, Text Box and click or drag the crosshair to create your first box.
2. Click Insert, Text Box and click or drag the crosshair to create your second box.

3. Click the first text box to select it, then click the Create Text Box Link button on the Text Box toolbar. The pointer turns into a little pitcher. Move the pointer into the second text box, and the pitcher pours its contents, as seen in Figure 14.14.
4. Click the second box with the spilling pitcher, and the Text Box link is established. When text fills up the first box, it flows automatically into the second box, as seen in Figure 14.15.

Q&A ***How come I don't see the Text Box toolbar?***

It should appear automatically when you insert a Text Box. If you don't see the Text Box toolbar when you insert a box, first click the box to select it. Then click View, Toolbars, Text Box to pop up the Text Box toolbar. You'll see the Text Box choice on the View, Toolbars menu only if a Text Box is selected.

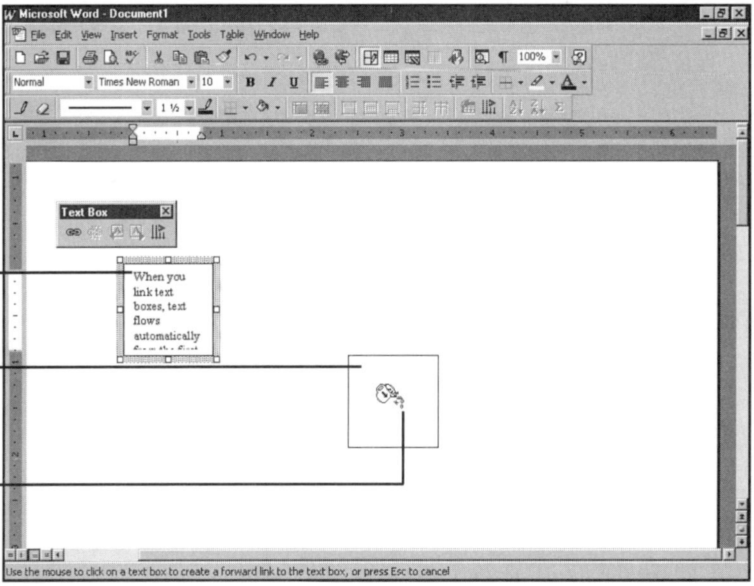

Fig. 14.14
When your pitcher appears to be pouring, you're about to set up your Text Box link.

Here's the first text box

This is the second text box

After the first box is selected and the Create Text Box Link button is clicked, the pitcher spills into the second box

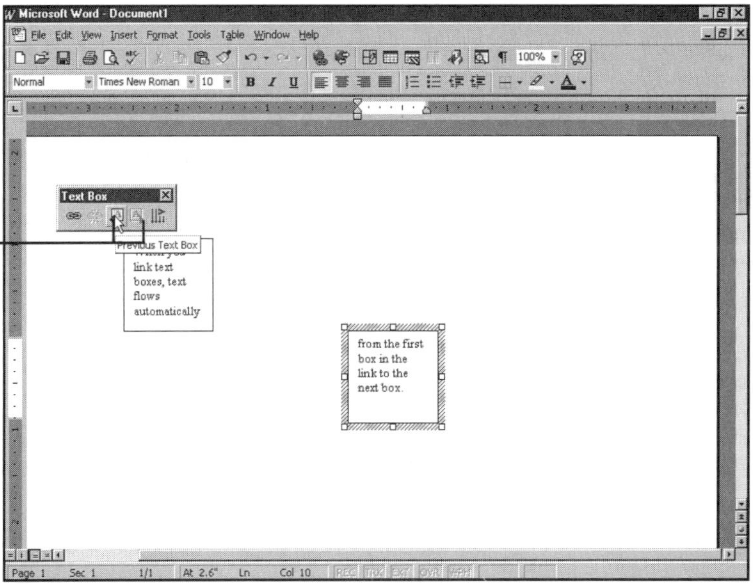

Fig. 14.15
Like a water clock, text pours from one box to another in Linked Text Boxes.

Click these buttons to move from box to box, handy if your linked boxes are on different pages

CAUTION **Formatting that you've applied to text within a linked text box** flows into the other boxes in the linked chain, right along with the text. So if you have a bottom border for your text in the first box, the border will be pushed into the second box. That's one good reason not to use bottom borders in linked text boxes.

Less is more: use white space for readable documents

Word provides many ways to jazz up documents. Borders, shading, Text Boxes—they're all great gadgets. But at the end of the day, you want a document that's a pleasure to read. After you've experimented with Word's fancy effects, you might find that adding a little white space gives you a more readable document.

The default right, left, top, and bottom margins that Word provides are probably fine for most uses. But if you want more white space around your document, just drag the margin boundaries at either end of the rulers.

TIP **If margin exactitude is required, double-click the margin** boundaries to pop up the Margins dialog box. That lets you set your margins within hundredths of an inch.

Adding more white space within the text of the document is like drawing open a window shade; you let in a little light. Here are two quick things you can do to add more white space:

- Add a blank line after all your paragraphs, including headings and subheadings. Just press Enter at the end of the last line in the paragraph.
- Increase **line spacing** (the blank space between the lines) from a single line to 1.5 lines. Select the paragraphs in which you want more white space. Then click Format, Paragraph, Indents and Spacing in the Indents and Spacing dialog box. Click the Line Spacing drop-down arrow and select 1.5 Lines.

TIP **If you set line spacing at 1.5 lines at the beginning of a new** document, you don't have to bother selecting the paragraphs first. If you've already written the document and you want line spacing of 1.5 lines for the whole thing, click Edit, Select All, then change the spacing.

Need a typesetter? It's you!

Many good page design artists and typesetters feel that the best-designed page is one in which the design elements are invisible. Not that they don't want the reader to read what's on the page. The idea is to make a readable page in which the reader is unaware of all the hard work that went into making it so.

Theirs is a specialized craft, with all the trappings of specialties—arcane jargon and painstaking technique. Word puts some of those techniques in the hands of the non-specialist. Once you get a handle on the jargon, using the features is a snap.

Look closely, and you kern see extra spacing

No, that's not a typo up there. **Kerning** is the typesetter's trick of adjusting the spacing between letter pairs to compensate for the different shapes of letters. Computers don't necessarily do that, which can result in extra space between certain letters. It's especially noticeable in large font sizes, as you can see in Figure 14.16.

If you're working with large font sizes, in a title for example, and these spacing problems bug you, Word gives you two ways to fix the problem.

Automatic kerning works with proportionally spaced TrueType fonts such as Times New Roman. If that's what you've got, try automatic kerning first:

1. Select the characters whose spacing you want to adjust.
2. Click Format, Font, Character Spacing for the Character Spacing dialog box.
3. Click the Kerning For Fonts check box and click OK.

If you're starting a new document and you plan to work with large font sizes, click the Kerning For Fonts check box before you begin typing.

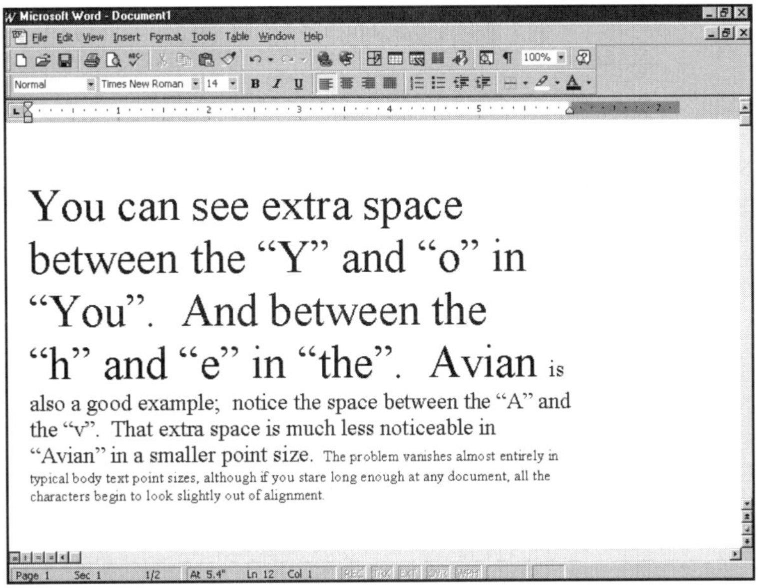
Microsoft Word - Document1
File Edit View Insert Format Tools Table Window Help
You can see extra space between the "Y" and "o" in "You". And between the "h" and "e" in "the". Avian is also a good example; notice the space between the "A" and the "v". That extra space is much less noticeable in "Avian" in a smaller point size. The problem vanishes almost entirely in typical body text point sizes, although if you stare long enough at any document, all the characters begin to look slightly out of alignment.

Fig. 14.16
Certain letter pairs in different fonts are prone to kerning problems.

Character spacing, for the typographical perfectionist

Automatic kerning doesn't work for all fonts, and the adjustment it makes is very slight. If you'd prefer to take matters into your own hands, use the Spacing option in the Character Spacing dialog box to force the issue.

Select the characters whose spacing you want to adjust and click Format, Font, Character Spacing for the Character Spacing tab of the Font dialog box. Click the Spacing drop-down arrow and select Condensed. Now click the down arrow in the By edit box to bring the selected letters closer together one tenth of a point at a time.

15 Picture This! Documents with Graphics

In this chapter:

- Where do I find Word's artwork?
- How do I insert this image in my document?
- I need to move and resize a picture
- Can I wrap text around a graphic?
- How do I put text inside a picture?
- Shadow and 3-D effects in a document? Why not!

A pick-me-up for dull documents, pictures can spice up even lively text. And if words, not pictures, are your bag, it's no problem. Word puts artwork within reach of nonartists . . .

Where art is concerned, everyone's a critic. Take Michelangelo's *David*. It's probably the most famous statue in the world; people travel to Florence just for a glimpse of it. *David* inspires a hush in even the loudest tourist.

Artwork you stick in a Word document probably won't inspire any reverential hushes. On the other hand, if any important critics object to your work, Word makes it easy to do alterations. And you can silence even the toughest critic with a simple dodge that Michelangelo couldn't have dreamed of: Just click the graphic, press Delete, and insert something else.

Where is Word's artwork, and how do I view it?

You don't have to be a great artist to insert pictures in a Word document. In fact, you don't have to be an artist at all. Word comes with a gallery of *clip art* images—small pictures and decorations that you can put right in your documents. Use clip art for logos, posters, or simply to jazz up a report.

When you installed Word, you also installed a folder packed with clip art images called—no surprises here—Clipart. Depending on the installation you chose (Custom or Typical), the bulk of Word's clip art might have remained on the Word or Office CD-ROM. In a typical installation, for example, only a fraction of Word's clip art is installed on your hard disk; the rest is stored on the CD.

If you want to browse all the available clip art, insert your Word or Office CD in your CD-ROM drive first. Then, click Insert, Picture, Clip Art. That pops up the Microsoft Clip Gallery 3.0 dialog box, with previews of Word's clip art files on both CD and hard drive. Select a category in the Microsoft Clip Gallery 3.0 dialog box, then scroll through the previews of clip art images, as shown in Figure 15.1.

If you see an image you like, double-click it. That pops the image right into your document at the insertion point.

Fig. 15.1
The Clip Gallery automatically tracks down graphics files on hard drive and CD and lists them in the dialog box.

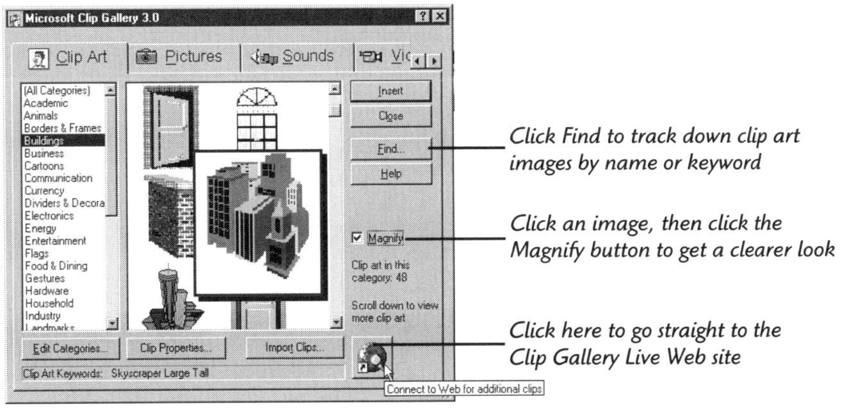

Want more clip art? Visit the Clip Gallery Live

Word includes hundreds of clip art images, but if you can't find exactly the image you want, hundreds more are available on the World Wide Web. The Microsoft Clip Gallery Live Web site has loads of additional photos, sound clips, videos, and images that you can download and add to the Microsoft Clip Gallery 3.0.

You'll need to have an account with an Internet provider (the Microsoft Network, for example), and either the Microsoft Internet Explorer 3.0 or Netscape 2.0 or later installed. If you have both an Internet account and either of the Web browsers, click the Connect to Web button in the Microsoft Clip Gallery 3.0 dialog box. You'll be connected to the Clip Gallery Live Web site automatically (see Figure 15.2).

Once connected to the Clip Gallery Live, choose either Browse or Search, and then click Go. Once you locate the Clip Art image you want, click the file name below the thumbnail of the image. If your browser prompts you to Open or Save the image, choose Open.

The selected image is automatically downloaded and added to the images on your hard drive. The next time you want that image, you don't have to reconnect to the Clip Gallery Live. You'll find your downloaded image installed with all the existing art work in the Microsoft Clip Gallery 3.0, in a new category called Downloaded Clips.

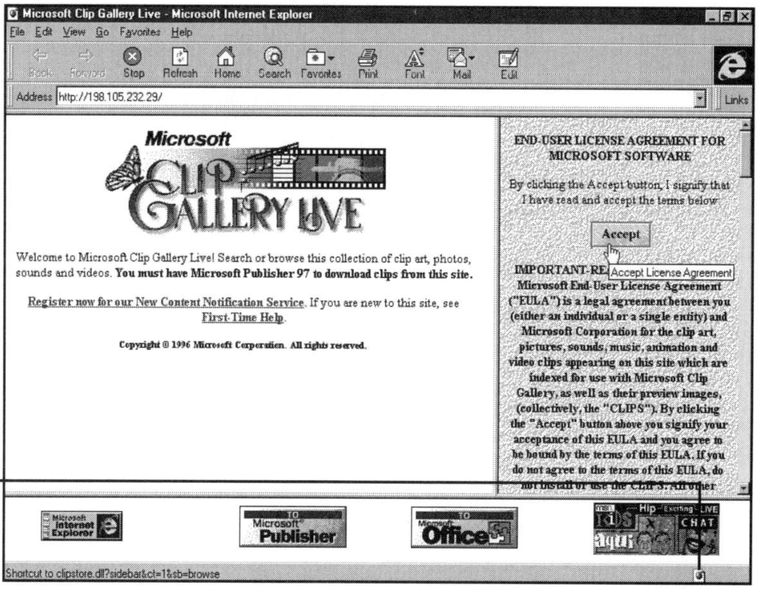
Microsoft Clip Gallery Live - Microsoft Internet Explorer
File Edit View Go Favorites Help
Back Forward Stop Refresh Home Search Favorites Print Font Mail Edit
Address http://198.105.232.29/
Links
Microsoft
CLIP GALLERY LIVE
Welcome to Microsoft Clip Gallery Live! Search or browse this collection of clip art, photos, sounds and videos. You must have Microsoft Publisher 97 to download clips from this site.
Register now for our New Content Notification Service. If you are new to this site, see First-Time Help.
Copyright © 1996 Microsoft Corporation. All rights reserved.
END-USER LICENSE AGREEMENT FOR MICROSOFT SOFTWARE
By clicking the Accept button, I signify that I have read and accept the terms below.
Accept
Accept License Agreement
Microsoft End-User License Agreement ("EULA") is a legal agreement between you (either an individual or a single entity) and Microsoft Corporation for the clip art, pictures, sounds, music, animation and video clips appearing on this site which are indexed for use with Microsoft Clip Gallery, as well as their preview images, (collectively, the "CLIPS"). By clicking the "Accept" button above you signify your acceptance of this EULA and you agree to be bound by the terms of this EULA. If you do not agree to the terms of this EULA, do
Microsoft Internet Explorer
Microsoft Publisher
Office
CHAT
Shortcut to clipstore.dll?sidebar&ct=1&sb=browse

Fig. 15.2
Microsoft's Clip Gallery Live Web site has a vast collection of document-enhancing clip art to download.

Click the Accept button to accept the license terms and access the Clip Gallery Live's clip art

CAUTION **Inserted graphics vastly increase the size of any document, an** important consideration for World Wide Web document publishers. Although graphics on a Web page will catch the eye of passing readers, they also slow the loading of the page into a Web browser. If you're planning to include graphics in a Web page, or in a Word document that you convert to HTML for posting on the Web, don't overdo it. More than a couple of graphics on the page may lose you readers too impatient to wait for the page to load.

What do I do with this image?

You can pop a clip art image into an existing document, or into a new file. Either way, it's easy to move and resize the inserted image.

To insert a clip art image into a document, resize it and move it into position:

1 Position the insertion point where you want your image to appear (you don't have to be precise about location, because you can move the graphic around later) and select Insert, Picture, Clip Art.

2 That gets you the Microsoft Clip Gallery 3.0 dialog box (refer to Figure 15.1). Double-click any of the thumbnail images to stick the image itself into your document.

3 Just like text inserted into a document, inserted images push existing text aside to make room. If you find that your document's spacing and alignment are out of whack after you insert a picture, resize and move it. Point at any of the handles and the pointer turns into a double-headed arrow. Now drag to resize the image, as shown in Figure 15.3.

TIP **Inserted images appear with the sizing handles displayed. If you** lose the handles (by clicking outside the image or pressing Esc), just click the image to make the handles reappear.

Fig. 15.3
If inserted clip art images are too large (or small) for your purposes, resize them.

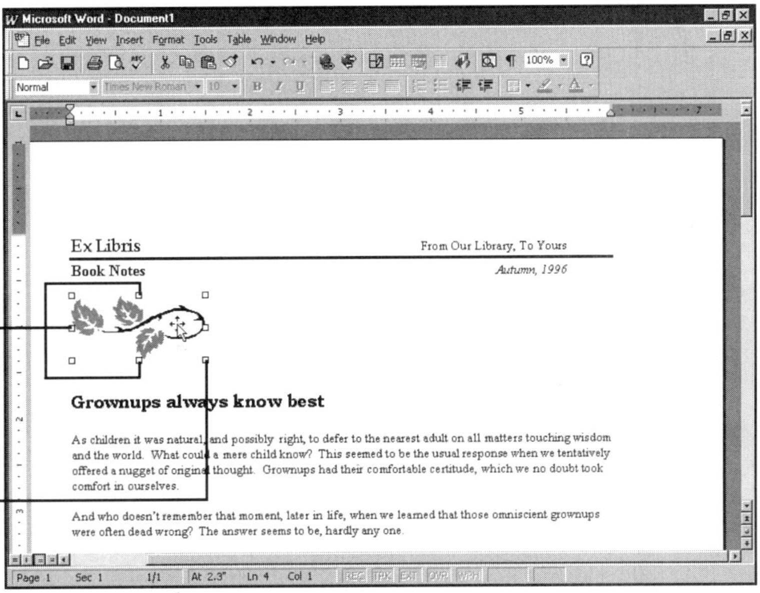
Microsoft Word - Document1
Ex Libris
From Our Library, To Yours
Book Notes
Autumn, 1996
Grownups always know best
As children it was natural, and possibly right, to defer to the nearest adult on all matters touching wisdom and the world. What could a mere child know? This seemed to be the usual response when we tentatively offered a nugget of original thought. Grownups had their comfortable certitude, which we no doubt took comfort in ourselves.
And who doesn't remember that moment, later in life, when we learned that those omniscient grownups were often dead wrong? The answer seems to be, hardly any one.
Drag one of the middle handles to stretch the image up, down, or sideways
Drag a corner handle to resize the image and keep the original proportions

4 To move the image, point at the image and drag with the four-headed arrow.

After all this, you might decide against inserting that graphic after all. To get rid of it fast, click the image once to pop up the handles. Then press Delete to instantly excise it from the document.

Really indecisive? Click the Undo button on the Standard toolbar to get just-deleted graphics back again.

I need to move this image to page 50!

Dragging is a convenient way to move things around in a Word document, but for long-distance moves, use the Cut and Paste buttons on the Standard toolbar.

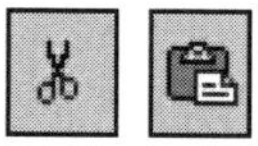

Click the image to select it, then click the Cut button. Move the insertion point to the new location, click the Paste button, and the graphic pops into place.

Want to marry text to image? Wrap it

Moving and resizing clip art is easy to do, but it'll only get you so far toward an attractive document. You'll also want to fit the text in your document to your newly inserted image. There's no need for drastic alterations; all you do is *wrap* text around the image. That fits the words to the picture in a way that makes the picture look like it really belongs on the page.

To wrap text around an inserted clip art image:

1 Right-click the graphic and choose Format Object (see Figure 15.4).

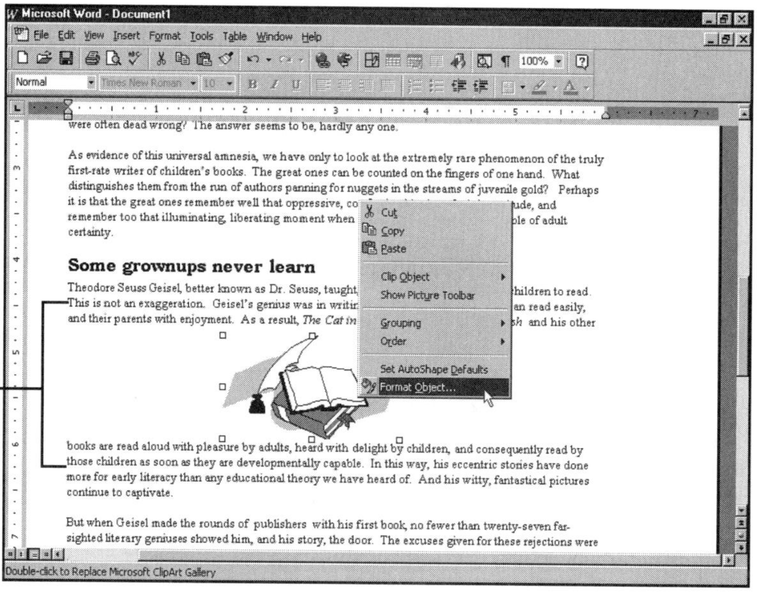
Microsoft Word - Document1
File Edit View Insert Format Tools Table Window Help
Normal
100%
were often dead wrong? The answer seems to be, hardly any one.
As evidence of this universal amnesia, we have only to look at the extremely rare phenomenon of the truly first-rate writer of children's books. The great ones can be counted on the fingers of one hand. What distinguishes them from the run of authors panning for nuggets in the streams of juvenile gold? Perhaps it is that the great ones remember well that oppressive, co
ude, and
remember too that illuminating, liberating moment when
ble of adult
certainty.
Some grownups never learn
Theodore Seuss Geisel, better known as Dr. Seuss, taught,
hildren to read.
This is not an exaggeration. Geisel's genius was in writin
an read easily,
and their parents with enjoyment. As a result, The Cat in
h and his other
Cut
Copy
Paste
Clip Object
Show Picture Toolbar
Grouping
Order
Set AutoShape Defaults
Format Object...
books are read aloud with pleasure by adults, heard with delight by children, and consequently read by those children as soon as they are developmentally capable. In this way, his eccentric stories have done more for early literacy than any educational theory we have heard of. And his witty, fantastical pictures continue to captivate.
But when Geisel made the rounds of publishers with his first book, no fewer than twenty-seven far-sighted literary geniuses showed him, and his story, the door. The excuses given for these rejections were
Double-click to Replace Microsoft ClipArt Gallery

Fig. 15.4
Inserting graphics images in body text can do odd things to text alignment.

The inserted image pushes this text out of whack

2 In the Format Object dialog box that appears, click the Wrapping tab shown in Figure 15.5.

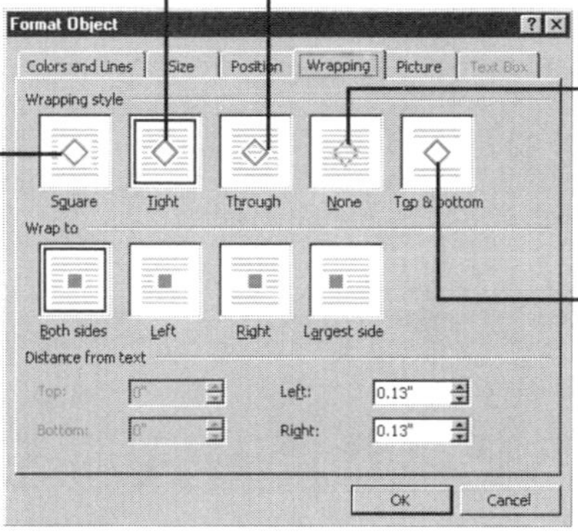
The text follows the contours of the graphic
Lines of text stop at, then continue past, the graphic
Places the graphic over the text
The default setting puts text above and below the graphic
Squares off the text next to, above, and below the graphic
Format Object
Colors and Lines
Size
Position
Wrapping
Picture
Text Box
Wrapping style
Square
Tight
Through
None
Top & bottom
Wrap to
Both sides
Left
Right
Largest side
Distance from text
Top:
Bottom:
Left:
Right:
0.13"
0.13"
OK
Cancel

Fig. 15.5
Text wrapping lets you arrange text around, on either side of, or even under your graphic.

3 Choose Wrapping Style and Wrap To options in the Wrapping tab of the Format Object dialog box. Figure 15.6 shows text wrapped with the Tight and Both Sides options.

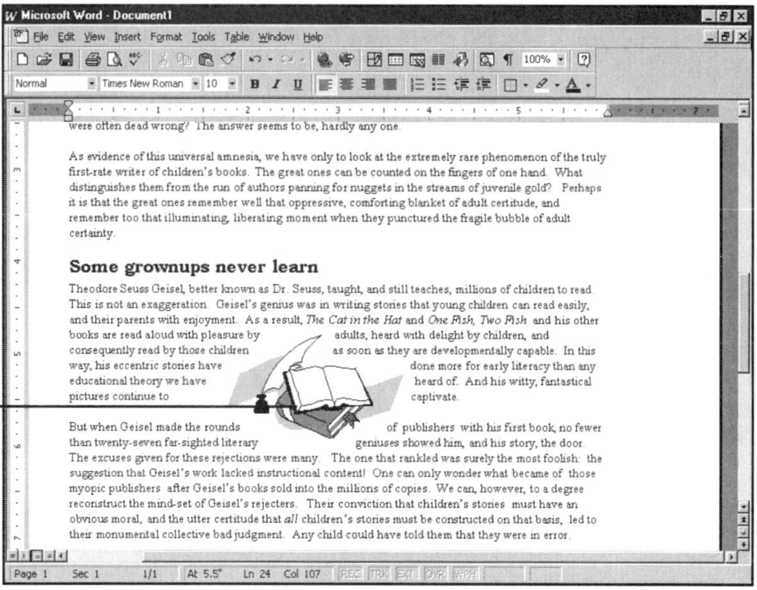
Microsoft Word - Document1
File Edit View Insert Format Tools Table Window Help
Normal
Times New Roman
10
were often dead wrong? The answer seems to be, hardly any one.
As evidence of this universal amnesia, we have only to look at the extremely rare phenomenon of the truly first-rate writer of children's books. The great ones can be counted on the fingers of one hand. What distinguishes them from the run of authors panning for nuggets in the streams of juvenile gold? Perhaps it is that the great ones remember well that oppressive, comforting blanket of adult certitude, and remember too that illuminating, liberating moment when they punctured the fragile bubble of adult certainty.
Some grownups never learn
Theodore Seuss Geisel, better known as Dr. Seuss, taught, and still teaches, millions of children to read. This is not an exaggeration. Geisel's genius was in writing stories that young children can read easily, and their parents with enjoyment. As a result, The Cat in the Hat and One Fish, Two Fish and his other books are read aloud with pleasure by adults, heard with delight by children, and consequently read by those children as soon as they are developmentally capable. In this way, his eccentric stories have done more for early literacy than any educational theory we have heard of. And his witty, fantastical pictures continue to captivate.
But when Geisel made the rounds of publishers with his first book, no fewer than twenty-seven far-sighted literary geniuses showed him, and his story, the door. The excuses given for these rejections were many. The one that rankled was surely the most foolish: the suggestion that Geisel's work lacked instructional content! One can only wonder what became of those myopic publishers after Geisel's books sold into the millions of copies. We can, however, to a degree reconstruct the mind-set of Geisel's rejecters. Their conviction that children's stories must have an obvious moral, and the utter certitude that all children's stories must be constructed on that basis, led to their monumental collective bad judgment. Any child could have told them that they were in error.
Page 1 Sec 1 1/1 At 5.5" Ln 24 Col 107
Text wrapped in the Tight style follows the shape of the image

Fig. 15.6
Text wrapped on both sides of a graphic in the Tight style contours the text around the graphic.

4 Text contoured around an image looks dramatic, but might make the text more difficult to read. For a more formal looking document, try the Square and Left options and click OK, for the result seen in Figure 15.7.

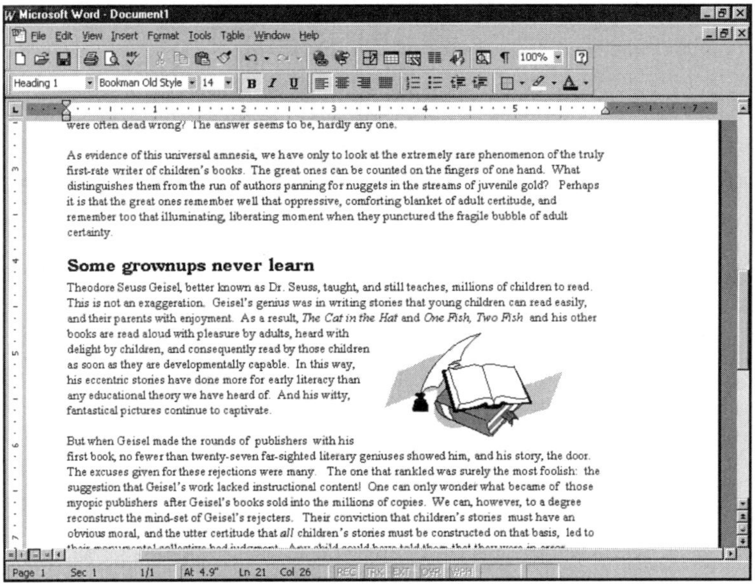
Microsoft Word - Document1
File Edit View Insert Format Tools Table Window Help
Heading 1
Bookman Old Style
14
100%
were often dead wrong? The answer seems to be, hardly any one.
As evidence of this universal amnesia, we have only to look at the extremely rare phenomenon of the truly first-rate writer of children's books. The great ones can be counted on the fingers of one hand. What distinguishes them from the run of authors panning for nuggets in the streams of juvenile gold? Perhaps it is that the great ones remember well that oppressive, comforting blanket of adult certitude, and remember too that illuminating, liberating moment when they punctured the fragile bubble of adult certainty.
Some grownups never learn
Theodore Seuss Geisel, better known as Dr. Seuss, taught, and still teaches, millions of children to read. This is not an exaggeration. Geisel's genius was in writing stories that young children can read easily, and their parents with enjoyment. As a result, The Cat in the Hat and One Fish, Two Fish and his other books are read aloud with pleasure by adults, heard with delight by children, and consequently read by those children as soon as they are developmentally capable. In this way, his eccentric stories have done more for early literacy than any educational theory we have heard of. And his witty, fantastical pictures continue to captivate.
But when Geisel made the rounds of publishers with his first book, no fewer than twenty-seven far-sighted literary geniuses showed him, and his story, the door. The excuses given for these rejections were many. The one that rankled was surely the most foolish: the suggestion that Geisel's work lacked instructional content! One can only wonder what became of those myopic publishers after Geisel's books sold into the millions of copies. We can, however, to a degree reconstruct the mind-set of Geisel's rejecters. Their conviction that children's stories must have an obvious moral, and the utter certitude that all children's stories must be constructed on that basis, led to
Page 1 Sec 1 1/1 At 4.9" Ln 21 Col 26 REC TRK EXT OVR WPH

Fig. 15.7
Text that's squared off against the left side of an image might be the most readable choice. Once you've settled on your text wrapping options, click OK in the Format Object dialog box. If you decide to move or resize the picture, text will wrap in the way you've selected wherever the picture moves. Click anywhere outside the graphic to get rid of the handles.

Q&A ***I returned to Normal View and now my picture's disappeared!***

It hasn't really disappeared, it's just out of sight. Graphics don't display in Normal View. Click the Page Layout view button in the status bar to redisplay your image.

This picture needs some minor alterations

The images in the Clip Art Gallery come already drawn, colored, and composed. That makes them ready-to-use, hence convenient. On the other hand, those instant, pre-fab clip art images might not be exactly to your taste.

If your inserted artwork is too bright, or too dark, or seems wanting in some other way, right-click the picture and choose Show Picture Toolbar on the shortcut menu. The Picture Toolbar appears, with a bundle of handy tools to alter an inserted graphic.

Here's one possible use for the Picture Toolbar: cropping white space from around an image. Many of the Clip Gallery pictures have excess space around them, which can make for unsightly gaps in a document. To get rid of some of that excess, click the Crop tool on the Picture Toolbar and drag a handle towards the center of the image. If you go too far and cut off some of the image itself, just drag the Crop tool back in the other direction (see Figure 15.8).

Fig. 15.8
The Crop tool only works if you drag a handle; dragging anywhere else will simply move the image.

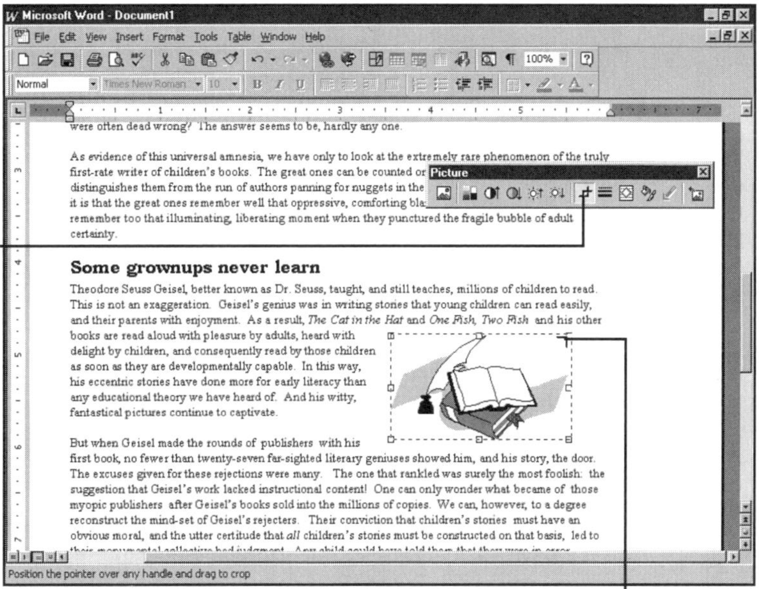

Click the Crop tool on the Picture Toolbar

Then drag a handle toward the center of the image to eliminate unwanted white space

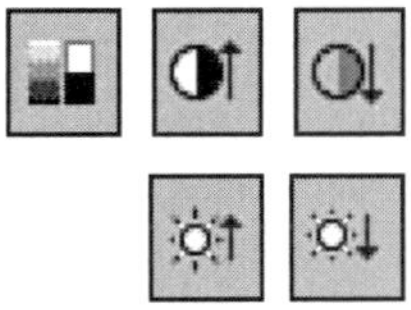

Click the contrast and brightness buttons on the Picture Toolbar to adjust the appearance of a picture. The Image Control button lets you convert color pictures to black and white or grayscale. For a border around your clip art, click the Line Style button and choose one of the many different lines.

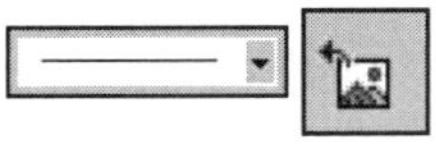

And if you find that all your modifications made the picture worse, not better, click the Reset Picture button to restore the image to its original state.

This picture needs major alterations!

The graphic artists responsible for creating the images in Word's clip art library spent a lot of time putting those pictures together. In seconds, you can disassemble, rearrange, color, and completely redo their good work.

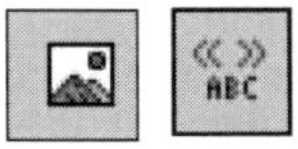

To edit a clip art image, insert it as a file, not from the Microsoft Clip Gallery 3.0. Click Insert, Picture, From File (or click the Insert Picture button on the Picture Toolbar). Either way, you get the Insert Picture dialog box, with a list of clip art images in editable file form. They're the same images you'll find in the Clip Gallery, but you're inserting them in a different format. To preview the image files, click the Preview button in the Insert Picture dialog box.

Select the image you want in the Insert Picture dialog box, then click Insert. That pops the image into your document. Now double-click the inserted image to summon up Word's built-in drawing program. The Drawing toolbar appears automatically at the top of the editing window, as shown in Figure 15.9.

Click Close Picture when you're finished editing

Click in here, then type a caption for your picture if you want one

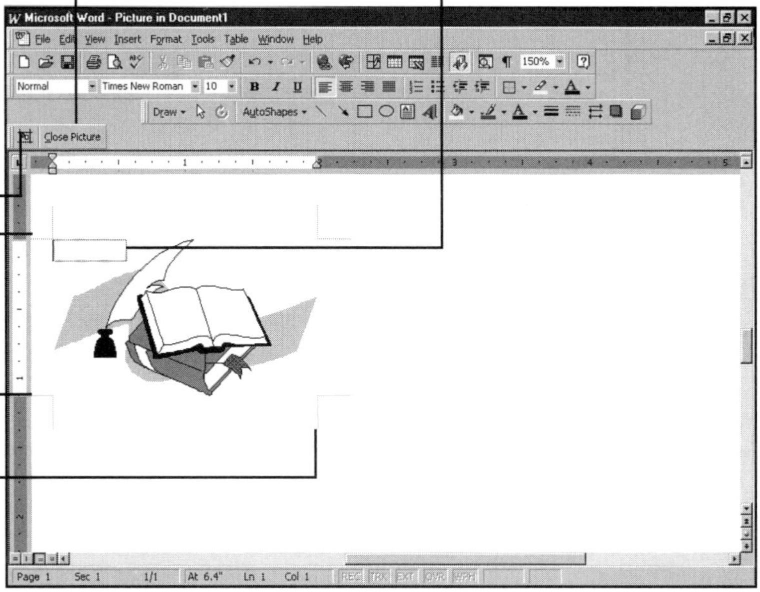

Fig. 15.9
The surrounding document disappears from view. It's still there, just hidden.

Adding, moving, or deleting objects can change the picture's size; click Reset Picture Boundary to fit the boundary to the changes

These lines are the Picture Boundary

Pull apart the old picture to get a new one

The graphic in Figure 15.8 is actually composed of many different objects. Each of those objects can be resized, moved, deleted, or copied. Click anything in the picture; one of the books, for example, or the quill pen. Handles pop up around the selected object, and you can do whatever you want to it.

Figure 15.10 shows the image disassembled, with its component objects dragged outside the picture boundary.

Fig. 15.10
This should appeal to the kid in anyone—pulling clip art apart is like tearing up an old coloring book.

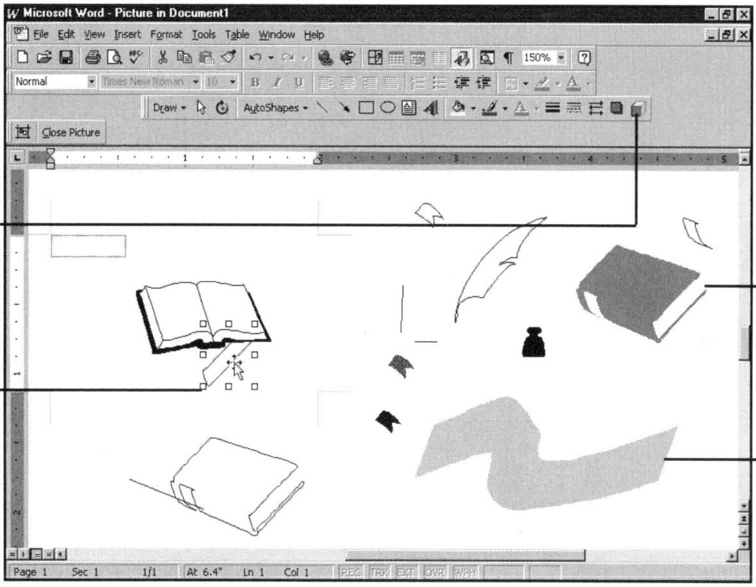

The Drawing toolbar has tools to change the object's fill color, orientation, and other attributes

Click an object to select it; the handles pop up

Drag an object out of the picture boundary, and it'll be left out of the picture

TIP **To select filled objects, like the ink well in Figure 15.10, just click** anywhere in the object. Select unfilled objects, like the feather, by clicking anywhere along their exterior lines.

Any object left outside the picture boundary will be left out of the picture itself when you return to the document. That's handy if you're not sure whether you want to keep one element of the image or not. Instead of deleting it right off the bat (press Delete to do that), just drag it outside the boundary and leave it until you make up your mind.

I want this image behind my text

Once disassembled, use the bits and pieces of a clip art image any way you like. One handy use: putting an image behind your text. You might want to create a *logo*, for example, with a company name on top of a section of a picture.

To put text inside a picture:

1. Click Insert, Picture, From File in the Insert Picture dialog box, and double-click the clip art file you want to insert in the active document.
2. Double-click the image itself. That pops up the built-in drawing program (refer to Figures 15.9 and 15.10).

> **Q&A** ***I'm double-clicking my picture, but I keep returning to the Clip Gallery!***
>
> If you insert a picture from the Clip Gallery, double-clicking the picture takes you right back to the Clip Gallery. To edit a picture, click Insert, Picture, From File and select an image in the Insert Picture dialog box. When you double-click the inserted picture now, you'll get Word's drawing program instead of the Clip Gallery.

3. Use the whole picture, or delete (or drag out of the picture boundary) the objects in the image that you don't want.

> **TIP** **If you're extracting several objects from a clip art image and you** want to keep them together, click the first object, then Shift+click each additional object. With several objects selected at the same time, click Draw, Group on the Drawing toolbar. That groups the objects together in one unit, which makes it easier to move and resize the whole thing. To break the grouped objects up again, click the group to select it, then click Draw, Ungroup on the Drawing toolbar.

4. Click the Text Box button on the Drawing toolbar. The pointer turns into a cross-hair. Position the cross-hair at the upper left corner of where you want the text in the graphic, and drag down to the lower right corner. That puts a text box right inside the picture.

5 You might want to change the text box fill to match, or contrast with, the fill color of the object under it. You can also get rid of the border around the text box. Just right-click the text box border for the shortcut menu and select Format Text Box, as shown in Figure 15.11.

Fig. 15.11
Choose the same fill color for the graphic and the text box, and the marriage of the two will look seamless.

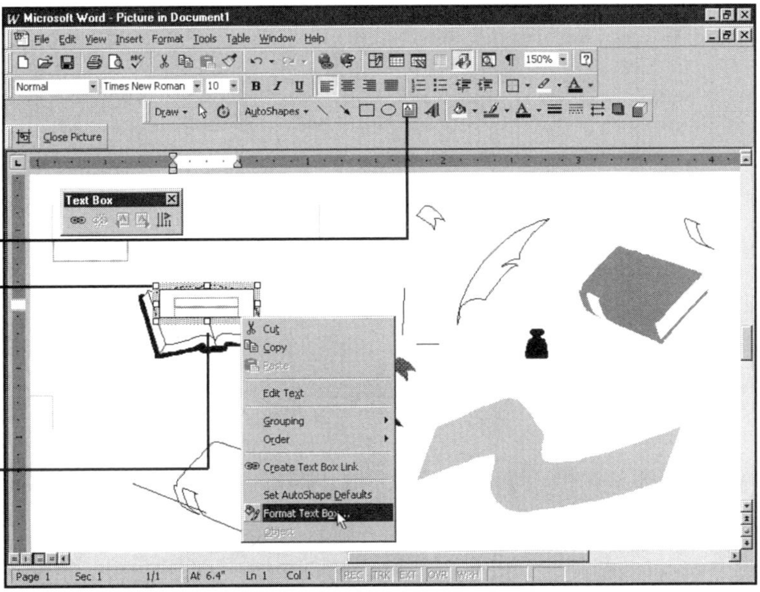

6 In the Format Text Box dialog box that pops up, click the Fill Color drop-down arrow and select No Fill. Then click the Line Color drop-down arrow and choose No Line.

7 Click OK in the Drawing Object dialog box. The insertion point is inside the text box; type your text, and use the Formatting toolbar to change fonts and attributes.

Q&A *I don't see the insertion point inside the text box!*

It's there, but it may be hidden within the text box border. Press the spacebar or Tab key to bring it out in the open. Or click the text box border and drag a handle to expand the box. A bigger box might be easier to work with, and it also exposes the insertion point to view.

8 When you're finished typing and formatting the text and editing the graphic, click Close Picture to return to your document. You'll wind up with something that looks like Figure 15.12.

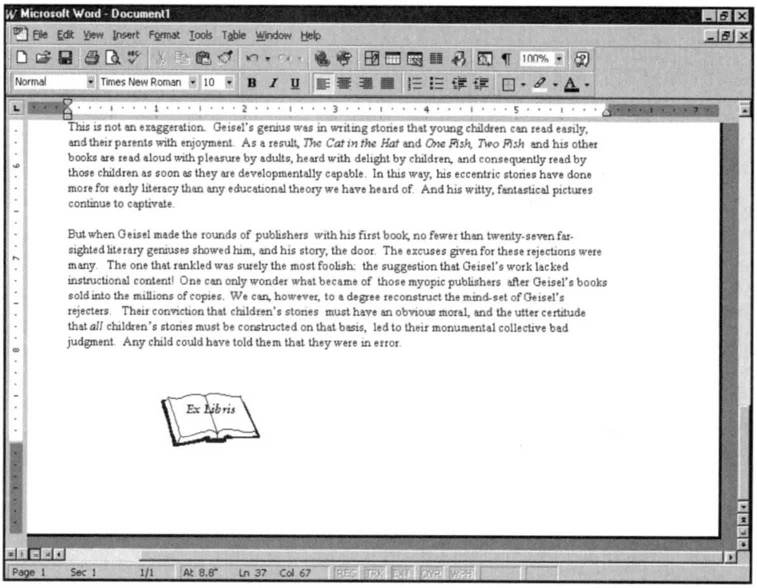
Microsoft Word - Document1
File Edit View Insert Format Tools Table Window Help
100%
Normal
Times New Roman
10
This is not an exaggeration. Geisel's genius was in writing stories that young children can read easily, and their parents with enjoyment. As a result, *The Cat in the Hat* and *One Fish, Two Fish* and his other books are read aloud with pleasure by adults, heard with delight by children, and consequently read by those children as soon as they are developmentally capable. In this way, his eccentric stories have done more for early literacy than any educational theory we have heard of. And his witty, fantastical pictures continue to captivate.
But when Geisel made the rounds of publishers with his first book, no fewer than twenty-seven far-sighted literary geniuses showed him, and his story, the door. The excuses given for these rejections were many. The one that rankled was surely the most foolish: the suggestion that Geisel's work lacked instructional content! One can only wonder what became of those myopic publishers after Geisel's books sold into the millions of copies. We can, however, to a degree reconstruct the mind-set of Geisel's rejecters. Their conviction that children's stories must have an obvious moral, and the utter certitude that *all* children's stories must be constructed on that basis, led to their monumental collective bad judgment. Any child could have told them that they were in error.
Ex Libris
Page 1 Sec 1 1/1 At 8.8" Ln 37 Col 67

Fig. 15.12
Instant logos like this can be created with a clip art image and a text box.

I already have text, and I want a picture behind it

When you hold a sheet of good-quality paper up to the light, you'll see a design stamped into the paper. That's a watermark. Put text on the sheet of paper, and the design will show, faintly, behind the text. You can create a similar effect in Word.

To make a watermark:

1. Click Insert, Picture, Clip Art and double-click the image you want to insert in your document.
2. Right-click the inserted image and choose Show Picture Toolbar if the Picture toolbar isn't already displayed.

3. Click the Image Control button on the Picture toolbar and select Watermark. That lightens the image so that text will be legible with the image behind it.
4. Drag the image to the location you want it in the document.

5. Click the Text Wrapping button on the Picture toolbar and choose No Wrapping. Your text will flow under the lightened image.

6 To make the text flow over, instead of under, the watermark, right-click the image and choose Order, Send Behind Text on the shortcut menu. That's the finishing touch, and Figure 15.13 shows the completed watermark.

Fig. 15.13
It takes a few steps to do it, but it is possible to create a watermark in Word.

To select the watermark again in order to make further alterations, click it with the four-headed arrow

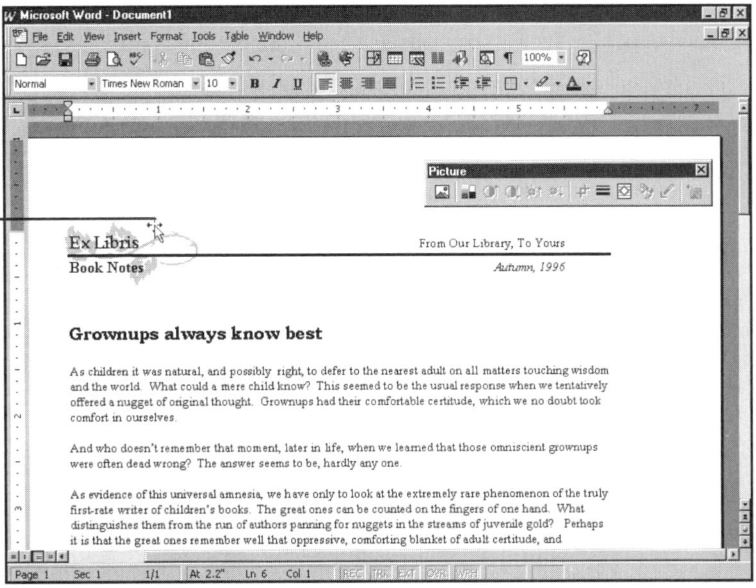
Microsoft Word - Document1
File Edit View Insert Format Tools Table Window Help
Normal
Times New Roman
10
100%
Picture
Ex Libris
From Our Library, To Yours
Book Notes
Autumn, 1996
Grownups always know best
As children it was natural, and possibly right, to defer to the nearest adult on all matters touching wisdom and the world. What could a mere child know? This seemed to be the usual response when we tentatively offered a nugget of original thought. Grownups had their comfortable certitude, which we no doubt took comfort in ourselves.
And who doesn't remember that moment, later in life, when we learned that those omniscient grownups were often dead wrong? The answer seems to be, hardly any one.
As evidence of this universal amnesia, we have only to look at the extremely rare phenomenon of the truly first-rate writer of children's books. The great ones can be counted on the fingers of one hand. What distinguishes them from the run of authors panning for nuggets in the streams of juvenile gold? Perhaps it is that the great ones remember well that oppressive, comforting blanket of adult certitude, and
Page 1 Sec 1 1/1 At 2.2" Ln 6 Col 1 REC TRK EXT OVR WPH

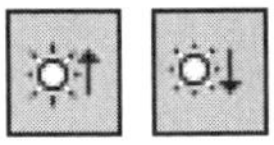

With the watermark still selected (the handles will be visible), use the More Brightness and Less Brightness buttons on the Picture toolbar for a darker or lighter image. If you need to reposition the watermark, drag it with the four-headed arrow.

Q&A ***I created a watermark, but with text in the way, I can't select the picture again!***

If your watermark is buried in a paragraph of text, selecting it in order to move or alter the picture is difficult, not to say impossible. Unless, that is, you clear away some of the text first. Click inside the paragraph over the watermark and press Enter to insert a blank line. Now click the watermark with the four-headed arrow, and you'll see the handles pop up. Move or alter the watermark, and don't forget to delete the inserted blank line.

Pink elephants? It wasn't necessarily that last martini...

Once you know your way around the Picture and Drawing toolbars, you'll find it easy to modify clip art images to suit yourself. For example, Word's Clip Gallery includes a brooding, faintly menacing elephant. But what if you prefer your elephants in dignified striped trousers, wearing a thoughtful pair of spectacles?

Nothing could be simpler. To customize a clip art image:

1. Select a graphic from the Insert Picture dialog box: Click Insert, Picture, From File, or click the Insert Picture button on the Picture toolbar. Double-click the selected picture to insert it into the document.

2. To make it easier to work with, drag a corner handle of the inserted picture to enlarge it. Now double-click the inserted picture to pop up the drawing program. Remember that each clip art image is made up of several discrete objects. Click an object inside the picture boundary to select it, then click the Fill Color drop-down arrow on the Drawing toolbar to change the colors and patterns.

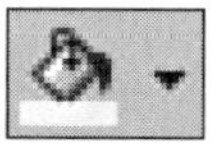

3. Choose a new color from the Fill Color palette, as shown in Figure 15.14.

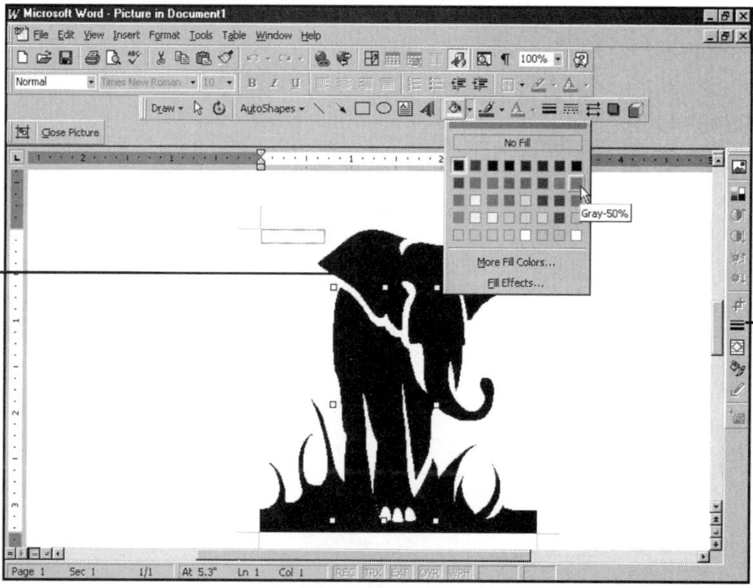

Fig. 15.14
The Drawing and Picture toolbars hold all the tools you need to edit clip art.

This is the selected object inside the picture boundary

If a toolbar gets in the way, drag it to the top, bottom, or sides of the editing window to dock it

4 Click the Fill Color drop-down arrow again and choose Fill Effects. In the Fill Effects dialog box that appears, click the Patterns tab and choose a pattern. To make the pattern stand out, click the Background drop-down arrow and choose a different background color (see Figure 15.15).

The Gradient and Texture tabs are worth exploring for a variety of startling visual effects

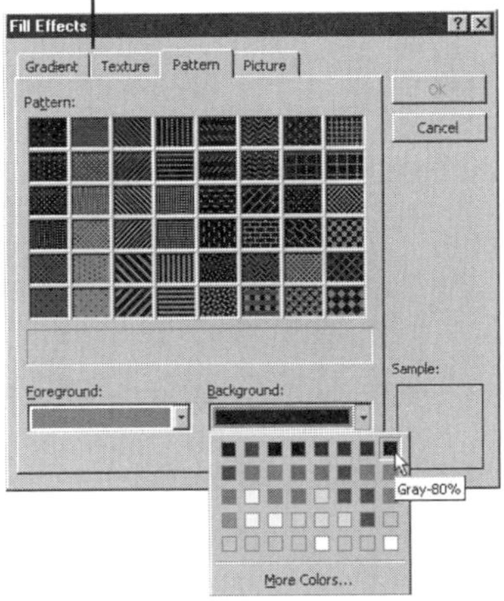

Fig. 15.15
Changing the background pattern and color customizes a graphic to suit.

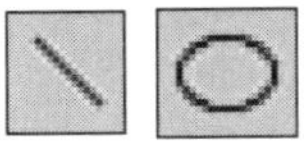

5 Click OK in the Fill Effects dialog box. Now use the Drawing toolbar to create your own objects. You'll find it easier to draw your objects outside the picture boundary. To draw the pair of spectacles shown in Figure 15.16, I clicked the Line button to draw a straight line with Line tool. To draw the lenses, I click the Oval button and drew two near-circles. I then selected the line and the circles and clicked the Line Style button to format them with a heavier line.

6 Once you've created your drawing, Shift+click each of the different objects in the drawing to select them all. Click the Draw button on the Drawing toolbar and select Group to meld the different objects into one unit.

7 Now drag the grouped object into position on the graphic, and click Close Picture to pop the image into your document. The result is shown in Figure 15.17.

Fig. 15.16
Professional graphic artists have little to fear, but you can create serviceable artwork with Word's drawing tools.

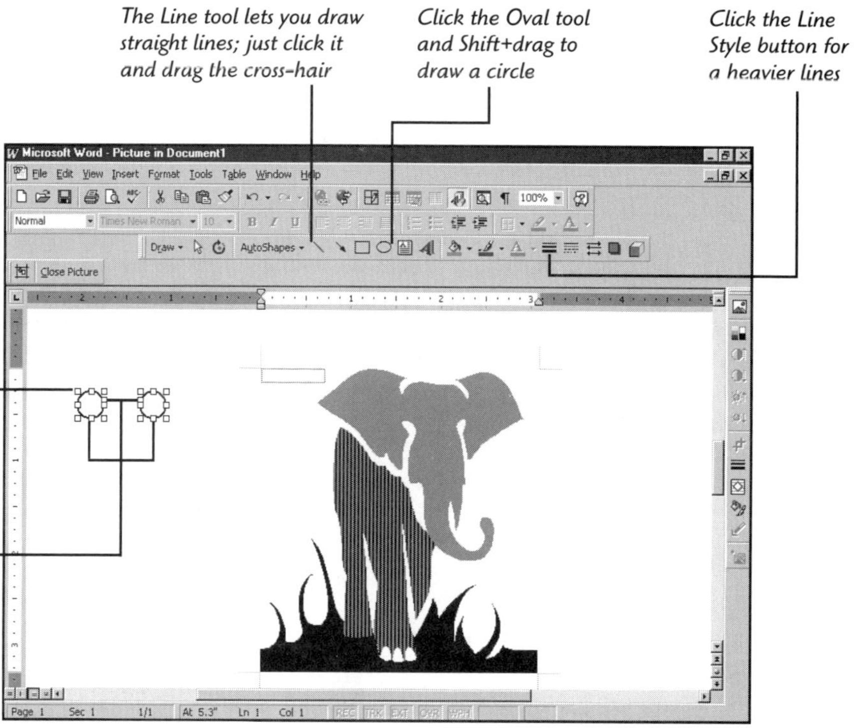
The Line tool lets you draw straight lines; just click it and drag the cross-hair
Click the Oval tool and Shift+drag to draw a circle
Click the Line Style button for a heavier lines
It's easier to do your drawing outside the picture boundary
Shift+click each object to select them all, then group them
Microsoft Word - Picture in Document1
Close Picture

Fig. 15.17
Babar's long-lost older brother?

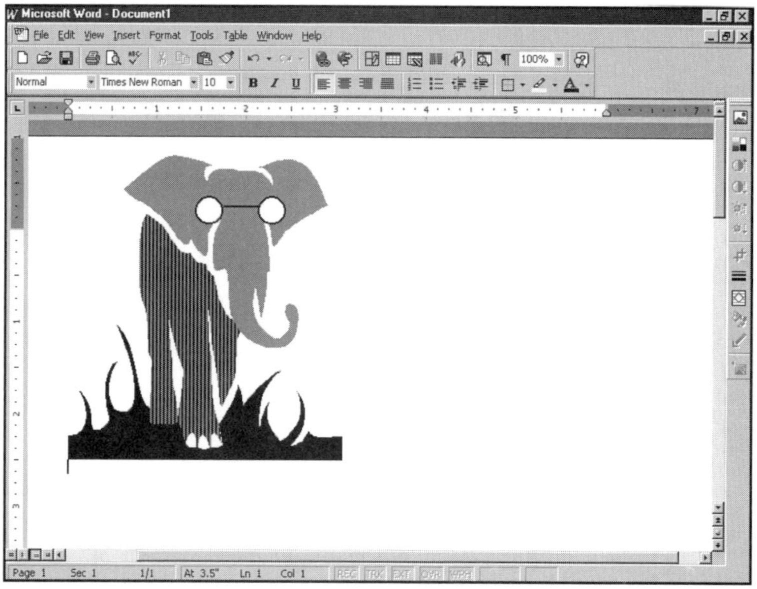
Microsoft Word - Document1

I need an instant shooting star

Word's Drawing toolbar is an amazing gadget. You can draw any conceivable shape, flawlessly, then format the shape with an array of special effects. Need a shooting star in your document? Here's how to create one:

1. Click the Drawing button on the Standard toolbar. On the Drawing toolbar that appears, click the AutoShapes button.
2. Choose Stars and Banners on the AutoShapes menu, and click a star shape on the palette.
3. The pointer turns into a cross-hair. Start in the upper left corner of where you want your star, then drag to the lower right corner. When you release the mouse button, the star pops into place.

4. With the star still selected, click the 3-D button on the Drawing toolbar and choose a 3-D style from the palette. For the shooting star effect, try 3-D Style 16 (see Figure 15.18).

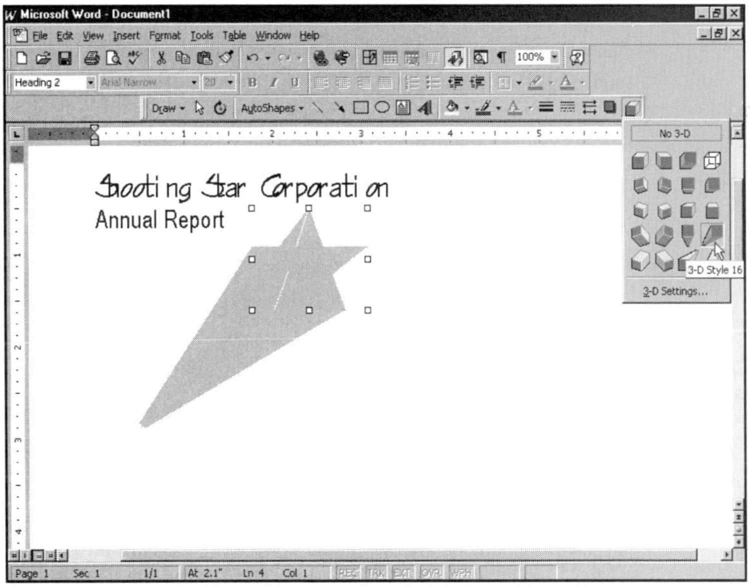

Fig. 15.18 Special effects in a Word document are easy to concoct with the Drawing toolbar.

You can tinker all you like with 3-D. With your object selected, click the 3-D button on the Drawing toolbar again and choose 3-D Settings. That pops up the 3-D settings toolbar, with gadgets to change the lighting, direction, and other attributes of your 3-D object.

How do I insert graphics from other programs?

Extensive though it is, Word's clip art collection may not have exactly what you want. Chances are, you'll have other programs lurking on your hard drive with different image collections.

TIP **If you come across interesting images on your travels across** the World Wide Web, you can stick those images in a Word document. Use your browser's File, Save As command to save the image in a standard format like .GIF, .JPG, or .BMP, then import it into Word by any of the ways described in this section. And see Chapter 25 for more on converting Web HTML documents to Word format.

If you want to stick an image from another program into a Word document, you have a few choices for how to go about it. The simplest way of getting artwork from another program into Word:

1. Select the object in the other program.
2. Click the Copy button in that program to copy the object to the Windows Clipboard.
3. Switch to Word, and click Edit, Paste Special.
4. In the Paste Special dialog box, choose Paste, As Picture, then click OK.

Once the graphic is inserted into Word, edit it, move it, or resize it, just as you'd do with Word's own clip art images.

CAUTION **Always save your Word document before you import graphics from** another program. Most likely, all will go well; in the event that it doesn't, you won't lose your work.

Part V: Organizational Tools

16 Hate Outlines? Outline View May Change Your Mind

In this chapter:

- **Do I really need an outline?**
- **OK, how do I create an outline from scratch?**
- **Collapse? Expand? Explain!**
- **I need to convert this outline to a document**
- **How do I squeeze an outline out of this document?**
- **AutoSummarize does document summaries, automatically**

Outlining is the best way to organize a document, but writing an outline has always been more of a duty than a pleasure. Word makes the procedure painless and quick. . . . .

When most of us sit down to write an outline, we have in mind a sketch of the final draft, the bare bones of a document, to be fleshed out whenever we can get around to it.

H.G. Wells wasn't most of us. The author of *The Time Machine*, *The Invisible Man*, and *The War of the Worlds* also wrote *The Outline of History*, nothing less than a popular account of the human species. No mere sketch, Wells envisioned his *Outline* as a kind of blueprint for a future world state. Three-quarters of a million words later, Wells' completed *Outline* was a huge success. No world state materialized, but *The Outline of History* helped make its author a rich man.

Although Wells wrote with pen and ink, he'd have enjoyed using Word's outlining tools. A Word outline is a convenient way to organize documents of all kinds, even if they don't run to hundreds of thousands of words. Outlines let you display or hide as much or as little detail as you like. They clarify your thinking as you write, and help to tighten your document when you're finished. Outlines are also easy to use, whether you're writing a humble report, or trying to sort out human history.

Why bother with an outline in the first place?

Outlines are like dental checkups—we know they're important, we know they're good for us, but we don't have anything to do with them unless we have to. If somebody hands you a writing assignment, you probably want to plunge right in. If deadlines are tight (aren't they always?), who wants to take the extra time to prepare an outline? It's just an extra step, taking time that might as well be spent writing the actual document.

Here's some good news: outlines in Word don't require an extra step at all. With Word, the outline *is* the document. And just like that visit to the dentist you've been shirking for the last six months, an outline can spare you a lot of future pain:

- Outlines force you to break your document down into topics, with headings and subheadings describing each topic. Outline headings are easily moved, promoted, or demoted. That helps you organize your material and present it in a coherent way.

- Word outlines are very flexible. You can convert a heading into body text, or body text into a heading, with a click of the mouse.
- It's easy to get lost in a tangle of words, even in a simple memo. Outlines let you see your way clearly, by hiding or displaying as much cluttering detail as you care to deal with. Shove your body text out of sight, and your topics jump right off the page. That makes it a lot easier to see the big picture of your document.

Organized documents start with an outline

Think of a Word outline as a document arranged in a hierarchy of topics and subtopics. Each topic is formatted in a different heading style, according to its importance in the context of the document. A topic in the Heading 1 style is more important than a topic in the Heading 2 style, and so on. You decide on the importance of your topics and subtopics, and Word applies the heading styles automatically.

Take a look at the figure on page 299 to see what outlines are all about.

Create an outline from scratch...

Word makes it a snap to create a new outline. And if you've written a report and the boss says, "Send me an outline," don't groan. It's just as easy to convert an existing document into outline form, with no retyping needed.

To create an outline:

1. Click the Outline View button down at the lower left corner of the Word window. The Outline toolbar pops up, the Styles box displays the Heading 1 style, and a fat minus sign appears in the left margin.
2. Type your first heading and press Enter at the end of the line. That'll be your first main topic, but you're not committed; if you decide to make it a subtopic later, it's easy to change things around.

3. Now type the first subtopic heading. It also gets the Heading 1 style, just like the first heading. Since you want it to be a subtopic, click the heading, then click the Demote button on the Outline toolbar. That makes it a Heading 2 style heading. Figure 16.1 shows the outline so far.

Close-Up: The Outlining toolbar

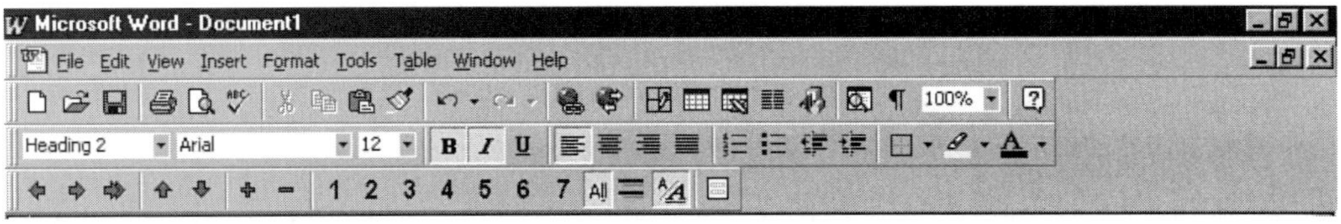

Promote
Changes a heading to a higher level.

Demote
Changes a heading to a lower level.

Demote to Body Text
Converts headings to body text.

Move Up
Moves a selected heading up one line.

Move Down
Moves a selected heading down one line.

Expand
Displays all the items under a selected heading.

Collapse
Hides the lowest level item displayed under a selected heading.

Show Headings
Click any of these numbered buttons to display only that heading level and the levels above it.

All
Displays all the headings and body text in the outline.

Show First Line Only
Toggles a display of either the first line of each paragraph of body text or all the text.

Show Formatting
Toggles the display of heading styles.

Master Document View
Pops up a toolbar to control the collapsing and expanding of large documents.

Anatomy of a Word outline

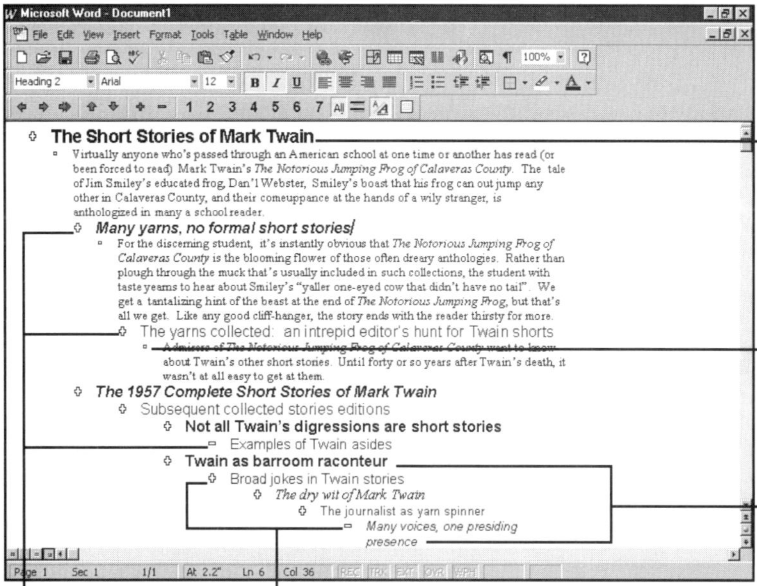
Microsoft Word - Document1
File Edit View Insert Format Tools Table Window Help
Heading 2
Arial
12
The Short Stories of Mark Twain
Virtually anyone who's passed through an American school at one time or another has read (or been forced to read) Mark Twain's The Notorious Jumping Frog of Calaveras County. The tale of Jim Smiley's educated frog, Dan'l Webster, Smiley's boast that his frog can out jump any other in Calaveras County, and their comeuppance at the hands of a wily stranger, is anthologized in many a school reader.
Many yarns, no formal short stories
For the discerning student, it's instantly obvious that The Notorious Jumping Frog of Calaveras County is the blooming flower of those often dreary anthologies. Rather than plough through the muck that's usually included in such collections, the student with taste yearns to hear about Smiley's "yaller one-eyed cow that didn't have no tail". We get a tantalizing hint of the beast at the end of The Notorious Jumping Frog, but that's all we get. Like any good cliff-hanger, the story ends with the reader thirsty for more.
The yarns collected: an intrepid editor's hunt for Twain shorts
Admirers of The Notorious Jumping Frog of Calaveras County want to know about Twain's other short stories. Until forty or so years after Twain's death, it wasn't at all easy to get at them.
The 1957 Complete Short Stories of Mark Twain
Subsequent collected stories editions
Not all Twain's digressions are short stories
Examples of Twain asides
Twain as barroom raconteur
Broad jokes in Twain stories
The dry wit of Mark Twain
The journalist as yarn spinner
Many voices, one presiding presence
Page 1 Sec 1 1/1 At 2.2" Ln 6 Col 36

The Heading 1 style is applied to your main topics

The little square indicates body text

These are subtopics in the Heading 4, 5, 6, 7, and 8 styles

Click outline symbols to select outline items; double-click to hide or display outline items

Each heading level is indented further into the page

Fig. 16.1
As you build your outline, you promote or demote headings depending on their relative importance

The minus sign changes to a plus, indicating that there are lower level items immediately below the heading

New headings take the style of the previous heading; click Demote or press Tab to change the heading to a lower heading level

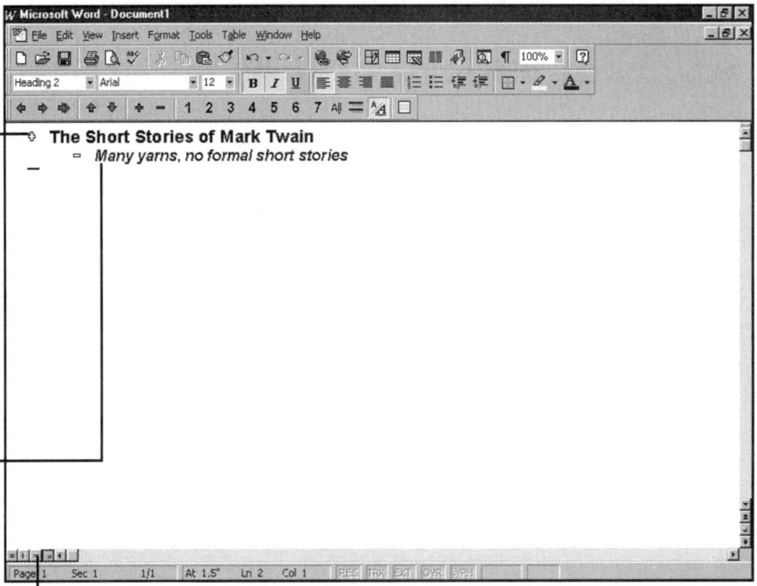

The Outline View button

TIP **Want to promote and demote outline headings without lifting** your fingers from the keyboard to click Outline toolbar buttons? Press Tab to demote headings, and Shift+Tab to promote headings.

4 Press Enter to go to the next line and type your next heading. It also takes the heading style of the previous heading; if it's a lower-level topic, click Demote again to make it a Heading 3 style heading.

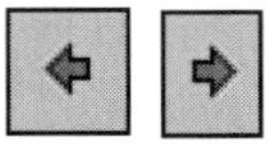

5 Type the rest of your topic headings. Click the Promote or Demote button and press Enter after each one. When you're done, you'll have a hierarchy of topic headings organized from level 1 on down. An outline, in other words, as shown in Figure 16.2.

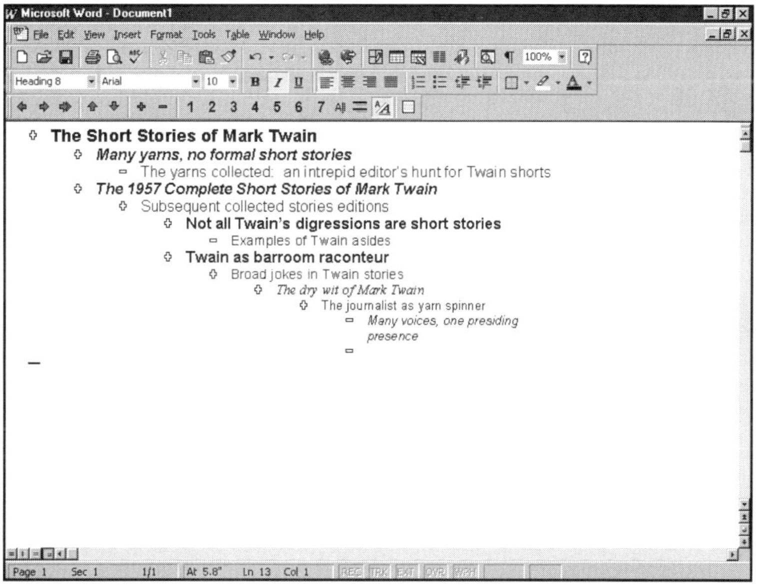

Fig. 16.2
If you change your mind about the importance of any of the headings, click the heading, then click the Promote or Demote button.

Want to promote a level 4 heading to level 2? Just click the heading and click the Promote button twice. To demote it back to level 4, click the Demote button twice.

I need to reorder these topics

Outlines show you the structure of the document, without the confusing detail of the document itself. That makes it easier to reorganize your work. An outline, like the girders supporting an office building, is the skeleton of the finished document. And just as in an office building, it's much easier to move a girder or two around *before* all the plumbing, wiring, and walls are added.

To move a heading up or down within the outline, just click the heading, then click the Move Up or Move Down button on the Outline toolbar.

Figure 16.3 shows a Heading 4 level topic moved up one line above a Heading 3 level topic.

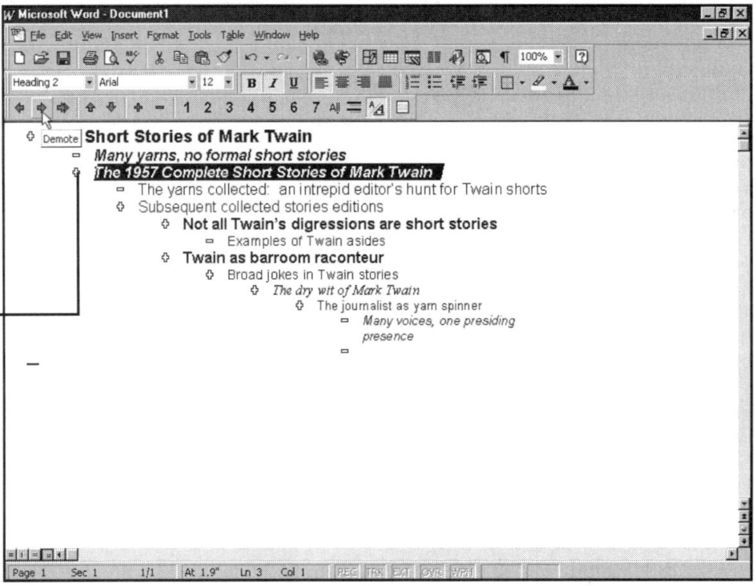

Fig. 16.3
When you move outline items up or down, they swap places with the items above or below them.

You don't have to select a heading to move it up or down; just click it. It's automatically selected when you click the Move Up or Move Down button.

CAUTION **Don't click the plus sign next to a heading to select it for a move.** When you do that, not only that heading but *all* the headings and the text under the headings are selected. Move the heading, and everything under it moves too (unless that's what you want to do, of course).

Once you move the outline item, you can promote or demote it, and promote or demote the item whose place it took, to restore the outline's order.

Where are my outline heading numbers?

You'll notice something about Word outlines right away: They don't have that progression of numbers and letters we were all taught to use. Those I's, 1's, a)'s and so forth were always a pain to keep straight (mine would usually get hopelessly out of sequence), but Word makes it easy to keep them in order.

Word not only lets you add those numbering schemes to your outlines, it lets you choose a scheme that suits you. Once you've finished typing your headings, click the first + sign in the outline to select the whole thing.

Click Format, Bullets and Numbering and click the Outline Numbered tab in the Bullets and Numbering dialog box that appears, as shown in Figure 16.4.

Select any of the outline numbering schemes

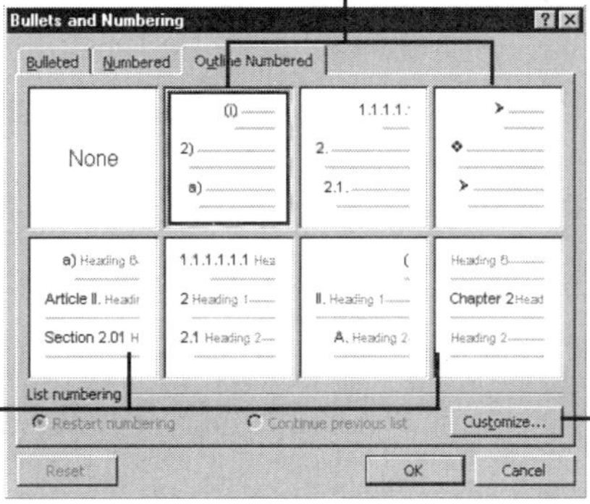

Fig. 16.4
Instant outline numbers and letters that are always in sequence make outlines painless.

These options format your headings as chapter or appendix titles

Click Customize to modify the heading numbering schemes

Select any of the outline numbering formats in the Outline Numbered tab and click OK. The selected numbering scheme is applied to the outline. Each heading level gets the correctly sequenced number or letter, as shown in Figure 16.5.

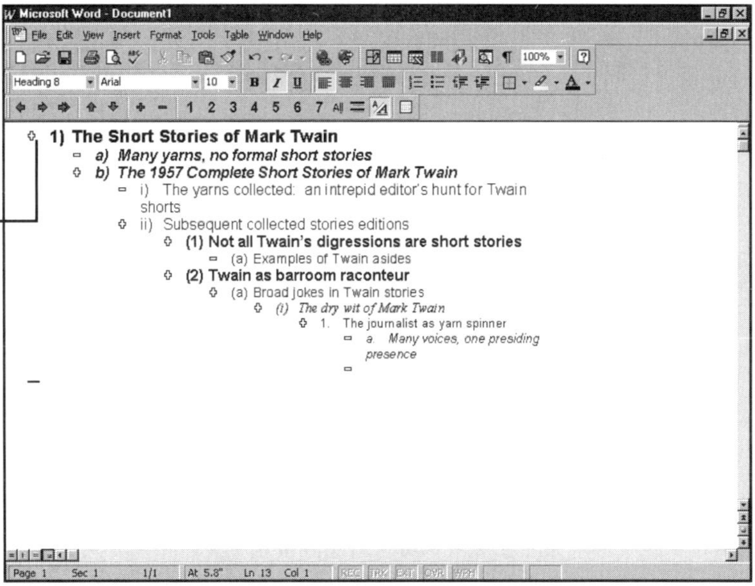

Fig. 16.5
Word automatically assigns numbers and letters in the order of the heading levels.

Click the first + sign in the outline to select the entire document

To get rid of heading numbers, which you'll want to do if you convert your outline headings to document headings (see below), click the first + sign to select the entire outline. Click Format, Bullets and Numbering and click the Outline Numbered tab in the Bullets and Numbering dialog box. Select None, and click OK.

What happens if I move numbered headings around?

If you decide to move your outline headings up or down after you've numbered them, you'll see that the heading number style is linked to the heading level. For example, if your level 7 heading is numbered (i), it'll retain that numbering level even if you move it up or down in the outline.

The heading is automatically renumbered to keep the heading numbers in sequence. So, if you move a heading numbered (i) below another heading numbered (i), Word renumbers the heading you moved to (ii).

TIP **It'll probably be less confusing to remove the heading numbers** before you start shuffling headings around. Make your moves, then reapply the numbers when you're done.

Surprise! Your outline is also your document

You need a formatted, numbered outline, something like the one in Figure 16.5? Typing, promoting and demoting, then ordering and numbering headings is all you need to do. But maybe you're responsible for the document as well as the outline. If you've finished your outline headings, you've also finished your document headings.

Those outline headings *are* document headings. Just add body text, and the document is done. To add body text to your outline headings:

1. If you've numbered your headings, click Format, Bullets and Numbering and click the Outline Numbered tab in the Bullets and Numbering dialog box. Select None, and click OK to get rid of the numbers. They can be reapplied again if you need to.
2. Click the Normal View button to switch to Normal view.

3 Position the insertion point at the end of a heading, press Enter to start a new line, and type your text. Use any paragraph formatting you like—tabs, indents, borders, whatever. Treat your former outline just like an ordinary document (it is an ordinary document).

4 Body text finished? Save the document and go home.

Figure 16.6 shows our existing outline headings, stripped of heading numbers, in Normal view and with body text added.

Position the insertion point after a heading in Normal view, press Enter, and type your body text

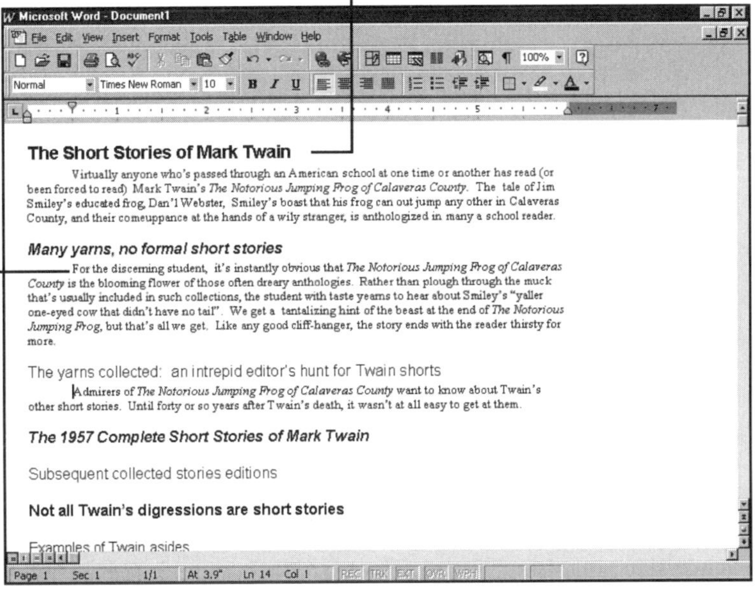
Microsoft Word - Document1
File Edit View Insert Format Tools Table Window Help
Normal
Times New Roman
10
100%
The Short Stories of Mark Twain
Virtually anyone who's passed through an American school at one time or another has read (or been forced to read) Mark Twain's The Notorious Jumping Frog of Calaveras County. The tale of Jim Smiley's educated frog, Dan'l Webster, Smiley's boast that his frog can out jump any other in Calaveras County, and their comeuppance at the hands of a wily stranger, is anthologized in many a school reader.
Many yarns, no formal short stories
For the discerning student, it's instantly obvious that The Notorious Jumping Frog of Calaveras County is the blooming flower of those often dreary anthologies. Rather than plough through the muck that's usually included in such collections, the student with taste yearns to hear about Smiley's "yaller one-eyed cow that didn't have no tail". We get a tantalizing hint of the beast at the end of The Notorious Jumping Frog, but that's all we get. Like any good cliff-hanger, the story ends with the reader thirsty for more.
The yarns collected: an intrepid editor's hunt for Twain shorts
Admirers of The Notorious Jumping Frog of Calaveras County want to know about Twain's other short stories. Until forty or so years after Twain's death, it wasn't at all easy to get at them.
The 1957 Complete Short Stories of Mark Twain
Subsequent collected stories editions
Not all Twain's digressions are short stories
Examples of Twain asides
Page 1 Sec 1 1/1 At 3.9" Ln 14 Col 1 REC TRK EXT OVR WPH

Fig. 16.6
Suddenly, our outline looks like a regular document. Just click the Normal View button to switch out of Outline view.

Paragraph formatting you add in Normal view, like indents or tabs, isn't displayed in Outline view. But it isn't removed, only hidden.

Q&A ***Why can't I just add body text in Outline view?***

You can. It's just easier to type body text in Normal view because you can see your paragraph formatting.

Use outline tools to tighten the final document

Outline view is handy for launching a writing project, as we've seen. Once you've got the document written, Outline view is just as useful for polishing the structure of the document.

Use the outline collapse and expand tools to see more or less document detail, and you'll have more control over the document's organization. Suppose you've written your body text, and now you'd like to display only your document headings again.

To hide body text and display only headings in Outline view:

1. Click the Outline View button to switch to Outline view.

2. Click a heading with body text under it. Don't select the heading; just put the insertion point anywhere within the heading.

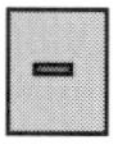

3. Click the Collapse button on the Outline toolbar. All the body text under that heading and the headings below it are hidden, as shown in Figure 16.7.

Fig. 16.7
When the trees of your document are hidden by a forest of text, put the text out of sight with the Collapse button.

To display heading levels 1 through 7 and quickly hide all the body text in the outline, click the Show Heading 7 button

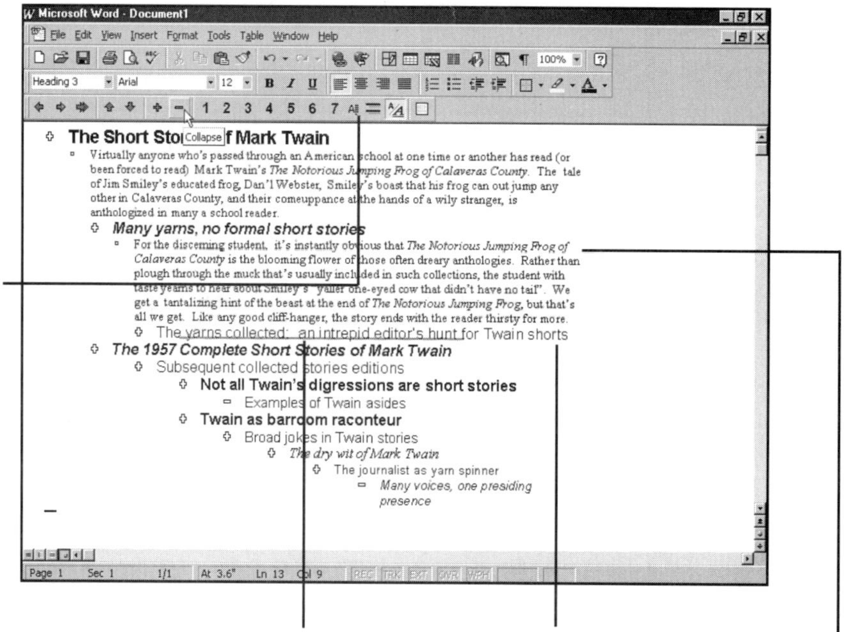
Microsoft Word - Document1
File Edit View Insert Format Tools Table Window Help
Heading 3
Arial
12
1 2 3 4 5 6 7
Collapse
The Short Sto f Mark Twain
Virtually anyone who's passed through an American school at one time or another has read (or been forced to read) Mark Twain's The Notorious Jumping Frog of Calaveras County. The tale of Jim Smiley's educated frog, Dan'l Webster, Smiley's boast that his frog can out jump any other in Calaveras County, and their comeuppance at the hands of a wily stranger, is anthologized in many a school reader.
Many yarns, no formal short stories
For the discerning student, it's instantly obvious that The Notorious Jumping Frog of Calaveras County is the blooming flower of those often dreary anthologies. Rather than plough through the muck that's usually included in such collections, the student with
one-eyed cow that didn't have no tail". We get a tantalizing hint of the beast at the end of The Notorious Jumping Frog, but that's all we get. Like any good cliff-hanger, the story ends with the reader thirsty for more.
The yarns collected: an intrepid editor's hunt for Twain shorts
The 1957 Complete Short Stories of Mark Twain
Subsequent collected stories editions
Not all Twain's digressions are short stories
Examples of Twain asides
Twain as barroom raconteur
Broad jokes in Twain stories
The dry wit of Mark Twain
The journalist as yarn spinner
Many voices, one presiding presence
Page 1 Sec 1 1/1 At 3.6" Ln 13 Col 9

The faint underlines indicates body text under this heading

With the insertion point in this heading, the Collapse button hides all the body text below it

Body text above the current heading remains on display

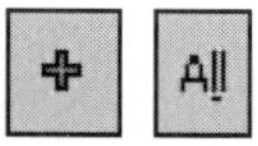

To redisplay the body text you've just hidden, click the Expand or All button on the Outline toolbar.

I don't want to see these headings

When you put the insertion point in a heading and click Collapse, you hide the body text below the heading, as we just did. But maybe you want to hide both the body text *and* the headings below a particular heading level.

There are two quick ways to hide both headings and body text:

3

- To display only a particular heading level and the levels above it, click one of the numbered buttons on the Outline toolbar. For example, to see only level 3 headings and above, click the Show Heading 3 button on the Outline toolbar.
- An even faster way is to position the pointer over the plus sign next to that level 3 heading, and it turns into a four-headed arrow. Now double-click; all the headings and body text below the level 3 heading are hidden, as shown in Figure 16.8.

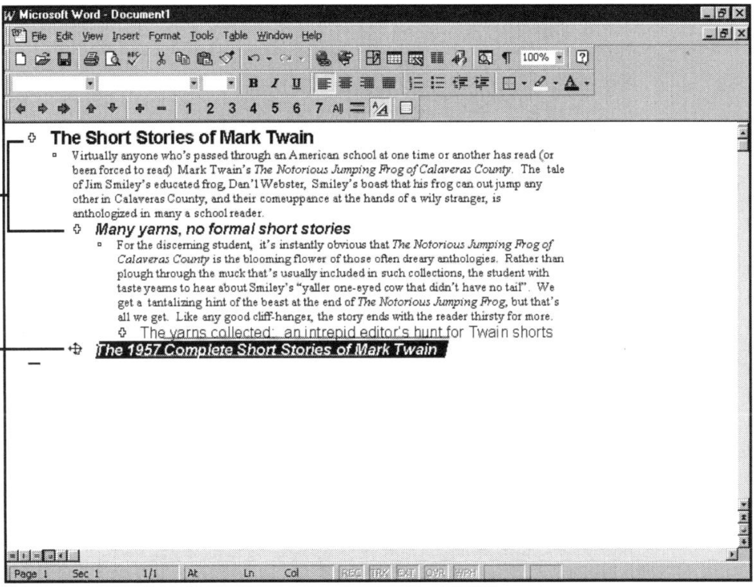
Microsoft Word - Document1
File Edit View Insert Format Tools Table Window Help
100%
1 2 3 4 5 6 7 All
The Short Stories of Mark Twain
Virtually anyone who's passed through an American school at one time or another has read (or been forced to read) Mark Twain's The Notorious Jumping Frog of Calaveras County. The tale of Jim Smiley's educated frog, Dan'l Webster, Smiley's boast that his frog can out jump any other in Calaveras County, and their comeuppance at the hands of a wily stranger, is anthologized in many a school reader.
Many yarns, no formal short stories
For the discerning student, it's instantly obvious that The Notorious Jumping Frog of Calaveras County is the blooming flower of those often dreary anthologies. Rather than plough through the muck that's usually included in such collections, the student with taste yearns to hear about Smiley's "yaller one-eyed cow that didn't have no tail". We get a tantalizing hint of the beast at the end of The Notorious Jumping Frog, but that's all we get. Like any good cliff-hanger, the story ends with the reader thirsty for more.
The yarns collected: an intrepid editor's hunt for Twain shorts
The 1957 Complete Short Stories of Mark Twain
Page 1 Sec 1 1/1 At Ln Col REC TRK EXT OVR WPH

Fig. 16.8
Double-click an outline's plus sign to speedily hide the outline items below it.

Double-click the plus signs, and all the outline items below them will be hidden

The pointer turns into a four-headed arrow when you place it over the outline symbol

To redisplay the outline items you've just hidden, double-click the outline symbol again.

Can't I just see my headings and some of my body text?

When you want to hide or display text and headings, Word outlines give you a lot of flexibility. That's good, because it lets you control precisely what you see. It can also be mildly confusing, because there are so many options. Just play around with it; since you're not making any changes to the document itself, you can hide, display, and hide again until you're comfortable with all the controls.

Here's one more outlining trick: Suppose you want to see all your headings, and the first line of each paragraph of body text. That's a handy way to get a bird's-eye view of a document's structure without losing sight of all the detail.

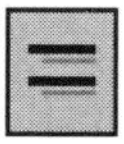

Just click the Show First Line Only button on the Outline toolbar. Figure 16.9 shows you how it looks.

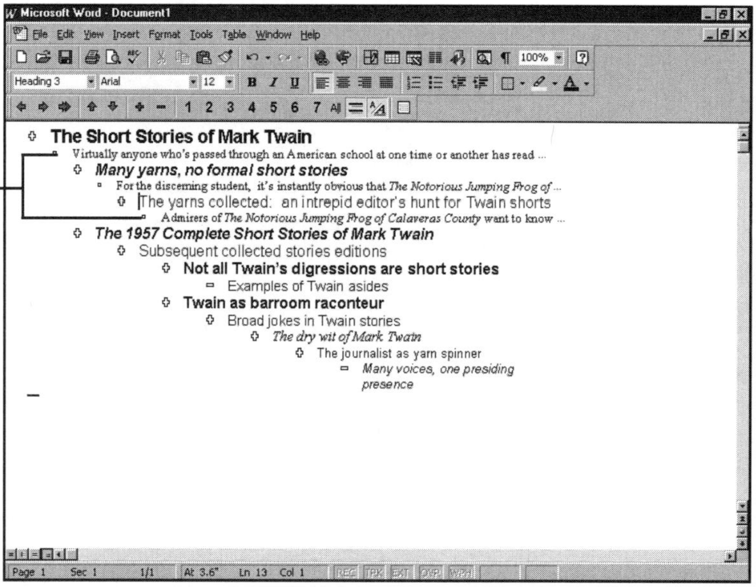

Fig. 16.9
Now you can see the trees, and some of the undergrowth, too.

The first line of each paragraph of body text gives you a clue about what's in the rest of the paragraph

Q&A *I just moved my outline heading up, but the body text below it got left behind!*

If you move headings around in an outline, you can wind up with orphaned body text, deserted by the parent heading when you moved it up or down. To avoid this, collapse the body text under the heading first, then move the heading. Collapsed body text accompanies a heading wherever you move it.

I need to turn this document into an outline

After hours of toil, your document is finally finished. You reach out a hand shaky with exhaustion and make the fateful phone call:

> You: "It's ready. Want me to send it up?"
>
> The boss: "Can't read the whole thing now. Just send me the outline." Click.
>
> You (talking to yourself, never a good sign): "I didn't do an outline. I didn't have time to do an outline. If that no-good so-and-so wants an outline, why then…"

Don't say it. With Word, you can craft an instant outline from an existing document. The fact that it's an afterthought is entirely between you and your conscience; no one else need ever know.

To turn an existing document into an outline:

- If you've used Word's built-in styles for headings (Heading 1…8 in the Style box) in your document, just click the Outline View button. Your outline is finished with one click. Add heading numbering if you want to, and send the outline on its merry way.
- Chances are, your document is a mix of body text, bolded headings, italicized subheadings, and so on. Now that you know your way around the outline tools, it's easy to turn that jumble of formatting into an outline. Click the Outline View button. Word ignores all your own paragraph formatting, and treats the whole document as body text. Use the Promote, Demote, and Demote to Body Text buttons on the Outline toolbar to turn selected text into outline headings and body text. A few minutes of work will see that pesky outline completed.

Text that you promote to headings in Outline view is formatted with those heading styles, even when you switch back to Normal view. If you like the formatting of your original document, save the document first, then switch to Outline view and make your promotions and demotions. Click File, Save As, and save the outline under a different name.

On the other hand, converting your document headings to the Word heading styles automatically gives your document a consistent, polished look. Going through the exercise of turning a document into an outline just might leave you with a better-looking document. That's another bonus of using Word's outline tools.

If you need a summary, AutoSummarize

Summaries of documents are, if anything, more irksome to prepare than outlines. Summaries force us to think about the substance of what we've written, extract it, and write it up in terse but lucid fashion. Of course, writing a summary can be a salutary exercise. It forces us to confront the question of "just what have I written about here?" which is surely a good thing to do. But then, so is a trip to the dentist.

Word users can entirely avoid the pain of preparing document summaries. The AutoSummarize feature combs through your document looking for headings, and for text that's directly relevant to those headings. AutoSummarize then displays its findings in the form of a summary, automatically.

To turn AutoSummarize loose on your document, open the document and switch to Normal View or Page Layout View if you're not there already. Then click Tools, AutoSummarize for the AutoSummarize dialog box shown in Figure 16.10.

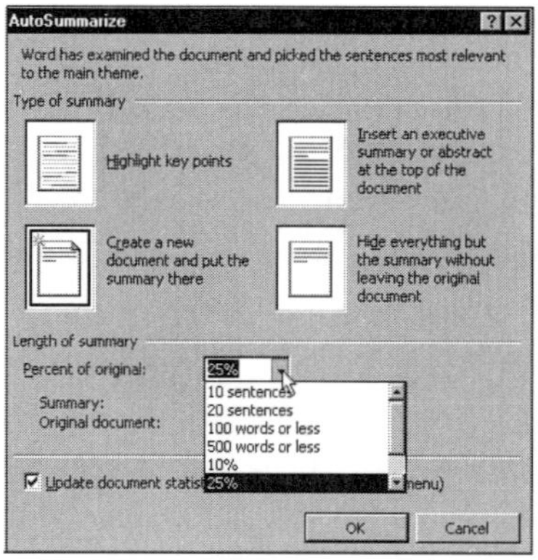

Fig. 16.10
If you hate outlines, you'll really hate summaries. Fortunately, there's AutoSummarize.

Select the Type of summary you want from the surprisingly self-explanatory options under that heading in the AutoSummarize dialog box. How long a summary do you want? Click the Percent of original drop-down arrow (refer to Figure 16.10) and make your choice. For a four hundred-page document, the default 25% will be more than you need; select a shorter option.

Click OK in the AutoSummarize dialog box, and you're off to the races. Shorter documents are summarized in no time at all; longer documents require a little patience. And although it's a great idea, AutoSummarize isn't perfect:

- For long documents without formatted headings (a novel, for example), AutoSummarize's summary will be gibberish.
- Short documents with no clear section headings also don't fare well at the hands of AutoSummarize. Letters, for example, yield summaries that won't necessarily illuminate the most important points.
- To get the most out of AutoSummarize, your document has to have clearly defined sections, headed with outline-style headings. If that describes your document, AutoSummarize will save you a lot of time.

Q&A ***Why is the AutoSummarize choice on the Tools menu dimmed?***

You're in Outline View. Switch to Normal View, and the AutoSummarize option will spring to life.

How do I change this outline formatting?

If the default heading styles don't appeal to you, just modify the styles. See Chapter 12 for details on how to change document styles. Or take the express route to outline formatting makeovers. With the insertion point anywhere in your outline, click Format, Style Gallery to pop up the Style Gallery dialog box. Your outline is shown in Normal view in the Preview window, as shown in Figure 16.11.

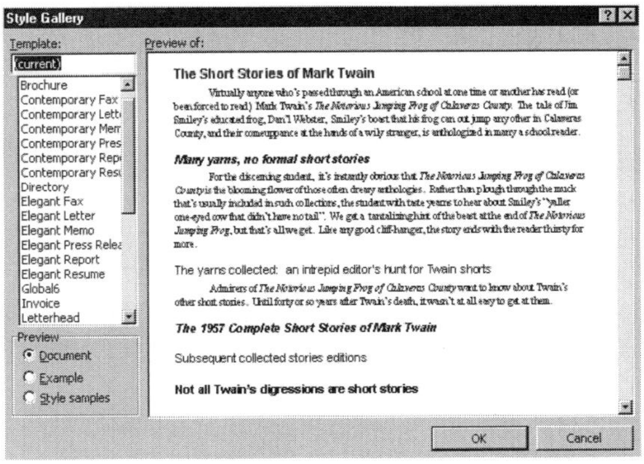

Fig. 16.11
Use the Style Gallery for instant outline formatting changes.

Even though you're previewing the outline in Normal view, it'll revert back to Outline view when you leave the dialog box. Now choose a new format from the Template list in the Style Gallery dialog box, then click OK. The outline is instantly reformatted in the styles of the new template. Figure 16.12 shows our outline formatted in the Elegant Report template styles.

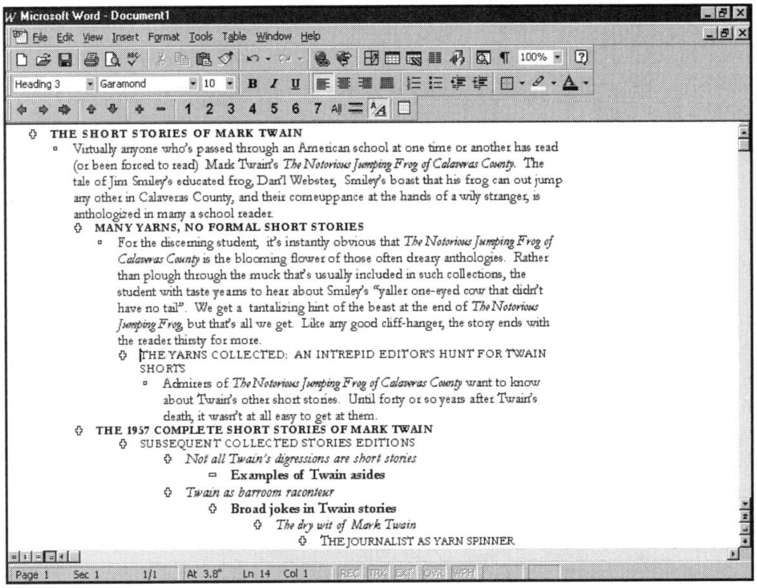

Fig. 16.12
Remember that when you reformat an outline, you're also reformatting the document.

I need to print this outline

Outline printing works like document printing, with a few twists:

- Those plus and minus outline symbols won't print. Ditto for the little squares indicating body text. Those symbols display only on the screen.
- You print as much outline detail as you have displayed when you click the Print button on the Standard toolbar. If you want to print only your headings, collapse the body text first, then click the Print button.
- Heading numbering does print; if you want heading numbering in the print job, just add it to the outline before printing.

17

Mastering Big Documents Is No Mystery

In this chapter:

- **Do big documents go in one file, or many smaller files?**
- **What are master documents, and when do I use them?**
- **I want to turn a long document into a master document**
- **How do I create a new master document?**
- **All these documents would be more convenient in one file**

A long report in a dozen parts, or a dozen different files? With a master document, you can consolidate them in one big file! . . . .

What do stereotomy (cutting solids into sections), Epicurus (the ancient Greek philosopher), and fruit vendors have in common? Nothing much, unless you happened to be fiction's first great detective, C. Auguste Dupin. Before Sherlock Holmes saw action, Edgar Allan Poe's Dupin followed those three clues to the perpetrator of *The Murders in the Rue Morgue.* And with that, the modern detective story was born.

Those unwieldy, biceps-testing mysteries and thrillers we lug to the beach are outsized descendants of Poe's compact tale. If you've ever fallen asleep over one and had it land on your chest, you might have been tempted to take the stereotomist approach to big books: cut them up into more manageable pieces.

That's exactly what Word master documents let you do to big documents. You can break up a long file into handier smaller files. What's more, you can put them back together again. Just try doing that with the latest best-seller.

Do I keep my work in one big file, or many little ones?

Painting the back porch? Chances are, you'll start with the railings, then do the steps, and so on. Any big chore is more manageable when you break it up into smaller parts, and big writing jobs are no different. Most of us tackle long reports or book-length documents one part or chapter or section at a time. That makes the job seem much less overwhelming. You also organize your material better when you focus on each section separately.

You *could* keep all your chapters or sections in one long document in Word. It's easier to keep the parts of a big document in separate files:

- Spell checking, finding and replacing, and even file saves all go more quickly in a smaller file.
- You'll want to print a single chapter every once in a while, not the whole document. That's not as easy to do if your chapter is buried inside a big document.

- Coworkers or editors may need to see a chapter or a section, not the whole document. It's easy to copy a file to floppy disk, or send it on the network. It's much more work to extract a chunk of big document first, before copying or sending it.
- If you're working on a single chapter and the rest of the document is unchanged, you don't want to have to back up the whole document just to preserve the changes in one section of it. If your chapter's in its own file, you can just back up the file.

Keeping your document parts in separate files is efficient, but there are some drawbacks to the strategy. There'll be times when you do want to work on the whole document instead of each part. You might want to print the whole document, or make global replacements. And pagination can be a chore when you've got loads of small files that are all part of a bigger document.

Master documents combine, then divide, smaller files

So what should we use for a long document, one long file, or many smaller ones? We'd rather have both at once: the parts of a large document in separate files, that we could combine into one large file whenever necessary. And when we needed to, we could break up the large file into its component parts again. Then recombine them when the urge struck.

That's exactly what we get with a **master document**. A master document is like an outline of a large document, akin to the outlines we looked at in Chapter 16, "Hate Outlines? Outline View May Change Your Mind." In a master document, the outline items are themselves smaller files, called **subdocuments**. Each subdocument is a section of the large document. When you expand the master document, you get your entire large file to edit or print. Collapse it again, and you can work on each subdocument individually.

The following graphics page shows a master document containing five subdocuments. Each subdocument is a section of a book manuscript.

Master big documents with master documents

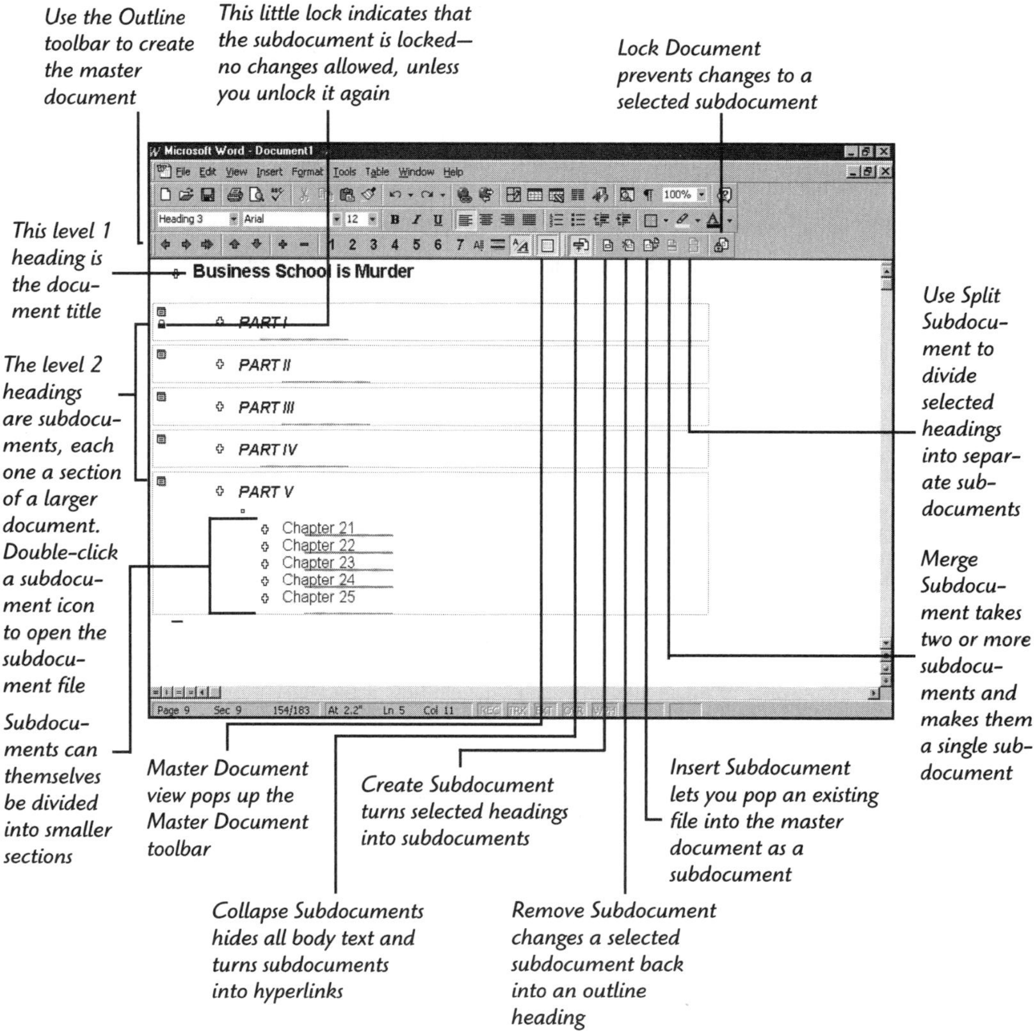
Use the Outline toolbar to create the master document
This little lock indicates that the subdocument is locked—no changes allowed, unless you unlock it again
Lock Document prevents changes to a selected subdocument
This level 1 heading is the document title
The level 2 headings are subdocuments, each one a section of a larger document. Double-click a subdocument icon to open the subdocument file
Subdocuments can themselves be divided into smaller sections
Use Split Subdocument to divide selected headings into separate subdocuments
Merge Subdocument takes two or more subdocuments and makes them a single subdocument
Master Document view pops up the Master Document toolbar
Create Subdocument turns selected headings into subdocuments
Insert Subdocument lets you pop an existing file into the master document as a subdocument
Collapse Subdocuments hides all body text and turns subdocuments into hyperlinks
Remove Subdocument changes a selected subdocument back into an outline heading
Microsoft Word - Document1
Business School is Murder
PART I
PART II
PART III
PART IV
PART V
Chapter 21
Chapter 22
Chapter 23
Chapter 24
Chapter 25

You can create a new document as a master document, or take an existing long document and turn it into a master document. You can even combine many existing document files into a single master document. We'll take a look at all three possibilities.

Like an electronic paper clip, master documents let you clip together a stack of document files. Pull the files out to work on them, then clip them together again when you're done. Master documents are just as easy to use as paper clips, with the advantage that no amount of use will bend them out of shape.

How do I create a master document for a new writing job?

Any writer embarking on a big writing project has to settle one question at the outset: where do I start? Plenty of writers throw up their hands and give up, unable to get past that point. Word master documents ensure that this calamity need never befall you. With a new master document, you always get your writing job off to a good start.

Suppose, for example, that we're planning to write a book in twenty-five chapters, divided up into five parts. Each of those five parts is going to be a subdocument, with five short chapters in each subdocument. Instead of staring at a blank screen, wondering what the heck to write, we'll get off to a solid start with a master document.

Master documents start with an outline

To create a master document for a new long document, you begin by creating an outline. Make it as detailed as you like. As long as you use Word's outline tools to format your headings and subheadings, the master document will come out perfectly.

To outline a new document:

1. Click View, Master Document. That switches you to Master Document view and pops up the Outlining and Master Document toolbars.

TIP **Or get to Master Document view like this: click the Outline** View button at the lower left corner of the screen to pop up Outline view and the Outlining toolbar. Then click the Master Document View button on the Outlining toolbar.

2 Type your document title. This will be the title for the long document itself. You don't have to have a title at all, but it's always a good beginning.

3 Press Enter to go to the next line, and type the first section heading. It's going to be our first subdocument. We'll call it **Part I**.

TIP **The headings that you turn into subdocuments will be saved as** separate files when you save the master document. Word uses the headings for file names, so it's a good idea to write headings that are also descriptive enough to work as file names. To avoid conflicts, Word may alter the heading text when it names the subdocument.

4 Click the Demote button on the Outlining toolbar (or press Tab) to demote the heading to Heading 2 level. Figure 17.1 shows the master document so far.

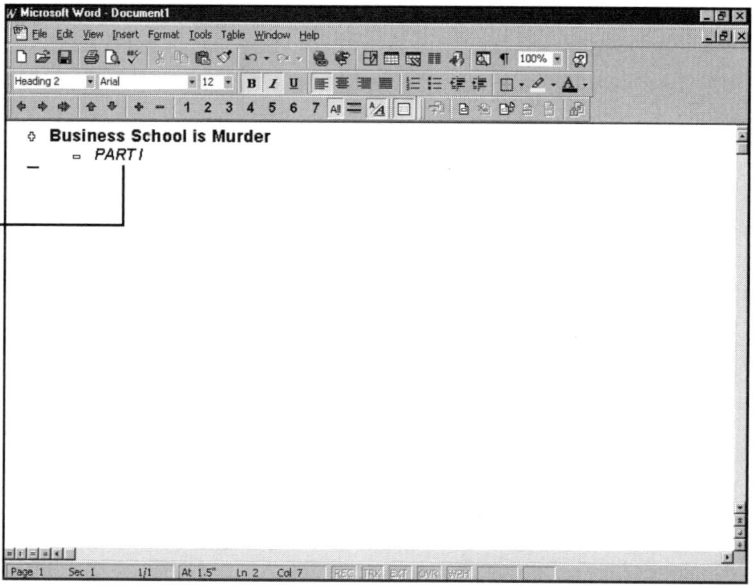

Fig. 17.1
Creating a master document is just like creating an outline.

This subheading under the document title will be the first subdocument

5 Now type the first subheading under Part I. We're calling it **Chapter 1**. Press Enter at the end of the line and type the next subheading, **Chapter 2**. Repeat the procedure for all the subheadings in Part I, through Chapter 5.

6 We want to demote those subheadings under Part I to Heading 3 level, so we'll take care of them all at once. Position the pointer over the minus sign next to Chapter 1, and it turns into a four-headed arrow. Click to select the subheading, Chapter 1.

7 Shift+click inside the last subheading in Part I, Chapter 5. That selects all the subheadings under Part I at once, as shown in Figure 17.2.

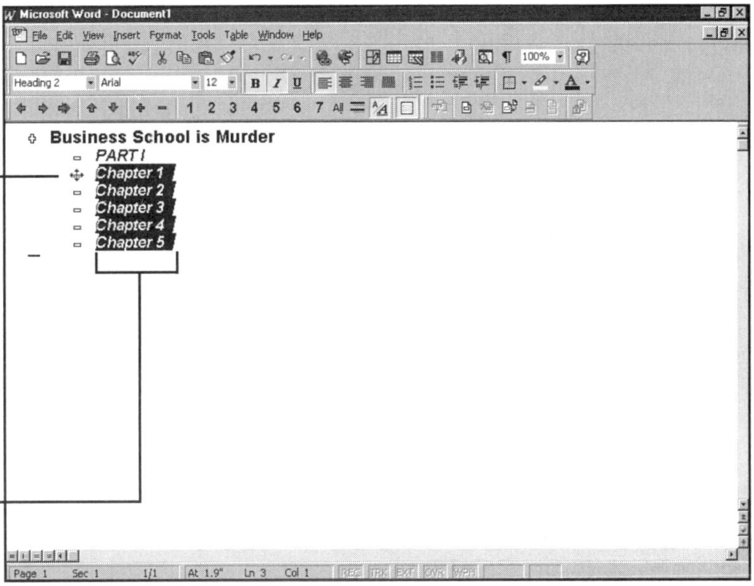

Fig. 17.2
Click the first subheading, then Shift+click the last subheading in a section to select them all.

The pointer turns into a four-headed arrow when you position it over the outline symbols. Click to select the first heading.

Shift+click inside the text of the last heading to select them all

8 Click the Demote button on the Outlining toolbar to demote all the selected subheadings to Heading 3 level.

9 Type the next subdocument heading, **Part II**. Click the Promote button on the Outlining toolbar to make it a Heading 2 level heading. Type the subheadings, Chapters 6 through 10, select and demote them, and repeat for Parts III, IV, and V. When you're through, it'll look something like Figure 17.3.

Fig. 17.3
One more benefit of using master documents: you're forced to write an outline before you start writing the document.

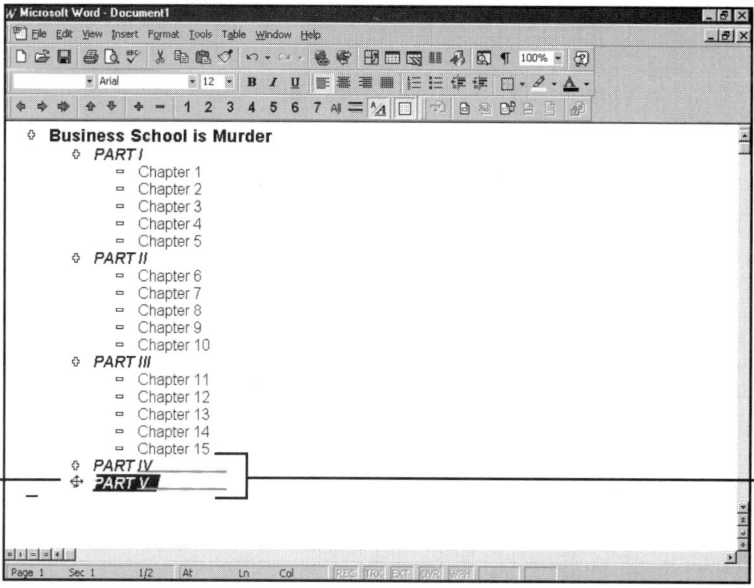

To collapse outline items under a heading, double-click the outline symbol with the four-headed arrow

This text is collapsed so you can see all the headings

Turn outlines into master documents with a click or three

Once the outline is completed, turning it into a master document is a snap. There's only one decision to make: what heading level to use as subdocuments. In the example in Figure 17.3, we only have one Heading 1 level heading, so the choices are between the Heading 2 and Heading 3 level headings.

Either one works; it's just a question of how many subdocuments you want to work with. Word will create separate document files for each heading we turn into a subdocument, based on the first heading in the selection. If you really wanted twenty-five different files, you'd make the first selected heading a Heading 3 level head. In this case, five separate files seems like plenty, so we'll make our first selection a Heading 2 level heading.

To create a master document from an outline:

1 Select all the headings that you want to turn into subdocuments. Click the first heading that you want for a subdocument, then Shift+click inside the text of the last heading. Figure 17.4 shows the selected headings.

Fig. 17.4
These selected Heading 2 heads will become subdocuments, with the Heading 3 heads below them as subheads in the subdocument files.

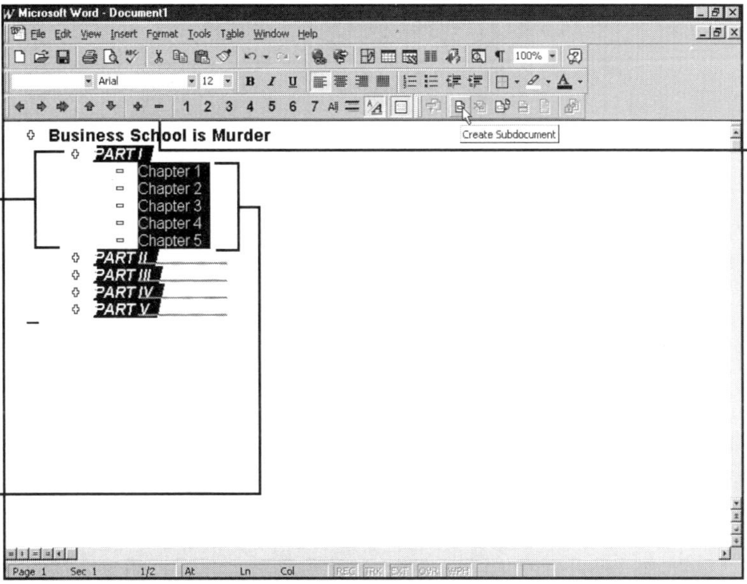

If you find the subheadings confusing, click the Collapse button to put them out of sight

Selecting the Heading 2 headings also selects the Heading 3 subheads, which become subsections in each subdocument

If you wanted subdocuments for each chapter, you'd make the first Heading 3 head your first selection

2 With the outline headings selected, click the Create Subdocument button on the Master Document toolbar. Since a Heading 2 level head was the first heading in the selection, Word creates a subdocument for every Heading 2 head it finds within the selected text, as shown in Figure 17.5.

Fig. 17.5
The Heading 2 level heads in the selected text created the subdocuments.

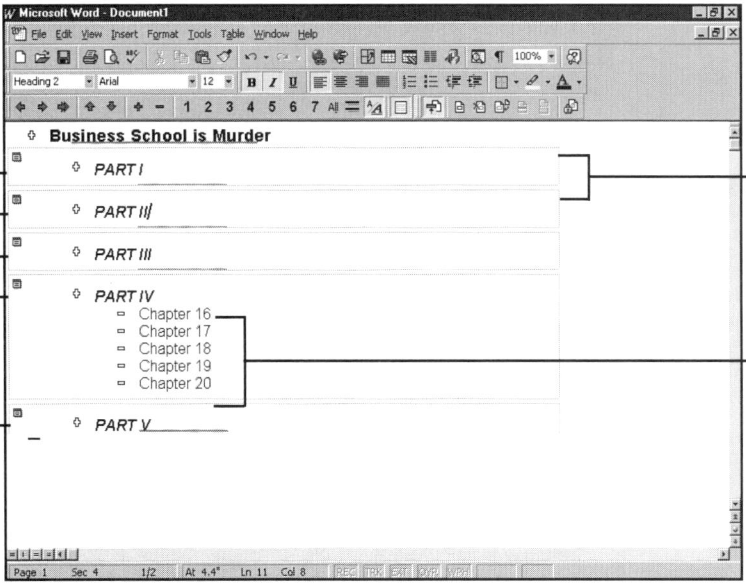

Word adds a border around each subdocument

These subdocument icons appear automatically; double-click one to open the subdocument

The subheads are within each subdocument

What happens when I save my master document?

With the master document created, all you have to do is save it (of course, there's still that little matter of actually writing the document). Click the Save button on the Standard toolbar and give your master document a name. When you click Save in the Save As dialog box, Word saves the master document, and all the subdocuments too. Each subdocument gets the heading text as a file name, as shown in Figure 17.6.

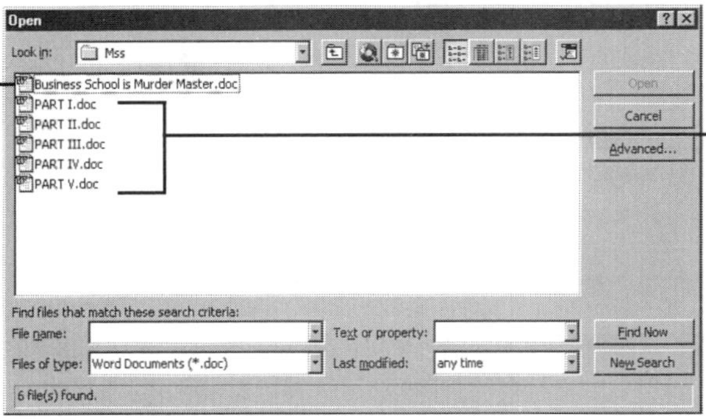

Fig. 17.6
The Open dialog box shows the saved master document file, and all the subdocument files with the headings as file names.

Here's our master document

These are the subdocuments, saved under the names of the outline headings

So what do I do with this master document?

Now we've got our document outlined, divided up into handy subdocuments, and named and saved. Just add text and call it a day. To add the text, double-click any of the subdocument icons in the master document. That opens the subdocument, and you can start typing. Format the text any way you like; the subdocument is an ordinary Word file, so treat it accordingly.

Figure 17.7 shows a windowed view of the master document and an open subdocument.

When you open a subdocument for editing, a padlock appears in the subdocument in Master Document view (refer to Figure 17.7), indicating that the master document subdocument is locked. You can edit all you want in the open subdocument file, but you can't make changes to the corresponding master document subdocument. If you want to do that, close the subdocument file first.

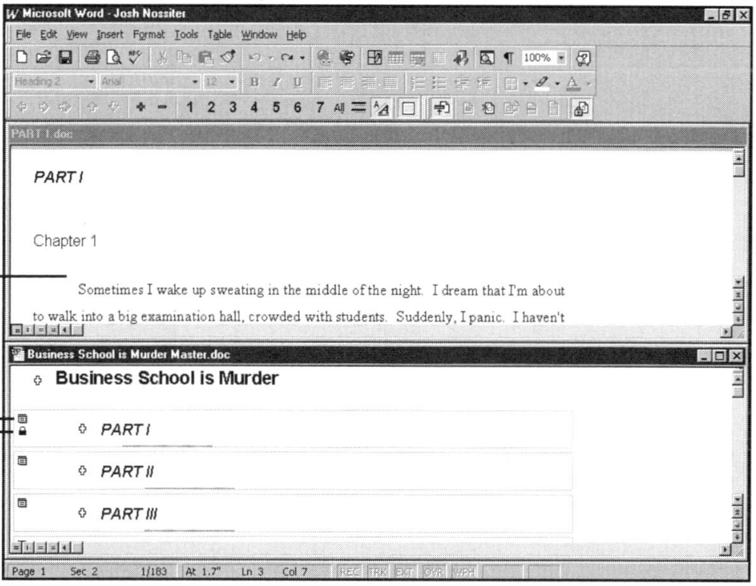

Fig. 17.7
A mere five chapters to write, and they're probably due tomorrow. At least the chapter headings are done.

...pops open the Part 1 document

Double-clicking the Part 1 subdocument icon...

The padlock in Master Document view appears when you open the subdocument

TIP **Text that you type in the subdocument also appears in the master** document. If you add additional subheadings in a subdocument, format them with the built-in Word heading styles (Headings 1...8). Formatted this way, the headings will show up in the master document *as* headings. That preserves the structure of your outline. To get the built-in headings, click the Style Box drop-down arrow on the Formatting toolbar.

What else should I know about master documents and subdocuments?

Although subdocuments are ordinary Word document files, they're linked to the master document. Because of that, there are a few things to keep in mind:

- If you want to delete a subdocument, do it from the master document, not the Windows Explorer or My Computer. Otherwise you'll get an error message from Word when you try to open a master document containing subdocuments that Word can't find.
- Double-click the subdocument icon in the master document and use the Save As dialog box to move or rename subdocuments. Moving or renaming subdocuments with the master document closed results in error messages when you try to reopen the master document.

- Editing changes you make within a subdocument automatically updates the subdocument in the master document. The reverse is also true: make changes to the subdocument from the master document, and when you open the subdocument, you'll find those changes in it as well.

How do I turn this long document into a master document?

There's nothing quite like finishing a big writing project. Fiction or non, book or report, for a writer "The End" is the most satisfying phrase in the language. But for most of us, The End is just the beginning: of rewriting, editing, and revising.

Converting a single big document file into a master document can help make the revisions phase of a writing project less arduous. Breaking up an existing document makes it easier to focus on problem areas one at a time. And if you have co-writers on the project, it's sometimes handier to send revised subdocument sections back and forth, rather than the entire document.

It's easy to turn an existing file into a master document:

1. Open the document and click View, Master Document.
2. Your document is displayed in Outline view. If you already have headings styled in the Heading 1 through Heading 8 styles, your outline is already done and you can skip down to step 5.

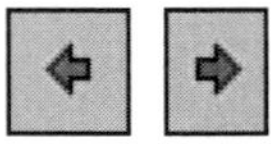

3. If you used your own formatting for headings, they appear as body text. Click the heading, then click the Promote and Demote buttons on the Outlining toolbar to format them in the various heading styles, as shown in Figure 17.8.
4. Work your way through the entire document, applying Word's heading styles to your headings. If you don't like the way they look, modify the heading styles (see Chapter 12, "Word Documents Are Never Out of Style," for details on how to do that).

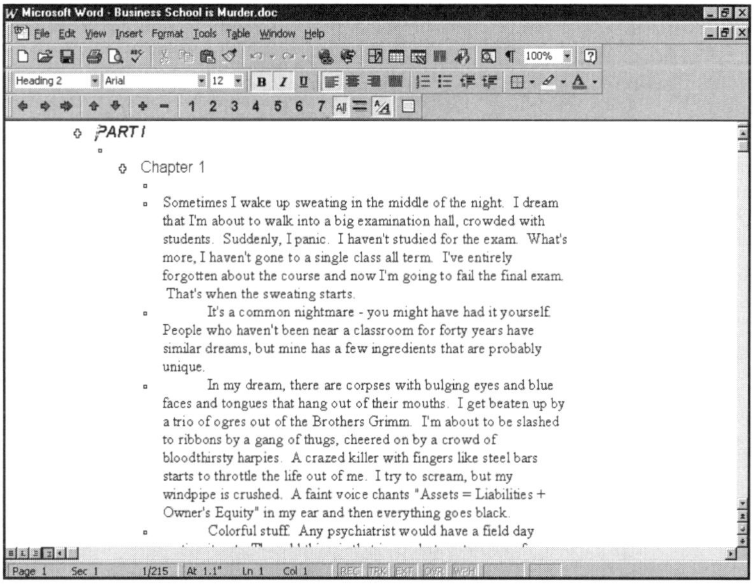
Microsoft Word - Business School is Murder.doc
File Edit View Insert Format Tools Table Window Help
Heading 2
Arial
12
100%
1 2 3 4 5 6 7 All
PART I
Chapter 1
Sometimes I wake up sweating in the middle of the night. I dream that I'm about to walk into a big examination hall, crowded with students. Suddenly, I panic. I haven't studied for the exam. What's more, I haven't gone to a single class all term. I've entirely forgotten about the course and now I'm going to fail the final exam. That's when the sweating starts.
It's a common nightmare - you might have had it yourself. People who haven't been near a classroom for forty years have similar dreams, but mine has a few ingredients that are probably unique.
In my dream, there are corpses with bulging eyes and blue faces and tongues that hang out of their mouths. I get beaten up by a trio of ogres out of the Brothers Grimm. I'm about to be slashed to ribbons by a gang of thugs, cheered on by a crowd of bloodthirsty harpies. A crazed killer with fingers like steel bars starts to throttle the life out of me. I try to scream, but my windpipe is crushed. A faint voice chants "Assets = Liabilities + Owner's Equity" in my ear and then everything goes black.
Colorful stuff. Any psychiatrist would have a field day
Page 1 Sec 1 1/215 At 1.1" Ln 1 Col 1 REC TRK EXT OVR WPH

Fig. 17.8
Converting an existing document into a master document starts with an outline.

TIP **The fast way to track down headings in a long document? Click** Edit, Find for the Find dialog box. Type the first few letters of your next heading in the Find What text box (type **chap** if you're looking for chapters, for example). Then click Find Next. When you get to your heading, don't close the Find dialog box. Click in the document, but outside the dialog box, then click the Promote or Demote button. That promotes or demotes the heading, and leaves the Find dialog box popped up. Click Find Next again to go the next heading, and repeat.

5 With all your headings properly promoted or demoted, it's decision time. Which heading level do you want at the beginning of each subdocument? Whichever heading you choose, Word will dump all the text between those heading levels into each subdocument you create. Here, we're going to create subdocuments at each Heading 2 level heading.

2

6 Click the Show Heading 2 button on the Outlining toolbar. That collapses all the text in between each Heading 2 heading, as shown in Figure 17.9.

Fig. 17.9
This step is not essential, but it's a lot easier to see what you're doing when only the critical headings are in view.

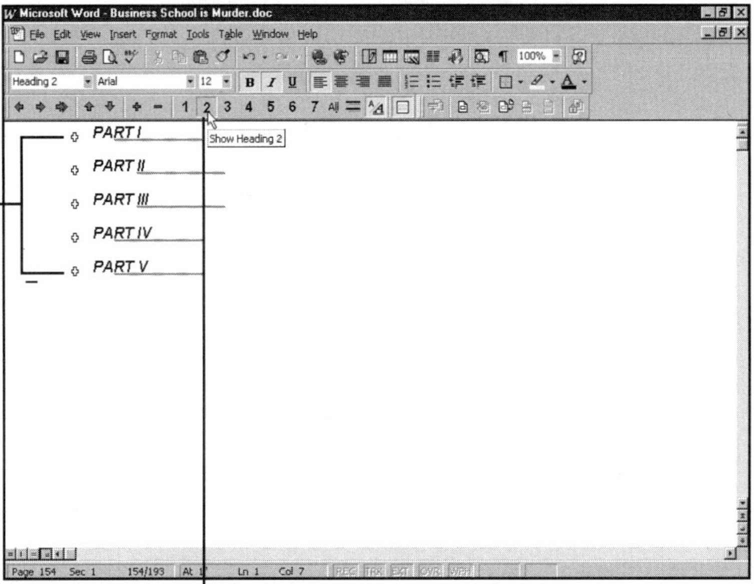

Clicking Show Heading 2 displays only the Heading 2 level heads (the faint underline tells you the text is collapsed)

Decide what heading level you want at the beginning of each subdocument, then click the corresponding Show Heading button

7 Position the pointer over the plus sign next to the first displayed heading and click to select it.

8 Now position the pointer inside the text of the last displayed heading, and Shift+click to select them all, as shown in Figure 17.10.

9 With all the headings selected, click the Create Subdocument button on the Master Document toolbar. The selected headings are enclosed in boxes, and the subdocument icons pop up beside each one, as shown in Figure 17.11.

All the text in between each Heading 2 head in Figure 17.11 is now dumped into separate subdocument files. The subdocument files are named after each heading, as in Part I.

To open each subdocument, double-click the corresponding subdocument icon. To view the entire document, click the Normal View button down at the lower left corner of the screen.

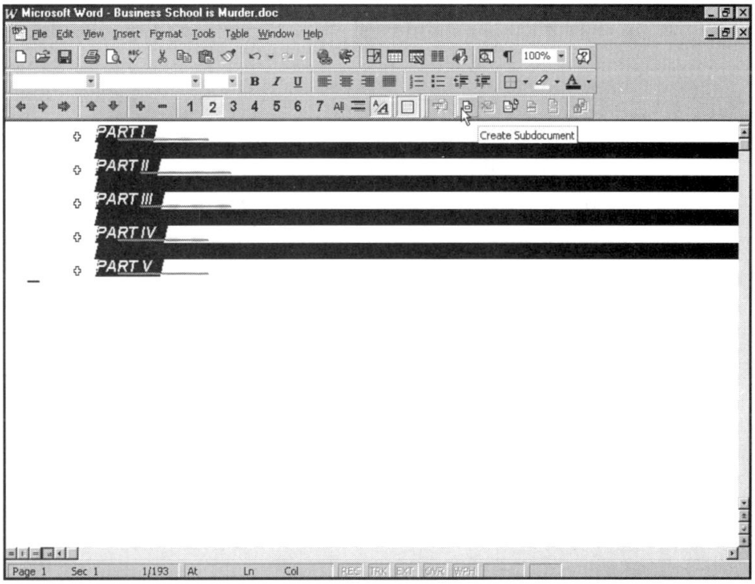

Fig. 17.10
Use the Shift+click combination to select all the headings at once.

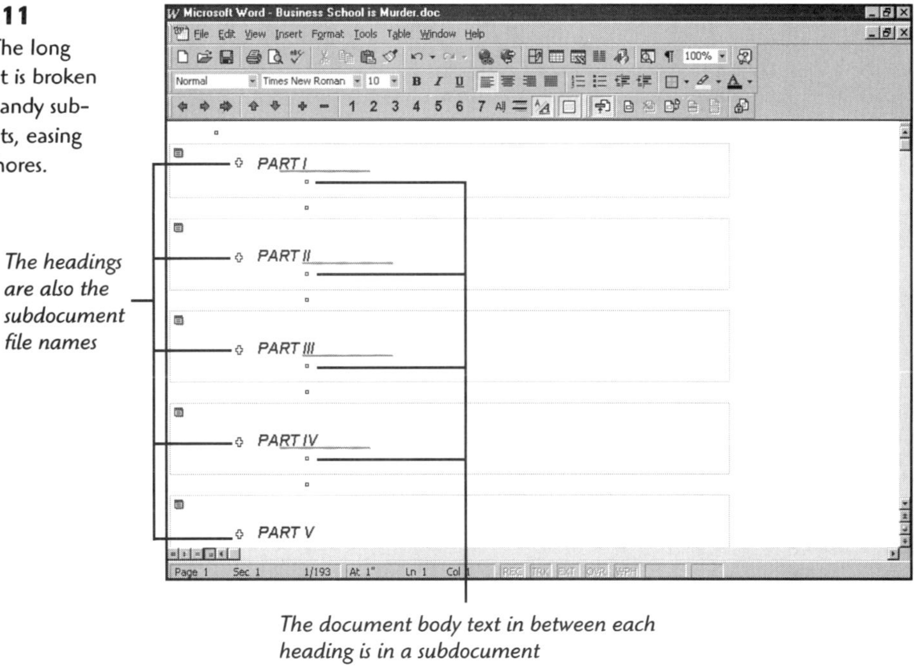

Fig. 17.11
Eureka! The long document is broken up into handy subdocuments, easing editing chores.

I'm drowning in a sea of Master Document text

Convenience is the main reason for creating a master document in the first place. You want to open your subdocuments fast whenever they need work, then put them away just as quickly when you're done. And when you need to work on the whole document at once, you want all your subdocuments to spring open with a single click.

Click the Collapse Subdocuments button on the Master Document toolbar, and each subdocument in the master document shrinks to a hyperlink. Click the button again, and all the subdocuments expand, displaying whatever text and graphics they contain. You can also click a subdocument hyperlink to open that subdocument. Figure 17.12 shows a master document with collapsed subdocuments.

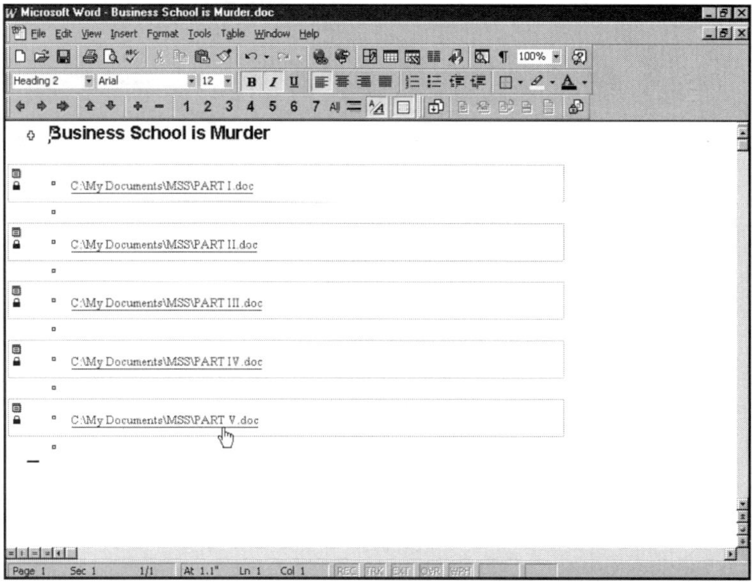

Fig. 17.12
Subdocument hyperlinks act just like links on the World Wide Web; click one to go right to the subdocument.

Plain English, please!

Hyperlinks are automated cross-references. Instead of a notation like "see page 50," a hyperlink connected to page 50 takes you to the page with a single click. Hyperlinks are familiar to anyone who's meandered along the byways of the World Wide Web. They're the underlined words or phrases that we click to travel from page to page on the global network. Word hyperlinks, like Web links, are underlined, and change color once they've been clicked.

Clicking a single subdocument hyperlink is just like double-clicking a subdocument icon. The real advantage of the Collapse (and Expand) Subdocuments button is that it collapses (and expands) all your subdocuments at once. If your master document is bulging with text, that's very convenient. And that, after all, is why we're here.

Q&A *I changed the master document's template, and now all the formatting in my subdocuments has changed!*

The more you look at a master document, the more inclined you might be to change the way it looks. The Format, Style Gallery command, for example, can give your master document a radically new appearance. That's fine, but the master document's template overrides the subdocuments' formatting. If you change the master template, the change is also applied to the subdocuments.

I want to print my master document

Here's one good reason to use master documents: they let you control exactly how much or how little of a document you print. You can print the whole document, or just bits and pieces of it, with ease:

- To print the entire document, click the Normal View button, then click the Print button on the Standard toolbar.
- If you want to print a subdocument, double-click the subdocument icon in the master document to open the subdocument file. Click the Print button, and only the open subdocument will print.

- To print several subdocuments, click the Open button on the Standard toolbar. Click the first subdocument you want to print to select it, then Ctrl+click each additional subdocument. Press the right mouse button and select Print from the shortcut menu. Click OK in the Print dialog box to print the selected subdocuments.
- To print selected sections of a long document, use Master Document view and the Outlining toolbar to display or hide as much of the document as you want to print. Click the Print button on the toolbar to print only the displayed text.

How do I turn these different files into a single master document?

You've been slaving away for weeks on a long document. You've dutifully saved each section or chapter of the opus in separate files, named Chapter 1 or Section 2, or something similar. Now that you've accumulated a collection of such files, you're beginning to wish the document was in one file after all. Maybe you need to make a global replacement or two, or print the whole document.

If a heap of separate files is a nuisance, use Word's electronic paper clip to gather them together. Just create a new master document, in which the subdocuments are your separate files.

To gather different files together in a master document:

1. Click View, Master Document to switch to Master Document view.

2. Click the Insert Subdocument button on the Master Document toolbar. That pops up the Insert Subdocument dialog box shown in Figure 17.13.
3. Double-click any file listed in the Insert Subdocument dialog box, and the file is popped into the master document as a subdocument.
4. Files inserted into master documents keep their existing file names. Add as many files as you like, then save the master document with its own file name.

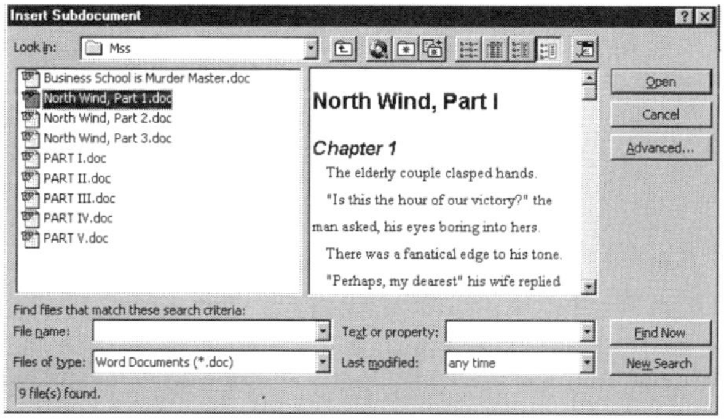

Fig. 17.13
The Insert Subdocument menu looks a lot like the Open dialog box. Just like its twin, it lists all your Word files.

If you insert a file as a subdocument and change your mind, just click the Undo button on the Standard toolbar.

CAUTION

Remember that the master document template overrides the formatting in subdocuments. If your master document is formatted in a template different from your inserted subdocument's template, the subdocument gets the master document's formatting.

18 Running a Tight Ship: Managing Your Files

In this chapter:

- **Avoiding file overload: creating new files**
- **Can I really create a list of the folders I use the most?**
- **Where did I put that file? How to find lost documents**
- **I need a system for organizing my files!**
- **Moving, copying, and renaming files**

With Word's simple file management tricks, you'll spend more time writing and less time trying to unearth misplaced documents. . . . .

It's an annual taxpayer's ritual. Each spring, you spend countless hours digging out the receipts, invoices, and canceled checks you tossed in drawers and shoe boxes during the last 12 months. And each spring you promise yourself that from now on you're going to keep your financial papers organized.

Your Word files are a lot like your personal paperwork. They're made up of many different kinds of documents—some big, some small, some important, some not, but too often tossed carelessly into whatever folder is available as you hurry from one task to the next.

Your computing life doesn't have to be that way. After all, you have a computer to make life simpler, not create more chaos. Why not let your computer do the work it's designed for?

Word 97 has a host of features whose purpose is to help you organize your documents. You can create folders; move easily among your folders; delete, move, and rename files; and find files by file name or by content.

Good file organization starts with good folder management. Once you learn how to create folders and subfolders, you'll begin to see how you can use those folders to develop a file-saving system. Who knows? It might even give you some ideas on how to prepare your financial records for next April.

Folder finesse

On most computers, Word is set up to save your files in a folder called Winword. But putting all of your documents in one folder is like tossing all your papers into one file drawer—convenient but sloppy. A much better strategy is to create subfolders by subject as you need them.

Since every computer is set up differently, you'll have to decide for yourself where you're going to put what folders for what documents. Later, we'll talk more about how to organize the documents on your hard drive. But for now, let's keep life simple and use the Winword folder as our base of operations.

Plain English, please!

A **folder** is a Windows 95 and Windows NT 3.51 term for what previous versions of Windows and MS-DOS called a directory.

Q&A *Why wouldn't I use Windows' Explorer for my file and folder management?*

Word's Open and Save As dialog boxes are designed to handle simple, routine file and folder management. Explorer has more functions, and it gives you better options for moving and copying files (for example, the ability to drag and drop). If you're familiar with Explorer and have to do extensive file management tasks, Explorer is probably the better option.

Creating a new folder

Your Winword folder will probably contain several folders already, such as Wordmail, Macros, and Startup. Let's assume you want to create a fourth folder called Expense Reports.

From the Save As dialog box, click the Create New Folder button. The New Folder dialog box appears like the one shown in Figure 18.1. `New Folder` is highlighted in the Name text box; type the name of the folder you want to create and click OK.

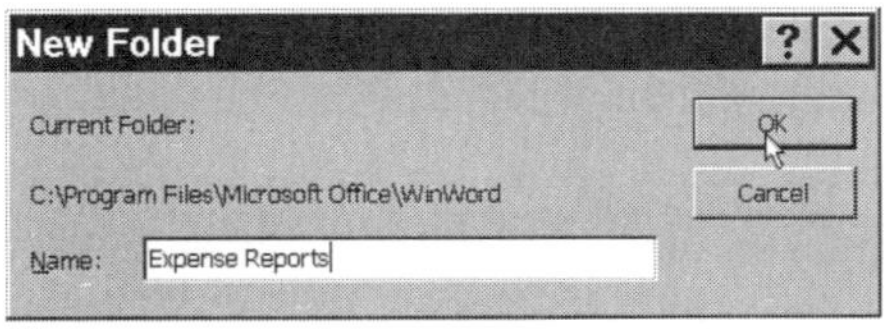

Fig. 18.1
To create a new folder, type its name in the Name text box and click OK.

TIP **You can create folders within folders. For example, the folder** Letters might in turn contain a folder for each month of the year. The second folder is often called a **subfolder**.

Q&A *When I create a folder, can I only use it for Word documents?*

Word is not actually creating the folder, it's instructing Windows to create it. Thus, your folder is available to all of your programs. Also, you can manage folders created in Word with Windows Explorer.

Moving to a folder

You move to your new folder by double-clicking it.

To return to the previous folder, click the Up One Level button to the right of the Save In text box.

TIP  **Click the Details button on the Save As dialog box toolbar** to get more information on the files in a folder. Word tells you if the item is a folder, Word document, or other item; when you last modified the folder or file; and, for files, the size.

Playing Favorites: creating a list of favorite folders

Urban rail commuters can usually choose between two types of transportation—the regular train, which stops at every station, or the express train, which goes straight to their destination.

The Save As dialog box has its own express train: the Favorites list. Click the Look In Favorites button on the Save As dialog box toolbar. Click a folder on the list, and Word goes directly to the folder, no matter where it is on your hard drive. The Favorites list can also include files, which you can open without first going to the proper folder.

Figure 18.2 shows a typical Favorites list, consisting of a file and two folders.

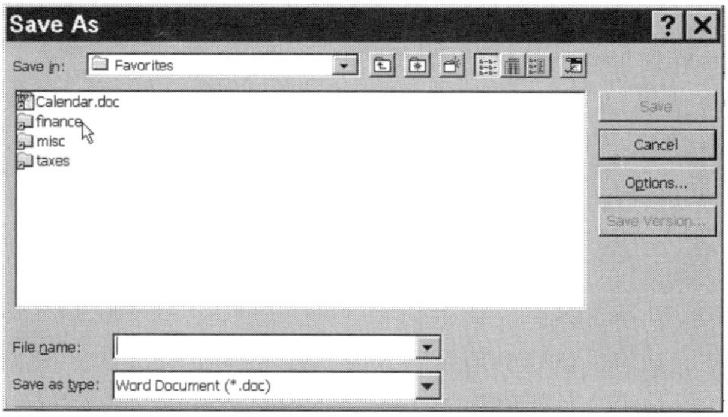

Fig. 18.2
For quick access to your most used folders and documents, use the Favorites list. The Look In Favorites button calls the list; the Add To Favorites button to the right adds to the list.

Your Favorites list is empty until you add folders and files to it. You can't add an item to your Favorites list from the Save As dialog box; you have to do it from the Open dialog box. Go to the appropriate folder and click the Add To Favorites button on the Open dialog box toolbar. A small selection box pops up, giving you two options:

- Add *folder name* To Favorites, where *folder name* is the folder in the Look In box, adds the folder that appears in the Look In text box to your list.
- Add Selected Item To Favorites adds the item you've selected in the list box. You can select any item, including documents and folders.

TIP **When you're in your Favorites folder, the Favorites button changes** into a Return To button. Click the button to return to the folder you came from.

List limitations

Favorites is a folder that contains shortcuts, called *links*, to the files and folders you see. (You can identify a shortcut by the little boxed arrow in the lower left-hand corner of the icon.) If you use the shortcut menu to delete an item in the Favorites list, you delete the link, not the actual file or folder. Similarly, copying or moving an item copies or moves the link, not the file or folder the item represents.

CAUTION **Be careful that you don't accidentally save a file into the Favorites** folder. You might mistake it for a link and accidentally delete it. Keep actual files in regular folders.

Changing your start-up folder

When you run Word, it always starts you in the same folder—a real inconvenience if you want to begin your work somewhere else. It's easy to change this start-up folder to one of your own choosing.

Select Tools, Options from the menu bar and click the File Locations tab. Highlight Documents in the File Types selection box, then click Modify.

A Modify Location dialog box appears, similar to the Open dialog box. Move to the folder you want as the default. Its name appears in the Folder Name text box. Then click OK.

Finding files

As long as you have only a handful of documents in a few folders, finding your files won't be hard. You can click folders and the Up One Level button to move around until you see the document in the Open list box.

But as you create new folders, and subfolders within folders, and subfolders within subfolders within folders, the day will come when you'll start to lose track of your files. Before long, you'll be wandering around your hard drive like a bewildered shopper in a mall, searching every shelf of every aisle for that old report your boss suddenly wants a copy of.

Word devotes a number of features to help you find files. But first, let's digress a bit and talk about disk drive organization.

Before you reach for the silver bullets and garlic cloves, be assured that this will not be a technical discussion of sectors, file allocation tables, and other such technical trivia. We'll keep the material simple and talk only about matters that relate directly to finding your documents.

How your drive is organized

It's much easier to find a store at the mall if you have a general idea of the mall's floor plan. You'll likewise have an easier time finding folders and files if you understand how they're placed on your hard drive.

The easiest way to get a sense of how your folders are structured is to click the Look In text box in the Open dialog box. Word shows you a tree similar to the one shown in Figure 18.3.

To simplify matters for now, we're going to forget about Desktop and My Computer and assume that the hard drive, `(C:)` in Figure 18.3, is at the top of the tree. Cascading from C: is a series of folders that eventually leads to the current folder, called Resolved.

TIP **On most computer systems, the floppy drive is drive A: the hard** drive, C:, and the CD-ROM drive, D: If you're on a network, the network drives will have other letter designations.

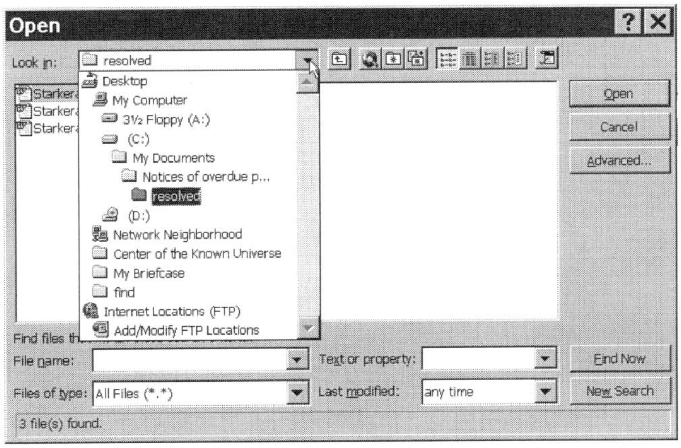

Fig. 18.3
Click the Look In text box to see how your folders are organized.

The tree reveals how the folders are nested within one another. My Documents Notices of Overdue Payment, which contains Resolved.

Clicking the Up One Level button takes us to the Notices of Overdue Payment folder. As Figure 18.4 shows, Resolved is one of three folders in Notices of Overdue Payment. Moving up another level would show that Notices of Overdue Payment is in turn one of seven folders in My Documents.

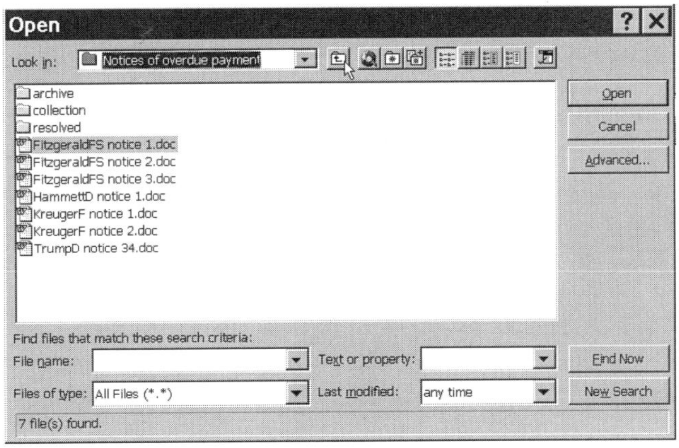

Fig. 18.4
Resolved is one of three folders nested in the Notices of Overdue Payment folder.

C: worthy

Eventually, if you go up enough levels, you'll get to the C: drive (see Figure 18.5).

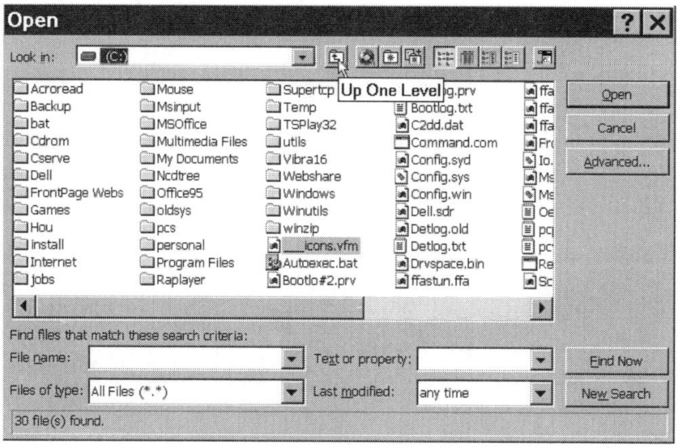

Fig. 18.5
At the top of the folder heap is C:, to which all folders belong.

To return to our shopping mall metaphor, C: is the mall's main atrium. Along with My Documents are a variety of other "stores," which variously contain programs (Acroread, WinZip, Vibra16), groups of programs (games, utilities), and system files (Windows). Most of these folders have nested folders similar to those inside My Documents.

If your computer is new, you probably don't have many folders in C:. But if you're a compulsive organizer, folders will start multiplying like the dust bunnies under your bed. A modest 380-megabyte drive might hold thousands of files in hundreds of folders.

Obviously, clicking folders and the Up One Level button to root around your hard drive looking for a file is impractical. In fact, it's a complete waste of time when you can automate the search with Word's file-finding features.

Finding a file anywhere on your drive

Here's a simple example of how to search your entire drive for a specific file. In this case, the search is for a document, containing "The Legend of Sleepy Hollow," whose file name includes the word "sleepy":

1. Open the Open dialog box (see Figure 18.6) and select the C: drive from the Look In text box.
2. Because the file might not have a .DOC extension, choose All Files in the Files Of Type text box.
3. Type **sleepy** in the File Name text box.

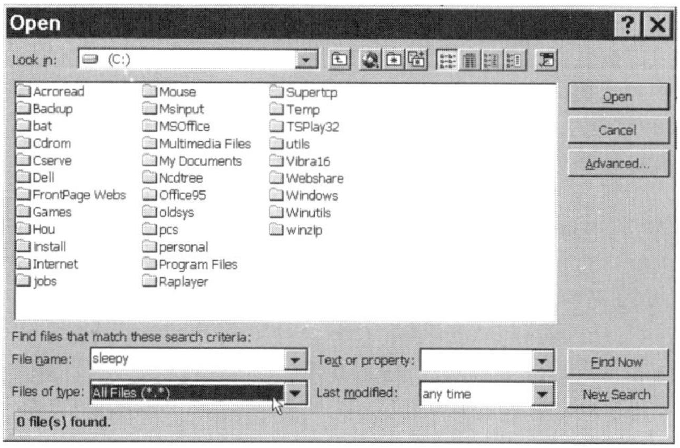

Fig. 18.6
Start a file search in the Open dialog box by entering a file name or part of a file name in the File Name text box and choosing what types of files to look for.

4 Click the Commands and Settings button and select Search Subfolders.

5 Click Find Now. Word searches the hard drive for all file names that include "sleepy" and presents a list.

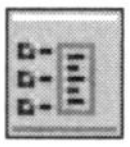

6 Click the Preview button to display the contents of the files and show what folders they're in (see Figure 18.7).

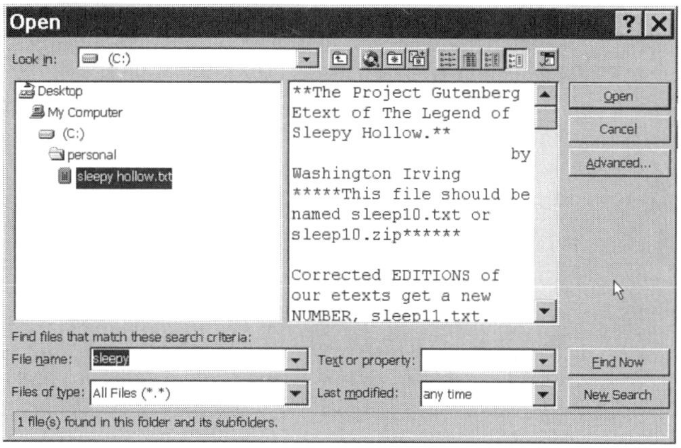

Fig. 18.7
When Word is done with its search, it shows you a list of all the files that match the search criteria.

TIP **Searching your entire hard drive can take a while. If you know the** file is somewhere in a certain set of folders, start your search from the top folder of the tree. You also can narrow your search by date; click the Last Modified text box and choose one of the options offered. And if you really want to get fancy, click the Advanced button; it opens the Advanced Find dialog box, which offers a variety of options for choosing search criteria.

Finding a file by its contents

A few years ago, Ed's mom sent him e-mail that included a quotation Ed now wants to use in a speech to the local literary club. But there's a problem—Ed can't remember the name of the file it's in.

Almost all of us have lost information this way. In such an instance, a file name search is futile. But Word has a solution: it can search the *contents* of your files.

A content search is almost identical to a file name search. The only difference is that you leave the File Name text box empty and put the text you want to find in the Text Or Property text box.

In Figure 18.8, for example, Word lists all files in the Personal folder that include the string "murder."

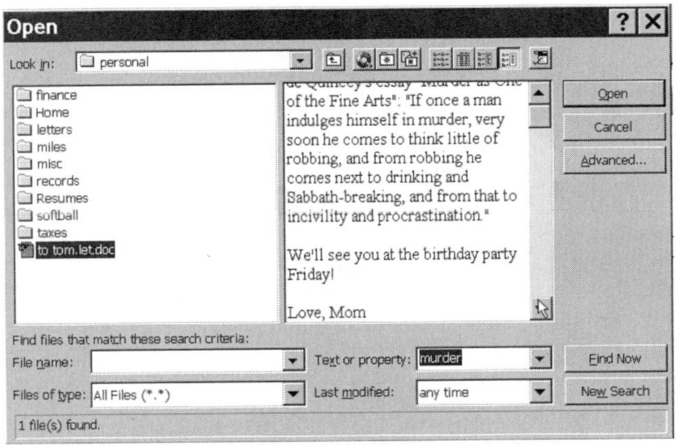

Fig. 18.8
Word lets you search for documents that include a specific string, which you type in the Text Or Property text box.

TIP **You can sort your file names by size, type, or date modified.** Select Sorting from the Commands and Settings menu.

Q&A ***I did a content search, and it took more than half an hour! Is there any way I can speed up my searches?***

You can take a couple of steps to make your searches go faster. First, don't search the entire drive unless you have to. If you know the file is in a certain tree of folders, search only those folders. And second, avoid using All Files in the Files of Type text box.

CAUTION **Don't forget to turn off Search Subfolders when you're done with** your search. Otherwise, Word will search all of your subfolders the next time you use the Open dialog box.

Barking up the right folder tree

Throughout this chapter, we've touched on how a hard drive organizes folders and files. We've also mentioned the importance of not putting all of your documents in the Winword folder.

But we haven't answered an important question: how do you decide what folders to create and where to put them?

This is not the place for a long discussion of file organization. However, because drives are as large as they are these days, you need a plan you can put into effect from the moment you save your first document.

Here is an overview of the two most popular models for file organization: Grouping files by subject and grouping them by file type.

Organizing files by subject

When you organize files by subject, you create a folder for each subject and folders for different parts of the subject.

For example, let's say you sell widgets for the Wellworthit Widget Company. For each client, you've got a variety of reports, correspondence, and proposals.

You might begin by creating a folder called Clients in drive C:. In that folder, you create subfolders for each client. And in each of those subfolders, you create subfolders for the type of document. The resulting tree would look something like this:

```
--Drive C:
  --Clients
    --Carbo
      --Budgets
      --Letters
```

```
  --Proposals
  --Reports
--Fisk
  --Budgets
  --Letters
  --Proposals
  --Reports
--Lee
  --Budgets
  --Letters
  --Proposals
  --Reports
--Rice
  --Budgets
  --Letters
  --Proposals
  --Reports
```

Mixing file types

When you organize by subject, you often mix file types. For example, in the tree above, the folder Proposals might include Word documents and Excel budget spreadsheets. This technique is becoming more practical as programs are able to use data of different formats.

Pros and cons of organizing files by subject

The advantage of this type of disk organization is that you can manage your files by subject. You can move, copy, and delete files and folders with minimum effort.

Also, while your documents are in many different folders, you can still manage them as a group by using the file-finding commands in the Open dialog box. For example, if you want to copy certain documents to a floppy disk, you search the drive for all document files, then select and copy the ones from the resulting list.

The disadvantage is that not all programs you use might have Word's ability to manage files. For example, if you're using a spreadsheet program that's a few years old, you might not like having your spreadsheet files scattered all over your hard drive.

Organizing files by type

When you organize your files by type, you set up folders to hold the data files for each of your programs.

The tree below shows a file structure for the Wellworthit Widget Company. Main folders have been set up for spreadsheets, Word documents, and databases. Each main folder has subfolders for different subjects:

```
--Drive C:

  --123 spreadsheets

    --Clients

      --Carbo

      --Budgets

    --Expense reports

  --Word documents

    --Clients

      --Carbo

        --Letters

        --Proposals

    --Meeting notes

  --Databases

    --Clients

      --Active list
```

```
    --Old list
    --Prospects
  --Vendors
  --Distributors
```

Pros and cons of organizing files by type

The upside of organizing by file type is that you can copy, back up, and delete all of your documents more easily. Your documents are also a little easier to find; you don't have to swing from tree to tree to find the files you want.

On the other hand, you might have files for a project scattered among several folder trees, so deleting or backing them up as a group can be inconvenient.

Besides their obvious jobs of saving and opening files, respectively, the Save As and Open dialog boxes can handle routine tasks such as copying, moving, deleting, and renaming files.

The important commands are packaged neatly in a shortcut menu (see Figure 18.9), which you get by selecting the file you want to work with and clicking the right mouse button.

Fig. 18.9
For common file management commands, select a file in the Open dialog box and click the right mouse button.

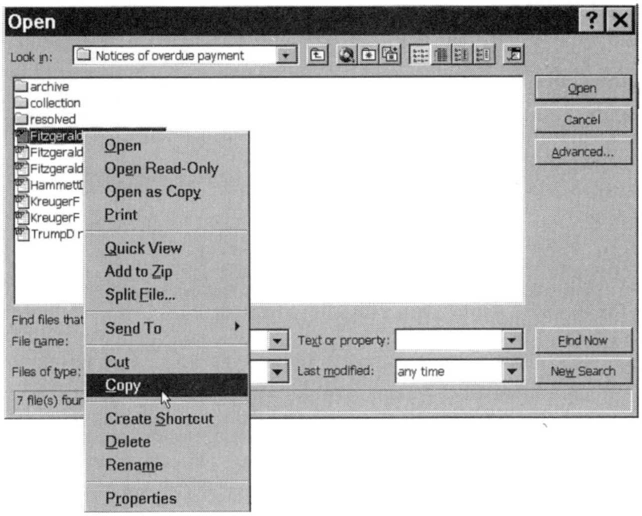

TIP **You can use the shortcut menu to copy, move, and delete folders** the same way you do files.

How to copy files

Word's copy functions lack many amenities, such as Explorer's ability to drag and drop a file. But the shortcut menu's Copy command can't be beat for quickly and efficiently copying a file to another folder.

Highlight the file you want to copy and choose Copy from the shortcut menu. Ignore the fact that absolutely nothing seems to happen, and go to the folder you want to copy the file to. Click the right mouse button on an empty part of the list box. Choose Paste from the shortcut menu, and a copy of the file appears.

TIP **To copy a file to a floppy disk, choose Send To on the shortcut** menu and select the floppy drive.

How to move files

You move files the same way you copy them, only you use Cut instead of Copy.

Highlight the file you want to move and choose Cut from the shortcut menu. Go to the destination folder and click the right mouse button on an empty part of the list box. Click Paste.

How to delete files

To get rid of a file, choose Delete from the shortcut menu. Word asks you to confirm the deletion, then tosses the file into the Recycle Bin.

TIP **You can copy, move, and delete several files at a time. Just select** the files you want, then click the right mouse button on any of the highlighted files to get the shortcut menu.

How to rename files

To rename a file, select the file name in the Open or Save As dialog box. Click the file name; it changes to a mini-text box with an insertion point. Type a new file name or edit the existing file name by pressing an arrow key and deleting and inserting text as you would in any text box.

CAUTION **You can rename items in your Favorites list. However, be aware** that you're renaming only the shortcut to a file or folder, not the file or folder itself.

Part VI: Advanced Topics

19 Document Signposts: Tables of Contents and Indexes

In this chapter:

- **Do I have to use Word's heading styles?**
- **I need a quick table of contents**
- **What happens if my document page numbers change?**
- **Can I really create an instant index?**
- **I want to add more entries to my index**
- **My document's so big I need a map to get around**

Just as road signs help us find our way around town, indexes and tables of contents help readers, and writers, find their way around documents . . . .

Imagine trying to find your highway exit without those big green road signs.

From flickering neon to shimmering constellations, signs show us where to go and what to do. Long before neon was even a bad idea, Constantine I, Emperor of Rome, was about to fight a crucial battle. According to the famous story, a glowing cross appeared in the sky, with the words "in hoc signo vinces"—"In this sign, conquer"—under it. Constantine's men duly painted crosses on their shields and won the battle.

Long documents, like highways and battles, sometimes need to be sign-posted. That's the job of indexes, cross-references, and tables of contents. They act like signs in a Word document, telling readers where to go to find things. What's more, Word indexes and tables of contents are a snap to create—no assistance from a higher power is needed.

Heading styles make fast tables of contents

Word's built-in heading styles are the backbone of the outlines and master documents we looked at in Chapters 16, "Hate Outlines? Outline View May Change Your Mind," and 17, "Mastering Big Documents Is No Mystery." You also use heading styles to generate speedy tables of contents.

TIP **Still not sold on Word's heading styles? Here's another reason to** use them: documents formatted in the default heading styles can take advantage of Word's new Document Map feature. Document maps are like dynamic tables of contents that update themselves as soon as you type a new heading and that take you to any of your topics with a single click. Click View, Document Map to see a map of your own document (and see page 366 in this chapter for more information on Document Maps).

Tables of contents help your readers find what they need. Like a summary outline, they display only headings and page numbers, and that makes them handy for your own reference as well. Tables of contents are also navigational tools. Click a page number in a table of contents, and you go right to that page in your document.

If you've already applied the built-in heading styles to your document, you're all set to create a table of contents. Otherwise, consider going through your document and applying the heading styles before generating a table of contents.

If you use the built-in heading styles, Word tables of contents automatically track down all the headings in your document. Then they display the heading text, with the corresponding page number, in a neat table.

Plain English, please!

A **style** is a collection of formatting commands that have been named and saved. The Heading 1 style is Arial 14-pt. bold, for example. See Chapter 12, "Word Documents Are Never Out of Style," for more information on creating, modifying, and applying styles.

Figure 19.1 shows Word's built-in heading styles as they're applied to a document.

Fig. 19.1
With Word's built-in heading styles in your documents, you can generate tables of contents with ease.

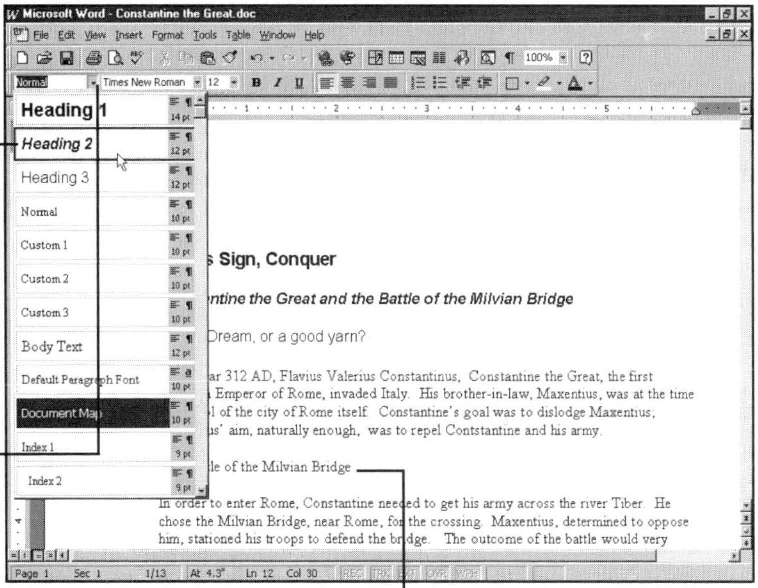

Microsoft Word - Constantine the Great.doc
File Edit View Insert Format Tools Table Window Help
Normal
Times New Roman
12
100%
Heading 1
14 pt
Heading 2
12 pt
Heading 3
12 pt
Normal
10 pt
Custom 1
Custom 2
Custom 3
Body Text
Default Paragraph Font
Document Map
Index 1
9 pt
Index 2
Sign, Conquer
ntine the Great and the Battle of the Milvian Bridge
Dream, or a good yarn?
ar 312 AD, Flavius Valerius Constantinus, Constantine the Great, the first
Emperor of Rome, invaded Italy. His brother-in-law, Maxentius, was at the time
l of the city of Rome itself. Constantine's goal was to dislodge Maxentius;
us' aim, naturally enough, was to repel Contstantine and his army.
le of the Milvian Bridge
In order to enter Rome, Constantine needed to get his army across the river Tiber. He
chose the Milvian Bridge, near Rome, for the crossing. Maxentius, determined to oppose
him, stationed his troops to defend the bridge. The outcome of the battle would very
Page 1 Sec 1 1/13 At 4.3" Ln 12 Col 30 REC TRK EXT OVR WPH

Select a heading style to apply it in the document

Click the Style Box drop-down arrow to display the heading styles

Click the heading where you want the style applied

TIP **If you're working with new text, don't forget about Word's** automatic headings. Type a heading at the left margin, then press the Enter key on the keyboard twice in rapid succession to format the heading in the Heading 1 style. To automatically apply heading styles 2 through 9, press Tab once for Heading 2, twice for Heading 3, and so on. Type the heading, then press Enter twice. Make sure your heading starts with a capital letter and contains no punctuation. Otherwise, automatic headings won't work.

For instant tables of contents, just add mouse clicks

There's nothing more frustrating than laboring over a long report, turning it in, and then having a reader come back to you with, "Why didn't you cover x, y, and z?" You *did* cover those topics; the reader simply missed the crucial passages. With a table of contents, all your readers will know exactly where to look for the information they seek.

Format your document with Word's built-in headings (see Figure 19.1). Then, to add a table of contents:

1 Put the insertion point where you want the table of contents to appear. A blank line at the very beginning or the very end of the document is a good choice.

2 Click Insert, Index and Tables, Tables of Contents. That gets you the Tables of Contents tab of the Index and Tables dialog box shown in Figure 19.2.

Fig. 19.2
Even though these are instant tables of contents, the options in the dialog box let you add custom touches.

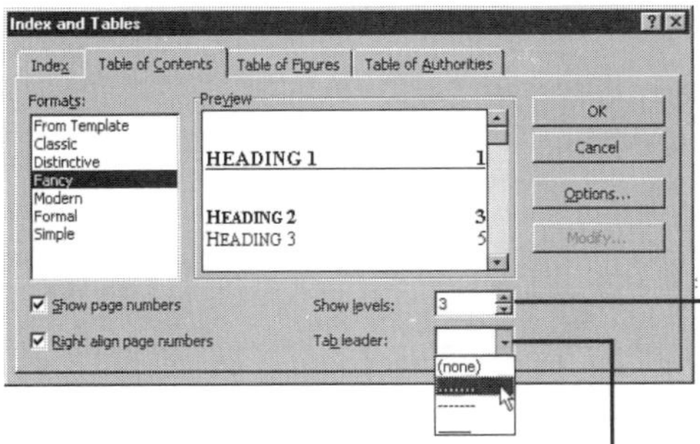

Click the Show levels arrows to control the heading levels displayed in the table of contents

Dots, thick dots, solid lines, or nothing at all? Take your pick of Tab leaders (also known as dot leaders)

3 Click any of the formats on the list in the Formats box, then view the result in the Preview window.

4 Tab leaders are the dots, lines, or spaces that separate headings from page numbers. Click the Tab leader drop-down arrow and choose one of the options, or don't do anything and use the selected format's default tab leader.

TIP **Use the Tab Leader options to modify the canned table of contents formats.** If, for example, you like the look of the Fancy format but you want tab leaders, click the format, then select one of the tab leader choices.

5 How detailed do you want your table of contents to be? Click the Show Levels arrows to decide what heading levels to display in the table.

6 Once you've made your choices, click OK in the Index and Tables dialog box. Your table of contents appears at the insertion point, as shown in Figure 19.3.

Fig. 19.3
Word tables of contents handle all the page numbering and formatting issues for you.

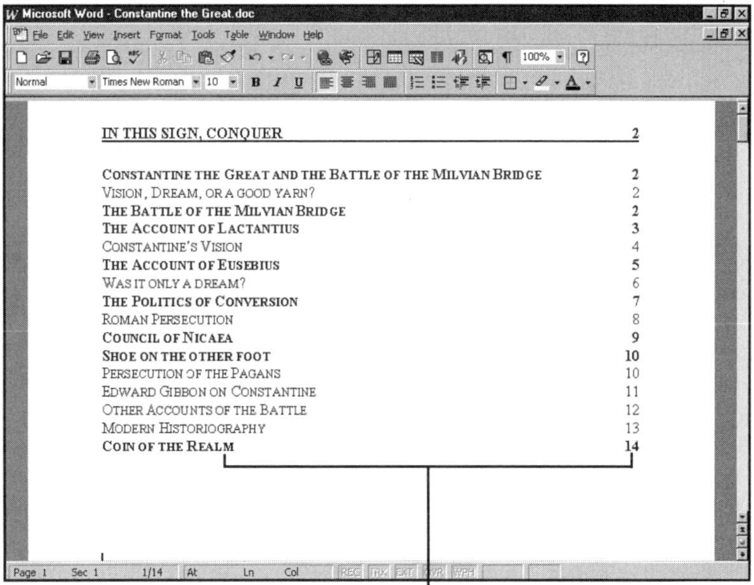

Word found all the document headings and their page numbers

If you decide you don't want a table of contents after all, just get rid of it. Select the entire table, either by dragging through it with the mouse or with the Shift+arrow key combination, then press Delete.

TOCs even do your scrolling for you

There are plenty of ways to get around in a Word document. Press Page Up and Page Down, click the scroll buttons or bars, roll or hold the IntelliMouse wheel—there's no lack of navigational variety in Word. With a TOC, you've got yet another way to navigate your pages of text. Point at a page number in your TOC, and the pointer turns into a pointing hand (see Figure 19.4).

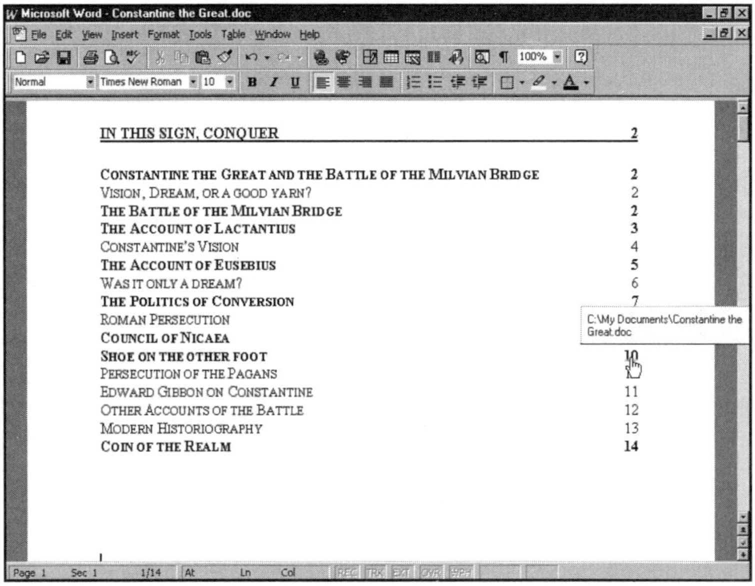

Fig. 19.4
With a Word TOC, just click the page you want to scroll to in a flash.

Click the TOC page number with the pointing hand, and the document scrolls right to that page.

Because TOC page numbers are hyperlinks, you'll also get the Web toolbar popping on to the screen. *Hyperlinks* are those automatic cross-references that you click to travel from document to document on the World Wide Web. Use the Web toolbar to open other documents, or to connect to the Web.

If you don't want the Web toolbar, just click the toolbar's Close button to put it away. If the toolbar is docked, right-click the toolbar and deselect it on the shortcut menu. The Web toolbar won't reappear on your subsequent TOC trips through the document, at least until you close and reopen the document again.

What happens to my table of contents if I change my page numbers?

Word tables of contents do a great job of finding your headings and their page numbers. But what if you create your table, and then move text around? You might also add or cut an entire section of the document. Those changes will alter the pagination in your document, but the table of contents won't reflect the new page numbers.

Not until you tell it to show the new page numbers, that is. To speedily update the page numbers in a table of contents:

1. Click anywhere in the table of contents. Word colors the table in gray shading to show it's been selected.

Q&A ***Why does Word shade my table of contents when I click in it?***

Tables of contents are peppered with special codes, called **field codes**, that Word uses to control features like indexes and tables of contents. Field codes are normally hidden, since they operate behind the scenes. Word will shade field-coded text, or not, at your option. To toggle the shading of field-coded text, click Tools, Options and click the View tab of the Options dialog box. Click the Field shading drop-down arrow and select an option from the list. Choose Never if you don't want shading when you click inside a table of contents. Click OK in the Options dialog box to save your changes.

2. Press F9. That pops up the Update Table of Contents dialog box shown in Figure 19.5.

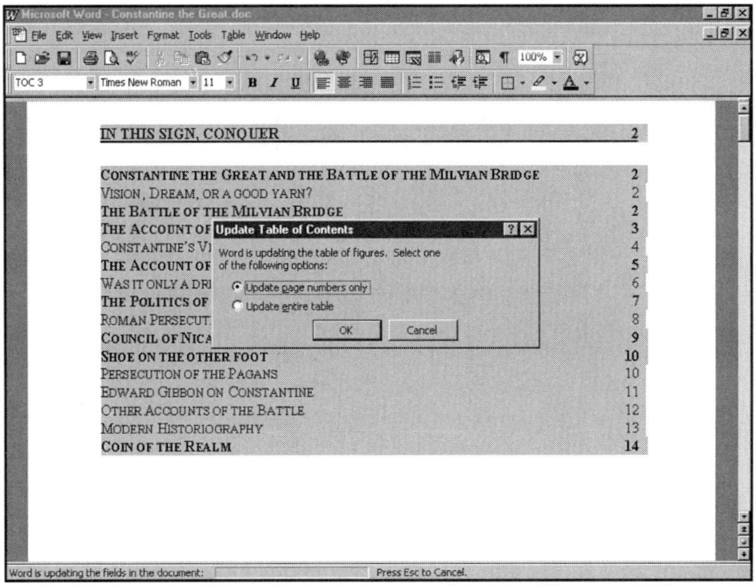

Fig. 19.5
The Update Table of Contents dialog box brings your table page numbers up to date after editing changes.

3 Select Update Page Numbers Only in the Update Table of Contents dialog box, then click OK. Word updates the page numbers in the table to reflect the new page numbers of the headings in the document, including any headings you've added or cut.

CAUTION **If you select the Update Entire Table option in the Update Table** of Contents dialog box, Word updates the heading page numbers and restores the table's formatting to the default for whatever table format you chose. If you've added your own formatting to the table of contents, it'll be wiped out.

I have my own heading styles, and I want a table of contents

Sturdy individualists who refuse to use canned headings aren't left out in the cold when it comes to creating tables of contents (although using canned heading styles is a bit easier). If you've created your own heading styles, you can use those to generate a table of contents without too much fuss.

For example, suppose you've created three heading styles and called them Custom 1, Custom 2, and Custom 3. To create a table of contents based on your own styles:

1. Put the insertion point where you want the table of contents to appear.
2. Click Insert, Index and Tables, Tables of Contents for the Tables of Contents tab of the Index and Tables dialog box (refer to Figure 19.2).
3. Click Options. That pops up the Table of Contents Options dialog box shown in Figure 19.6.

Fig. 19.6
You can create tables of contents based on your own styles; it's just a little extra work.

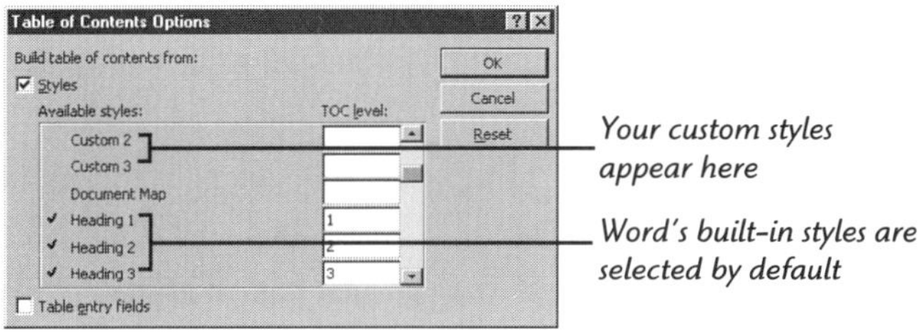

4. Deselect the built-in heading styles by deleting the numbers in the TOC Level edit boxes. You'll notice the check marks by the built-in styles in the list of Available Styles disappear.
5. Enter TOC Level numbers of your own in the edit boxes next to your custom styles. Type a **1** for your first level heading, a **2** for the second level, and so on. It should look like Figure 19.7.

Fig. 19.7
Once you assign TOC levels to your own heading styles, you can generate a table of contents based on those styles.

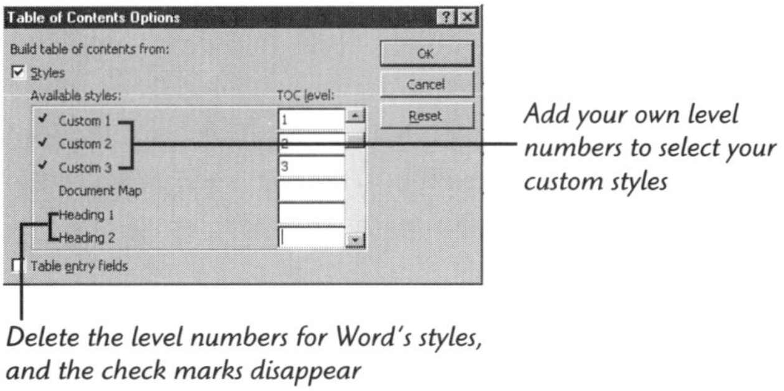

6. Click OK in the Table of Contents Options dialog box.
7. Make your selections in the Table of Contents dialog box, then click OK to generate the table of contents.

Research assistant on vacation? Index your own document

For some people, creating an index is truly effortless. University professors with graduate students at their beck and call, or law partners with a team of paralegals standing by, simply summon the hapless victim and say, "Do me an index, please" (we hope they say please). For the rest of us, indexes are a little more work. If you're using Word, the extra work really is only a little.

There are two steps to creating an index:

- Go through your document marking the text you want to appear in the index.
- Select a format and generate the index based on the marked text.

Word automatically lists any marked text with its corresponding page number in an index. The index pops up in its own two-column section at the end of the document.

TIP **Want your index to appear in the table of contents? Title the** index, and apply one of the heading styles to the title. Click the table of contents, press F9 to update it, and the title of your index appears with the correct page number.

First, mark your index entries

The hard labor involved in creating an index is deciding what to put in it. And even that's not too much of a sweat; all you do is select the text. Important names, recurring topics, key theories; they're all candidates for inclusion in an index. Don't worry if you mark the same text more than once. Word automatically removes duplicate entries.

To select and mark text for an index:

1. Select the first text you want in the index and press this combination of keyboard keys: Alt+Shift+X.
2. The Mark Index Entry dialog box pops up, with the selected text displayed in the Main Entry edit box, as shown in Figure 19.8.

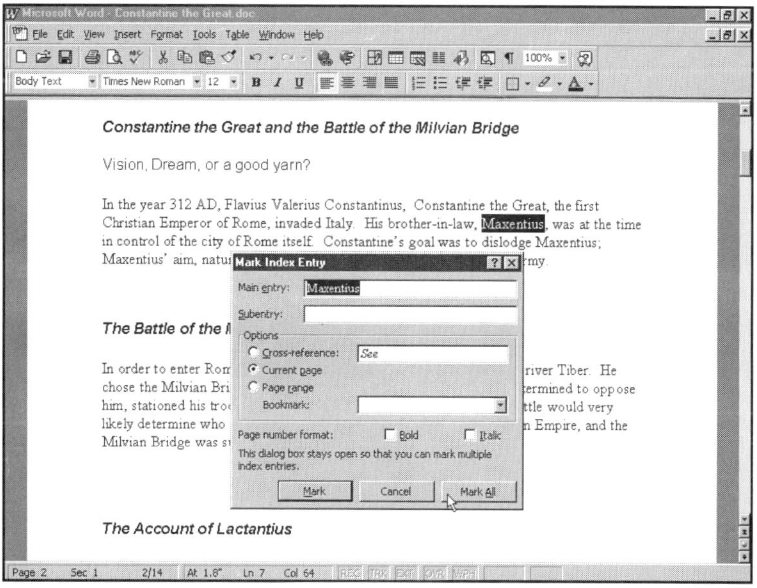

Fig. 19.8
If you want to edit the index entry text, make your changes in the Main Entry edit box.

3 Click Mark in the Mark Index Entry dialog box. If it's text that recurs throughout the document, click Mark All to mark every occurrence of the text.

4 Word displays the XE index entry code next to the selected text. That's one of Word's normally hidden codes, which are scattered (though out of sight) throughout your documents. Click anywhere outside the dialog box, and select the next text you want in the index. The Mark Index Entry dialog box stays open, and you can scroll the document and select text while it's popped up.

Q&A ***I selected my next index entry, but the Mark button in the Mark Index Entry dialog box is still grayed out!***

Click the Main Entry edit box. You have to do that for every index entry you select.

5 With the next text selected, click the Main Entry edit box. The text appears in the box, and you can make any necessary changes to it there.

6 Click Mark or Mark All. Click outside the dialog box, select the next text, click the Main Entry edit box, then click Mark or Mark All again.

7 Continue to select and mark all the text you want in the index.

8 When you've marked all the index text, click Close in the Mark Index Entry dialog box.

Generate the index from the marked text

Once all your text is marked, generating the index is easy. To create an index of text entries you've already marked:

1 Click Insert, Index and Tables, Index for the Index tab of the Index and Tables dialog box.

2 Select a format for the index from the list of Formats (Modern is a good choice). The Preview window gives you an inkling of how the index will look, as shown in Figure 19.9.

Fig. 19.9
The index formats automatically add an index heading letter above each alphabetical group of entries.

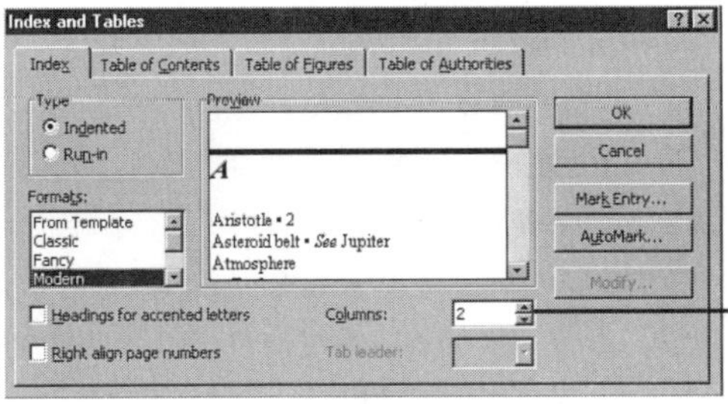

Select the number of columns for your index; 2 columns is the default

3 Click OK, and the index appears at the end of the document in its own section.

Word automatically alphabetizes your index entries and displays them in columns, with their corresponding page numbers. Figure 19.10 shows a completed index in Page Layout view.

Fig. 19.10
If your readers still can't find their way around a document after you've added a TOC and an index, tell them to wait for the movie.

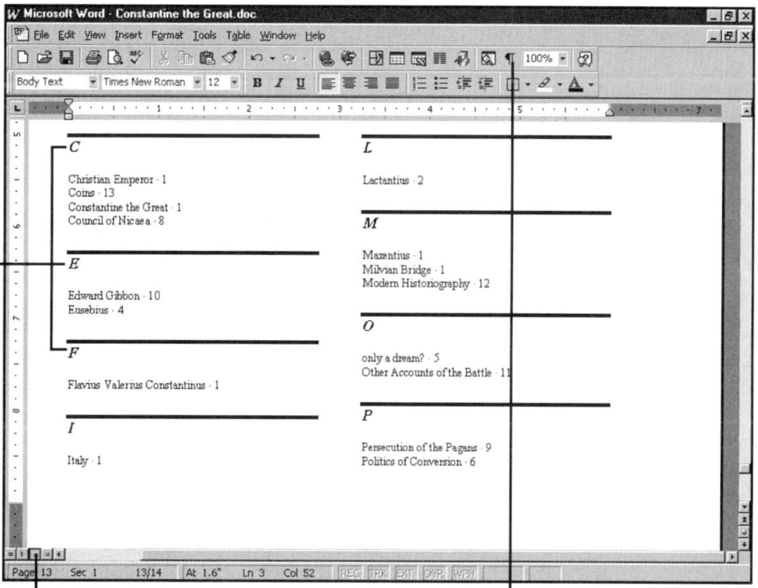

Word automatically alphabetizes the entries and supplies these headings for each letter

Switch to Page Layout view to see the index's columnar format

Click the Show/Hide button to hide Word's formatting codes

How do I add entries to an existing index?

It's easy to miss entries as you scroll through a document marking text. No need to redo the index—once you've created your index, you can easily add anything that's been missed.

Press Shift+Alt+X to pop up the Mark Index Entry dialog box. Select the additional text, click Mark, and repeat until you've added all the new entries. Click Close in the Mark Index Entry dialog box, put the insertion point in the index, then press F9.

Your index is automatically updated to include the new entries.

Q&A ***My document is littered with field codes! How do I get rid of them?***

If you select text and press Shift-Alt-X to mark it as an index entry, Word displays all the index field codes in the document. To hide the codes again, press the Show/Hide¶ button on the Standard toolbar.

Document Maps, for a running TOC

Word's indexes and tables of contents are easy to create, and flexible enough to change at will. As we've seen, Word TOCs also make good navigational tools to get you around long documents. There's only one catch to using a TOC as document navigator: you have to update the TOC each time you make changes in the document. What you really need is a dynamic TOC, one that's updated automatically, and that sends you to distant pages of the document with a single click.

TOCs don't really fit the bill, but Document Maps do. A Document Map gives you a window on the structure of the document, and a fast means of jumping from topic to topic within the document.

To see a map of your document, click View, Document Map, or click the Online View button at the bottom of the screen. The editing window splits into two panels. Every heading you've formatted in Word's heading styles appears in the left panel. The document itself is displayed in the right-hand panel. Click a topic in the left-hand panel, and the right-hand panel instantly scrolls to the corresponding heading in the document, as shown in Figure 19.11.

Document Maps update instantly. Add a new heading formatted in one of the default heading styles, and it appears in the map.

TIP **Like an outline, you can control the heading levels that are** displayed in the map panel. Right-click any heading in the Document Map for a shortcut menu, and select the heading level you want to display.

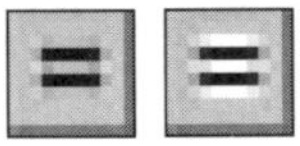

If you want to resize the Document Map, drag the divider between the two panels left or right. To close the Document Map, double-click the divider. Or click View, and choose Normal or Page Layout. If you're not in Online View, you can also click the tiny Normal View or Page Layout View buttons at the bottom of the screen. In Online View, those buttons disappear—from view.

Only headings formatted in Word's heading styles appear in the map window

Fig. 19.11
Document Maps are both instant outlines and navigational tools for long documents.

Click the [-] and [+] symbols to hide or display the sub-headings under the selected heading

Click a topic in the map panel, and the document scrolls right to that topic in the document panel

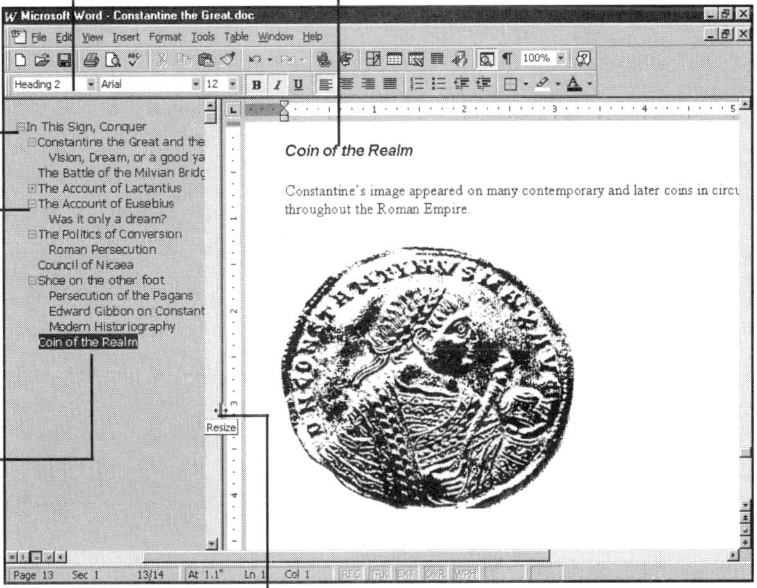

Drag the divider to resize the Document Map window

20 Text as Art, Numbers as Pictures: Charts and WordArt

In this chapter:

- What is WordArt, and where do I find it?
- These WordArt special effects are attention-getters!
- How can I make a quick chart
- What kind of chart should I use?
- This chart needs a complete makeover

With WordArt and Microsoft Graph, documents need never be boring—even if the content doesn't exactly scintillate . . . .

Personal computers do remarkable things with text and numbers. Colorful images, exotic fonts, startling charts—they're all just a mouse click or two away. So why are so many documents so boring? Content has something to do with it. Invoices, tax forms, and the latest corporate decree might all be terminal cases. But if your document has a flicker of life, Word has a couple of tricks to fan the flicker into a flame. Microsoft Graph takes boring rows of numbers and turns them into colorful pictures. WordArt stretches and bends text into arresting shapes.

Shake up your fonts with WordArt

WordArt takes fonts and stretches, shadows, and shapes them. Use it to create logos, posters, and banners. WordArt is also great for getting a rise out of the office font connoisseur. Figure 20.1 shows you what a WordArt object looks like.

> ### *Plain English, please!*
>
> **Objects** can be charts, maps, pictures, spreadsheet tables, even Word documents. An object is anything in your computer that can be edited, moved, or inserted into an application. Why are they called objects? Probably because "things" would have sounded a bit vague.

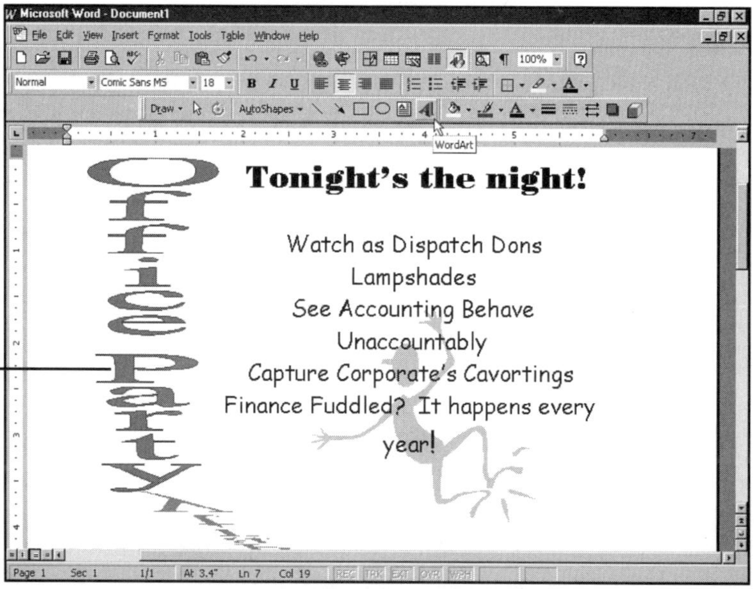

Fig. 20.1
When ordinary fonts won't do, get some attention with a little WordArt.

WordArt objects are inserted into Word documents, just like pictures or any other objects

Make a poster with WordArt

There you are minding your own business, trying to put a dent in your work, reasonably content with life in general. Then you get one of those phone calls from upstairs. "We need a poster for the office party. Oh, and we need it by four o'clock."

"Do it yourself" is on your lips, but you're a good soldier. You hold your fire and fire up WordArt instead. To create a poster with WordArt:

1 Click the Drawing button on the Standard Toolbar to pop up the Drawing toolbar. If the Drawing toolbar is in your way in the editing window, double-click the toolbar's title bar to dock it at the top of the screen.

2 Click the WordArt button on the Drawing toolbar. The WordArt Gallery appears, as shown in Figure 20.2.

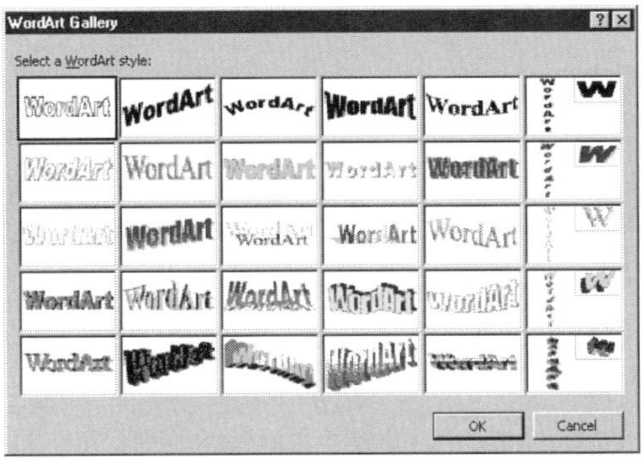

Fig. 20.2
When you type your own text, it'll take the color and shape of any WordArt style you choose here.

3 Your own text will replace the word "WordArt" in any of the shapes and colors on view in the WordArt Gallery. Double-click any WordArt style that strikes your fancy.

4 The Edit WordArt Text dialog box pops up. Type your own text in the Text edit box, and select a new font and font size if you want them (see Figure 20.3.)

5 Click OK in the Edit WordArt Text dialog box when you're finished typing and formatting your text. The WordArt object is inserted into the active document, and the WordArt toolbar pops up. Like any Word graphic object, WordArt can be resized and moved around the page. Drag a handle to resize, and drag the object with the four-headed arrow to move it (see Figure 20.4)

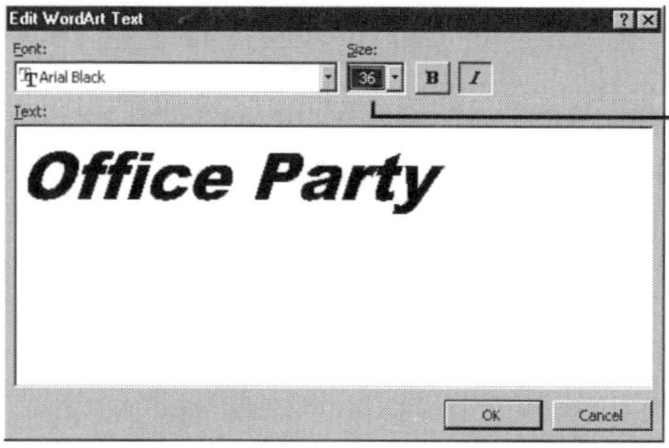

Fig. 20.3
You can type any text you like in here, but try to keep it short; longer text distorts the WordArt characters.

If your text runs longer than a word or two, try selecting a smaller font size

Once you've inserted, moved, and resized your WordArt, you might be completely satisfied with what you've got. If you're not satisfied, WordArt can be altered to suit you in almost any way you can think of. To do that, read on.

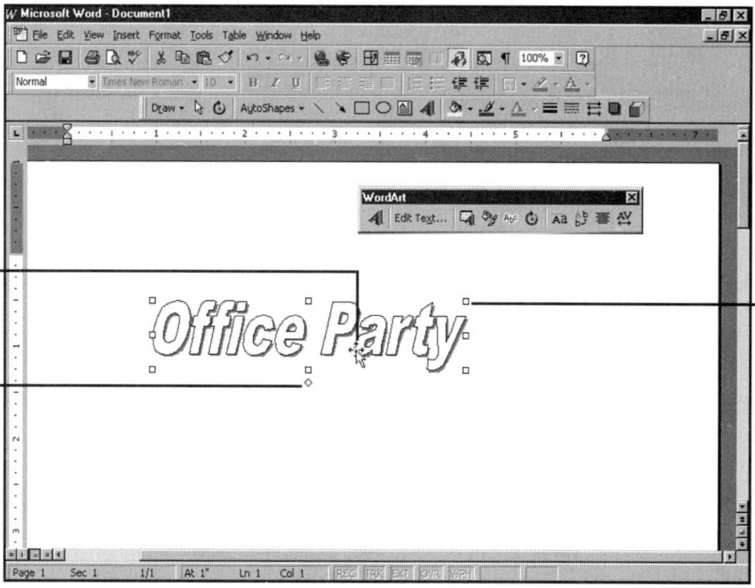

Fig. 20.4
WordArt is easily moved and resized; think of it as a graphic rather than ordinary text.

Drag with the four-headed arrow to move WordArt around the page

Drag the diamond to skew—shift sideways—the WordArt characters

Drag a handle to resize the object

My WordArt needs some work

Between the Drawing and WordArt toolbars, you've got all the tools you need to transform one of the stock WordArt styles into a custom creation. Change the shape, the colors, add shadow and 3-D effects—the possibilities are limited only by the amount of time you have for playing around with this.

To customize an inserted WordArt object:

1 WordArt is inserted into a document with the sizing handles and WordArt toolbar displayed. If you lose the handles and the toolbar, just click the WordArt object to get them back.

2 Want to stretch and bend those WordArt characters into a different shape? Click the WordArt Shape button on the WordArt toolbar and choose a new shape from the menu, as shown in Figure 20.5.

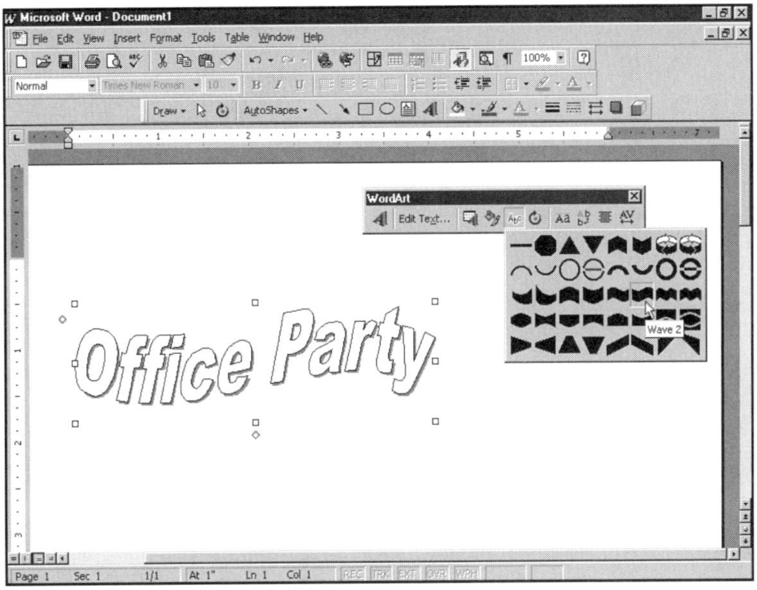

Fig. 20.5
Some of these shapes may not be exactly shapely, but they're certainly startling.

TIP

If you change the WordArt shape and you don't like the results, click the Undo button on the Standard toolbar to restore the WordArt object to it's original shape. Then try a different option on the WordArt Shape button menu.

3 If horizontal text seems a tad conventional, click the WordArt Vertical Text button to flip the characters to the vertical.

4 Don't leave your WordArt object in the shade; click the Shadow button on the Drawing toolbar and select a shadow style from the menu.

5 Or click the 3-D button on the Drawing toolbar and take your pick of effects from the menu. Click the 3-D button again and choose 3-D Settings to pop up the 3-D Settings toolbar. Click the Lighting button and choose the direction from which your 3-D effect is lit, as shown in Figure 20.6.

Fig. 20.6
Of all the nifty new Word features, this one stands out—even the menu is interesting.

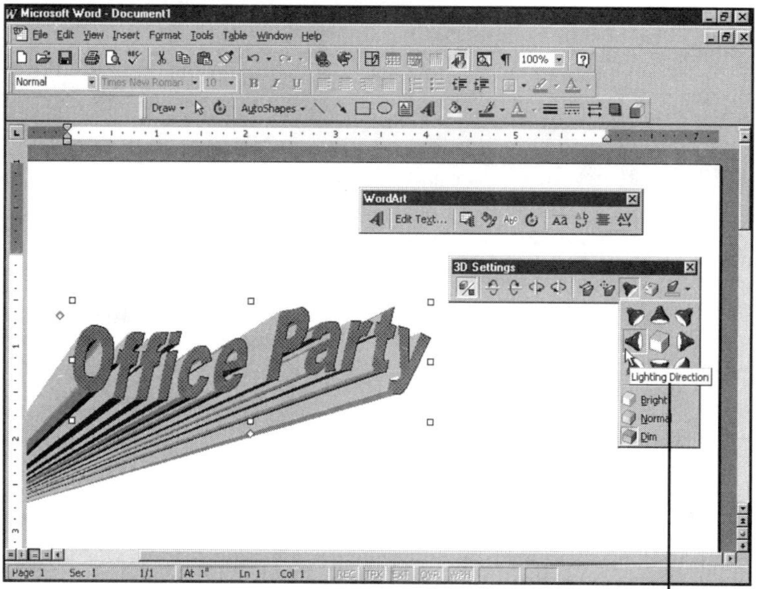

Select a lighting direction, then see the effect on the cube in the middle of the menu

CAUTION **Not all WordArt's shapes and styles lend themselves to 3-D** effects. Some will be illegible if you add 3-D. Trial and error is the way to go here; you just have to tinker until you're satisfied.

6 At the end of the day, you'll wind up with a poster, or any document trying to make a splash, that's sure to get a little attention (see Figure 20.7).

Experimentation is the ticket with WordArt. Try the different effects on for size, and have a little fun doing it. That, after all, is the best revenge for being saddled with assignments like the office party poster.

Fig. 20.7
When you're called on to produce home-made graphics, WordArt can save the day.

To wrap text around the WordArt object, click the Format WordArt button on the WordArt toolbar and make your choices on the Wrapping tab

How do I further edit an inserted WordArt object?

It's easy to make more changes to a WordArt object. Just click it to pop up the handles and the WordArt toolbar.

And if you decide to get rid of the WordArt object entirely, click it once to select it, then press Delete.

Can I make charts in Word?

Charts make numbers come alive. Since Word makes creating charts a snap, use them whenever your document includes numerical data. Charts can supplement your data, or even replace it.

> **"** ***Plain English, please!***
>
> **Chart** or **graph**, which is it? Either, or both. The terms are interchangeable. Word's online help mentions Microsoft Graph, which has a Chart Type button to let you change chart types, so I call them charts below. If you prefer to call them graphs, feel free. **"**

Use Word's built-in chart for fast results

Word has a ready-made sample chart built right into the program. Just enter your own numbers and labels, and you've got an instant chart.

Suppose we're preparing a billing report for a small accounting practice. We want a chart that shows the billings generated by each of the four partners in the first quarter of 1995.

To put Word's sample chart to work on your own data:

1 Click Insert, Picture, Chart. Word's sample data and chart pop up, together with the Graph toolbar, as shown in Figure 20.8. Column charts like the one in Figure 20.8 display data along two or more arms, called **axes**. The axes correspond to the columns and rows of the datasheet:

- The vertical y axis represents **data series**, those numbered rows of data in the datasheet. That's why it's also called the series axis. In a column chart, a group of columns of the same color is the graphical way of showing a data series.

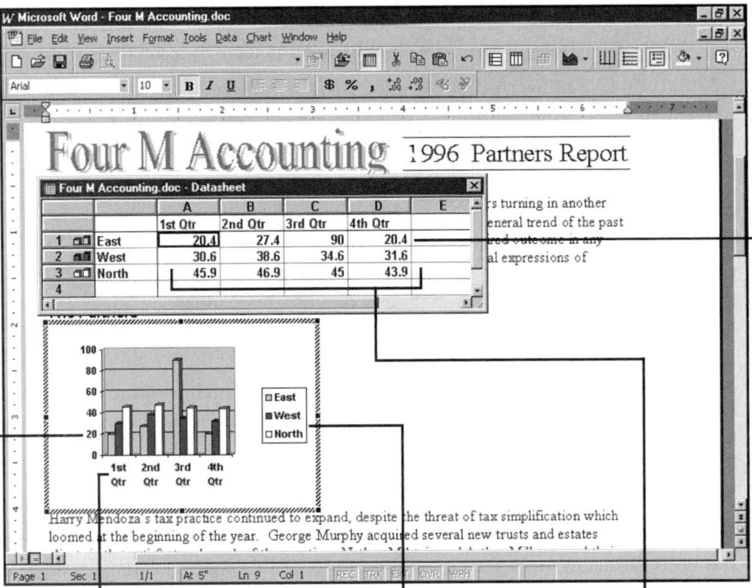

Fig. 20.8
The labels and numbers in the datasheet produce the chart. Just drag the data sheet window out of the way to see the chart.

The values in each cell are data points

3-D charts like this one have a z axis to display data series values. In a 2-D chart, it's called the y axis.

The x axis shows the categories in the datasheet columns

The chart legend is the key to the chart

The data in each row is a data series

- A 3-D chart has a second vertical axis, called the z axis, which displays the values in the rows of data in the datasheet. Each value in a row is represented by a single column in a column chart. That's called a **data point**.
- The horizontal x axis represents the categories in the datasheet. In Figure 20.8, the categories are each of those lettered columns in the datasheet. The category labels appear at the top of each column in the datasheet, and also along the x, or **category axis**, on the chart. In Figure 20.8, the categories are 1st Qtr, 2nd Qtr, and so on.

2 The sample chart reflects the data and the labels in the sample datasheet. All we need to do is enter our own data in the rows and columns of the datasheet. Type the numbers or text in each cell, right over the sample data, then press Enter, Tab, or an arrow key. Every press of the key updates the chart, as shown in Figure 20.9.

Fig. 20.9
Enter your own labels and values in the datasheet to create your own chart.

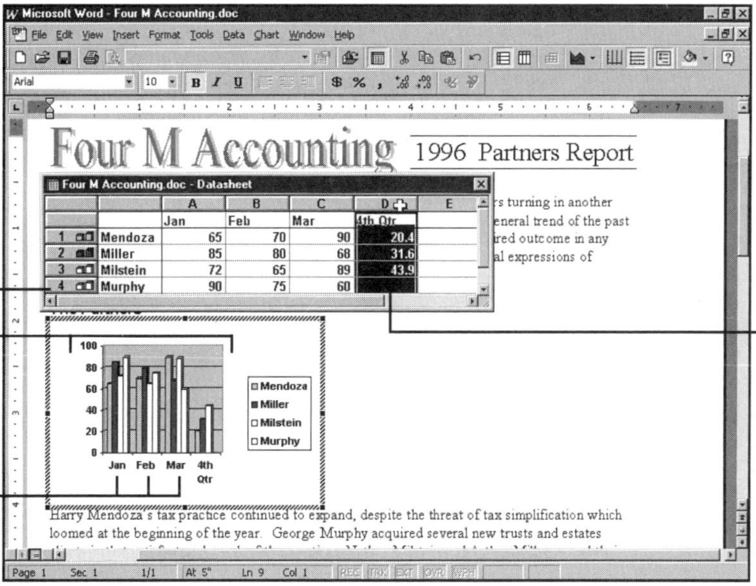

When you add another row, Word automatically formats the data series

The chart columns adjust to reflect the new data

The x axis labels change to show the new column headings

To get rid of this entire column of sample data, click the column header to select the whole column, then press Delete

3 To format the numbers and text in the datasheet, drag through the cells you want to format and click a button on the Formatting toolbar. If you want to display your numbers with dollar signs, for example, drag through the cells to select them, then click the Currency Style button on the Formatting toolbar, as shown in Figure 20.10.

4 Now that our numbers are formatted, we need to tell the reader what the numbers mean with chart and z axis titles. Click Chart, Chart Options and the Chart Options dialog box pops up.

5 Click the Titles tab in the Chart Options dialog box shown in Figure 20.11.

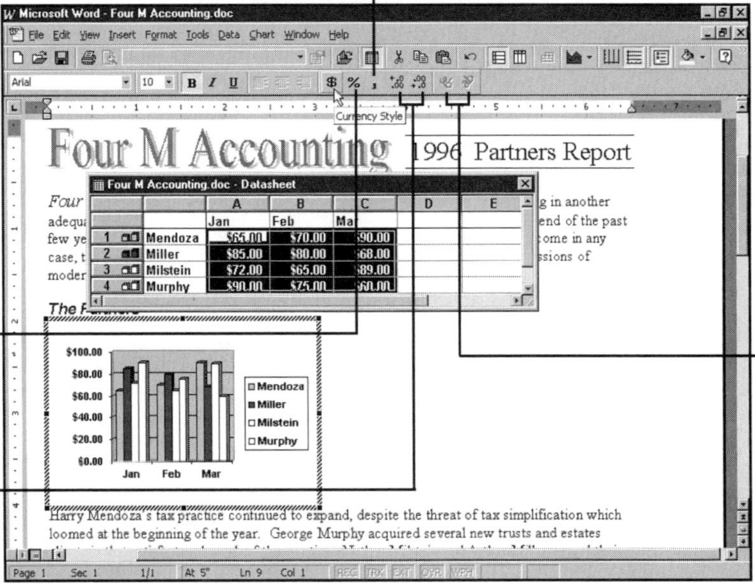
Click Comma Style to format numbers with commas and two decimal places
Click Percent Style to format numbers as percentages
Click Increase Decimal and Decrease Decimal to more, or fewer, decimal places
These buttons angle labels in the chart upward or downward
Microsoft Word - Four M Accounting.doc
Currency Style
Four M Accounting
1996 Partners Report
Four M Accounting.doc - Datasheet
Mendoza
Miller
Milstein
Murphy
Jan
Feb
Mar

Fig. 20.10
Formatting numbers in the datasheet is just like formatting characters in the Word editing window.

Q&A *I clicked outside the chart and the datasheet and now I seem to be back in a Word document!*

You just discovered the quick way to close Word's charting program, Microsoft Graph 8. Just double-click the chart to return to the charting program.

6 Type your titles, then click OK in the Chart Options dialog box. The titles appear in the chart, as shown in Figure 20.12.

Fig. 20.11
Chart titles tell readers everything they need to know about the chart.

The chart title will go here

The z axis title will go here

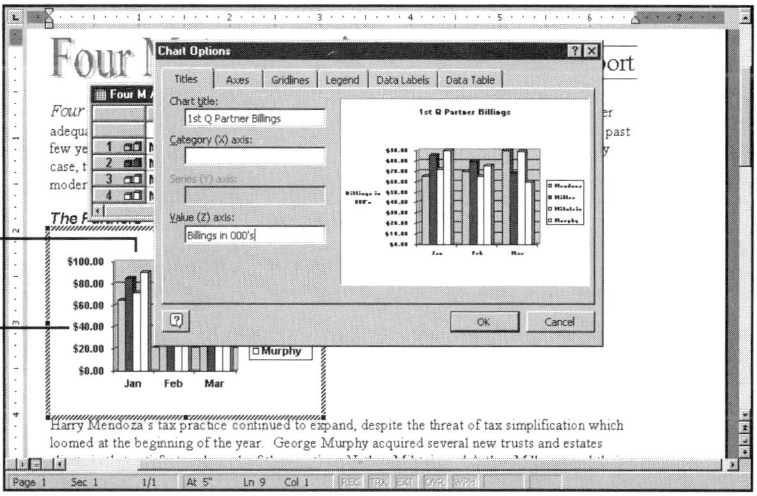

Fig. 20.12
With informative titles and labels, the reader knows at a glance what the chart is all about.

Click View Datasheet to toggle the datasheet display

Drag a handle to resize the chart

The chart title

Here's the z axis title; right-click to format it

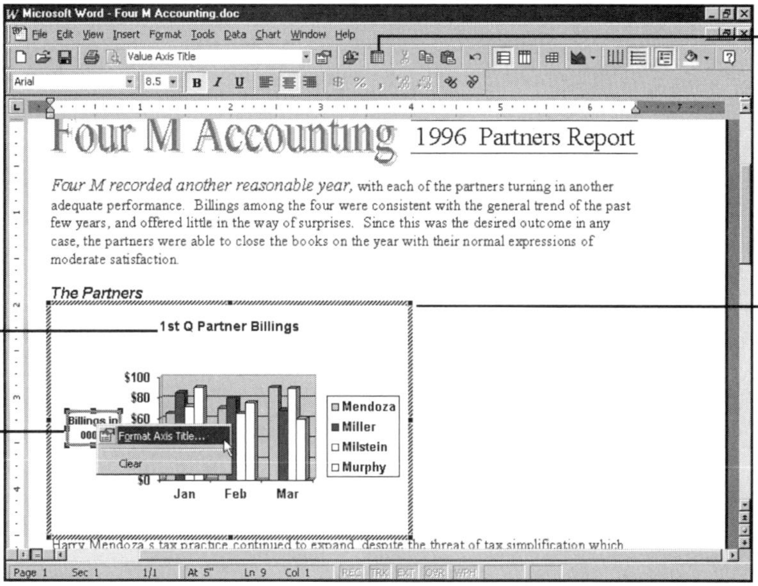

TIP **To align a z axis title parallel with the z axis, right-click the title to** get the shortcut menu. Choose Format Axis Title on the shortcut menu; that pops up the Format Axis Title dialog box. Now click the Alignment tab in the Format Axis Title dialog box, shown in Figure 20.13.

7 With your own data and titles, the sample chart is now *your* chart. Click anywhere outside the chart and the datasheet to pop thc chart into your document.

8 Once the chart is in your document, drag with the four-headed arrow to move it into position, and drag a handle to resize the chart. To wrap text around the chart, right-click it, then select Format Object on the shortcut menu. Choose a text wrapping option on the Wrapping tab of the Format Object dialog box, and click OK. Figure 20.14 shows the chart in the document with text wrapped Tight and Left.

To edit the chart further, just double-click it to return to Microsoft Graph 8.0.

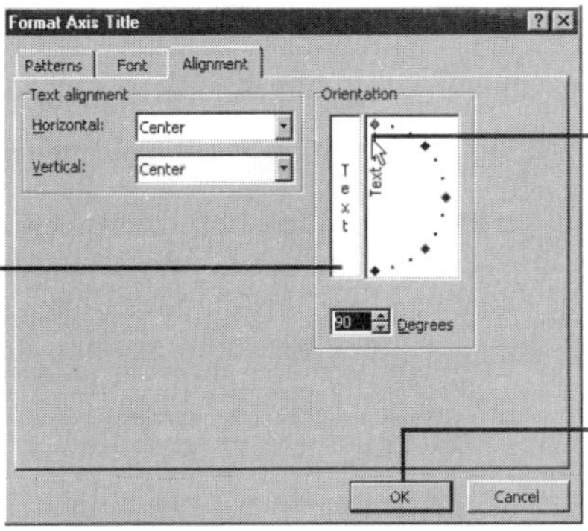

Fig. 20.13
Click the Font tab to change title fonts and sizes.

Click in here to align the text vertically

Drag the clock hand up or down to change the angle of the text. With the hand at 12 o'clock, text will be at 90 degrees.

Click OK when you're done

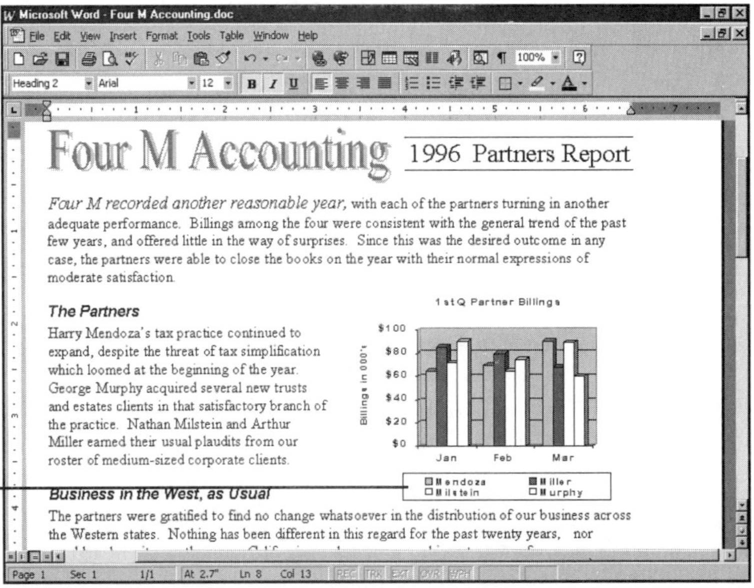

Fig. 20.14
Wrapping text fits the chart to the page.

Everything in the chart can be moved around; just double-click the chart and drag objects like the legend wherever you want them

This chart's not my type: formatting tips and tricks

Modified with your own data, Word's sample chart is perfectly acceptable. But if acceptable isn't good enough, you don't have to settle for it. A few clicks can completely transform Word's canned chart.

Changing the chart type is the most radical transformation you can make. It's also the easiest. The default type is a 3-D column chart.

To change the chart type, double-click the chart if it's already in your document. That returns you to Microsoft Graph 8.0. Now click the Chart Type drop-down arrow on the Graph toolbar for a palette of chart types. Click any one of them to change your chart type, as shown in Figure 20.15.

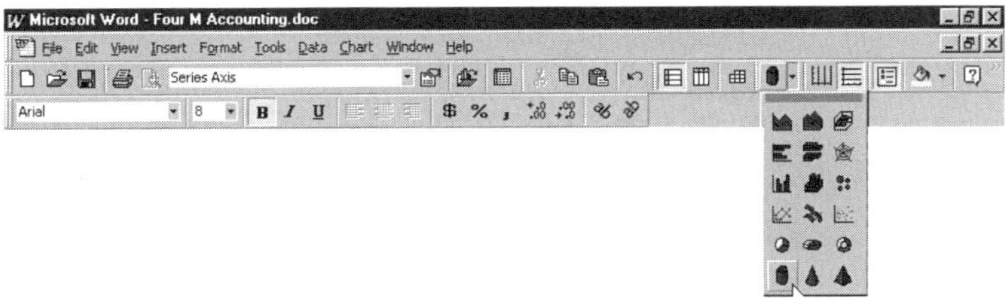

Fig. 20.15
The Chart Type button gives you a fast chart makeover.

What chart type should I use?

With all the available chart types, you're probably wondering what type is best. Some chart types work for certain types of data, some don't. To see all the available chart types, click Chart, Chart Type to pop up the Chart Type dialog box shown in Figure 20.16.

Click any of the Chart types in the Chart Type dialog box, then double-click a Chart sub-type to instantly transform your chart. Click Custom tab to see charts with formatting added. Some chart sub-types are 2-D, some are 3-D. The difference between them is mostly aesthetic. In either case, the best choice of chart depends on your data:

- **Cylinder charts** like the one in Figure 20.14 show comparisons among different items in one period of time, or changes in different items over several periods (annual sales and expenses for one year or several, for example). **Conc**, **Pyramid**, **Bar**, and **Column** charts are close cousins, and are used for the same type of data.

- **Pie charts** are used to show the relationship between the parts and the whole. Pie charts only show one data series (different budget items as parts of the total budget, for example).
- **Line charts** show changes over time for one item or several (your stock's performance over the past six months against the Dow, for example).
- **Area charts** show changing values over time, like line charts, and proportional relationships, like pie charts.
- **Scatter charts** are often used in statistics to show the strength of the relationship between single values and a mean value.
- **Bubble charts** are scatter charts that also display the value of a third variable, represented by the size of the bubble.
- **Radar charts** illustrate differences between each data series, and between many data series simultaneously. They're sometimes used in complex project management applications.
- **Doughnut charts** are like pie charts; they show the relationship of the parts to the whole. The difference is that doughnuts show multiple data series. Each ring of the doughnut corresponds to a different row of data on your datasheet.

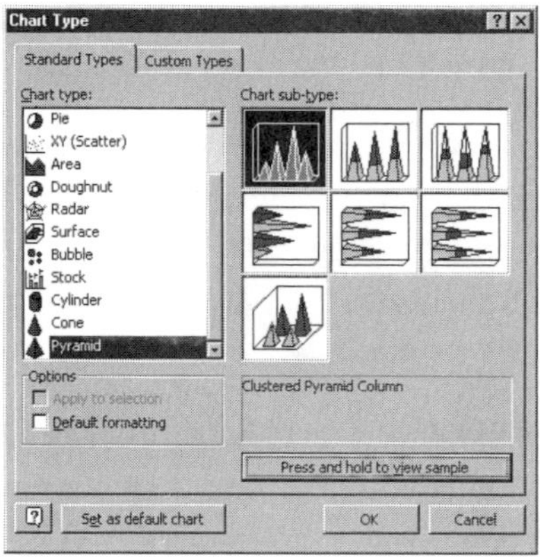

Fig. 20.16
Word has a chart for every type of data, and each chart type has several subtypes to choose from.

Chart interior makeovers with a click or two

Ever move your furniture around for a change of pace? You can do the same kind of thing with the interior of your chart. Everything in the chart—axes, titles, legends, data series, and points—can be altered to suit.

No matter what the alteration, the basic principle is the same: click the object in the chart to pop up the handles. Then either drag the object to move it, or right-click for the shortcut menu and choose a formatting option. Change the colors of your bars, the fonts of your titles, or the appearance of the chart background.

Figure 20.17 shows a selected data series and the shortcut menu that pops up when you right-click the selected object.

These are the chart walls. Right-click the walls or floor for the shortcut menu

Click to hide the legend if you no longer want it

Fig. 20.17
Click an object to select it, then make any changes you want from the shortcut menu.

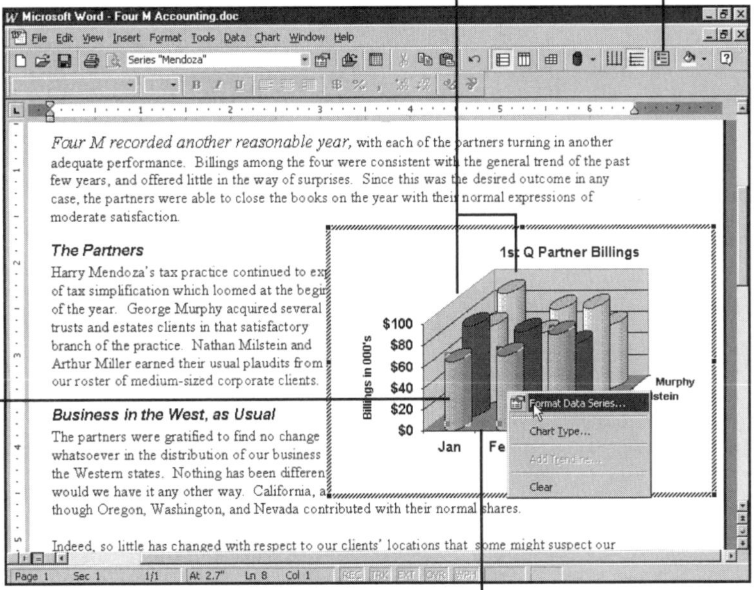
Microsoft Word - Four M Accounting.doc
File Edit View Insert Format Tools Data Chart Window Help
Series "Mendoza"
Four M recorded another reasonable year, with each of the partners turning in another adequate performance. Billings among the four were consistent with the general trend of the past few years, and offered little in the way of surprises. Since this was the desired outcome in any case, the partners were able to close the books on the year with their normal expressions of moderate satisfaction.
The Partners
Harry Mendoza's tax practice continued to ex
of tax simplification which loomed at the begi
of the year. George Murphy acquired several
trusts and estates clients in that satisfactory
branch of the practice. Nathan Milstein and
Arthur Miller earned their usual plaudits from
our roster of medium-sized corporate clients.
Business in the West, as Usual
The partners were gratified to find no change
whatsoever in the distribution of our business
the Western states. Nothing has been differen
would we have it any other way. California, a
though Oregon, Washington, and Nevada contributed with their normal shares.
Indeed, so little has changed with respect to our clients' locations that some might suspect our
1st Q Partner Billings
Billings in 000's
$100
$80
$60
$40
$20
$0
Jan
Fe
Murphy
lstein
Format Data Series...
Chart Type...
Clear
Page 1 Sec 1 1/1 At 2.7" Ln 8 Col 1

Click any of the cylinders to select the data series, right-click for the shortcut menu, then change the patterns or colors

This is the chart floor

21

Customizing Word

In this chapter:

- **How do I change what I see on the screen?**
- **Adding and removing toolbar buttons is more like a snap**
- **I need a toolbar for what *I* do in Word**
- **What's a macro?**
- **I could use some instant stationery**
- **How can I tell one dialog box from another?**

Does your desk look like it's been hit by a hurricane? Or maybe it's as tidy as a Swiss village. Whatever your work habits, you can make Word as comfortable as your own desktop. . . . .

"Build to suit" say the property for-sale ads. Three words that tell us a lot about the way we like to rearrange our surround-ings to please ourselves.

One big benefit of the computer age: if you confine your alterations to the screen, they won't harm so much as a blade of grass. Furthermore, you can undo your changes whenever you like. Word has all kinds of options for adjusting the program to your tasks and preferences. You can also restore the original settings if you don't like your alterations. When you build Word to suit, the only lasting impact is on your work habits.

Fit the editing window to the job

Word accommodates itself to your style; crowd the screen with tools, or work in a completely bare editing window. Your chore might dictate your choice. If you're writing a long, plain-text document, clear the screen of everything but text to see more of your work. For a document loaded with graphics, keep your tools at your fingertips.

Change your views

To see more document and fewer tools, click View, Full Screen. Everything disappears from the screen except your document and the Full Screen button, as shown in Figure 21.1.

To restore the toolbars and all the other screen elements, click the Close Full Screen button or press Esc.

You can still apply Word's formatting commands in full-screen view. Just use the keyboard shortcuts. Press Ctrl+B, for example, to apply boldface to text, Ctrl+I for italics, or Ctrl+U for underlining. You can also move the pointer to the top of the screen to make the menu bar reappear, and choose commands from the menus. And you can always right-click and choose commands and options on the shortcut menu.

If you like to see all your tools, make the tools easier to see. Click View, Toolbars, Customize to pop up the Customize dialog box. Click the Options tab and select Large Icons. For another twist, select Show shortcut keys in ScreenTips if you'd like to learn how to do without the icons at all.

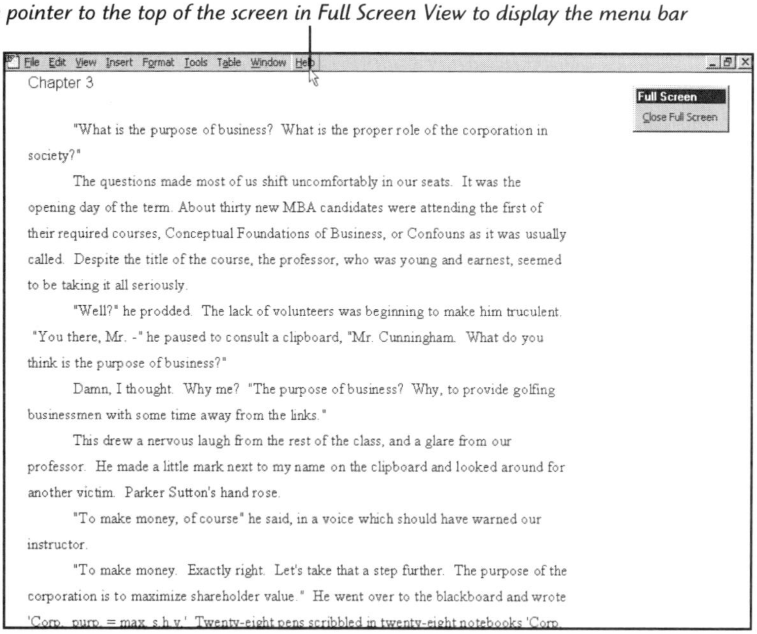
Slide the pointer to the top of the screen in Full Screen View to display the menu bar
File Edit View Insert Format Tools Table Window Help
Chapter 3
Full Screen
Close Full Screen
"What is the purpose of business? What is the proper role of the corporation in society?"
The questions made most of us shift uncomfortably in our seats. It was the opening day of the term. About thirty new MBA candidates were attending the first of their required courses, Conceptual Foundations of Business, or Confouns as it was usually called. Despite the title of the course, the professor, who was young and earnest, seemed to be taking it all seriously.
"Well?" he prodded. The lack of volunteers was beginning to make him truculent. "You there, Mr. -" he paused to consult a clipboard, "Mr. Cunningham. What do you think is the purpose of business?"
Damn, I thought. Why me? "The purpose of business? Why, to provide golfing businessmen with some time away from the links."
This drew a nervous laugh from the rest of the class, and a glare from our professor. He made a little mark next to my name on the clipboard and looked around for another victim. Parker Sutton's hand rose.
"To make money, of course" he said, in a voice which should have warned our instructor.
"To make money. Exactly right. Let's take that a step further. The purpose of the corporation is to maximize shareholder value." He went over to the blackboard and wrote

Fig. 21.1
It's still Word, but full-screen view looks like a sheet of typewriter paper, about right for a novel or long report.

Open or split windows to shed light on documents

Even in full-screen view, Word only displays about half a page at a time. You can compensate for this minor nuisance by either splitting the screen, or by opening a new document window.

To split the screen so that you can see two parts of the current document at once:

1. Click Window, Split. The gray split bar appears across the screen, and the pointer turns into a double-headed arrow.
2. Slide the split bar up or down the screen by moving the mouse; don't drag, just slide. The split bar follows the pointer as you move the mouse.
3. When you've got the split bar where you want it, click to split the screen. The editing window is divided in two. Scroll the parts independently to see two different sections of your document at once, as shown in Figure 21.2.

Fig. 21.2
Split-screen view is handy for long documents, or to see the top and bottom of the page at the same time.

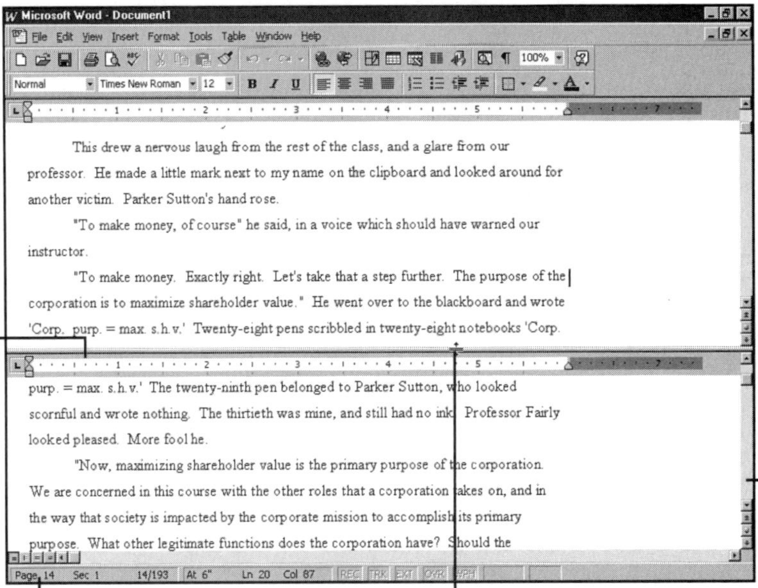
Microsoft Word - Document1
File Edit View Insert Format Tools Table Window Help
Normal
Times New Roman
12
100%
This drew a nervous laugh from the rest of the class, and a glare from our
professor. He made a little mark next to my name on the clipboard and looked around for
another victim. Parker Sutton's hand rose.
"To make money, of course" he said, in a voice which should have warned our
instructor.
"To make money. Exactly right. Let's take that a step further. The purpose of the
corporation is to maximize shareholder value." He went over to the blackboard and wrote
'Corp. purp. = max. s.h.v.' Twenty-eight pens scribbled in twenty-eight notebooks 'Corp.
purp. = max. s.h.v.' The twenty-ninth pen belonged to Parker Sutton, who looked
scornful and wrote nothing. The thirtieth was mine, and still had no ink. Professor Fairly
looked pleased. More fool he.
"Now, maximizing shareholder value is the primary purpose of the corporation.
We are concerned in this course with the other roles that a corporation takes on, and in
the way that society is impacted by the corporate mission to accomplish its primary
purpose. What other legitimate functions does the corporation have? Should the
Page 14 Sec 1 14/193 At 6" Ln 20 Col 87 REC TRK EXT OVR WPH

Double-click the split box to remove the split. When the screen is split, the split box looks like part of the split bar.

The second view gets its own scroll bar

The status bar displays your position in the section of the split that holds the insertion point

The pointer becomes a double-headed arrow when you point at the split bar. Drag the bar to resize either window.

Click in either portion of the split to edit that section of the document. To get rid of the split again, double-click the split bar (refer to Figure 21.2) or click Window, Remove Split.

TIP **If you have sharp eyes and a steady hand with the mouse, here's** the fast way to split the screen: the split box lives at the top of the vertical scroll bar in the Normal, Page Layout, or Outline view. You know you've found it when the pointer turns into a double-headed arrow. Drag or double-click the split box to split the screen. The split box is still functional when you split the screen; it just moves down the vertical scroll bar as you move the split bar (refer to Figure 21.2).

Open windows extend your view

Working on several documents at once? You can view them simultaneously in separate windows by opening each document and clicking Window, Arrange All. Figure 21.3 illustrates how viewing multiple documents on the screen may not always be helpful.

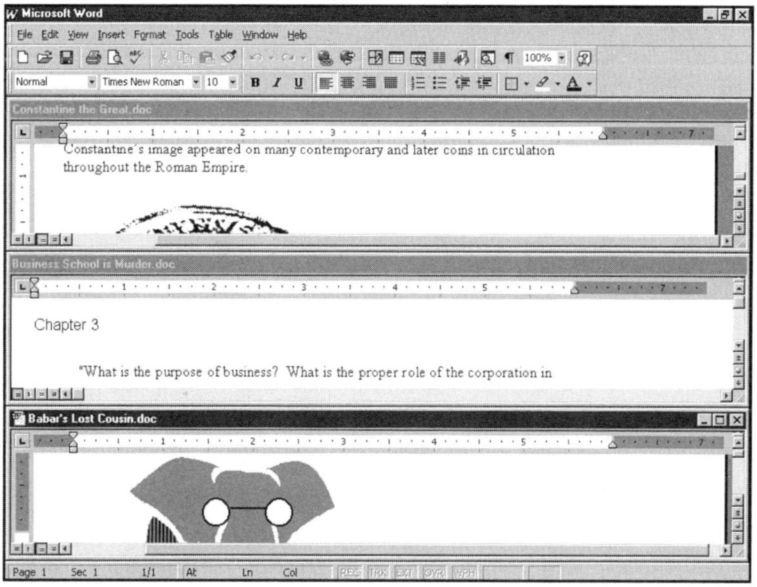

Fig. 21.3
The more documents you put on the screen, the less you see of each document.

Between the ruler, the title bar, and the scroll bars, you don't get to see too much of the actual document. To put these various screen elements out of sight:

1 Before you open your documents, click View, Ruler to get rid of the ruler.

2 Click Tools, Options, View and clear the check boxes for the Horizontal and Vertical Scroll Bars.

3 Click OK in the Options dialog box, and the scroll bars drop out of sight.

Now open your various documents and arrange the windows on the screen. You'll see a little more document with the scroll bars and ruler out of sight. This is especially handy for IntelliMouse users, who really don't need the scroll bars anyway.

Make your own toolbars

Between the Standard and the Formatting toolbars, you'll probably find that most of the tools you need are right under your nose. But maybe not all the tools you need are where you can see them. And you just may not have any use for some of the tools on the existing toolbars.

Word comes with a library of extra tools that you can add to the toolbars. And you can tear off tools you don't need and discard them. You can even make your own toolbar.

Make room for me! Removing a toolbar button

We all use Word in different ways. Some might insert loads of Excel tables in their documents; others might never do that at all. Maybe those non-Excel users find themselves producing a lot of envelopes instead.

If you're in the latter camp, get rid of the Insert Excel Worksheet button on the toolbar, and put the Envelopes and Labels button in its place.

First, to get rid of a toolbar button:

1. Click View, Toolbars, Customize to pop up the Customize dialog box.
2. In the Customize dialog box, click the Commands tab.
3. With the Customize dialog box active, any toolbar button is fair game; just drag the button off a toolbar to get rid of it (see Figure 21.4).
4. Click Close in the Customize dialog box, and your toolbar changes are saved in the current template.

TIP **Do you want your new toolbar button available to all your documents,** or do you need it only in a particular template? If you want the button in a template other than the default, Normal template, open the other template first. Click File, New and select one of the templates in the New dialog box, for example. Then follow the steps to add and remove toolbar buttons. When you're done, click the Save Changes In drop-down arrow in the Customize dialog box and select a template (refer to Figure 21.4).

Fig. 21.4
If there are toolbar buttons you never use, drag them to oblivion.

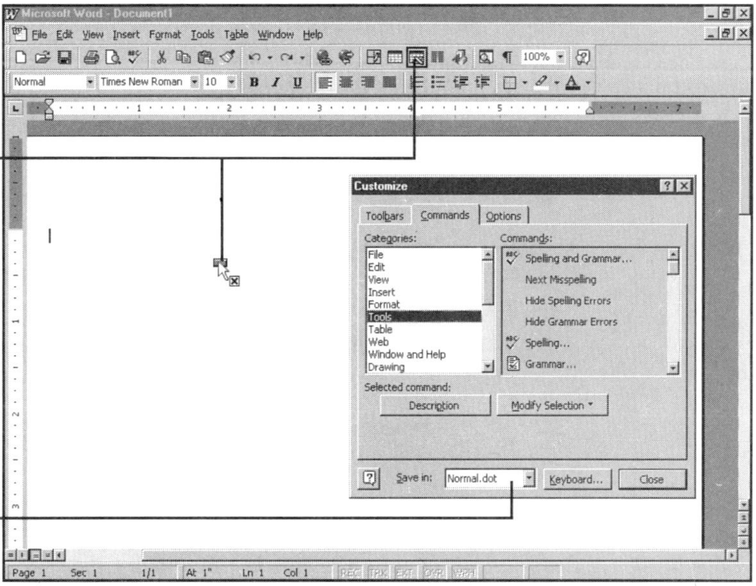

Drag a button off a toolbar, and it vanishes when you release the mouse button

To save your toolbar changes to the active document only, or to a different template, click here

Let me in! Adding a toolbar button

To add a button to a toolbar:

1. Click View, Toolbars, Customize to pop up the Customize dialog box. Or take the direct route: point at any toolbar and right-click for the shortcut menu. Choose Customize on the shortcut menu for the Customize dialog box. Choose the Commands tab in the Customize dialog box.

2. Click any of the Categories on the Commands tab in the Customize dialog box, and the buttons in that category appear in the Commands box. To see what the buttons do, click one, then click Description.

3. When you locate the button you want, drag it onto a toolbar. You can only add buttons in between existing buttons, or adjacent to the last toolbar button. The blank space past the end of the toolbar can't be used.

4. Once the button's in place, click Close in the Customize dialog box. You'll find that the newly added button not only works, it even has its own ScreenTip.

Add or remove as many buttons as you want to the existing toolbars. If you add more buttons than there's room for on the toolbar, some of the buttons will be pushed out of sight. To see those hidden buttons, point at the toolbar's handle and double-click or drag to float the toolbar onto the editing window (see Figure 21.5).

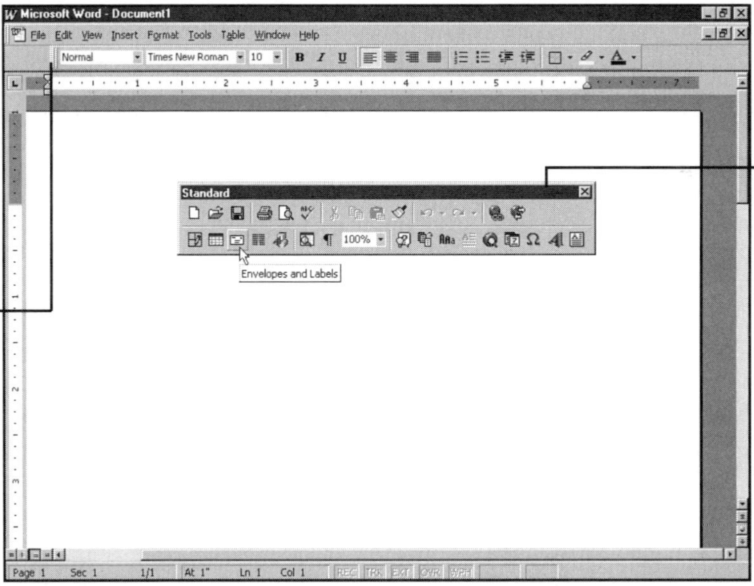

Fig. 21.5
Toolbar buttons are handy, but the more you add, the less room you'll have in the editing window.

Once the buttons are in sight again, you can use the Customize dialog box to add, remove, or rearrange them.

Q&A ***How do I get the original toolbars back again?***

You might have so much fun dragging buttons around that you wind up with toolbars that are not as functional as you'd like. To restore the toolbars to their original state, right-click a toolbar and choose Customize on the shortcut menu. Click the Toolbars tab in the Customize dialog box and choose Reset. When you close the Customize dialog box, all your button additions and subtractions are erased, and your toolbars are back to where they started.

The Letters toolbar is born

If you often find yourself doing the same chore in Word, build a specialized toolbar to help speed your work. For frequent letter writers, here's how you'd create a Letters toolbar:

1 Right-click any toolbar and choose Customize on the shortcut menu. Select the Toolbars tab in the Customize dialog box and click New.

2 The New Toolbar dialog box appears. In the Toolbar Name edit box, type a name for the new toolbar, as shown in Figure 21.6.

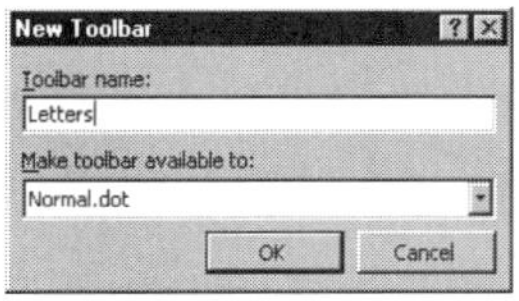

Fig. 21.6
The new toolbar's name will appear on the toolbar shortcut menu when you right-click a toolbar.

3 Click OK in the New Toolbar dialog box, and an embryo toolbar appears on the screen. Click the Commands tab of the Customize dialog box, and drag buttons onto the new toolbar.

4 As you add buttons to the new toolbar, it grows to accommodate them (see Figure 21.7).

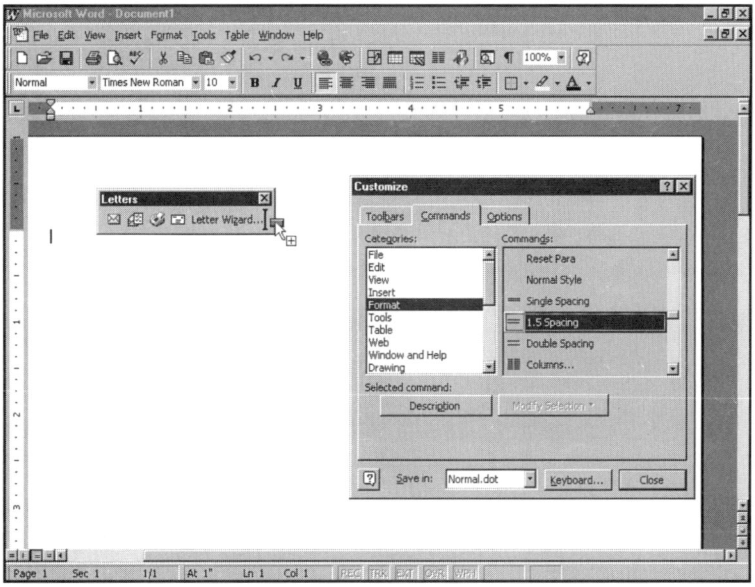

Fig. 21.7
New toolbars expand to hold as many buttons as you care to add.

5 Click Close in the Customize dialog box when you're done, and the new toolbar is finished.

You can't delete Word's own toolbars, but you can get rid of any new ones you create. Click View, Toolbars, Customize and choose the Toolbars tab. You'll see your new toolbar on the list of Toolbars. Select it, and the Delete button springs to life. Click Delete, Yes to delete your new toolbar.

Macros turn Word into a robot assistant

Creating something new is always exciting. Doing the same old thing over and over again is just plain dull. Word has a great gadget to save you from the tedium of repetitive chores: **macros**. Recording a macro is like dictating a memo to a high-speed dictation expert; your every keystroke and mouse click are faithfully taken down. When you run a macro, all your keystrokes and mouse clicks are played back again, just as you performed them.

> ***Plain English, please!***
>
> Macro is a familiar prefix, meaning large or long; think of macroeconomics, or even macrostylous (long-styled, as in prosy authors). In computer lingo, a **macro** is a single command that executes a large number of other commands.

Use a macro for any repetitive task involving more than a couple of keystrokes:

- Text that you type often, like a company name and address.
- Formatting commands that you use and reuse. Macros are especially handy for combining often-used text and formatting commands—your company name in a particular font, for example.
- File searches, especially if you find yourself hunting for the same group of documents all the time.

There are three easy steps to creating a macro: turn the macro recorder on, perform the chore, and turn the macro recorder off.

Need a letterhead? Let a macro do it for you

Word comes with a choice of letter templates that you can use to craft good-looking correspondence. To view them, click File, New, Letters & Faxes and double-click any of the template icons. I find it faster to use my own macro for letterhead stationery. I can set up the letterhead exactly the way I want it, and with a macro, I only need to set it up once; thereafter, I just run the macro to produce instant stationery.

To create a letterhead macro (or any macro) of your own:

1 Click Tools, Macro, Record New Macro. Type a name and description for the macro, as shown in Figure 21.8.

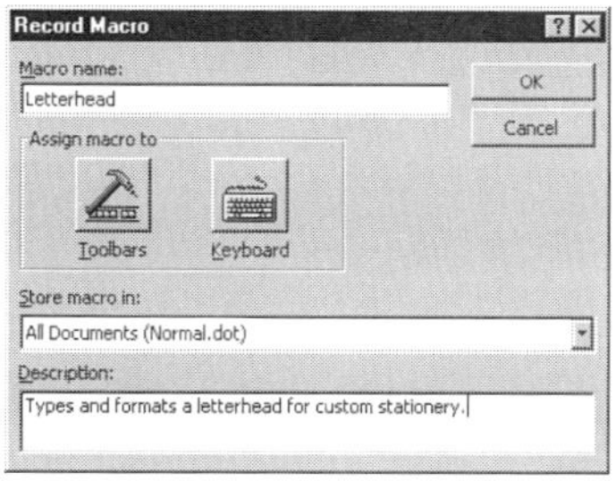

Fig. 21.8
Adding a description is a good idea; otherwise, you might forget what the macro is for.

2 You can assign a macro to a toolbar or a keyboard shortcut from here, but for now we won't bother. Just click OK in the Record Macro dialog box.

3 The Record Macro dialog box drops out of sight, and you get the Stop Recording toolbar instead. The pointer acquires a little cassette icon, to remind you that whatever actions you take are being recorded. Whatever your Word chore, perform it just as you would ordinarily.

For letterhead like the one shown in Figure 21.9, click View, Header and Footer, type your text in the header, change fonts, add an inside border, and align some of the text flush right.

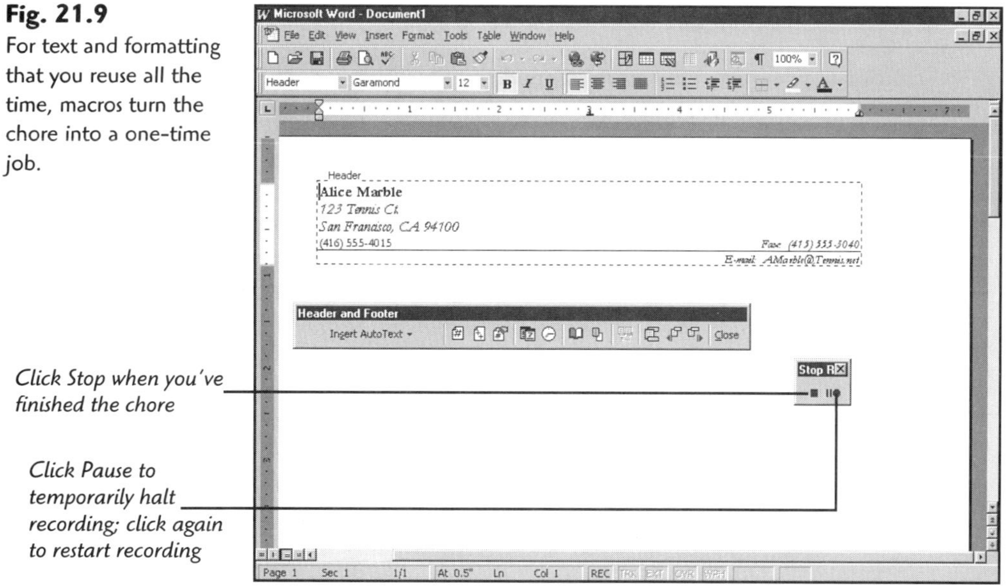

Fig. 21.9
For text and formatting that you reuse all the time, macros turn the chore into a one-time job.

4. Click the Stop button on the Record Macro toolbar when you've finished the chore you're recording. That puts the Record Macro toolbar away, and you can go back to work.

TIP **Here's another way to start and stop recording a macro: double-**click REC on the status bar to pop up the Record Macro dialog box. Double-click REC again to stop macro recording.

If you make a mistake while you're recording the macro, just correct it as you would ordinarily. When it's time to play back the macro, even though your errors are recorded, the corrections are recorded too. The end result should be fine.

Make sure that you perform all your repetitive keystrokes and commands while recording the macro. For example, if you click the Tables and Borders button on the Formatting toolbar to add borders during macro recording, click the button again while the macro is still recording to put away the Tables and Borders toolbar. Same thing with headers and footers. If you include either one (or both) in your macro, click the Close button on the Header and Footer toolbar while macro record is on to exit the header or footer.

Q&A ***I'm trying to select text while recording this macro, but I can't seem to do it with the mouse!***

That's because you can't select text with the mouse while recording a macro. Use the Shift+arrow key combination instead. The mouse does work for toolbar buttons and menu commands during macro recording.

Macro recorded? Run it

The only labor involved in creating macros is performing the chore you're recording. Once that's done, playing the macro is a snap.

To play back a macro:

1. Click Tools, Macro, Macros (or press Alt+F8) for the Macros dialog box.
2. Your newly recorded macro appears on the list under Macro Name; select the macro, then click Run. That runs the macro, inserting any text and formatting you've recorded at the insertion point.

If you recorded a letterhead macro, just run the macro any time you want letterhead stationery. That saves you a lot of typing and formatting, to say nothing of a trip to the printer.

A macro mistake! Can I fix it?

The last thing anyone needs is another of life's minor irritations. Sometimes that's just what you get with a macro. After you go to the trouble of recording it, playing back a macro might reveal a flaw or two in your creation.

If the flaws seem more like major errors, you can always delete the macro. Click Tools, Macro, Macros for the Macros dialog box, select the offending macro, and click Delete to do that. You can sort out what went wrong, then record a new, error-free macro.

But if it's just a question of a minor bug, squash it. Word includes some handy tools for editing macros, and it doesn't take a programming expert to put them to work. Suppose that letterhead macro we just created was fine in all respects, but we got a digit wrong in the phone number's area code. It's a lot easier to fix a small mistake like that than it is to rerecord the whole macro.

To edit a macro:

1. Press Alt+F8 or click Tools, Macro, Macros for the Macros dialog box, select the macro, and click Edit.
2. That pops up the Microsoft Visual Basic window and toolbar. If the macro appears as a minimized icon, click the Maximize button to display it. The macro text and codes appear as shown in Figure 21.10.
3. The Visual Basic Standard toolbar can be used to add commands to a macro, or debug a troubled macro. For a simple text fix, we don't need it. Text that you type while recording a macro appears in quotes in the macro editing window (refer to Figure 21.10). Simply locate the text you want to change, use Backspace or Delete to clear the mistake, and type in the correction.
4. When you've corrected your macro, click File, Close and Return to Microsoft Word. Your changes are saved automatically.

The Find button on the Visual Basic Standard toolbar is handy for fixing text in the macro editing window. The Find dialog box it summons up not only helps you locate and fix mistakes, Find and Replace also ensure that you don't accidentally delete any of the Visual Basic commands and punctuation. Each of those quotation marks, for example, is a vital part of the macro. If you zap one by mistake, your macro won't run properly.

Click View Microsoft Word to see your document, handy if you want to watch a macro being run while you're in the Visual Basic window

These tools are to modify macros, and squash macro bugs

Fig. 21.10
Here's what our macro looks like in Word's programming language, Visual Basic.

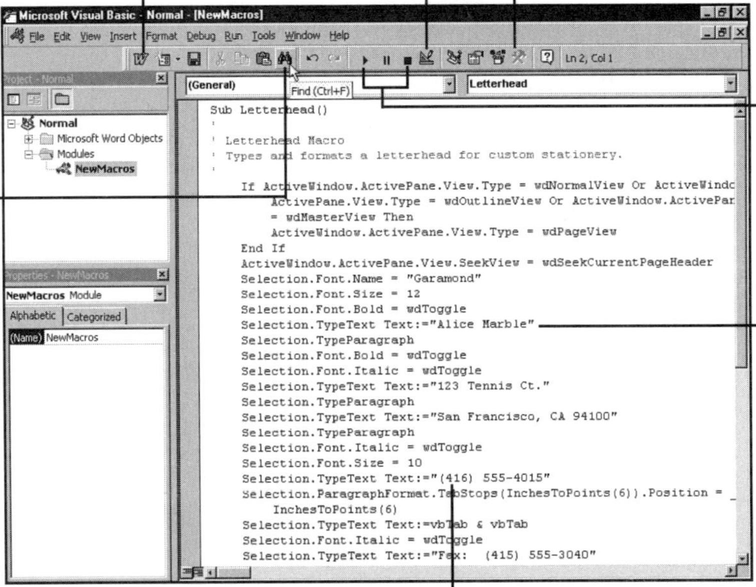

Run, Pause, or Stop a macro

Click Find to search for text or codes in the macro

Text typed while the macro was recording is in quotes

The offending area code. Delete the 6, type a 5, and no one will ever know there was a mistake.

Custom buttons, menus, and keyboard shortcuts

Word puts a lot of menu commands, toolbar buttons, and keyboard shortcuts at your disposal. You'll probably have no need to add your own, but you can if you want to. The handiest use for these custom additions is to link a macro to a button, or a menu command, or even a keyboard shortcut.

Take our letterhead macro. Instead of running it from the Macro dialog box, we can assign it to a button, command, or a key combination, like Shift+Alt+L, and run it with a click or keystroke.

Stick a macro on its own button

Remember that Letter toolbar we created? A button to run a letterhead macro would make a great addition to it.

To assign a macro to a button and stick it on a toolbar:

1. Right-click a toolbar and select Customize on the shortcut menu for the Customize dialog box. On the list of Toolbars, click the check box for the toolbar to which you want to add the macro button. If you're adding the button to the Standard or Formatting toolbar, they're already checked.

2. Click the Commands tab in the Customize dialog box. Scroll down the list of Categories and select Macros.

3. A list of Macros appears next to the Categories list. Point at the macro you want and drag it to a toolbar, as shown in Figure 21.11.

Fig. 21.11
By default, only the macro name, Letterhead, will appear on the toolbar; the generic macro icon does not.

The I-beam shows where on the toolbar the addition will go

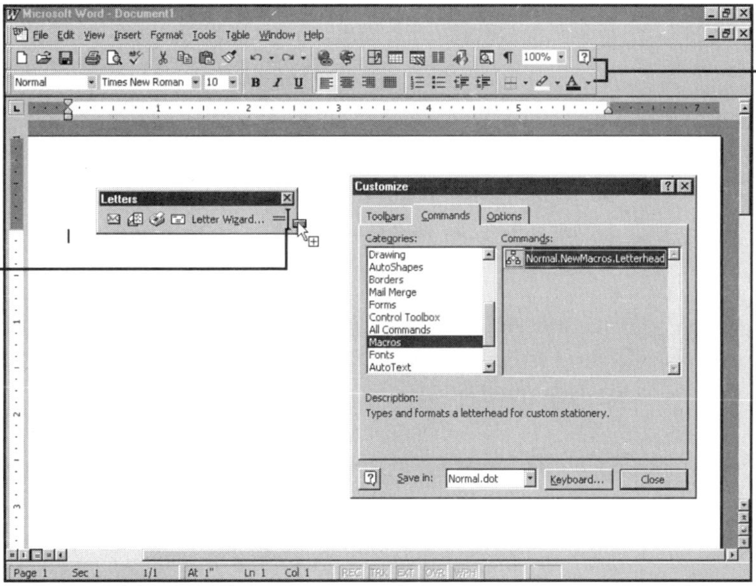

If you don't have another toolbar displayed, you can drag a macro to the Formatting or Standard toolbar

4. When you drop the dragged macro onto a toolbar, it appears as a text button. To add an icon to the text button, click Modify Selection on the Commands tab and choose Change Button Image as shown in Figure 21.12.

Fig. 21.12
This collection of buttons doesn't do anything yet, but assign them to macros, and they'll do whatever you want.

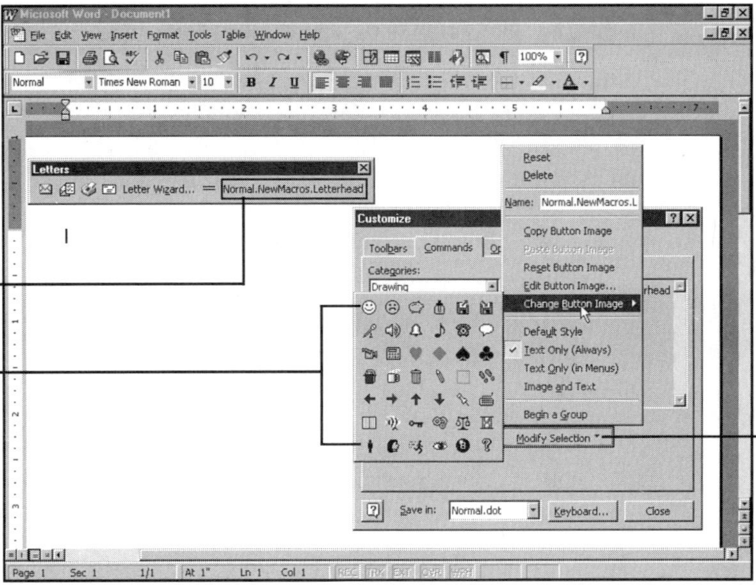

Here's the text button, soon to be joined by a picture

Click any of the icons to transform your text button

The Modify Selection choice only appears when you drag a command to a toolbar

5 Select any of the icons on the Change Button Image menu, and the selected icon joins the text on the toolbar button. If you don't want the text to display along with the icon, choose Text Only (In Menus) on the Modify Selection menu.

6 Click Close in the Customize dialog box, and your macro is safely installed behind a toolbar button, complete with its own SmartTip. Now whenever you want to run the Letterhead macro, just click the button.

You can assign any macro, command, style, or font to a button with the method we just used. Return to the Customize dialog box, select a category, and drag the item you want onto a toolbar.

TIP **To draw your own toolbar button, drag the macro name out of** the Customize dialog box and onto a toolbar. Click Modify Selection, Edit Button Image, then draw your button in the Button Editor dialog box. Don't forget to select a Modify Selection menu option that displays images—either Text Only (In Menus) or Image and Text will work—so that you'll see your creation on a toolbar.

I'd rather have a keyboard shortcut for my macro

Word has dozens of existing keyboard shortcuts, those key combinations like Ctrl+B for boldface. I can't keep them straight, but if you can, and want still more keyboard shortcuts to remember, add as many as you like.

To assign a macro to a keyboard shortcut:

1. Right-click a toolbar for the shortcut menu, then select Customize for the Customize dialog box.
2. Click the Commands tab in the Customize dialog box.
3. Click Keyboard. In the Customize Keyboard dialog box that appears, select Macros from the list of Categories, then click your macro on the Macros list.
4. Click the Press New Shortcut Key edit box, then press the key combination you want to use. For the Letterhead macro, Shift+Alt+H (Shift+Alt+L is already in use by Word) is a good choice; just press those keys on the keyboard.
5. The key combination you pressed appears in the Press New Shortcut Key edit box; if it looks right, click Assign.
6. Click Close in the Customize Keyboard dialog box, and you're done.

Now whenever you want to run the macro, press the key combination you assigned to it—if you can remember the keys.

TIP **If you do forget the key combination, return to the Customize** Keyboard dialog box, select your macro, and view the assigned key combination in the Current keys box.

22 Mail Merge, for Homemade Mass Mailings

In this chapter:

- **Just what is mail merge?**
- **I've got a letter and a dozen folks to send it to—now what?**
- **Main document? Data source? Explain, please!**
- **I'm only sending letters to Indiana**
- **How about some labels and envelopes?**

Really clever goods look hand-crafted, even when they're not. Like Word's mail merge documents—they're mass-produced, but they don't look it. . . . .

Ransom E. Olds' 1901 Oldsmobiles were successful—until people started driving them. Olds' cars didn't last on roads designed for the horse and buggy. Henry Ford came along and designed a car tough enough for rough roads; the only problem was producing enough of them to satisfy demand.

Ford's answer was the assembly line, thanks to which the Model T was a historic success. But eventually, the car passed into history. Its problem? Every Model T was identical; they were mass-produced, and they looked it.

Buyers began demanding cars that at least gave the illusion of individuality. And that's still true. Our cars can be identical, but we're happier if mine is red and yours is green. That's why you'll like Word's mail merge feature. You get mass-produced documents, letters by the hundreds if you want them, that look entirely personalized. Your assembly-line letters may not make history, but your readers will appreciate the personal touch, however illusory.

Why do I need mail merge?

A dozen identical letters to write, a dozen people to send them to, and you've got the makings of a really tedious chore—but not if you use mail merge. In a merge, you write a single letter in one document, enter all your recipients' names and addresses in another document, and then merge the two to produce as many personalized letters as you need. Magic? Not really. Convenient? You bet.

What happens in a merge?

Like Ford's assembly line, mail merges take the shell of the finished product, add parts as needed, then roll out the completed goods.

There are three parts to a merge:

- You enter items like your recipients' names and addresses in a handy **data form**. All the information you enter in the data form, such as last names, first names, street addresses, and so on, is saved in a table, called the **data source**. The data source supplies all the spare parts for your assembly line document. If you use Microsoft Exchange or Windows Messaging, you can draw on your Personal Address Book as a data source.

- Once you've entered all your data, you write the letter itself. The body of the letter is text formatted any way you like. But instead of typing in names and addresses, you insert **merge fields**. Just like that space on a tax form labeled LAST NAME, merge fields are labeled spaces that look like this: <<LastName>>. You choose the merge fields you need from a list, and click to insert them in the appropriate spots in your letter. The document containing the merge fields is called the **main document**. It's the shell of the final product, ready to be filled in along the assembly line.
- When you perform the merge, the spare parts from the data source, those names and addresses, are plugged into the corresponding merge fields in the main document, turning a shell of a document into the final product. Last names replace all the <<LastName>> merge fields, and so on. You get as many letters as you have names and addresses in the data source.

Use mail merges whenever you have one document to send to more than a couple of recipients. You can also use a merge to produce dozens of labels and envelopes, each one neatly addressed with the names and addresses you entered in the data source.

Figure 22.1 shows you what a typical main document and data source look like.

Plain English, please!

A **data source** is a database, an orderly list of information. Databases have their own jargon (doesn't everything?), a smattering of which you'll need to know. **Records** are like Rolodex cards; each record holds all the information for one of your letter recipients. The items of information in a record—last names, first names, and so on—are called **fields**. In a Word data source table, the rows of the table are records, and the columns are fields. The top row of the table (the **header row**) labels each column, or field.

These are the merge fields. They're replaced by the data in the corresponding fields in the data source.

The main document holds the body text of your letter

Fig. 22.1
You probably won't need to tinker with the data source itself, but as you step through the mail merge, it's helpful to know what the jargon refers to.

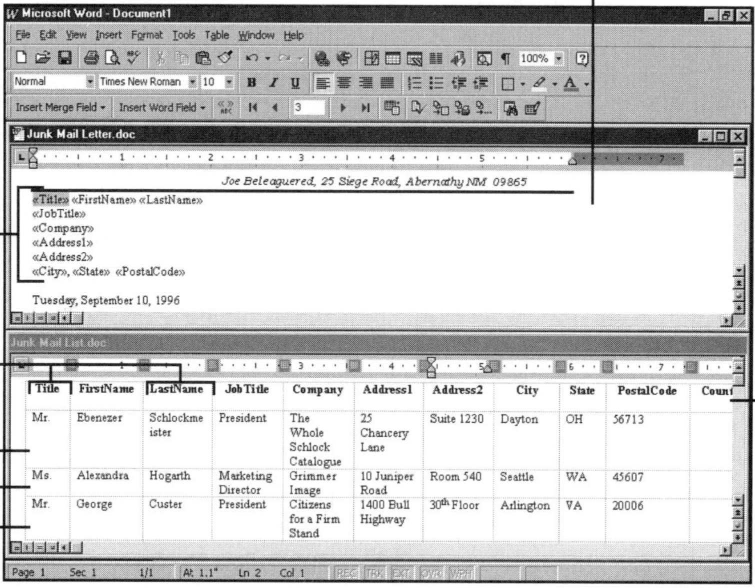

Each column is called a field, containing items of data such as last names

The data source is a table that Word creates; each row is like a Rolodex card of information

The header row has the names of each field

Mail merges made easy

Is your mail box as crowded with junk mail as mine? Catalogs, fund-raising letters, political statements—we're bombarded with mass mailings. Mail merges give you the chance to strike back. You create your own form letter, Word fills in the blanks, and then produces a blizzard of completed letters that you can send to as many recipients as you care to.

Mail merges start with a data source

Use mail merge to send newsletters, product announcements, change of address letters, whatever you like. Another possible use for mail merge: gather a few days' worth of junk mail, clip out the senders' names and addresses, and send them all a letter asking them not to send you any more letters. If your missives are addressed to the senders by name, they might even get results.

To produce a mass mailing with mail merge, first create the data source, the file for your recipients' names and addresses:

1 In a new blank document, click Tools, Mail Merge. The Mail Merge Helper pops up.

2 Click Create in the Mail Merge Helper for the list of options shown in Figure 22.2.

Fig. 22.2
We'll tackle envelopes and labels later. For now, we want a stern letter.

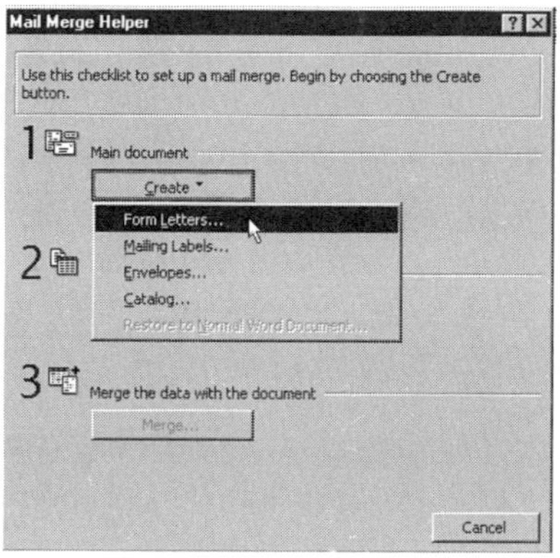

3 Click Form Letters on the Create drop-down list, and a message from Word pops up, prompting you to choose the location of your main document. Since we started from a new blank document, click Active Window.

4 That takes us back to the Mail Merge Helper. Click Get Data and choose Create Data Source. The Create Data Source dialog box pops up, as shown in Figure 22.3.

Fig. 22.3
Remember the header row? Here's where you get to pick what goes into it.

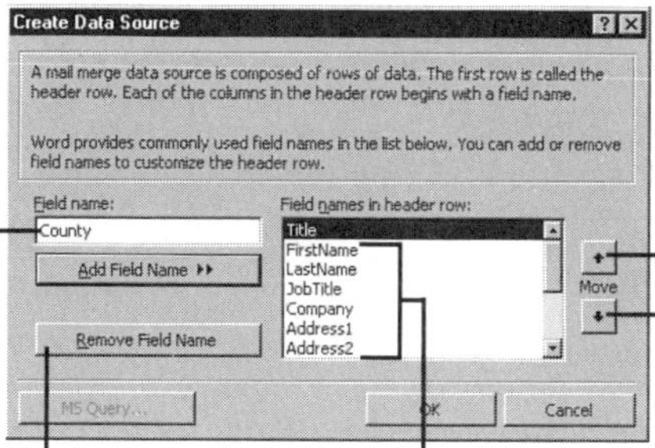

To add a field name of your own, type it here and click Add Field Name

Select a field name, then click these buttons to move it up or down in the list

Select any field name you don't need, then click Remove Field Name to discard it

These field names appear in the header row of the data source

TIP **Microsoft Exchange or Windows Messaging users with their ad-**dress data in an Address Book can choose Get Data, Use Address Book in the Mail Merge Helper dialog box. Select the address book you want to use, then skip down to "The next step: make your own form letter," which is the next section in this chapter.

5 The Create Data Source dialog box is where you decide just what items of information to put in your Data Source. If the names in the list of Field Names have your data covered, do nothing in the Create Data Source dialog box. And any field names that you have no use for are ignored in a merge anyway, so you needn't be concerned with excess fields. But if you want to tinker with your field names, try one of these options:

- Scan the list of Field Names In Header Row. If any of the field names don't apply to your data, select them and click Remove Field Name. If you're sending letters in the U.S., for example, you might not need the Country field name.
- None of the field names on the list apply to your data? Type your own field name in the Field Name edit box, then click Add Field Name to add it to the list.
- If you want to reorder the field names, click a name, then move it up or down the list with the Move arrows.

TIP **The main document determines what data is included in your** letters, and where the data will go *in* the letter. That being the case, you don't have to worry too much about your choices in the Create Data Source dialog box.

6 Click OK in the Create Data Source dialog box, and the Save As dialog box pops up. Type a name for your Data Source file in the File Name edit box and click Save.

7 Another message from Word appears, with the helpful information that the data source you just created contains no data (I like to yell "I KNOW that!" at this point, but that's optional). Click Edit Data Source.

8 The data form pops up. There are edit boxes for each of the field names you included in the Create Data Source dialog box. Enter your first record, typing the data in the appropriate box. Click the box you want, or press Tab to go from box to box. Figure 22.4 shows the data form completely filled in, but you don't have to fill in every field in every record. Word ignores any blanks when it performs the merge.

Click Add New when you're ready to add another record

Fig. 22.4
It takes a few steps to get here, but the data form is a handy way to enter information

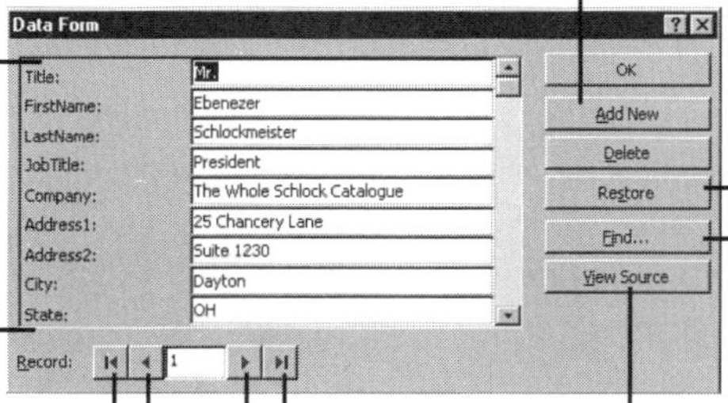

Use Restore with caution—see the caution below

Click Find to search for records, or fields in records

These are the field names from the Create Data Source dialog box

Click these buttons to jump from record to record

View Source takes you to the table Word creates for your data

CAUTION **The Restore button on the data form restores your entries to the** way they were when you last saved them. If you click Restore before saving a record, any entries in that record are wiped out. You "restore" the blank edit boxes! Helpful, no? If you call up an existing record, edit it, and make a mistake during the edit, use Restore to restore the original record. Restore also won't restore deleted records, by the way.

9 When you've finished typing the fields for your first record, click Add New in the data form. That saves your first record, and clears the edit boxes so you can add the next record. Enter all your records, clicking Add New for each one.

10 Once you've entered all your records, click OK. The data form drops out of sight, and you're in the main document, with the Mail Merge toolbar parked above it. At the moment, the document is blank, but we'll change that.

Q&A ***How come I don't see that data source table Word created?***

It's there, but you don't need to bother with it. The data source lurks in the background, supplying data as needed. If you want to examine the data source, click the Edit Data Source button on the Mail Merge toolbar for the data form, then click View Source.

The next step: make your own form letter

No matter how cleverly the "personalized" name and address is slipped in, it's usually easy to spot a form letter. That stilted, unnatural language, the carefully noncommittal constructions, it's all a dead giveaway. When you get one of those magazine subscription letters that begin "You Jane E. Smythe have a unique opportunity…" you can practically see the merge code where your name was inserted.

Here's your chance to improve on the standard boilerplate. Form letters in Word are still form letters, but at least they're of your own writing. To create the mail merge form letter:

1. Once you've clicked OK in the data form (see step 10 previously), you're in a blank document with the Mail Merge toolbar displayed above it. Click the Insert Merge Field button on the Mail Merge toolbar, and a list of your field names drops down, as shown in Figure 22.5.
2. There's a merge field for every one of the data source field names. Click a merge field, and it pops into the document at the insertion point. Insert a title where you want a title, and so on. If you want your data separated by a space or a blank line, be sure to press the space bar or the Enter key after inserting the merge field. The salutation and recipient's address part of the form letter might look like Figure 22.6.

3. Once you've inserted a few merge fields, click the View Merged Data button on the Mail Merge toolbar to preview the merged document. The merge fields are replaced by data from the data source, as shown in Figure 22.7.

Fig. 22.5
You saw them in the Create Data Source dialog box, and in the data form, and here they are again as merge fields: the ubiquitous field names.

Click any of the merge fields to insert them at the insertion point

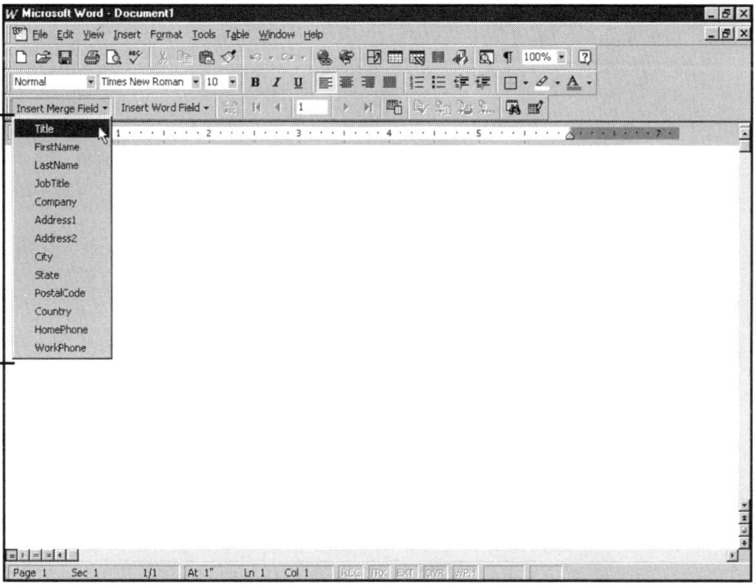

Insert spaces between merge fields where you'd want spaces between words in your text

Fig. 22.6
Insert a merge field from the Insert Merge Field list wherever you want the corresponding data.

Press Enter to put merge fields on a new line, just as though you were entering text on a new line

Don't forget to include punctuation between or after merge fields, like commas or periods

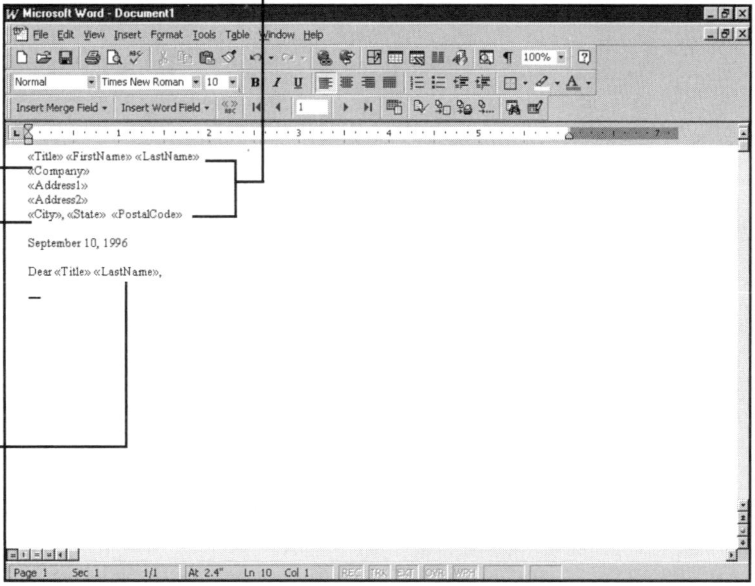

Click View Merged Data for a preview of the merged document

Click these buttons to preview additional records from the data source—they only work if you click the View Merged Data button first

Want to find a particular record? Click Find Record to ferret it out

If you need to change a record, click Edit Data Source to display the data form

The information from the data source replaces the merge fields when you view merged data

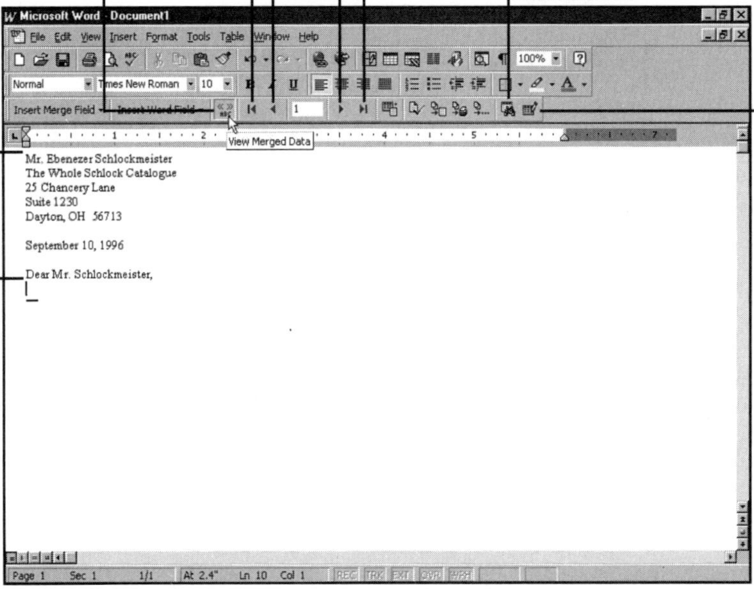

Fig. 22.7
You haven't committed yourself to the merge yet; the View Merged Data button just gives you a sneak preview.

Q&A *I inserted a merge field I didn't want!*

It's easy to click the wrong merge field. Or you might decide you don't want a particular field in a particular spot in your document. Either way, double-click the merge field to select it. Word shades the merge field to show it's been selected; press Delete to get rid of it.

CAUTION **Don't try to type merge fields by hand; Word will ignore any such** attempts. For merge fields to work, they have to be inserted with the Insert Merge Field button on the Mail Merge toolbar.

4 Once you've got your merge fields where you want them, type the letter body text. Insert merge fields throughout the letter if you like. Add a letterhead, save the document, and the finished form letter will look something like Figure 22.8.

Fig. 22.8
Somehow a form letter always winds up sounding like a form letter, no matter how you try to disguise it.

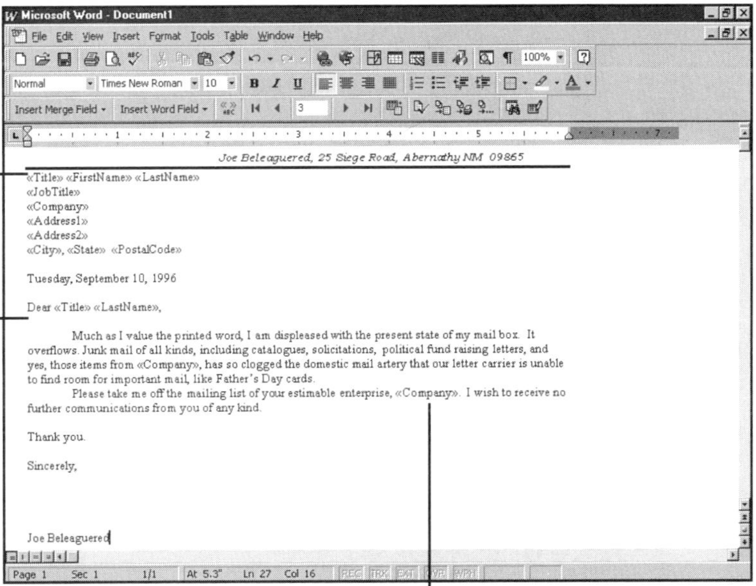
Microsoft Word - Document1
File Edit View Insert Format Tools Table Window Help
Normal
Times New Roman
10
100%
Insert Merge Field
Insert Word Field
Joe Beleaguered, 25 Siege Road, Abernathy NM 09865
«Title» «FirstName» «LastName»
«JobTitle»
«Company»
«Address1»
«Address2»
«City», «State» «PostalCode»
Tuesday, September 10, 1996
Dear «Title» «LastName»,
Much as I value the printed word, I am displeased with the present state of my mail box. It overflows. Junk mail of all kinds, including catalogues, solicitations, political fund raising letters, and yes, those items from «Company», has so clogged the domestic mail artery that our letter carrier is unable to find room for important mail, like Father's Day cards.
Please take me off the mailing list of your estimable enterprise, «Company». I wish to receive no further communications from you of any kind.
Thank you.
Sincerely,
Joe Beleaguered
Page 1 Sec 1 1/1 At 5.3" Ln 27 Col 16

You can use the same merge field as many times as you like

Merge fields can go anywhere in the main document, including in the body text

Data done? Form finished? Merge maneuvers come next

Assembling data and writing the form letter is the labor-intensive part of mail merges. The actual merge is handled by Word, so it's pretty easy. How easy?

With your data entered, and your form letter completed, click the Merge to New Document button on the Mail Merge toolbar. Word merges your data and form letter, and gives you multiple copies of your letter with the data filled in, one copy for each record in the data source, as shown in Figure 22.9.

You'll want to print a sample page or two before turning your printer loose on all the merged documents. That way you can check to make sure that all the merge codes are in the right place, and that you haven't made any data-entry errors when you set up the data source.

Word gives your merged document a temporary file name, but there's no need to save the file

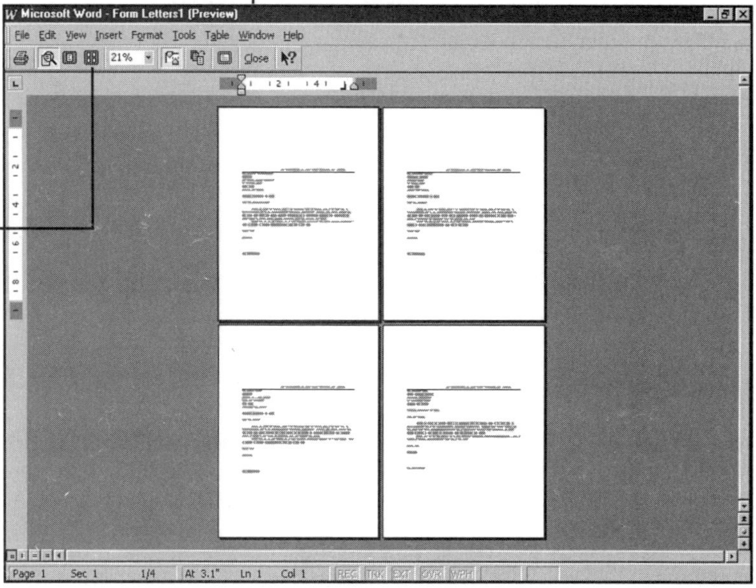

Fig. 22.9
Instant custom letters. Mail merge sure beats retyping the same letter a dozen times.

Print Preview mode, with the Multiple Pages button selected

To print a preview document, click File, Print. In the Print dialog box, click the Current Page option, then click OK. That prints a single page of the merge file; eyeball the printout carefully before sending the entire file to the printer.

If you want envelopes or labels addressed to your recipients, read on.

TIP **There's no need to save the new document containing the merged** letters—that just takes up hard disk real estate. Since you've saved your data source file and your form letter, you can merge them again any time you want to.

What if I don't want to merge all my data?

Maybe you don't want to send a letter to everyone in your data file. No problem. Click the Mail Merge button on the Mail Merge toolbar to pop up the Merge dialog box shown in Figure 22.10.

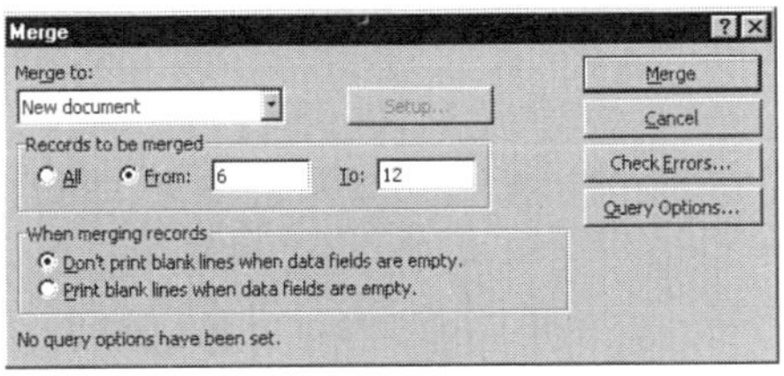

Fig. 22.10
All your records are numbered, from 1 to whatever. Just enter the range of records you want to merge in the Merge dialog box.

Click From in the Merge dialog box, then enter the range of record numbers you want to merge. If you have twelve records, for example, and you want to merge only the last six, enter From 6 to 12, then click Merge in the Merge dialog box.

Can't remember which record is numbered what? Click Close in the Merge dialog box. Then click the View Merged Data button on the Mail Merge toolbar and use the Previous Record and Next Record buttons to browse your records. The record numbers appear in the Go To Record box, in between the Next Record and Previous Record buttons.

I'm only sending letters to Kansas

Merging only a range of records isn't the most refined way of orchestrating your mass mailing. What if you only want to send letters to folks in a single town or state? Or maybe you only want to send letters to doctors. Either way, you can **filter** your records to extract exactly the ones you want, and just merge those extracted records.

To filter data source records:

1. Click the Mail Merge Helper button on the Mail Merge toolbar (if the toolbar isn't displayed, choose Tools, Mail Merge).
2. In the Mail Merge Helper, click Query Options to pop up the Query Options dialog box.
3. Click the Filter Records tab in the Query Options dialog box, then click the Field drop-down arrow.
4. That gets you a list of those familiar field names we've seen in various guises. Select a field name from the list; if you're sending mail to Kansas only, choose the State field name from the dropped-down list.

5 By default, the Comparison is Equal To. In English, that means that only those records in which the State field contains exactly what you type in the Compare To edit box will be chosen. For our Kansas mailing, we'd type **Kansas** in the Compare to Edit box. Figure 22.11 makes it all more comprehensible.

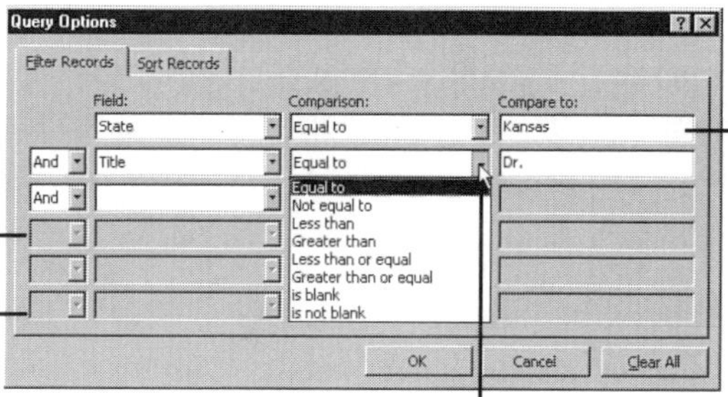

Fig. 22.11
The Query Options dialog box is a powerful search tool, and after you play around with it a little, it's pretty easy to use.

You can refine the filter further by adding additional fields and criteria

Only those records with Kansas in the State field will be merged. If you used state abbreviations in your data, type abbreviations and not state names here.

Click here for the other comparison operators, like Not Equal To or Less Than

6 Refine the filter still more if you want to. For letters to doctors in Kansas, leave the default And operator at the beginning of the second row, click the Field drop-down arrow in the second row and choose Title. Still on the second row, set the Comparison to Equal To, and type **Dr.** in the Compare To edit box.

7 Click OK when you're done, then go ahead and merge. Only the records that match the criteria you've set will be merged into your main document.

How about those envelopes and labels?

We just merged our data into a form letter; it's just as easy to merge the same data into envelopes or mailing labels.

TIP **Word gets your envelope return address from the User Info tab** of the Options dialog box. If you want to change the return address, click Tools, Options, User Info. Then type a new address in the Mailing Address box and click OK.

Envelopes by the bushel

To create mail merge envelopes:

1. Click the Mail Merge Helper button on the Mail Merge toolbar. In the Mail Merge Helper, click Create, Envelopes.
2. If you've already merged your form letters, a Word message pops up asking if you want to convert the merged document into envelopes, or open a new document for your envelopes. You'll probably want to do the latter, so click New Main Document.
3. Now we're back to the Mail Merge Helper. Click Get Data and choose Open Data Source.
4. The Open Data Source dialog box pops up. It should look familiar—it's close kin to the Open and Save As dialog boxes. Double-click the file name of your data source file.
5. That gets you another Word message box. Click Set Up Main Document in the message box.

   It took a while to get here, but that pops up the Envelope Options dialog box. Click OK in the Envelope address dialog box.
6. Eureka! We've arrived at the Envelope address dialog box. Click Insert Merge Field, and select merge fields to insert in the Sample Envelope address box, as shown in Figure 22.12.

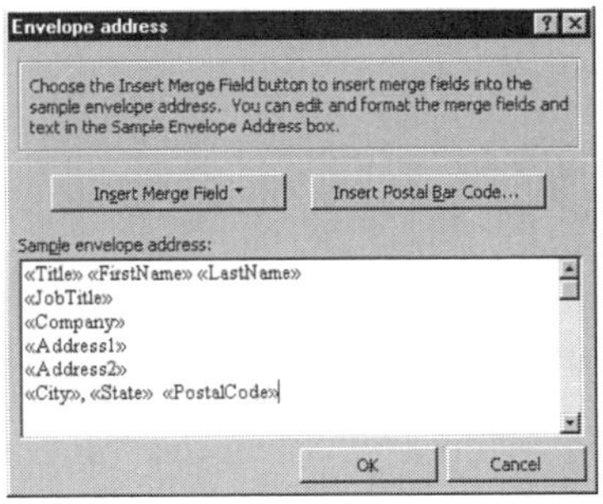

Fig. 22.12
This is just like inserting merge fields in the form letter; click a field on the list, and it pops in at the insertion point.

7. Don't forget spaces, blank lines, and punctuation in between the merge fields. Click OK in the Envelope address dialog box when you're done.

8 We've come this far, and we're back to the beginning: the Mail Merge Helper reappears. But the work is done. Just click Merge in the Mail Merge Helper, and the Merge dialog box pops up (refer to Figure 22.10).

9 Choose all your records or a range of records. Click Merge in the Merge dialog box. Word merges your data into envelopes and displays them in Page Layout view. Look them over to make sure that all is right, then go ahead and print the envelopes.

If you want labels instead of envelopes, go back to step 1 and click Create, Mailing Labels. Then work your way through the same steps we took to create envelopes. Word automatically formats the labels for a variety of standard Avery label types. Just check your label package for the model number, and choose the same type of labels when you get to the Word Label Options dialog box.

Part VII: Word and the Rest of the World

23 Pony Express It's Not: Sending Data In and Out of Word

In this chapter:

- **Can I open old word processor files in Word?**
- **I want my Excel chart in a Word document**
- **The chart's in Word. Now how do I update and edit it?**
- **How do I use menus in Windows?**
- **How do I get my PowerPoint slide in Word?**
- **I can send faxes and e-mail, right from Word?**

Exchanging data between applications on your hard drive, or between offices across the continent, just isn't what it used to be. Thank goodness for that!

The next time you get a Federal Express delivery, spare a thought for FedEx's ancestor: the Pony Express. The daredevil riders of the famous mail service raced letters from Missouri to California—almost two thousand miles—in eight days, twice as fast as the regular mail.

Their route was no milk run. Besides rough terrain and bad weather, two- and four-legged dangers lurked at every pass. The "pony-riders'" greatest admirer was Mark Twain, who reported that there was "but little frivolous correspondence" in a Pony Express mail bag. Only important business letters justified the hefty (in 1860) five-dollar charge.

Heroics aren't required to send important letters, or any other kind of data, in and out of Word. A few quick mouse clicks, and the job is done. And it doesn't take much more time than that for Word to dispatch faxes or e-mail to anywhere, from California to Missouri and beyond. About the only danger you face exchanging data in and out of Word is missing the exchange; look away for a moment, and it's already happened.

What do I do with my old files?

Summer in Europe. Sunshine, fountains, outdoor cafes—and phrase-book-studying tourists bumping into walls. We might be among them. Without those handy phrase books, how could we convert unfamiliar words into plain old English?

Word has its own phrase books built right into the program. They're called **filters** and **converters**. Word uses them to translate files from other applications into its own terms. The translation is automatic; just open your file, and Word puts its phrase books to work. You don't have to do a thing.

Word's translation isn't perfect. Just as that French you try to speak to the cabby at the airport may not sound exactly *comme il faut*, files from other applications may look a little different when you open them in Word. Fonts, spacing, and page layouts may not turn out exactly the way you want them to. It depends on your original application, and on how heavily formatted your document happens to be:

- Documents from older versions of Word will convert to Word for Windows 95 or Windows NT with few, if any, changes. Just open your document.

- If you're using the Internet Explorer 3.0, convert any Web page on the World Wide Web to a Word document. Just click Edit on the Internet Explorer toolbar.
- Documents created in other Windows word processors, like WordPerfect for Windows, may undergo some formatting changes when you open them in Word. Chances are, the changes won't be too drastic, and you can put all the Word formatting tools to work on any necessary repairs.

Word's file translations will be close to the original, even for files in older DOS word processors. Figure 23.1 shows a file created in WordPerfect 5.0 in one window, and the same file in the Word editing window.

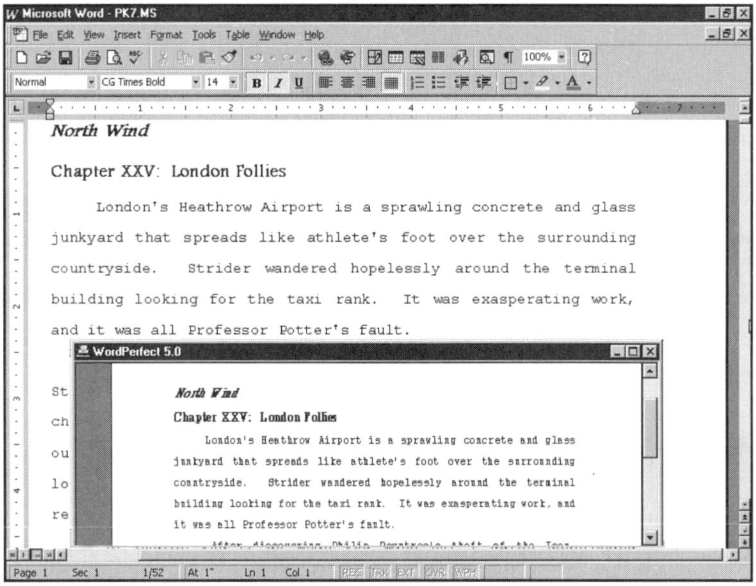
Microsoft Word - PK7.MS
File Edit View Insert Format Tools Table Window Help
Normal
CG Times Bold
14
North Wind
Chapter XXV: London Follies
London's Heathrow Airport is a sprawling concrete and glass junkyard that spreads like athlete's foot over the surrounding countryside. Strider wandered hopelessly around the terminal building looking for the taxi rank. It was exasperating work, and it was all Professor Potter's fault.
WordPerfect 5.0
North Wind
Chapter XXV: London Follies
London's Heathrow Airport is a sprawling concrete and glass junkyard that spreads like athlete's foot over the surrounding countryside. Strider wandered hopelessly around the terminal building looking for the taxi rank. It was exasperating work, and it was all Professor Potter's fault.
Page 1 Sec 1 1/52 At 1" Ln 1 Col 1

Fig. 23.1
The fonts changed slightly when the WordPerfect 5.0 document was opened in Word, but not much.

This imported file isn't behaving

If you're in France, naturally you grab a book of French phrases. Word does the same thing when you import a file from another word processor; the right converter or filter is chosen for you automatically. And just as you would if you were translating foreign words into English, Word makes some judgment calls about the best way to render a "foreign" file in Word.

Word's decisions can sometimes give odd results. Documents imported from certain versions of WordPerfect, for example, may give you a lot of trouble if you try to format them with balanced newspaper columns in Word. It's a bit like a Frenchman teaching an English course, and insisting that "a veal is a dead calf" (true story). Technically correct, but...

Although that Frenchman will probably never see the error of his ways, Word is more flexible. If your imported document seems to be misbehaving in Word, click Tools, Options for the Options dialog box. Click the Compatibility tab, shown in Figure 23.2.

On the Compatibility tab:

- It's unlikely to happen, but if Word made an entirely wrong guess about the origins of your imported file, click the Recommended Options drop-down arrow and select the appropriate file format.
- If your import is acting up, clear the Options check boxes. Then click OK to return to your document.

Can I use Word to edit my system files?

Windows 95 and Windows NT 3.51 handle most system settings automatically. Back in the days of DOS, you might have spent a fair amount of time fiddling with device drivers and AUTOEXEC.BAT and CONFIG.SYS files. Users of prior versions of Windows may have gotten more familiar with files like WIN.INI than they really cared to. You probably won't have to peer into the innards of Windows 95 in the same way. The new operating system does a much better job of keeping those painful computing details out of sight and mind.

If for some reason you do need to take a closer look at the inner workings of your PC, Windows 95 and Windows NT have a handy system file editor called Sysedit. Use it instead of Word if you have to change your system settings by hand.

To run the Windows System Configuration Editor, Sysedit:

1. Click the Start button and choose Run to get the Run dialog box.
2. In the Open edit box, type **sysedit**.
3. Click OK, and the System Configuration Editor pops up, with all your system files in separate windows. Click the window with the file you need, and edit away. Just be sure you know what you're doing before you make any changes.

- Word substitutes the closest match among your installed fonts for imported documents that use fonts not installed in your copy of Windows. If you don't like the choices Word made, click the Font Substitution button and select different proxy fonts. But you might find it easier to simply change fonts using the Word Formatting toolbar.

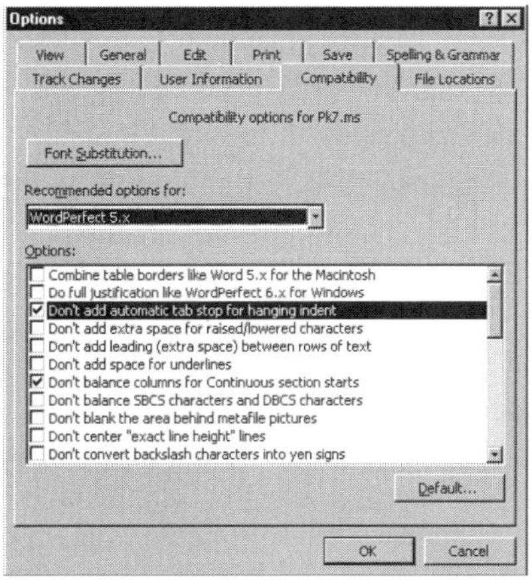

Fig. 23.2
On the Compatibility tab, Word makes certain decisions about how to translate your import into Word-ese, but you can alter them.

How to put a chart in your document

Word has a charting feature of its own called Microsoft Graph (see Chapter 15 for details). But if you're a serious number-cruncher, you probably use a spreadsheet program like Lotus 1-2-3, Quattro Pro, or Microsoft Excel.

When you stick a chart created in one of those programs into a Word document, you get a pretty snappy document. And sticking a chart into Word is a simple job. Select the chart in the spreadsheet program, copy it, then paste it in Word.

That's the basic idea, anyway. There are a few wrinkles that you should know about. To illustrate them, we'll take an Excel chart and pop it into a Word document.

Stick Excel charts in Word documents the fast way

There are a few things you can do to simplify inserting Excel charts in Word documents:

- Excel chart sheets are too big for Word documents. Chart sheets are what you get when you select the As new sheet option in the last step of Excel's Chart Wizard. They're designed to fill the page, so they'd be out of scale inserted in a page of text in Word. That doesn't mean you *can't* insert a chart sheet in Word. You just have to resize the chart in Excel before shipping it over to Word.
- Embedded charts are the kind you get when you choose As object in the final step of Excel's Chart Wizard. You probably won't have to resize an embedded Excel chart as drastically as a chart sheet before inserting it in Word. You do have to select the embedded chart with care, however. When you select the chart in Excel to copy it, just click it. Double-clicking the chart in Excel, and then copying it, causes problems if you subsequently try to resize the chart in Word.
- Do your chart editing and resizing in Excel, before you insert the chart in Word. You *can* tinker with Excel charts from within Word, but you'll find it easier to do your tinkering in Excel first.

CAUTION **Save your work before copying and pasting between applications.** Windows 95 is much more stable than previous incarnations of Windows, especially for maneuvers like these. Unexpected things can still happen, though, and there's nothing worse than losing a morning's work because your application decides to go south on you.

To resize an Excel chart sheet and paste it in a Word document:

1. With both Word and Excel running, switch to Excel. Click your chart sheet tab to display the chart, then click the Chart Area to select the chart.
2. Click File, Page Setup on the Excel menu bar for Excel's Page Setup dialog box.
3. In the Page Setup dialog box, click the Chart tab and select the Custom option, as shown in Figure 23.3.
4. Click OK in the Page Setup dialog box, and you'll see that your chart is surrounded by a broken-line border, labeled Chart Area in the lower right-hand corner.

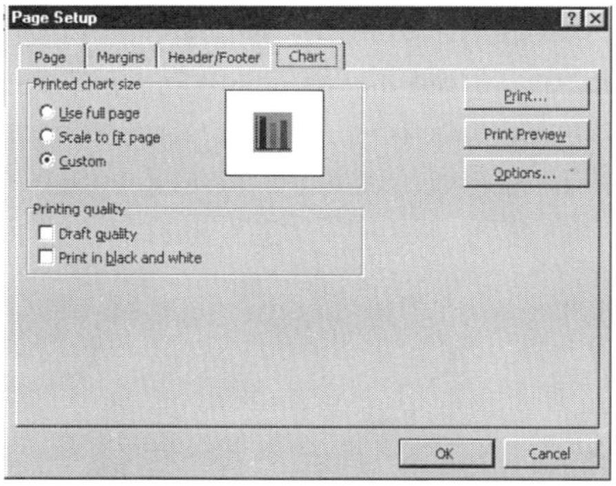

Fig. 23.3
Even though you're not printing the chart, you can only resize chart sheets with the Page Setup Custom option.

5 Click the broken-line border around the chart; the border changes from broken line to patterned, and handles pop up around it. Now drag any handle to resize the chart, as shown in Figure 23.4.

TIP **To keep the chart in proportion as you resize it, drag the corner** handles.

6 You'll have to resize the chart title, legend, and axes fonts. Right-click each of them in turn and select Format Axis (or Title or Legend, depending on what you've right-clicked) on the shortcut menu. In the Format dialog box that pops up, click the Font tab, select a smaller font size, and click OK.

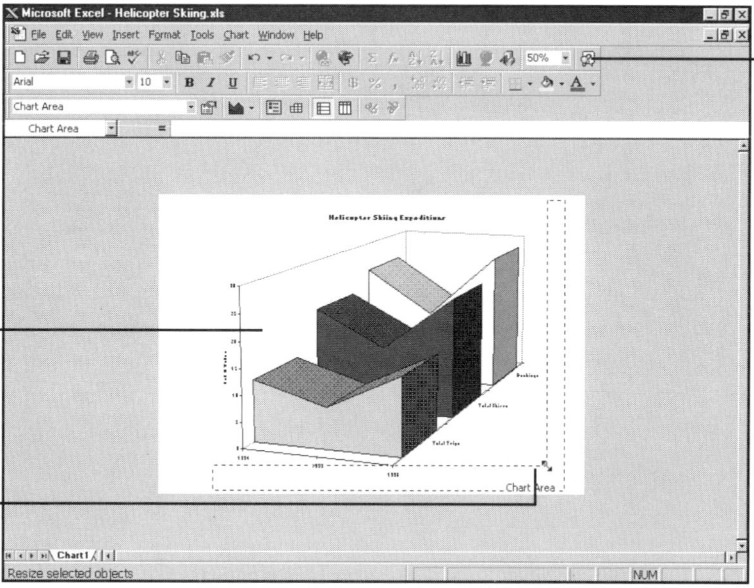

Fig. 23.4
As you drag a handle, the border changes to a dotted line. Quirky, but it works.

Remember that chart sheets aren't displayed at 100% magnification, so this chart looks smaller than it really is

If resizing the Chart Area does odd things to your chart's appearance, click the Plot Area to select it, then drag to resize it

When you're finished sizing your chart, click the Print Preview button to check your chart's actual size on the page

7 Once you've dragged the chart down to size, click the Zoom Control drop-down arrow on the Standard toolbar (refer to Figure 23.4) and select 100% so you can see your chart's actual size. Drag to resize further if you have to; you'll want the chart small enough to fit on a page full of text.

8 Got your chart resized? The handles around the Chart Area should still be displayed; if they're not, click the chart to get them back. Then click the Copy button on the Excel toolbar. That copies the chart to the Windows Clipboard.

9 Now switch to Word. Put the insertion point where you want the chart and click the Paste button on the Word Standard toolbar. The chart pops right into your document, as shown in Figure 23.5.

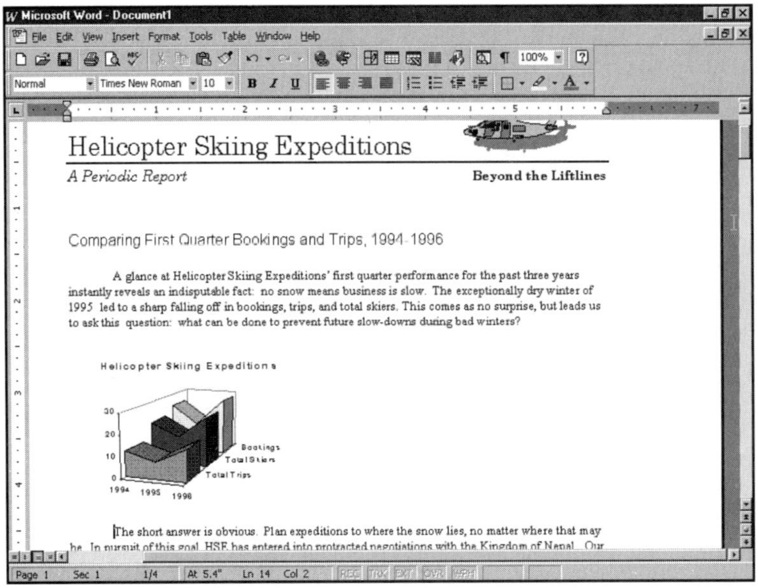

Fig. 23.5
Inserting a chart is just like inserting text; everything around it gets shoved aside to make room.

As you can see in Figure 23.5, just plopping a chart into the middle of a document may not give you exactly what you want. Existing text gets unceremoniously pushed aside by an inserted object, and the result is as you see. It's easily fixed.

I want text to flow around my chart

Charts look like they really belong in documents when text flows around them. Otherwise, a reader will think you just pasted in the chart any old way (which is exactly what we just did).

To wrap text around an inserted chart:

1. Right-click the inserted chart in your Word document and select Format Object on the shortcut menu.
2. Click the Wrapping tab in the Format Object dialog box that pops up.
3. Choose a Wrapping style and a side to Wrap to, and click OK. When you're through moving, resizing, and wrapping, your document will look something like Figure 23.6.

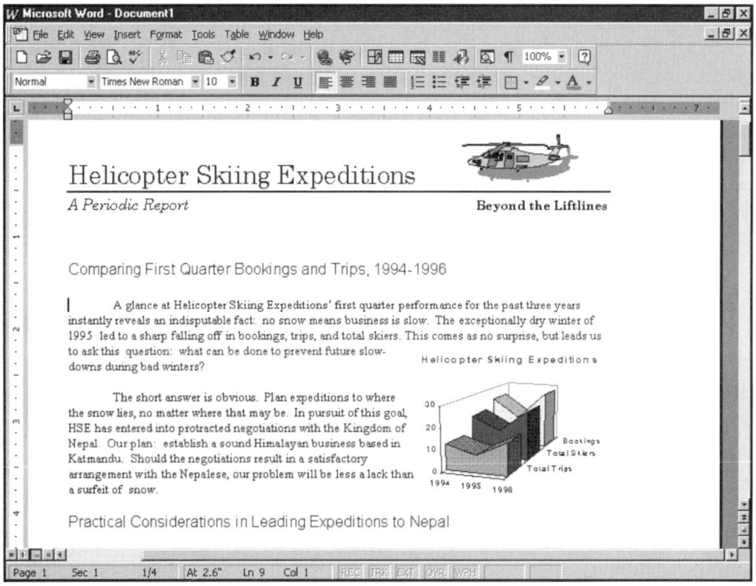

Fig. 23.6
With text wrapped around it, the chart looks like it belongs here.

What if I want to insert an embedded Excel chart?

Charts embedded in Excel worksheets can be inserted into Word documents just as easily as chart sheets. Select the chart in Excel, click the Copy button on the Excel Standard toolbar, then paste the chart in Word.

How to edit and update your Excel chart in Word

Click a chart in Excel, copy it, and paste it in Word. As we've just seen, the maneuver is easy, barring a few pitfalls (which we now know to avoid). When you copy and paste like that, you **embed** the chart in Word. An embedded object takes a chunk of the program that created the object with it. That lets you edit the embedded object with all the original tools you used to create it. For an Excel chart embedded in a Word document, that means you can edit the chart with all the Excel chart-formatting features, right from within Word.

> ### *Plain English, please!*
>
> An Excel chart *embedded in Word* is not to be confused with an **embedded Excel chart**. Embedded Excel charts are charts plopped onto your worksheet in Excel; they're the kind you create with the ChartWizard button on the Excel toolbar (as opposed to chart sheets). A chart or any object embedded in Word is an inserted object that can be edited with the program that created it, right from within Word. I don't make this stuff up, I promise.

To edit your chart in Word, just double-click it. The Word toolbars are replaced by the Excel toolbars, as shown in Figure 23.7.

Fig. 23.7
We've got Excel running right from Word; that's handy if you want to put Excel's charting features to work on your inserted chart.

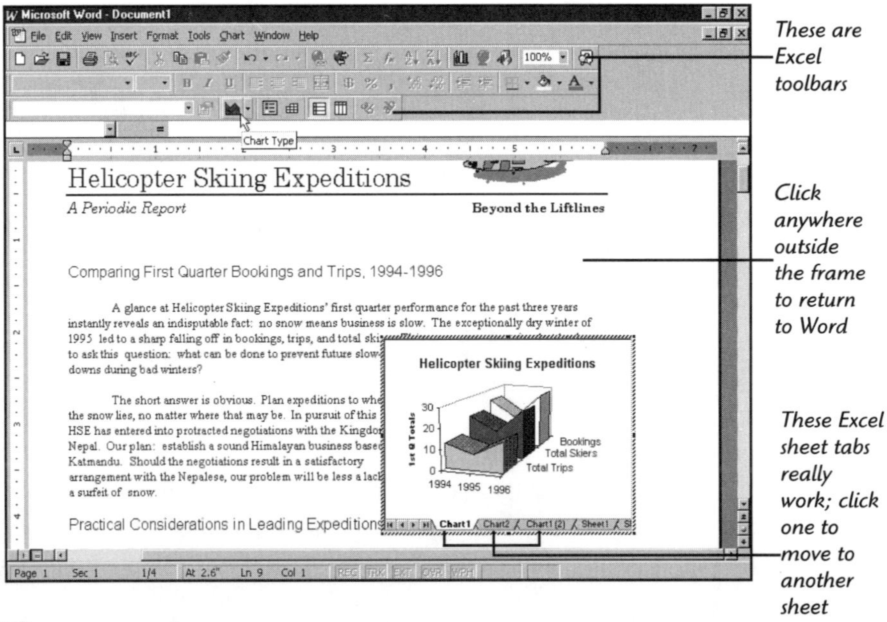

Now go ahead and edit the chart as much as you want. All the Excel tools are available for the job, just as if you were using Excel proper. When you're done editing, click outside the frame; that shuts down Excel and returns you to your Word document.

The changes you make to an embedded object don't affect the original. That Excel chart you copied in the first place remains unchanged, no matter how much you edit the embedded copy in Word.

How do I get rid of this chart?

You've copied and pasted, resized, moved, edited, and wrapped, and you still want to delete your chart in Word? At least this job's uncomplicated. To delete an embedded object in Word, click it, then press Delete.

My Excel data is changing; I want my Word chart to show the changes too

Embedding a chart in Word is a neat trick. But what if the data underlying your original Excel chart keeps changing? Excel updates the Excel chart automatically. If you want your Word chart updated as well, paste it as a **link**. With a Word copy linked to the Excel original, all the changes you make in Excel are automatically made to the Word copy.

To link an Excel chart to a copy of the chart in Word:

1. With both Word and Excel running, select the chart in Excel and click the Copy button on the Excel Standard toolbar.
2. Switch to Word, and click Edit, Paste Special on the Word menu bar.
3. That pops up the Paste Special dialog box. Click Paste Link, as shown in Figure 23.8.

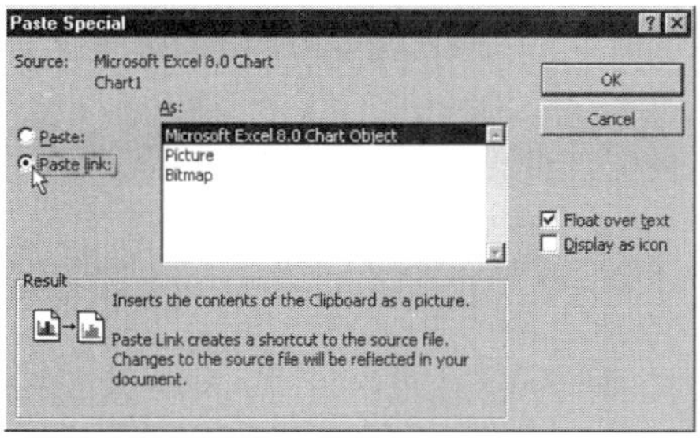

Fig. 23.8
Pasting as a link updates the pasted copy whenever you make changes in the original.

4 The Paste Special dialog box gives you a few other pasting options:

- Pasting As a Microsoft Excel Chart Object gives you an embedded object that you can edit with Excel's charting tools. That's just like the pasted chart we got with the Copy and Paste buttons earlier, with one big difference: pasted as a link, changes in the original chart update the embedded object copy. That doesn't work both ways, though. If you edit a linked, embedded object in Word, the Excel original is unaffected.
- Pasting As Picture gets you a simple copy of the chart. A picture uses less memory than an embedded copy, but you can't use Excel's tools to edit the chart in Word. A Picture pasted as a link *will* be updated by any editing you do in Excel.
- Pasting As Bitmap gives you an exact duplicate of your original chart. This option uses a lot of memory and disk space, and it can make Word irritatingly slow to use. Chances are, you won't notice any difference in the appearance of a bitmap copy anyway.
- The Display As Icon option inserts the chart in Word, but it appears as an icon. That results in the fastest Word performance and uses the least memory, but you don't see the way the chart looks in your document. You can double-click the icon to edit the chart.

Make your choices in the Paste Special dialog box, then click OK.

No matter which type of object you chose to insert in the Paste Special dialog box, if it's pasted as a link, it'll be updated automatically whenever you change the original chart or data.

Can I copy my Excel table to a Word document?

Best of 97

Excel lists and numerical tables are easily copied to Word. Just select the Excel data you want, click the Copy button, and paste it in Word. The data appears at the insertion point, formatted as a Word table. If you want to link the Word copy to the original list or table, use the Paste Special command in Word to paste as a link, just as we did earlier.

Once pasted, treat your copied table like any other pasted object. You can move it, frame it, or use any of Word's table formatting features to format it.

Turn a Word outline into an instant PowerPoint slide show!

Microsoft Office users get a snappy presentations program called PowerPoint. PowerPoint is used to create slide shows and fancy overhead projection transparencies, and it comes with an array of image editing tools and a big selection of clip art images. All you need to do is add text, and that's where Word comes in.

Any Word document formatted with the built-in heading styles can be turned into an instant PowerPoint slide presentation. Each Heading 1 style head becomes a separate slide. The sub-headings and body text beneath the Heading 1 head appear on the same slide. If you've created an outline in Word (see Chapter 16, "Hate Outlines? Outline View May Change Your Mind," for all you'll need to know about turning documents into outlines), it's a natural for a PowerPoint slide show. Figure 23.9 gives you the idea.

Fig. 23.9
Word outlines are no mere aid to composition—they're also instant slide shows.

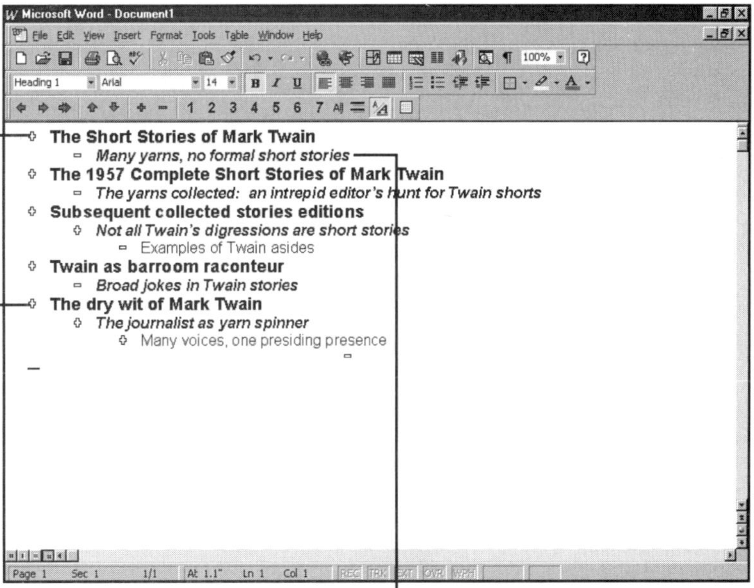

Heading 1 style heads become separate slides

Sub-heads appear on the same slide as the Heading 1 head above them

TIP **If you don't want your body text to appear in PowerPoint slides,** delete the body text from your Word outline, then save the outline with a new name before sending it to PowerPoint.

To turn your outline into a slide show, open the outline document and click File, Send to, Microsoft PowerPoint. PowerPoint loads, and in moments you'll see your Word outline transformed into a PowerPoint outline. Click the Slide Sorter View button in PowerPoint to view the new slides, as shown in Figure 23.10.

Now that you've created a series of new slides from your Word outline, put the PowerPoint formatting and graphics tools to work to dress them up. You'll have whipped up a quick presentation, with absolutely no extra typing.

Since editing text in Word is so easy, you might want to begin any Power-Point presentation with a Word outline. You get instant titles and slide text. Just add graphics and call it a show. For more information on creating presentations with PowerPoint, pick up a copy of Que's *Using Power-Point 97*.

Each Heading 1 style head created a new slide

Fig. 23.10
Here's the raw material for a presentation, which you can dress up any way you like with PowerPoint's tools.

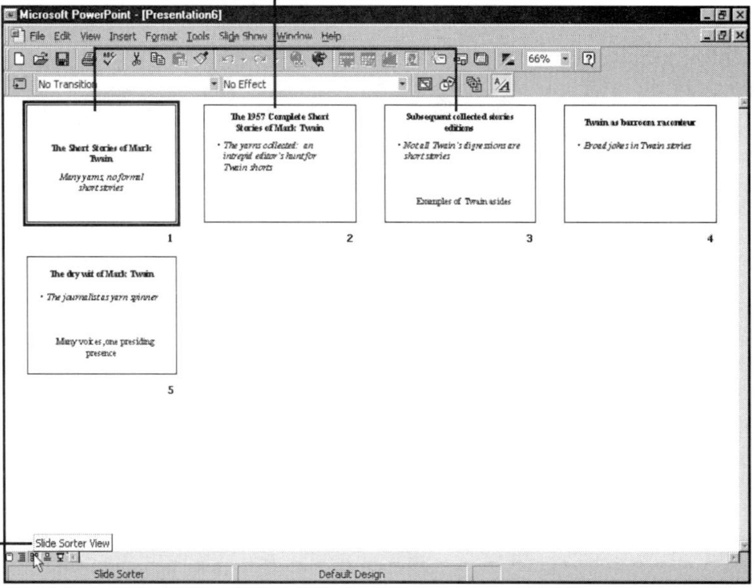

Click Slide Sorter View to see multiple slides

Word and the rest of the world: faxing and e-mail

Never thought there was any drama in sending mail? Mark Twain described the passing of a Pony Express rider like this: "…a wave of the rider's hand, but no reply, and man and horse burst past our excited faces, and go winging away like a belated fragment of a storm!"

Truth to tell, sending mail isn't very dramatic, at least not when you use Word. If you've set up the Window's fax software and The Microsoft Network, you can send faxes and e-mail right from Word.

Save your document first. In case the transmission goes awry, you don't want to lose any work.

With the document open, click File, Send To. Choose a recipient—either mail, fax, routing or a Microsoft Exchange folder. If you choose a mail recipient, with an icon of the active document displayed, as shown in Figure 23.11.

Fig. 23.11
On my system, the Message box takes a while to appear, but it's still faster than the Pony Express.

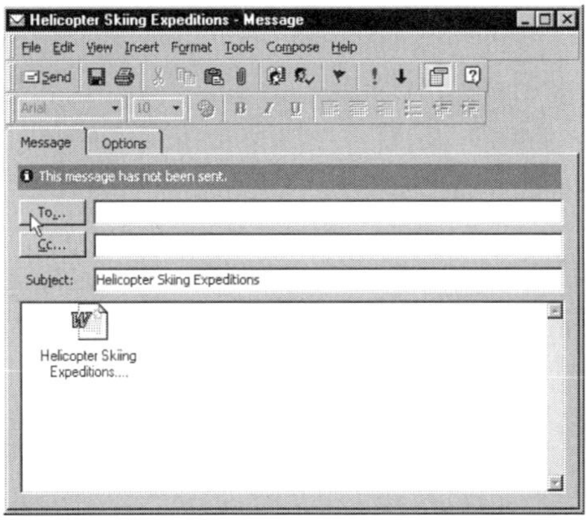

Click the To button and select a recipient from your address book (or add one if you need to). Click the Send button, and your mail is on the way. Depending on your recipient's address in the address book, it goes as either fax or e-mail.

Not romantic, but efficient.

24

All Together Now—Using Word in Your Workgroup

In this chapter:

- **Got an opinion? Add comments to a document**
- **Mark my words! Tracking revisions and edits**
- **New! One document, many versions**
- **War of the Words: Overcoming incompatibilities**
- **Learning how to share: Setting up your computer for several users**

Developing a report with your coworkers doesn't take as much effort as building a cathedral, but it still requires teamwork. Here's how Word simplifies revising and tracking documents in the workgroup. . . . .

Notre Dame at Paris took about 172 years to build. Needless to say, its construction required more than one contractor. But despite a succession of kings, carpenters, and popes, the cathedral was finished pretty much according to plan.

Most proposals and reports don't take quite as long to complete. But their architects and builders face many of the same problems. How can everyone in your workgroup contribute ideas in an orderly fashion? How do you track changes to the original blueprint? For that matter, how do you keep the blueprints from getting lost?

The answers lie with Word 97's assemblage of workgroup features. Microsoft has taken something old, added something new, and packaged them all into one convenient toolbar. Among these features, you'll find a command that lets everyone add their comments to a document, tools for tracking edits, and a new option that lets you save different versions of a document in a single file.

Exploring the Reviewing toolbar

Before you go any further, get familiar with the Reviewing toolbar, shown in Figure 24.1. You'll learn how to use its tools in the following sections.

You display the toolbar by choosing View, Toolbars, Reviewing from the main menu. You probably won't need the toolbar when you're adding occasional comments or simply tracking changes, but you'll want to display it when you're adding a bunch of comments all at once, editing and reviewing comments, or reviewing tracked changes.

Fig. 24.1
The Reviewing toolbar helps you make and track changes in your documents.

Comments, anyone?

In many offices, a routing slip is tantamount to a declaration of war. By the time half a dozen people have finished adding their illegible scrawls in the margins and on sticky notes, your beautifully formatted proposal looks more like a New York subway car.

Word offers an elegant solution to the clutter: Comments. Using this command, you and your coworkers can annotate to your heart's delight without turning the document into an unreadable mess.

Word indicates comments with a highlight, and the comments appear only when you touch the highlight with your mouse pointer. In Figure 24.2, the words "new breakthrough" in line one were highlighted in light yellow, but when touched with the mouse pointer, they become bright yellow, and the comment is displayed in a ScreenTip.

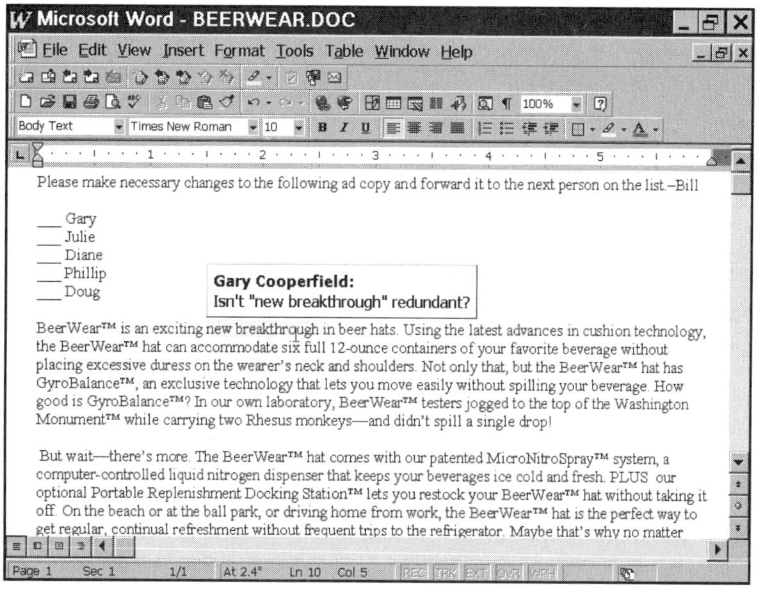
Microsoft Word - BEERWEAR.DOC
File Edit View Insert Format Tools Table Window Help
Body Text
Times New Roman
10
100%
Please make necessary changes to the following ad copy and forward it to the next person on the list.–Bill
___ Gary
___ Julie
___ Diane
___ Phillip
___ Doug
Gary Cooperfield:
Isn't "new breakthrough" redundant?
BeerWear™ is an exciting new breakthrough in beer hats. Using the latest advances in cushion technology, the BeerWear™ hat can accommodate six full 12-ounce containers of your favorite beverage without placing excessive duress on the wearer's neck and shoulders. Not only that, but the BeerWear™ hat has GyroBalance™, an exclusive technology that lets you move easily without spilling your beverage. How good is GyroBalance™? In our own laboratory, BeerWear™ testers jogged to the top of the Washington Monument™ while carrying two Rhesus monkeys—and didn't spill a single drop!
But wait—there's more. The BeerWear™ hat comes with our patented MicroNitroSpray™ system, a computer-controlled liquid nitrogen dispenser that keeps your beverages ice cold and fresh. PLUS our optional Portable Replenishment Docking Station™ lets you restock your BeerWear™ hat without taking it off. On the beach or at the ball park, or driving home from work, the BeerWear™ hat is the perfect way to get regular, continual refreshment without frequent trips to the refrigerator. Maybe that's why no matter
Page 1 Sec 1 1/1 At 2.4" Ln 10 Col 5 REC TRK EXT OVR WPH

Fig. 24.2
Touching the highlight displays the comment in a ScreenTip.

Write here!

Comments are easy to add. With the Reviewing toolbar displayed, place the insertion point where you want the comment to appear. If you're commenting on several words or a paragraph, highlight the text first. Click the Insert Comment button on the Reviewing toolbar. If the Reviewing toolbar isn't displayed, choose Insert, Comment from the main menu. Word opens a comments window at the bottom of the screen, as in Figure 24.3.

Fig. 24.3
Word highlights the text you're commenting on and lets you type your comments in a separate window.

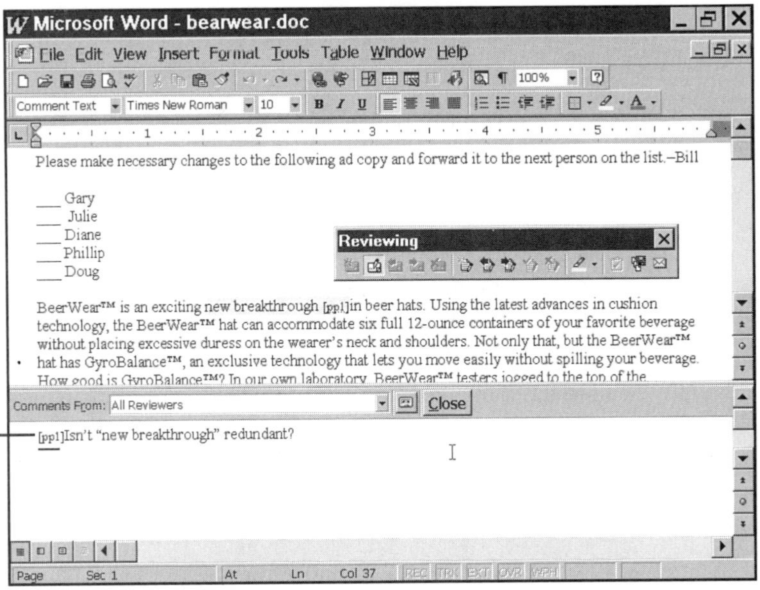

This field code identifies the author of the comment

Word automatically inserts the field code for the user's initials at the beginning of the comment. Type your comment after the initials and choose Close.

Don't like what you said or have something you'd like to add? No problem. Click the Edit Comment button on the Reviewing toolbar or right-click the highlighted text and choose Edit Comment from the shortcut menu. Word reopens the comments window. Use Word's standard editing tools to add and delete text.

Q&A ***How does Word know the user's initials and name?***

They're stored as part of the user information. Choose Tools, Options and click the User Information panel. You'll see text boxes for your name and initials. If you want a different name or initials to appear with your comments, change them and choose OK.

Q&A ***What if I want to add a comment to text that's already been commented by someone else?***

Add your comment the same way explained previously. When you touch the comment highlight, both comments will appear.

Read 'em and weep

After you get your commented document back, Word lets you choose among several ways to read what other people have to say about your deathless prose:

- Touch a comment highlight. The comment appears along with the person's full name, which Word expands from the user's initials.

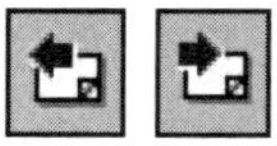

- Use the Previous Comment and Next Comment buttons on the Reviewing toolbar to jump from one comment to another.

- Open the comment window by clicking the Edit Comment button on the Reviewing toolbar or choosing Edit Comment from the shortcut menu. You'll see a complete list of comments like the one in Figure 24.4. When you click a comment, Word takes you to the commented text in the document window.

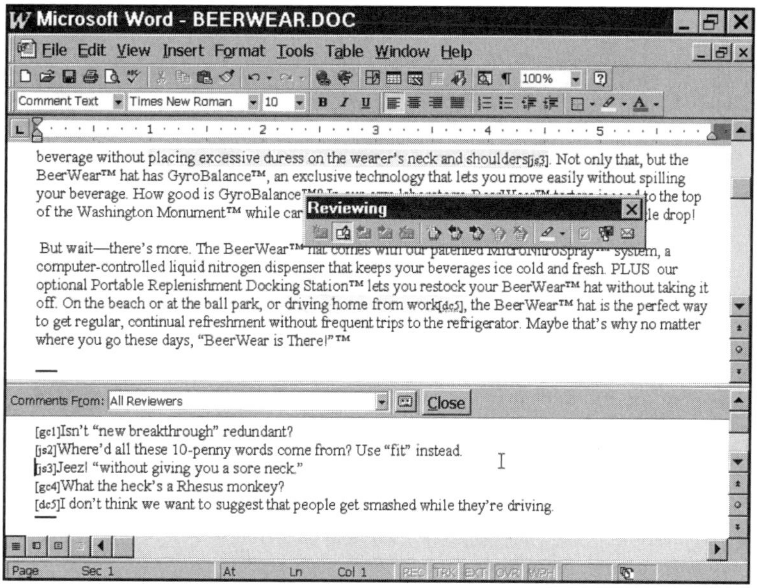

Fig. 24.4
Click a comment in the comment window to jump to the corresponding text in the document window.

Deleting comments

Delete a comment by choosing Delete Comment from the Reviewing toolbar or right-clicking the comment highlight and choosing Delete Comment from the shortcut menu. Comments also disappear when you delete the text to which they're attached.

You cannot delete a comment from the comments window.

Choose your commentator

Perhaps you're discussing your document with a colleague and want to see only her comments. Or maybe you want to review only your own comments. Word has an easy way to screen out everyone else's annotations.

Click the Edit Comment button to open the Comment window. Click the Comments From box, and select the person whose comments you want to read, as shown in Figure 24.5. Then choose Close. Only that person's comment highlights will be visible.

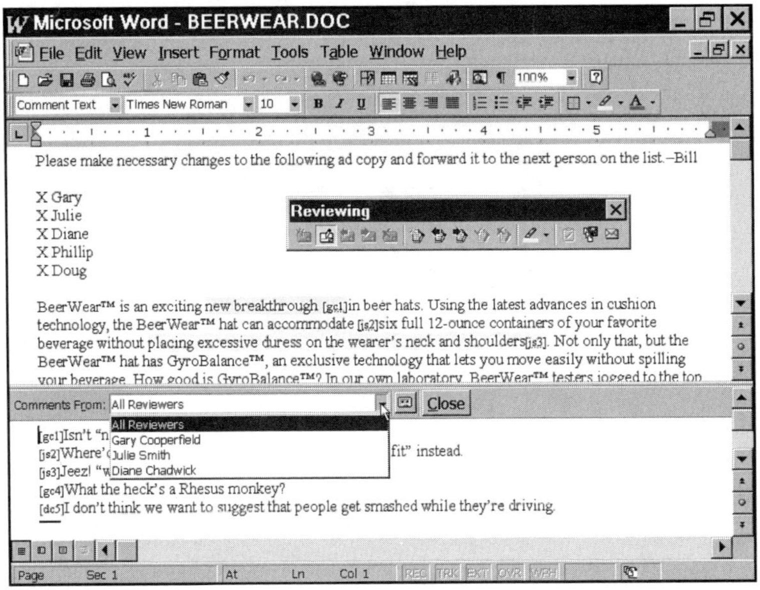

Fig. 24.5
You can choose to read everyone's comments or only those of one person.

Q&A ***I share a computer with a coworker. How do we each get our own initials and names in our comments?***

Word offers three solutions, each with its own purpose. The first is a temporary fix. Before you start commenting your document, choose File, Properties and click the Summary tab. Replace the name in the Author text box with your own and choose OK. Word uses your name for the rest of the session. The next time Word is run, it reverts to the original author name.

The second solution is more permanent. Before commenting, choose Tools, Options and click the User Information tab. Enter your own name and initials in the Name and Initials text boxes and choose OK. Word saves the information and uses it for subsequent sessions.

The problem with both solutions is that your coworker must use one of the same methods to use his or her name. Mistakes are inevitable, and sooner or later someone will end up getting credit for someone else's comments.

The third, and best, long-term solution is to give each of you your own individual Windows desktop. Essentially, you split your computer into two different computers, each with its own version of Word. The section "One machine, many users," later in this chapter, explains how.

Revisionist history: tracking your edits

Here's a scenario familiar to anyone in a workgroup:

You send a document to a coworker for editing. A few weeks later, it comes back with a note that reads, "Made a few changes. Let me know if they're ok." Problem is, you don't recognize the document anymore. What parts are yours and what parts have been edited? The only way to know is to dig out a copy of your original—if you can find one.

The problems get worse if you decide you want to reinsert that introductory paragraph your coworker summarily dumped. Not only do you have to find the original file, but you have to copy and paste the deleted material from the original to the edited version. Either that, or retype the paragraph.

No doubt about it; this is a job for Word's Track Changes tools. Your coworker can make all the insertions and deletions she wants, and you'll be able to see them side-by-side with the original text. What's more, you'll be able to accept or reject her changes.

Making Tracks

The fastest way to turn Track Changes on when you're editing a document is to click the TRK mode button on the status bar. If the Reviewing toolbar is showing, you can click the Track Changes button.

From then on, Word runs a line through text you delete, underlines text you add, and adds a color to all changes (see Figure 24.6).

If more than one person edits the document, each person's changes appear in a different color. Word has enough colors for eight different reviewers, after which it starts reusing colors.

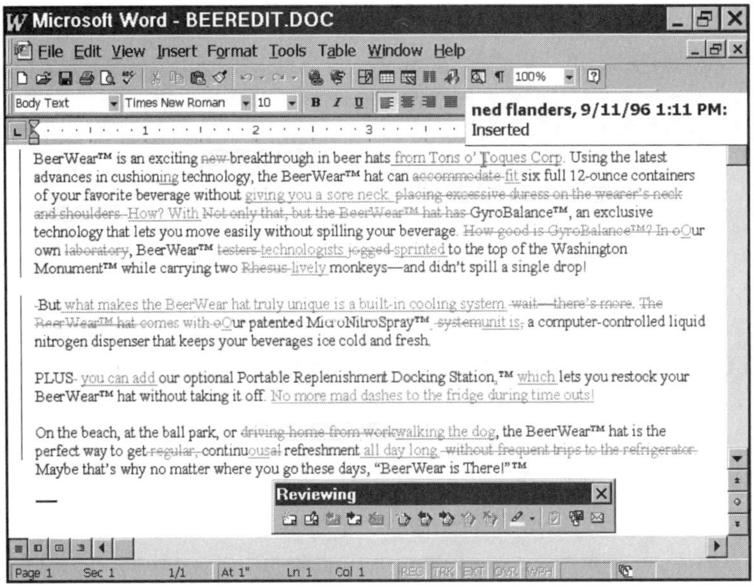
Microsoft Word - BEEREDIT.DOC
File Edit View Insert Format Tools Table Window Help
Body Text
Times New Roman
10
100%
ned flanders, 9/11/96 1:11 PM:
Inserted
BeerWear™ is an exciting new breakthrough in beer hats from Tons o' Toques Corp. Using the latest advances in cushioning technology, the BeerWear™ hat can accommodate fit six full 12-ounce containers of your favorite beverage without giving you a sore neck. placing excessive duress on the wearer's neck and shoulders. How? With Not only that, but the BeerWear™ hat has GyroBalance™, an exclusive technology that lets you move easily without spilling your beverage. How good is GyroBalance™? In oOur own laboratory, BeerWear™ testers technologists jogged sprinted to the top of the Washington Monument™ while carrying two Rhesus lively monkeys—and didn't spill a single drop!
But what makes the BeerWear hat truly unique is a built-in cooling system. wait—there's more. The BeerWear™ hat comes with oOur patented MicroNitroSpray™, systemunit is, a computer-controlled liquid nitrogen dispenser that keeps your beverages ice cold and fresh.
PLUS- you can add our optional Portable Replenishment Docking Station,™ which lets you restock your BeerWear™ hat without taking it off. No more mad dashes to the fridge during time outs!
On the beach, at the ball park, or driving home from workwalking the dog, the BeerWear™ hat is the perfect way to get regular, continuousal refreshment all day long. without frequent trips to the refrigerator. Maybe that's why no matter where you go these days, "BeerWear is There!"™
Reviewing
Page 1 Sec 1 1/1 At 1" Ln 1 Col 1 REC TRK EXT OVR WPH

Fig. 24.6
When you track changes in a document, Word highlights deleted text with a strikethrough and inserted text with an underline.

TIP **You can get information about a change by touching it; the** person's name, along with the date, time, and nature of the change, appear in a ScreenTip, as in Figure 24.6. If you don't see a ScreenTip, choose Tools, Options, click the View tab, and put a check next to ScreenTips.

I don't like what you did!

When you get a document with tracked changes, you'll probably want to look at each edit and decide whether to accept it. The easiest way to review track changes is with the Reviewing toolbar.

Start at the top of the document and click the Next Change button. Word highlights the first change—in Figure 24.6, the deleted word "new."

If you want to accept the edit, click the Accept Change button.

If you prefer the original text, click the Reject Change button.

Q&A ***I accepted a change, but changed my mind. What do I do?***

You can undo the change by clicking the Undo button on the Standard toolbar or pressing Ctrl+Z.

In one fell swoop

You get an edited document from Eddie, the knucklehead in marketing, who has never made a useful suggestion in his life. No point in reviewing his edits; you might as well reject them in toto.

Right-click any tracked change in the document and choose Accept or Reject Changes from the shortcut menu. Word displays the Accept or Reject Changes dialog box in Figure 24.7. Click the Reject All button. Word asks you if you really want to remove all signs of Eddie's handiwork. Choose Yes, and you're done.

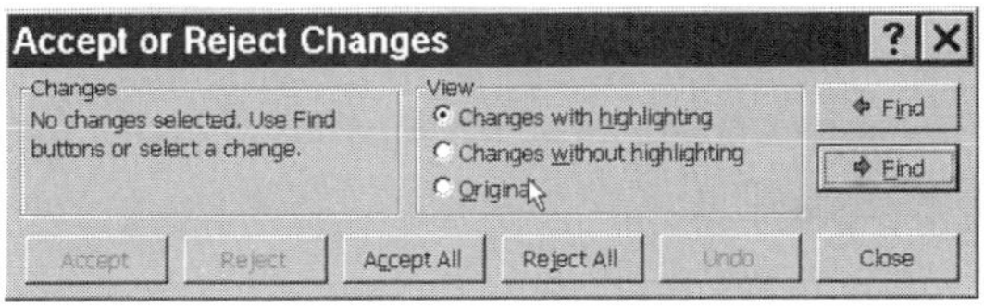

Fig. 24.7
Use the Accept or Reject Changes dialog box to accept or reject all changes in one step.

If, on the other hand, you want to accept all changes, click the Accept All button instead.

What'll it look like?

Reading a document with lots of track changes can be like reading street signs through a bug-spattered windshield. You can get a better view of what your document will look like with all changes accepted or how it looked originally. You can do both from the Accept or Reject Changes dialog box.

To look at the document with no edits—that is, as it will be if you click Reject All—click the Original button. If you want to view the document with all edits accepted, click the Changes Without Highlighting button.

Word also provides another way to preview a document before accepting any changes. Right-click the TRK mode button on the status bar and choose Highlight Changes from the shortcut menu. Word displays the Highlight Changes dialog box, as in Figure 24.8. Remove the check next to Highlight Changes on Screen and choose OK.

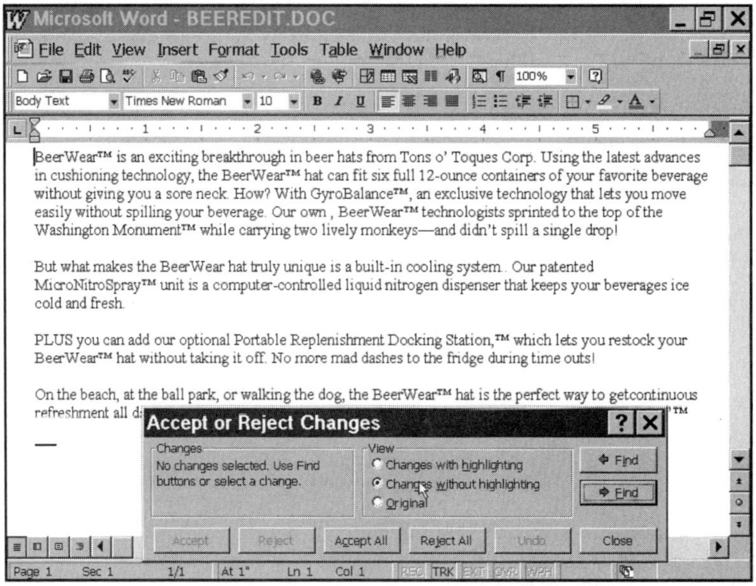
Microsoft Word - BEEREDIT.DOC
File Edit View Insert Format Tools Table Window Help
100%
Body Text
Times New Roman
10
BeerWear™ is an exciting breakthrough in beer hats from Tons o' Toques Corp. Using the latest advances in cushioning technology, the BeerWear™ hat can fit six full 12-ounce containers of your favorite beverage without giving you a sore neck. How? With GyroBalance™, an exclusive technology that lets you move easily without spilling your beverage. Our own , BeerWear™ technologists sprinted to the top of the Washington Monument™ while carrying two lively monkeys—and didn't spill a single drop!
But what makes the BeerWear hat truly unique is a built-in cooling system.. Our patented MicroNitroSpray™ unit is a computer-controlled liquid nitrogen dispenser that keeps your beverages ice cold and fresh.
PLUS you can add our optional Portable Replenishment Docking Station,™ which lets you restock your BeerWear™ hat without taking it off. No more mad dashes to the fridge during time outs!
On the beach, at the ball park, or walking the dog, the BeerWear™ hat is the perfect way to getcontinuous
Accept or Reject Changes
Changes
No changes selected. Use Find buttons or select a change.
View
Changes with highlighting
Changes without highlighting
Original
Find
Find
Accept
Reject
Accept All
Reject All
Undo
Close
Page 1 Sec 1 1/1 At 1" Ln 1 Col 1 REC TRK EXT OVR WPH

Fig. 24.8
You can see what your document will look like with all changes accepted by right-clicking the TRK mode button and deselecting Highlight Changes on Screen.

Q&A ***Can I print my document without the highlighted changes?***

Yes. Right-click the TRK mode button on the status bar and choose Highlight Changes from the shortcut menu. Remove the check next to Highlight Changes in Printed Document and choose OK.

Version Territory

As a reviewed document gets bent, folded, spindled, and mutilated by each author, vital information often is distorted or disappears entirely. The results are often grim.

The standard method for keeping track of document versions is by saving each to a separate file. But this is an inefficient system. You can't be sure everyone in the office has a complete set of all versions, or that they have the correct versions. Reviewing old versions means digging out the right documents.

Now there's a better way. Word's new Versions command lets you save all of your versions in a single document. The versions pass from one user to the next, and anyone can look at a previous version simply by clicking it.

Figure 24.9 is the Versions dialog box for a document that contains three versions. Bill Williams created the first draft on September 11. Phil Phillips changed pricing information in a second version saved on September 13. Then, an hour later, he saved a third version that corrected errors in version 2.

We'll look at how to view versions and version comments in a moment. But first, let's go over the steps you take to save versions.

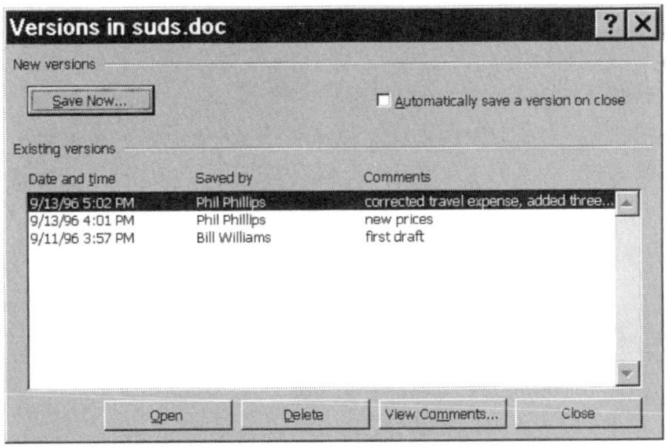

Fig. 24.9
Three versions of SUDS.DOC are stored in a single file.

Take a picture

When you've got a version of your document ready to save, choose File, Versions from the main menu. Word displays the Versions dialog box in Figure 24.9, only it won't have any entries under the Existing Versions heading. Choose Save Now, and Word opens the Save Version dialog box in Figure 24.10. Type your notes in the Comments on Version text box and choose OK.

Fig. 24.10
When you save a version of your document, add any comments that might help identify the version when it's reviewed at a later date.

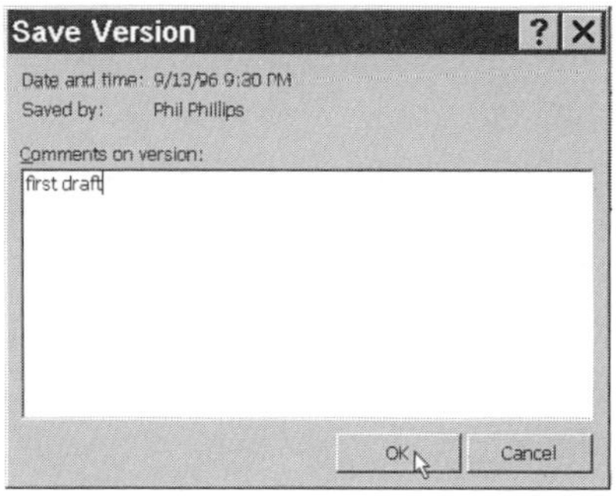

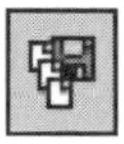

Once you're familiar with the procedure, you can skip the Versions dialog box and go straight to the Save Version dialog box by clicking the Save Version button on the Reviewing toolbar.

If you haven't saved your document, Word opens the Save As dialog box; give the document a name and save it as you normally would. If the document has already been named and saved, Word closes the Versions and Save Version dialog boxes and takes you back to your document.

Word automatically stamps the version with the current time and date, and it takes the name in the Saved By column from User Information. As is the case with comments, you can use a different name. Choose Tools, Options from the main menu, click the User Information panel, and type a new name in the Name text box. See the section on Comments and the "One Machine, Many Users" section, later in this chapter, for details.

TIP **You can instruct Word to automatically save a version of your** document when you close the document. Put a check next to Automatically Save a Version on Close in the Versions dialog box. Word saves a new version only if you've made changes to the document since the last version. You can see in the Versions dialog box which versions are ones that Word has saved automatically; they've got the words "Automatic version" in the Comments column.

CAUTION **Remember: A version is a still photo of your document at the time** you save the version, not the document. If you make more changes to the document and save it, the versions you save remain the same. If you want a version that reflects your changes, save another version.

Total recall: reviewing your versions

Let's say that Bill Williams gets the proposal with Phil's changes, but he doesn't remember the details of his original memo. No problem. He chooses File, Version from the main menu, selects the version with "first draft" in the comment column, and chooses Open. Word presents him with the split screen in Figure 24.11, current version on top and previous version on the bottom.

The two versions look, feel, and behave like two separate documents. That's because they are. You can resize, minimize, and close either document independent of the other.

You also can revise your previous version any way you like. But there's one caveat: You can't save changes back into the original document. In Figure 24.11, for example, you can edit the file called "Suds, 9-11-96 3-57 PM version," but you can't resave the document as part of the file suds.doc. If you want to preserve changes you make to the old version, you have to save the version as a new file.

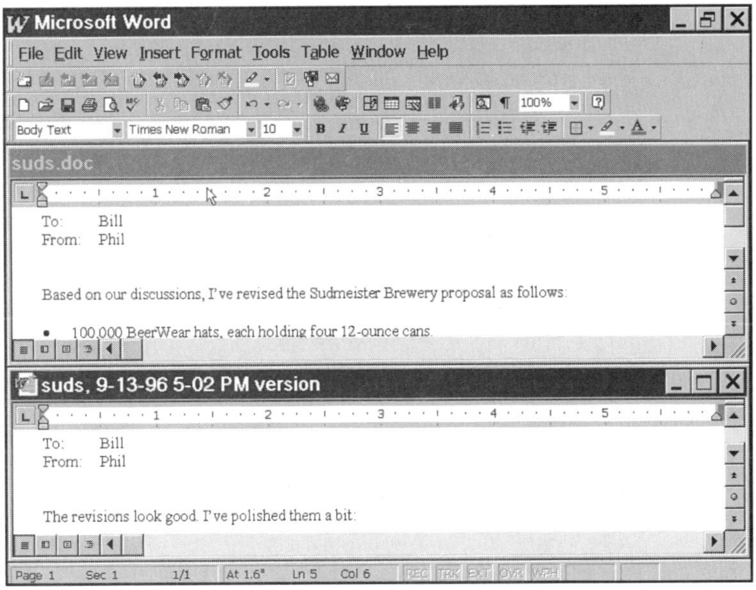

Fig. 24.11
When you open a previous version, Word handles them as two separate documents, but you can't save changes to the old version back into the document.

TIP **It's a good idea to delete any versions that you don't need.** Too many versions can fatten a document, eating disk space, and taking more time to e-mail. To delete a version, select it in the Versions dialog box (refer to Figure 24.9) and choose the Delete button.

TIP **To see the rest of a comment that doesn't fit the Versions dialog** box's Comments column, choose View Comments to display the View Comments dialog box.

The war of the Words

Variety may be the spice of life, but it's the sourball of the workplace. Different operating systems, different versions of Windows, different versions of Word—why can't we all just get along?

Of course, every business wants to take advantage of the bells and whistles the latest software has to offer. But that's little consolation to you when Judy down the hall can't read your Word 97 files, or Ed in El Paso doesn't know what you're talking about when you tell him to read a saved version of a document.

While you can't overcome every incompatibility problem you'll run into, Microsoft does offer various solutions that make it easier to share documents. You just need to know a bit about what's in your spice rack.

Welcome to the Version Zone

Let's say you get a call from Smudgley, asking for the same Hopper report you sent to Smithers. You ask Smudgley what word processor he uses. "Word," he says. "Great," you say, and send him the file through office e-mail.

A few hours later, Smudgley calls again. He says he opened the file and got several screens full of hieroglyphics characters. "I asked for a Word file," he says. "I gave you a Word file," you protest. "What version are you using?" he asks. "Version?" you answer.

Welcome to the Version Zone, a cockeyed world in which Word on one computer is apparently something else on another.

Actually, there's a simple, if not entirely satisfactory, explanation. Different versions of Word save in different formats. That is, each version embeds its own special codes that control the look, feel, and behavior of its documents. Earlier versions of Word don't understand Word 97's codes and translate them into garbage.

So what's the solution? Use Word 97's ability to save documents in other formats. You'll lose some of Word 97's features in the translation, but that's the price you pay for being on the cutting edge of technology.

A version primer

First, you need to know what versions of Word your colleagues are using. Here are the four you're most likely to encounter:

- *Word for Windows 2.x.* The first version of Word for Windows. Can't convert or read documents created in later versions.
- *Word for Windows 6.0.* Reads Word 2.x documents. Reads Word 97 documents with a special converter.
- *Word for Windows 95.* Uses the same format as Word 6.0.
- *Word 97.* Automatically converts and reads Word 2.x and 6.0/95 files.

The trick, then, is to use the lowest common denominator when saving your files. If coworkers are using Word 2.x and Word 6.0/95, save your files as Word 2.x files. If everyone's using Word 6.0/95, save them as Word 6.0/95 files.

So how do I convert?

You don't have to do anything special to convert; Word 97 does the work for you.

When you're ready to save your file, choose File, Save As to display the Save As dialog box. Choose the Save As Type selection box and click the format you want (see Figure 24.12). Then choose Save. Word 97 does the rest.

Q&A ***The format I want doesn't show up in the File Type box. What's wrong?***

The converter has been moved or deleted, or it wasn't installed. To get help, choose Help, Contents and Index from Word's main menu, click the Find tab, and search for "I can't find the converter I need."

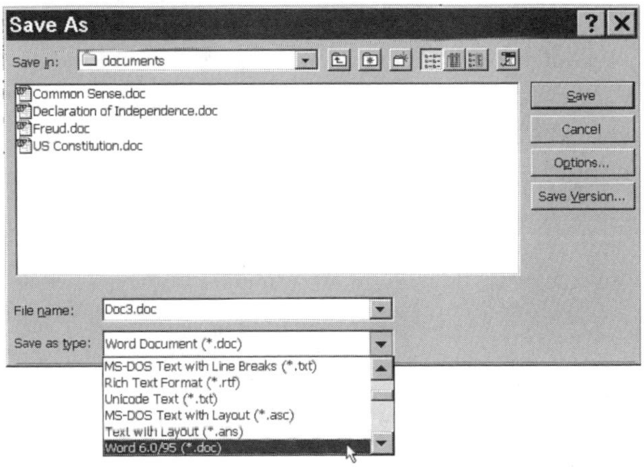

Fig. 24.12
Use the File Type selection box to choose a different file format.

Automatic conversion

Word 97 includes a new feature that lets you change the default format. Use this trick if you save your documents exclusively in a format other than Word 97's:

1. Choose Tools, Options from the main menu.
2. Click the Save tab.
3. Choose the appropriate file format in the Save Word Files As selection box.
4. Choose OK.

Remember: If you use this option, you might lose data or formatting during the conversion. Here are some of the more important losses you'll experience when converting to Word 6.0/95:

- Page character, and paragraph borders
- Character shading
- Animated text
- Embossed and engraved characters
- Vertically merged table cells
- Vertically aligned text in table cells
- Hyperlinks

- Tracked changes for properties, paragraph numbers, and display fields
- Password protection of documents

If you're not sure of what you're going to lose, save the file in the foreign format. Close the file and reopen it. Don't forget to save it first as a Word 97 document, in case you lose data during your conversion to the foreign format.

Another option for Word 6.0/95 users

Mindful of the woes it's creating with so many formats, Microsoft is giving away a Word 97 converter for Word 6.0/95 users. It's called wrd97cnv.exe, and is available on the Office 97 CD-ROM. You also can get it from Microsoft Support on the World Wide Web at **http://www.microsoft.com/support** or from the Microsoft Software Library on the Microsoft Network online service. For more information, Choose Help, Contents and Index from Word's main menu and search for wrd97cnv.exe in the Find panel.

Helpful hints for the Word warrior

Covering every software incompatibility you might face in the office would take a book in itself. But here are a few other pointers that will help you coexist with your neighbors:

- If you're not sure what version a coworker has, save in Word 3.x-5.x for MS-DOS format. This is a sort of protoformat that all other versions of Word understand.
- Long file names are ok if you're saving in Word for Windows 95 format. Otherwise, the file name can't have more than eight characters. See Chapter 4, "Saving and Managing Your Documents," for more on using long file names.
- If you're not sure the other person is even using Word, provide a plain-text file as well (the Text Only option). The document's formatting instructions will be removed, but at least your colleague will be able to read the file.

One machine, many users

When people write about workgroups, they usually assume that everyone in the group has his own computer. Each person has set up Word with his own name, initials, and address. (You can view your own information by choosing Tools, Options from the main menu and clicking the User Information Panel.)

In the real world, of course, single computers often are shared by several people. If the computer isn't set up properly, many of the features discussed in this chapter become impractical to use, because everyone shares the same user information.

For example, Word automatically inserts the user name when you add comments to a document. So if the user name is Diane Johnson, she's the one to whom all comments are attributed, no matter who is using the computer.

But many users don't realize that Windows 95 has a feature that lets each person set up her own desktop. You can set up Word with your user information, Diane on the night shift can do likewise, and Joe the new guy can have his own setup. When it comes time to add comments to a document you wrote, Joe's comments will be attributed to Joe, not Diane.

Before you decide to take this step, make sure that everyone using your computer participates. Otherwise, someone might not be able to log on the next time they turn on the computer.

You are your own user

First, your computer might already be set up for multiple desktops. It's easy to figure out: You see a Welcome to Windows dialog box when you turn on your computer. If so, setting up another desktop is easy. Reboot your computer. When the Welcome to Windows dialog box appears, take the following steps:

1 Type a new name in the User Name text box (see Figure 24.13).

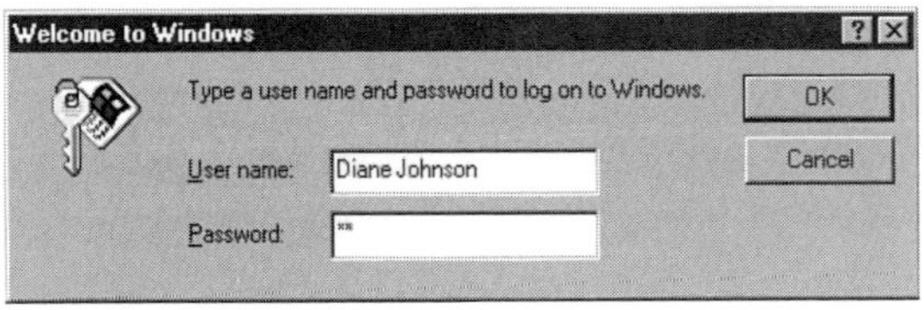

Fig. 24.13
To create your own desktop, type your name and a password in the Welcome to Windows dialog box. The password is optional.

2 Type a password in the Password text box. If you don't want a password, leave this box blank. Choose OK.

3 Word asks you to confirm the password; type it again and choose OK.

4 Word asks you if you want to retain your settings for future log-ons Choose Yes.

Setting up from scratch

If you don't get the Welcome to Windows dialog box, then you need to take a few extra steps.

1 Select Settings from the Windows Start menu.

2 Click Control Panel and select Passwords.

3 In the Passwords Properties dialog box under the User Profiles tab (see Figure 24.14), click the Users Can Customize Their Preferences and Desktop Settings button.

4 Make sure both options under User Profiles Settings are on.

5 Select OK.

6 Windows asks whether you want to restart your computer; select Yes.

From here on, follow the four steps in the previous section.

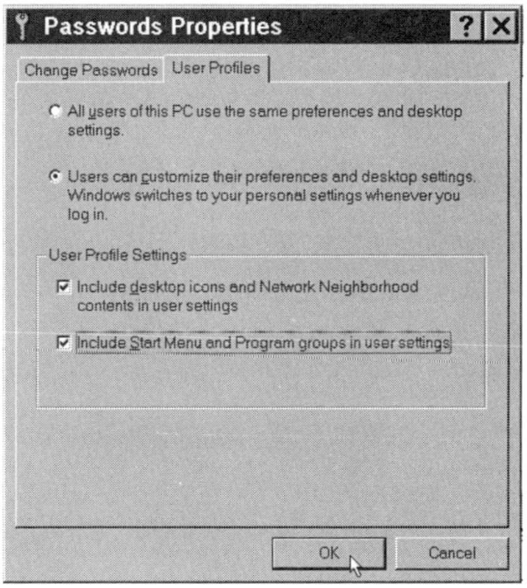

Fig. 24.14
These options set up your computer so that each user can have his or her own setup.

Making Word your own

All that's left to do is enter your user information into Word. This is the easiest part:

1 Choose Tools, Options from the main menu and click the User Information panel.

2. Type your name in the Name text box, and your initials in the Initials text box. Add your mailing address if you use Word for printing labels and envelopes.
3. Choose OK.

You're done! Now, all of your documents will have your name on them, as well as your comments and saved versions.

Using your own desktop has added benefits. Each person can set up Word's options to his or her own liking, without worrying about someone else changing them.

Word's faxing and e-mail

If you've set up the Window's fax software and The Microsoft Network, you can send faxes and e-mail right from Word. Save your document first. In case the transmission goes awry, you don't want to lose any work. Then with the document open, click File, Send To. Choose a recipient—either mail, fax, routing or a Microsoft Exchange folder. If you choose a mail recipient, a Message box pops up with an icon of the active document displayed, as shown in Figure 24.15.

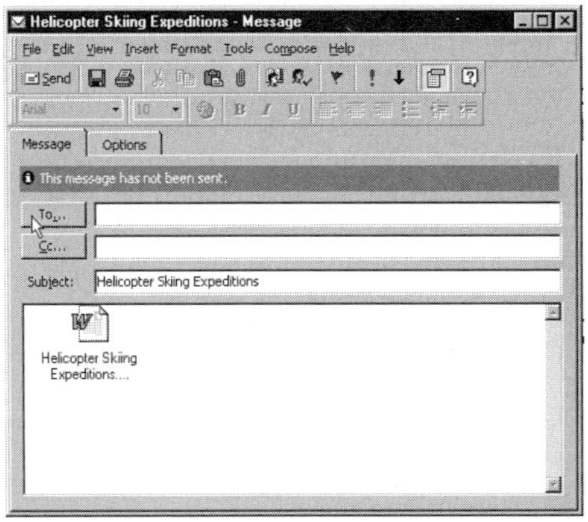

Fig. 24.15
On my system, the Message box takes a while to appear, but it's still faster than the Pony Express.

Click the To button and select a recipient from your address book (or add one if you need to). Click the Send button, and your mail is on the way. Depending on your recipient's address in the address book, it goes as either fax or e-mail.

25 The Word on the Web

In this chapter:

- **Cyberspace? URL? Hyperlinks? Explain, please!**
- **I want this Word document on the Internet (or an intranet)**
- **My Web page needs a makeover**
- **How can I cook up a fast Home Page?**
- **This page is missing links**

The jet plane brought the world as close as the nearest airport. Now comes the Internet, which puts the world right on your desk. . . . .

Back when the globe was vast, Ptolemy, the 2nd century astronomer, proved that the Earth was at the center of the universe. Nowadays, astronomers relegate us to an outlying spiral of a mere galaxy.

As our idea of the universe has grown, our own little planet has shrunk in proportion. When Stanley Livingstone disappeared into the far reaches of unexplored Tanzania, the *New York Herald* sent Henry Stanley to find him. Stanley's heroically casual "Dr. Livingstone, I presume?" gave their encounter all the drama of a chance meeting on a walk around the block.

Explorers like Stanley and Livingstone helped trim the world to neighborhood-like proportions: the Internet, 125 years later, shrinks the globe even more and fits it into your computer. Bitten by the exploration bug? Click the Word's Web toolbar button, enter the address **http://www.mungopark.com**, and your expedition to the wilds is launched. Well, virtually launched. You'll visit *Mungo Park*, an online magazine devoted to wilderness exploration, and named for another explorer who lost himself in Africa. Word puts the Internet's World Wide Web on your desk, and that gives you the whole world on a plate, or at least a computer screen. Internet explorations in Word may lack the heroics of Stanley, Livingstone, and Mungo Park, but at least you can't get lost.

The Web in a word (or two)

When handed fat reports laden with jargon and acronyms, United Nations officials are sometimes afflicted with a condition they call MEGO, or My Eyes Glaze Over. Reading about the Internet can induce a similar condition. Even the best-intentioned writing about the great international network of computers that makes up the Internet slips against its will into a sea of references to *URLs*, *browsers*, and *cyberspace* (see the sidebar for definitions). The murky tangle of Internet terms obscures the fact that the Net, and especially its user-friendly graphical face, the *World Wide Web*, can be practical, and fun. For research, technical support, news, and entertainment, the Internet is an unparalleled resource.

Q&A ***Why do I get an "Unable to open http://..." message when I try to connect to the Internet?***

Have you installed the Internet Explorer yet? Word's (or Office's) installation program put a Setup for Microsoft Explorer 3.0 icon on your Windows desktop. Double-click the icon and follow the directions for installing Explorer in your system. If you *have* installed Microsoft Explorer 3.0 and you're getting this error, save any open documents, close Word, and restart the program. Try the Web connection again, and it should work.

Need technical support? Try the Web

How practical is the Web? Technical support for computer users, as essential as a reliable power supply, is not always easy to reach by phone. If you've installed a Web browser like Netscape Navigator or the Microsoft Internet Explorer, and you have an Internet account set up with a service provider (the Microsoft Network or AT&T WorldNet, for example), you can avoid inane music-on-hold. Try tech support on the Web instead! For help with Microsoft Word, just click Help, Microsoft On the Web, Online Support. For any other hardware or software questions, visit the handy TechHelper Web page:

1. Click the Web toolbar button on the Standard toolbar.

Go

2. Click any text in the Address box on the Web toolbar to select it, and type **http://www.techhelper.com** (see Figure 25.1). That's the address of a useful Web page that makes a good starting point for technical support searches on the Web.

Web
Favorites
Go
http://www.techhelper.com
Search the Web takes you to a Web page full of useful search tools
The Address box; type an address and press enter to go directly to the page
Start Page takes you directly to Microsoft's Start Page, a good jumping off point for Web explorations

Fig. 25.1
Here's the direct path to the Web page of your choice; if you know the address of the page you want, just type it in.

Plain English, please!

What's in a **URL**? Uniform Resource Locators on the Web have some things in common. All share the http://www. prefix, and though the other elements of the URL vary, they give you clues as to what a Web site might be about. The bit that follows the www. in the prefix is called the **domain name**. In the URL **http://www.mcp.com**, mcp.com is the domain name. The domain name is the giveaway: the .com in mcp.com stands for commercial organization (that happens to be Macmillan Computer Publishing's Web site). If the domain name has an .edu suffix, it's an academic institution like a college. Nonprofits like National Public Radio have an .org suffix, and government sites have domain names that end in .gov.

3 Press Enter. Your service provider's connection box pops up; click Connect, and after the usual whistling and wailing modem noises, the TechHelper page appears.

I'm Lost in Cyberspace

Like any other subculture, the Internet has its own language and customs. Take the language. Please. Words like "hot" and "cool," "zine" and "cyberspace," and the many variants of "to surf," are seen at every turn. The jargon of the Internet is a strange brew of California beach town and science fiction, which isn't surprising. Although the World Wide Web was invented in Europe (at CERN, the European particle physics lab), many of its devotees hail from our own left coast. Science fiction being the reading of choice among computer adepts, the mingling of sci fi and Beach Boys was inevitable. **Cyberspace** is a word invented by William Gibson, author of a science fiction yarn called *Neuromancer* (Gibson himself reportedly doesn't use computers at all). It usually refers to the whole realm of computers linked together on the global Internet network. To **surf** the Web means to browse, more or less aimlessly, among the millions of documents posted on the World Wide Web. A **zine** is an electronic magazine, along with its variants **e-zine** and **webzine**. If you're drawing a blank at any of the terms in common use on the Web, visit one of the many glossaries or **FAQ**s (acronym for frequently asked questions). The Microsoft Web page has both a good FAQ and a glossary. The **URL** (Uniform Resource Locator, or address) for the Microsoft Web site is **http://www.msn.com**. Click Help, Microsoft on the Web, Frequently Asked Questions to go straight there. You can also enjoy and profit from the World Wide Web without knowing anything about its arcana; it's pretty user-friendly, which is why it was invented in the first place.

4 On the TechHelper Web page, enter a search term for the support you're after, or choose a software or hardware category to browse. Most of the links take you directly to the Web sites of your hardware and software vendors. Figure 25.2 shows the TechHelper Web page.

Fig. 25.2
Every Web page looks a little different, but they all have certain elements in common.

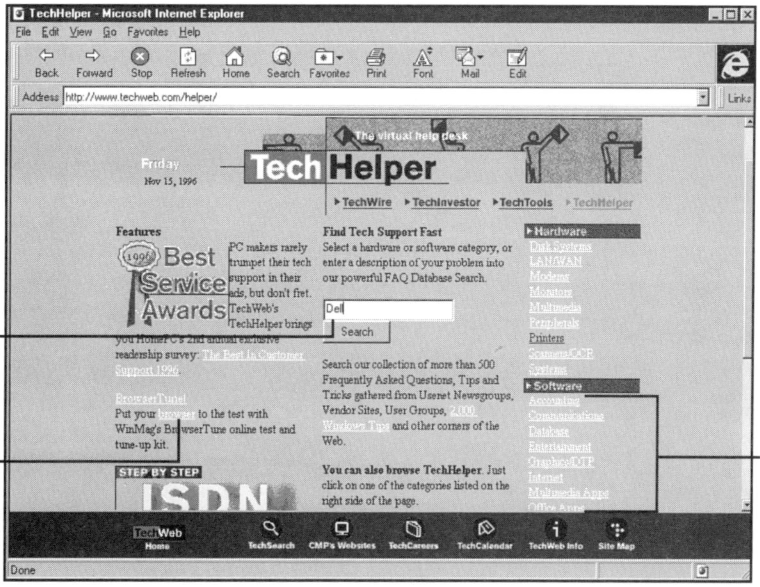

Type the beginning of your vendor's name and click Search to search for a vendor

When you click a link, it typically changes color to let you know you've visited the linked page

Click any of the underlined links for a list of Vendors' Web sites

5 Although every Web page is different, well-designed pages have **links**—those underlined words or phrases—to other sites. If there are many links on the page, you'll often find a search feature as well. Scroll down the TechHelper vendor list or use the Search for a Company box to locate your vendor's link. When you find it, click the link to go straight to your hardware or software vendor's Web page.

TIP

When you visit a Web page that you plan to revisit, add the page to your list of Favorites. Click the Favorites button on the browser toolbar and select Add to Favorites. For your next visit, click the Favorites button and select the added site from the list.

6 To return to the TechHelper page after you've visited a vendor or two, either click the Back button on your browser's toolbar, or click the Address drop-down arrow and choose **http://www.techhelper.com** on the list.

7 Of course you can go anywhere else on the Web as well. Try the Search button on the browser's toolbar; if you're using Microsoft Explorer 3.0 as a browser, that takes you to the invaluable Find it Fast page. Type a few words that describe what you're looking for, and click Search, as shown in Figure 25.3.

Fig. 25.3
Microsoft's Find it Fast page puts all the top Web search services, and more besides, in one place.

Search engines are search services provided by various Internet companies. Experiment with them to see which suits you best.

Although they're not underlined, these are all links; click any that look interesting

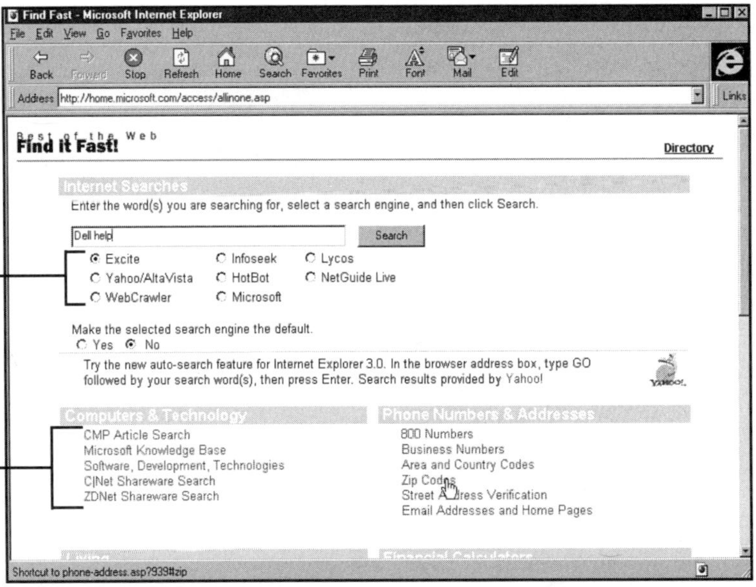

TIP **Web hyperlinks don't always look like hyperlinks. Instead of** underlined words, you might see graphics, text buttons, or plain text. If you're in doubt, point at any object on a Web page. If your pointer turns into a little hand, the object is a link.

8 When you're through browsing the Web, click your service provider's icon on the Windows Taskbar and choose Disconnect. Microsoft Network subscribers can right-click the MSN icon on the Taskbar and select Sign Out on the shortcut menu. Click the Close button in the browser window to shut down Microsoft Explorer or Netscape Navigator, or whatever you happen to use.

Now that I'm on the Web, where do I go?

A typical ramble on the World Wide Web involves exactly the kind of hopping from Web site to Web site we've just sampled. Getting around is easy—just click a link. Finding what you want is more challenging. For standard fare like the news, sports and stock quotes, and for reference information such as ZIP Codes, Bartlett's, and Roget's, the links on Microsoft's Find Fast page are more than adequate.

Use search engines like Yahoo, InfoSeek, and AltaVista for more esoteric matter. They're all accessed from the Find Fast page, and each one works in a different way. Yahoo organizes the Web by category, which narrows the choices and makes it easy to use. AltaVista is broader. AltVista searches typically return many (many!) documents, most of which will be completely irrelevant, though you'll strike the occasional vein of gold as well. There are millions of documents on the Web, and although many of them are of interest only to their creators, there's plenty of compelling reading and viewing to be found.

Here are a few other sites to consider:

- If you're writing financial reports of any kind, *The Wall Street Journal* (**http://www.wsj.com**) has stock quotes, company financial data, stock charts—and almost all the text in the daily edition of the newspaper. Although the *Journal* charges a subscription fee to Internet users, Microsoft Internet Explorer 3.0 users get a free ride, at least at the time of this writing.
- Word users writing research papers will want to visit Oxford University's Bodleian library, which has an amazing service called BARD (**http://www.bodley.ox.ac.uk/bardhtml/bard.html**).BARD puts a vast compendium of Web information sources in one place. If research is your bag, BARD is your site.
- Writing a letter in Word that's destined for foreign climes? Research-It (**http://www.itools.com/research-it/research-it.html**) is another good place for the information hungry. You can look up a word in Italian, Japanese, German or Spanish, conjugate French verbs, or even find English rhymes.

- For general information to include in any Word document, there are hundreds of magazines on the Web, both online versions of print magazines and journals that you won't find on any conventional newstand. You'll find a thorough listing on the Dominis eZines Database (**http://www.dominis.com/Zines**).

That's not even the beginning of a tiny sampling. Don't overlook the Internet discussion group network, Usenet, where you can read, and respond to, posted messages on every topic from all corners of the globe. And if the overwhelming variety of topics on the Web has you slightly bewildered, click Links, Best of the Web on the Internet Explorer 3.0 toolbar. If you're in Word, click the Start Page button on the Web toolbar. Either way, you'll go to the Internet Explorer Start Page shown in Figure 25.4, which is as good a jumping off point as any.

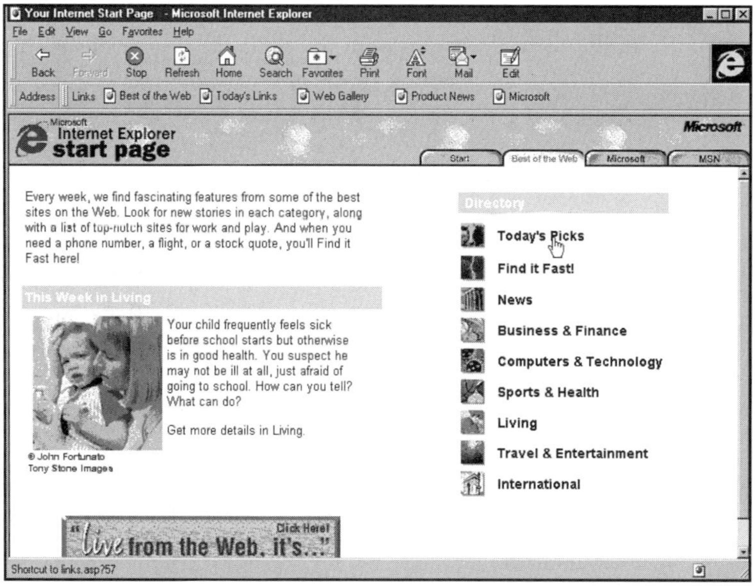
Your Internet Start Page - Microsoft Internet Explorer
File Edit View Go Favorites Help
Back Forward Stop Refresh Home Search Favorites Print Font Mail Edit
Address Links Best of the Web Today's Links Web Gallery Product News Microsoft
Microsoft Internet Explorer start page
Microsoft
Start Best of the Web Microsoft MSN
Every week, we find fascinating features from some of the best sites on the Web. Look for new stories in each category, along with a list of top-notch sites for work and play. And when you need a phone number, a flight, or a stock quote, you'll Find it Fast here!
This Week in Living
Your child frequently feels sick before school starts but otherwise is in good health. You suspect he may not be ill at all, just afraid of going to school. How can you tell? What can do?
Get more details in Living.
© John Fortunato Tony Stone Images
Directory
Today's Picks
Find it Fast!
News
Business & Finance
Computers & Technology
Sports & Health
Living
Travel & Entertainment
International
Click Here!
"Live from the Web, it's..."
Shortcut to links.asp?57

Fig. 25.4
Where to start? Investigate the links on the Internet Explorer Start Page.

This document deserves a million readers

Writing is hard enough without having to drum up readers as well. Even writers whose words flow like mountain streams in spring may not be quite as prolific at finding readers. Word, however, can change all that. The World Wide Web puts millions of readers right on the other side of your monitor.

Your local intranet might have several hundred users. Publish a document on either one, and even if you don't get millions of readers, you'll surely get some.

> ***Plain English, please!***
>
> An **intranet** is a local computer network that uses the same standards for displaying and sharing documents in use on the World Wide Web.

Word uses its own special codes and conventions to format documents, and The World Wide Web has an entirely different set of codes and conventions. Word's Internet publishing tools convert Word documents to the World Wide Web format, **HTML** (Hypertext Markup Language). Word also converts HTML documents into Word format, and lets you create an HTML document from scratch.

> ***Plain English, please!***
>
> **Hypertext Markup Language**, or HTML, is what makes the World Wide Web tick. It's a formatting language that allows the insertion of special codes to link documents together. Hypertext links are like cross-references in an encyclopedia—they direct you to another page with related information. Hypertext links are automatic though: click the links in a hypertext document (they're usually underlined words), and you travel automatically to other documents. Those document addresses are embedded in the link. Word lets you insert the hypertext links of your choice in any Web documents you create.

If this stew of jargon and acronyms is beginning to make your eyes glaze over, it's not surprising. What is surprising is the ease with which you can put a Web page together in Word:

- Open the document you want to publish on the Web. It can be pretty much anything that's neither libellous nor otherwise likely to get you in trouble. The Web is a large-spirited place, but there are laws and limits.
- Save your Word document as an HTML document. It's automatically displayed in HTML format. Use the Word Standard toolbar to add hypertext links.
- Post your document on the Web through your Internet service provider.

Not all Word's formatting features can be converted to HTML. Columns, drop caps, fill, headers and footers, page numbering, tabs and indents, vertical lines, and watermarks won't make the transition. Nor will borders. You'll want to bear that in mind as you create your document.

To convert a Word document into an HTML document:

1. Click the Save button to save your Word document in Word format.
2. With the document still open, click File, Save as HTML.
3. In the Save As HTML dialog box that pops up, give the document a new name if you want to. Otherwise, click Save. If you don't change the name, the original document is unaffected, and it'll remain DOCUMENT NAME.doc. You'll also have a new document called DOCUMENT NAME.html, the HTML version of the original.
4. Click OK in any Word message boxes that pop up (you may be warned that your document's formatting will change, for example), and the HTML document appears in the editing window.

Figure 25.5 shows a document before it's converted to HTML in one window, and the document saved in HTML format in the other window.

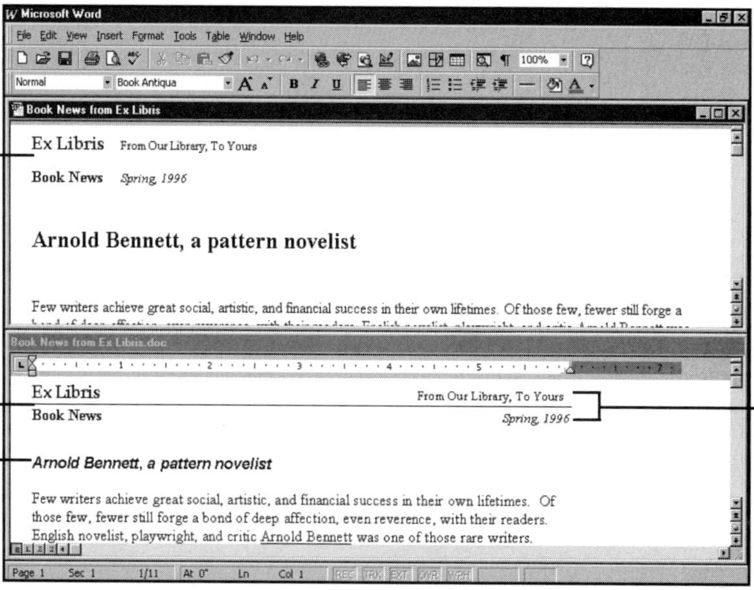
Microsoft Word
File Edit View Insert Format Tools Table Window Help
Normal
Book Antiqua
100%
Book News from Ex Libris
Ex Libris From Our Library, To Yours
Book News Spring, 1996
Arnold Bennett, a pattern novelist
Few writers achieve great social, artistic, and financial success in their own lifetimes. Of those few, fewer still forge a
Book News from Ex Libris.doc
Ex Libris
From Our Library, To Yours
Book News
Spring, 1996
Arnold Bennett, a pattern novelist
Few writers achieve great social, artistic, and financial success in their own lifetimes. Of those few, fewer still forge a bond of deep affection, even reverence, with their readers. English novelist, playwright, and critic Arnold Bennett was one of those rare writers.
Page 1 Sec 1 1/11 At 0" Ln Col 1 REC TRK EXT OVR WPH

Fig. 25.5
Documents converted to HTML (like the one shown in the top window) lose something in the translation, but Word has tools to fix it.

Borders in Word documents won't convert to HTML

Fonts will change in the HTML conversion

Tabs don't work in HTML, so these right-aligned tabs are lost in the HTML translation

CAUTION **Although converting Word documents to HTML format is a snap,** the translation pushes Word's resources to the limit. Word's codes are stripped from the document, and HTML codes are inserted by the bushel. It can lead to the occasional crash, so always save your documents in ordinary Word format before attempting a conversion to HTML.

TIP **HTML is like a clumsy word processing language, in which you** insert special codes for every formatting effect in the document. Word's Internet publishing tools spare you from having to learn the HTML codes, but if you want to see what they look like, click View, HTML Source. Click the Online View button on the Status bar to hide the HTML codes again.

How do I format my HTML document?

Word's HTML conversion will alter your document's formatting, but it's easy to format the HTML document so that it looks more or less like the original. To format a converted HTML document like the one in Figure 25.5:

1. Columns and tabs don't work in HTML documents, but tables do. And tables are excellent for positioning text and graphics on an HTML page. Click the Tables and Borders button on the Standard toolbar. Start at the upper left corner of where you want your table, and drag to the lower right corner with the table drawing tool.

2. Release the mouse button, and the outer borders of the table appear. Now drag inside the table wherever you want vertical and horizontal gridlines, as shown in Figure 25.6.

3. Click the Draw Table button on the Tables and Borders toolbar to get rid of the table drawing tool. Now drag through a section of text (or click a graphic) to select it. Drag the selection into a cell on the table; when you release the mouse button, the selection pops into place (see Figure 25.7).

TIP **Drawing a table and dragging items into it works for both text and** graphics. If you've only got text to deal with, select the text, then choose Table, Convert Text to Table. Choose the number of columns and rows you want, then click OK in the Convert Text to Table dialog box. That puts your text inside table cells automatically. You might still have some dragging to do if text didn't wind up where you wanted it inside the table.

Drag inside the table with the table drawing tool for vertical and horizontal gridlines

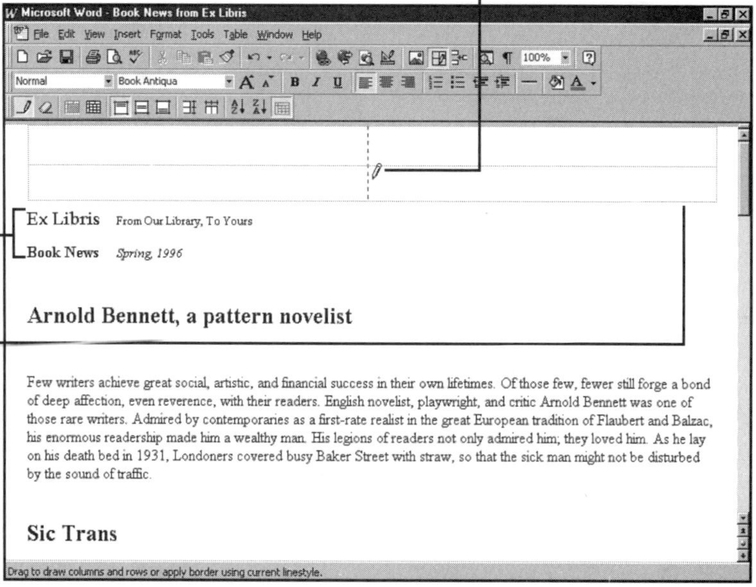
Microsoft Word - Book News from Ex Libris
File Edit View Insert Format Tools Table Window Help
Normal
Book Antiqua
100%
Ex Libris
From Our Library, To Yours
Book News
Spring, 1996
Arnold Bennett, a pattern novelist
Few writers achieve great social, artistic, and financial success in their own lifetimes. Of those few, fewer still forge a bond of deep affection, even reverence, with their readers. English novelist, playwright, and critic Arnold Bennett was one of those rare writers. Admired by contemporaries as a first-rate realist in the great European tradition of Flaubert and Balzac, his enormous readership made him a wealthy man. His legions of readers not only admired him; they loved him. As he lay on his death bed in 1931, Londoners covered busy Baker Street with straw, so that the sick man might not be disturbed by the sound of traffic.
Sic Trans
Drag to draw columns and rows or apply border using current linestyle.

Fig. 25.6
When you want to align text and graphics in HTML documents, draw a table.

Existing text or other material on the page is pushed aside to make room for the table

The initial drag operation gave us the table's outer border

You can also move the whole table around on the page. Drag through the table to select it, then drag the table into position.

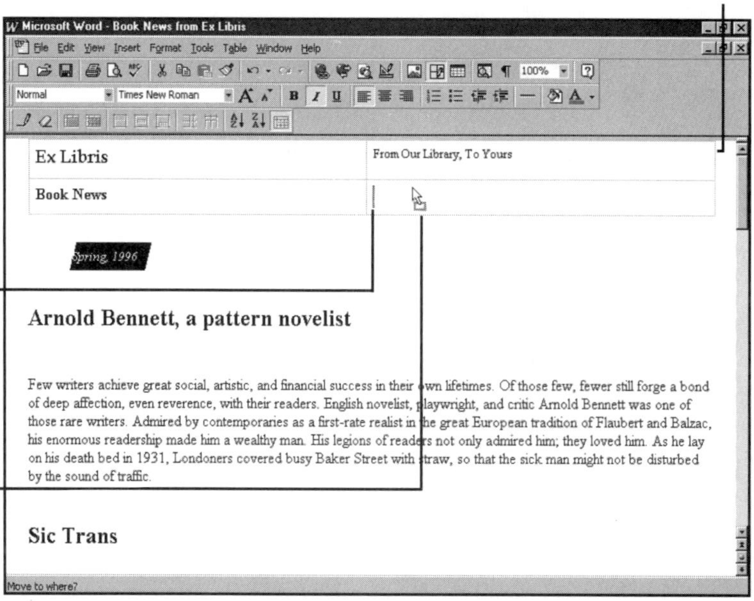
Microsoft Word - Book News from Ex Libris
File Edit View Insert Format Tools Table Window Help
Normal
Times New Roman
100%
Ex Libris
From Our Library, To Yours
Book News
Spring, 1996
Arnold Bennett, a pattern novelist
Few writers achieve great social, artistic, and financial success in their own lifetimes. Of those few, fewer still forge a bond of deep affection, even reverence, with their readers. English novelist, playwright, and critic Arnold Bennett was one of those rare writers. Admired by contemporaries as a first-rate realist in the great European tradition of Flaubert and Balzac, his enormous readership made him a wealthy man. His legions of readers not only admired him; they loved him. As he lay on his death bed in 1931, Londoners covered busy Baker Street with straw, so that the sick man might not be disturbed by the sound of traffic.
Sic Trans
Move to where?

Fig. 25.7
You can drag text or graphics into table cells. Once inside the table, alignment and positioning are a breeze.

An outline of the cursor shows you where your dragged selection is going

This frame follows your pointer around as you drag

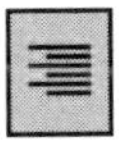

4 Select any table cells with text that you want right-aligned and click the Align Right button on the formatting toolbar. Now choose Table, Hide Gridlines, and presto! Text that used to be formatted with right-aligned tabs in the Word document is now right-aligned inside an HTML document table. With the gridlines turned off, it's hard to tell the difference.

5 Click a blank line outside the table to put the cursor in the document. Now click the Horizontal Line button on the Formatting toolbar, and a Horizontal line is inserted.

6 Click the line and drag a handle to extend or shorten it; drag the line with the four-headed arrow to move it into position. For a perfectly straight line, shift and drag a handle. After all that work, we've now got an HTML document that looks very much like our original Word document (see Figure 25.8).

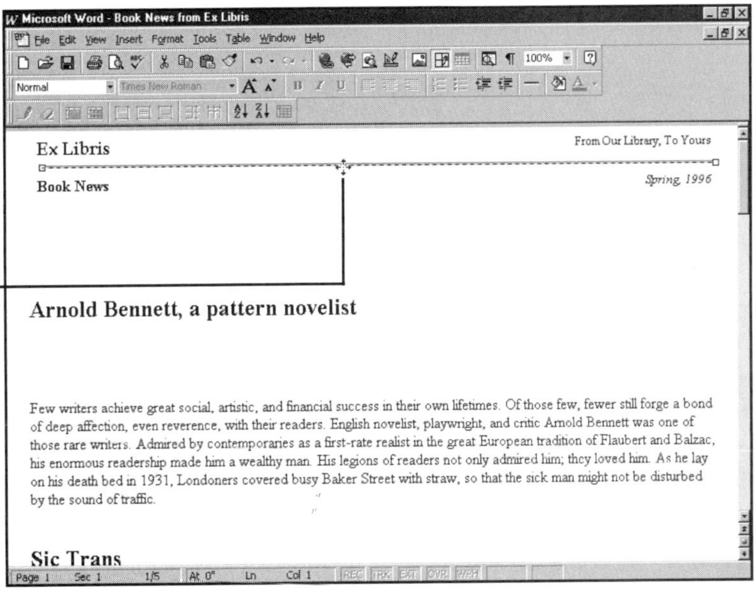

Microsoft Word - Book News from Ex Libris
File Edit View Insert Format Tools Table Window Help
Normal
Ex Libris
From Our Library, To Yours
Book News
Spring, 1996
Arnold Bennett, a pattern novelist
Few writers achieve great social, artistic, and financial success in their own lifetimes. Of those few, fewer still forge a bond of deep affection, even reverence, with their readers. English novelist, playwright, and critic Arnold Bennett was one of those rare writers. Admired by contemporaries as a first-rate realist in the great European tradition of Flaubert and Balzac, his enormous readership made him a wealthy man. His legions of readers not only admired him; they loved him. As he lay on his death bed in 1931, Londoners covered busy Baker Street with straw, so that the sick man might not be disturbed by the sound of traffic.
Sic Trans
Page 1 Sec 1 1/5 At 0" Ln Col 1

Fig. 25.8
It takes a little more work, but HTML documents can be formatted to look a lot like Word documents.

Like other objects, horizontal lines can be moved and resized with a little dragging

You can take any Word document and convert it to HTML. Once your document is formatted, it's ready for publication on the Web, or on your local intranet. Although many Internet service providers post their subscribers' HTML documents on the Web as part of the service, not all do. Contact your own provider for information on how to publish your page on the Web.

Give me a home (page) where the Net surfers roam

Books have covers and tables of contents. Web sites have home pages to serve the same purpose. Home pages are designed to catch the eye of passing Net surfers, or to get attention on an intranet. They also display the contents of their sites. Home pages usually include links to other pages on the Web, or to HTML documents on the site. Word makes it easy to set up home pages complete with links and other Web gadgets.

You can cook up a home page from scratch and save it as an HTML document. Or you can save yourself some time and effort and use Word's home page templates, a bit like home pages in a can. Add your own text and links, and it's ready for publication on the Web.

Summon up the Web Page Wizard for custom home pages

To create your own home page, call on the Web Page Wizard:

1. Click File, New, Web Pages. Double-click the Web Page Wizard icon, and the Web Page Wizard dialog box pops up over a sample page, as seen in Figure 25.9.

2. Make a selection from the types of pages on the list, and click Next. Choose a style for your page in this next step of the Web Page Wizard. Click a style, and the editing window displays a preview.

3. Click Finish, and you're left with a canned home page filled with sample text and dummy hypertext links that don't go anywhere—yet. Click the Save button, and give your home page a name. HTML format is selected by default in the Save as type box, so all you have to do is type a file name.

4. Drag through the sample text to select it, and type your own. That includes the dummy hypertext links that the Web page is peppered with; change the link text, or delete it. Delete any other text you don't want. Many of the Web Page Wizard templates use tables; click inside the table and choose Table, Show Gridlines so that you can see what you're doing.

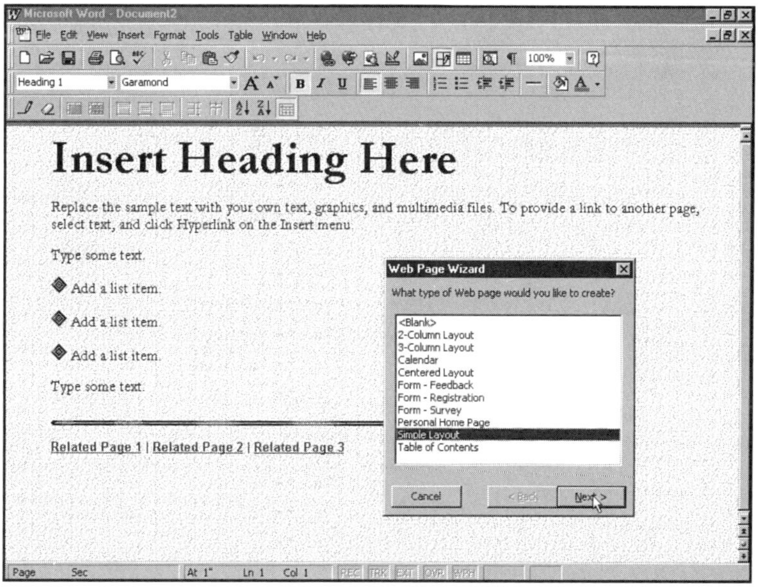

Fig. 25.9
Click a choice on the list, and the editing window displays the corresponding Web page template.

5 Click Insert, Picture, Clip Art and insert graphics if you want. To change the background, choose Format, Background, Fill Effects for the Fill Effects dialog box shown in Figure 25.10.

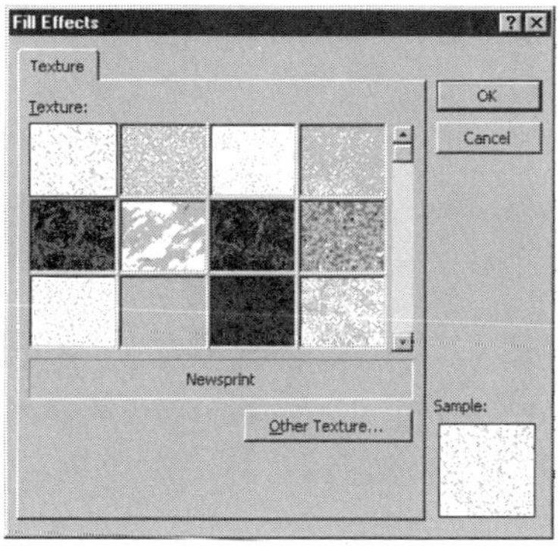

Fig. 25.10
If you choose one of these darker textures, be sure to change the font color to a lighter shade; otherwise the page will be unreadable.

CAUTION **Anyone who's waited forever for a graphics-laden Web page to** appear knows how irksome that can be. A graphic or two is a fine addition to a Web page, but don't add too many. Try opening your Web page once you've uploaded it to the server. If you get impatient waiting for it to load, you know that you've added too many graphics.

6 Add any other formatting touches you care to, and save your finished page.

Missing links? Add them

The Web Page Wizard's canned pages are peppered with hypertext links. They look convincing, but they don't go anywhere. You'll want to add your own links to other documents on your own site, and to other pages on the Net. You can also link text within an HTML document, to take readers on quick trips to sections of the page that aren't immediately in view.

To add hypertext links to other documents and pages:

1 Select the link text. It can be either the dummy links in a Web Page Wizard home page, or any other text in the document.

2 Click the Insert Hyperlink button on the Standard Toolbar. The Insert Hyperlink dialog box pops up, as seen in Figure 25.11.

Click the drop-down arrow and select any Web pages you've visited recently

Fig. 25.11
Hyperlinks take readers on quick trips across a document, or around the world.

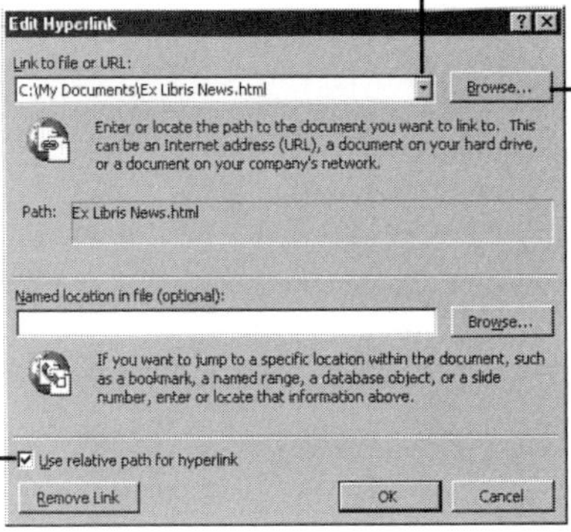
Edit Hyperlink
Link to file or URL:
C:\My Documents\Ex Libris News.html
Browse...
Enter or locate the path to the document you want to link to. This can be an Internet address (URL), a document on your hard drive, or a document on your company's network.
Path: Ex Libris News.html
Named location in file (optional):
Browse...
If you want to jump to a specific location within the document, such as a bookmark, a named range, a database object, or a slide number, enter or locate that information above.
Use relative path for hyperlink
Remove Link
OK
Cancel

Click Browse to view the contents of your hard drive or network

Make sure the Use relative path box is checked. That way if you move the document you're linking, the hyperlink will still work.

3 Click inside the Link to file or URL edit box, and type the address or path of the document you want to link. Click the Browse button to see the contents of your hard drive or network, then double-click a file to pop its address or path into the box. Or click the drop-down arrow and select a Web site from a list taken from your Web browser's history file, or from a recently opened HTML document.

TIP **The first item on the drop-down list is a blank http:// address.** Select it, then type the rest of the address. That saves you from typing and retyping that annoying World Wide Web prefix.

4. Click OK, and the link is established. As long as the Use relative path for hyperlink box is checked (see Figure 25.11), the link will work even if you move the linked file. The link in Figure 25.11 points to a document on my hard drive. If both the linked documents are moved to another location, the Web for example, or an intranet, the link will still work.

5. Point at the link, and the pointer turns into a little hand. Click the link, and you'll go straight to the linked document (see Figure 25.12).

Fig. 25.12
When you point at a link, you even get a reminder of where the link will take you.

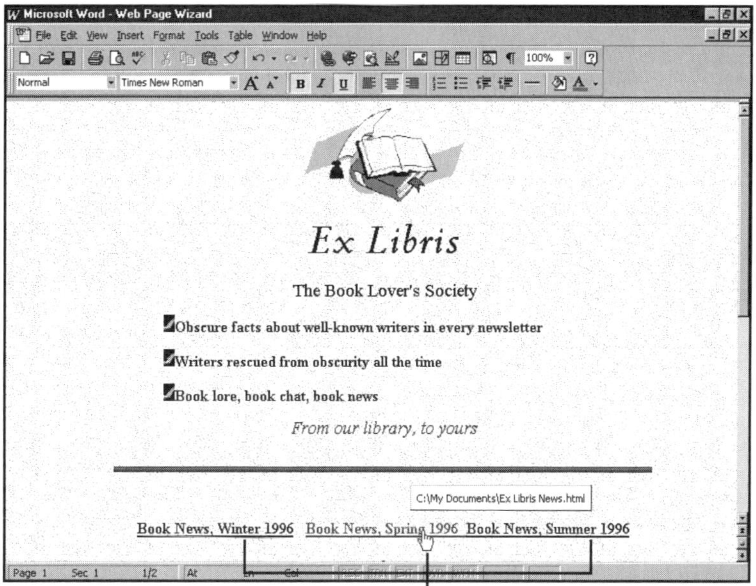

To edit the link text, use the arrow keys to move the insertion point into the link

Q&A ***I can't click a link without traveling to the document it's linked to. So how do I edit link text!?***

Since you can't click the link without activating it, use the arrow keys to move the insertion point inside the link text. Then press Delete and Backspace and type new text, just as you would ordinarily.

To edit the hyperlink, right-click the link and choose Hyperlink, Edit Hyperlink. To delete the link, select it with the Shift+arrow key combination and press Delete.

I need links within this long page

The great drawback to reading documents on a computer monitor is that we can see so little of them at any one time. Reading long Web pages requires a lot of scrolling. You can relieve your readers' scrolling blues with links within the page itself. Link, for example, text at the top of the page with text that's out of the monitor window at the bottom of the page.

To link text within a page:

1. Select the text you want readers to go to when they click the link. Text, for example, at the bottom of the page.
2. Click Insert, Bookmark. In the Bookmark dialog box that pops up, type a name in the Bookmark name edit box and click Add.
3. Select the text you want for the link. This will be the underlined hyperlink text that readers will click to go to the bookmark we've just created.

4. Click the Insert Hyperlink button. In the Insert Hyperlink dialog box, click the Browse button next to the Named location in file edit box. Double-click the bookmark name in the Bookmark dialog box that appears.
5. Click OK in the Insert Hyperlink dialog box, and the link is established. When readers click the link, the window will jump straight to the bookmarked text. The split screen view in Figure 25.13 gives you the idea.

Fig. 25.13
Bookmark links make handy automated cross-references in long Web pages.

When this link at the top of the page is clicked...

...the page scrolls automatically to this bookmarked text at the bottom of the page

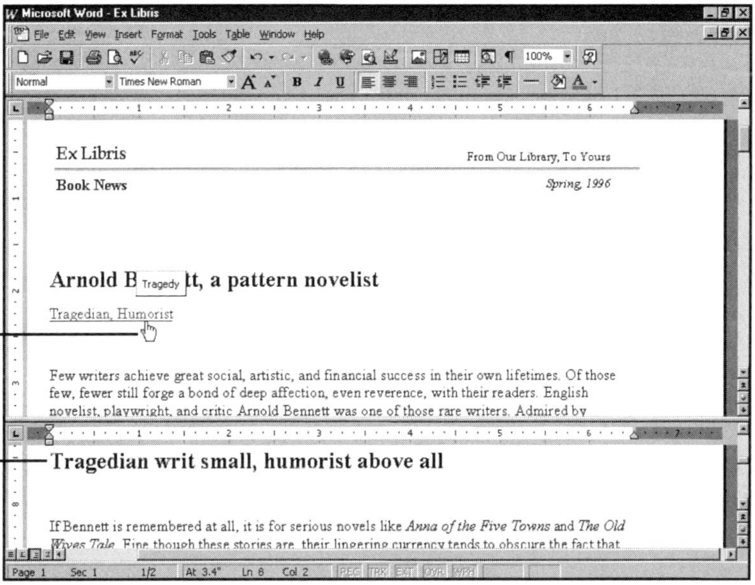
Microsoft Word - Ex Libris
Ex Libris
From Our Library, To Yours
Book News
Spring, 1996
Arnold B Tragedy tt, a pattern novelist
Tragedian, Humorist
Few writers achieve great social, artistic, and financial success in their own lifetimes. Of those few, fewer still forge a bond of deep affection, even reverence, with their readers. English
Tragedian writ small, humorist above all
If Bennett is remembered at all, it is for serious novels like Anna of the Five Towns and The Old

Well-designed Web pages usually have a link at the bottom of the page that takes readers back up to the top. With Word's bookmarks and hyperlinks, it's easy to add a gadget like that to your own Web pages.

Index

Symbols

A

B

D

E

G

H

I

J-K

N

O

P

Q-R

U

V

W-X-Y-Z